Dedication

We would like to dedicate this book to the memory of family and friends whom we wish were here to read it: Davida R. Trope, Edwin Upchurch, Richard Applebee, Dorothy Bednarowska, Sam Beatson, Susan Fillman, Art Leff, Leon S. Lipson, Madeleine Lejwa and John Nitta.

Acknowledgments

We owe a debt of gratitude to several professionals whose comments, criticism, insights and suggestions improved the final manuscript.

Lt. Colonel John Bickers, Elliot Brown, Colonel Nathaniel Causey, Generaladvokaten Arne Willy Dahl, Orrie Dinstein, Nelson Dong, John Gregory, Candace Jones, Lynne R. Malina, Professor Stefan Markowski, Michael McGuire, Leah Montange, Dr. Charles Palmer, Vince Polley, E. Michael Power, Chuck Resor, David Rosenblum, Thomas Schramm, Art Spitzer, Professor Margaret Stock, Gwan Tan, and Cynthia Trope.

Dr. Monique Witt rigorously edited the manuscript before its submittal to the American Bar Association. Her efforts clarified our arguments, improved their cogency, and contributed perspectives we had overlooked. For all the hours she invested and for all that she accomplished, we are deeply grateful.

We would also like to thank the ABA Cyberspace Committee for its firm support of our efforts, and our editors at the ABA, Ms. Suzy Bibko and Ms. Joani Orr Taylor, for their patience, understanding and contributions. We owe a special thank you to M. A. Witt and Dev Avidon for the original graphic design of the cover, and to Ms. Jill Tedhams, Art Director for ABA Publishing, for the final design of the cover.

To the extent that this book achieves its objectives, those we have thanked deserve a generous portion of the credit and no share in the blame for errors, deficiencies or shortcomings.

Lastly, the writing of a book involves many negotiations with family, who are continually asked to make compromises and concessions, with the tacit understanding that completion of the manuscript will restore order. Our families have been extraordinarily patient with the time the book has taken from them, while providing us with unstinting support. They have our deepest thanks.

Summary of Chapters

Contents

Glossary

ABR: Anti-Boycott Regulations

AECA: Arms Export Control Act

BIOS: Basic Input and Output System

BIS: United States Department of Commerce's Bureau of Industry and Security

BSA: Bank Secrecy Act

CBP: Dutch Data Protection Authority

CCL: Commerce Control List

CFIUS: Committee on Foreign Investment in the United States

CSI: Container Security Initiative

CSR: Cuban Sanctions Regulations

DDTC: United States Department of State's Directorate of Defense Trade Controls

DHS: United States Department of Homeland Security

DISA: United States Defense Information Systems Agency

DoD: United States Department of Defense

DoS: United States Department of State

DPA: Definitive Purchase Agreement

EAR: Export Administration Regulations

ECA: United Kingdom's Export Control Act of 2003

ECCN: Export Control Classification Number

EPCI: Enhanced Proliferation Control Initiative

EU: European Union

FATF: Financial Action Task Force

FDIC: United States Federal Deposit Insurance Corporation

FEMA: Canadian Foreign Extraterritorial Measures Act

FFIEC: Federal Financial Institutions Examination Council

FTC: United States Federal Trade Commission

GAO: United States General Accounting Office

GTSR: Global Terrorism Sanctions Regulations

HIPAA: Health Insurance Portability and Accountability Act

HPC: High performance computer

IACR: Iranian Assets Control Regulations

IDS: Intrusion Detection System

IEEE: Institute of Electrical and Electronic Engineers

IEEPA: International Emergency Economic Powers Act

IG: Inspector General

ILSA: Iran and Libya Sanctions Act of 1996

IM: Instant Messaging

INA: Immigration and Nationality Act

IP Phone: Internet Protocol Phone

ITAR: International Traffic in Arms Regulations

ITR: Iranian Transactions Regulations

JSF: Joint Strike Fighter

MoD: Ministry of Defence

M2M: Machine-to-machine

NASA: United States National Aeronautics and Space Agency

NATO: North Atlantic Treaty Organization

OECD: Organisation for Economic Co-Operation and Development

OFAC: United States Department of Treasury's Office of Foreign Assets Control

OPPA: California Online Privacy Protection Act of 2003

PDPA: Dutch Personal Data Protection Act

PIPEDA: Canadian Personal Information Protection and Electronic Documents Act

POTS: Plain Old Telephone System

PSTN: Public Switched Telephone Network

P2P: Peer-to-peer

QATT: Qualified Anti-terrorist Technology

QoS: Quality of Service

RIAA: Recording Industry Association of America

SAFETY Act: Support Anti-Terrorism by Fostering Effective Technologies Act of 2002

SALSA: Syrian Accountability and Lebanese Sovereignty Act of 2003

SAO: Security Advisory Opinion

SARBOX: Sarbanes-Oxley Act of 2002

SDGT: Specially Designated Global Terrorist

SDN: Specially Designated Nationals

SEC: Securities and Exchange Commission

SSN: Social Security Number

SSR: Sudanese Sanctions Regulations

STIG: Voice Over Internet Protocol Security Technical Implementation Guide

TAL: Technology Alert List

TSR: Trade Sanction Regulations

U.K.: United Kingdom

USML: United States Munitions List

USSC: United States Sentencing Commission

WMD: Weapon of Mass Destruction

VoIP: Voice over Internet Protocol

INTRODUCTION

Surveying the Problem: The Risks of Cross-Border Transactions in Cyberspace

Our intention in writing this book is to help parties and their counsel complete cross-border transactions with the minimum unnecessary regulatory costs and risks and the maximum certainty. This is a deceptively complex undertaking, in the context of the extensive regulatory schema that currently applies to such transactions, and the increasingly complicated compliance requirements in conjunction with such regulations. Our primary focus will be on creating compliance checks that can be used effectively both for on-going in-house review and for early identification of regulatory risks and issues in connection with individual transactions. The premise of early and on-going attention to these issues is that, when compliance requirements are addressed late (particularly in the context of a cross-border transaction), already complex issues can become onerous burdens that ultimately hamper the successful and cost-effective completion of the deal, requiring time-consuming and costly remediation. This is in no one's best interest. Our hope therefore is to provide a kind of roadmap that will allow counsel to negotiate the layered and often redundant scopes of the relevant regulations and, in some instances, to structure around the more onerous ones by avoiding certain "transfers" or "releases" of funds, supplies, products, information, technical data and software.

In our practice, we have observed that cross-border transactions are often impeded by prolonged delays and substantial cost increases, when parties do not check for potential noncompliance with laws and regulations that control transfers of, access to, or use of, advanced technologies, technical data, personally identifiable information and patented inventions. To reduce these risks, we recommend the early development of what we call "checkpoints." Each checkpoint is designed to examine a proposed transaction for compliance with a body of laws and regulations that parties tend to overlook or to be unaware of, but which can easily jeopardize the transaction and imperil the parties. Such checkpoints are useful for any cross-border transaction. But they are especially helpful in averting the additional risks that arise in complex transactions (mergers, acquisitions, strategic alliances and outsourcings), particularly when the parties negotiate by e-mail and instant messaging through cyberspace.

Early attention also facilitates the business negotiations by alerting all parties to potential risks. When confronted late in a deal with unexpected compliance issues, both U.S. and non-U.S. parties often question the applicability of the relevant laws or underestimate the gravity of the risks of their violation. They will express the justifiable and indeed reasonable concern that the deal's momentum will be sacrificed, if technical violations sidetrack the negotiations, and will contend that whatever remediation is required can be postponed until after closing, or alternately made a condition to closing.

Because the issues we are addressing fall under the rubric of risk management, parties will often initially believe that they can elect to absorb the risk, as they do under many other statutory/regulatory schemes, and will attempt a straightforward cost/benefit analysis of non-compliance or delayed (postponed) compliance. Such an analysis, however, is neither practicable, nor particularly helpful in the context of the overlapping laws we are discussing. We will try to demonstrate that early compliance is the least burdensome, most efficient and most cost-effective strategy in virtually all cross-border transactions.

While postponement of remediation may have a superficial appeal, that appeal diminishes rapidly when one understands the full scope of the legal risks: investigation by multiple federal enforcement agencies, substantial fines, prolonged loss of export privileges (ten years is not uncommon) and personal liability (which for certain violations can include criminal indictment and lengthy imprisonment). Moreover, in this field, the maxim *where there's one there's likely to be many*, is frequently correct. If a firm commits one violation of the export control laws, for example, it is likely to commit a number in the same transaction, related transactions and follow-up transactions, or pursuant to a course of business conduct. In the latter context, violations can accumulate very rapidly, and will often be charged individually rather than aggregated. As a result, relatively minor violative behavior (such as a deemed reexport of low level, technical information pursuant to an e-mail to a foreign national of a U.S. ally) can give rise to substantial monetary fines very quickly. If a firm is not actively structuring its business dealings to avoid such violations, it will not establish a credible record for claiming mitigating circumstances, if it is subsequently charged. Under the regulatory framework being considered, such mitigation can be all-important in avoiding prosecution. As will become apparent, the cost of penalties quickly exceeds the cost of remediation, making the risks uneconomic. And the further prospects of imprisonment, or the ordeal of a trial, make the risks wholly unpalatable to responsible company officers and directors. When these factors are considered in the context of a pending acquisition or outsourcing, post-closing compliance will not be acceptable to a U.S. firm.

The hard sell for any counsel seeking to facilitate the expeditious completion of a transaction involving such laws and regulations will be the need to consider *pre-signing* remediation. Post-signing, pre-closing corrections do not always solve compliance problems, and run the risk of leaving many others to be discovered only later after closing, when the substantial costs of any remediation are shifted to the party least well-positioned to address them or to defend against an enforcement action. Overseas firms may promise, in good faith, to disengage from transactions prohibited to a U.S. person, and to complete such disengagements prior to closing, but they often underestimate the logistical realties of unwinding long-term economic relationships under compressed time schedules. Months after formal termination of a relationship with a supplier or customer, there can still be shipments of goods, transfers of technical data, or placements of orders that, having been in the pipeline, continue to flow in spite of best efforts. (Sometimes such relations continue because the overseas firm hopes to extract the maximum benefit from such transactions before the U.S. firm compels it to disengage.) Thus, short-term economic interests will ordinarily trump regulatory requirements, unless the real long-term costs of non-compliance are explained and factored into the business calculus.

As a result, a U.S. acquirer may discover after closing that it is still receiving shipments from, and delivering shipments to, parties with whom U.S. persons are prohibited from dealing by the applicable export and trade sanction laws.[1] Moreover, certain provisions of those laws

---

1. One list of parties that U.S. persons are generally prohibited from dealing with, the Specially Designated Nationals list maintained by the Treasury Department's Office

make it a violation to facilitate such dealings either directly or indirectly, and can be interpreted by federal authorities as violated when a U.S. person signs a definitive acquisition agreement, thereby facilitating the overseas firm's ability to complete its performance of transactions that benefit prohibited parties. (Not surprisingly, such signings often lead to accelerated performance, thereby further facilitating the very activities that the applicable laws seek to interdict.) Hence, pre-signing remediation becomes the safest course, but the hardest to recommend, since resistance to such advice will come from both sides of the table. Overseas firms will see early remediation as compelling them to sacrifice valuable economic relationships and opportunities; and U.S. firms will see it as an excess of caution that threatens to delay or derail the transaction. We understand and appreciate that commercial parties accustomed to agreeing on remediation as a condition to closing will find it counter-intuitive that trade sanction regulations can be violated simply by signing a definitive agreement, by entering into negotiations with a prohibited party, or by starting to collect, transfer or use personal data during pre-signing due diligence. But this is in fact the scope of the applicable enforcement. And we have found that it is more efficient and effective to be aware of the breadth of the potential risks early.

While licenses can be obtained for certain forms of proscribed pre-signing conduct, these can also create different risks, include ambiguous conditions, and thus provide little legal certainty. A U.S. acquirer (or outsourcer) will usually conclude that pre-signing remediation is the only safe course. Having determined that, however, the U.S. party is still faced with the challenge of persuading the overseas party that, upon completion of such remediation (at substantial costs to the overseas party), the U.S. party will in fact sign and go through with the acquisition or outsourcing. In our experience, overseas parties respond better to such requests, if the request comes early, and not after they have been forced to wade through a long checklist in an initial due diligence request.

Two other factors aid in making the case for early detection of such problems and, when required, pre-signing remediation. *First*, the task of ascertaining whether certain activities contravene the U.S. Export Administration Regulations is heavily fact driven and requires carefully

---

of Foreign Assets Control, included as of July 25, 2000, more than 30,000 such entities and individuals. *Nunn-Wolfowitz Task Force Report: Industry "Best Practices" Regarding Export Compliance Programs*, July 25, 2000, p. 6.

mapped and timed diligence.[2] *Second,* in the current post-9/11 enforcement environment, there is increasing evidence that the U.S. government is interpreting and enforcing the applicable export control, trade sanction and defense trade control laws aggressively. Many governments have tightened the enforcement of their security laws, export control laws and other laws applicable to cross-border transactions.[3] In light of such shifts in enforcement, businesses must re-assess how they address the risk of inadvertently contravening laws that have unusually broad extra-territorial reach. This book is designed to assist counsel in doing so. We have adopted the position that, if the momentum to do a deal is to be sustained, early detection of compliance problems and their early remediation is the best course, despite the challenges posed by such course. Cross-border compliance issues are best addressed through early, enhanced due diligence, because there is a far greater probability that the proposed remediation will be efficient and cost-effective, and will have the least disruptive impact on the transaction.

Failure to address such issues early (in a pre-signing due diligence) can impose burdensome transactional costs and can ultimately cause an acquisition or strategic merger (one clearly in the best economic interests of both parties) to be unwound at the eleventh hour. This was amply illustrated in the attempted merger of Lockheed Martin Corporation ("Lockheed") and Titan Corp. ("Titan"). The deal, originally

---

2. As commentators have observed: "Interpreting and applying the export laws can be difficult because some terms in the regulations are undefined or ill-defined. The application of some definitions to particular information requires judgment calls of technological and legal complexity. For example, it is especially challenging for companies to know when furnishing public domain information to a foreign person ceases to be allowable, unlicensed communication and, crossing a significant legal line, becomes "assistance" for which a license is required. ("Assistance" is an important but undefined term in the export control regulations.) Therefore, companies need to develop means to reach necessary judgments while effectively operating in a fast-paced, competitive business environment." *Nunn-Wolfowitz Task Force Report: Industry "Best Practices" Regarding Export Compliance Programs,* July 25, 2000, pp. 6–7.

3. A similar trend is occurring also in the cross-border enforcement of the securities laws by the Securities Exchange Commission: "As financial markets grow more global, the SEC is increasingly working with foreign regulators to track down wrongdoing at companies listed in the U.S. . . . The SEC's increased global role is in part a legacy of the September 11, 2001 attacks. . . . [T]he Sarbanes-Oxley act . . . gave the agency a broader mandate and more resources for investigations, including overseas ones." Schroeder, Michael, and Ascarelli, Silvia, *New Role for SEC: Policing Companies Beyond U.S. Borders,* THE WALL STREET JOURNAL, July 30, 2004, p. A-1 and A-6.

valued at $2.4 billion (including Lockheed's assumption of approximately $580 million of Titan's debt) was signed and announced in mid-September of 2003, and was scheduled to close in early 2004.[4] The Boards of Directors[5] of both companies had approved it[5] (but the deal was still subject to approval by Titan's shareholders, government regulatory review and other closing conditions included in the definitive merger agreement).[6] Lockheed, the nation's largest defense contractor (whose Skunk Works had developed stealth technology for combat aircraft) had recently developed its information technology services into "one of its fastest growing lines,"[7] and was keenly interested in acquiring Titan (whose portfolio included valuable government contracts for research and development,[8] classified information technology services, aerospace and homeland security, and was further augmented by "8,700 employees with coveted federal security clearances").[9] Titan was a major part of a team (led by Accenture Ltd.) selected to provide the U.S. government with "virtual borders," a system to monitor foreign visitors to the United States (valued in excess of $10 billion).[10]

Although Titan had net losses in seven of the past ten years,[11] and had lost $271.5 million on revenues of $1.39 billion in 2002, its stock had recently more than doubled, climbing from $7 per share (on April 11, 2003) to over $16 per share by September 2003. The apparent reason for that climb was Titan's success in winning certain lucrative government contracts. In the 18 months preceding Lockheed's offer, Titan had

---

4. Hardy, Michael, *Lockheed to Buy Titan*, FCW.com, September 16, 2003, accessed at www.fcw.com/fcw/articles/2003/0915/web-lm-09-16-03.asp.

5. Id.

6. Wait, Patience, *Lockheed Martin Snaps up Titan*, Washington Technology, September 29, 2003, accessed at www.washingtontechnology.com/news/18_13/federal/21770-1.html.

7. Karp, Jonathan, *Playing Defense: As Titan Mutates to Meet Needs of Pentagon, Risks Become Clear*, THE WALL STREET JOURNAL, June 28, 2004, p. A-1.

8. Titan had been awarded the National Security Agency's Enterprise Architecture and Decision Support program and a Special Operations enterprise network management and engineering services contract. Wait, Patience, *Lockheed Martin Snaps up Titan*, Washington Technology, September 29, 2003, accessed at www.washingtontechnology.com/news/18_13/federal/21770-1.html.

9. Id.

10. Karp, Jonathan, *Playing Defense: As Titan Mutates to Meet Needs of Pentagon, Risks Become Clear*, THE WALL STREET JOURNAL, June 28, 2004, p. A-1 at A-7.

11. *Titan Shares May Drop 40% with Collapse of Sale to Lockheed*, Bloomberg.com, June 25, 2004, accessed at http://bloomberg.com/apps/news.

won more than 12 such contracts whose aggregate value exceeded $100 million.[12]

Lockheed agreed to pay a premium to acquire Titan in an acquisition that was valued at 16.4 times Titan's estimated 2003 earnings (before interest, taxes, depreciation and amortization) for cash and stock totaling $22 per share[13] (approximately 130% of Titan's then current share price of $16.96). Titan's stock price rose 25% on announcement to roughly $21.

The deal offered significant advantages to both companies. Lockheed would gain a significant presence in the growing fields of homeland security, information technology (including a half-billion-dollar project for the National Security Agency)[14] and information security. For Titan, it represented the climax of over two decades of growth from its founding in 1981 to a multi-billion dollar defense conglomerate.[15]

The merger agreement contained the customary contingencies for "break up" and "unwind," including a $60 million liquidated payment, if Titan walked away from the deal post-signing. There was no comparable penalty for Lockheed's failure to close.[16] The asymmetry of these walk-away penalties reflected Lockheed's strong interest in concluding the transaction (and its unequal bargaining power).

The first indication of an impediment to completing the transaction occurred just before the initially scheduled closing date. Lockheed's due diligence included Titan's acquisition in 2001 of a satellite and radio communications product maker, Datron World Communications ("Datron"), and of an information-services company, BTG Inc., that had contracts with intelligence agencies. It also included Titan's "risky bid" in 2002 to develop wireless telephone networks in Asia, Africa and Latin America.[17] Titan had pursued business opportunities in developing

---

12. Hwang, Jeff, *Lockheed Gets Titan*, TheMotleyFool.com, September 16, 2003, accessed at www.fool.com/News/mft/2003/mft03091613.htm.

13. Wait, Patience, *Lockheed Martin Snaps up Titan*, Washington Technology, September 29, 2003, accessed at www.washingtontechnology.com/news/18_13/federal/21770-1.html.

14. Karp, Jonathan, *Playing Defense: As Titan Mutates to Meet Needs of Pentagon, Risks Become Clear*, THE WALL STREET JOURNAL, June 28, 2004, p. A-1 at p. A-7.

15. Brickley, Peg, *Holders Sue Titan Execs over Lockheed Deal Breakup*, The Wall Street Journal Online, July 1, 2004, accessed at http://online.wsj.com/article/0,,BT_CO_20040701_007973-search,00.html?collection = autowire%2F30day&vql_string = %27holders + sue + titan%27%3Cin%3E%28article%2Dbody%29.

16. Id.

17. Karp, Jonathan, *Playing Defense: As Titan Mutates to Meet Needs of Pentagon, Risks Become Clear*, THE WALL STREET JOURNAL, June 28, 2004, p. A-1.

countries with reputations for corruption: Indonesia, Saudi Arabia and Benin (in West Africa). Due diligence belatedly revealed evidence of actions potentially in violation of the Foreign Corrupt Practices Act of 1977 ("FCPA"). Lockheed had good reason to be alert to such findings. The FCPA was enacted in response to charges that several U.S. companies (particularly defense contractors) routinely made illegal payments to foreign government officials. In 1995, Lockheed Corp. had paid a $24.8 million penalty for violating the FCPA in connection with a questionable payment to an Egyptian politician.[18] Lockheed clearly wanted to avoid a reoccurrence, when it was confronted by evidence of potential violations on the part of Titan that posed a substantial risk of successor liability. The only acceptable course of action for Lockheed was to investigate the conduct thoroughly, report any evidence of violations to the enforcement agencies, and conclude any enforcement proceedings arising from such violations *prior* to closing. Lockheed did not want to give the impression of impeding or obstructing an investigation, if the government enforcement agencies started their own investigation. In an unusual but appropriate stratagem, the parties decided to disclose what they knew (and suspected) to the federal government before completing their diligence.

On February 13, 2004, Titan and Lockheed announced that they had jointly informed the Securities Exchange Commission ("SEC") and the Justice Department that the companies "were conducting their own internal review of some of Titan's foreign operations" related to the sale of Titan military radios.[19] Statements by spokesman for both companies suggested that nothing untoward had been found, and that the internal investigation was just a prudent precaution:

Titan: "Neither company has found any wrongdoing. . . . But because of the context and the size of the merger, Titan and Lockheed shared the view that everything should be reviewed."[20]

---

18. Karp, Jonathan, *SEC Probe May Delay Titan Sale*, The Wall Street Journal Online, February 17, 2004, accessed at http://online.wsj.com/PA2VJBNA4R/article/0,,SB107697880004530999-search,00.html.

19. Id.

20. Statement by Titan Spokesman Wil Williams, quoted in Karp, Jonathan, *SEC Probe May Delay Titan Sale*, The Wall Street Journal Online, February 17, 2004, accessed at http://online.wsj.com/PA2VJBNA4R/article/0,,SB107697880004530999-search,00.html.

Lockheed: "[W]e noticed that Titan had contracts in certain countries that have historically been associated with international consultant payment issues—unlawful payments."[21]

However, the precipitous timing of the joint disclosure suggests strongly that Lockheed had insisted on it for at least two reasons: (i) to avoid any appearance of impropriety by its personnel; and (ii) to ensure that if enforcement action did occur, it would be concluded prior the closing, thereby insulating Lockheed against successor liability. (Later disclosures revealed that Lockheed's due diligence had found potential bribe payments involving a Datron unit selling two-way radio systems for security forces.)[22] While the SEC did in fact launch an investigation in February 2004,[23] the companies expressed confidence that the deal would be successfully and timely completed.[24]

Both companies later provided the authorities with further information concerning possible improper payments identified by the due diligence, but continued to take the position publicly that it was unclear whether such remunerations were illegal. In early March of 2004, however, the Justice Department commenced an investigation.[25] Because Titan's shareholders were scheduled to vote on the transaction on March 16, 2004, the companies doubted whether they or the Justice Department could finish their respective investigations by the voting date. In response to this development, Lockheed released a statement that, if the investigations could not be completed, "Lockheed Martin will need to determine whether the conditions to the merger have been satisfied."[26]

On March 22, 2004, *The Wall Street Journal* reported that Titan's own investigation had found evidence of "millions in illegal pay-

21. Statement of Lockheed Spokesman, Tom Jurkowsky, quoted in Karp, Jonathan, *SEC Probe May Delay Titan Sale*, The Wall Street Journal Online, February 17, 2004, accessed at http://online.wsj.com/PA2VJBNA4R/article/0,,BT_CO_20040626_000170-search,00.html.

22. Karp, Jonathan, *Playing Defense: As Titan Mutates to Meet Needs of Pentagon, Risks Become Clear*, THE WALL STREET JOURNAL, June 28, 2004, p. A-1 at A7.

23. Id.

24. Karp, Jonathan, *Lockheed Says Probe Jeopardizes Takeover of Titan*, The Wall Street Journal Online, March 8, 2004, accessed at http://online.wsj.com/PA2VJBNA4R/article/0,,SB107868747819648509-search,00.html.

25. Id.

26. Karp, Jonathan, *Lockheed Says Probe Jeopardizes Takeover of Titan*, The Wall Street Online, Journal Online, March 8, 2004, accessed at http://online.wsj.com/PA2VJBNA4R/article/0,,SB107868747819648509-search,00.html.

ments."[27] At this point, the parties renegotiated the merger agreement, reducing the offering price, extending the closing date, and conditioning the closing on complete remediation:

- Lockheed's offer was reduced from $22 per share to $20 per share[28] (reducing the value of the deal from $2.4 billion to $2.2 billion);[29]
- The offer was restructured as an all cash transaction (no longer cash and stock);[30]
- The closing date was extended twice—from its original date of March 16, 2004[31] to April 20, 2004,[32] and then to June 25, 2004;[33]
- If the deal did not close by June 25, 2004, either Lockheed or Titan could end the pact unilaterally, provided that the party seeking to terminate the deal was not "then in material breach of its obligations in a manner that has contributed to the failure to complete the merger by that date;"[34]
- The closing conditions now included that Titan must obtain written confirmation that the "Justice Department considers its investigation of these allegations resolved and doesn't intend to pursue

---

27. Pasztor, Andy, and Karp, Jonathan, *Titan Foreign Payments Scrutinized*, THE WALL STREET JOURNAL, March 22, 2004, accessed at http://online.wsj.com/PA2VJBNA4R/article/0,,SB107991361923261391-search,00.html, and Forbes.com reported earlier that on March 5, 2004, Titan had admitted the payments were illegal. See Berman, Phyllis, *Will Lockheed Blink?*, Forbes.com, March 10, 2004, accessed at www.forbes.com/business/2004/03/10/cz_pb_0310titan.html.

28. Murphy, Tara, *Lockheed Won't Extend Titan Deadline*, Forbes.com, June 25, 2004, accessed at www.forbes.com/markets/2004/06/25/cx_tm_0625video1.html.

29. Souder, Elizabeth, *Titan: New Deal with Lockheed Makes Closing More Certain*, The Wall Street Journal Online, April 7, 2004, 10:37 a.m. .

30. Karp, Jonathan, and Pasztor, Andy, *Lockheed Trims Bid for Titan amid Bribery Inquiry*, The Wall Street Journal Online, April 8, 2004, accessed at http://online.wsj.com/PA2VJBNA4R/article/0,,SB108138112563377406-search,00.html.

31. Berman, Phyllis, *Will Lockheed Blink?*, Forbes.com, March 10, 2004, accessed at www.forbes.com/business/2004/03/10/cz_pb_0310titan.html.

32. Pasztor, Andy, and Karp, Jonathan, *Titan Foreign Payments Scrutinized*, March 22, 2004, THE WALL STREET JOURNAL accessed at http://online.wsj.com/PA2VJBNA4R/article/0,,SB107991361923261391-search,00.html.

33. Dow Jones Newswires, *Lockheed Lowers Offer to Buy Titan*, The Wall Street Journal Online, April 7, 2004, accessed at http://online.wsj.com/PA2VJBNA4R/article/0,,SB108134247816776597-search,00.html?collection = autowire%2Farchive&vql_string = lockheed + and + titan%3Cin%3E%28article%2Dbody%29.

34. Id.

any claims against Titan, or Titan must have entered into a plea agreement with the the [sic] Justice Department and completed the sentencing process."[35] In that event, Lockheed would not view the allegations and government proceedings (including costs and expenses) as having a material adverse effect on Titan[36] (apparently a condition that would entitle Lockheed to abandon the deal).

Titan released a statement expressing the view that, as renegotiated, "There's a higher certainty that the deal will close,"[37] and a Lockheed spokesman observed that the revised agreement "ensures that Titan will dispose of issues that occurred on its watch, before we close the transaction."[38] At this juncture, Lockheed was able to quantify its increased risk and to adjust the purchase price accordingly. However, the ongoing investigation uncovered additional improprieties that were not easily quantified, that were open-ended (in terms of potential liability), and that magnified Lockheed's risk substantially:

- In May of 2004, a U.S. Army investigation into abuse of prisoners at Abu Ghraib prison in Iraq "implicated a Titan [employed] translator, Egyptian-born Adel Nakhla" and a translator who worked for a Titan subcontractor. Such charges focused on Titan's largest single contract in 2003—the provision of translators for the U.S. Army (for which billings had amounted to $558 million).[39]
- Later, Titan agreed to reduce translator billings by $937,000 for "accounting deficiencies," and by $178,000 for the two translators implicated in the Army's investigation.[40]
- The translators' contracts were scheduled for renewal in July 2004, and were estimated to be worth $1.5 billion.[41]

35. Id.
36. Id.
37. Souder, Elizabeth, *Titan: New Deal with Lockheed Makes Closing More Certain*, The Wall Street Journal Online, April 7, 2004.
38. Karp, Jonathan, and Pasztor, Andy, *Lockheed Trims Bid for Titan amid Bribery Inquiry*, The Wall Street Journal Online, April 8, 2004, accessed at http://online.wsj.com/PA2VJBNA4R/article/0,,SB108138112563377406-search,00.html.
39. Karp, Jonathan, *Playing Defense: As Titan Mutates to Meet Needs of Pentagon, Risks Become Clear*, THE WALL STREET JOURNAL, June 28, 2004, p. A-1 at A7.
40. Id.
41. Id.

- Titan eventually disclosed that the alleged illegal payment practices extended beyond Datron's activities in Indonesia, and included Titan Secure Systems (for military communications work in Saudi Arabia) and Titan Wireless (for commercial telephone-network contracts in Benin).[42]

- Titan set aside $3 million (a remarkably small amount)[43] to pay potential penalties that might be imposed by the U.S. enforcement agencies, and commenced settlement talks with the Justice Department.[44]

- In early June 2004, the SEC surprised the market, however, by announcing that it would recommend civil enforcement action against Titan.[45]

- On June 7, 2004, Titan announced that its shareholders had approved the merger with Lockheed.[46]

- Both companies suggested that a settlement with the Justice Department would be forthcoming.[47]

- On June 24, 2004, Titan announced that it could not meet the amended merger agreement's June 25, 2004 deadline to conclude a plea agreement with the Justice Department.[48]

---

42. Id., and Karp, Jonathan, *Lockheed-Titan Deal Appears to Collapse as Deadline Looms*, THE WALL STREET JOURNAL, June 25, 2004, p. A-2.

43. The amount not only looks small in hindsight, it appeared so when disclosed. As one contemporaneous commentator observed: "We already know that Titan does not anticipate huge fines being levied upon it by either the DoJ or the SEC. The company has, after all, only set aside $3 million in anticipation of such fines. Yet Lockheed is decreasing its offer by not $3 million, but $150 million." Smith, Rich, *Lockheed's Titan Markdown*, TheMotleyFool.com, April 8, 2004, accessed at www.fool.com/News/mft/2004/mft04040807.htm.

44. Id.

45. Karp, Jonathan, *Titan Could Face SEC Legal Action in Bribery Probe*, The Wall Street Journal Online, June 7, 2004, accessed at http://online.wsj.com/PA2VJBNA4R/article/0,,SB108655597899713006-search,00.html.

46. Dow Jones Newswires, *Titan Stockholders OK Merger with Lockheed Martin*, June 7, 2004, accessed at http://online.wsj.com/article/0,,BT_CO_20040607_005045-search,00.html?collection=autowire%2F30day&vql_string=titan+and+lockheed%3Cin%3E%28article%2Dbody%29.

47. Karp, Jonathan, *Lockheed-Titan Deal Appears to Collapse as Deadline Looms*, THE WALL STREET JOURNAL, June 25, 2004, p. A-2.

48. Id.

• Titan requested another extension of the deadline but Lockheed declined, explaining that "We made every possible effort to make this happen, but it just reached a point where we didn't want the uncertainty surrounding this to continue indefinitely."[49]

The deadline expired. Lockheed abandoned the deal. Titan's stock dropped (from $18.24 at time of the announced collapse down to $12.84 a few days later,[50] and within two weeks had dropped 35% from its pre-announcement high).[51] Titan shareholders filed suit against Titan officers and directors, alleging that they had failed to disclose the results of internal investigations into potential FCPA violations and improper revenue inflation, causing Lockheed to walk away from the deal.[52]

Under the proposed settlement, the Justice Department required that Titan (or its subsidiaries) plead guilty to multiple felony counts and pay fines substantially in excess of the $3 million that Titan had earlier set aside. Charges against senior Titan officials were not included in the proposed settlement.[53] However, it is clear from the discrepancy (between what Titan set aside for fines and the amounts ultimately assessed in penalties) that it radically underestimated the gravity of the risks and the magnitude of its exposure. This failure to understand and

49. Statement by Lockheed spokesman, Tom Jurkowsky, quoted in *Lockheed Martin Terminates Merger Accord with Titan*, The Wall Street Journal Online, June 26, 2004, accessed at http://online.wsj.com/PA2VJBNA4R/article/0,,BT_CO_20040626_000170-search,00.html?collection = autowire%2Farchive&vql_string = lockheed + and + titan%3Cin%3E%28article%2Dbody%29.

50. The Titan Corp., stock quotation for close of business, July 2, 2004, FINANCIAL TIMES, accessed at http://mwprices.ft.com/custom/ft-com/quotechartnews.asp?osymb = &ocountrycode = &pageNum = &company = NEW&industry = &region = &extelID = &isin = &ftep = &sedol = &FTSite = FTCOM&symb = TTN&countrycode = &t = e& s1 = &s2 = &q = TTN.

51. Karp, Jonathan, *Titan Acts to Restore Confidence*, THE WALL STREET JOURNAL, July 9, 2004, p. A-3.

52. Brickley, Peg, *Holders Sue Titan Execs over Lockheed Deal Breakup*, The Wall Street Journal Online, July 1, 2004, accessed at http://online.wsj.com/article/0,,BT_CO_20040701_007973-search,00.html?collection = autowire%2F30day&vql_string = %27holders + sue + titan%27%3Cin%3E%28article%2Dbody%29.

53. To date there is no suggestion that Titan has the "public authority" defense available to it (described by a U.S. District Court as arising "when a defendant commits an illegal act in reasonable and sincere reliance on a statement or act of a government agent with actual legal authority to empower the commission of that illegal act. . . ."). See *United States v. James H. Griffen*, (S.D.N.Y. 2004), reprinted in NEW YORK LAW JOURNAL, July 12, 2004, p. 22.

appreciate the enforcement risks clearly contributed to the failure of the merger.

The FCPA is a well-known compliance obligation for corporations, and is particularly well known in the defense contract community. That Titan would have had three units in serious violation of the FCPA, suggests systemic failures in its compliance program. If Titan's senior officers did not know of the FCPA violations, when the merger agreement was signed in September of 2003, that would suggest systemic failures in its reporting system and internal auditing as well. Companies can experience good faith lapses in compliance, when their internal compliance programs are not periodically reviewed and up-dated to address the rapidly changing enforcement climate. The most troubling consequence of this, in Lockheed's deal, was the belated discovery of problems that neither time, expense nor determination could resolve before the proposed merger unraveled (in spite of the clear and substantial economic benefits for both parties, and the fact that both parties were committed to completion).

Without second guessing Lockheed's due diligence (which accomplished a key objective by finding, assessing and reporting the problems, and showed fortitude in reporting them promptly to the Justice Department and the SEC), it is reasonable to assume that earlier compliance review diligence would have offered the parties valuable alternatives that might have increased the chances for successful completion of the merger. Pre-signing diligence would have discovered the same problems and enabled the parties to postpone signing until the full scope of potential violations had been ascertained, the risks assessed and the necessary remediation completed (settlements with the Justice Department and the SEC).

Moreover, a delayed signing, under these circumstances, would have caused far less "turbulence" in the stock value (and market value) of both companies than that caused by repeatedly postponing the closing. Such turbulence in itself can destabilize a transaction, particularly where the consideration (or deal price) is partially in stock. Fluctuations in the stock price cause fluctuations in the deal price, changing the economics of the deal (particularly, as was the case here, where the stock being offered increases in value relative to the value of the stock being purchased) and threatening authorizations, if the transaction includes a "collar," or restrictions on the absolute movement of the stock price in either direction after announcement but before closing. Usually market movement beyond the accepted margin of risk will trigger "unwind" provisions, and will jeopardize the deal's successful completion even in the absence of a regulatory violation. Moreover, in this posture, Titan was forced to negotiate with the Justice Department with a gun to its head, when a successfully concluded plea agreement was added as a condition to Lockheed's closing. From Lockheed's perspective, it could have pursued other business opportunities in the interim, without tying up financial and legal resources for nine months while pursing incompatible objectives—attempting to determine if there were any further problems and attempting to reduce the uncertainty that any such discoveries would create. The failure of the Lockheed/Titan merger was, in all probability, a preventable one, and holds lessons for pre-signing diligence in the areas of trade sanctions, export controls, defense trade controls and data protection laws as well.

In hindsight, Titan's reserve of only $3 million for possible penalty payments reflected a remarkable misunderstanding of the gravitas of the offense, the enforcement environment and the Justice Department's (and other agencies') determination to impose fines of a magnitude that punish and deter (and cannot easily be absorbed as a mere cost of doing business). As confirmation, note that on July 6, 2004, a few days after the collapse of the Lockheed/Titan merger, two subsidiaries of ABB (a Swiss-Swedish engineering giant) pled guilty to charges of foreign bribery and agreed to pay fines in the amount of $10.5 million. The subsidiaries, Houston-based ABB Vetco Gray, and Scottish based ABB Vetco Gray UK, admitted to violating the FCPA. Concurrently, their parent, ABB, entered into a settlement agreement with the SEC on parallel bribery charges and paid $5.9 million. The SEC had charged that ABB's subsidiaries had paid $1.1 million in bribes to officials of the governments of Nigeria, Angola and Kazakhstan, respectively, between 1998 and 2003, to influence acts and decisions by such officials with the aim of obtaining and retaining business. The SEC alleged that management-level officials at the subsidiaries knew of and approved the illicit payments, that ABB improperly accounted for such payments, and that it lacked internal controls "to detect or prevent" such payments. As part of the settlement, ABB was not required to admit to wrong-doing. However, the *Financial Times* reported that counsel familiar with the FCPA concluded that "the total fines paid by ABB—$16.4m—were relatively high given the size of the alleged bribery, just over $1m."[54]

---

54. Catan, Thomas, *Illicit Payments: ABB Units Admit Foreign Bribe Charges*, Financial Times, July 7, 2004, p. 20.

Titan's actual exposure to penalties emerged more clearly on July 8, 2004 when it announced it would reserve "between $26 million and $32 million, in addition to $3 million previously set aside" for potential penalties from the bribery investigation by the Justice Department and SEC.[55] Potential penalties of such magnitude must be factored into the risk calculus, when counsel evaluates the risks of delayed due diligence.[56]

During the negotiation of the Lockheed/Titan transaction and subsequent enforcement action, Norway's major oil company encoun-

---

55. Karp, Jonathan, *Titan Acts to Restore Confidence*, THE WALL STREET JOURNAL, July 9, 2004, p. A-3, and Bowe, Christopher, *Titan to Post Loss in Second Quarter*, FINANCIAL TIMES, July 9, 2004, p. 20.

56. Note that a similar risk appears to cloud General Electric's attempted acquisition of InVision Technologies, a bomb detection and baggage screening equipment manufacturer. On July 29, 2004, InVision voluntary disclosed to the Justice Department and the SEC that it had been internally investigating "possible offers of improper payments by distributors in connection with foreign sales activities" (and thus possible violations of the Foreign Corrupt Practices Act). The merger agreement (under which GE has agreed to acquire InVision for $900 million) contains a provision that if, by October 31, 2004, all regulatory approvals have not been obtained, either party can terminate the agreement. InVision press releases, July 30, 2004, accessed at http://investor.invision-tech.com/ReleaseDetail.cfm?ReleaseID = 140716, and March 15, 2004, accessed at http://investor.invision-tech.com/ReleaseDetail.cfm?ReleaseID = 131195.

Note also that in early February 2004 reports emerged that the U.S. Treasury's Office of Foreign Assets Control had reopened an investigation into whether Halliburton contravened federal regulations by its dealings with Iran via a foreign subsidiary. See *US Treasury Asks Halliburton about Iran Dealings*, THE NEW ZEALAND HERALD, February 12, 2004. In mid-July of 2004, this investigation was elevated into a criminal investigation as a grand jury in the southern district of Text subpoenaed the company to present documents "related to a Cayman Islands subsidiary that serves the Iranian National Oil Company." Chaffin, Joshua, *Halliburton Admits to Criminal Probe*, FINANCIAL TIMES, July 21, 2004, p. 3. In addition, Halliburton has come under investigation for alleged improper payments of up to $180 million by one of its subsidiaries in Nigeria. See Catan, Thomas, *Illicit Payments: ABB Units Admit Foreign Bribe Charges*, FINANCIAL TIMES, July 7, 2004, p. 20. Later reports indicate the SEC is investigating TSKJ, a consortium jointly owned by Technip, Halliburton, and two other companies in connection with potential bribes paid to win a construction project contract in Nigeria. See Michael, Adrian, and Catan, Thomas, *SEC Investigates Halliburton's French Partner in Nigerian Deal*, FINANCIAL TIMES, July 9, 2004, p. 3.

As of this writing the Justice Department and the SEC have also launched investigations into possible violations by Lucent of the Foreign Corrupt Practices Act in connection with telecommunications contracts with the Government of Saudi Arabia. Rhoads, Christopher, *Lucent Faces Bribery Allegations In Giant Saudi Telecom Project*, THE WALL STREET JOURNAL, November 16, 2004, p. A-1.

tered comparable problems of illicit foreign payments with similarly adverse consequences.

Statoil ASA ("Statoil") is Norway's largest firm and the largest operator on the Norwegian continental shelf. In 2002, the Government of Norway owned 82% of Statoil's outstanding shares (but was under a parliamentary mandate to reduce state holdings to 66.6%).[57] Statoil's remaining shares are traded publicly on world exchanges, including the Oslo Stock Exchange and the New York Stock Exchange, and are therefore subject to the rules of those exchanges and to the relevant enforcement agencies (such as the SEC.) Although Norway is a major oil exporter, Statoil had pursued oil development contracts in Iran since 1999, and in 2002 won a contract to assist Iran in developing its offshore South Pars gas field.[58] Statoil was keenly interested in competing for a concession to develop Iran's largest oil field (the Azadergan Field). As a result of the failure of a Japanese consortium to reach agreement with Iranian authorities to develop the Azadergan Field, Iranian authorities invited other oil companies (including Statoil) to bid for the development contract. Statoil felt it needed assistance to compete effectively, and took actions that raised significant regulatory issues:

- In late 2002 or early 2003, Statoil entered into a consultancy agreement with a London-based firm (registered in the tax haven of Turks & Caicos), Horton Investments Ltd ("Horton" and the "Horton Agreement");
- The Horton Agreement's terms lacked the transparency required by Statoil's internal standards and contained several questionable features:
  - ➤ The "benefits" provided by Horton to Statoil were not spelled out explicitly but included "consultancy services" for a term of 11 years;
  - ➤ The price for such unspecified benefits was substantial (and later deemed excessive)—USD 15.2 m;

---

57. George, Nicholas, *Norway Raises Nkr8bn from Statoil Stake*, FINANCIAL TIMES, July 8, 2004, p. 16.

58. *Oil & Gas: Statoil Lost out on Iraq* [sic] *Engagement*, THE NORWAY MAIL, February 19, 2004, accessed at www.norwaypost.no/content.asp?folder_id = 6&cluster_ id = 24616. Note that the article title should read "Iran," not "Iraq."

> ➤ Horton's services would be tendered in connection with Statoil's pursuit of petroleum contracts with the Government of Iran;[59]

> ➤ Payment was heavily front-loaded—before the end of the first year, Statoil would pay USD 5 m;

> ➤ Payments were not to be made to Horton, however, but to a different company, in a different country (Dillinger Company Finance Inc.) via a Swiss bank account;

> ➤ One Horton official, an Iranian national, was simultaneously employed by a subsidiary of the National Iranian Oil Company;

> ➤ The complicated financial dealings also involved Mehdi Hashemi Rafsanjani, son of the former Iranian president Ali Akbar Rafsanjani;[60]

> ➤ As Norwegian government enforcement officials later explained, the deal was "'in reality, an offer of excessive incentives' so that 'Rafsanjani Junior and others' would exert their influence in Statoil's favour;"[61]

> ➤ Statoil's Chief Executive Officer, Olav Fjell, approved the Horton Agreement, but did not disclose it to other senior management at the company.[62]

• Receipt of an invoice from Horton in March 2003 triggered an internal audit at Statoil.

• The internal auditors submitted a report to senior management (including Statoil's Chairman Leif Terje Loedessoel) criticizing the payments under the Horton Agreement and recommending its termination. Statoil's Chairman allegedly rejected the auditor's report,[63] and its CEO decided instead to change the payment procedure.

---

59. Økokrim, *Penalty Notices in the Statoil Case*, June 29, 2004, accessed at www.okokrim.no.

60. *Scandal Puts Top Statoil Jobs on the Line*, AFTENPOSTEN, September 15, 2003, accessed at www.aftenposten.no/english/business/article625641.ece.

61. *Ex-Statoil Bosses Escape Indictment*, AFTENPOSTEN, June 29, 2004, accessed at www.aftenposten.no/english/business/article819219.ece.

62. Id.

63. *Scandal Puts Top Statoil Jobs on the Line*, AFTENPOSTEN, September 15, 2003, accessed at www.aftenposten.no/english/business/article625641.ece.

- Senior management was by then aware of the Horton Agreement. When a new anti-corruption law came into force on July 4, 2003, Statoil management continued the Horton Agreement, but did not disclose it publicly.

- In early September of 2003, the Norwegian financial daily, *Dagens Naeringsliv*, published a report that Statoil had paid millions of U.S. dollars in "consulting fees" into a Swiss bank account controlled by Horton to influence Iranian oil officials.[64]

- The *Dagens Naeringsliv* report of the Horton Agreement and its terms drew widespread attention, and further reports quickly followed in other Norwegian publications.

- Statoil terminated the Horton Agreement on September 10, 2003 "following exposure by the newspaper *Dagens Naeringsliv*."[65] The same day, the Økokrim (Norwegian National Authority for Investigation and Prosecution of Economic and Environmental Crime)[66] launched an investigation (on its own initiative, but expressly "based on" the articles in *Dagens Naeringsliv*),[67] raided Statoil's offices and seized the relevant documents.

---

64. Id.

65. Id.

66. The Økokrim, established in 1989, is a special unit for white-collar crime. It is both a national police unit and a prosecution authority, as explained at www. okokrim.no. When Statoil ASA signed a consultancy agreement with a foreign consultant company, the Økokrim's Corruption Team initiated an investigation that led to Statoil being formally charged with violation of the Norwegian General Civil Penal Code provision concerning illegal influencing of foreign government officials. See Økokrim *Press Release: Investigation of Statoil ASA*, September 12, 2003, accessed at www. okokrim.no/aktuelt_arkiv/pressemeldinger/eng.pm_Statoil_120903.pdf.

The Økokrim investigates, among other violations, money laundering, stock market and securities violations, environmental, computer crimes (such as hacking), and information handling offenses. It was the Økokrim that investigated and prosecuted 19-year-old Jon Lech Johansen, for copyright violation in reverse engineering a bypass of DVD DeCSS code protection. See *"DVD-Jon" Faces Retrial,* Aftenposten, January 20, 2003, accessed at www.aftenposten.no/english/local/article474756.ece. Its scope includes cooperating with anti-terrorism efforts, as occurred when the U.S. government accused Mullah Krekar of planning terror actions (suicide missions) by signals distributed on the Internet—as a result of which, the Økokrim confiscated large amounts of recordings of Mullah Krekar's activity on the Internet. See *CIA Misinformed about Ansar*, Nettavisen, January 8, 2004, accessed at http://pub.tv2.no/nettavisen/english/article170292.ece.

67. Økokrim, *Penalty Notices in the Statoil Case*, June 29, 2004, accessed at www.okokrim.no/.

- The public protests prompted a meeting of the Board of Directors on September 15, 2003, which criticized the CEO for his weak evaluation of the Horton Agreement, but both the CEO and the Chairman were allowed to remain in office.

- Norway's Oil & Energy Minister (who officially represented the state's 82% stake in Statoil) was criticized for not taking action on the initial reports of the Horton Agreement.[68]

- As more information about the arrangement appeared in the media, Board members convened a second meeting, on September 22, 2003, and determined that the CEO should resign. The Chairman was forced to resign later.[69]

- The Økokrim conducted an extensive investigation (from September 2003 through June 2004), including unannounced searches for documents in Statoil's offices, the taking of statements from 50 individuals, and review of "a considerable number of documents, especially documents in electronic format."[70]

- In the fall of 2003, the SEC launched its own investigation of Statoil's conduct under the Horton Agreement.

- In February 2004, before the Økokrim completed its investigation, the Iranian government signed a $2 billion contract with a Japanese consortium regarding the Azadergan Field.[71]

- Statoil belatedly engaged outside auditors and counsel to conduct an internal investigation.[72]

---

68. *Cabinet Minister Backs Statoil Bosses,* Aftenposten, September 16, 2003, accessed at www.aftenposten.no/english/business/article626483.ece.

69. *Statoil Scandal: Company Says Internal Audit Unit Ignored,* Morningstar.com, October 31, 2003, accessed at http://64.233.161.104/search?q=cache:gYai4eKxYGQJ:news.morningstar.com/news/DJ/M10/D31/1067616662866.html+morningstar+and+%22statoil+scandal%22&hl=en.

70. Økokrim, *Penalty Notices in the Statoil Case,* June 29, 2004, accessed at www.okokrim.no. (Note: under Økokrim's procedures, there is no administrative hearing prior to a determination of culpability and imposition of a fine or recommendation of criminal proceedings.)

71. *Oil & Gas: Statoil Lost out on Iraq* [sic] *Engagement,* The Norway Post, February 19, 2004, accessed at www.norwaypost.no/content.asp?folder_id=6&cluster_id=24616. Note that the article title should read "Iran," not "Iraq."

72. *Statoil Clears Itself of Corruption,* Aftenposten, June 18, 2004, accessed at www.aftenposten.no/english/business/article812642.ece.

- Counsel concluded in mid-June of 2004 that there were violations of Statoil's code of ethics but no wrong-doing.
- Counsel based its reasoning in part on the fact that the younger Rafsanjani did not have the power to influence Iranian oil contract awards and that no evidence of any effort to do so had been found. He concluded from this that the Horton Agreement did not violate the applicable Norwegian law, before or after July 4, 2003, and that there was no basis for criminal liability on the part of the company or any of its officers.
- Counsel acknowledged that the Horton Agreement violated Statoil's rules of ethics and of transparency, because it did not mention Rafsanjani's name. Horton was registered in an overseas tax haven, and thus Statoil had "little idea of who it was dealing with."[73] This conclusion, however, omits to address the underlying issue of why Statoil was willing to commit such a substantial sum (USD 15.2 m) for unspecified services. Statoil immediately released the findings of the report to the press.[74]
- On June 29, 2004, the Økokrim published its own findings to the contrary, fined Statoil 20 m NKr (USD 2.9 m) and the former head of Statoil's international division 200,000 Nkr (USD $29,400).[75]
- The Økokrim added this clarification: "There is reason to stress that the investigation has not provided a basis for concluding that there was in fact any influencing of decision-making processes on the Iranian side. *Nor do any of the relevant anti-corruption provisions require this to be the case.*"[76]

The Økokrim analyzed the case from two perspectives: potential violations under the pre-July 4, 2003 law, and under the post-July 4, 2003 law. The prior law, Section 128 of the Norwegian Penal Code, made it a punishable offense for any person who

"by granting or promising a favour seeks to **induce** a public servant illegally to perform or omit to perform an official act. . . . "[77]

---

73. Id.
74. Id.
75. *Statoil Wants More Time to Weigh Appeal*, AFTENPOSTEN, June 30, 2004, accessed at www.aftenposten.no/english/business/article820168.ece.
76. Økokrim, *Penalty Notices in the Statoil Case*, June 29, 2004, accessed at www.okokrim.no/.
77. Id. [Emphasis added]

There were three post-July 4, 2003 provisions that replaced existing provisions: Section 276(a) of the Penal Code (corruption), Section 276(b) (serious corruption) and Section 276(c) (trading in influence). These three sections combined have a broader scope and a lower threshold for commission of the predicate offense than those contained in the prior law. Section 276(a) makes it a punishable offense for any person who:

"confers on or offers another person an improper advantage **in connection with** a post, office or commission."[78]

And Section 276(c) makes it a punishable offense for any person who:

"confers on or offers another person an improper advantage **in return for influencing the performance** of a post, office or commission."[79]

These provisions apply to a "post, office or commission" in a foreign country, and apply to corruption both in the private and public sectors. The Økokrim found no violation of the pre-July 4, 2003 laws or of Section 276(a) (which came into force on July 4, 2003); but it did find that Statoil had violated Section 276(c) by not terminating the Horton Agreement before that section came into force on July 4, 2003. It concluded that the Horton Agreement actually involved an offer of improper advantages to Iranian officials (Mehdi Hashemi and/or others) who "were or would be involved in decision-making processes relevant to Statoil's commercial activity in Iran, including administrative acts concerning the award of contracts in the oil and gas sector."[80] Failure to terminate constituted a criminal violation. The Økokrim found the former Director of Statoil's International Department liable for having failed to arrange for termination of the Horton Agreement "as soon as possible after 4 July 2003," and found the company liable "as represented by the Chairman of the Board."[81]

In retrospect, the behavior of Statoil and its management suggests that it believed that the following risks (posed by this course of conduct) were acceptable in the context of the potential benefits to be derived:

78. Id. [Emphasis added]
79. Id. [Emphasis added]
80. Id.
81. Id.

- Disclosure of the Horton Agreement (with its implicit linkages to Iranian oil officials and the pending award of a major development contract) would clearly provoke Iranian officials;
- Whatever benefits Statoil thought to obtain from its substantial payments under the Horton Agreement, the confidentiality of such payments/benefits was at best uncertain, and once disclosed would certainly draw negative media attention;
- A controlled disclosure by Statoil of the Horton Agreement would undermine Statoil's efforts to win the Azadergan Field contract, but an uncontrolled disclosure by the media of a surreptitious attempt to influence the award of the concession would in all probability ruin Statoil's bid for the lucrative contract;
- Statoil's Chairman and CEO, having rejected the internal auditors criticism, would be vulnerable, if the Økokrim investigation concluded that the Horton Agreement violated Norway's new anti-corruption law;
- Statoil's Board, by initially taking no action, took the risk that the company's reputation and business prospects would be best protected by "not rocking the boat," a decision that the Board soon reversed, compounding Statoil's public relations debacle;
- The ambiguous purpose of the belated (and redundant) internal investigation could only further tarnish the company's public image;
- If the internal investigation concluded that violations of Norwegian law had occurred, it is doubtful that Statoil would have published such findings; it is reasonable to infer therefore that Statoil hoped that an exonerating report could be published and might indirectly affect the Økokrim's deliberations or might position Statoil to appeal any adverse findings by the Økokrim.

This last point is crucial, because failure to appeal would be viewed as a tacit admission of guilt, and would probably lead to a more substantial fine by the SEC. At this time (September, 2004), Statoil has until October 18, 2004 to consider whether it will appeal those penalties.[82]

---

82. In the meantime, US regulators continue to investigate Statoil. See Boxell, James, *Chief keeps Statoil's strategy*, FINANCIAL TIMES, September 27, 2004, p. 18.

Statoil's failure to understand the scope of the applicable Norwegian law ultimately cost the company the resignations of two senior officers, the loss of a USD 2 billion contract, fines of $2.9 million, exposure to further fines by the SEC, nine months of adverse publicity, and losses comparable to those suffered by Lockheed and Titan in their failed merger. Statoil's most significant loss, however, was the loss of an important business opportunity (the Iranian concession) and not a drop in its stock price (like that suffered by Titan). Statoil's share price, in fact, reached an all-time high of Nkr 91 in April 2004, and the Norwegian government sold 100 million of its shares in July 2004 at Nkr 84.30 to Lehman Brothers.[83]

Statoil's problems, and those of Lockheed/Titan, were largely avoidable, but only with a culture of rigorous compliance and early, enhanced due diligence. In light of this and similar experiences, we would encourage the early deployment of transactional checkpoints and their rigorous enforcement to enable counsel and companies to detect such problems, and to help their officers to recognize that more often than not the risks of deferred compliance are outweighed by the benefits of prompt remediation. This will help to avoid the loss of business opportunities and destruction of "good will" (in the form of share value) that occurred in the Lockheed/Titan and Statoil debacles. Our concern in this book is not with the FCPA (or the comparable Norwegian anti-corruption statutes), which seldom involve *inadvertent* violations, but rather with those laws and regulations that are not easily summarized, that change frequently (creating moving compliance and enforcement targets), that apply redundantly and unexpectedly to cross-border transactions, that often impose strict liability and that are enforced aggressively (particularly since 9/11). The enforcement and compliance contexts are further complicated by the fact that these laws and regulations apply as well to the new trade routes of cyberspace, and thus present challenges by virtue of the rapid changes in cyberspace and communications technologies. Businesses are continuously adjusting to such changes, developing customs and practices that can capitalize on opportunities while minimizing risks. By contrast, the law tends to lag behind in adjusting to such changes, and imposes rules that often do not adequately reflect or accommodate business realities. The efficiencies of the electronic medium often obscure risks of noncompliance

---

83. George, Nicholas, *Norway Raises Nkr8bn from Statoil Stake*, FINANCIAL TIMES, July 8, 2004, p. 16.

that are more easily discerned in face-to-face communications and negotiations. They also obscure the ease with which company personnel can transmit volumes of sensitive technical data with a mouse click, and thereby commit multiple violations of applicable export, reexport and trade sanction regulations.

Transactional checkpoints are not a new concept, but we think the traditional placement of checkpoints, and the compliance concerns that have historically been their focus, need substantial improvement in the context of cross-border transactions in cyberspace. By properly managing such checkpoints, parties conducting transactions through cyberspace, or in reliance on communications and negotiations transmitted through cyberspace, will have greater certainty, and will be able to manage and quantify their risks more effectively. As defense industry commentators have cautioned:

> "A company's export compliance responsibilities span the entire life cycle of a merger, acquisition or divestiture and impact a company's obligations long after the transaction closes. From the time that a potential transaction is first suggested, through the finalization of post-closing documents by the attorneys, companies need to recognize that each phase of activity is accompanied by specific responsibilities. . . . The complexity of today's business environment and the creativity applied to structuring mergers, acquisitions and divestitures, *counsels strongly that companies include export reviews and regulatory analyses as early in the process as possible.* . . . Because companies maintain the flexibility to negotiate acceptance of certain liabilities and responsibilities, ensuring that an entity fully understands those obligations is key to avoiding surprises and the need to devote extraordinary resources to clean up post-closing violations."[84]

To illustrate such concealed risks, this book's opening chapter surveys the potential legal exposure of parties to cross-border transactions conducted in cyberspace. It analogizes cyberspace to a trade route, and maps the legal risk points for parties seeking to use cyberspace to facilitate the completion of their transactions.

We have selected for detailed examination those bodies of law and regulations that meet one or more of the following criteria: their con-

---

84. Society for International Affairs, Mergers, Acquisitions & Divestitures, *Guidance and Advice for Defense Trade Export and Legal Professionals*, 2003, p. 49.

travention results in strict liability; they impose severe penalties that can include substantial prison terms for officers and directors who knowingly participate in violations; and customary business practices (such as indemnification) provide inadequate protection for the firm and its officers. In this context, solutions like indemnification can be used to argue or demonstrate that the parties were aware that the risk of violation was not remote and thus to establish that the violation in question was intentional or willful. We have also chosen laws that are changing rapidly as a direct result of technological developments in cyberspace. As technological advances make circumvention of certain laws easier, those laws are being amended and/or supplemented, with the result that well-intending transactors are at greater risk of inadvertent yet serious violations. Applying those criteria, the following bodies of law deserve particular attention:

(i) U.S. export controls (the Export Administration Regulations or "EAR");[85]

(ii) U.S. trade sanctions (the various trade sanction regulations or "TSR");[86]

(iii) U.S. defense trade controls (the International Traffic in Arms Regulations or "ITAR");[87]

(iv) Personal data protection and privacy laws (in The Netherlands, Norway, Canada, and Japan);[88]

(v) Information security laws (expressed or implied in the EAR, TSR, ITAR and personal data protection and privacy laws);[89] and

(vi) U.S. patent laws.[90]

Because of its potential impact on foreign acquisitions of U.S. high tech firms, we have also included the hidden risks posed by the Exon-Florio Amendment,[91] particularly in light of the fact that executives abroad may not be aware that an Exon-Florio review can result in an Executive Order requiring the post-signing or post-closing unwinding of an acquisition.

---

85. Discussed in Chapter 2.
86. Discussed in Chapter 3.
87. Discussed in Chapter 4.
88. Discussed in Chapter 5.
89. Discussed in Chapter 6.
90. Discussed in Chapter 7.
91. Discussed in Chapter 4 (Subchapter 4.6).

All such laws involve control of access to valuable assets, technologies, information or resources. Export and defense trade regulations deny adversaries access to items, technologies and data that could be used to harm the national security of the United States and its allies. Trade sanction regulations deny adversaries access to the economic benefits of transacting business with U.S. persons. Personal data protection laws seek, in part, to deny unauthorized persons access to such data. Information security laws similarly seek to deny unauthorized persons (and malicious code packages) access to systems and data that could be compromised, altered, damaged or destroyed thereby. And finally, patent laws grant a monopoly on the use of the inventions they cover (allowing the inventor to refuse to commercialize the patented invention), and thereby deny competitors access to use of the invention for the term of the patent. For convenience, we refer to these laws collectively as "Access Control Laws."

To facilitate an appreciation of specific risks, we have explored the problems of compliance posed by the Access Control Laws in the context of a hypothetical acquisition of Troll (a Norwegian defense contractor) by Agile-Wing (a U.S. defense firm). While no transaction will have the Job-like panoply of problems that arises from our hypothetical, we have used it throughout in creating a uniform fact pattern. (We have similarly focused on compliance problems from which there is no relief in available exceptions to the EAR and TSR.) By noting the consequences to the transaction of belated discovery of compliance problems, we hope to make the case for enhanced due diligence and the deployment of rigorous checkpoints that will enable parties to detect and remedy early the problems that can arise from non-compliance with the Access Control Laws. It is important to understand from the onset that these areas of the law are *not checklist law*, and should not be approached that way.

Investment in rigorous checkpoints and on-going internal review helps to remove such legal impediments before they can delay or disrupt transactions or put transactors at risk of personal liability. The budget for such investment should include funding for periodic internal audits and annual training of senior management to ensure that compliance efforts are updated on an on-going basis.

We invite readers to use this book to develop compliance solutions that will enable their companies or clients to achieve their transactional goals.

Roland L. Trope
Gregory E. Upchurch

CHAPTER **1**

The Case for Mapping Risk Points and Deploying of Checkpoints

1.0 Trade Route of Cyberspace.

Trade routes have historically developed to cope with distance. They enable parties to conduct economic transactions over great distances, and help to reduce risks and impediments to those who transact business through them. Cyberspace is a kind of trade route. Like the Silk Road before it, it serves to draw transactors into markets, transactions and relationships.[1] It can expose those who transact on it to risks that, if not removed or removed only at great cost, can jeopardize the successful completion of transactions. Often such risks go unnoticed, unappreciated or unreported. When the unforeseen risks do surface, they

---

1. The Silk Road (a term coined in the 19th century) refers to an exchange of products that occurred along it from the 2nd century B.C.E. through the 14th century C.E. (See Kennedy, Richard, *The Silk Road: Connecting Cultures, Creating Trust* accessible at www.silkroadproject.org/smithsonian/*program/default.htm*.) The Silk Road was not a single route but several multi-branched routes linking Japan, China, and Europe—and thus the cities of Nara, Xi'an, Samarkand, Constantinople, and Venice. Caravans carried precious commodities in both directions. Barter—one good exchanged for another—occurred along the way, as did plunder since caravans, no less than cyberspace, attracted those seeking to take what others did not adequately police and protect. Also not unlike cyberspace, thoughts, ideas, and beliefs may have been the most significant commodity, as Buddhism reportedly came from India to China along that trade route. See Wild, Oliver, *The Silk Road* 1992, accessible at www.ess.uci.edu/~oliver/silk.html. See also *The Silk Road Connecting Cultures, Creating Trust*, 36th Annual Smithsonian Folklife Festival, June–July 2002, accessible at www.silkroadproject.org/smithsonian.

1

usually do so by virtue of the question: will the transaction imperil the transactors? The question can cause a transaction to stall before take-off. Our focus in this book will be on certain risks presented by the cyberspace trade route: contraventions of the Access Control Laws.

To explore these risks we need a venturer, a Marco Polo, who will report such risks and some ways to leverage the lessons learned.[2] As our venturer, we have taken Agile-Wing LLP ("Agile"), a hypothetical company engaged in aerospace acquisitions. Agile participates in cyberspace transactions from its website, and engages in robust cyber-driven transactions (*i.e.,* those that use exchanges of e-mail and attachments as substitutes for face-to-face negotiations, on-site visits and in person "due diligence"). After introducing Agile and its most recent contemplated acquisition, we will explore the need for increased use of transactional checkpoints to avert the risks of violating the Access Control Laws. We will then consider the concealed risks that Agile initially failed to discern which, without timely remediation, would have threatened to trigger federal investigations and substantial monetary penalties.[3]

---

2. As trade routes evolve they confer advantages on entities that can position themselves to control access, portals, gateways, and other chokepoints along the routes. For example, if the flow of goods must pass through a narrow channel, well-positioned parties and entities can apply pressure and turn the passageway into a potential chokepoint. As a result, traders may have to sacrifice goods or funds to pass through or proceed. A gateway city like Petra (and some Nabatean ports) took advantage of its position on the trade route for frankincense and myrrh and allowed traders to pass only upon payment of a substantial tax (sometimes up to 25% of the value of their goods). A similar development may be occurring in the competition for strategic position at the portals or gateways to cyberspace (among ISPs and, more recently, among search engines and telecommunications carriers).

It should be remembered, however, that the strategic position on a trade route depends on the commercial need for the route (which may decline if demand for, and trade in, the goods declines) and on the emergence of technologies that make other routes more competitive. Thus Petra's advantages declined when the demand for frankincense and myrrh subsided and when improvements in nautical technology opened new sea routes and made the overland routes and camel caravans of the Arabian Peninsula through Petra obsolete. Its people failed to find a way to replenish their lost advantages. We may be seeing a similar cycle in cyberspace as firms invest billions in broadband routes, bandwidth dependent technologies, and Voice-over-Internet-Protocol (VoIP) to position themselves for the expansion of cyberspace through such routes, which may cause the decline in the advantages enjoyed by firms controlling established landline telephones connections.

3. Although regulatory approval remains a major risk in cross-border transactions, particularly if transactors in one jurisdiction underestimate or mishandle objections of

Fortunately, Agile learned of such problems before federal action would have been warranted; however, the issue of remediating such problems mid-course on the cyberspace trade route presents its own unique challenges.

1.1 Premise—The Need for Increased Use of Transactional Checkpoints When Dealing Through the Cyberspace Trade Route.

There is an emerging need for companies that transact in cyber-space,[4] or that engage in cyber-driven transactions,[5] to improve their policies and procedures for determining whether such transactions will bring the company and its management[6] into contraventions of Access Control Laws. Foremost among such improvements should be judicious use of the increasingly available technologies that enable transactors to know who they are dealing with in connection with the cyberspace trade route. Such knowledge would include whether the person (individual or entity), and the country that person logs on from, are targeted by the TSR, EAR or ITAR. In such cases, U.S. persons would be prohibited from transacting business with them under the express terms of such Access Control Laws. We can anticipate that the recent trend of tightened enforcement of the TSR and EAR will in all likelihood continue. Such trend toward heightened scrutiny and enforcement is exemplified by the Bureau of Industry and Security's ("BIS") heightened scrutiny of applications for export licenses, and its recent efforts to impose successor liability for violations of the EAR.[7]

---

authorities in another jurisdiction, our hypothetical transaction addresses risks that arise before customary requests for regulatory approval are submitted. These risks cannot be comprehensively addressed by applying for licenses (which require disclosures firms often do not wish to risk, a process that can be cumbersome, and timing that may not fit the expeditious needs of doing a deal). Notice of enforcement action may unfortunately be the first word the transactors receive of overlooked or unreported risks.

4. By sales or leases from company website, supply-chain websites, or auction sites.

5. By mergers, acquisitions, outsourcings, joint ventures, long-term supply agreement.

6. The term "management" will be used to refer to officers, directors, partners, and other persons in positions of authority in the company.

7. On tightened enforcement, consider the remarks of the Under Secretary of Commerce, BIS: "We have an independent responsibility to protect the national security of the United States. And since September 11, everyone in the government has been more

In addition, the federal government has begun to abandon its assumptions that website transactions are opaque, that website customers are anonymous, and that website owners and operators do not have meaningful access to information regarding their customers. These assumptions, derived from the early days of cyberspace, have historically had the effect of equating a website purchase with a purchase at a McDonald's drive-up window: a single point transaction, with an anonymous purchaser. Such a transactional paradigm, however, is not one that the Treasury Department's Office of Foreign Assets Control ("OFAC") deems relevant or appropriate for enforcement purposes under the TSR.[8] The paradigm that OFAC employs is closer to the negotiated model that is operative when a U.S. firm seeks to acquire an overseas company. In the latter instance, the TSR clearly require the acquirer to ascertain that it is not acquiring interests in property owned by a sanctioned party, or transacting with such a party (or anyone working on its behalf). "Due diligence"[9] investigations provide adequate op-

---

highly focused on ways to increase the security of our country. This heightened attention to security issues has some consequences. Export license applications are receiving a higher level of scrutiny by agencies to make sure that we are not approving items or technologies that could be used against our armed forces, or that could be diverted for use in proliferation activities." Juster, Kenneth I., *Keynote Address at the Update 2002 Export Controls and Policy Conference*, October 10, 2002, accessible at www.bxa.doc.gov/news/2002/ken2u@update02.htm. On BIS efforts to impose successor liability, see discussion in Section 1.1.

8. Although counsel and commentators sometime refer to the "McDonalds exception" to the TSR, the expression is potentially quite misleading. Apart from the fact that it does not derive from any known or alleged violation by the McDonalds corporation, it is not an exception but a point on a continuum of likely enforcement action. It should be remembered that OFAC may take enforcement action for something seemingly small to the offender (e.g., accepting goods or services in Cuba *without* paying for them or an offer of products over the Internet to a TSR-targeted country), or it may take action against substantial transactions that would seek to include transfers of property blocked under the TSR. Note that OFAC has come to the position "that even a person who accepts good or services in Cuba without paying for them is in fact engaging in a prohibited dealing in property in which Cuba or a Cuban national has an interest." OFAC, *Recent OFAC Actions*, June 16, 2004, accessed at www.ustreas.gov/offices/eotffc/ofac/actions/20040616.html.

Similarly, the BIS has announced a rule that limits the delivery of gift parcels to Cuba containing items other than food to "once per month per household" instead of the former rule of once per month per recipient (and defines "household" for purposes of such parcels as "all individuals living in common at a unique address" and restricting "recipient" to "grandparent, grandchild, parent, sibling, spouse, or child of the donor"). 69 FEDERAL REGISTER 119, June 22, 2004, at pp. 34565–34567.

9. We use the term "due diligence" to refer to the investigation of one party to a

portunity to gain the information needed to comply with the TSR. And the acquiring party would not consider trying to hide behind the "opaqueness" of country borders. Increasingly, it can no longer hide behind the presumed opacity of cyber borders either.

Although the TSR, in fact, prohibit McDonalds (like any other U.S. person) from dealing with any sanctioned person, the prohibition will not be enforced—unless McDonalds had a *reason to know* that its customer was an OFAC sanctioned person.[10] It cannot know this from the order or from the cash payment. As it turns out, OFAC targets funds more than goods, on the assumption that no goods can flow without funds. Interdicting fast food sales will not disrupt a terrorist group. Blocking terrorists' access to funds, by contrast, is potentially quite disruptive (if comprehensive and well coordinated).

Section 312 of the USA Patriot Act reinforces OFAC's strategy, by requiring "enhanced due diligence" on the part of financial institutions in connection with private banking and correspondent bank accounts. Section 312 states, in pertinent part:

> "Each financial institution that establishes, maintains, administers, or manages a private banking account or a correspondent account in the United States for a non-United States person, including a foreign individual visiting the United States, or a representative of a non-United States person shall establish appropriate, specific, and, where necessary, *enhanced, due diligence* policies, procedures, and controls that are reasonably designed to detect and report instances of money laundering through those accounts."[11]

Thus, on a continuum of OFAC's enforcement priorities, those who should be most concerned to avoid violating the TSR are those engaged in activities that potentially provide the greatest financial benefit to sanctioned persons, and those who have the greatest opportunities to check thoroughly the identity and business relationships of the other

---

transaction by another, with the aim being to verify facts in order to determine if representations and warranties the investigated party makes are accurate and to otherwise know the background and business relationships of that party.

10. Although it would not be a good allocation of OFAC's limited resources to enforce such violations, the fact that OFAC's published civil settlements reveal penalties as low as $2,500 should dispel any suggestion that there is a *de minimis* threshold amount below which a U.S. person can violate the TSR.

11. Uniting And Strengthening America By Providing Appropriate tools Required to Intercept And Obstruct Terrorism (USA Patriot Act) Act of 2001, Public Law 107–56. [Emphasis added.]

parties to a proposed transaction. On that continuum, cyberspace trans-actions have historically tended to be viewed as more analogous to the domestic fast-food sale than to the cross-border transaction involving significant financial transfers. We believe, however, that OFAC will ad-just its enforcement policies in light of the following:

(i) Emerging and available technologies that make it increasingly possible and cost-efficient for website owners to "know" im-portant and relevant information about their customers and to apply "enhanced due diligence" procedures at the appropriate checkpoints;[12]

(ii) The increasing value and usefulness to sanctioned persons of the goods they can procure in cyberspace transactions;

(iii) The fact that the anonymity of cash transactions is not dupli-cated in cyberspace (credit card transactions give the vendor access to the customer's identity and to service providers who have considerable customer information); and

(iv) The fact that, as pressure to protect homeland security in-creases, website operators can use interdiction software to deny access to a transaction by sanctioned customers in the same manner that financial institutions can interdict prohibited deal-ings when they process fund transfer requests.

To achieve their purpose, however, checkpoints must offer transac-tional efficiencies and benefits that offset the costs of deploying and enforcing them. Just as a fishnet's meshes are designed to capture spe-cific targeted items and to permit passage of everything else, becoming chokepoints only for what the user seeks to control, so border-crossing enforcement controls on the cyberspace trade route need to be cali-brated accordingly. Our proposal does not mean that every transactional checkpoint will necessarily become a transactional chokepoint. The Ac-cess Control Laws already require extensive compliance, yet transactions flow smoothly if compliance is anticipated and built into the structure of doing business. With technologies increasingly available to operate

---

12. Enhanced due diligence for firms engaged in cyberspace transactions would not have the background information that financial institutions are required to obtain before opening accounts. However, enough information is increasingly available for a seller in cyberspace to conduct a cost-effective and properly calibrated enhanced due diligence to ensure compliance with the EAR, TSR, and ITAR.

checkpoints, it is highly probable that commercial companies will be required to adopt enhanced due diligence in the near future. The software that facilitates this will make compliance increasingly cost-effective and efficient. Our focus should therefore be on what causes otherwise effective checkpoints to fail. Those failures, and their consequences, become the true chokepoints in cross-border transactions, and the costs related to them justify the increased scrutiny along the cyberspace trade route.

Although not all goods sold on the cyberspace trade route deserve equal attention, the TSR apply to all such transactions (even seemingly *de minimis* transactions), particularly now that technology (software code) puts cyberspace vendors in the position to have *reason to know* whether they are dealing with parties and projects sanctioned by the TSR, EAR or ITAR. The TSR prohibit U.S. persons from dealing with (or transferring property or interests in property belonging to) any sanctioned party—a prohibition that applies:

(a) To U.S. persons, wherever located, and

(b) To any such property or interests in such property in the possession or control of U.S. persons or that thereafter comes into their possession or control.

Auction sites, for example, are markets in cyberspace where sanctioned parties can earn considerable sums. It seems highly improbable that OFAC will overlook such opportunities, now that the auction site operators have available the technologies to ensure compliance with the TSR. Judicial decisions have begun to take account of the availability of such technology, and federal enforcement agencies can reasonably be expected to rule in accordance with such judicial notice of such technology. In light of this, an adjustment of OFAC's enforcement priorities seems probable.

For firms engaged in cyberspace transactions, improved compliance and anticipatory review of the requirements of the Access Control Laws should start with implementation of "enhanced diligence" checks, performed virtually in real-time, to determine whether the customer placing an order, agreeing to a license or submitting a bid (or that customer's organization, home country, etc.) is targeted by such laws. U.S. financial institutions, processing millions of transactions each day, perform such checks routinely to avert violations the TSR and EAR.

Improved compliance or anticipatory compliance should thus begin with a recalibration of the scope and timing of an entity's "diligence" investigations. What this does is effectively "buy time" by identifying the risk of non-compliance early in a transaction. Certain TSR, EAR, ITAR and privacy laws can be violated not only on closing, but weeks or months earlier—on signing the definitive transactional document(s). In certain circumstances, violations can occur as early as the commencement of negotiations with EAR, TSR or ITAR targets, or in disclosing personal information at the start of negotiations across borders (where to do so violates applicable privacy or personal information protection laws). Such risks are not remote, but are often overlooked, and the resulting penalties can be substantial.[13] **Moreover, intent to violate is not always a predicate element of a civil violation.**

To the surprise of many transactors, enforcement action by OFAC, the BIS or the State Department's Directorate of Defense Trade Controls ("DDTC"), can include seizure of product, orders that ships return to port to off-load contravening cargo,[14] blocking of funds owed under letters of credit,[15] and the rendering of a transaction "null and void." Willful violations can result in substantial fines or worse, imprisonment of any U.S. person involved for up to ten years on each count. In the

---

13. For example, under the Iranian Transaction Regulations, for each criminal violation the corporate penalties can be up to $500,000; similarly, for each criminal violation, the individual fine can be up to $250,000 and the individual can be sentenced to a maximum of 10 years, or both. Civil penalties up to $11,000 per count can also be imposed. See OFAC, *An Overview of O.F.A.C. Regulations Involving Sanctions against Iran,* accessed at www.ustreas.gov/offices/eotffc/ofac/sanctions/t11iran.pdf.

14. See *Pakistan National Shipping Corporation v. A Cargo of 2,733.82 M/T of Heavy Steel Scrap,* 159 F. Supp. 2d 942 (S.D. Texas, 2001) in which the court notes that 15 C.F.R. §758.8(b) provides that "where there are reasonable grounds to believe that a violation of the Export Administration Regulations has occurred . . . with respect to a particular export from the United States . . . the U.S. Customs Service may order any person in possession or control of such shipment, including the exporting carrier, to return and upload the shipment."

15. See *Itek Corporation v. The First National Bank of Boston,* 704 F.2d 1 (1st Cir., 1983) involving a regulation preventing a final judgment extinguishing Iran's interest in standby letters of credit. As the court notes, "standby letters of credit, have from the onset of the national emergency [declared by President Carter on November 14, 1979 relating to Iran], been assets over which the Executive has exercised control in order to effectuate the purposes of the President's blocking order." The Iranian Asset Control Regulations (31 C.F.R. § 535.201 et seq.), should not to be confused with the Iranian Transaction Regulations, which implemented President Carter's blocking order, prohibiting the unauthorized transfer of property in which Iran had an interest.

course of complex or extended negotiations, the distinction between unwitting and willful violations of the TSR, EAR or ITAR can easily become blurred. That is particularly true when, as often happens:

(i) The evidence of negotiations and other transactional conduct is preserved in injudiciously phrased e-mails and instant messages without the benefit of review by counsel (a strikingly different scenario than when clients are accompanied by counsel and engage in face-to-face negotiations, video conferences, etc.);

(ii) The same e-mails and instant messages (with increasing frequency) pass through federal agency surveillance checkpoints with no indication (to sender or recipient) that they have been scanned;

(iii) Those e-mails and instant messages are also under continuous surveillance by Internet service providers seeking to detect spam and viruses (or by employers seeking to detect misuse of computer networks and telecommunications systems by employees—who might be wasting time surfing the World Wide Web or compromising their employers by transferring its trade secrets);

(iv) Companies increasingly develop and market and/or use technologies that scan the contents of e-mails;[16] and

(v) U.S. persons enter into negotiations with parties whose countries may have few, if any, laws that support the TSR, EAR or ITAR or, conversely, whose countries may have far broader laws for protection of personal privacy than those found in the United States. Moreover, such countries may have "blocking laws" prohibiting cooperation with certain U.S. trade embargoes. They may also have "clawback laws" granting their na-

---

16. For example, Google's offer of Gmail includes a feature only the purchaser of the product would know, that Google deploys algorithms that scan each e-mail (supposedly while retaining anonymity) but that retrieve information for use by marketers. Gmail's scans clearly pose privacy risks to anyone who sends a Gmail user an e-mail and is not aware of such features and has not consented to such scanning of their transmittals. See Waldmeir, Patti, *Google's E-mail Snooping Is a Test Case for Privacy*, FINANCIAL TIMES, May 24, 2004, p. 8, and Delaney, Kevin J., *Will Users Care if Gmail Invades Users Privacy?*, THE WALL STREET JOURNAL, April 6, 2004, p. B-1. Google's announcement of Gmail has provoked suits against it by privacy advocates.

tionals a right to sue to recover damages caused by enforcement of such embargoes.

The trail of such dealings (in commercial relationships, executory contracts and contracts currently requiring future performance, etc.), if not discerned at an early checkpoint, can become a hidden risk that imperils the transaction and the transactors. Similarly, the opening of new relationships, encouraged by a country's efforts to overcome differences with an adversary (such as South Korea's "sunshine policy"), can draw U.S. persons into dealings that may support transactions prohibited by the EAR, TSR or ITAR. Violations by certain overseas parties can suddenly lead to their being added to the target set of persons sanctioned by the EAR, TSR or ITAR (with the onerous economic consequences of being embargoed from dealings with U.S. individuals and entities). The prohibition against dealings by U.S. persons with such sanctioned parties takes effect immediately, creating new risks that must be vigilantly monitored on an on-going basis to avert violation. Thus, in a truly maddening regulatory pattern, a party previously reviewed and found to be free of sanction risk can present a new risk midway through a transaction by virtue of his unrelated business dealings. (In addition, U.S. persons run the risk of substantially higher penalties, if their violations of the EAR are committed during times when the Export Administration Act is in effect.)[17] Cyberspace thus has risks that virtually line the trade route, but that remain concealed or not apparent, unless checkpoints are deployed early and rigorously enforced.

These are the lessons we hope are demonstrated by the fact pattern we have created for Agile-Wing. Whether it can extricate itself from such risks without, in the process, contravening the TSR, EAR or ITAR, or other nations' privacy or personal information laws, and without infringing on patents, will in some instances remain an open question, depending upon what enforcement action (if any) follows.

---

17. While the Export Administration Act is at the time of this writing in lapse, violations when it is in effect can be subject to a maximum civil penalty of $120,000 for each violation. That accounted, in part, for the substantial penalty ($647,000) that Morton International and its affiliates (located in France and Japan) agreed to pay to settle charges in connection with exports and reexports to Mexico, Singapore, and Taiwan in violation of the EAR. The number of violations (over 100 alleged) contributed also. See BIS, *Illinois Company and Two Foreign Affiliates Settles Charges Relating to Illegal Exports*, February 24, 2004, accessed at www.bis.doc.gov/News/2004/MortonIntl2 _24.htm.

1.2 Hypothetical: A Cross-Border, Cyber-Driven Acquisition by Agile-Wing.

Agile, a New York firm, with overseas branches in several European and Asian capitals, specializes in investments in aerospace, pharmaceuticals and chemical products. Agile owns controlling interests in aerospace units that manufacture high-performance hydraulic parts, fly-by-wire software and flight-line maintenance chemicals. Agile products are installed on civilian passenger aircraft and military jets (including the new F-35 or Joint Strike Fighter). Agile also owns controlling interests in pharmaceutical units, specializing in production of antidotes for biochemical toxins and weapons. It controls certain chemical and software-for-chemical companies that (since the first World Trade Center bombing) have been developing devices to detect and intercept illegally transported or imported explosives and bio-chemical terrorist weapons. Since the second attack, Agile's chemical units have been responding to requests for proposals from the nascent Department of Homeland Security. Agile maintains an active website on which it advertises its product lines, contracts with suppliers and, in some instances, makes "product" software available for download. In compliance with ITAR §122.1,[18] Agile holds a current registration with the Directorate of Defense Trade Controls.

Agile's partners recently approved plans to expand into new markets, specifically Department of Homeland Security contracts for anti-terrorist technologies. Acquisition of overseas software houses, and pharmaceutical or chemical research and development firms (whose capabilities can fill gaps in Agile's), will improve its chances of winning such contracts. Agile has an excellent reputation for timely delivery of developmental products that meet demanding specifications. It also has an excellent reputation for its approach to acquisitions. It conducts rigorous examinations of a company before agreeing to a definitive purchase agreement; it typically places its partners on the target company's Board of Directors; and, as a result, it usually improves the management

---

18. ITAR §122.1 requires that "any person who engages in the United States in the business of either manufacturing or exporting defense articles or furnishing defense services is required to register" with the U.S. State Department's Directorate of Defense Trade Controls.

and operation of the companies it acquires. Acquisition by Agile therefore significantly enhances a company's future financial prospects.

Agile's Board has selected a new target for a friendly acquisition: a privately owned, limited liability company—Troll Digisonde A/S,[19] headquartered in Trondheim, Norway ("Troll"), its wholly owned subsidiary, A. Brugge BioPharm A/S, headquartered in Tromsø, Norway ("Brugge"), and its recently purchased majority interest in Ijsselmeer Biometrie NV, headquartered in Eindhoven, The Netherlands ("Ijsselmeer," pronounced "aay-sill-mere"). The latter is a joint venture formed by students and faculty at three academic institutions:

(i)   The Technische Universiteit Eindhoven (Technical University of Eindhoven) in The Netherlands,

(ii) The Biomedical Engineering Department (University of Ontario Medical School) in Toronto, Canada, and

(iii) The Humanoid Robotics Institute (Waseda University) in Tokyo, Japan.[20]

Troll designs and develops reconnaissance systems, target mapping software (for Norwegian produced AGM-119 "Penguin" missiles),[21] geo-locating software, and classified encryption and encryption-attacking software. Troll's first and best customer is the Royal Norwegian Ministry of Defence ("MoD"). Troll has performed MoD software maintenance and repair contracts in support of Norwegian peace-

---

19. Under Norwegian law—in particular, its Limited Liabilities Act—a privately owned, limited liability company is referred to as a private "Aksjeselskap," and is identified by any of the following abbreviations: "A.S." or "A/S" (in contrast to a public company "Allmennaksjeselskap," identified by abbreviation "ASA"). See the Royal Norwegian Embassy, *Doing Business and Investing in Norway*, accessed at www.cairo2.mfa. no/Norway/Doing + business + in + Norway/Doing + business + in + Norway.htm.

20. Since none of Troll's affiliates is a registered U.S. subsidiary, the ITAR §122.4(b) requirements for notice to the Directorate of Defense Trade Controls 60 days prior to the closing do not apply to Agile's contemplated acquisition of Troll.

21. Penguin missiles are relatively long-range missiles, which can be fired against small combatants and surfaced submarines in the littoral environment. The first customer for Penguin missiles was the Royal Norwegian Navy. A folded wing version for deployment on helicopters is in the U.S. inventory and referred to as AGM-119B. Another version was adapted for launching from F-16s. See *Kongsberg Penguin*, accessible at www.eurofighter.starstreak.net/common/AG/penguin.html, and Parsch, Andreas, *Directory of U.S. Military Rockets and Missiles: AGM-119*, accessed at www.designation-systems.net/dusrm/m-119.html.

keepers in the Middle East and East Asia. Moreover, it has used such in-country opportunities to make friends, engage local agents and land contracts from Middle Eastern, African and East Asian firms, some of which are owned or controlled by the national governments.

Since much of Troll's work for the MoD is classified, Troll has traditionally relied on "trade secret" protections rather than patents to protect its inventions. As a result, Troll tends to do little if any investigation of patents when developing new, cutting edge technological products.

Brugge manufacturers a wide range of medicaments, broad-spectrum antibiotics and vaccines (including one tested successfully against weapon-grade anthrax). Brugge also has a distributor relationship with German and Italian pharmaceutical companies and, as a result, deploys a large sales force in Eastern European countries that border the Baltic (Poland, Estonia, Lithuania and Latvia) as well as in India and South-East Asia. It has a well-developed pharmaceutical patent portfolio, but has moved aggressively into the production of generic medicines, sometimes well before the expiration of patents held by some of the world's largest pharmaceutical companies.

Ijsselmeer operates three small "new technology" units:

- One develops biometric sensors and algorithms for biometric detection, identification and authentication systems;
- One develops polymer thick-film sensors for use as biometric sensors for smartcards (for protecting sensitive personal data, signing of electronic documents and verification of transactions); and
- One develops machine-to-machine ("M2M") and RFID technologies for security systems, and is seeking to create personal mobile gateways and platforms, *i.e.*, clusters of geographically dispersed devices that would change dynamically as the context and needs of the user change.

Agile's Denmark based partners, one a U.S. citizen and one a Danish citizen, will negotiate the acquisition. Agile's transaction counsel are Danish lawyers. Troll's counsel are Norwegian lawyers. Agile and Troll have already agreed that Danish law will govern their agreements. When Agile's Danish counsel completes its initial diligence review and submits its reports, it identifies no serious impediments to the deal, except that it cautions that Ijsselmeer's technologies probably pose issues under personal data protection laws of the EU, The Netherlands, Canada (federal) and Japan. These issues are enhanced by the fact that Agile wants the right to relocate some of Ijsselmeer's production and research facilities to the United States. As part of its due diligence, Agile plans to have its engineers assess Ijsselmeer's technologies by evaluating existing test reports that include extensive personal data of the test subjects. (Thus Agile will need the right to transfer personally sensitive data from The Netherlands, Canada and Japan into the United States.) Agile hopes to use Ijsselmeer's operations to pursue anti-terrorism technology contracts with the U.S. Department of Homeland Security and DARPA. Agile's Danish counsel asks whether Agile has anticipated this issue and, specifically, whether it has applied to participate in the U.S.-EU Safe Harbor Framework. The company had briefly considered participating, but determined that it was not worth the investment at that time. Such action, moreover, would not have solved all the privacy issues arising in The Netherlands, Canada and Japan.[22] Agile begins to consider whether to require Troll to divest itself of Ijsselmeer before the closing ("Closing"). (The parties held intermittent exploratory talks beginning in December of 2002. Serious negotiations began a year later, and by spring of 2004, the parties were close to an agreement. During this period, Agile's general counsel monitored developments that might affect the transaction, particularly the due diligence that Agile would need to conduct.)

1.2.1 Recent Changes in the Enforcement Environment at the Departments of State, Treasury, and Commerce.

On January 2, 2003, the U.S. State Department issued a Press Briefing. It described, among other things, a "charging letter" dispatched by the State Department to Hughes Electronic Corporation ("HEC") and Boeing Satellite Systems (formerly Hughes Space and Communications, an entity that Boeing purchased from Hughes Electronics in January of 2000). The "charging letter" listed 123 charges involving violations of

---

22. Moreover, in view of the availability of the Standard Contractual Clauses for the Transfer of Personal Data (accessed at http://europa.eu.int/comm/internal_market/privacy/modelcontracts), companies need to consider carefully whether to qualify for the Safe Harbor or use the Standard Contractual Clauses.

the Arms Export Control Act ("AECA") and the ITAR. These occurred in connection with misconduct by those corporations following the 1995 and 1996 failed launches of the People's Republic of China Long March rockets carrying the APSTAR II and Intelsat 708 spacecrafts, respectively, and the transfer of detailed data relating to the Astra 1G and Astra 1H satellites.

The Boeing Company took the position that Boeing bought the branch from HEC (a unit of General Motors) "after all this had happened" and thus had "nothing to do with the violations."[23] However, State Department spokesman Richard Boucher responded unequivocally that Boeing was "still the responsible party to respond to these claims about the unit and what it did."[24] The State Department imposed compliance obligations on Boeing (and on HEC), required Boeing's management, Boeing Satellite Systems and HEC to sign the consent agreement and imposed fines and penalties against Boeing and HEC.

The State Department position is clear: successor liability for violations of the AECA and ITAR is not cut off by an acquisition. As defense industry commentators have observed, "it is highly likely that this trend will continue and the Government will impose fines and penalties on both the divesting and acquiring entities."[25] The Commerce Department's BIS adopted a similar position in a major case only a few months earlier.[26] Seeing an emerging regulatory trend, Agile's General

23. U.S. Department of State, press release, January 2, 2003, accessed at www.state.gov/r/pa/prs/dpb/2003/16309.htm, accessed on February 4, 2003, and June 23, 2003. Issuance of a "charging letter" gave each company 30 days to respond or within seven days of the service of that response each could request an oral hearing.

24. Id.

25. Society for International Affairs, MERGERS, ACQUISITIONS & DIVESTITURES: GUIDANCE AND ADVICE FOR DEFENSE TRADE EXPORT AND LEGAL PROFESSIONALS, 2003, p. 50.

26. See, for example, $1.76 million penalty agreed to by Sigma-Aldrich Corporation of St. Louis, Missouri, and two of its subsidiaries to settle 366 charges involving illegal exports of biological toxins. BIS press release, November 4, 2002, accessed at www.bxa.doc.gov/press/20 . . . gmaAldrichPays4Acquisition.html, accessed on December 16, 2002. See also the Department of Commerce, then Bureau of Export Administration "charging letter" to Sigma-Aldrich, dated March 21, 2001, accessed at http://efoia.bis.doc.gov/ExportControlViolations/E740.pdf, accessed on June 23, 2003. The penalty followed a decision by an administrative law judge that companies can be held liable for export control violations that have been committed by firms that they acquire. See also BIS postings of export violations dating from January 1, 1997, through the present date accessed at http://efoia.bis.doc.gov/ExportControlViolations/TOC ExportViolations.htm.

Such publications on the BIS's website and on OFAC's website (which discloses civil

Counsel did not want his company to be adversely affected. The Commerce Department's BIS, the State Department's Directorate of Defense Trade Controls, and probably the Treasury Department's OFAC, appeared likely to give serious consideration to the imposition of successor liability in the acquisition context. Agile would, therefore, need to conduct diligence into Troll's and Brugge's historical, current *and contemplated* commercial activities and relationships, in order to evaluate accurately the risk of successor liability. If successor liability was a potential risk, Agile would need to know prior to completing negotiations of the definitive purchase agreement ("DPA") for its acquisition of Troll, Brugge and Troll's interest in Ijsselmeer. The later it raised those issues in the negotiation, the more likely it was that it would encounter resistance from Troll (and quite reasonably so), and the less leverage it would have for obtaining the protections it would need before signing the final text of the DPA.

General Counsel also noted the widespread coverage and adverse publicity that accompanied State Department publication of the terms of the "charging letter" (relating to Boeing) and references in news articles to comparable violations by other companies within the last year.[27] Such adverse publicity could impede efforts to complete a deal, because transactions that violate certain TSR are "null and void" from inception. And because BIS and the State Department can withhold licenses altogether, or grant them only with severe limitations, parties can be forced to put a deal on hold or abandon it.[28]

---

penalties assessed and settlements) permit due diligence teams, upon being alerted to a contemplated transaction, to check if a company has a recent history of violations of the EAR and TSR. See OFAC website at www.ustreas.gov/offices/eotffc/ofac/civpen/index.html. Disclosure and maintenance of such penalties on a website for several years adds another dimension to the risks of adverse publicity, since the problem remains accessible to future potential transactors. Many companies that value their reputation will find such records an increasingly powerful disincentive to taking risks of violating the EAR and TSR.

27. See Gerth, Jeff, *U.S. Says 2 Companies Gave Data to China*, THE NEW YORK TIMES, January 1, 2003, at p. A-6. For more substantial penalties within the last three years, see, for example, (1) agreement by Loral Space and Communications to pay $20 million in a case "involving one of several satellite issues in the case against Boeing and Hughes;" and (2) agreement by Lockheed Martin Corporation to pay $13 million in fines in 2000 in relation to its alleged provision of technical assistance and space-related information to a Hong-Kong based company "with ties to Beijing."

28. Agile's General Counsel also noted that as part of its enforcement strategy the U.S. Government used "sting" operations where federal agents, posing as purchasing representatives of a fictitious company from a country to which U.S. defense articles

General Counsel has been monitoring penalties imposed for violation of EAR and TSR. Since April 2003, pursuant to promulgation of a new rule, OFAC now publishes detailed civil penalty enforcement information on its website monthly, including disclosure of the violator's identity (corporate or individual), its address, the particular TSR violated, whether "voluntary disclosure" by the violator had preceded investigation by OFAC, the amount of the penalty, and whether it reflected an assessed penalty or a settled amount.[29] This new policy has made OFAC processes more transparent. However, it has also increased OFAC's leverage over potential and alleged violators. Once published on OFAC's website, the information becomes accessible to the public and subject to widespread media attention and potential distortion. Each month's disclosures can be scanned by reporters. In the first six months of 2004, OFAC published civil penalty enforcement information that included the following significant fines:

Figure 1. OFAC Civil Penalties Enforcement Information (Concerning Entities)

Name of Entity	Sanctions Program	Actual or Alleged Violation	Amount
Chiron Corporation Ltd.	Cuba	1999–2002 Exportation of goods to Cuba	$168,500
IEPS Electronic, Inc. by Smart Power Systems, Inc.	Iran	1995–1997 Brokerage services to Iran and importation of financial services into the United States	$100,000

(continued)

could not be exported without a license, would seek to buy such articles and entrap persons willing to circumvent ITAR. In one such operation in 2003, federal agents posed as representatives of a fictitious Chinese company, Sino-American Aviation Supply, purportedly based in Shenyang, China, and successfully sought to purchase ITAR-controlled military components for F-4 Phantom and F-5 Freedom-Fighter/Tiger II fighter jets from two individuals who operated United Aircraft & Electronics in Anaheim, California. The U.S. Government eventually arrested the two sellers, seized the parts before they departed the U.S. and indicted the sellers for violations of the ITAR, the Arms Export Control Act, as well as for conspiracy and causing an act to be done. See press release, Department of Homeland Security, *Two Charged and Arrested in Scheme to Illegally Export U.S. Fighter Jet Components to China*, July 24, 2003, accessed at www.dhs.gov/dhspublic/display?content = 1091.

29. OFAC civil penalties information is accessible at www.ustreas.gov/offices/eotffc/ofac/civpen/penalties/index.html.

**Figure 1. OFAC Civil Penalties Enforcement Information
(Concerning Entities) (Continued)**

Name of Entity	Sanctions Program	Actual or Alleged Violation	Amount
Alpha Pharmaceutical, Inc; ICN Farmaceutica S.A. de C.V.; and Laboratorios Grossman, S.A.	Cuba	1998–2003 Importation and exportation of goods to/from Cuba	$198,711
Bank of New York	Iraq	1999 Funds Transfer	$137,500
JP Morgan Chase & Co.	Cuba, Iran, Libya, & Sudan	2000–2002 Funds transfers & letter of credit	$73,281[a]

[a]Office of Foreign Assets Control, *Civil Penalties Information*, January 2, 2004–June 4, 2004, accessed at www.ustreas.gov/offices/eotffc/ofac/civpen/penalties/index.html.

Agile's partners do not want their company (or their own names) to appear on OFAC's or the BIS's websites, and thereby to be accessible from search engines worldwide. The seriousness of such a risk is easily demonstrated: a Google search for documents including the terms "OFAC" and "Citibank" or "JP Morgan" produced OFAC Civil Penalties Enforcement Information naming "Citibank, N.A." twice, albeit for very small penalties (each less than $3,000), and "JP Morgan Chase & Co." twice, for amounts of $73,000 and $17,000. The appearance of an entity on such list makes it a simple task for others worldwide to find out if a particular company or individual has recently been the subject of an enforcement action under the TSR, what the alleged violation involved and its seriousness (as measured by the magnitude of the penalty).[30]

On February 11, 2003, the Financial Times reported on shareholder resolutions filed to force General Electric, Halliburton and Conoco-Phillips to "end their operations in Iran and Syria." Although, reportedly, GE and Halliburton "skirt[ed] . . . US laws that prohibit direct dealings with terrorist-sponsoring states" such as Iran, and Conoco-Phillips had invested in Syria through a UK subsidiary, GE responded that it did "'a very limited amount of business in Iran and all of it is compliant with US law."[31] Far from being "nuisance suits," these resolutions were filed by the pension fund manager for the New York City's

---

30. Accessed at www.treas.gov/offices/eotffc/ofac/civpen/penalties/04042003.pdf.

31. Alden, Edward, *Companies Pressed to Cut Ties with "Terror states*," FINANCIAL TIMES, February 11, 2003, at p. 17.

fire and police forces, further adding to the negative publicity for the companies involved.[32]

On February 28, 2003, the State Department posted a new release on its website, describing a settlement agreement with Raytheon Corporation.[33] Raytheon had been charged with committing fraud against the Customs Service and the State Department in a scheme to export mobile truck mounted military communications equipment to Pakistan from 1990 to 1997 without a State Department license in violation of the ITAR. Raytheon, an experienced and sophisticated defense contractor, is well aware of the ITAR, its scope and the risks of violating it. Raytheon had submitted an application to export military communications equipment to Pakistan in 1993. The State Department's DDTC denied Raytheon's request, due to sanctions imposed by the Pressler Amendment.[34] Raytheon was aware that there was a Canadian exemption to the ITAR that, under certain circumstances, allowed exports of defense articles on the U.S. Munitions List from the United States to Canada without an export license.

Apparently believing it could circumvent the ITAR, Raytheon arranged to assemble and sell essentially the same equipment to the same end user (in Pakistan) through its Canadian subsidiary. The Canadian exemption to the ITAR was not intended as an end run to the ITAR, but rather as a means of facilitating defense trade solely between U.S. sellers and Canadian end users. The violation resulted in charges against Raytheon. Under the terms of the 2003 settlement, Raytheon agreed to pay a **$25 million** civil penalty ($20 million to U.S. Customs Service in lieu of forfeiture claims, $3 million to settle administrative charges and $2 million dedicated to remedial compliance measures). The settlement also required the appointment of a Special Compliance Official to oversee Raytheon's military communications business (and its export control practices generally) for an indefinite period.

On May 20, 2003, Agile was alerted (by *The Wall Street Journal Online*) that Stolt-Nielsen SA (a Luxembourg-registered conglomerate,[35]

---

32. See also Alden, Edward, *Top US Companies Gave to Charity Linked to al-Queda*, FINANCIAL TIMES, January 31, 2003, p. 1, noting that such donors included "Microsoft, UBS, and Compaq."

33. Department of State, *Settlement of Raytheon Export Control Violation Case*, February 28, 2003, accessed at www.state.gov/r/pa/prs/ps/2003/18086.htm.

34. Id.

35. Bandler, James, *Stolt Won't Discipline Officials on Possible Collusive Activities*, The Wall Street Journal Online, March 4, 2003 accessed at http://online.wsj.com/article_print/0,,SB1046741658720775280,00 . . . , accessed on May 20, 2003.

and one of the world's largest chemical-shipping companies) had disclosed payment of a $95,000 fine in settlement of a U.S. Government investigation of its dealings with the Sudan. OFAC was also reportedly probing the company's business with Iran.[36]

1.2.2 Agile's Response to the New Enforcement Environment—Enhanced Due Diligence Before Signing the Definitive Acquisition Agreement.

Agile's concern was obvious: did Troll have similar issues? Since Troll was a major Scandinavian defense industry participant, performing contracts for the MoD of a NATO ally, Agile's partners had not thought it necessary to ask if Troll was involved in dealings prohibited to a "U.S. person." Local counsel do not customarily have such issues on their "due diligence" checklists.

General Counsel, however, has a strong entrepreneurial interest. He joined the Company at its inception, and quickly became a Vice-President and Chief Compliance Officer. As such, he has a heightened sensitivity to the financial ramifications of such violations. He has been a vocal advocate of a comprehensive written compliance policy with respect to the Access Control Laws. Nevertheless, Agile is still more concerned with the potential loss of flexibility that written policies create than with what it perceives as the need for increased compliance. Agile provides no formal training or briefing for its partners on Access Control Laws compliance, and relies primarily on counsel to ensure that such problems are addressed. Neither does Agile conduct internal audits to ensure such compliance: Agile has not thought it worth the investment of time. Despite credible efforts by its outside counsel, Agile's General Counsel is Agile's primary line of defense against inadvertent or unwitting violations of Access Control Laws. And in spite of his diligence, his efforts would likely fall short by OFAC standards of qualifying as a "mitigating factor" in the event of a violation.

---

36. Bandler, James, *U.S. Probes Whether Shipper Acted to Bust Trade Embargoes,* The Wall Street Journal Online, May 20, 2003 accessed at http://online.wsj.com/article_print/0,,SB105337481158720800,00.html, accessed on May 20, 2003.

As Agile's General Counsel reviews the recent developments in Access Control Laws, and the information about Troll and Brugge from e-mail reports of Agile's Danish partners running the deal, he grows increasingly concerned that a possible violation could trigger an OFAC or BIS investigation, generate adverse publicity (as it has for Stolt-Nielsen for over a year), severely damage Agile's reputation, expose it to possible fines and raise the specter of criminal prosecutions by the Justice Department. The latter could result in imprisonment for culpable individual "U.S. persons." A patent infringement (actual or apparent) poses a second important risk. Agile's U.S. defense competitors have become even more aggressive in enforcing their patents (as a result of the high risk investments they reflect and the revenue streams they must generate to justify such front-end investments financially). Companies losing market share to competitors have increasingly resorted to patent suits, if they suspect that infringements are in any way implicated in such loss. For example, Reuters recently filed a patent infringement suit against Bloomberg.[37]

In addition, companies whose businesses critically depend on their website operations and transactions, have become uncertain and apprehensive about the extent to which their websites must comply with the TSR and EAR, and what errors in compliance might attract the attention of the BIS or OFAC. Many have voluntarily raised their standard of compliance. Monster.com (without notice or caution from OFAC, but purely out of a concern to avert a violation of the TSR) elected in April of 2003 to "remove references to Iran, Iraq, Cuba, Libya, North Korea, the Sudan and Syria from its standard format for resumes, thereby preventing individual job seekers in these countries, regardless of their nationality, from looking for jobs in the United States."[38] While this is clearly a factually driven decision, what is significant is that Monster believed it was appropriate to take an additional step not required by either the TSR or EAR. Monster removed those countries "from the drop down box under the 'Education' section of online resumes, pre-

---

37. However, Reuters also reportedly denied the action had resulted from a loss of market share or international customers to Bloomberg. See Burt, Tim, *Reuters Sues Bloomberg over Patents,* FINANCIAL TIMES, published July 11, 2003, updated July 12, 2003, accessed at http://news.ft.com/servlet/ContentServer?pagename = FT.com/StoryFT/FullStory&c = StoryFT&cid = 1057562343171&p = 1012571727088.

38. *NIAC Seeks Meeting with Monster.com,* PRWeb, May 14, 2003, accessed at www.prweb.com/releases/2003/5/prweb65888.php, accessed on June 23, 2003.

venting individuals educated in these countries from listing the locations of the institutions where they were educated."[39] It is interesting to note that the U.S. Government would probably want such background information to continue to be accessible.[40] Later, Monster reversed its policy.[41] A *Wall Street Journal Online* article on Monster pointedly observed: "the situation is an example of a new puzzle: How far must online and information companies go to comply with sanctions? . . . Monster . . . and other companies that trade solely in information— and depend on widespread accessibility—are now struggling to try on the sanctions slipper. It doesn't always fit comfortably."[42]

After carefully weighing those and other examples, Agile's General Counsel decides to take preemptive precautionary action. He recommends a second due diligence review, this time by U.S. counsel, this one narrowly focused on the risks of violating the Access Control Laws. A number of partners initially perceive this as an excess of caution not warranted by a quick cost/benefit analysis. They reason that divestment of Ijsselmeer would arguably avoid most of the data protection law problems (discussed below) that counsel has identified, and would be far more cost-effective. Counsel's recommendation also encounters stiff resistance from one of Agile's Danish partners. Her reasoning, (which she circulates in an e-mail) is that the deal has delicate timing issues, and that these in turn have a direct impact on the future economic health of the company. Troll hopes to become Norway's first subcontractor to the Joint Strike Fighter ("JSF"). If Troll is successful in this endeavor, it will raise a host of export license issues with the State De-

---

39. Id.

40. The deletion of countries from resumes was reported by Monster to be a "system'glitch.'" Agile's general counsel thought it unusual, if not implausible, for software code to have a TSR-sensitive "glitch." It seemed more probable to Agile's General Counsel that the change resulted from the rewriting of software code. To call it a "system'glitch'" appeared an effort at spin: it placed blame on the system, not the system operators.

41. McCullagh, Declan, *Monster.com's Resume Purge Draws Fire*, CNET News.com, April 23, 2003, accessed at http://news.com.com/2102-1022-998118.html?tag = ni_ print, accessed on June 3, 2003.

42. *Sanctions Force E-Businesses to Rethink Global Strategies*, The Wall Street Journal Online, May 29, 2003, accessed at http://online.wsj.com/article/ 0,,SB105423088353710300-search,00 . . . The article quotes a former official at OFAC, Michael Malloy, stating, "Figuring out the boundaries of sanctions'gets complicated when you move into the electronic age.'"

partment's DDTC (prompted, in part, by the desire of the U.S. manufacturer of the JSF to restrict access to its trade secrets, and to maintain control over the project and any spin-off technologies). Both Danish partners believe that the inevitable delays and transactional costs created by an additional checkpoint, and the potential disruption to the negotiations, outweigh any potential compliance benefit. They also believe that the reduction in risks to Agile will prove insignificant. Their American partners should not press the extraterritorial reach of U.S. law, particularly not in Europe, where the presumption is that U.S. embargoes and other action directed at Middle East countries do not deserve European support. The extraterritorial enforcement of U.S. laws by U.S. federal agencies (and particularly by the Securities Exchange Commission) was recently reported in *The Wall Street Journal* to be creating "resentment at a time when many countries are chafing at U.S. heavy-handedness on issues ranging from climate change to Iraq,"[43] prompting some European companies and their counsel to refer to such enforcement as "'U.S. regulatory imperialism.'"[44] The European Commission has formally expressed its opposition to the extra-territorial application of U.S. regulatory laws, noting in its *Report on United States Barriers To Trade And Investment* that:

"The application of U.S. legislation outside the U.S. territory is a long-standing feature of the U.S. legal system manifesting itself in fields such as environment, banking and export control. While the EU may share some of the objectives underlying such laws, it is opposed, as a matter of law and principle, to the exterritorial application of such domestic legislation insofar as it purports to force persons present in—and companies incorporated in—the EU to follow U.S. laws or policies outside the United States. . . . In particular, the EU opposes the exterritorial provisions of certain U.S. legislation that hampers international trade and investment by seeking to regulate EU trade with and investment in third countries [such as Cuba and Iran]."[45]

43. Schroeder, Michael, and Ascarelli, Silvia, *New Role for SEC: Policing Companies beyond U.S. Borders*, THE WALL STREET JOURNAL, July 30, 2004, p. A-6.

44. Id, quoting Ralph Ferrara, a former SEC general counsel who represented Shell in its dealings with the SEC.

45. European Commission, *Report on United States Barriers to Trade and Investment*, 2003, p. 10, accessed at http://trade-info.cec.eu.int/doclib/docs/2003/december/tradoc_115383.pdf.

1.2.3 Troll's Response to a Request for Enhanced Due Diligence.

Agile's Danish partners ultimately put the request to Troll, which predictably opposes it. Its Norwegian counsel objects to any suggestion that U.S. law could be relevant to a transaction to be consummated by Troll in Trondheim and the Danish branch office of Agile in Copenhagen. They think the emphasis should instead be on reviewing the personal data protection and privacy laws, which they believe Agile is underestimating. Otherwise, they make the typical arguments of sellers who believe themselves to be beyond the reach of the TSR, EAR and ITAR. They believe that Agile's concerns can be addressed after the signing of the DPA through provisions for indemnification by Troll or some other post-signing (*ex ante*) cost adjustment mechanism. Their arguments are not unreasonable; however, they are shortsighted. Such indemnification could later be construed as evidence of willful contravention (cold comfort to Agile's personnel who could face criminal charges for violations of the EAR, TSR or ITAR).

Troll's counsel is particularly upset by duplicative document requests for commercial and banking documents, some of which have already been produced in the initial due diligence, but have not been reviewed for these purposes. In his view, Agile (like most American firms) sees the world as full of traps and snares. Their compliance concerns are, as Troll's executives would say, "*å lage storm i ett vammglass*" (to make a storm in a glass of water). They recommend that Troll consider other offers. It has received others during the negotiations with Agile, and there was never a letter of intent with Agile barring Troll from considering such offers. However, Troll eventually rules out such a course of action, noting that the next best offer is also from a U.S. firm. Problems with the TSR, EAR and ITAR, if they exist, will draw the other company's attention, and perhaps at an even earlier stage.

1.2.4 Findings and Consequences of the Enhanced Due Diligence.

Ultimately, Troll complies with the diligence request, and sends the documents to Agile's U.S. counsel, who reviews them, and submits a comprehensive report prefaced with an executive summary, an excerpt from which reads.

"If Agile signs the purchase agreement before our recommended corrective actions are taken by Troll and its affiliates, Agile will likely come into violation of several TSR, EAR and ITAR provisions. Certain violations, set forth below, would occur upon Closing; other violations would occur earlier, upon the signing of the DPA. Signing may also trigger patent infringement suits from certain competitors of Agile, because Troll and Brugge have products that, if sold or offered for sale in the United States, would infringe their existing U.S. patents, if those products were intended for the U.S. market."

General Counsel and his Agile partners adopt the memorandum's detailed recommendations. They inform Troll's negotiators that requests will be sent to them detailing corrective actions, leaving it to Troll to decide how it wishes to achieve them. The general objective, however, is disengagement from a large number of dealings by Troll and Brugge— disengagements that they propose be completed and certified as completed *before* Agile signs the DPA. Anyone with even small transactional experience will realize immediately that the future financial cost of such divestiture (in lost business opportunities) will have to be weighed against a relatively "inchoate" yet real risk that the transaction will not be completed and there will be no benefit to "offset" against the clear cost of divestiture. Agile's partners understand that the request is extraordinary, but wish to avoid all risk of liability now that they appreciate the magnitude of the risk. They try to provide as much certainty as possible (within the constraints of what partners are permitted to bind themselves to without breaching their obligations to the Firm) with assurances that, upon Troll's completion of these disengagements, Agile will sign the DPA. Agile's priority, however, is to avert any such violations, which makes pre-signing removal of all recognized problems a potential deal-breaker. When Troll reluctantly agrees, it invites Agile's Danish partners to participate in the disengagements negotiations to ensure that they are done to Agile's ultimate satisfaction. However, General Counsel and Agile's Outside Counsel, adamantly advise against lending such assistance.

What does counsel find so problematic? The answer to that question is multi-layered and requires a nuanced understanding of the TSR and EAR. As we set forth the answer, we will develop our case for adding checkpoints to avert the risks of such violations and infringements.

In the next section, we review some of the risks that violations of the TSR, EAR and ITAR pose to transactions and transactors. We explore evidence that vendors in cyberspace remain insufficiently aware that their transactions can readily contravene the TSR, EAR and ITAR, and that participants in cyber-driven transactions are increasingly exposed to such risks. We conclude the section with a discussion of the need to adopt counter-measures and pre-emptive compliance to avert such risks.

1.3 Evidence that Cyberspace Vendors Appear to Underestimate the Risks of Violating the TSR and EAR.

A cyberspace vendor's interests can be fairly accurately assessed from what the vendor posts on its website, by the activities it invites in seeking to attract visitors to its site, and by the measures it takes (if any) to police and control activity on its site. Judged by those standards, many U.S. vendors in cyberspace do not invest seriously in measures to avert violations of the TSR, EAR or ITAR. The most obvious evidence of this is the vendor's posted "Terms and Conditions," "Terms of Use," "Disclaimers," "Legal Notice," or other postings that reflect an effort to improve the vendor's position in the event of a legal dispute or government investigation.

There are currently many commercial websites, hosted by computers in the United States, with "Terms of Use" that do little more than recognize the existence of cross-border risks or the obligation of vendors to comply with Access Control Laws. Many "Terms of Use," in fact, attempt to shift the burden of compliance to the visitor (perhaps a carry-over from drafting the "contracts of adhesion" for transactions conducted at websites). Websites seldom provide any useful information for anyone unfamiliar with the referenced regulations. Promises to comply with laws as to which the promisor is ignorant, and with respect to which it receives no guidance, are without legal force or merit and, in fact, are evidence of an attempt to delegate non-delegable legal duties (similar to a disclaimer of negligence). They are also fundamentally misconceived: if a vendor engages in a "deemed export" of controlled technology or software by posting it on its website, and permitting it to be downloaded by foreign nationals located within the United States, it is the vendor who is initially and primarily guilty of the violation. Nonetheless, most such "Terms of Use" purport to shift responsibility and culpability to the visitors (which would be true only with respect to any subsequent reexport by such persons).

What constitutes appropriate website "Terms and Conditions" (or "Terms of Use") has been a recurrent issue, as cyberspace transactions and transactors enter the gravitational pull of U.S. terrestrial laws. In overlapping succession, the following issues have attracted attention from the bar and the courts: enforceability of click-wrap software licenses; enforceability of copyrights to musical works and cinematic works of authorship fixed in digital media; access to, and disclosure of, personally identifiable data; and avoidance of securities laws violations (resulting in the frequent inclusion of "forward looking statement" disclaimers on websites), among others. Often one finds website "Terms and Conditions" modified (sometimes seriously, sometimes speciously) to adjust to developments and anticipated developments in such rulings and adjudications. When one selects at random several website "Terms and Conditions," and views their discussion (if any) of the Access Control Laws, one finds little consistency. Moreover, there is a great deal of misinformation, and an occasional effort by website owners and/or operators to convert their own representations of compliance with the EAR and TSR into representations of purported compliance by users of the website. The result (in the overwhelming majority of the websites we have examined) is:

(i) A failure to address TSR, EAR and ITAR compliance;

(ii) Naïve efforts at ensuring such compliance (often mere pretensions of doing so); and/or

(iii) Serious yet incomplete efforts to address such requirements (which nonetheless do little to avert the risk of contravening the TSR, EAR and ITAR). As noted earlier, the advent of technologies that make it possible to know the identity, location and other pertinent facts about website visitors will inexorably bring with it liability, initially under the rubric of constructive knowledge (having *reason to know*), and eventually pursuant to inferences of deliberate disregard of facts and deemed actual knowledge.

Consider a few recent examples of website "Terms and Conditions" that purport to address TSR or EAR compliance. The first is taken from a site whose "Terms and Conditions" give only a deferential nod to EAR compliance, do not mention TSR, and merely ask the licensee to agree that some kind of EAR exists and applies somewhere to someone:

> "LICENSEE AGREES THAT THE EXPORT OF GOODS AND/OR TECHNICAL DATA FROM THE UNITED STATES MAY RE-QUIRE **SOME FORM OF EXPORT CONTROL LICENSE** FROM THE U.S. GOVERNMENT AND THAT FAILURE TO OBTAIN SUCH EXPORT CONTROL LICENSE MAY RESULT IN CRIMI-NAL LIABILITY UNDER U.S. LAWS. This software is exported from the United States in accordance with the Export Administration Regulations. Diversion contrary to U.S. law is prohibited. At the time of the creation of this license, export of the software to Cuba, Iran, Iraq, Libya, North Korea, Sudan, and Syria is prohibited without a license, and is also prohibited for citizens of these countries to use the software without a license."[46]

Curiously, while these "Terms and Conditions" admit that they cover transactions that include the export of goods or technical data, they imply that the obligation to obtain the requisite license is the duty of the licensee. This reflects a fundamental misconception: the belief that the sole risk point is that the licensee will violate the EAR by failing to obtain the requisite license. The more immediate (and antecedent) risk point is that the website operator will violate the EAR by failing to obtain a license to export controlled, U.S.-origin goods and technology to the licensee. Since the website facilitates exports from the U.S., the "Terms and Conditions" should:

(i) Disclose whether the website owner or operator believed it needed to obtain an export license;

(ii) If so, confirm that it has obtained it;

(iii) Identify any conditions that would affect the recipient (such as limitations on reexport);

(iv) Determine whether the site exercises any control to prevent "diversion" to licensees in any of the proscribed countries or to any citizens of such countries. They should also alert the licensee that the EAR can be violated by an unauthorized export (*e.g.*, if the licensee obtains the goods or technical data in the

---

46. Accessed on June 30, 2003.

United States and then exports them, or engages in a "deemed export," without the requisite license); and

(v) Alert the licensee to its obligations to comply with the EAR in any reexport of such items it engages in, or that it has reason to know the next transferee might engage in.

More serious efforts at creating satisfactory website terms and conditions are in use. These recognize that the risk point for noncompliance with the EAR and TSR occurs in any transaction at the website. These efforts typically entail a "blind" representation that the buyer or licensee does not intend to provide the product or technology to persons or countries targeted by the applicable EAR. However, no accompanying effort is made to qualify the website transaction itself in a similar manner. Moreover, the terms and conditions do not mention the applicability of the TSR, although they expressly refer to OFAC's key list of targeted entities—the "Specially Designated Nationals" list:[47]

> "X software contains technology that is subject to the U.S. Export Administration Regulations . . . and other U.S. law. X software is not to be exported or reexported to certain non-class 1 countries (currently including Afghanistan, Cuba, Iran, Iraq, Libya, North Korea, Serbia, Sudan and Syria) or to persons or entities prohibited from receiving U.S. exports (including Denied Parties, entities on the Bureau of Export Administration Entity List, and **Specially Designated Nationals**). BY DOWNLOADING X SOFTWARE PROGRAM YOU AGREE THAT THE SOFTWARE IS NOT INTENDED FOR USE BY AN ABOVE GOVERNMENT OR IDENTIFIED END-USER, AND THAT YOU WILL ABIDE BY ALL U.S. AND OTHER APPLICABLE EXPORT AND IMPORT LAWS. For more information on the . . . EAR see 15 C.F.R. Parts 730-774. For more information on the EAR and the Bureau of Export Administration ("BXA"), please see the BXA homepage and the EAR index."[48]

Most visitors to the website would be unfamiliar with the "Specially Designated Nationals" list, and the site provides no clarification or guidance for those who wish to obtain such information. The text suggests that the "Specially Designated Nationals List" relates to the EAR and

---

47. Non-mention of the ITAR is more understandable, presuming that the object being sold or licensed does not contain any items governed by the ITAR.

48. Accessed on June 30, 2003. [Emphasis added.]

comes under the jurisdiction of the Bureau of Export Administration—
the only agency mentioned. In actuality, the list is linked to the TSR
and comes under OFAC's jurisdiction. It is important to note that the
"BXA" ceased to be known by that name in April of 2002; its new name
is the Bureau of Industry and Security (or "BIS"). The outdated reference makes clear that updates to address EAR compliance are neither
frequent or not comprehensive. Finally, such Terms and Conditions do
not disclose whether the website operator or owner makes any efforts
to fulfill its obligation to prevent exports that could violate the referenced regulations, lists, etc.

To the extent that a visitor to the site might interpret the quoted
terms as imposing a "representation," it is doubtful that the visitor
would understand its import. Further, in our experience, overseas parties are extremely reluctant to make such broad representations. Such
parties have no reliable way of knowing the applicable U.S. export control and trade sanctions laws and regulations, and understandably do
not want a post-closing remedy triggered by violation of one of them
(whether technical or substantive). Representations concerning the TSR
and EAR in cross-border agreements tend to be heavily negotiated,
uniquely tailored to each transaction, and remarkably varied from transaction to transaction. And their coverage is likely to be notably incomplete, if the U.S. person lacks leverage, is unaware of the inherent risk
points or underestimates them. There is also a certain transactional
fatigue that occurs in response to foreign party resistance to inclusion
of references (in representations or elsewhere) to the applicable TSR or
EAR, particularly when the governing law clause states that the agreement will be governed by the laws of a country other than the United
States.

Websites operated by the most sophisticated and experienced exporters—such as those in Agile's defense contract community, who
know that their products, technologies and services are subject to the
TSR, EAR or ITAR—continue to reflect a kind of "incantatory" quality,
as if one could comply with applicable law merely by reciting them.
Such websites represent that they comply (or are required to comply)
with the TSR, EAR and/or ITAR. However, they do not appear to make
any effort to police the website's usage to ensure such compliance (by
specifically interdicting transactions that would contravene those regulations). As a result of the mergers in the 1990's, and the substantial
reduction in number of remaining defense contractors, one would expect significant uniformity in website "Terms and Conditions" con-

cerning EAR, TSR and ITAR compliance. This does not appear to be the case, however, as is suggested by the following two examples. The first example, quoted from a firm's "site terms," states, in pertinent part:

"BY ACCESSING, BROWSING, AND USING THIS SITE, YOU AGREE TO BE BOUND BY THE TERMS AND CONDITIONS DESCRIBED BELOW . . . IF YOU DO NOT AGREE TO THESE SITE TERMS OR ANY SUBSEQUENT MODIFICATION, DO NOT ACCESS, BROWSE OR OTHERWISE USE THIS SITE . . . Any software and all underlying information and technology downloaded from this Site ("Software") by you may be subject to U.S. export controls, including the Export Administration Act . . . and the . . . EAR . . . and may be subject to export or import regulations in other countries. You are responsible for complying with all trade regulations and laws both foreign and domestic. Except as authorized by law, you agree and warrant not to export or reexport the Software to any country, or to any person, entity, or end-user subject to U.S. export controls, including without limitation persons or entities listed on the U.S. Department of Commerce Bureau of Export Administration's Denied Parties List and the U.S. Department of Treasury's Specially Designated Nationals. You further represent and warrant that no U.S. federal agency has suspended, revoked, or denied your export privileges."[49]

A sophisticated firm should not speculate that its software "may be subject" to the EAR, when it is in the best position to know and verify that fact. If certain of its software products are *subject to* the EAR (and we think a number of them might be), it should apprise visitors to the website of that fact. Assertions that the visitor is "responsible" for EAR and TSR compliance are not accompanied, as they should be, by acknowledgements that the website operator has primary responsibility for such compliance in transactions at its website. If a license is required, the obligation to obtain it is the sole responsibility of the site operator. (A single operator license, with the appropriate provisos or limitations, could be drafted to cover all such sales, and would be far less burdensome to the BIS and OFAC than many license applications, each submitted by a prospective visitor to the vendor's website.) The website firm no doubt has internal compliance procedures and policies that prohibit "releasing" any data subject to the EAR or ITAR in face-to-

49. Accessed on June 30, 2003.

face meetings with persons who are not U.S. citizens. The website, however, does not disclose whether the firm enforces any such policies or polices the use of its website for potential violations of the EAR, TSR and ITAR. Website operators often seek to make their online licenses enforceable and secure against repudiation. To do so, they typically implement express assent procedures, and block the transaction if the visitor does not complete them (*e.g.,* by clicking one or more "I AGREE" buttons on the website). The omission of such procedures for compliance with the applicable EAR, TSR and ITAR suggests that such compliance continues to be taken far less seriously than the risk of non-enforcement of the online agreement, although the risks of non-compliance with the former continue to escalate.

A head-to-head competitor of the defense contract firm whose "site terms" were quoted above takes a very different approach, one that suggests that its priorities rest with its intellectual property, not with compliance with the EAR, TSR, ITAR or property belonging to others. This firm's site "Disclaimer" asserts that those who access the site thereby "agree" to the posted terms and conditions (a browse-wrap agreement of dubious or limited enforceability). The "Disclaimer" then devotes unusual attention to the firm's trademarks: it lists in bold type over 400 of the firm's marks, and prohibits infringement of them. The "Disclaimer" includes a representation that the firm is not providing investment advice on its website, a warning not to rely on the stock price information available at the website, and a disclaimer of "forward-looking information." Quite sensible stuff. There is, however, no mention of the applicability of the EAR and TSR and, despite the elaborate notice about trademarks, no caution against infringement of the company's patents (which could just as easily have been listed by number on the website to give clear notice to all visitors). Perhaps the second firm trusts that it will provide nothing that can be accessed or downloaded that could violate the EAR and TSR. But it is more probable that the issue did not appear on the radar screens of the website's development and audit teams.

To summarize, companies with considerable experience in cross-border transactions rely on "Terms and Conditions" that reflect misconceptions of the website owner's obligations to comply with the EAR, TSR and ITAR. Such "Terms and Conditions" reflect an apparent effort to shift to visitors the owner's obligations to comply with the EAR, TSR and ITAR with respect to the use of certain information. At the same time, such "Terms and Conditions" understate the visitors' obligations, particularly with respect to "deemed exports" within the United States, reexports outside of the United States, and a broad spectrum of prohibitions set forth in the applicable TSR, EAR or ITAR. Such "Terms and Conditions" thus radically underestimate the risks of violating the Access Control Laws.[50]

1.4 Misconceptions That Obscure the Risk of Violating the EAR and TSR.

Companies often bring to cyberspace certain misconceptions that make them reluctant to deploy Access Control Law checkpoints early in a transaction. One commonly held misconception is that the EAR only applies to cross-border transactions. The parties then reason that if no international border has been crossed, no export has occurred, and they are beyond the reach and perceived scope of export control or trade sanction regulations. The EAR applies, however, when a statutorily defined "export" occurs, and that *does not require a transaction, shipment or transfer of goods or technologies to traverse an international boundary.*

Under the EAR, exports can readily occur without the controlled item leaving U.S. soil. Consider, for instance, U.S.-controlled technical data. If such technical data fits within an enumerated category on the Commerce Control List (and thus has civilian and potential military uses or so-called "dual use"), it is clearly "subject to" control by the EAR.[51] Releases of such data to non-U.S. citizens are "deemed ex-

---

50. We recognize, of course, that while a website can put its visitors on notice about required compliance with the EAR, TSR, and ITAR, its operator or owner does not want to be deemed to be giving definitive legal advice on which the users can subsequently rely for exculpation of their conduct. Such concerns should not prevent a website from directing a visitor to sources for guidance, such as the BIS and OFAC websites, which provide excellent, up-to-date resources and interpretative guidance.

51. The Commerce Control List ("CCL") contains entries called Export Control Classification Numbers, or ECCNs, which are used in determining whether a license from the BIS is required for certain exports and reexports. It is important to note, however, that the CCL also describes some items that are subject to the export licensing jurisdiction of the State Department's DDTC and thus to tighter controls on their export and on foreign nationals' access to such items and related technical data. The DDTC has export licensing authority over items that have been specifically designed, developed, configured, adapted, or modified for military application and do not have predominantly civil applications or that have significant military or intelligence applications. BIS, by contrast, has export licensing authority over items that have predominantly civil uses, although they also may be used by the military.

ports."[52] A U.S. aerospace client who shows a blueprint, printout, diagram or PowerPoint slide containing such data to visiting executives from another country (even if only for marketing purposes) is deemed by the EAR to have just "exported" the information to such executive's home country or countries. Doing so (without first obtaining the requisite license from the Commerce Department, assuming such a license would be granted) contravenes the EAR. There are also exports with respect to which there is a presumption of denial for license applications with regard to certain end-users in countries targeted by the EAR.[53]

Website construction seldom includes an appreciation of the EAR's domestic application. As a result, releases of technology and software from a website risk contravening the EAR, regardless of whether the release is to a U.S. or foreign national outside the United States, or to a foreign national within the United States. Curiously, a few websites reflect an awareness of the risk, only to ignore it by seeking to shift responsibility to the visitor for compliance with the EAR. In one instance, a major defense contractor's site asserts that if a visitor wishes to disclose any information from the website to a "foreign national," such visitor would first have to obtain the appropriate approvals. The website, however, does not prevent "foreign nationals" from accessing the site and downloading information directly. The site's "Terms and Conditions of Use" state, in pertinent part:

> "This information is subject to all laws, regulations and administrative acts, now or hereafter in effect of the U.S. government regarding the exportation and/or reexportation of information. The **recipient of this information acknowledges that they will be responsible for compliance** as necessary with such laws, regulations and administrative acts. **Prior to the disclosure of information presented on this website to any foreign national, the recipient will obtain any such approvals** in a manner consistent with the terms and conditions of this agreement."[54]

---

52. The EAR defines "export" to mean "an actual shipment or transmission of items subject to the EAR out of the United States, or release of technology or software subject to the EAR to a foreign national in the United States. . . ." 15 C.F.R. §734.2(b). Any such release is deemed an export to the "home country or countries of the foreign national" under what is termed the "deemed release" rule. 15 C.F.R. §734.2(b)(2)(ii).

53. If such presentation also included data identified on the U.S. Munitions List (22 CFR Part 121), and the client did not obtain the requisite license from the State Department, the client will also have contravened the International Traffic in Arms Control Regulations.

54. Accessed on June 15, 2004. [Emphasis added.] As with earlier examples of

Similarly, a firm can inadvertently violate the ITAR by failing to understand when its activities come within the ITAR's scope. For example, a firm that previously made products solely for civilian or consumer use, may decide to modify for homeland security or potential military use. **Prior to production, it is required to register with the U.S. State Department's DDTC.** Such modified items are not necessarily controlled by the Department of Commerce. If the item is on the U.S. Munitions List, it is subject to the ITAR, and requires the firm to register with the DDTC before production or export. Even when a firm does not export, but merely manufactures components (on the U.S. Munitions List) solely for inclusion in defense articles sold to other U.S. defense contractors, it must register with the DDTC.[55] If personnel of the firm meet in the United States with foreign nationals to discuss a problem the foreign national is having using an item controlled by the ITAR, and offer suggestions to reduce, remedy or work around that problem, they have just "exported" a "defense service." If this is done without first obtaining a license from the DDTC, this activity violates the ITAR.[56] Such violations can occur just as easily, in casual exchanges by e-mail or instant messaging between personnel at a contractor's facilities in the United States responding to complaints from a customer about a product on the U.S. Munitions List. Increasingly, the DDTC's concerns are less about unlicensed sales of hardware and more about "a CD-ROM full of advanced software and design data being sent across borders with the click of a computer mouse."[57]

Cyberspace transactions and cyber-driven transactions have historically proceeded on the assumption that what we have termed the Access Control Laws did not need to be reviewed at a pre-transactional checkpoint. Although communications and commerce in cyberspace initially occurred beyond the domain of national borders, legal jurisdictions and territorial regulations, as the Web has developed, there has been a corresponding re-formulation of these concepts and of their applicable

---

"Terms of Use" reviewed in previous sections, it would not serve a useful purpose to identify the site.

55. Id.

56. Cf. 22 CFR §120.9 (definition of "defense service") and 22 CFR §127(1)(a)(1) (prohibiting unlicensed export of "defense service").

57. *Remarks by Assistant Secretary Lincoln P. Bloomfield, Jr. on the Occasion of the Inauguration of the Allied Command Transformation*, Norfolk Beach, Virginia, June 19, 2003, accessed at www.state.gov/t/pm/rls/rm/22158.htm.

domains. U.S. persons who participate in cyberspace transactions and cyber-driven transactions can now no longer reliably assume that they do not need to know about the commercial dealings and relationships of the parties with whom they transact business. This tension, and the resulting lack of compliance sensitivity, is not solely a cyberspace phenomenon. The U.S. National Aeronautics and Space Agency ("NASA"), for example, has found itself under the same conflicting pressures as the Commerce Department: the obligation to prevent unauthorized exports can become subordinated to the drive to share information for scientific and commercial objectives. NASA's recognition of the need to ensure compliance with the EAR and the ITAR did not occur until 1995, when NASA finally established an Export Control Program.[58] Nonetheless, a 1999 Inspector General Audit of NASA's supervision of export-controlled technologies concluded that: "NASA may not have adequate control over export-controlled technologies to preclude unauthorized or unlicensed transfers."[59] Evidence of inadequate training, lack of appropriate audits, and incomplete identification of all export-controlled technologies in NASA's possession (among others) supported that conclusion.[60] Consider the procedures NASA was "supposed" to adhere to:

> "When NASA needs to export a controlled technology,[61] the Agency takes special steps to ensure compliance with the Arms and Export Regulations. NASA uses the Denied Persons List to screen the foreign party recipient for clearance. After determining that the foreign party has a clearance, the item is classified as to whether it is governed by either the Munitions List or by the Commerce Control List, if either, and is classified accordingly. After another series of screenings, if required, NASA submits the request for an export license to either the Department of State or the Department of Commerce. The NASA Headquarters Export Administrator serves as a liaison between NASA and the two Federal Departments, as well as

---

58. NASA treats as export-controlled technology any item that appears on the U.S. Munitions List or on the Commerce Control List.

59. *Final Report on Audit of NASA Control of Export-Controlled Technologies, Assignment Number A9901200, Report Number IG-99-020*, March 31, 1999, p. i, accessible at www.hq.nasa.gov/office/oig/hq/ig-99-020.pdf.

60. Id.

61. Note that such "export" would, of course, include a "deemed export" to one of the foreign nationals participating in a NASA program or visiting a NASA controlled facility or communicating with NASA by phone or e-mail.

other agencies with export control roles. Once a license is obtained, NASA may export the item."[62]

It is not surprising that, if NASA gives only belated attention to compliance with the EAR, gives no attention to the TSR,[63] and only partially implements its own internal compliance procedures, participants in cyberspace will be even slower to recognize the need for enhanced diligence.

That need will become acute, we believe, because the distinction between cyberspace transactions and cyber-driven transactions is rapidly narrowing.[64] As that distinction narrows, the risk of incurring liability (sometimes-strict liability for civil offenses) is rising to a level that poses substantial financial and "good will" risks to any company that invests in and relies on its brand name(s). Such good will risks include having the firm's name appear in connection with enforcement actions on the OFAC and BIS websites and in newspaper and online articles that would in all probability be critical of the firm. The more serious the violations, the more adverse the resulting publicity and the greater

---

62. *Final Report on Audit of NASA Control of Export-Controlled Technologies, Assignment Number A9901200, Report Number IG-99-020,* March 31, 1999, p. 1, accessed at www.hq.nasa.gov/office/oig/hq/ig-99-020.pdf.

63. Although not noted by the Inspector General, checking only the Denied Persons Lists (a list maintained by the BIS and accessible at its website) is an incomplete checking of all the applicable lists—both those maintained by the BIS and the SDN List maintained by the OFAC.

64. Cyberspace transactions appear to be becoming increasingly complex. For example, aerospace and chemical industry firms have established websites for supply contracts, previously the kind of activity that would be regarded as potentially cross-border, but strictly on terra firma. As corporate transactions rely increasingly on cyberspace substitutes for activities formerly carried out in person, in country, and on-site, such cyber-driven transactions will come to resemble certain key features of cyberspace transactions. Some bridging of the remaining gap, of course, occurs when parties negotiate via videoconferencing, as many companies resorted to for business in East Asia during the outbreak of SARS. Nonetheless, such conferences, while offering substantial cost reductions, are not without their substantial drawbacks. Just as one never really knows who else is on-line (and in the room) when a negotiation occurs by conference call and one of the participants insists on using their speaker phone, so too one never knows who else is in the room beyond the field of view captured by the videoconferencing camera, nor whether such negotiations are being recorded and available as evidence in a subsequent litigation or as leverage in a pre-litigation dispute negotiation. Since videoconferencing too can be a transmission vehicle for unauthorized exports in violation of the EAR, firms that use such communications in cross-border transactions need checkpoints in place to avert such risks.

the resultant damage to the firm's good will (both in terms of on-going commercial relations and in terms of future business opportunities). Yet such risks are still not an important part of the "risk calculus" of U.S. persons engaged in cross-border cyberspace transactions, even though such risks, when discerned in connection with a particular transaction, invariably elicit a response like: "we don't want our company to get anywhere near a violation or infringement; make sure we don't."

The reasons are obvious. First and foremost, violations can result in imprisonment of the responsible individuals, and there is no corporate shield, indemnification, insurance or other protective mechanism that can be interposed either post-violation or pre-emptively. The prospect of indictment and public criticism (even without consideration of a potential prison term) is virtually guaranteed to have a chilling effect on the future financial success of the firm.

In addition, violation of the TSR or the ITAR can result in imprisonment for up to ten years *for each count.* Violations of the TSR, EAR and ITAR can also result in heavy fines (both corporate and personal), seizure of property, blockages of assets and interests in assets, voiding of transactions, deprivation of export privileges and being declared a party with whom no "U.S. person" is permitted to transact or have any other dealings. Civil penalties and settlements are published monthly on the OFAC's website, and similar information appears on the BIS' website.

Such liability poses a real threat to the economic viability of most companies. Nonetheless, many companies need to improve their understanding of such risks and of the need to deploy carefully tailored, systematic precautions to avert the risk of contravening the Access Control Laws (whose existence is often not well known or understood). While compliance reviews for securities laws are routine, such reviews have not yet become routine for a set of laws with comparably draconian penalties, and whose net is cast arguably even more broadly.

In this section, we have explored certain misconceptions that can hinder recognition of the TSR, EAR and ITAR risks to cyberspace transactions, cyber-driven transactions and the U.S. persons involved in such transactions. In the next section, we will consider certain trends in cyber-driven transactions that make it increasingly likely that such risks will not be detected, or detected too late for remediation, substantially increasing the transactional costs and putting the transactors at personal and economic risk.

1.5 Emerging Need to Deploy Checkpoints Sufficiently Early to Detect and Defuse the Access Control Law Risk in Cyberspace.

Agile's partners continuously engage in multiple simultaneous cross-border transactions. To the extent that such transactions are cyber-driven, Agile gains transactional efficiencies. Face to face meetings are often replaced in on-going commercial relationships by cost-effective time-saving e-mail negotiations. E-mail preserves the discourse of negotiation across dislocated time zones.

In a strategic acquisition of an overseas company by a U.S. firm, the convenience and transactional efficiencies, however, have hidden costs. Certain objectives can only be achieved face-to-face, in country or on-site at the target company. On-site visits are often necessary to appreciate the real nature of a company's commercial dealings. One has the opportunity to engage in conversations with personnel who run the day-to-day commercial operations, to become familiar with how the company deals with personnel in countries to which it reexports controlled U.S.-origin items, and to evaluate potential risks of reexport, thereby creating a data base from which to map the risk points under the Access Control Laws. Counsel can then pursue enhanced, finely guided, due diligence from which the Company will reap the greatest benefits and which will justify any additional costs.

Unfortunately, perceived benefits of cyber-intensive negotiations and routine commercial dealings and evolving transactional customs have increasingly altered the way clients want their deals done. While the cost-savings are obvious, the potential liability off-setting such savings is often concealed. The benefits of first person negotiations consist largely in increased understanding of the terms of the transaction and in the ability to resolve multi-party disputes. If negotiations by e-mail reach an impasse, a telephone conference or a face-to-face meeting may need to be arranged to facilitate a resolution. Long meetings often accomplish through fatigue what e-mail cannot. The cost, however, is the tangible cost of transporting and tying up personnel through long, often unproductive meetings.

The costs of cyber-negotiation are less obvious and often largely concealed. They consist of:

(i) Restricted or inefficient use of counsel;

(ii) Unrestricted (and unreviewed) communications by e-mail and instant messaging; and

(iii) The difficulty of extricating a client after the fact from actual violations (whether willful or unwitting), including violations imputed to a U.S. person by virtue of the target's conduct.

Another largely concealed cost of cyber-negotiation for Agile (as for other U.S. companies engaged in cross-border acquisitions) is that the "due diligence" review has become more attenuated as a result of increased use of overseas counsel, reduced use of on-site visits and increased cyber communication. What has been lost as a result are the opportunities to see and evaluate what never appears on paper: the attitudes, customs and practices that provide the informative business context. As a result, there is little to prevent counsel from assuming that business is conducted, relationships are structured, in short, things are done, in a foreign jurisdiction in precisely the same manner as they are in the United States. Without face-to-face contact, it is far too easy to miss the "red flags" of potential problems and improprieties and to fail to make the necessary enhanced due diligence. Cyber-driven transactions fall at the opposite end of the diligence continuum from those characterized by ample opportunity to gain access to detailed on-site information. The more such opportunities are sacrificed, the more likely the company will enter into transactions where it may be held liable for having *reason to know* that it would be contravening the TSR, EAR or ITAR, but elected willfully to blind itself. That the resulting violation was unwitting will provide no defense when strict liability applies.

Negotiations that proceed by e-mail or instant messaging ("IM") with few restrictions create additional risk points. New risk points proliferate to the extent that cross-border contract performance is re-routed into cyberspace and reconfigured to occur as a cyber-transaction (*e.g.,* performed by actions electronically processed and recorded at a commercial website). They also proliferate to the extent that more complex transactions become cyber-driven. Negotiations by e-mail or IM create an informal discourse, often marked by premature communications with insufficient review. And unlike face-to-face negotiations, where there is no formal record, the e-mail and IM trail of negotiation positions is frequently preserved, and contains risks that counsel may not be aware of unless copied on all correspondence (which is no longer feasible). As a result of these and other tendencies in cyber-driven transactions, TSR, EAR and ITAR risk points slip past formal checkpoints or encounter no checkpoints at all and remain concealed.

When legal risk points do not correlate with appropriately staffed and enforced checkpoints, impediments to the successful completion of a transaction are unlikely to be detected early. Each delay in detection reduces the opportunity for timely, effective remediation, and with each transactional delay, the associated costs rise sharply. When companies are engaged in aggressive cost cutting, as they are currently, there is a structural/institutional tendency to cut back on transactional checkpoints. This has the counter-productive result that counsel becomes more removed as the transaction becomes more cyber-driven. The more negotiations occur by e-mail and IM or by videoconference (potentially recordable in the latter case, unlikely to be deleted in the former), the more unlikely it becomes that counsel or the customary checkpoints will achieve early detection of the risks posed by the Access Control Laws. *The later the discovery of such risks, the more costly it will be to prevent them from imperiling the transaction and the transactors.*[65]

In the context of the Access Control Laws, the closer the client comes to committing a violation or infringement, the harder it is to extricate the client without concomitantly engaging in conduct that could lead to charges of evading such laws, contributing to an infringement or committing a vicarious infringement. Moreover, it can be particularly difficult for counsel to persuade its client to take appropriate corrective action, when such action is required prior to, and as a pre-condition of, signing the definitive transactional agreements. If the risks of violating the Access Control Laws are not detected before signing, however,

---

65. The business persons running cyber-driven transactions, particularly between parties separated by the Pacific or Atlantic oceans, may often be tempted to relax requirements for "due diligence," to be satisfied with overseas local counsel's selection and review of documents, and to be satisfied with summaries that comment chiefly on corporate and financial condition. As a result, such "due diligence" efforts often do not ask to review the kinds of documents that typically contain evidence that, for example, a target company in an acquisition is engaged in dealings that would be prohibited under the TSR, EAR or ITAR if engaged in by a "U.S. person." Such documents often include: primarily documentation of commercial transactions, agency agreements, letters of credit agreements, and other commercial documents that could easily contain evidence that a U.S. person with access to such documents had "reason to know" that its conduct by doing the deal would contravene the Access Control Laws. Without such review, the outcome, as seen in Agile's hypothetical acquisition of Troll, Brugge and Ijsselmeer can be a failure to address such risks adequately before the U.S. person has inadvertently contravened the Access Control Laws.

signing may itself cause U.S. persons to be drawn into violations of such laws. That fact is perhaps the one most frequently overlooked. More often than realized, remediation must *precede* signing of the definitive transactional agreements.

For example, if Troll has a contract to provide defense services to the Government of Sudan, and the service contract extends for three additional years, Agile's signing of an agreement to acquire Troll indirectly facilitates Troll's performance of the service contract by improving Troll's financial prospects (which Troll could use to obtain loans to help it perform its contractual obligations to the Government of Sudan prior to the Closing). The Sudanese Sanction Regulations prohibit the direct or indirect facilitation of the export of goods, technology or services to Sudan. Without a license, a U.S. person would be taking a considerable risk that OFAC would view such action as a prohibited, indirect "facilitation." Moreover, the longer that such services to Sudan continue after signing, the more likely that indirect facilitation will become direct facilitation. Once signing has occurred, there is an increasing likelihood that Troll's directors will confer with Agile's partners on how business should be conducted and, to the extent that such discussions involve issues of the Sudanese service contract, further violations of the TSR become highly probable if not unavoidable. If the target firm agrees to complete its disengagements from the proscribed entities or persons prior to signing, the U.S. persons must still avoid becoming involved in direct or indirect negotiations with the very parties they seek to avoid (Troll's invitation to Agile's Danish partners to help negotiate the disengagements poses precisely that risk).

It is a matter of simple business sense that parties will be reluctant to agree to requests from U.S. persons to disengage from profitable dealings before a definitive agreement (for a merger, acquisition, outsourcing, etc.) has been signed. If they agree, they run the risk of losing valuable business opportunities with no enforceable agreement to compensate them for taking such risk. One available solution is straightforward but often unpalatable to U.S. persons—that is, to seek a license for any suspect transactions or dealings. Companies more often than not find such solution unacceptable, because:

(i) There is no assurance that a license will be granted;

(ii) Few companies are willing to disclose the considerable information that OFAC, BIS or the DDTC would require as a condition for granting such a license;

(iii) A license might contain burdensome conditions; and/or

(iv) The processing time for a license (four to six months, and often longer) creates much too great a delay for time-sensitive transactions.

Anything less, however, provides no protection for the U.S. persons.

An impasse on this issue can be anticipated, unless the parties come to an understanding on the significant terms and conditions of the proposed acquisition. In the latter context, the prospect of swiftly and successfully completing the deal can be used as an incentive for the target company to proceed promptly with the required disengagements. In effect, disengagement can be built into the deal timetable and checklist as one more step toward completion, if the need to disengage is identified sufficiently early. Any preliminary pre-offer diligence to evaluate potential acquisition targets should include a basic understanding of these issues. If compliance issues are found in a target (once identified), the acquirer must make a convincing case that the transactions are clearly prohibited by the TSR, EAR or ITAR, that violation by U.S. persons will occur upon signing, and that the acquisition cannot proceed before the required disengagements have been completed (which requires not only that termination agreements be executed, but that all shipments in the pipeline cease, and that no deliveries of goods, acceptances of orders or receipts of payment occur thereafter). Ultimately, the deal will probably proceed if the overseas (target) firm understands that, while it risks losing certain business opportunities, the U.S. firm's potential exposure is open-ended liability for which there is no protection except proscription of the prohibited dealings. While one can have considerable sympathy for the burdens, distractions, disruptions and associated costs of disengagement, the inescapable fact remains that, for most U.S. companies (and those who run them), multiple violations of the EAR, TSR or ITAR are unacceptable costs of doing business or of doing a deal.

Thus, contrary to the customary approach to cross-border transactions, such checkpoints should be in place "anticipatorily" in advance of the final negotiations of definitive agreements (on a merger, acquisition, outsourcing, joint venture, long term supply agreement, etc.). Early deployment and strong enforcement of such checkpoints are crucial for ensuring that by signing a definitive transactional agreement U.S. persons will not thereby violate the TSR, EAR or ITAR. They are also crucial for ensuring that U.S. persons negotiating or advising on a cross-border, cyber-driven transaction do not (unwittingly or wittingly) enter into negotiations that violate such regulations, thereby imperiling the transaction, their company and themselves.

In this section we reviewed certain trends that make it increasingly likely that U.S. persons engaged in cyberspace transactions or cyber-driven transactions will be unaware of the risks of violating the Access Control Laws. In the next section we explore certain challenges to the deployment of Access Control Law checkpoints for transactions in and through cyberspace. In light of those challenges, we will argue that deployments of those checkpoints should be designed to respond to checkpoint failures that could potentially result in Access Control Law violations. Doing so positions firms facing "worst case" scenarios to avert misguided and inefficient, late "damage control," to distance themselves from conduct that would in all probability be deemed "aggravating factors" by enforcement agencies and instead to qualify for "mitigating factors."

1.6 Challenges of Implementing Checkpoints for the Access Control Laws.

While the monitoring of border crossings tends to pose only a linear problem (one key moment at one key location), susceptible to a linear solution, guiding a cross-border transaction through its many different phases of negotiations and completion tends to pose multi-layered, recurring (often amplifying) problems with multiple crossings involving the interface of personnel and expertise in multiple global locales. Mapping risk points is a continuous process, as is the structuring and enforcement of the related checkpoints. To avert violations of TSR, EAR and ITAR, one cannot simply focus on the Closing (although there will be tremendous pressure to do so). If a "U.S. person" delays its checkpoints for compliance with the TSR until Closing, it will run a high risk of finding itself already in violation. The TSR were not drafted to accommodate the standard transactional scenario of signing followed months later by a Closing. The TSR were drafted (and continue to be drafted) for immediate effect, and often bar even the most preliminary dealings in connection with a proposed or contemplated future transaction—the early discussions to explore the feasibility and potential benefits of a deal. Such tentative "feelers" customarily do not even rise to the level of certainty that would require disclosure for SEC reporting purposes in quarterly filings of the company. However, the regulatory framework we are looking at has a much more sensitive trigger, and comes into play at a much earlier stage. Agile's concern for its reputation dictates that it be attuned to this law enforcement threshold. Its policy is to avert the risk of contravening the TSR, EAR and ITAR (rather than to attempt to skirt such risks or to find ways to circumvent those regulations and develop a rationale after the fact).

To avert the risks of TSR, EAR and ITAR violations, counsel should try to imagine the range of hypothetical exposure, from inadvertent violations to violations resulting from the seller's failure to disclose relevant information. In addition, because such a risk-management strategy will often involve delays in business negotiations, negotiating personnel should probably be carefully directed (scripted with bullet points) and monitored periodically. Business persons are often required to compromise to conclude the negotiation of definitive agreements. Many of the definitions of conduct prohibited by the TSR do not include an "intent" to commit such violation, but merely "commission" (although some, such as action to evade such regulations, will be harder to defend in the face of evidence of such intent). Many definitions also do not include knowledge that such conduct constitutes a violation. Most troubling to Agile's General Counsel is the provision that knowledge can be imputed to Agile and its partners, if they had *reason to know* that an action or inaction violated the TSR. Here Agile must confront what we would refer to as a *transparency paradox*: the greater a "U.S. person's" access to information about other parties to a transaction, the more likely that person will be deemed to be in a position to have had *reason to know* of any conduct or dealings engaged in by such parties that would be illegal or in violation of the TSR if performed by a U.S. person.[66] Such increased access, however, also promotes effective due diligence.

Agile's negotiation of "due diligence" access to Troll, Brugge and Ijsselmeer, accentuates the impact of this paradox: it will thereby be

---

66. Although civil violations of the EAR can incur strict liability, there is less clarity when one looks at the *mens rea* element of a criminal violation of the EAR. Part of the difficulty derives from whether the EAR are authorized at the time in question by the Export Administration Act of 1979 (EAA), which from time to time has been allowed to lapse, or by the IEEPA. The EAA provides penalties for violations committed "knowingly" and different, severer penalties for violations committed "willfully." See 50 U.S. C. app. §§ 2410(a) and (b).

deemed by OFAC to have had *reason to know* of actions by these parties that could bring it into violation of the TSR. The TSR also create a *knowledge paradox* for Agile: the greater a "U.S. person's" knowledge of the TSR, the more likely it will be deemed to be in a position to have had *reason to know* of any conduct or dealings engaged in by such persons that would be illegal or in violation of the TSR if performed by a U.S. person. Both paradoxes would seem to encourage willful ignorance of the other parties to a transaction and of their business dealings—a policy that, from a purely commercial standpoint, makes little sense. However, ignorance of the TSR will *not* provide Agile with greater benefits than knowledge of it. It is therefore not advisable to rely primarily on overseas counsel, who may not be familiar with the TSR, or who may have only a poor appreciation of their content and scope.

If the penalties for EAR, TSR and ITAR violation could be written off as "costs of doing business" (as often occurs with other kinds of violations),[67] counsel would find it difficult to persuade Agile to con-

---

67. We have in mind, for example, the ways in which defense contractors can engage in activity that closely approximates that prohibited by the Foreign Corrupt Practices Act, but which is condoned by the U.S. Government if such activity is dubbed a negotiated "offset." For example, when the United Arab Emirates sought to combine military purchases with expansions of their local economy, it negotiated with U.S. defense contractors—Boeing, Northrop Grumman, and Lockheed Martin—to promise to provide "offsets" in exchange for purchase of defense materiel. Such offsets included expenditures or investments of millions of dollars in projects ranging from financing a medical diagnostic center linked by satellite to the Mayo Clinic to staging a laser-printer recycling business to helping with oil-spill cleanups to construction of a shipyard. As noted recently, "In another era, these gifts might be considered bribes. Now they are called offsets. Bribes were outlawed under the Foreign Corrupt Practices Act of 1977. . . . But offsets, while little known [outside the defense contract community], are a legal and, companies say, necessary part of the international arms trade not only in the emirates but around the globe." Wayne, Leslie, *A Well-Kept Military Secret*, THE NEW YORK TIMES, section 3, February 16, 2003, at pp. 1 and 11.

Some countries will refuse to award a contract unless offsets match or approximate the contract price. For example, when Boeing won a $4.4 billion South Korean contract for 40 F-15 fighter jets, Boeing offered $3.3 billion in offsets. As of this writing, however, U.S. House Armed Services Committee Chairman Duncan Hunter has introduced (and the House of Representatives has passed) controversial legislation that would bar U.S. purchases of systems and components from any country that requires offsets. In a June 16, 2004 response, U.K. Defence Secretary Geoff Hoon warned that such legislation could result in a U.K. review "to consider whether we were prepared to continue to place significant defense contracts with U.S. suppliers . . . ." See Chuter, Andrew, *U.K. Threatens Limits to U.S. Firms' Access*, DEFENSENEWS, June 28, 2004, pp. 1 and 8. In a letter to Defense Secretary Rumsfeld, Secretary Hoon warned that the U.K. was prepared

sider voluntary disclosure of an EAR, TSR or ITAR violation. But the penalties for TSR and EAR violations include substantial fines, voided transactions and imprisonment for up to ten years for *each* violation. Moreover, violations are not aggregated into one count per transaction. Instead, each act in violation of such regulations constitutes a separately punishable count. If a firm lets ten deliveries of its goods be sold under contract, shipped to a targeted party and paid for by a Letter of Credit issued by a targeted bank, that firm (and potentially the officers and directors or partners involved) would face the prospect of strict liability for 30 counts—one for each of the ten separately negotiated prohibited contracts, the ten prohibited deliveries and the ten prohibited draws on the Letters of Credit. Voluntary disclosure in such circumstances becomes a valuable "mitigating factor," particularly since such disclosure will only be treated as a "mitigating factor" by the OFAC or the BIS if the firm discloses the violations *before* the OFAC issues a pre-penalty notice or before the BIS takes comparable action. Counsel should, therefore, give strong consideration to structuring checkpoints defensively to position the company to defend itself optimally in the event it or its personnel become the subject of an OFAC or BIS investigation and enforcement action. In this context, we will review the recent changes made by the OFAC in what it will include as possible "mitigating" and "aggravating" factors in the next section.

1.7 Positioning a Firm to Qualify for "Mitigating" Factors and to Distance it from "Aggravating" Factors Under the TSR.

OFAC has for many years evaluated apparent TSR violations in terms of "mitigating factors" and "aggravating factors." Until recently, OFAC's guidelines for such factors were not published or publicly disclosed. There are now at least two versions of these "factors:"

   (i) The Penalties Guidelines authorized by OFAC's Director, R. Richard Newcomb, dated May 25, 1995, intended for "internal use only"[68] (these were never published by OFAC, but were

---

to retaliate by steering military contracts away from U.S. military contractors if U.S. protectionist policies were not reversed. Spiegel, Peter, *Hoon Warns US of Retaliation against Arms Deal Protectionism*, FINANCIAL TIMES, July 30, 2004, p. 1.
   68. Director Newcomb's cover memorandum for these guidelines notes that they

provided by it in 2001 to the Judicial Review Commission on Foreign Assets Control);[69] and

(ii) An updated version, published by OFAC in the Federal Register on January 29, 2003, as a proposed rule with requests for comments (the **"Internal Economic Sanctions Enforcement Guidelines"** or **"Enforcement Guidelines"**).[70]

The updated version of the Penalties Guidelines appears to be only partial, and would not appear to supersede other information contained in the Penalties Guidelines that was not updated by the Enforcement Guidelines. Of significant interest to Agile's General Counsel is the fact that the Penalties Guidelines explain that: "Intentional violations of the regulations and violations which involve gross negligence *will always result in formal penalty proceedings."*[71] Also of interest is the Penalties Guidelines' description of OFAC's approach to violations for civil penalty purposes. Such violations are described as falling into one of four classes (described below) "according to:

(i) The significance of the violation (including its'visibility') with respect to the sanctions objectives of the program involved, and

(ii) The nature of the violator's actions in committing the violation."[72]

The four classes of violations are:

(i) "Class I Violations"—where the evidence suggests intentional commission with knowledge of the pertinent OFAC regulations, and which contravene substantive (nontechnical) prohibitions or requirements;

(ii) "Class II Violations"—covering any other violation intentionally committed with knowledge of the pertinent OFAC regula-

---

should "not be copied or released" nor "given to anyone outside OFAC." To his and OFAC's considerable credit, OFAC under leadership has changed its policy from nondisclosure to disclosure of such guidelines.

69. Judicial Review Commission on Foreign Assets Control, *Documents from the Office of Foreign Assets Control, Final Report to Congress* (*"Final Report"*), January 2001, Appendix C, accessed at www.law.stetson.edu/JudicialReviewCommission.

70. 68 FEDERAL REGISTER, 19, January 29, 2003, at pp. 4422–4429.

71. Penalties Guidelines, in *Final Report*, Appendix C, p. 2. [Emphasis added.]

72. Id.

tions *or* "under circumstances in which the violator *should have known* of the regulations," or where evidence of transactions suggest that "gross negligence rather than willful conduct is involved;"

(iii) "Class III Violations"—those involving ordinary negligence, but with respect to which issuance of a "warning letter or other nonpenalty action is inappropriate;" and

(iv) "Class IV Violations"—those where the violation was "unintended," and which "could not have been reasonably foreseen by the violator," and thus where an "educational warning letter to the violator can be expected to achieve the same result as a monetary penalty insofar as future compliance with OFAC regulations is concerned."[73]

Agile's General Counsel is most concerned with Class II Violations, where circumstances could suggest that Agile "*should have known* of the regulations," or where the violation might result from gross negligence. This is because the opportunity to conduct a second "due diligence" investigation of Troll and Brugge by counsel familiar with the TSR may paradoxically increase the chances that OFAC will view a subsequent violation in connection with the transaction as involving the applicable threshold level of negligence described in the Penalties Guidelines. If Agile finds evidence that Troll engages in transactions prohibited by the TSR, or discovers "red flags" that suggest the need to inquire further into the possibility of such transactions, Agile will be compelled to expand its due diligence even further, and to press Troll to take corrective action, because Agile's conduct will arguably have crossed the line from *could not have known* to *knew* or *should have known*. In addition, depending on the mitigating or aggravating factors present, penalties proposed for violations may be mitigated 25–75% according to the Penalties Guidelines, in the discretion of OFAC, although with less mitigation afforded for Class I and II violations.[74] For that reason, Agile's General Counsel has given special attention to "mitigating" and "aggravating" factors in developing a strategy for addressing potential violations of the TSR. In case of a failure to avert TSR violations, and particularly in instances where Agile should have known of the violation, Agile needs to ensure that it will qualify for the benefits of "mit-

---

73. Id, pp. 2–3.
74. Id, p. 12.

igating" factors and avoid having "aggravating" factors outweigh those benefits.

The charts below (Figures 2 and 3) provide a comparison of typical "mitigating" and "aggravating" factors that may be considered by OFAC, as set forth in the two versions of its Guidelines. We have marked with an asterisk the mitigating and aggravating factors from 1995 that do not appear among the 2003 Enforcement Guidelines, and have set in italicized text the new factors that appear to have been modified or added in the 2003 Enforcement Guidelines. Omission of a factor from the 2003 Enforcement Guidelines, while indicative of a significant change in policy by OFAC, should not be exaggerated, because OFAC has emphasized in both the Penalties Guidelines and the Enforcement Guidelines, that:

(i) The mitigating and aggravating factors listed are those that *might* be taken into account when OFAC determines *civil* penalties for a violation (OFAC would not appear obligated by its own rules to take such factors into account, and could be expected not to take them into account where circumstances and the objectives of a particular TSR would be better served thereby); and

(ii) The lists of such factors are not exhaustive.[75]

Figure 2. Mitigating Factors That OFAC Might Take Into Account

1995 Penalties Guidelines[a]	2003 Enforcement Guidelines[b]
1. "First offense"	1. "Voluntary disclosure"
2. "Voluntary disclosure"	2. "First offense . . ."
3. "Compliance program in place at time of violation"	3. "Compliance program in place at time of violation"

(continued)

---

75. OFAC clearly is best served by maintaining a flexible policy, particularly since the national security and foreign policy objectives it serves require OFAC to be capable of rapid adjustment to rapidly changing circumstances. Though deals may go sour or crater in relatively brief periods of time, such changes do not present the challenges for rapid adjustment that emerging threats create for a country's national security and foreign policy. Responses to those changes often appear quite rapidly in changes to the TSR and EAR. Note also that OFAC may modify the 2003 Enforcement Guidelines in light of comments it received during the comment period.

Figure 2. (Continued)

1995 Penalties Guidelines[a]	2003 Enforcement Guidelines[b]
4. "If no compliance program, institution of one upon self-discovery or OFAC[c] notification of violation"	4. "If no compliance program, implementation of one upon the respondent's discovery of or OFAC notification of the violation"
5. "Other remedial measures taken"	5. "Other remedial measures taken"
6. "Useful enforcement information provided in response"	6. *"Provision of a written response to a prepenalty notice"*
7. "Cooperation with OFAC during investigation"	7. *"Useful enforcement information provided during an OFAC audit, investigation, or penalty proceeding"*
8. "History of cooperation with OFAC in the past"*	8. "Part of a comprehensive settlement with U.S. Customs Service"
9. "Part of comprehensive settlement with USCS"[d]	9. *"Other U.S. government enforcement action already completed"*
10. "Clerical error, inadvertence or mistake of fact"	10. *"Lack of relevant commercial experience"*
11. "Licensable transaction"[e]	11. "Clerical error, inadvertence, or mistake of fact"
12. "Language barrier or other impediment to understanding of regulations (individuals only)"	12. *"Evidence in the administrative record that a transaction(s) could have been licensed by OFAC under an existing licensing policy had an application been submitted"* [a clarification of Penalties Guidelines #11]
13. "Humanitarian transaction"	13. *"Apparent language barrier or other impediment to understanding of regulations (individual only)"* [a clarification of Penalties Guidelines #12]
14. "Such other matters as justice may require"	14. "Humanitarian nature of transaction"
15. "Administrative considerations: • Litigation risk • Early settlement"*	15. "Such other matters as justice may require"

[a]Id, pp. 12–13 for all quotations in table of Penalties Guidelines.
[b]68 FEDERAL REGISTER 19, January 29, 2003, at p. 4427.

(continued)

Figure 2. Mitigating Factors That OFAC Might Take Into Account (Continued)

[c]"FAC" appears to signify "Foreign Assets Control" or OFAC.
[d]I.e., "USCS" appears to signify "United States Customs Service."
[e]I.e., required a license but not obtained prior to violation.

Figure 3. Aggravating Factors That OFAC Might Take Into Account

1995 Penalties Guidelines[a]	2003 Enforcement Guidelines[b]
1. "Intentional misconduct"	1. "Willfulness"
2. "Second or more offense"	2. "Second or subsequent offense . . ."
3. "Concurrent offense of other relevant laws or regulations"*	3. "Apparent disregard of prior notice from U.S. government concerning transactions at issue"[c]
4. "Knowledge of regulations"	4. "No remedial measure taken after notice or discovery"
5. "Deliberate effort to hide or conceal goods"	5. "Deliberate effort to hide or conceal the violation"
6. "No remedial measures taken (repeated offenses)"	6. "Extraordinary adverse economic sanctions impact"
7. "Lack of cooperation, including verbal abuse and threats; concealing information"*	7. "Useful enforcement information provided during an OFAC audit, investigation, or penalty proceeding"
8. "Sanctions damage (completed transaction)"	8. "Familiarity with economic sanctions programs"[d]
9. "Lack of compliance program (may be applicable to certain first offenses by banks and other businesses)"*	
10. "Relevant commercial experience"*	

[a]Penalties Guidelines, in Final Report, Appendix C, pp. 12–13 for all quotations in table of Penalties Guidelines.

[b]68 FEDERAL REGISTER 19, January 29, 2003, at p. 4427.

[c]OFAC on occasion issues "cautionary letters," where an OFAC audit or civil investigation results in insufficient evidence to conclude that a violation occurred but indicates activity that could eventually lead to a violation. OFAC also on occasion issues "warning letters," where OFAC concludes a violation has occurred but determines that such warning would achieve the same objective as imposition of a financial penalty. See Enforcement Guidelines, 68 FEDERAL REGISTER 19, January 29, 2003, at p. 4426.

[d]Using knowledge of the TSR as an "aggravating factor" is potentially counterproductive, and has been criticized by commentators. See Letter of American Bankers to OFAC, March 31, 2003, p. 2, accessed at www.ustreas.gov/offices/eotffc/ofac/interim/enf_docs/aba.pdf.

The most significant changes in the typical "mitigating factors" from 1995 to 2003 are in the increased emphasis that OFAC now places on voluntary disclosure of violations, and on providing a written response to a pre-penalty notice (which, to be responsive, would probably require complete disclosures of all potentially relevant facts related to the alleged violation that would be of interest to OFAC in understanding the surrounding circumstances). Actions aimed at ensuring compliance (or averting violations) can be expected to qualify as "mitigating factors." In addition, the company should distance itself from actions and inaction that could be viewed as "aggravating factors." Examples of mitigating factors include having a compliance program in place prior to a violation, or implementing one promptly in the event of discovery of a violation. The underlying theme of such mitigation is that a company that errs should demonstrate that it sought in good faith to comply; that, upon discovering a violation, it sought to prevent further violations (by implementing a compliance program, if it did not have one); that it made efforts to prevent prohibited parties from receiving any benefits; and that it brought the matter to OFAC's immediate attention so that it could implement further action if necessary.

OFAC's changes to typical "aggravating factors" appear more significant than those made to "mitigating factors." Of particular interest to Agile's General Counsel is OFAC's apparent de-emphasis of knowledge of the relevant TSR from fourth (in 1995) to eighth (in 2003), and its increased emphasis on the lack of appropriate response to self-discovery and to notices from OFAC. Where a post-discovery implementation of a compliance program may count as a "mitigating factor," a failure to take corrective action with respect to the particular violation is likely to be viewed as an "aggravating factor." Moreover, we think that whatever benefit a pre-discovery "mitigating factor" might bring to a company, it would be more than offset by post-discovery conduct that qualifies as an "aggravating factor," *e.g.,* a violation that results from a clerical error might cease to deserve to be a "mitigating factor," if discovery of the violation did not prompt timely efforts to prevent financial benefits accruing to a targeted party, and if the violator sought to hide or to conceal the violation.

The Enforcement Guidelines reinforce the importance of positioning Agile, if the need arises, to qualify for "mitigating factors" and to distance itself from "aggravating factors," by noting that OFAC "encourages evidentiary submissions indicating the presence or absence of a mitigating or aggravating factor."[76]

The aggravating factor that poses the greatest challenge to any company is the one involving "Deliberate effort to hide or conceal the violation," because voluntary disclosure is often contrary to the business culture. Moreover, since the next most serious aggravating factor is a "Second or subsequent offense," there is a built-in incentive to view non-disclosure as a virtue: each undisclosed violation enables the company to claim credibly that its subsequent offense was a "first" offense. However, non-disclosure has the opposite incentive as well: accumulating undisclosed offenses can put pressure on a company to be less concerned with preventing violations than with concealing them. The slide from preventing violations (and making voluntary disclosure) to ignoring violations (and trusting that non-disclosure will ensure non-discovery) may seem gradual over time, and only appear precipitous in hindsight. Such conduct can lead to institutional resistance to compliance, or what can be described as *"mettle fatigue"* (refusal to respond swiftly or appropriately). This can undermine any compliance program in place, and any attempts at remediation of the risks discerned by enhanced due diligence review.

Even if "mettle fatigue" is not present, voluntary disclosure can become the most problematic "mitigating factor" for a firm's counsel. No company would want confidential commercial activities scrutinized by federal agents of any agency, whether OFAC, BIS, DDTC or Justice. Assuming that the company has "nothing to hide," it would still not be anxious to have its confidentiality compromised, its management distracted for prolonged periods by deliberations over the investigation and responses to it, and its transactional opportunities delayed or put in doubt. Once word hits the street (or global cyberspace) that a company is under investigation by OFAC, other companies will become reluctant to deal with it, fearing that they might thereby become subjects of an OFAC investigation. Moreover, a firm's officers, directors and/or partners may fear that voluntary disclosure will trigger an investigation by OFAC or the Justice Department, whereas prompt corrective action (without disclosure to OFAC) might mitigate any harm and avoid the adverse consequences of an OFAC or Justice Department investigation. The appeal of such reasoning makes counsel's job all the more difficult.

---

76. *Enforcement Guidelines*, 68 FEDERAL REGISTER 19, January 29, 2003, at p. 4427.

Moreover, OFAC has anticipated such considerations. The Enforcement Guidelines indicate that when a party voluntarily discloses an apparent violation to OFAC, OFAC's proposal of a penalty "generally will be mitigated by **at least 50%** from the amount that would otherwise be proposed under these Guidelines."[77] **Voluntary disclosure, however, if not timely made, is not deemed "voluntary" by OFAC:**

> "Notification to OFAC may not be considered to be a voluntary disclosure if OFAC previously received information concerning the transactions from another source, including but not limited to another regulatory or law enforcement agency or another person's blocking or funds-transfer rejection report."[78]

What is alarming is the opportunity that such policy creates for OFAC to disqualify a firm from "voluntary disclosure," if it receives information concerning a prohibited transaction from a disgruntled employee, a firm's strategic competitors (or allies), or a major stockholder at a target company who opposes its acquisition by the "transgressing" firm. The prospect of this makes it essential that a firm (whether it transacts in cyberspace or engages in cyber-driven transactions) have a clear and reliable analytic approach to identifying transactional points where it needs to avert or minimize its exposure to Access Control Law risks.

Recent changes to the U.S. Sentencing Guidelines and the EAR enforcement policies and procedures reinforce that need, and make it imperative that companies consider implementing a "defense-in-depth" approach to the checkpoints that are deployed on an on-going basis and that are enforced in connection with any cross-border transaction. Even entry into very preliminary negotiations (whether or not they result in an agreement) can constitute violations of the TSR, EAR and ITAR. A rigorous compliance program, including the early deployment of transactional checkpoints (if built into the institution's commercial

---

77. *Enforcement Guidelines*, 68 FEDERAL REGISTER 19, January 29, 2003, at p. 4427. [Emphasis added.] The Enforcement Guidelines also point out that proposed penalties for apparent violations that constitute a first offense "generally will be mitigated at least 25%" unless "aggravating factors are also present" or the apparent violations involve willful misconduct or gross negligence. Id.

78. Id. OFAC further notes in these guidelines that certain actions will not qualify as a voluntary disclosure of a violation: (1) submission of a license application; and (2) response to an administrative subpoena or other inquiry from OFAC.

approach), will not add costs, but rather will reduce both cost and risk (as well as uncertainty). The latter is achieved primarily by sparing the company and its management the costs of the delays required to remediate problems that could have been avoided, the costs of thwarted transactions that could have been successfully completed, and the costs of defending a post-closing investigation into violations or successor liability that would not have been overlooked had effective checkpoints been in place at the proper time.

If the costs of rigorous compliance (and the checkpoints we recommend) are weighed against the short-term savings of superficial compliance, what tips the balance heavily in favor of rigorous compliance is not the dollar amount of potential financial penalties as much as the transactional consequences of lax enforcement: a major acquisition unravels as a result of belatedly discovered compliance problems (as occurred in the failed Lockheed/Titan merger), or the benefits of a completed acquisition are deferred or diminished by belatedly discovered successor liabilities. In short, rigorous compliance is cost effective, because it increases the certainty of successfully completing transactions. Avoiding the alternative—a thwarted transaction or a spectacularly public meltdown of a company (like that which occurred to Arthur Anderson or Enron)—adds to the benefit side of the cost/benefit calculus of enhanced compliance. And if litigation is required to exonerate the firm from charges of wrongdoing, the full-court press required for a successful defense of the company and its management will accumulate costs that dwarf those of a ten-year budget for an effective compliance program. Last, but not least, there is the psychic strain that develops during an investigation of a company's management by a federal enforcement agency, which is redoubled if there is also a trial of senior personnel on criminal charges. The costs entailed in avoiding such strains are modest; the costs of surviving them are substantial, in the event of an acquittal, and incalculable, in the event of a conviction. While no compliance program can guarantee that there will be no inadvertent or technical violations of the EAR, TSR or ITAR, a rigorous compliance program will, in all probability, keep OFAC (or other relevant agency) from referring a matter to the Justice Department, because such program will have increased the likelihood of averting willful violations and provided the company and its management with solid grounds for demonstrating that the violations did not occur through gross negligence.

1.8 Changes to the EAR Enforcement Policies and Procedures Increase the Need for a Compliance Program that Includes a "Transactional Checkpoint EAR."

On February 20, 2004, the Department of Commerce's Bureau of Industry and Security ("BIS") published a final rule (dated February 11, 2004) that amended the EAR by incorporating guidance on how BIS makes penalty determinations (when settling administrative enforcement cases), and how it responds to violations of the EAR (the "Penalty Guidance").[79] At the same time, the BIS provided responses to comments it had received regarding the proposed rule on such matters, dated September 17, 2003. The BIS' responses offer illuminating insights into BIS policies that are not easily discerned from the final rule, including the following:

- Although voluntary self-disclosure of a violation may be viewed as a mitigating factor, a firm should not expect such disclosure to exonerate it. The BIS emphasizes that no single factor, not even voluntary self-disclosure of a violation, will carry a presumption that the BIS will not seek a penalty.[80]

- Acquiring firms cannot expect to avoid liability for violations of the EAR committed by a target firm. However, when an acquirer takes reasonable steps to uncover, correct and disclose to the BIS the conduct by the target firm that gave rise to violations prior to the acquisition, the BIS typically will not take such violations into account in settling other violations by the acquiring firm (in effect, only by uncovering, correcting and disclosing such violations by the target firm can the acquirer avert having those treated as aggravating factors in any of its own violations).[81]

---

79. 69 FEDERAL REGISTER 34, at p. 7867, February 20, 2004, accessed at www.nacua.org/ documents/Enforcement_of_ExportAdministrationRegulations.pdf.

80. 69 FEDERAL REGISTER 34, at p. 7868, Response 1(f).

81. 69 FEDERAL REGISTER 34 at p. 7869, Response 4(d). Note, however, that does not dispel the problem for acquirers of the potential "successor liability" that may be imputed to them as a result of a target firm's prior (and perhaps continuing) violations. See discussion of the *Sigma Aldrich* case, in Section 1.3.0.

- Although the BIS now lists in the EAR specific mitigating and aggravating factors, that list is non-exhaustive. The BIS will, therefore, consider a party's contention that other circumstances be treated as mitigating factors in the context of a particular case.[82]

The Office of Export Enforcement ("OEE") investigates possible violations of the Export Administration Act of 1979, the EAR and any order, license or authorization issued thereunder. It pursues dual objectives in each instance of an apparent violation—appropriate penalties and deterrence. Its investigations may lead to:

(i)   A warning letter,

(ii) A civil enforcement proceeding, and/or

(iii) A referral to the Department of Justice for criminal prosecution.

OEE issues a warning letter (explaining an apparent violation and urging compliance), when it believes that the violation was technical and that the violator made good faith efforts to comply with the applicable law and cooperated with the investigation. OEE may also issue warning letters, when a violator's self-disclosure brought the matter to the OEE's attention and caused it to investigate, *provided* that no aggravating factors exist.[83] OEE seems to have overlooked, however, the dilemma that such provision creates for general counsel who has labored to create an effective compliance program and must, on occasion, decide on short notice whether to recommend that its firm either make a voluntary self-disclosure of the violations the compliance program has uncovered (but not prevented), or attempt to limit the damage by curing the violation (or putting an end to such conduct) but not disclosing it to the OEE, in the hopes of averting an investigation and adverse publicity.

General counsel will not always be in a position to know whether any aggravating factors exist that could severely limit or nullify the benefits of voluntary self-disclosure. There may not be time to conduct a thorough investigation, or counsel may fear that voluntary self-disclosure triggering an OEE investigation will uncover aggravating factors. Since firms have a positive obligation to make voluntary self-disclosure,

---

82. 69 FEDERAL REGISTER 34 at p. 7869, Response 5(b).
83. 69 FEDERAL REGISTER 34, at p. 7871.

it would seem counter-productive for OEE to deny a firm the full mitigation of such disclosure if it happens that, despite a firm's good faith investigation, aggravating factors escaped its notice and were subsequently uncovered by the OEE. Moreover, the OEE's position could undermine its own efforts to encourage voluntary self-disclosure.

If the OEE determines to pursue a civil enforcement, it will issue a charging letter. The result can be one or more of three types of administrative sanctions: civil penalty, denial of export privileges (which can apply to all the firm's privileges[84] or be narrower in scope),[85] and exclusion from practice before the BIS. The significant risk of incurring a civil penalty is less the amount of the fine that might be imposed than the fact that each pattern of violative conduct tends to produce multiple violations. Violative conduct seldom occurs in isolation, but tends to be an inadvertent consequence of the way a firm transacts business.[86] As a result, a firm whose activities contravene the EAR may suddenly be facing scores of counts, and a monetary penalty can be assessed for each such count. For example, UCAR International, Inc. ("UCAR") of Nashville, Tennessee, in the brief period from September 1995 through March 1996, allegedly exported U.S.-origin Grade ATJ graphite from the United States to Australia, Brazil, Chile, France, Japan, South Africa and South Korea, on 38 separate occasions without the validated licenses that were required, and thereby committed 38 violations of the EAR. In addition, on 40 occasions, on or about May 31, 1996 and on or about August 12, 1997, UCAR, exported U.S.-origin ATJ Grade graphite from the United States to Australia, Brazil, Columbia, France, Japan and South Africa without the export licenses that were required by the EAR, and thereby committed 40 further violations of the EAR—for a total of 79 violations. At that time, the maximum penalty that could be imposed per violation was $10,000, but the multiple violations brought the maximum up to $790,000.[87] Such rapidly magnifying exposure undoubtedly

---

84. For the standard denial of export privileges, see the EAR, part 764, Supplement No. 1.

85. See the EAR §764.3(a)(2).

86. The Enforcement Guidance gives, as an example, an exporter who mis-classifies an item on the Commerce Control List. As a result of that error, the exporter fails to obtain the required export license when exporting the item and submits a Shipper's Export Declaration that gives an inaccurate applicable Export Control Classification Number and inaccurately identifies the export as qualifying for the "no license required" designation, thereby committing three violations from one error. 69 FEDERAL REGISTER 34, at p. 7871.

87. Letter of U.S. Department of Commerce, Bureau of Export Administration

provides the Commerce Department with leverage for negotiating a settlement, which, in the case of UCAR, resulted in an agreement to pay a civil penalty of $237,000. (Note that while the most commonly known uses for graphite are solely for consumer goods such as pencil 'leads', the Commerce Department controls ATJ grade graphite because of its use in rocket nozzles and re-entry vehicle nose tips (*i.e.*, warhead nose cones for long range ballistic missiles)).

The BIS considers six factors when determining the appropriate administrative sanction for a settlement:

(i) **Degree of Willfulness.** If the violation involves simple negligence or carelessness, BIS typically seeks a settlement involving payment of a civil penalty. Greater willfulness in the violation, however, leads to greater sanctions. If the violation involves gross negligence, willful blindness to the EAR requirements or knowing or willful violations, the BIS tends to curtail or cut off the firm's ability to engage in cross-border transactions by denying export privileges, excluding it from practice, and/or requiring it to pay an enhanced civil penalty.[88]

(predecessor to the BIS) to UCAR International, Inc., dated May 22, 2001, accessed at www.efoia.bis.doc.gov/ExportControlViolations/e698.pdf.

88. Although violation of some EAR provisions requires a degree of knowledge or intent as an element of the offense, the BIS can infer from the facts and circumstances of a case that the violator's actions amounted to a knowing (or willfully blind) violation. For example, if the BIS finds that the violator should have recognized the presence of certain indicia of unlawful diversions—so-called "red flags"—specified in Supplement no. 3 to EAR part 732 and that the party did not make much, if any inquiry, after such red flags were noticed or should have been noticed, such conduct tends to make the case for a willful or willfully blind violation. The red flags listed in Supplement no. 3 include the following:

(i) The customer or purchasing agent is reluctant to offer information about the end-use of a product.

(ii) The product's capabilities do not fit the buyer's line of business; for example, a small bakery places an order for several sophisticated lasers.

(iii) The product ordered is incompatible with the technical level of the country to which the product is being shipped. For example, semiconductor manufacturing equipment would be of little use in a country without an electronics industry.
. . . .

(v) The customer is willing to pay cash for a very expensive item when the terms of the sale call for financing.

(vi) The customer is unfamiliar with the product's performance characteristics but still wants the product.

(ii) **Destination.** If the violative export or reexport involves countries subject to anti-terrorism controls,[89] or destinations specifically targeted by that type of export control (*e.g.*, export or reexport of items subject to nuclear controls to a country that engages in nuclear proliferation), or destinations that "implicate" harm to national security or other essential interests protected by the export control system, then the BIS is more likely to seek increased monetary penalties and/or denial of export privileges or exclusion from practice.[90]

(iii) **Related Violations.** If a firm commits multiple related violations, the BIS has discretion to charge the firm with separate violations, but to settle the case for a smaller penalty than would be appropriate if each violation were unrelated. It may also charge fewer than the full number of violations, and pursue a settlement based on that charging decision. Of course, the BIS will tend to exercise lenience in instances where the violations do **not** result from knowing or willful conduct, willful blindness to the requirements of the EAR or gross negligence, or from different underlying errors or omissions, or that do not cause distinguishable or separate harm.[91]

(iv) **Multiple Unrelated Violations.** Conversely, if a firm commits multiple **unrelated** violations, BIS is more likely to seek severe penalties, *i.e.*, a denial of export privileges (which, for most firms, is far more costly than a fine), exclusion from practice and/or substantial monetary penalties. BIS justifies this approach on the grounds that multiple, unrelated violations tend to indicate serious compliance problems and a high risk of future violations, and may require simply denying the offending party the privilege of exporting.[92] Note that a denial of export privileges is not simply a slap on the wrist—the frequently used

---

(vii) Routine installation, training or maintenance services are declined by the customer.

. . . .

(xi) When questioned, the buyer is evasive or unclear about whether the purchased product is for domestic use, export, or reexport."

89. See EAR §742.1(d).
90. 69 FEDERAL REGISTER 34, at p. 7871.
91. Id.
92. Id.

brief debarment that the DoD imposes on defense contractors who have violated procurement regulations. BIS denial of export privileges tends to be for a period of one to two decades, virtually excluding the disciplined party from the export market, and effectively destroying its business and good will.[93]

(v) **Timing of Settlement.** Since early settlement saves resources, BIS may take early settlement into account when determining which settlement penalties to seek.[94]

(vi) **Related Criminal or Civil Violations.** BIS cautions against inferring any precedent from a civil settlement. If a firm enters a guilty plea to a criminal charge, for example, the BIS may view its acceptance of responsibility favorably, regard the criminal penalty as a sufficient deterrent and reduce the administrative sanction accordingly. Conversely, the BIS may seek greater administrative sanctions in those enforcement actions where no criminal penalty is likely. To many counsel, this may appear counter-intuitive, and Agile's General Counsel faces no small task in trying to explain it to Agile's European counsel.[95]

---

93. Denial of export privileges also extends to a prohibition that bars any party from assisting such firms in export activity and thus reaches far broader than most penalties. It poses substantial risks to firms that fail to check if counterparties to a transaction are subject to a denial of export privileges, since a firm that assists a firm prohibited from engaging in exporting could find itself charged and facing the risks of being subject to a similar ban.

94. 69 FEDERAL REGISTER 34, at p. 7871.

95. Id. Note that this is merely one of many such challenges for Agile's General Counsel in alerting his European counterpart to risks from U.S. regulations. European counsel not infrequently view the EAR, TSR, and ITAR as inappropriate extra-territorial reaches of U.S. law and not only object on that ground but may misreport the gravity of the potential offense to U.S. counsel, who, on such misinformation, may advise European counsel to resist corrective measures. Only belatedly may U.S. counsel realize that by such advice they are in peril of appearing to have supported a circumventing of such regulations, which is a separate offense. Counsel should not underestimate the risks of tacking too close to the noncompliance line when advising clients. See Sherwood, Bob, *Morgan Lewis Sued over Cuba Trading Advice*, FINANCIAL TIMES, February 13, 2004, p. 4, reporting that a major U.S. law firm faces a $40 million malpractice suit from a former client, Purolite (a privately owned water purification resin manufacturer based in the U.S.) for allegedly advising it to continue trade between itself (through a British subsidiary) and "entities affiliated with Cuba"—advice that allegedly was contradicted by the law firm's own internal research memoranda.

The BIS considers not only the above-mentioned general factors, but also the presence or absence of mitigating and aggravating factors, when determining what sanctions to apply in a given settlement. Note that the list provided in the Penalty Guidance, summarized in the tables below, is viewed by the BIS as not exhausting the factors it may consider in a given case. The BIS differentiates the amount of weight it gives to these factors, labeling some of "GREAT WEIGHT." However, such differential treatment can be overestimated by counsel, as BIS merely notes that "such a factor should ordinarily be given considerably more weight than a factor that is not so designated." Clearly, if counsel is in a position to recommend specific compliance precautions, a company's investment is better allocated to deploying precautions that will qualify for "GREAT WEIGHT" mitigating factors, and for avoiding "GREAT WEIGHT" aggravating factors. We therefore group the "GREAT WEIGHT" factors in Figure 4, and all others in Figure 5 below.

Since BIS has increased its enforcement of successor liability (liability imposed on an acquirer for pre-acquisition violations by the target firm), the Penalty Guidance also states that, if the acquirer takes reasonable steps to *uncover, correct and disclose* to BIS the conduct that caused the violations by the target firm, BIS "typically will not take such violations into account in settling other violations by the acquiring firm."[96] BIS also disclosed that, when deciding whether to impose the ultimate sanction of denial of export privileges, it deems the following factors as of particular relevance:

- The presence of any "great weight" mitigating or aggravating factors;
- The degree of the violator's willfulness;
- The extent to which senior management participated in or knew of the violative conduct;
- The probability of future violations (determined, in part, from the quality of violator's export compliance program, if any), and
- Whether a monetary penalty will likely have a sufficient deterrent effect.

---

96. 69 FEDERAL REGISTER 34, at p. 7278.

Figure 4. "GREAT WEIGHT" Factors in BIS Penalty Guidance

Mitigating Factors	Aggravating Factors
1. Voluntary self-disclosure of the violation,[a] particularly of violations that no existing BIS investigation would have been reasonably likely to discover otherwise.	1. Violator deliberately hid or concealed its violation(s).[b]
2. Violator has an "**effective export compliance program**"[c] and its overall export compliance efforts have been of high quality, *i.e.*, extent to which such program complies with principles set forth in BIS' recommended compliance program—the Export Management System (available for download at the BIS website).[e] (The BIS notes it will consider whether such compliance program discovered the violation, whether it thereby prevented further violations, and whether the organization took steps, "reasonably calculated to be effective" to improve its compliance program in light of such violation.)	2. Violator's conduct exhibited serious disregard for its export compliance responsibilities.[d]
	3. Violation considered significant because it involved sensitive items and/or sensitive reasons for controlling them to the destination, *i.e.*, when the violation implicates a substantial national security interest or other essential interest protected by the U.S. export control system.[f]

[a]But such disclosure must satisfy the requirements of EAR §764.5.

[b]69 Federal Register 34, at p. 7872.

[c]**Note:** the term "effective export compliance program" has two features that deserve close attention. First, in this context there is not necessarily a contradiction between a firm that contravenes the EAR and the same firm's claims that it has an "effective export compliance program," *provided* the firm can show that it learned of the violation from the routine operation of that compliance program and not from a report from an outside third party (such as a financial institution whose interdiction software may have detected the violation).

Second, proposed amendments to the U.S. Sentencing Guidelines, which were submitted in April 2004 for Congressional approval only a few months after the publication of the BIS's Penalty Guidance, are intended to provide improved guidance to organizations and courts

(continued)

(Continued)

regarding the criteria for an "effective compliance program" to prevent and detect violation of the law. Neither the BIS's Penalty Guidance nor the proposed amendments in 2004 to the U.S. Sentencing Guidelines mention or cross-reference each other, but we think counsel would benefit from borrowing the criteria provided in such amendments when advising an organization on the full panoply of precautionary checkpoints needed to ensure the organization will qualify for a mitigating factor in the event of an EAR violation. A similar argument would be appropriate when reporting to the BIS a voluntary self-disclosure of a violation. See discussion in next section of the proposed amendments to the U.S. Sentencing Guidelines.

[d]69 FEDERAL REGISTER 34, at p. 7872.

[e]See www.bxa.doc.gov/ExportManagementSystems/Default.htm.

[f]69 FEDERAL REGISTER 34, at p. 7872. Examples would include violations of controls on nuclear, biological, and chemical weapon proliferation, missile technology proliferation, and national security concerns and exports banned under EAR, part 744.

Note: BIS hereby makes clear that there are not only more great weight aggravating factors than great weight mitigating factors, but it is harder to qualify for great weight mitigating factors than it is to be implicated in great weight aggravating factors.

Figure 5. Other Factors in BIS Penalty Guidance

Mitigating Factors	*Aggravating Factors*
1. Violation was isolated occurrence, or resulted from a good-faith misinterpretation.[a]	1. Violation likely involved harm that the applicable regulatory provision was principally designed to avert.[b]
2. In instances where a license was required, but not obtained, the violator would likely have been granted such license if it had requested it.[c]	2. Violator exported so large a quantity or high a value of items, that an enhanced penalty may be needed to achieve an appropriate punishment or deterrence, or "to make the penalty proportionate to those for otherwise comparable violations involving exports of lower quantity or value."[d]
3. Except for antiboycott matters (under EAR part 760), the violator: (a) has never been convicted of an **export-related *criminal* offense**;[e] (b) in the past five years, the violator has not entered into a settlement of an "export-related" administrative enforcement case with BIS or another U.S. Government agency or been found liable in such a case brought by any such agency;[f]	3. Violation concurrently contravenes a law or regulation enforced by an agency other than the BIS.[i]

(continued)

Figure 5. Other Factors in BIS Penalty Guidance (Continued)

Mitigating Factors	*Aggravating Factors*
(c) in the past three years, the violator has not received a warning letter from BIS;[g] (d) in the past five years, the party has not otherwise violated the EAR.[h]	
Other Mitigating Factors	*Other Aggravating Factors*
4. Violator provided exceptional cooperation with BIS investigation of its violation.[j]	4. Except for antiboycott matters (under EAR part 760), the violator: (a) has been convicted of an **export-related *criminal* offense**; (b) in the past five years, the violator has entered into a settlement of an "export-related" administrative enforcement case with BIS or another U.S. Government agency or been found liable in such a case brought by any such agency;[k] (c) in the past three years, the violator has received a warning letter from BIS;[l] or (d) in the past five years, the party has otherwise violated the EAR.[m]
5. Violator provided substantial assistance to BIS investigation of another person who may have violated the EAR.[n]	
6. Violation not likely to pose harm of the kind that the EAA, EAR or other authority (such as a license condition) are designed to protect against.[o]	
7. When committing the violation, the violator was **both** inexperienced in exporting and unfamiliar with export practices and requirements.[p]	

[a]69 FEDERAL REGISTER 34, at p. 7872.
[b]Id.
[c]69 FEDERAL REGISTER 34, at p. 7872.
[d]Id.

(continued)

(Continued)

[e]"Export-related" should not be interpreted narrowly to be only a criminal violation of the EAR. It probably would be viewed by the BIS to include such violations of the TSR and ITAR and arguably may extend to other cross-border violations, provided they serve the same ultimate objectives as the EAR, TSR, and ITAR. We doubt, for example, that such argument would apply to violations of the patent laws or a privacy law unless the result of such violation adversely affected national security or a similar objective. However, a violation of the Economic Espionage Act of 1996, although it concerns a company's trade secrets, would probably involve an export and might well count as an "export-related" criminal offense. Counsel needs to investigate such possibilities diligently to avoid being alleged by the BIS to have failed to be forthcoming or candid in its submittals to the BIS.

A curious omission from the Penalty Guidance, in an era of multi-national organizations, is whether the BIS would include in "export-related" criminal violations such a violation of another country's laws or whether it intends to consider only violation of U.S. laws. Since avoidance of circumvention of the EAR is a high priority, and since the EAR, and to a larger extent the TSR and ITAR, depend on cooperation by governments of other countries, it would seem that the BIS should clarify this point. If it does, we do not expect the BIS to include criminal violations of other countries' export laws (although we think to do so would be appropriate), because in the next subparagraph of this list of mitigating factors the BIS uses the term "export-related" in a way that clearly restricts it to violations of U.S. laws and regulations.

[f]69 FEDERAL REGISTER 34, at p. 7872.

[g]Id.

[h]Id. Agile's General Counsel also makes a mental note of a comment in BIS's Penalty Guidance: that, where necessary to effective enforcement, BIS may impute to a firm the prior involvement in export violations by any of the firm's owners, directors, officers, partners, or other related persons in determining whether the four noted criteria (criminal violation, settlement, warning letter, or other violation) are satisfied. See 69 FEDERAL REGISTER 34, at p. 7872.

[i]Id.

[j]69 FEDERAL REGISTER 34, at p. 7872.

[k]69 FEDERAL REGISTER 34, at p. 7872.

[l]Id.

[m]Id.

[n]Id. Of the several mitigating factors, this one seems of dubious efficacy and merit, since a party could qualify by providing information even about a person who did not violate the EAR.

[o]69 FEDERAL REGISTER 34, at p. 7872.

[p]Id. Note that if the BIS finds the violator engaged in willful blindness of the applicable regulations, the violator would not qualify for this mitigating factor.

Several important conclusions can be drawn from reviewing BIS' Penalty Guidance. First, the most frequently occurring factor in the Guidance is the presence or absence of an effective compliance program. Agile's General Counsel infers that an audit or a spot check of Agile's compliance program would be prudent prior to any major cross-border acquisition (if a regularly scheduled audit has not occurred within five months of commencement of the acquisition). Several reasons support this policy: it enables General Counsel to demonstrate the seriousness of its compliance program to BIS, if the need arises; it increases the chances that the transaction will receive the due diligence warranted; it reduces the likelihood of inadvertent violations due to personnel being unaware of recent changes in applicable regulations (whose pace of change has increased during the past five or six years); and, for all those reasons, it increases the probability that Agile will detect and correct problems that might otherwise be imputed to it from pre-acquisition or pre-Closing conduct of the target company. It should be noted that all these have ancillary transactional benefits as well, and those benefits should be factored into any cost/benefit analysis of acquisition driven compliance.

Agile's General Counsel, however, takes a dim view of the BIS requirement that, to qualify for certain mitigating factors, a firm must not only detect and correct the violation but must also take the far more risky step of voluntary self-disclosure. Many directors and officers will oppose such step. They will question the cost of inevitably triggering an investigation that will almost certainly delve into matters beyond any violation, and thus into particulars of the firm's transactions that it has valid reasons for wanting to keep confidential. And they will probably weigh these costs unfavorably against the less quantifiable and more long-term benefits of compliance. Once again, the tension this creates in any analysis arises from the divergent time frames of the relevant costs vs. the relatively inchoate benefits. Counsel must be able to articulate short-term benefits as well as long term costs, to offset the obvious short-term costs and the understandable perception that any benefits must be "discounted" based on the uncertainty of their being realized. Arguably it would have served BIS' ultimate objectives far better if, instead of requiring voluntary self-disclosure, it had permitted a firm, when investigated, to then disclose its previous violations, without the risk of incurring additional liability (thereby engaging in a presumption of good faith).

The BIS' Penalty Guidance and OFAC's Enforcement Guidelines combine to increase substantially a firm's cross-border transactional risks (and costs). In the aftermath of the attacks of September 11, 2001, it is understandable that the enforcement environment could be expected to change and, in the interests of homeland security, become more aggressive. In the United States and other countries (such as Spain, after it suffered the attacks of March 11, 2004), major terrorist attacks have tended to usher in a new enforcement paradigm—one that shifts efforts towards pre-emptive attempts to improve security, and that relies increasingly on "an intelligence-gathering form of policing through the use of powerful mass surveillance technologies."[97] Ironically, such shifts often have the adverse effect of causing people to believe that heightened enforcement efforts actually (and paradoxically) reduce their sense of security, because such efforts quickly become intrusive, reducing personal privacy and the confidentiality of transactions.

Agile's General Counsel has observed that during the period in which Agile-Wing and Troll explored the possibility of Agile acquiring Troll—a 16-month period from roughly January 2003 through May 2004—the business environment became increasingly more difficult for the following reasons:

- US policies to tighten immigration controls have antagonized many countries, particularly those who view themselves as U.S. allies;

- Since the United States does not have the broad privacy protections found in the EU or Canada, the expansion of surveillance powers under the USA Patriot Act seem particularly aggressive, and may prompt Europeans and Canadians to insist ever more forcefully on respect for their respective privacy laws and regulations;

- The invasion of Iraq (a military action whose legitimacy has been questioned) has been uniformly unpopular in Europe, creating psychological impediments to business that have made issues of compliance with the extra-territorial application of U.S. laws more contentious (one perceived over-reach—the pre-emptive doctrine in Iraq—causing business resistance to other forms of apparent over-reaching);[98]

---

97. Institute for Prospective Technological Studies, *Security and Privacy for the Citizen in the Post-September 11 Digital Age: A Prospective Overview, Report to the European Parliament Committee on Citizens' Freedoms and Rights, Justice and Home Affairs (LIBE)*, EUR 20823 EN, July 2003, Executive Summary, Section 2. That report also observes that: "the events of September 11 can be regarded as the occasion rather than the cause of the introduction of a new security paradigm. The main characteristic of the new paradigm is a shift from 'reactive' to 'pro-active' modes of security protection using ICT[information and communications technologies]-based systems to facilitate data collection and sharing between multiple sources in support of intelligence gathering."

98. The crisis of legitimacy that divided the United States and its traditional liberal European allies has created tensions that influence efforts to negotiate corrective measures during a transaction to ensure compliance with U.S. federal laws and regulations.

- Such policies appear unilateral to Europeans, a departure from the consensual approach of the U.S. in the 1990's (under former Presidents Bush and Clinton) and, as explained by one scholar, reminiscent of the more

  "Aggressive and unilateralist tactics pursued under President Reagan. With few exceptions, Europeans and others resisted the entreaties of the Reagan administration [for sanctions against Libya] in part because they perceived U.S. policy toward Libya in the 1980s to be largely driven by domestic factors. At the time, U.S. sanctions were viewed as a manifestation of American desires to project U.S. power and influence in the world in the wake of a series of defeats, including the Soviet invasion of Afghanistan, the Islamic revolution in Iran, and the still recent American losses in Vietnam . . . .also by the American pursuit of regime change—a goal that was viewed by many outside of the United States as being far out of proportion to the threat posed by Qadhafi."[99]

- When U.S. counsel emphasize the need for compliance with the EAR, TSR and ITAR, they are increasingly asked to provide more extensive (and often political and ethical) justifications for such

---

When allies divide, both sides lose. That Europe criticizes U.S. action in Iraq as illegitimate is, as Robert Kagan cogently points out, a double standard applied by Europeans who ignored the illegitimacy of their own advocacy of military action in Kosovo. As Kagan observes, "It is difficult to avoid the conclusion that when Europeans, and Americans, claim that American action in Iraq was 'unilateral,' they do not really mean that the United States lacked wide international support. They mean the United States lacked wide European support . . . that the United States did not have the full support of all its traditional European allies . . ." Kagan, Robert, *Of Paradise and Power*, Vintage Books, 2004, p. 147. The pre-invasion loss of the support of Berlin and Paris, and the post-invasion loss of support of Madrid (after the train bombings of March 11, 2004) raises the standard that U.S. counsel has to meet when trying to persuade European counsel in a target firm that certain dealings must cease in order to comply with U.S. laws.

99. O'Sullivan, Meghan L., *Shrewd Sanctions*, Brookings Institution Press, 2003, p. 219. Young executives may not remember the Reagan policies, but senior executives recall them, and the resumption (however cyclical) of unilateral action by the U.S. causes concern among U.S. allies (just as the ebbing of such action, followed by the opposite extreme—isolationism—would also cause concern). Whether the NATO members will find in "out of theatre" action the cohesion that existed during the Cold War is a sensitive question whose resolution is not irrelevant to U.S. efforts to avert military action by recourse to strong economic sanctions nor to U.S. firms' efforts to comply with such sanctions when engaged in cross-border, cyber-driven transactions.

regulations, and more persuasive arguments for compliance. However, the clearest arguments for such regulation are often the most quickly rejected overseas (*e.g.*, the political justifications of anti-terrorism and non-proliferation, and the economic argument of strict liability); and

- U.S. incarceration and interrogation policies and procedures have alienated allies whose citizens have been held at Guantánamo Naval Base (under conditions the U.S. Government insists are beyond the reach of the Geneva Convention on the treatment of prisoners of war),[100] and the revelations (particularly in digital photos accessible on the World Wide Web) of the treatment of prisoners at Abu Ghraib prison in Baghdad, Iraq, have intensified an increasingly common reluctance to cooperate with extra-territorial application of U.S. laws and regulations.[101]

In short, Agile's General Counsel is keenly aware that his firm faces

---

100. That U.S. citizens are similarly detained and incarcerated does not diminish overseas' objections to the use of such procedures. At this writing, it is too early to ascertain what effect, if any, the U.S. Supreme Court decisions on the Guantánamo detainees will have on such objections, but it is helpful that Justice O'Connor's majority opinion in *Hamdi v. Rumsfeld* declares clearly (in the case involving indefinite detention of a U.S. citizen) that:

"'In our society liberty is the norm,' and detention without trial 'is the carefully limited exception.' . . . .Moreover, as critical as the Government's interest may be in detaining those who actually pose an immediate threat to the national security of the United States during ongoing international conflict, history and common sense teach us that an unchecked system of detention carries the potential to become a means for oppression and abuse of others who do not present that sort of threat . . . .We therefore hold that a citizen-detainee seeking to challenge his classification as an enemy combatant must receive notice of the factual basis for his classification, and a fair opportunity to rebut the Government's factual assertions before a neutral decision maker . . . .We have long since made clear that a state of war is not a blank check for the President when it comes to the rights of the Nation's citizens." *Hamdi v. Rumsfeld*, Slip Opinion, 124 S.Ct. 2633 [2004] at pp. 2646, 2647, 2648 and 2650.

101. As Professor Wedgewood and former CIA Director Woolsey note in their criticism of the January and August 2002 memos by the Justice Department's Office of Legal Counsel to the White House, titled "Application of Treaties and Laws to al Qaeda and Taliban Detainees" and "Standards of Conduct for Interrogation" (the "OLC memos"): "In the wake of the Abu Ghraib scandal, it is clear that maintaining humanitarian standards for those we take prisoner is central to the good name of the United States . . . . Most troubling is the narrow account [by the OLC memos] of the ban on

a broader range of U.S. regulations at home, an increasingly aggressive enforcement environment, and an increasingly punitive approach towards those found to have contravened such regulations (greater surveillance by the government's police powers and greater insistence by the U.S. Attorney General for strict application of the U.S. Sentencing Guidelines). Outside of the United States, where Agile pursues acquisitions, there is increasing opposition to pre-Closing compliance and pre-signing measures to ensure that a U.S. person does not contravene the EAR, TSR or ITAR. The tension between these two trends requires that Agile's General Counsel look carefully at recently proposed amendments to the U.S. Sentencing Guidelines, since these will become relevant, if a firm violates the criminal provisions of these regulations.

1.9 Proposed Amendments to the U.S. Sentencing Guidelines Concerning an "Effective Compliance Program."

The U.S. Sentencing Guidelines (the "Sentencing Guidelines") determine penalties imposed on individuals, organizations and officers and directors for noncompliance with certain U.S. laws, rules and regulations.[102] Congress delegated to the United States Sentencing Commission (the "Sentencing Commission") authority to identify factors that a judge must take into account in setting a sentence. The Sentencing Commission, a White House appointed panel of six judges and attorneys, reviews the Guidelines periodically and votes to propose new Guidelines and amendments thereto to Congress. As recently described by one U.S. District judge:

---

torture . . . . Curiously, the OLC opinion bends over backwards to limit the definition of 'severe pain or suffering' in a way that only Savoranola could love. In a non-Hippocratic application of hospital emergency medicine rules, the OLC explains that only 'death, organ failure, or serious impairment of body functions' should serve as the measure of 'severe pain.' This diminished definition of the crime of torture will be quoted back at the United States for the next several decades." Wedgwood, Ruth, and Woolsey, R. James, *Law and Torture*, THE WALL STREET JOURNAL, June 28, 2004.

102. In the Sentencing Reform Act of 1984, Congress created the United States Sentencing Commission as an independent agency within the federal judiciary and gave it the task of generating guidelines for federal sentencing proceedings. The commission issued such guidelines first for individual defendants in November 1987.

"Under this scheme, a sentencing judge's conclusion that a particular factor exists results in a certain number of points (or levels), which in turn places the defendant on the vertical axis of a sentencing grid. The horizontal axis evaluates the defendant's recidivism. The intersection point on the grid identifies what has become known as the "guideline" sentence. The guideline sentence is the defendant's "presumptive" sentence under the federal sentencing scheme. . . . "[P]resumptive" means just that—the sentence is not automatic; the presumption can be overcome . . . a federal judge can depart either up or down from the presumptive sentence, although we are not supposed to do that with any great frequency, lest we incur the wrath of Congress by refusing to allow the USSG [U.S. Sentencing Guidelines] to 'fetter the discretion of sentencing judges.'"[103]

The Commission issued guidelines initially applicable only to individual defendants in November of 1987. Those guidelines re-structured the Federal District Court sentencing discretion to ensure that similar offenders who committed similar offenses received similar sentences. Four years later, in November of 1991, the Commission issued guidelines for the sentencing of organizations, which became Chapter 8 of the *Federal Sentencing Guidelines Manual* (the "Organizational Guidelines"), in order to provide incentives for organizations to report violations, cooperate in criminal investigations, discipline culpable employees and take the steps needed to prevent and detect improper conduct by their agents.[104]

The Organizational Guidelines require high fines for organizations that have no meaningful programs (*i.e.*, compliance programs) to prevent and detect criminal violations of U.S. federal law in which management was involved or of which it was willfully ignorant. The Commission did not limit the Organizational Guidelines to corporate or business entities, but applied them to "any person other than an individual," and explained that such term included "corporations, partnerships, associations, joint-stock companies, unions, trusts, pension funds, unincorporated associations, government and political subdivi-

---

103. Judge McMahon in *U.S. v. Paul G. Einstman*, 325 F.Supp. 2nd 373, 376 [S.D.N.Y., 2004].

104. Federal Judges rely on the Guidelines Manual when determining what penalties to impose on companies and other organizations that have violated criminal provisions of applicable laws.

sions thereof and non-profit organizations."[105] The Commission concluded that existing organizational sentencing was incoherent and inconsistent, and that the fines imposed were too low, often with the paradoxical result that the sanctions were less expensive than the costs of compliance to avert liability.[106]

Penalties imposed for wrongdoing by a corporation or other organization usually have two components: a remedial part (reflecting what the organization's violation caused in the way of gain to the organization or harm to third parties), and a punitive part (representing the computation of a number representing the seriousness of the offense multiplied by a number representing the culpability or blameworthiness of the organization).

A. Remedial Component.

The Commission recommended, and the Organizational Guidelines explain, that "the court must, whenever practicable, order the organization to remedy any harm caused by the offense."[107] This remedial component of an imposed sentence is not designed to punish the offending corporation or organization, but rather to make the injured party whole, and the remedy will usually be in the form of an order of restitution "for the full amount of the victim's loss." It may also entail a remedial order requiring the organization "to remedy the harm caused by the offense and to eliminate or reduce the risk" that the offense will cause further harm. Where, however, the applicable statute or regulation sets a maximum sentence, that maximum will supersede any sentence, calculated in accordance with the Guidelines, that exceeds the statutory maximum. As a result, the maximum remedial penalty that can be imposed on a corporation or other organization for a given count or single violation is the greatest of:

(i) The amount, if any, established by the law that creates the offense,

---

105. USSC Section 8A1.1, App. Note 1.

106. *Report of the Ad Hoc Advisory Group on the Organizational Sentencing Guidelines*, November 2003, p. 12.

107. *Amendments to the Sentencing Guidelines*, May 10, 2004, (unofficial text of the amendments submitted to Congress on April 30, 2004), Section 8, Introductory Commentary, accessed at www.ussc.gov/2004guid/RFMay04.pdf.

(ii) $500,000, if the organization is convicted of a felony, and

(iii) Not more than twice the gross gain obtained by the organization through its violation, or twice the gross loss caused by the
organization's violation (unless imposition of such fine would
unduly complicate or prolong the sentencing process). The
"twice gross gain or loss" rule is the sentence customarily imposed in cases where the defendant corporation or organization
has profited significantly from its violation or caused significant
harm thereby.

B. Punitive Component.

There are important categories of organizational violations that are
not *yet* covered by the Organizational Guidelines. Examples include
environmental offenses and export control violations. However, in exports and in cross-border transactions, organizations often inadvertently violate other important applicable laws that carry criminal penalties, including, for example, trade sanction violations and violations
of privacy and security regulations. Because it is important to minimize
that risk, Agile needs to understand the punitive component of all applicable laws in order to protect its interests.

If a violation requires imposition of a fine on the corporation or
organization, the Organizational Guidelines provide for a series of com-
putations that take into account the gravity of the violation as well as
mitigating (exculpatory) conduct by the corporation that may qualify
it for a substantial reduction in penalty. The court is required to mul-
tiply a number that reflects the *seriousness* or gravity of the violation
(known as the "Base Fine") times a number that reflects the culpability
of the defendant corporation or organization. The seriousness of the
defendant corporation's violation, reflected in the Base Fine, is the greatest of:

(i) The amount from a table,

(ii) The amount of financial gain obtained by the defendant corporation from the violation, and

(iii) The loss caused by the defendant corporation's violation, to the
extent that such loss was intentionally, knowingly or recklessly
caused.

The culpability of the defendant corporation's violation (the extent to which it deserves the blame for committing, or permitting the commission of, the violation) is determined by the court through a computation of what is known as the organization's "Culpability Score."[108] That computation begins by adopting a base score of **five culpability points**. The court then adds (or subtracts) points depending on its determination of the presence (or absence) of factors that, in the Commission's view, aggravated the offense (these add points and increase the penalty), or mitigated the offense (these subtract points and decrease the penalty).

1. Aggravating Factors.

A court may add a range of points to the penalty calculation to reflect the size of the organization and the rank and "degree of discretionary authority" of the individuals who were involved in (or who condoned) the violative conduct. The Report notes, for example, that a court will add five points, if the organization had 5,000 or more employees, and the culpable individuals (those involved, or those who condoned or were "willfully ignorant" of the offence) included persons within the organization's high-level personnel. By contrast, if the same offense were committed by an organization with only 200 employees, the court would add only three points.

2. Mitigating Factors.

Organizational defendants may seek reduction in their culpability score under two provisions:

(i) If the offense occurred *despite* the existence of an effective program to prevent and detect violations of law; and

(ii) If the organization self-reported the violation, cooperated with enforcement authorities and accepted responsibility for the offense.

3. Effective Program to Prevent and Detect Violations.

The Commission's Report emphasizes the importance to an organization of implementing an effective program to protect itself from inadvertent violations committed by employees, agents and others whose conduct may be imputed to that organization. The Report notes

---

108. Guidelines Manual, Section 8C2.5.

that an organization must take care not to disqualify itself from mitigation under this provision. Any credit that an organization could otherwise earn may not apply if "highly-placed officials within the organization participated in, condoned, or were willfully ignorant of the offense."[109] Credit will also not apply if an organization becomes aware of an offense and then unreasonably delays reporting the offense to appropriate governmental authorities.[110] (Note that this loss of reduction is styled as a presumption that a defendant can try to rebut, although that would be difficult, and the Guidelines do not specify what evidence would be required to rebut such presumption.)

The Organizational Guidelines previously included an explanatory note that "due diligence" could only be evidenced by the organization's having taken a minimum of seven specified steps. As explained below, the proposed amendment now makes those seven steps part of the formal provisions of the Guidelines, thereby emphasizing their importance. If an organization can prove that it met all seven steps, it will currently gain three mitigation points (*i.e.,* its culpability score will be reduced by three points).

4. Cooperation with Enforcement Authorities.

The number of credits gained (in mitigation) depends on the extent of an organization's cooperation. If an organization accepts responsibility (*i.e.,* pleads guilty to the violation), it receives one point of credit. However, if before being investigated by the authorities, the organization reports its violation to the governmental authorities, fully cooperates and pleads guilty, it will receive five mitigation points (*i.e.,* its culpability score will be reduced five points).

The Commission concluded, however, that there was an imbalance in these two crediting provisions: the preventative conduct earned fewer credits than the post-violation cooperation. That is not consistent with the Organizational Guidelines objectives. Moreover, most organizations are far more likely to invest in implementing and maintaining a compliance program (to avert or reduce the risk of committing an offense) than to self-report a violation or to cooperate to the full extent the authorities require. The Commission therefore included (in its commentary on the proposed amendment) a request for public comment

---

109. Report, p. 18.
110. Id.

on whether there should be more than three mitigation points awarded for companies that implement and maintain an effective compliance program.

Most importantly, (according to the Report), the U.S. Justice Department has confirmed that it has "*declined prosecutions based on the existence of an effective compliance program.*"[111]

However, since 1991, enforcement policies issued by the Department of Justice, and amendments to the Sentencing Guidelines, have placed increasing pressure on companies to cooperate with investigative authorities, to reduce support for personnel who are under investigation or are accused of wrong-doing, and to position the company before and after violation of the law to qualify for leniency. Companies engaged in cross-border transactions, therefore, need to adjust their compliance programs and to anticipate defenses to the changes in the Guidelines and the enforcement policies. Those changes include:

1991—Amendment to the Organizational Guidelines, requiring organizations to cooperate with prosecutors in order to qualify for leniency;

1999—Justice Department memorandum advising U.S. prosecutors to take into account an organization's willingness to waive the attorney-client privilege (which could include, of course, the findings of a company's own internal investigations) and to identify "culprits within the corporation;"[112]

2003—Justice Department memorandum, by Deputy Attorney General Larry D. Thompson, revising the principles for federal prosecution of business organizations ("Thompson Memo")[113] to increase "emphasis on and scrutiny of the authenticity of a corporation's cooperation."

The Thompson Memo proceeds from the perspective that "Too often business organizations, while purporting to cooperate with a De-

---

111. Report, p. 27. [Emphasis added.] The Report further notes that an effective compliance program puts organizations in a position to make early detections of violations and thereby give them the opportunity to self-report and qualify for lenient treatment under government policies. Id.

112. Cohen, Laurie P., *Prosecutors' Tough New Tactics Turn Firms against Employees*, THE WALL STREET JOURNAL, June 4, 2004, p. A-1, at p. A-8.

113. Thompson, Larry D., *Memorandum on Principles of Federal Prosecution of Business Organizations*, January 20, 2003, accessed at www.usdoj.gov/dag/cftf/business_organizations.pdf.

partment investigation, in fact take steps to impede the quick and effective exposure of the complete scope of wrongdoing under investigation." Federal prosecutors should, therefore, determine which corporate governance mechanisms "are truly effective rather than mere paper programs."[114] The Thompson Memo encourages the prosecution of individuals for the reason that "imposition of individual criminal liability may provide the strongest deterrent against future corporate wrongdoing."[115] (However, such policies also tacitly encourage "scapegoating.") To implement this approach, and to provide some guidance for making such a subjective determination of the good faith of compliance efforts and efforts to cooperate, the Thompson Memo advises federal prosecutors to gauge the extent of a "corporation's cooperation" by using the following criteria:

- Timely and voluntary disclosure of wrongdoing;
- Willingness to cooperate with the investigation;
- Willingness to identify the culprits within the corporation (including senior executives);
- Willingness to make witnesses available;
- Willingness to disclose the complete results of its internal investigation;
- Willingness to waive attorney-client and work product protection; and
- Willingness to withdraw measures that protect *culpable* employees and agents.[116] (It should be noted that the latter presumes guilt before any definitive determination has been made.)

The pressure to obtain waivers of privilege, and to withdraw support for accused personnel, are expressed without any countervailing emphasis on the need to protect the presumption of innocence or the civil rights of the accused individuals. As a result, the Justice Department's policies, as expressed in the Thompson Memo, create significant incentives for a corporation to decide early, and perhaps prematurely, whether its personnel (including senior officers) have engaged in wrongdoing and, on that basis, to decide whether to seek leniency by cutting off support for such personnel.

---

114. Id, p. 1.
115. Id, p. 2.
116. Id, p. 6.

There is a serious risk that the line between impeding an investigation and protecting personnel's entitlement to a presumption of innocence will be shifted in favor of the government and away from individual rights and social justice. What results is a kind of mini-trial by a corporation under investigation to determine whether any protection should be provided, or whether the Justice Department's allegations must be taken as a pre-trial judgment that can be ignored only at the corporation's peril. This gives the government extraordinary coercive power. Indictment of a corporation or firm can ruin its reputation as well as its ongoing financial/economic viability (recall Drexel Burnham Lambert, which collapsed, and Arthur Andersen LLP, which was reduced to a fraction of its pre-indictment size and value).

However, unwarranted action against a company's personnel leaves the company (and arguably its officers) open to civil suits for deprivation of rights and unlawful taking (with respect to destruction of reputation and loss of employment and livelihood) that could be equally damaging. It is well established that employees have a property right in their continued employment and good vocational reputations.

It should be observed in this context that the Justice Department has been somewhat reluctant to apply the full coercive force of these measures to prosecute defense contractors, and has instead settled for less severe punishments for such firms. The consolidation in the defense industry has left the United States with too few contractors capable of prime contractor's responsibilities. As a result, although defense contractors are not infrequently threatened with debarment from government contracts, imposition of such penalties against major contractors is often followed rapidly by the lifting of such penalties, because the government needs the work that it has contracted to such firms.[117]

Agile's General Counsel, however, cannot assume that Agile will benefit from such pragmatic and *ad hoc* leniency, because Agile is not in the first tier of defense firms, and would therefore be at greater risk from the Justice Department's more stringent enforcement policies. Agile needs to be prepared to make more decisive and potentially painful decisions, if investigated for alleged wrongdoing. Although the Thompson Memo states that the Justice Department does not consider waiver of attorney-client and work product protections to be absolute or inflexible requirements, it nonetheless urges that such factors be con-

---

117. The one-year debarment of Enron, which was not a defense contractor, was a rare instance of the debarment of a large firm.

sidered in evaluating a corporation's cooperation "when necessary to provide timely and complete information."[118] Although the Thompson Memo suggests (with less precision) that cases will differ depending on the circumstances, it emphasizes that a "corporation's promise of support to culpable employees and agents, either through the advancing of attorneys fees, through retaining the employees without sanction for their *alleged* misconduct, or through providing information to the employees about the government's investigation pursuant to a joint defense agreement, may be considered by the prosecutor" in assessing the corporation's cooperation.[119] Companies have understandably responded to such pressure. One company under investigation, KPMG, has reportedly conditioned payment of partners' and employees' legal fees on agreement to talk to prosecutors, and KPMG apparently has agreed to report to prosecutors the documents that such personnel request in their defense, thereby giving the prosecution unusually early insight into defense strategies.[120] This should give counsel pause, as it raises serious constitutional concerns. Moreover, as federal prosecutors gain such concessions, they are more likely to demand them in future investigations, and to treat them as common practice or to "require" them, as one U.S. Attorney explained: "once the prosecutor has gotten cooperation of a certain level, that level becomes what we all now consider cooperation."[121]

As the enforcement policies have tightened, so have the Sentencing Guidelines. The Sarbanes-Oxley Act, Section 805, directed the Commission to review and amend the Organizational Guidelines and related policy statements to ensure that they would continue to be sufficient to deter and punish organizational violations of the law. In response, the Commission conducted a review of the Organizational Guidelines. Based on that review, in October of 2003, an Ad Hoc Advisory Group submitted its final report to the Commission (the "Report"). The Report concluded that the Organizational Guidelines had induced many organizations to focus on compliance, and to create programs to prevent

---

118. Thompson, Larry D., *Memorandum on Principles of Federal Prosecution of Business Organizations*, January 20, 2003, accessed at www.usdoj.gov/dag/cftf/business_organizations.pdf, p. 7.

119. Id, p. 8.

120. Cohen, Laurie P., *Prosecutors' Tough New Tactics Turn Firms against Employees*, THE WALL STREET JOURNAL, June 4, 2004, p. A-1, at p. A-8.

121. Id, quoting U.S. Attorney in Birmingham, Alabama, Alice Martin.

and detect violations of the law. But it also recommended amending the Organizational Guidelines to achieve the following objectives:

- Promote an organizational culture that encourages a commitment to compliance;
- Require *compliance training* at all levels of the organization;
- Define high-level personnel's responsibilities for compliance programs;
- Require programs to provide anonymous reporting mechanisms for potential violations of law; and
- *Require ongoing risk assessments* as an essential component of the design, implementation, and modification of an effective [compliance] program.[122]

The most significant amendments recommended in the Report concern a new guideline to define an "effective program to prevent and detect violations of law" by companies and other organizations. At the end of 2003, the Commission published its latest proposed amendments to the Sentencing Guidelines for public comment.[123] It held hearings on the proposed amendments on March 17, 2003, subsequently modified some of the Report's recommendations, and submitted amendments (as modified) to Congress on April 30, 2004.[124] Unless Congress votes to veto or change them, the proposed amendments will become law on the effective date specified by the Sentencing Commission— November 1, 2004.[125] However, a decision by the U.S. Supreme Court in 2004, that struck down a state's comparable sentencing guidelines has persuaded several District and Circuit Courts to refrain from applying the Sentencing Guidelines on the grounds that the Supreme Court's reasoning makes the Guidelines presumptively unconstitutional.

The Supreme Court issued its decision in *Blakely v. Washington* (No. 02-1632) on June 24, 2004, which invalidated the criminal sentencing

---

122. U.S. Sentencing Commission, "New Release," October 8, 2003, p. 1. [Emphasis added.]

123. 68 FEDERAL REGISTER 249, at p. 75340.

124. *Amendments to the Sentencing Guidelines*, May 10, 2004, cover page, accessed at www.ussc.gov/2004guid/RFMay04.pdf.

125. *Amendments to the Sentencing Guidelines, Policy Statements, and Official Commentary*, May 1, 2004, p. 1 accessed at www.ussc.gov/2004guid/2004cong.pdf.

guidelines of the State of Washington, and held that those guidelines (which permitted judges to make findings that increased a convicted defendant's sentence beyond the ordinary range for the crime) were unconstitutional, because the "State's sentencing procedure did not comply with the Sixth Amendment."[126] Although Justice Scalia's notes in his majority opinion that "The Federal Guidelines are not before us, and we express no opinion on them,"[127] Justice O'Connor's dissenting opinion observes that, in view of the Court's decision, "the hard constraints found throughout chapters 2 and 3 of the Federal Sentencing Guidelines, which require an increase in the sentencing range upon specified factual findings, will meet the same fate [as those of Washington State that the Court struck down]."[128] Commentators quickly suggested that *Blakely* put the constitutionality of the Federal Sentencing Guidelines in doubt.[129]

The uncertain status of the Sentencing Guidelines increased on June 29, 2004, when a U.S. District Court in *United States v. Crawford* struck down the Sentencing Guidelines as violative of the defendant's Sixth Amendment right to a jury trial, observing: "the inescapable conclusion of Blakely is that the federal sentencing guidelines have been rendered unconstitutional in cases such as this one. . . . A sentence may not be enhanced when doing so requires the judge to make factual findings which go beyond the defendant's plea or the verdict of the jury."[130] One day later, a U.S. District Court judge in the District of Columbia reduced

---

126. *Blakely v. Washington*, Slip Opinion, 124 S.Ct. 2531 (2004) at p. 2540, 2004 WL 1402697 (June 24, 2004).

127. *Blakely v. Washington*, Slip Opinion, 124 S.Ct. 2531 (2004) at p. 2540, footnote 9.

128. *Blakely v. Washington*, Slip Opinion, 124 S.Ct. 2531 (2004) at p. 2543 (Justice O'Connor, dissenting).

129. See Greenhouse, Linda, *Justices, in Bitter 5-4 Split, Raise Doubts on Sentencing Guidelines*, THE NEW YORK TIMES, June 25, 2004, pp. A-1 and A-19, and Cohen, Laurie P., and Fields, Gary, *Court Ruling Causes Tumult in Sentencings*, THE WALL STREET JOURNAL, June 28, 2004, p. B-1 and B-2.

130. *United States v. Coxford*, Case No. 2-02-CR-00302PGC, 2004 WL 1462111 (D. Utah June 29, 2004), quoted in Manson, Pamela, *Utah Federal Judge: Sentence Guidelines Unconstitutional*, THE SALT LAKE TRIBUNE, June 30, 2004, accessed at www.sltrib2002.com/2004/Jun/06302004/utah/179981.asp. The fact that the judge, U.S. District Court Judge Paul G. Cassell, has a conservative reputation and expressed reluctance in reaching this conclusion strongly suggests that unless Congress takes further action, judicial pressure will continue toward interpreting the Guidelines as inconsistent with the Supreme Court's decision in *Blakely*.

a defendant's sentence only a week after imposing it, and explained from the Bench, "The Supreme Court has told me that what I did a week ago was plainly illegal."[131]

In response, Deputy Attorney General James Comey issued a July 2, 2004 memorandum instructing federal prosecutors on new indictments, pending indictments and plea agreements. With respect to new indictments: they "should immediately begin to include in indictments all readily provable [sentencing] guidelines" that could be used for upward adjustments in a defendant's sentence "to protect against the possibility that such allegations in indictments will be held necessary."[132] With respect to pending indictments that have not resulted in a guilty verdict or a plea agreement, they should obtain new indictments that allege all "readily provable" factors that could be used to justify upward adjustments in sentences.[133] And with respect to plea agreements already concluded, they should "immediately" seek waivers "from all defendants who agree to plead guilty to bar them from later using" *Blakely* as a basis to challenge their plea agreement.[134] By August of 2004, several additional opinions had issued addressing the constitutionality of the Sentencing Guidelines under *Blakely*, including:

- *United States v. Khan*—in which Judge Weinstein (Eastern District of New York) opined that unless "*Blakely* is made retroactive—which seems highly unlikely in view of the chaos which would result—it is probable that this decision [*Blakely*] will have little impact on practice in federal district courts;"[135]

- *United States v. Booker*—in which Judge Posner, writing for the

---

131. Statement from the Bench by Judge Thomas Penfield Jackson, quoted in Cohen, Laurie P. and Fields, Gary, *Judge Rejects Federal Rules on Sentencing*, THE WALL STREET JOURNAL, July 1, 2004, p. B-1 at B-6. For an analysis of potential consequences of these decisions, see Vinegrad, Alan, and Sack, Jonathan, '*Blakely*': *The End of the Sentencing Guidelines?*, NEW YORK LAW JOURNAL, July 6, 2004, pp. 4 and 8.

132. Cohen, Laurie, *Sentence Ruling Prompts Memo to Prosecutors*, THE WALL STREET JOURNAL, July 7, 2004, p. B-1 at B-8.

133. Id.

134. Id.

135. See Hamblett, Mark, *Sentencing Guidelines Not Doomed, Weinstein Says*, NEW YORK LAW JOURNAL, July 26, 2004, pp. 1–2, quoting Weinstein, J., in *U.S. v. Khan*, 02-CR-1242. At approximately the same time, the U.S. Senate passed a concurrent resolution urging the U.S. Supreme Court to act "expeditiously" to "end inconsistence in the sentencing system triggered by *Blakely* . . . ." Senate, *Judges Urge 'Blakely' Redux*, NEW YORK LAW JOURNAL, July 26, 2004, p. 2.

United States Court of Appeals for the Seventh Circuit, concluded that the courts could not simply adhere to the Sentencing Guidelines until the Supreme Court clarifies its position;[136]

- *United States v. Montgomery*—in which the Sixth Circuit held that the Sentencing Guidelines were merely guidelines, not mandatory, and directed District Court Judges in that Circuit to apply indeterminate sentencing in all cases;[137] and

- *United States v. Einstman*—in which U.S. District Court Judge McMahon cogently reasoned that:

"To ask that the judges who are constrained to sentence those real people [sic] ignore what appear to be the inescapable constitutional consequences of a decision of the United States Supreme Court until that Court addresses it directly is, frankly, to ask too much. . . . We . . . risk the ultimate fate of countless defendants whose convictions and sentences will inevitably be finalized while this issue percolates through the usual channels— defendants who may not have an opportunity to assert latterly found Sixth Amendment rights because new pronouncements of law are not retroactive for defendants whose convictions are final. . . . I seriously doubt that today's district judges will fail to consult the Guidelines, or fail to be guided by them in most cases, simply because those provision [sic] are now in fact *guidelines* rather than mandates. . . . There is far too much wisdom in the Guidelines, practical as well as theoretical, for any sensible jurist to ignore them."[138]

Because the Sentencing Guidelines may well survive (if Congress takes remedial action to bring them into conformance with the *Blakely* decision or if the U.S. Supreme Court decides to uphold their constitutionality),[139] and because even if they do not survive they will continue

---

136. *United States v. Booker*, 2004 WL 1535858 (7th Cir. July 9, 2004).

137. *United States v. Montgomery*, 2004 Fed. App. 0226(p) (6th Cir. July 20, 2004).

138. *United States v. Einstman*, printed in the NEW YORK LAW JOURNAL, July 20, 2004, pp. 21–22.

139. As this book was going to press, the U.S. Supreme Court issued its decision in *United States v. Booker*, 124 S.Ct., 2005 WL 50108 (Jan. 12, 2005). The Court held the Sixth Amendment requires juries, not judges, to find facts relevant to sentencing, and, as a remedy, severed and excised the statutory provisions that require courts to impose a sentence within the applicable U.S. Sentencing Guidelines range and set forth standards of review on appeal. The Court explained that sentencing judges are now required to *take account* of the U.S. Sentencing Guidelines (together with other sentencing goals) when determining a sentence.

to exert a non-binding influence as a "guide" to sentencing, Agile's General Counsel has studied the proposed amendments to confirm that Agile's compliance program meets the Sentencing Guidelines requirements. Failure could have severe consequences for Agile and its partners. The following suggests a possible strategy (in response to the proposed amendments) to implement a program that would meet the Guidelines' criteria for an "effective compliance program."

1.10 Proposed Amendments to the Sentencing Guidelines.

The proposed amendments make several significant changes to the Sentencing Guidelines.

- **Seven Criteria—A New Guideline.** Incorporates the seven minimum steps for a compliance program into a new guideline as Section 8B2.1
- **Key Terms and Purposes.** Provides clarifications and definitions of key terms, and defines the obligations and purposes of an effective compliance program.
- **Establishes Scope.** Defines the scope of a compliance program to:

  "Exercise due diligence to prevent and detect criminal conduct,"[140] but adds the commentary that "prevention and detection of criminal conduct, as facilitated by an effective compliance and ethics program, will assist an organization in encouraging ethical conduct and in *complying fully with all applicable laws*."[141]

---

140. *Amendments to the Sentencing Guidelines, Policy Statements, and Official Commentary,* May 1, 2004, Section 8B.2.1(a)(1), p. 76, accessed at www.ussc.gov/2004guid/2004cong.pdf. This version reflects a substantial reduction in the scope of the Report's proposed amendment which read: ""preventing and detecting violations of any law, whether criminal or noncriminal (including a regulation), for which the organization is, or would be, liable." As commentators noted, that version was criticized at the March 17 hearings in the belief it "would prove too onerous to large, diverse corporations or corporations operating in highly regulated industries." See Liman, Lewis J., and Brodsky, David E., *Amendments to the U.S. Organizational Sentencing Guidelines,* NEW YORK LAW JOURNAL, June 16, 2004, p. 3.

141. *Amendments to the Sentencing Guidelines,* Introductory Commentary to Chapter 8, Part B, p. 75, accessed at www.ussc.gov/2004guid/2004cong.pdf. [Emphasis added.]

- **Compliance Culture.** Adds a new requirement that an organization shall also "otherwise promote an organizational culture that encourages a commitment to compliance with the law."[142]
- **Culpability Score—Two Changes in Factors.** Previously, the Guidelines precluded an organization from obtaining the compliance program's three credits if:

  (i) Any of certain categories of high-level personnel had participated in, condoned, or been willfully ignorant of, the organization's offense; or

  (ii) If an individual considered to be "substantial authority personnel" (such as a member of a Board of Directors, a plant manager or someone with authority to negotiate prices) participated in an offense.[143] The proposed amendments replace this automatic bar with the following: "an offense by an individual within high-level personnel of the organization results in a *rebuttable presumption*" that an effective compliance program did not exist.

In addition, commentary to the proposed amendments provides that an organization's waiver of attorney-client and work product privileges "is *not a prerequisite* to a reduction in culpability score under subsection (g)," but in some circumstances "may be required in order to satisfy the requirements of cooperation."[144] If properly implemented, this provision will mean that organizations will not be forced to waive protections (and face the uncertain consequences of such a waiver) in order to qualify for the cooperation credits in all cases. Presumably, an organization will only face that prospect if, for example, it appears (from

---

142. Proposed Amendment, Section 8B2.1(a)(2), accessed at www.ussc.gov/2004guid/2004cong.pdf.

143. The term "substantial authority personnel" means "individuals who within the scope of their authority exercise a substantial measure of discretion in acting on behalf of an organization. The term includes high-level personnel of the organization, individuals who exercise substantial supervisory authority (e.g., a plant manager, a sales manager), and any other individuals who, although not a part of an organization's management, nevertheless exercise substantial discretion when acting within the scope of their authority (e.g., an individual with authority . . . to negotiate or set price levels or . . . to negotiate or approve significant contracts)." *Guidelines*, Section 8A1.2, Application Notes, 3(c).

144. *Proposed Amendments*, Commentary to Section 8C2.5, p. 83, accessed at www.ussc.gov/2004guid/2004cong.pdf.

all evidence provided by the Government) that the organization is not fully disclosing the extent of its offenses in reporting a violation.

Implementing an Effective Compliance Program.

Under the proposed amendments as noted above, an organization must at a minimum "exercise due diligence to prevent and detect violations of law" and "otherwise promote an organizational culture that encourages a commitment to compliance with the law." An organization is required to take each of the following seven steps in order to qualify for the compliance program credit (or to persuade the Justice Department, where relevant, to decline to prosecute it or its officers):

(i) **Establish Standards.** Establish compliance standards and procedures to prevent and detect violations of law.

(ii) **Make Leadership Knowledgeable.** Ensure that its leadership is knowledgeable about the content and operation of the program to prevent and detect violations of law ("**Compliance Program**"). To fulfill this step, the organization must:

   a. Ensure that its governing authority is knowledgeable about the content and operation of the Compliance Program and exercises *reasonable oversight* of the Program's implementation and effectiveness;

   b. Assign to specific individual(s) within high-level personnel of the organization the *direct, overall responsibility* to ensure such implementation and effectiveness;
   Note: Such individual(s) must be given adequate resources and authority to carry out such responsibility, and they must **report directly** to the governing authority of the organization or an appropriate subgroup of the governing authority regarding the implementation and effectiveness of the Compliance Program.

(iii) **Exclude Violators from Positions of Authority.** Use reasonable efforts not to include within the substantial authority personnel of the organization any individual whom the organization knew, *or should have known* through the exercise of due diligence, has a history of engaging in violations of law *or other conduct inconsistent* with the Compliance Program (*i.e.,* unethical conduct).

(iv) **Require Compliance Training of Governing Authority of Organization.** Take reasonable steps to communicate in a practical manner the organization's compliance standards and procedures to the "members of the governing authority [*i.e.,* Board of Directors], high-level personnel, substantial authority personnel, the organization's employees, and, as appropriate, the organization's agents"[145] by conducting *effective training programs* and otherwise disseminating information appropriate to such individuals' respective roles and responsibilities.[146]

(v) **Audit the Compliance Program.** Take reasonable steps:

    a. To ensure that the organization's Compliance Program is followed, *including monitoring and auditing systems* that are designed to prevent and detect criminal conduct; and

    b. To **evaluate periodically** the effectiveness of the organization's Compliance and Ethics Programs, and require individuals with "operational authority" to report on such effectiveness to "high-level personnel and, as appropriate, to the governing authority, or an appropriate subgroup of the governing authority;"[147] and

    c. To have a Compliance Program that the organization *publicizes* and that ensures that the organization's employees and agents may report or seek guidance regarding potential or actual violations of law without fear of retaliation, *including mechanisms that allow for anonymous reporting.*[148]

(vi) **Promotion Compliance.** Promote and enforce the organization's Compliance Program consistently through appropriate incentives to act in accordance with such program (and institute disciplinary measures for conduct that constitutes violations of law or failure to take reasonable steps to prevent or detect violations of law).

---

145. Id, Section 82B.1(b)(4)(B), p. 77.

146. Id, Section 82B.1(b)(4)(A).

147. Id, Section 8B2.1(b)(2)(C), p. 77.

148. As the *Amendment* states: organizations shall make a reasonable effort "to have and *publicize* a [compliance] system, which may include mechanisms that *allow for anonymity or confidentiality,* whereby the organization's employees and agents may report or seek guidance regarding potential or actual criminal conduct without fear of retaliation." *Proposed Amendments,* Section 8B.2.1(b)(5)(c), accessed at www.ussc.gov/ 2004guid/2004cong.pdf. [Emphasis added.]

(vii) **Respond to Detected Violations.** Take reasonable steps, after a violation of law has been detected, to respond appropriately to the violation of law and to prevent further similar violations of law (including any necessary modifications to the organization's Compliance Program).

The Sentencing Guidelines add that the organization shall conduct **ongoing risk assessments,** and take appropriate steps to design, implement and/or modify each of the seven above-mentioned steps to reduce the risk of violations of law identified by such assessments.

1.11 Summary of Proposed Amendments to Sentencing Guidelines.

In Agile's situation, the proposed amendments require it to consider enhanced due diligence for its contemplated acquisition of Troll, as well as to review of its existing compliance procedures.

The following table highlights some of most significant changes contemplated by the proposed amendments:

Figure 6.

Subject Matter	Pre-Amendment Guidelines	Post-Amendment Guidelines
1. Compliance program	Objective is mainly to prevent crime	Objective is to promote "an organizational culture that encourages ethical conduct and a commitment to compliance with the law" §8B2.1(a)(2)
	The seven steps of an effective compliance program are only commentary to the Guidelines.	§ 8B2.1(b) elevates the seven steps to being "seven minimum requirements" of an effective program that encourages compliance with the law and ethical conduct, and provides additional guidance.
2. Prevention and detection of criminal conduct.	Required compliance program to "prevent and detect" criminal conduct	§8B2.1(b)(1) requires organizations to establish "standards and procedures to prevent and detect criminal conduct."

(continued)

Figure 6. (Continued)

Subject Matter	Pre-Amendment Guidelines	Post-Amendment Guidelines
		Note 1 adds that such standards and internal controls must be "reasonably capable of reducing the likelihood of criminal conduct."
3. Senior responsibility for compliance	Required that specific high-level individuals of the organization be assigned overall responsibility to oversee compliance (but did not specify who must oversee the organization's compliance program)	§8B2.1(b)(2) defines specific roles and reporting relationships. Requires an organization's governing authority (*e.g.,* Board of Directors) to "be knowledgeable about the content and operation of the compliance and ethics program" and must exercise "reasonable oversight" of its implementation and effectiveness.
4. Day-to-day responsibility for compliance	Not specified.	§8B2.1(b)(2)(C) requires assignment to specific person of the day-to-day responsibility for compliance. If the task is delegated to someone below the governing authority, such person must submit reports on the compliance program to the governing authority at least annually.
5. Background checks of senior officers	Required screening of substantial authority personnel for their "propensity to engage in violations of law"	§8B2.1(b)(3) requires that the organization "use reasonable efforts not to include within the substantial authority personnel of the organization any individual whom the organization knew, or should have known through the exercise of due diligence, has engaged in illegal activities or other conduct inconsistent with an effective compliance and ethics program.

(continued)

Figure 6. (Continued)

Subject Matter	Pre-Amendment Guidelines	Post-Amendment Guidelines
6. Compliance and ethics training	Not required.	§8B2.1(b)(4) Require compliance and ethics training, and that such training must also extend to the upper levels of an organization, including the governing authority and high-level personnel. Such training must not be a one-time only exercise, but must be ongoing, with "periodic" updates.
7. Compliance audits	Requires reasonable steps to achieve compliance. Requires reporting the "criminal conduct . . . of others" Requires "reporting systems without fear of retribution"	§8B2.1(b)(5) Requires organizations: (i) to use auditing and monitoring systems designed to prevent and detect criminal conduct; (ii) to periodically evaluate the effectiveness of compliance and ethics programs; and (iii) to have a "system, which may include mechanisms that allow for anonymity or confidentiality,[a] whereby the organization's employees and agents **may report or seek guidance** regarding potential or actual criminal conduct without fear of retaliation"
8. Risk assessment	None.	§8B2.1(c) requires organization to periodically assess the risk of the occurrence of criminal conduct. Application Note 6 provides various factors to be addressed in such assessments, *e.g.,* nature and seriousness of potential criminal conduct,

(continued)

Figure 6. (Continued)

Subject Matter	Pre-Amendment Guidelines	Post-Amendment Guidelines
		likelihood that certain criminal conduct may occur because of the nature of the organization's business, and prior history of the organization.
9. To qualify for downward adjustment in penalty for having "fully cooperated in the investigation"	Current text reads:"(g) Self-Reporting, Cooperation, and Acceptance of Responsibility If more than one applies, use the greatest: (1) If the organization (A) prior to an imminent threat of disclosure or government investigation; and (B) within a reasonably prompt time after becoming aware of the offense, reported the offense to appropriate governmental authorities, **fully cooperated in the investigation**, and clearly demonstrated recognition and affirmative acceptance of responsibility for its criminal conduct, **subtract 5 points**; or (2) If the organization **fully cooperated in the investigation** and clearly demonstrated recognition and affirmative acceptance of responsibility for its criminal conduct, **subtract 2 points**;[b] or (3) If the organization clearly demonstrated recognition and affirmative acceptance of responsibility for its criminal conduct, subtract 1 point."	Cooperation must be "thorough and timely." To be "thorough" the organization must disclose all pertinent information it knows. The test is whether law enforcement personnel can identify the nature and extent of the violations, and the individual(s) responsible for the culpable conduct. Cooperation is to be measured by the organization's cooperation, not any individual's cooperation. **Note:** In Note 12 to subsection (g) [quoted in the column to the left], the Commission added a very controversial guidance: **"Waiver of attorney-client privilege and of work product protections is not a prerequisite to a reduction in culpability score under subdivisions (1) and (2) of subsection (g)** *unless such waiver is necessary in order to provide timely and thorough disclosure of all pertinent information known to the organization."*[c]

(continued)

Figure 6. (Continued)

[a]The Commission acknowledged it was aware of inherent limitations in systems that provide anonymity to reporters of wrongs (such systems "may hinder an organization from engaging in effective dialogue with the potential whistleblower to discover additional information that might lead to a more efficient detection of the wrongdoing") or that seek to provide confidentiality to reporters of wrongs ("the ability of organizations to ensure total confidentiality may be limited by legal obligations relating to self-disclosure, law enforcement subpoenas, and civil discovery requests."). See *Amendments to the Sentencing Guidelines, Policy Statements, and Official Commentary,* May 1, 2004, p. 111 accessed at www.ussc.gov/2004guid/2004cong.pdf.
[b]Emphases added.
[c]Id.

1.12 Potential Problems in Proposed Amendments to the Sentencing Guidelines—Risks to the Attorney-Client Relationship.

Difficulties are created, however, by the proposed linking of "co-operation" with enforcement personnel (and downward adjustment in penalty) to waiver of the attorney-client privilege and work product protections ("to provide timely and thorough disclosure of all pertinent information known to the organization"). While the Commission commentary expressly states that "The Commission expects that such waivers will be required on a limited basis," the limitation may prove illusory in light of recent Congressional legislation (the Feeney Amendment to the PROTECT Act),[149] and the propensity of the current Attorney General to deprive judges of their discretion to grant downward adjustments in penalties.[150] Since the judge would ordinarily make the determination as to whether such waivers were warranted in a given case, general counsel would be forced to make a recommendation without knowing which judge would be ruling. Uneasiness with these provisions is widespread: "Critics said that forcing a corporation facing a criminal probe to waive attorney-client privilege would have a negative impact on employees and senior level officers who routinely go to company attorneys for advice on issues that arise."[151]

---

149. The Feeney Amendment severely limits judges' discretion.

150. Attorney General John Ashcroft, in memoranda dated July 28, 2003 and September 22, 2003, ordered prosecutors to notify the Justice Department whenever a federal judge issues a sentence with a downward departure. See www.usdoj.gov and Morvillo, Robert G., and Anello, Robert J., *Sentencing Guidelines in 2004,* NEW YORK LAW JOURNAL, February 3, 2004, pp. 3 and 6.

151. Fields, Gary, *Sentencing Panel Adds Hurdle for Companies to Get Leniency,* THE WALL STREET JOURNAL, April 9, 2004, p. B-3.

Federal prosecutors have further increased the pressure on companies and their counsel by indicting three former high-ranking executives of Computer Associates for, among other offenses, obstruction of justice in connection with their actions (statements) during meetings with company counsel conducting an internal investigation. Prosecutors charged that each defendant made "false statements and conceal[ed] material information" from company counsel while knowing that by doing so they would obstruct and impede the government's investigation.[152] As one commentator observed, the government's decision to base an obstruction of justice charge on false statements to counsel conducting an internal investigation:

"Reinforced an already resonating message that internal investigations are becoming extensions of the government's investigations. . . . In the past, company counsel conducting those investigations— even where a company has committed in advance to report the results to the government—have not seen the role of counsel as being functionally the same as the role of the prosecutor. Yet as the[se]. . . . prosecutions suggest, a lie to company counsel who is reporting to the government on the progress of the internal investigation can be made the legal equivalent of a lie to the prosecutor."

Such language sweeps very broadly, and arguably disciplines not only "lies" (or deliberate misstatements), but omissions to state facts later deemed relevant. It would seem that employees need to employ independent counsel before speaking to company counsel, and should have the rights (and constitutional guarantees of the 5th Amendment) to decline to speak on grounds of self-incrimination. However, declining to speak will raise the dual specters of non-cooperation and obstruction.

At this point, the company's interests and those of its employees will diverge markedly. A company seeking to avert risks will attempt to ensure prospectively that it will qualify for mitigating factors (in the event of a violation) and will distance itself from aggravating factors. If company counsel is tasked to conduct an internal investigation of a potential criminal violation of the Access Control Laws, the standard pre-interview cautions to company employees (that counsel represents the company, not its employees, that the attorney-client privilege is the com-

---

152. Strauss, Audrey, *Company Counsel as Agents of Obstruction*, New York Law Journal, July 1, 2004, p. 5.

pany's and may be waived by the company, and that the employee may want to engage independent counsel before talking to company counsel) may need to be supplemented (depending on the jurisdiction) by a further caution that any false statements or concealment of information could be interpreted by federal prosecutors as grounds for an indictment for obstruction of justice.[153]

1.13 "Armageddon" Scenarios Highlight Need for Pre-Negotiation Checkpoints.

Being charged with "obstruction of justice" is clearly the "worst case" scenario. But in any legal analysis, it is useful for counsel to look at the "Armageddon" scenario in order to appreciate the full scope of the risk, even if the company chooses not to structure its compliance strategy around that scenario. This is preferable to the post-violation "damage control" mode, which attempts to minimize exposure by shifting risks instead of reducing their causes. The result of the latter is more often conduct that will be deemed an aggravating factor, when a better decision taken at the same moment, could have instead qualified as a mitigating factor. Moreover, as one commentator observed, "Practitioners should look to the recent amendments" to the Guidelines "defining an 'effective' corporate compliance program **more as a means of avoiding indictment than mitigating a sentence.**"[154]

Following our analytic approach, a company and its counsel should insist on the establishment of checkpoints (for TSR, EAR, ITAR, privacy, information security and patents) **prior to entry into negotiations**. This is imperative, because (as noted above) such signings can constitute a violation of certain of those regulations, as can entry into negotiations with a targeted party (which can result in strict liability). If counsel encounters institutional resistance, the next best time to establish such checkpoints is immediately after the signing of a letter of intent or other preliminary agreement that does not bind the parties to complete the

---

153. Strauss suggests that giving such cautions could unduly chill the investigation and asks whether a more appropriate caution might be a subtle suggestion that anything said to counsel might be disclosed in a report to the federal enforcement authorities.

154. Devaney, William H., *Corporate Compliance Programs and the Sentencing Guidelines*, NEW YORK LAW JOURNAL, July 21, 2004, p. 4.

contemplated deal. At that checkpoint, counsel needs to define the potentially extensive reach of the Access Control Laws.

In the next section, we review recent developments that suggest that the risk of being investigated and held liable for such laws and regulations (sometimes strictly liable) appears likely to increase substantially in the near future.

1.14 Ten Recent Developments that Have Raised the Risks of Liability for Cyberspace Transactors and Cyber-Driven Transactions.

Currently, cyberspace transactions customarily employ only two checkpoints. Each operates independent of national boundaries (unless a dispute arises over the agreement on the jurisdiction whose laws should apply).[155] These are limited to contractual checkpoints ordinarily imposed and monitored by a seller in the form of:

(i) Buyer's execution of a sale or license agreement (usually a seller's clickwrap contract of adhesion), and

(ii) Buyer's or licensee's provision and seller's verification of payment information.

No other checkpoints are commonly used. Apparently, no others were perceived to be either required or advantageous.

Early cyberspace transactions typically involved a commercial sale of brand-name items by highly visible sellers to relatively opaque customers. Identities of customers initially had limited importance: to ensure the reliability of payment and correct delivery of the purchased goods or services. Gradually, the ability to identify customers expanded, as sellers wanted to market their goods more efficiently and cost-effectively. To meet that need, sellers revised their commercial websites to deposit "cookies" and other customer monitoring devices. We do

---

155. For discussion of jurisdiction in disputes arising in cross-border transaction, see Gilman, Jeremy, *Personal Jurisdiction and the Internet: Traditional Jurisprudence for a New Medium*, 59 BUSINESS LAWYER 395 (November 2000) at pp. 409–411. See also, Rice, Dennis T., and Gladstone, Julia, *An Assessment of the Effects Test in Determining Personal Jurisdiction in Cyberspace*, 58 BUSINESS LAWYER 601 at pp. 644–652.

not regard such devices as transactional checkpoints, but merely as monitoring devices of convenience, reporting on customer activity in cyberspace, but not on their commercial and other economic relationships. Historically, sellers evidenced no serious interest in knowing a customer's business partners, dealings, associations or relationships, and buyers evidenced no serious interests in knowing such facts about sellers.

In short, neither party to a cross-border cyberspace transaction treated the activity as subject to liability for violation of the TSR, EAR and ITAR, although such concerns had long been a high priority in corporate and financial cross-border transactions (*e.g.*, mergers and acquisitions, loans, joint ventures) and in long-term relational contracts (*e.g.*, design and development contracts for digital based, high-tech systems). The initial era of cyberspace, in which the parties operated extrajudicially, and with relatively opaque transactors, involved primarily simple buy/sell or lease transactions. That era is gone. A confluence of forces is causing the change, accelerating its pace and widening its effects. We identify ten causal forces that, at the time of this writing, appear to be the predominant causes for the substantial increase in Access Control Law risks to U.S. persons engaged in cyberspace transactions and cyber-driven transactions.

1.14.1 Heightened Scrutiny of Cross-Border Transactions.

Nations are increasingly reluctant to ignore transactions that cross their borders via cyberspace. They have begun to pursue enforcement of their applicable jurisdictional laws, rules and regulations relating to taxes, privacy, trade sanctions, export controls, money laundering, etc. One recent example is the European Union Directive (effective, July 1, 2003) requiring the Member States of the EU to "begin collecting the VAT, or value-added tax, on sales of digital goods and other electronic transactions from U.S. and other non-EU companies."[156] Doing so, however, will require verification of a customer's identity, with the added problem that "Sophisticated Internet users can mask their loca-

---

156. Krebs, Brian, *EU Stirs up Internet Sales Tax Debate*, June 9, 2003, accessed at www.washingtonpost.com/wp-dyn/articles/A36150-2003Jun9.html.

tions in order to escape paying sales taxes or make it look like they live in an EU country with a low VAT rate."[157] (See our observations below concerning expanded use of geo-locating software.)

This trend has been observed both in the U.S. and overseas:

> "Prior to 2001, due diligence laws were only enforced patchily in the UK. But as the result of recent anti-terrorism legislation and money laundering regulations, more organizations are boosting their due diligence. In addition to banks and financial companies, since last year [2003], lawyers, accountants, estate agents, casinos and dealers in significant sums of money (such as auction houses) have been obliged to perform basic checks on their clients. They must be able to verify the identity of customers; maintain records of the information used to verify that identity; and ensure an account holder is not on lists of suspected terrorists (maintained on the Bank of England website).[158] As a result, the bizarre spectacle of City of London law firms asking their clients for utility bills and proof of address details has become routine."[159]

---

157. Id. Countries are also becoming increasingly vigilant and willing to cooperate to detect and defeat online cross-border fraud and other commercial practices harmful to consumers. See *Organization for Economic Cooperation and Development: OECD Guidelines for Protecting Consumers from Fraudulent and Deceptive Commercial Practices across Borders,* June 17, 2003, accessed at www.oecd.org/pdf/M00041000/M00041835. pdf, which includes among its recommendations that "to address the speed at which those engaged in fraudulent and deceptive commercial practices can victimise large numbers of consumers, for example, through the Internet, member countries should work together to develop fast, efficient methods for gathering and sharing information . . . ," and, "Member countries should work towards enabling their consumer protection enforcement agencies to share the following information with consumer protection enforcement agencies in other Member countries in appropriate instances: . . . 3. Information about addresses, telephones, Internet domain registrations, basic corporate data, and other information permitting the quick location and identification of those engaged in fraudulent and deceptive commercial practices." At pp. 14 and 16.

158. The Bank of England's website includes a "Financial Sanctions" page which acts as an index to all material relevant to the Bank's financial sanctions related to Afghanistan and terrorist financing, including a consolidated list of targeted parties subject to notices issued by the Bank to the effect that all relevant institutions holding funds of such persons must ensure that such funds are not made available to any person except under the authority of a license granted by the UK Treasury. See Bank of England, *Financial Sanctions,* accessed at www.bankofengland.co.uk/sanctions/main.htm.

159. Overell, Stephen, *Due Diligence: The Constant Search for Skeletons in the Closet,* FINANCIAL TIMES, Special Supplement on "Understanding Corporate Security," July 14, 2004, p. 5.

Heightened diligence is not only driven by economic motives, but by security concerns.[160] In such instances, the enforcing government tends to apply increasingly severe penalties. For example, Japan's Financial Services Agency, on September 17, 2004, ordered Citibank NA (a subsidiary of Citigroup Inc.) to *close* its private-banking operations in Japan within a year as a penalty for having committed serious violations of the country's banking laws,[161] including "suspicious transactions linked to possible criminal activity by clients," and referred details of the investigation to a unit within the agency for possible investigation of money laundering.[162]

The U.S. Government is seeking to enhance security by improved surveillance and control of the flow of persons and products into the United States.[163] Such measures rely heavily on collecting and comparing data, and on making the results available to customs and immigration officials through networked computers.[164]

For example, in response to its perception of increased risks of terrorism in cross-border transactions, the United States has pursued a policy of deploying defense-in-depth initiatives and technologies (*i.e.,*

160. Adversaries can dispatch malware through the Internet to disable U.S.-based computers or damage the data stored within them. They can also use the World Wide Web for propaganda, whether broadcasting video (such as the awful beheading of Nick Berg in May 2004) or publishing calls to action. As noted by Jane's Terrorism and Security Centre, the Internet has probably become the main global source of literature promoting jihad or "holy war." See Huband, Mark, *Web Sends Call for Jihad Round the Globe in Moments,* FINANCIAL TIMES, June 17, 2004, p. 4.

161. Wighton, David, *Another Blow for Citigroup,* FINANCIAL TIMES, September 20, 2004, p. 19. See also Pacelle, Mitchell and Fackler, Martin and Morse, Andrew, *For Citigroup, Scandal in Japan Shows Dangers of Global Sprawl,* THE WALL STREET JOURNAL, December 22, 2004, p. A-1.

162. Morse, Andrew, and Pacelle, Mitchell, *Japan Orders Citibank to Halt Private Banking,* THE WALL STREET JOURNAL, September 20, 2004, p. A-3 at p. A-16.

163. Note that China has now implemented what commentators refer to as the "Great Firewall of China"—a system of devices and measures that limit access within the country to websites deemed objectionable to the Chinese government. Such devices and measures include: (1) the Chinese instant messaging service, QQ, which filters out more than a thousand objectionable words and phrases (such as "democracy," "Christian," "Falun Gong," and "Taiwan independence"); (2) "Routers that connect networks are encoded with the unique numerical addresses for the websites China deems objectionable, blocking, for example, purveyors of uncensored news, such as the BBC's Chinese and English news sites . . . ." Hutzler, Charles, *China Finds New Ways to Restrict Access to the Internet,* THE WALL STREET JOURNAL, September 1, 2004, p. B-1.

164. Unfortunately, the federal government's efforts to improve cybersecurity of the United States appear to lag far behind.

methods of checking persons and cargoes as far from the U.S. border as possible), relying on the checkpoint of customs and immigration officers only as a final defense. To address the risks of terrorist devices planted in cargo containers, U.S. Customs and Border Protection has sought, since January 2002, to gain acceptance by other countries of its Container Security Initiative ("CSI").[165] The primary purpose of CSI is to "protect the global trading system and the trade lanes between CSI ports and the U.S."[166] CSI has four core elements:

(i) Use of intelligence and automated information to identify and target containers that pose a terrorism risk;

(ii) Pre-screening of those targeted containers at their port of *departure* (and thus before they arrive at U.S. ports);

(iii) Use of detection technology to pre-screen targeted (high risk) containers efficiently and quickly;[167] and

(iv) Use of "smart," tamper-evident containers.[168]

In an unusual practice, each port that has agreed to participate in CSI allows the forward-deployment of U.S. Customs and Border Protection officers in the host port to work with port authorities to pre-screen and, when necessary, inspect containers suspected of posing a terrorism risk.[169] If a decision is made to inspect a container, the host port's au-

165. U.S. Bureau of Customs and Border Protection, Department of Homeland Security, PowerPoint presentation on CSI Ports, accessed at www.customs.ustreas.gov/ ImageCache/cgov/content/import/cargo_5fcontrol/csi/ csi_5fport_5fmaps_5f030904_2eppt/v1/csi_5fport_5fmaps_5f030904.ppt. As of this writing, the following ports participate in CSI: in Canada, Montreal, Halifax, and Vancouver; in Europe, Antwerp, Rotterdam, Bremerhaven, Hamburg, Le Havre, Felixtowe, Götteborg, Genoa, and La Spezia; in Africa, Durban; and in Asia, Yokohama, Busan, Hong Kong, Singapore, Port Kelang, and Tanjong Pelepas.

166. *Fact Sheet: Container Security Initiative*, March 8, 2004, accessed at www.customs.ustreas.gov/ImageCache/cgov/content/import/cargo_5fcontrol/csi/ csifactsheet030804_2edoc/v1/csifactsheet030804.doc. Two-thirds of all containers that arrive by sea to the U.S. come from or through 20 ports (the 19 that have joined CSI, plus one other).

167. Such technologies include non-intrusive inspection equipment; for example, gamma or X-ray imaging equipment and radiation detection equipment.

168. Id.

169. Forward deployment of U.S. officials is not a new idea—what is new is the scope and that such deployment will not be limited to countries that share a land border with the U.S. For example, since 1894, U.S. immigration inspectors have operated beyond U.S. borders in Canada, inspecting persons heading for entry into the U.S. Immigration inspectors were much later deployed to Canadian airports to clear U.S.-

thorities (in deference to international law, issues of sovereignty, and political sensitivities in the post 9/11 environment) conduct the inspection; the U.S. officials merely observe. Ultimately, the effectiveness of CSI depends largely on whether the host port has conducted a sufficiently thorough port assessment (to ascertain its vulnerabilities), whether it has corrected any vulnerabilities identified by such assessment, and whether it pursues such assessment further (with the same tenacity and audacious imagination that a terrorist group would employ to circumvent CSI, without which any such assessment amounts to little more than a placebo). CSI seeks also to serve as a deterrent to terrorism but, until it proves an effective detector of terrorist acts, it is unlikely function as such.

The complement to CSI, providing defense-in-depth against terrorists seeking to enter the U.S., is the Department of Homeland Security ("DHS") program entitled "US-Visit," which seeks to deploy a so-called "virtual border" beyond the U.S. border.[170] Like CSI, the virtual border would be placed at points of origin for travel to the United States. More specifically, at each location abroad where people seek visas to enter the United States, there would be biometric sensors to identify (and perhaps begin tracking) applicants for entry. The data gathered at such points would be transmitted into networks of computer databases. Reportedly, when the applicant visitor arrived at "checkpoints, including those at the Mexican and Canadian borders," such visitor would face "real-time identification" (or, more accurately, re-identification) to confirm that identity and to confirm that the information provided at such checkpoints contains no discrepancy from the information provided in the visa application.[171]

---

bound passengers through U.S. passport controls of flights from abroad connecting through Canadian airports. Thus U.S. Customs and Border Protection officials inspect persons at the Vancouver and Toronto airports who arrive on flights from Japan and will continue on subsequent flights into the U.S. See Koslowski, Rey, *International Cooperation to Create Smart Borders*, prepared for presentation at the Conference on North American Integration: Migration, Trade and Security, April 2004, accessed at www.irpp.org/events/archive/apr04/koslowski.pdf.

170. The terms of reference keep changing because the plans remain in flux; for example, on March 22, 2002, the U.S. and Mexico announced plans to create a "smart border" between the two countries; "virtual borders" seems a broader application of that concept.

171. Lichtblau, Eric, and Markoff, John, *U.S. Nearing Deal on Way to Track Foreign*

As one bidder explains, the virtual border endeavors to push "as many decisions away from the physical border as possible, so the guy standing at the border becomes the last line of defense . . ."[172] Our narrative's Marco Polo (Agile's General Counsel) anticipates that there will be considerable red-tape (additional regulations, rules and hassles) associated with CSI and "virtual borders," and finds such efforts—in motivation (fear for security), magnitude (in miles and potential threats) and allocated resources—reminiscent of the Great Wall of China, which similarly served as an early warning and first line of defense.[173] Instead of deterring attacks by creating a physical barrier, however, the "virtual border" security system will seek to deter attacks by creating a "virtual" informational barrier, in which the system will compile "integrated traveler folders" containing personal and biometric data (and perhaps digital images, fingerprints, voice-prints, etc.). Those will be deployed at 211 early-warning watchtowers—posts that issue visas overseas—and will form a global net. The information gathered there will be linked and compared with databases containing profile data, intelligence and watch lists, in order to identify trends or patterns in emerging risks of terrorist attacks.[174]

Visitors, THE NEW YORK TIMES, May 24, 2004, p. A-1 at p. A-21. Note that although the DHS has set a maximum of $10 billion for bids to create the "virtual borders" system, once the usual inefficiencies take effect the cost will likely double.

172. Id, quoting Eric Stange, managing partner for defense and homeland security at Accenture.

173. Whether "virtual borders" and CSI will be as successful a protection against external threats as the Great Wall of China is far too early to predict. The Great Wall, however, could not protect China from internal weakness, which is what permitted the Mongols in the 13th century and the Manchurians in the 17th century to seize power in China. We should add that the original Marco Polo makes no mention in *The Travels* of the Great Wall of China, which was only just beginning to take on its current form when Marco started on his journeys.

That virtual borders relies on the design, development, and deployment of a complex computer system funded by the federal government makes its success quite uncertain. Such systems tend to undergo repetitive changes as they attempt to keep pace with perceived threats, and code design often is insufficiently disciplined and is allowed to become unnecessarily complex and hard to maintain. These factors often result in cost overruns that could doom a project whose initial cost estimates have already swelled to $15 billion over an optimistically forecast 10-year program. In short, "the government has had a bad record in building computerized systems based on unproved technology." See Markoff, John and Lichtblau, Eric, *Gaps Seen in "Virtual Border" Security System*, THE NEW YORK TIMES, May 31, 2004, p. C-1.

174. See Alden, Edward, Morrison, Scott, and Bowe, Christopher, *Accenture Wins US Border Security Deal*, FINANCIAL TIMES, June 2, 2004, p. 3.

1.14.2 Increasingly Aggressive Action Against Infringers of Intellectual Property.

Companies are becoming increasingly vigilant and aggressive in the face of apparent infringements of their intellectual property in cyberspace and cyber-driven transactions. Plaintiffs no longer pursue only an alleged "gatekeeper"[175] for contributory and vicarious infringement (*e.g.,* MP3.com, Napster, Grokster and Aimster).[176] Increasingly, they

---

Software maintenance and cybersecurity for the virtual border security system will probably be its twin Achilles heels. Moreover, to suggest that the system will link to intelligence databases may underestimate the problem we have had from the start: to allow links to sensitive intelligence risks compromising it and to limit such links nullifies the promised benefits. There is, in short, a technological hubris at work in a country attempting to protect itself by building a system that probably will not adjust as fast to threats as needed and gives short shrift to the effectiveness achieved by highly trained human security teams. We doubt that virtual borders, for all its promise and expense, will provide U.S. airports, for example, the security that some countries achieve at airport checkpoints with young, highly motivated and determined security interviewers who watch, ask, and scrutinize each traveler and can be briefed and updated in many respects more efficiently than computers.

As the GAO noted in its review of seven technologies for use in border control (facial recognition, fingerprint recognition, hand geometry, iris, retina, signature, and voice recognitions), "Whether the financial and nonfinancial costs are warranted by the benefits of greater security is a policy issue that should be determined before biometric technologies are implemented in a border control system." GAO report *Technology Assessment: Using Biometrics for Border Security,* November 2002, at p. 6, accessed at www.gao.gov/new.items/d03174.pdf. Or, as one commentator notes, "Though the government must try any reasonable idea to counter terrorism, in the next round of security improvements to come there will be serious limits to practicality and affordability." Easterbrook, Gregg, *In an Age of Terror, Safety Is Relative,* THE NEW YORK TIMES, June 27, 2004, Section 4, p. 1. Moreover, such computer systems may lead to less vigilant border security personnel, who think that the system has relieved them of certain tasks and who may be so distracted by false positives and false negatives that they will be less attentive to cues visible to a vigilant interviewer. These are hidden risks that the technology will probably not address.

175. We borrow the term "gatekeeper" from Wu, Timothy, *When Code Isn't Law,* 89 VIRGINIA LAW REVIEW 101 (June 2003), at p. 130.

176. Each of those four defendants may have sought to avoid litigation. If so, that effort, of course, was unsuccessful. They may also have sought to avoid losing such suits by the technologies they used. If so, then that effort, too, has been unsuccessful—for MP3.com, Napster, and Aimster. Grokster recently won in the District Court and the Ninth Circuit, but the U.S. Supreme Court has granted *certiorari,* and Grokster's chances of prevailing are far from clear.

appear willing to invest in costly and time-consuming lawsuits against alleged individual infringers.[177] Plaintiffs set the stage for such action, in the months preceding this writing, by sending demands to third-parties (specifically colleges and universities), insisting that they assist in policing those who use their computer systems (such as the enrolled students), and in providing access to the identities of alleged violators.[178] Since June 2003, the Recording Industry Association of America ("RIAA") has implemented a strategy of searching "Internet file-sharing networks to identify users who offer'substantial' collections of MP3 music files for downloading."[179] It has filed numerous lawsuits seeking fi-

---

177. Their willingness increases as the long-predicted convergence of audio, video, and data communications "into a single source, received on a single device, delivered by a single connection" accelerates towards its achievement. See Forman, Peter, and Saint John, Robert W., *Creating Convergence*, SCIENTIFIC AMERICAN, November 2000, p. 50. Examples of such convergence include the increasing adoption of Voice over Internet Protocol (telephony by Internet) and services that will combine capabilities for downloading of music with downloading of videos and TV programming, such as that announced by Sony for its Sony Connect service. Burt, Tim, *Sony Plans to Add Video Downloads to Online Music Service within Year*, July 14, 2004, p. 1.

178. Examples in the 12 months from July 2002 to July 2003 include the October 3, 2002, letter from the Recording Industry Association of America (RIAA), the Motion Picture Industry of America, the National Music Publishers' Association, and the Songwriters Guild of America to university and college presidents urging them to address "student piracy on your network." Letter formerly accessible at www.riaa.com/pdf/Universityletter.pdf (copy on file with authors). That letter apparently precipitated the U.S. Naval Academy's decision to seize on November 21, 2002, approximately 100 laptop computers from midshipmen to check if they had been used to download infringing music and other intellectual property. One can only wonder at the unintended effects of such seizures. A check for infringing music might, for example, turn up only non-infringing music and, in addition, non-infringing pornographic materials, the possession of which, however, might raise other issues under certain military regulations.

Subsequently, the RIAA filed a lawsuit against Verizon to compel it to disclose the identities of two subscribers suspected of illegally downloading copyrighted music. Verizon was ultimately successful in its argument that the Digital Millennium Copyright Act §512(h) barred the issuance of a subpoena to an Internet service provider (like Verizon) when it acted only as a conduit for the peer-to-peer system communications (being used to infringe) and did not store the infringing materials on its servers and thus could not "remove" such materials nor "disable access" to such materials. See *RIAA v. Verizon*, 351 F.3d 1229 (D.C. Cir. 2003); see also Raysman, Richard, and Brown, Peter, *Copyright and File-Sharing: Identifying Anonymous Defendants*, NEW YORK LAW JOURNAL, July 13, 2004, p. 3, and Mark, Roy, *Verizon Ordered to Reveal Names of Music Pirates* and *Verizon Must Reveal Name of Alleged Online Pirate*, June 4, 2003 and January 21, 2003, respectively, accessed at http://dc.internet.com/news/article.php/2217371.

179. *Music Labels to Sue Hundreds of Internet Users Sharing Songs*, Wall Street

nancial damages.[180] Verizon, which filed an appeal to the District Court decision compelling it to divulge the names of four subscribers alleged by the RIAA to have illegally trafficked in copyrighted music, reportedly expressed the fear that "the record industry would issue hundreds of thousands of similar subpoenas, forcing US Internet service providers to divulge the identities of suspected file swappers."[181]

Contemporaneous with the start of RIAA's campaign, Universal Pictures successfully initiated criminal action against an individual who threatened the commercial prospects of its film, *The Hulk*.[182] The defendant, who pleaded guilty on June 25, 2003, was swiftly traced, because a digital "tag" had been inserted into the pre-release version of *The Hulk* that he had obtained and uploaded to a chat room in The Netherlands, where it was subsequently downloaded. This downloaded copy provoked widespread pre-release criticism of the film's special effects (thereby threatening to reduce interest in the film before it was publicly screened). The fact that only three weeks had elapsed between commission of the copyright crime and entry of a guilty plea in the

---

Journal Online, June 25, 2003, accessed at http://online.wsj.com/article/0,,SB105656218791307000,00.html. See also *Statement from RIAA on File-Sharing*, Wall Street Journal Online, accessed at http://online.wsj.com/article/0,,SB105656559944720700,00.html?mod = article-outset-box.

180. In June 2004, RIAA brought an additional 482 copyright infringement suits against file-sharers. See RIAA press release *New Round of File Sharing Lawsuits Brought by RIAA*, June 22, 2004, accessed at www.riaa.com/news/newsletter/062204.asp.

181. Morrison, Scott, Larsen, Peter Thal, and Burt, Tim, *Music Industry to Hunt down Online File Swappers*, FINANCIAL TIMES, June 26, 2003, p. 1. Although the RIAA has used the subpoena power granted it under the Digital Millennium Copyright Act, it (and others seeking to enforce similar rights) may also be using geo-locating software (described below) to track down apparent infringers.

Note that the International Federation of the Phonographic Industry (IFPI), a global trade body for music, issued a call in July 2003 for 10 countries to enact more stringent laws on enforcement of anti-piracy laws to reduce the making of counterfeit CDs. The 10 countries are Brazil, China, Mexico, Paraguay, Poland, Russia, Spain, Taiwan, Thailand, and Ukraine. The IFPI reportedly claims that sales of pirate CDs have doubled since 1999 and now amount to $4.6 billion a year. See Milne, Richard, *Record Industry Asks 10 countries to Curb Piracy*, FINANCIAL TIMES, July 11, 2003. It is unclear from that report, however, the extent to which such pirated CDs might increase the amount of music downloaded from the Internet in violation of copyrights, but one would think that as pirated CD sales increase, the music from such CDs would tend to make its way onto the hard drives of computers accessed by participants in P2P systems.

182. Weiser, Benjamin, *Hulk Vanquishes an Evildoer for Bootlegging His New Film*, THE NEW YORK TIMES, June 26, 2003, Section B, p. B-3.

New York District Court demonstrates the remarkable reach that intellectual property rights enforcers have now acquired.[183]

Although most enforcers of intellectual property rights do not have the financial resources of Universal Pictures (nor the now-or-never urgency to interdict), it appears that, at least temporarily, momentum and advantage are shifting from infringers to intellectual property rights enforcers. Infringers (formerly secure in the presumption that they could hide in cyberspace opacity) are increasingly at risk of being identified and located by intellectual property rights enforcers who are now armed with the "Subpoena to identify infringer" powers enacted in 17 U.S.C. § 512(h), and digital technologies that enable them to pinpoint, through tracing or heightened surveillance, the trail of links back to the violators access point to the Internet and, in turn, to the violator's address for service of process or arrest on criminal charges.[184]

In June of 2004, the U.S. Senate passed two bills and has a third pending that (if enacted) would substantially increase the enforcement pressure on alleged copyright infringers. The two bills passed by the Senate are: the Pirate Act (to enable the Justice Department to bring civil copyright infringement actions) and the Art Act (to allow civil actions for piracy of pre-release works, and to prohibit camcorder recording of motion pictures for unauthorized redistribution). Pending

---

183. This trend of increased enforcement of intellectual property is not, of course, limited to cyberspace. It tends to occur whenever a new technology facilitates both infringing and non-infringing activities. For example, invention of DVD recorders and programming of the software code to create DVD copies (with no loss in quality) has predictably prompted the film studios and Macrovision to file separate suits against one such software producer, 321 Studios, based in St. Louis, Missouri. As of this writing, District Courts in California (in February of 2004) and New York (in May of 2004) have decided such suits against the defendant and issued injunctions. See *321 Studio v. Metro Goldwyn Mayer Studios, Inc., et. al.*, February 10, 2004, accessed at http://news.findlaw.com/hdocs/docs/mgm/321mgm22004ord.pdf, *Paramount Picture Corp. v. 321 Studios*, 2004 U.S. Dist. LEXIS 3306, No. 03 Civ. 8970, 2004 WL 402756 (S.D.N.Y. March 3, 2004), alleging that 321 Studio's software when used to copy a DVD infringed Macrovision's patented anti-copy methods (the suit also alleged copyright violations).

184. Moreover, there are efforts to develop technological means to disrupt unauthorized downloading of copyright protected works. In an interview given to THE WALL STREET JOURNAL, Bertelsmann's Chief Executive Officer, Gunter Thielen, observed: "I think the downloading problem won't be solved until we're able to electronically interfere with the process. There are some new technologies being tested and I think they'll be ready pretty soon. . . . In one or two years, we'll have taken care of the problem." Karnitschnig, Matthew, *Bertelsmann's Latest Tune*, THE WALL STREET JOURNAL, September 27, 2004, p. B-1.

in the Senate is the Inducing of Infringements of Copyright Act, which would make it illegal to induce someone to infringe a copyright. At this writing, it is not clear whether any of these bills will be enacted, but the impetus for such legislation appears to be increasing.[185]

The federal authorities tasked with reinforcing homeland security, and waging the multi-front war against terrorism, are not likely to overlook the shift, not only in technological advantage, but in legal presumption. Courts appear increasingly susceptible to arguments that persons should be held liable on the basis of knowledge imputed to them, where they had *reason to know* that their actions were wrongful, or where they recklessly risked committing wrongful harm.[186] (Although the press and other media have focused on disputes and threats to copy-

---

185. An ominous recent development has been the introduction in 2004 of several versions of an Inducing Infringement of Copyright Act (e.g., S. 2560) which, unfortunately, would put at risk the inventors of new technologies. See McBride, Sarah, *Antipiracy Bill Divides Studios and Tech Companies*, September 27, 2004, p. B-1. In the meantime, the owners of copyright-protected sound recordings encountered a sharp setback when the Ninth Circuit in August 2004 affirmed *Metro-Goldwyn-Mayer Studios, Inc. v. Grokster Ltd.*, No. 03-56236, (9th Cir. August 19, 2004), holding that Grokster defendants lacked the requisite "knowledge" for contributory infringement and lacked the requisite "material contribution" to infringement. It concluded that they were not contributorily nor vicariously liable for copyright infringements committed by users of its peer-to-peer file sharing software.

186. Courts in online copyright infringement cases have focused, in part, on the alleged infringing website operator's access to, and disregard of, the identity of those who download infringing copies from such website. In such instances, some courts have drawn inferences adverse to an alleged infringer's defense. For example, in the Ninth Circuit decision of the record companies' suit against Napster, the Court found probative of Napster's contributory infringing conduct the fact that Napster had knowledge "both actual and constructive" of direct infringement by visitors to and users of its website and noted that the District Court had found actual knowledge because "a document authored by Napster co-founder Sean Parker mentioned 'the need to remain ignorant of users' real names and IP addresses 'since they are exchanging pirated music.'" *A&M Records, Inc. v. Napster, Inc.*, 239 F.3d 1004 (9th Cir., 2001) at p. 1020. Such actual knowledge was cited by the Court as the basis for holding Napster liable, not because its technology made infringement possible but because with such knowledge, linked to demonstrated infringing use of the Napster system which Napster could have blocked and did not, Napster was liable for contributory infringement. 239 F.3d 1004 at 1021.

The Ninth Circuit reasoned that liability is incurred when a website operator has powers to block and does not use them: "to escape imposition of vicarious liability, the reserved right to police must be exercised to its fullest extent. Turning a blind eye to detectable acts of infringement for the sake of profit gives rise to liability." 239 F.3d 1004 at 1023. We think that OFAC and the BIS may well make similar arguments to

right-protected works in digital formats, litigation involving patents far exceeds copyright litigation—in number of cases and in the potential magnitude of damage awards.)

---

those made by the Ninth Circuit in *Napster* as commercial website operators increasingly gain the technology to know if prospective transactors seeking to use their website can be identified as located in countries targeted by the TSR and EAR. Ironically, the Ninth Circuit also found Napster's deliberate disregard of the identities of infringing users of its website also undermined Napster's claim to a fair use defense: "The district court determined that Napster users engage in commercial use of the copyrighted materials largely because (1) "a host user sending a file cannot be said to engage in a personal use when distributing that file to an anonymous requester. . . ." 239 F.3d 1004 at 1016.

Similarly, in *In Re: Aimster Copyright Litigation*, the District Court rejected defendant Aimster's contention to have no knowledge whatsoever of when its users were exchanging copyrighted music files, who among its users were doing so, or what files were being exchanged. Defendants based that contention on the fact that Aimster supposedly provided its users complete privacy in their online transaction by use of encryption software. In short, Aimster argued that its encryption should be held to shield it from liability for knowing the identities of infringers and policing their activity on its website. Screen shots provided by plaintiff RIAA, however, identified the individual users who possessed the offending files; each individual had to log on to the Aimster system with a password and user name provided by Aimster. As the court observed: "it is disingenuous of Defendants to suggest that it [sic] is unaware of which users are using its system and what files those users are offering up for other users to download at their whim. It is also disingenuous of Defendants to suggest that they lack the requisite level of knowledge when their putative ignorance is due entirely to an encryption scheme that they themselves put in place." 252 F. Supp. 2d 634 (N.D. Ill., 2002) at p. 651.

In affirming that decision, on June 30, 2003, the Seventh Circuit, in an opinion by Judge Posner, rejected Aimster's defense that its encryption services prevented it from having the requisite knowledge for contributory infringement. Judge Posner reasoned that where a defendant should have suspected widespread infringing uses of its website services its efforts to avoid learning how its services were being used constituted criminal intent—which the court substituted for the knowledge required for contributory infringement: "Willful blindness is knowledge, in copyright law (where indeed it may be enough that the defendant *should* have known of the direct infringement. [citations] One who, knowing, or strongly suspecting that he is involved in shady dealings, takes steps to make sure that he does not acquire full or exact knowledge of the nature and extent of those dealings is held to have a criminal intent [citation], because a deliberate effort to avoid guilty knowledge is all that the law requires to establish a guilty state of mind [citations] ('to know, and to want not to know because one suspects, may be, if not the same state of mind, the same degree of fault).' [citation]" *In Re: Aimster Copyright Litigation*, Slip Opinion No. 02-4125 (7th Cir., 2003) at p. 11 [Emphasis in original.]

The keystone in the Seventh Circuit's argument is that the panel, like the District Court, *suspects* the defendant had to have known of the illegal activity, since his website's services (and Aimster Club and its user tutorial) *invited* visitors to the site to engage in

1.14.3 Tougher Enforcement Action for Failure to Safeguard Privacy and Personal Data.

With the prodigious expansion of the use of peer-to-peer ("P2P") exchanges (*e.g.,* KaZaA, Grokster and Morpheus) has come increasing disclosure by participants of personal and highly sensitive data over such networks, and the insertion in the enabling software of so-called spyware or adware programs. As noted by European commentators,

> "The pervasive nature of on-line information management systems makes it extremely difficult for end-users to identify abuse of their personal data. Not only that; the multiple identification and authorization processes involved in Internet transactions lead to a growing quantity of personal information collected and stored in an ever greater number of information systems, with a consequent increase in the risk of privacy abuse. . . . [M]ost of the technologies used to monitor or profile individuals, and the interactions they make possible, are invisible to the Internet user. Data collection, data aggregation and data mining carried out by third-party organizations, and their use for marketing purposes, are therefore greatly facilitated. . . . Citizen rights are in fact better protected against governmental infringements than they are against infringements from other citizens or from the private sector."[187]

Default settings on some programs provide outsiders access to the "My Documents" folder on a transactor's hard drive and thus to its

---

illegal downloading of copyrighted music. They are probably right, and their reasoning is clever, but it is also potentially perilous: if an avoidance of knowledge is too readily stretched into equivalence with actual knowledge, there may be other instances where such substitution will be made. Defendants who deny knowing and did not know of their wrong doing, may find that they are held to have had *reason to know* because they appear to have avoided doing much to know more than they did. Just as we think that geolocating software will tend to make website owners increasingly obligated to know considerable details about their customers, so the Seventh Circuit's reasoning in *Aimster* will, if followed by other Circuits, tend to make courts more willing to hold website operators to have had *reason to know* where they did little to learn what they could have about their customers.

187. Institute for Prospective Technological Studies, *Security and Privacy for the Citizen in the Post-September 11 Digital Age: A Prospective Overview, Report to the European Parliament Committee on Citizens Freedoms and Rights, Justice and Home Affairs (LIBE)*, EUR 20823 EN, July 2003, Section 4.

contents.[188] Users of programs, such as that provided by KaZaA, may not realize that by designating their computer's "C" drive as the download destination, they thereby give KaZaA search and copy access to all files on that drive.[189] Other programs have reportedly been secreted in KaZaA software.[190]

Exposure of personal and highly sensitive data occurs also at many websites for consumer goods, where the failure to protect such data is drawing Federal Trade Commission enforcement action. Such enforcement actions were initiated against clothing designer and accessory marketer Guess, Incorporated[191] ("Guess"), against record, book and video vendor Tower Records ("Tower"),[192] and against educational products vendor Gateway Learning Corp. ("Gateway").[193] In June of 2003, the

188. See, *Statement of the Honorable Patrick Leahy, United States Senator, Vermont,* in *The Dark Side of a Bright Idea: Could Personal and National Security Risks Compromise the Potential of P2P File-Sharing Networks?,* hearings conducted by the United States Senate Committee on the Judiciary, June 17, 2003, accessed at www.senate.gov/~judiciary/member_statement.cfm?id = 623&wit_id = 50.

189. See, Carney, David W., *Senate Committee Holds Hearing on P2P Networks,* Tech Law Journal Daily E-Mail Alert, June 18, 2003, reporting testimony of Nathaniel Good (a graduate student at University of California at Berkeley) to the United States Senate Committee on the Judiciary, June 17, 2003. Good reportedly testified that in a limited study of KaZaA users "only 2 correctly identified that KaZaA installation had been set to share all files on the hard drive."

190. As of April 30, 2002, KaZaA Media Desktop software contained Altnet, a Trojan software created by Brilliant Digital Entertainment, a California-based multimedia company. Upon a signal from Sharman Networks, Altnet would be activated and would reportedly harness the spare processing storage and communications power of the millions of computers that were connected to the KaZaA FastTrack network. See *KaZaA Users Brace for Hijack,* accessed at www.smh.co . . . s/2002/04/26/1019441306209.html accessed on March 26, 2003.

191. See *Guess Settles FTC Security Charges; Third FTC Case Targets False Claims about Information Security,* Federal Trade Commission, June 18, 2003, accessed at www.ftc.gov/opa/2003/06/guess.htm, where FTC reports that Guess "agreed to settle Federal Trade Commission charges that it exposed consumers' personal information, including credit card numbers, to commonly known attacks by hackers, contrary to the company's claims. The agency alleges that Guess didn't use reasonable or appropriate measures to prevent consumer information from being accessed at its Website, Guess.com. The settlement will require that Guess implement a comprehensive information security program for Guess.com and its other Websites."

192. Federal Trade Commission, *In the Matter of MTS, Inc. d/b/a Tower Records/ Books/Video,* Docket No. C-4110 and Decision and Order (May 28, 2004), accessed respectively at www.ftc.gov/os/caselist/0323209/040602comp0323209.pdf and www.ftc.gov/os/caselist/0323209/040602comp0323209.pdf.

193. Federal Trade Commission, *In the Matter of Gateway Learning Corp.,* Com-

Federal Trade Commission ("FTC"), in its third case targeting companies that "misrepresent the security of consumers' personal information," reached a settlement with Guess. The FTC charged that Guess exposed consumers' personal information (including credit card numbers) to "commonly known attacks by hackers," and that Guess "didn't use reasonable or appropriate measures to prevent consumer information from being accessed at its website, Guess.com."[194] Guess had represented to visitors to its website that "This site has security measures in place to protect the loss, misuse, and alteration of information under our control;" and that "All of your personal information, including your credit card information and sign-in password, are stored in an unreadable, encrypted format at all times."[195]

In May of 2004, the FTC reached a settlement with Tower of charges that, in December of 2002, Tower's revision of the software code for its website created an eight-day vulnerability during which personal information (names, billing and shipping addresses, e-mail address, phone number, etc.) relating to approximately 5,225 customers was accessed by unauthorized users. The FTC noted that Tower failed "to implement procedures that were reasonable and appropriate to detect and prevent vulnerabilities in their website and applications."[196] Tower's website had represented that "TowerRecords.com is committed to safeguarding your privacy online. We will never share your personal information with anyone for any reason without your explicit permission."[197]

In July of 2004, the FTC agreed on a settlement with Gateway of charges that, despite representations that it would not share such customer's personally identifiable information with third parties without a customer's prior consent, and that it would not share any information about children under the age of 13-years-old, Gateway nonetheless began (in April of 2003) to rent to third parties the personal information provided by consumers on the Gateway Learning website without hav-

---

plaint and Agreement Containing Consent Order, File No. 042-3047, July 7, 2004, accessed at www.ftc.gov/os/caselist/0423047/040707cmp0423047.pdf.

194. Federal Trade Commission, *Guess Settles FTC Security Charges; Third FTC Case Targets False Claims about Information Security,* June 18, 2003, accessed on February 12, 2004, accessed at www.ftc.gov/opa/2003/06/guess.htm.

195. Id.

196. Federal Trade Commission, *In the Matter of MTS, Inc. d/b/a Tower Records/Books/Video,* Complaint, Docket No. C-4110 and Decision and Order (May 28, 2004), accessed respectively at www.ftc.gov/os/caselist/0323209/040602comp0323209.pdf and www.ftc.gov/os/caselist/0323209/040602comp0323209.pdf.

197. Id.

ing sought or obtained the consent of such consumers. Such information included consumers' first and last names, address, phone number, purchase history and the age range of their pre-teenage children. The third party purchasers used such information to send direct mail and make telemarketing calls to Gateway's online consumers. In June of 2003, Gateway revised its online representations, stating that it was sharing such information with third parties, and offering consumers the opportunity to "opt-out" of having their information disclosed. Gateway, however, took no further measures to notify its customers of this change in its privacy policy. The FTC deemed such practices to be false or misleading and therefore an unfair act.[198]

The *Guess, Tower* and *Gateway* cases illustrate that governmental regulatory agencies are prepared to hold commercial firms liable for failing to provide adequate protection for the confidential information entrusted to them and that they solicited by promises of security. Software manufacturers may view the *Guess, Tower* and *Gateway* cases as merely instances of companies failing to fulfill explicit written privacy representations, but each case suggests the increasing likelihood that courts will also hold a firm liable for failing adequately to secure the software it sells—either at the time it first releases it, or at a subsequent time, when it should have learned of and corrected vulnerabilities in that software.[199] Thus, the risk of liability is no longer hypothetical or speculative. And that risk increases dramatically with increases in the sensitivity and quantum of confidential information gathered, stored and used by a commercial firm.[200]

Companies engaged in cross-border transactions face additional risks, if their presumed software security has multiple vulnerabilities.

---

198. Federal Trade Commission, *In the Matter of Gateway Learning Corp.*, Complaint and Agreement Containing Consent Order, File No. 042-3047, July 7, 2004, accessed at www.ftc.gov/os/caselist/0423047/040707cmp0423047.pdf.

199. We also note the remarkable development in the UK whose Office of Fair Trading is increasingly enforcing rules that would surprise most U.S. companies. See, for example, the OFT's recent success in persuading Micro Anvika Ltd, an online computer seller, to undertake not to "exclude liability for mistakes or inaccuracies on its website" or "exclude or limit liability for defective software" (each of which is a common disclaimer on U.S. vendor websites). See Office of Fair Trading, *Computer Companies Warned over Unfair Contracts and Sales Methods*, June 13, 2003, PN 77/03, accessed at http://www.oft.gov.uk/News/Press + releases/2003/PN + 77-03.htm, accessed on June 23, 2003.

200. For further discussion of such risks and possible ways for software vendors to reduce them, see Trope, Roland L., *A Warranty of Cyberworthiness*, IEEE SECURITY & PRIVACY, March/April 2004, pp. 73–76.

The information that may be leaked, accessed or pilfered without authorization can potentially bring them into contravention of the much more stringent privacy protection laws and regulations of other jurisdictions. Such laws include the EU Data Protection Directive 95/46/EC and EU Directive 97/66/EC Concerning the Processing of Personal Data and the Protection of Privacy in the Electronic Communications Sector (together with the implementing legislation of each of the Member States). They also include the privacy provisions of Canada's Personal Information Protection and Electronic Documents Act (which came fully into effect for all commercial purposes on January 1, 2004), and the privacy legislation of several Canadian provinces (such as Quebec and Alberta).

1.14.4 Proliferation of Malicious Code.

Cyberspace intrusive products are proliferating rapidly. Although users of cyberspace had historically assumed that they could browse the World Wide Web with relative anonymity (or at a minimum with self-chosen pseudo-anonymity), the technology and structure of cyberspace is quickly making anonymity available only to those who invest in appropriate shielding mechanisms, and even those appear increasingly vulnerable to military and other government funded-surveillance (such as "Carnivore" and "Echelon"). Two years ago a security expert observed:

> "The [then] new Intel Pentium III—class microprocessors have unique serial numbers that can be tracked, as do Ethernet network cards. Microsoft Office documents automatically contain information identifying the author. Cookies track people on the web; even anonymous e-mail addresses can theoretically be linked back to the real person by tracking IP addresses."[201]

Recent proposals for hardwire products from Cisco System promise even more enhanced capabilities to conduct surveillance on the Internet. The reported rationale is that "Cisco's customers, not just in the United States but in many countries, are finding themselves served with subpoenas to mandate lawful intercept functionality."[202] (Those apparently take the form of a request saying: "We want to look at a person.")

---

201. See Schneier, Bruce, SECRETS & LIES: DIGITAL SECURITY IN A NETWORKED WORLD, Wiley, 2000, p. 64.

202. McCullagh, Declan, *Inside Cisco's Eavesdropping Apparatus,* CNETNews.com, April 21, 2003, accessed at http://news.com.com/2102-1071-997528.html. The reader

Prior to development, Cisco received inquiries from its customers specifically requesting such capability.[203] Cisco's "lawful interception" product would take the form of a software upgrade.[204] Such products respond not only to customer's express needs, but to multilateral agreements and domestic laws that "require production of investigative or evidentiary information by telecommunication or information network providers."[205] Microsoft's Word has long been known automatically to record and to give access to the identity of the author (to the extent and in such form such "author" was provided when loading Word software), as well as to information about a document's creation, revision and identity of contributors. Recipients of a Word file need only peer into the file's metadata to extract such information relatively easily.[206]

---

may find opaque the jargon "mandate lawful intercept functionality." We venture that it means to enable law enforcement personnel to conduct surveillance of communications traffic on the Internet. It may, however, have a broader significance that only Cisco, its customers, and such law enforcement personnel fully appreciate.

203. McCullagh, Declan, *Inside Cisco's Eavesdropping Apparatus*, CNETNews.com, April 21, 2003, accessed at http://news.com.com/2102-1071-997528.html, (quoting Fred Baker, a Cisco fellow and former chairman of the Internet Engineering Task Force in an interview about his work on the "lawful interception" draft). See also Baker, Fred, *Intercept and Intelligence: Hopefully Lawful*, PowerPoint presentation accessed at www.soi.wide.ad.jp/soi-asia/pkg1/materials/02.pdf, accessed on June 23, 2003. For text of Cisco draft, see Baker, Fred; Foster, Bill; and Sharp, Chip, *Cisco Support for Lawful Intercept in IP Networks*, Internet Engineering Task Force, Internet Draft, April 2003, accessed at http://cryptome.org/cisco-vile.txtn, accessed on June 23, 2003 (note that draft expires on September 30, 2003).

Note, however, that Cisco Release Notes to the Cisco Cache Engine Version 2.0.2, dated September 1999, states for the "custom web catch" feature: "In Version 2.0.2, this feature provides support for transparent interception on HTTP traffic on any configurable port (1 to 1,600). It is now possible to transparently intercept HTTP traffic on any port." Accessed at www.cisco.com/en/US/products/sw/conntsw/ps547/prod_release_note09186a00800eaa50.html.

See also the U.S. Justice Department's controversial use of Carnivore and the Domestic Security Enhance Act, a proposed but not yet introduced legislation that would substantially expand its powers to conduct surveillance on the Internet. Accessed at www.pbs.org/now/politics/patriot2-hi.pdf. For the EU perspective, see the EU Convention on Cybercrime, particularly Articles 20 (real-time collection of traffic data) and 21 (interception of content data).

204. Id.

205. See *Proposal on Lawful Access/Interception*, at Global Cooperation and Collaboration Conference, Ottawa, Canada, April 28–May 1, 2003 (latest version dated 23 June 2003), accessed at www.oasis-open.org/apps/group_public/email/legalxml-intercept/200304/msg00003.html, accessed on June 23, 2003.

206. See discussion of problem and suggested solutions in Krause, Jason, *Guarding*

Commensurately intrusive products have emerged from software and hardware designers. Examples include *spyware* (a program that takes up residence in a hard drive and records confidential information the user has not authorized for disclosure, such as keystrokes, passwords and the history of the user's visits to websites) and *adware* (a program that causes advertisements to appear, without the user's request or permission, upon the user's screen). Of the two, the more problematic is spyware, some of which "creeps onto a computer's hard drive unannounced, often by piggybacking onto other software programs that people download or by sneaking through backdoor security gaps in web browsers when consumers visit certain sites."[207]

"Key-logger" software can be unobtrusively introduced into a computer, enabling surveillance and recording of each keystroke (thereby monitoring the user's online activities). Hardware products, such as those sold by Keyghost, are tiny self-contained plug-in units that can purportedly record "every keystroke, even those typed in the critical period between computer switch on and the operating system being loaded."[208] The fact that such devices have multiple contrary functions—to monitor a computer not owned by the monitoring person, or to determine if one's own computer is subject to unauthorized use—does not change the basic fact that the technology exists to provide increasingly intrusive reaches. The result is not an enhancement of privacy. The common American perception of the paramount importance of privacy is no longer borne out by the ease with which people are willing to relinquish it in exchange for the promised benefits of products

---

the Cyberfort, ABA JOURNAL, July 2003, p. 46. The article also highlights a converse problem: the frequent failure to archive communications transmitted by instant messaging and the resulting loss of information parties may need to have available (and cannot retrieve) in subsequent litigation.

207. O'Brien, Timothy L., and Hansell, Saul, *Barbarians at the Digital Gate*, THE NEW YORK TIMES, September 19, 2004, Section 3, p. 1 at p. 4. As O'Brien and Hansell note, such programs burden a PC's resources by forcing the PC to react to random commands and uncontrollable processes ordered by the spyware from the hard drive (causing the PC to process information more slowly and to respond sluggishly to commands from the user). Proliferation of spyware has created a market for anti-spyware programs (such as Spybot-Search & Destroy, Spy Sweeper, and Adaware) that promise to detect and disable spyware. However, sometimes such programs themselves are a form of spyware disguised as anti-spyware (such as Virtual Bouncer from Spyware Labs Inc.).

208. See Keyghost's product descriptions, accessible at www.keyghost.com/sx/key-logger-uses.htm and www.keyghost.com.

and activities that compromise privacy to an extent rarely fully appreciated (because such compromises remain largely hidden).

Some of the most recently developed intrusive products reduce e-mail confidentiality and, as a direct result, the privacy of sender and recipient. Consider two such products announced in 2004. Google's "Gmail" offers the inducement of a free web-based e-mail service (with substantially more storage space than competitor's services). However, there is a trade-off: the Gmail service scans each e-mail's text, compares keywords of such text with potentially related products and services that vendors wish to advertise (and presumably pay Google to promote), and attaches such vendors' advertisements to the e-mail which displays it prominently when the e-mail is opened. In initial public beta tests, these attached advertisements appear on the messages received by Gmail "subscribers," regardless of whether the sender is a subscriber. Thus the intrusive product scans e-mails that a non-subscriber sends to a Gmail subscriber without the consent or knowledge of the non-subscriber, who has a legitimate expectation of privacy. It is unclear whether scans are also of e-mails that a Gmail subscriber sends to a non-subscriber. Most importantly, because the non-subscriber is not alerted to the scans it cannot shield the message or know to self-censor the text. To allay concerns over propriety, Google officials assert that the service will not permit certain products or services to be advertised, if they involve words related to sex, dating, guns, drugs, and other topics that Google deems "off-limits."[209] Although counsel routinely sends confidential messages by e-mail (often without encryption), any e-mail sent through the Gmail service risks being viewed as presumptively non-confidential (on the basis of the characteristics of the service as explained to date by Google) and thus unsuitable for any transmittal that seeks to retain attorney-client and work-product protections. Google seeks to refute this, by explaining: "The matching of ads to content is a completely automated process performed by computers. No humans read your email to target the ads, and no email content or other personally identifiable information is ever provided to advertisers."[210] However, it is not clear whether unauthorized users could gain access to e-mails or their content.[211]

---

209. Hansell, Saul, *The Internet Ad You Are about to See Has Already Read Your E-Mail*, THE NEW YORK TIMES, June 21, 2004, p C-1 at C-8.

210. Gmail by Google, *About Gmail*, accessed at http://gmail.google.com/gmail/help/about.html#ads.

211. Some commentators assert that because e-mail is scanned by employers (for

While G-mail pries into message content, Rampell Software's new service—*DidTheyReadIt*—arguably goes further in its intrusion on individual privacy, reviewing when and where the recipient opened an e-mail and how long it was kept open. *DidTheyReadIt* is reportedly the "first [service] to keep such notification secret from the recipient, as well as the first to report on where the message was read."[212]

(**Note:** Rampell overstates its service's capabilities: it has no way of knowing if the recipient actually "reads" the e-mail, only if the recipient opens it or merely clicks on it; however, Rampell clearly seeks to persuade prospective customers that its service can determine if the recipient "read" the e-mail.)

DidTheyReadIt operates by embedding a graphic file (known as a "Web bug") in each e-mail message sent using the service. The "Web bug" is minute and cannot be seen. When the recipient opens such e-mail, the "Web bug" is downloaded (without asking for the recipient's permission) and transmits back to the *DidTheyReadIt* server the time at which the recipient opened the e-mail and the recipient's "approximate geographic location," which the server in turn transmits to the sender. When the recipient closes the e-mail (or clicks a different one), another message is sent to the *DidTheyReadIt* server, which transmits a second message to the sender stating the amount of time that the e-mail

---

porn and discriminatory remarks), by Internet service providers (for spam, viruses, and worms) and by the federal government (for terrorist activities) that "The notion that e-mail is a purely private medium is a quaint illusion" or that the intrusiveness of Gmail is mitigated by the fact that the subscriber must consent to the monitoring. Waldmeir, Patti, *Google's E-mail Snooping Is a Test Case for Privacy*, FINANCIAL TIMES, May 24, 2004, p. 8. We disagree. Such scans do not entitle employers, ISPs, or the government to publish the contents of messages that do not violate laws or regulations. Moreover, if privacy is utterly lost when one sends e-mail, that would severely undermine the rationale for laws and regulations that make it a punishable offense to gain unauthorized entry to computers and to review, copy, alter, or damage the information contained therein. Although stored messages can be now accessed by federal enforcement officials with a search warrant instead of having to comply with the more burdensome procedures to obtain a wire tap order (a change effected by the USA Patriot Act), the fact that stored e-mails are deemed less sensitive than those intercepted in real-time further suggests that it is far from "quaint" to regard e-mail as having substantial claims to privacy protections and to be concerned when vendors offer inducements to compromise not only the purchaser/subscriber's privacy but that of those communicating with them by e-mail.

212. Glass, Mark, *Tracking the E-mail You Sent*, International Herald Tribune Online, June 5, 2004, accessed at www.iht.com/articles/523394.html.

was open. Rampell claims that its service provides such information regardless of whether the recipient opens the e-mail in a computer or in a web-mail viewer, and that each time that e-mail is forwarded (regardless of the number of recipients) the original sender will be notified of the opening time, geographic location, and duration of viewing for each successive recipient. There is, at present, only one defense to prevent such disclosures: some e-mail services can be configured to preclude the downloading of "Web bugs."[213] However, since the service is not detected by e-mail programs, a user cannot know whether any particular e-mail contains Rampell's invasive "Web bug." Individual privacy is thus easily compromised unless a user's service has been programmed to protect against "Web bugs," and the user has configured the protective feature correctly.

Similarly, software is now available that purports to makes information about transactors, their conduct on websites and their geographic locations accessible to the operator of a commercial site. The extent to which a precise geographic location can be pinpointed with such software is unclear, but it reportedly can determine the "locales of the server computers that corporations and Internet service providers use to connect individual PC's to the Net. Often the geotargeting software can identify the ZIP code of the end user."[214] This is reminiscent of Hollywood movie renditions of phone trace technology. We can almost see the line progressing across a world map in real time. Users of such software can conduct crosschecks, relying on additional information (such as user's credit card billing address) to reduce the probability that the geotargeting software has provided an erroneous output about the surveillance location.[215] Examples of vendors that offer geotargeting software are Quova[216] and Akamai Technologies.[217] Akamai's website claims:

> "Knowing where and how users access the Internet can provide companies with the information required to . . . customize content

---

213. Id.

214. Tedeschi, Bob, *E-Commerce Report: The Market Is Growing for Software That Finds Internet Users' Locations*, THE NEW YORK TIMES, June 16, 2003, p. C-7.

215. Id.

216. Headquartered in Mountain View, California.

217. Headquartered in Boston, Massachusetts, and founded by Daniel M. Lewin, an Israeli who perished on the American Airlines jet that crashed into the World Trade Center on September 11, 2001.

to provide more relevant information or protect their goods and information from unauthorized users. EdgeScape [an Akamai product] . . . accurately identif[ies] a visiting user's geographic location, actual connection speed and corporate identity in real time."[218]

"EdgeScape enables enterprises to validate every end user's location, ensuring that information and goods are delivered only to trusted users in authorized geographies."[219]

Quova's website similarly claims that its "Geo-location" software is "effective, accurate and privacy-safe."[220] Quova provides an example of the use of its product that suggests that such products will allow cyberspace transactors to comply with the TSR and EAR. The example cites a Salt Lake City-based software company, Sorenson Media™, that provides an automated web casting service enabling users to deliver "globally rich media" or software over an integrated "Content Distribution Network." Sorenson joined with three other providers (Akamai, Speedera and Cable & Wireless) to deliver large digital assets (such as movie trailers) to so-called "Vcast" users. Quova's website notes, however, that:

"[P]roducers of digital video assets that are being delivered on the Internet want to know who their consumers are, where they are and what bandwidth they are using to receive the product. Software providers, in particular, whose products fall under certain State Department restrictions,[221] must be able to block downloads to embargoed nations, and therefore must know what country a customer

---

218. Akamai, *EdgeScape*, web page, accessed at www.akamai.com/en/html/services/edgescape.html.

219. Id.

220. Privacy advocates, however, will probably want to closely examine whether companies that offer geo-targeting or geo-locating software actually do not violate privacy rights, an issue that may prove particularly problematic for companies using such software with visitors from an European Union member state where rules prohibiting intrusions on individuals' privacy and personal data tend to be more comprehensive than those enforced in the United States.

221. The reference to the State Department suggests some confusion by Quova, since State enforces controls over items on the Munitions List, and the digital video assets (such as movie trailers) described by Quova's website are probably not on the U.S. Munitions List. They are more likely found on the Commerce Control List, but without more information that is unclear. Note too that the website makes no mention of the TSR, which clearly would apply regardless of whether the Quova product were on the Commerce Control List or the Munitions List.

is in when downloading a file in order to meet those embargo requirements."

"**The Challenge.** State Department regulations prohibit software distribution to or downloads in certain nations suspected of terrorism or espionage.[222] When Sorenson Media decided to market its Vcast application . . . the company already understood the necessity and value of geo-location to software customers who must block delivery to embargoed countries. . . ."

"**The Result** . . . If the prospective software buyer is in an embargoed country, the download is cancelled and his IP address and location are noted and logged . . . The customer [in a country not embargoed] is . . . able to complete the sales process . . . while remaining fully compliant with State Department restrictions."[223]

Other companies have recently adapted geolocating software to their product offerings, *e.g.,* RealNetworks offers games and movies but restricts such offerings to certain countries; certain vendors code their websites to ensure that potential customers see prices displayed in the currency that matches the country in which they access the web; and Google directs foreign visitors to home pages that match their country.[224]

To the extent that claims by such vendors remain valid, despite the inevitable efforts to disable, circumvent or cause the geo-locating software to produce erroneous or unreliable results, the enforcing agencies of the TSR and EAR (the OFAC and the BIS) could reasonably adopt the view that any operator of a commercial website must take comparable precautions. As banks and other financial institutions know, the ready availability at reasonable cost of so-called "interdiction" or "trans-

---

222. The Sorenson website's reference to regulations would appear to be an error: what would appear to be the applicable regulations for civilian and for "dual use" (civilian and military) software are actually the EAR, which are under jurisdiction of the Department of Commerce and its Bureau of Industry and Security.

223. Quova, *Sorenson Media,* web page, accessed at: www.quova.com/solutions/sorenson_media.html. Quova's website also states: "For the imposing challenges of geographic regulatory compliance and digital rights management, Quova's GeoPoint is the solution of choice . . . [it] enables these . . . enterprises to conduct business with confidence without inadvertently breaking the rules." *The Challenge for Online Compliance and Territory Rights Management,* accessed at www.quova.com/shtml/solutions/sol_solutions_compliance.shtml.

224. *Geolocation Tech Slices, Dices the Web,* SiliconValley.com, July 9, 2004, accessed at www.cnn.com/2004/TECH/internet/07/12/borders.online.ap.

action blocking" software is already presumed for entities that process transfers of funds. OFAC has taken enforcement action when a bank fails to interdict prohibited transfers of funds (which should only occur if the bank is not using interdiction software effectively, or if its staff fails to make appropriate inquiries after being alerted to a potential problem by such software).[225] As a result, website operators can no longer claim to be without knowledge of whether sales or licenses to a particular customer would contravene the TSR or EAR (or comparable regulations). With knowledge of geographic location and rudimentary payment information will inevitably come responsibility for knowing (or "having reason to know") a transactor's identity for purposes of compliance with such laws.

1.14.5 Increased Ability to Interdict Prohibited Transactions.

Commentators, such as Tim Wu, have amply illustrated the many ways in which software code writers seek to find loopholes in copyright and other laws. As Wu observes:

> "Code design . . . is a mechanism of *avoidance* rather than a mechanism of *change*. Nothing the code designer does rewrites laws. Instead, code design defines behavior to avoid legal sanctions. This description of how code "works" to influence law's effects, I suggest, fits most of the major efforts to use code for legal advantage."[226]

---

225. Note, however, that compliance with the TSR imposes considerable transactional costs on banks. "Any bank of significant size or with significant international operations will spend millions of dollars each year on OFAC compliance [i.e., compliance with the TSR promulgated and enforced by OFAC]. These costs include the costs of legal, compliance, and other personnel devoted to OFAC compliance; acquiring, maintaining, and updating the software that screens transactions; . . . researching transactions that are identified as having possible OFAC implications; compensation paid to other parties for delays involved when a transaction is cleared of OFAC taint but is completed late; court costs and expenses of litigation when banks are involved in suits for the recovery of blocked property." Smith, David B., *Additional Views of Commissioner David B. Smith*, JUDICIAL REVIEW COMMISSION ON FOREIGN ASSET CONTROL, January 23, 2001 at p. 51.

226. Wu, Tim, *When Code Isn't Law*, 89 VIRGINIA LAW REVIEW 101, June 2003, at pp. 127–128.

"As a general rule, code design will depend on identifiable weaknesses in legal enforcement."[227]

Wu's examples include junk e-mail (a strategy designed to circumvent laws regulating unsolicited advertising by mail and fax) and P2P file sharing (a strategy designed to circumvent copyright laws and to take advantage of the fact that, until recently, as Wu notes, "copyright has no record of enforcement against end-users").[228] Concurrently, other code writers are bringing products to market that can be expected to shift to website owners and operators the liability for failing to block or interdict transactions with targeted parties, governments and organizations. Software code is already in widespread use at financial institutions that process a multitude of transactions each day, primarily because the mandate to do so is integrated into their examination procedures manuals.[229] Such screening can only be accomplished without a substantial loss of commercial efficiency through the use of interdiction software, modules of which can scan letters of credit, securities and foreign exchange, as well as unstructured fields in telexes and e-mails. With slight customization, these products will run on a variety of operating systems.[230]

The core code of such interdiction software is thus not only reusable (and flexible in its potential applications),[231] but serves also as a mobile checkpoint. Manual checks using OFAC's online SDN List, for example, may suffice for due diligence, if used continuously (since updates occur

---

227. Id, at p. 130. Wu notes two weaknesses in copyright law: its "dependence on a gatekeeper enforcement regime" and "a severe and unusual lack of normative support among the regulated."

228. Id.

229. As noted by OFAC Director R. Richard Newcomb: "In the U.S., all federal, and many state, bank regulatory agencies are mandated to annually: (1) determine whether each bank has policies and procedures in place for complying with OFAC law and regulations; (2) determine whether each bank maintains a current listing of prohibited countries, entities, and individuals; (3) determine whether the OFAC information is disseminated to all offices; (4) determine whether new accounts (i.e., fiduciary, discount, or other securities brokerage transactions), new loan customers, wire transfer, or other new bank transactions are compared to the OFAC listings prior to opening accounts or conducting transactions; and (5) determine whether established accounts and other customer transactions are regularly compared to the current OFAC listings." Newcomb, R. Richard, *Targeted Financial Sanctions: The U.S. Model*, accessible at www.smartsanctions.ch/Papers/I2/2usmodel.pdf.

230. Id.

231. Id.

continuously). Electronic checking should expedite this. As OFAC's Director has cogently argued, the electronic movement of funds across the globe has made "sanctions implementation easier not harder,"[232] because code has been written that can swiftly interdict efforts to move funds through electronic channels.[233] OFAC's strategy presumes that interdicting the flow of funds, and thus the availability of money to pay for prohibited activities, will impede the flow of goods: "The goods won't ship if the seller isn't confident he will get paid."[234] We think that, in the near future, similar requirements may be imposed on U.S. persons operating commercial website where credit card purchases can be similarly subjected to scanning, with the additional wrinkle that unlike the bank's scanning of funds transfers, a website operator may also be expected or required to deploy geolocating software that can alert it to customers who are seeking to transact on behalf of TSR or EAR targeted persons, governments and organizations.

1.14.6 Increased Surveillance by Law Enforcement Agencies.

Law enforcement and defense agencies of the United States increasingly invest in the development of surveillance, "data mining," and data warehousing[235] technologies to detect and connect traces of terrorist and criminal activity (including copyright infringement).[236] The rapid de-

---

232. Id.

233. The *halwa* system of moving funds proves the converse: if one avoids electronic channels, then one avoids the checkpoints where electronic, code-enabled interdiction can be applied.

234. Newcomb, R. Richard, *Targeted Financial Sanctions: The U.S. Model*, accessed at www.smartsanctions.ch/Papers/I2/2usmodel.pdf.

235. "Data warehousing" denotes linking datasets from disparate sources—*e.g.*, a website's transactional data and demographic data procured from companies such as Axciom and Experian—and then searching for pre-identified types of patterns in the data that may evince or hint at illicit activity. Two analytic methods currently predominate: (1) detecting deviations from predetermined norms of online conduct; and (2) working from a predetermined pattern or signature that tends to co-occur with illicit activity and looking for indicia of or activity that matches that signature. Kumagai, Jean, *Mission Impossible?*, IEEE SPECTRUM, April 2003, p. 29. See Mena, Jesus, INVESTIGATIVE DATA MINING FOR SECURITY AND CRIMINAL DETECTION, Digital Press, 2003.

236. Kumagai, Jean, *Mission Impossible?*, IEEE SPECTRUM, April 2003, p. 28. One of the correlative objectives is to ascertain and verify identity. "Today, we use digital

ployment of intensive surveillance technology has in certain instances prompted Congress to bar its use, as occurred recently when, with no dissent, Congress prohibited the Department of Defense from searching for terrorists by using its "Total Information Awareness" system to mine Internet mail and financial and travel data.[237] Nonetheless, Federal police agencies can now rely on recently enacted laws, which authorize potentially intrusive probes into the identities and dealings of those who communicate, negotiate or transact in cyberspace, when pursuing anti-terrorism objectives.[238]

---

representations of who we are—name, address, Social Security Number, driver's license. It's become increasingly clear that identity is very vulnerable. You may not be what that digital identity represents you to be. The next major transformation is going to be biometric identity, which will tell us definitively. . . ." Coppola, Vincent, *Derek Smith's Brave New World*, Georgia Trends, accessed at http://216.239.37. 100/search?q = cache:q43xKYKB_QYJ:www.choicepoint.net/news/gatrend.html + choicepoint&hl = en&ie = UTF-8, accessed on July 4, 2003, quoting Derek V. Smith, CEO of ChoicePoint, Inc., a company that gathers personal records and sells the background information derived from them to prospective employers of such persons. See ChoicePoint Online at https://www.choicepointonline.com/default.asp, accessed on July 4, 2003.

237. See Clymer, Adam, *In the Fight for Privacy, States Set off Sparks*, THE NEW YORK TIMES, Section 4, p. 1, July 6, 2003, at p. 3. Regrettably, the Total Information Awareness ("TIA") project was poorly described by DARPA and the DoD to Congress. However, it would seem likely that some elements of the TIA project continue to be developed, because usually such strong promotion of a project, followed by Congressional disapproval, only drives such projects beyond the reach of Congressional oversight into a nonetheless well-funded, black box program.

238. In support of its TIA program, DARPA made several contract awards; for instance, a $4.6 million contract to ISX Corporation for Agent-assisted, Context-based, Collaboration across Information Spaces (AXIS). See Electronic Privacy Information Center, *Approved Contractors for BAA-02-08: Total Information Awareness*, accessed at www.epic.org/privacy/profiling/tia/contractors_table.html, accessed on April 7, 2003. See also the Combating Terrorism Technology Support Office's request for research proposals, including those for a "Counter-Encryption Tool" that would "Upgrade and expand an existing developmental software application that shall run 'behind the scenes' on a computer network and utilize the unused processing power of the network to attack protected data." *Technical Support Working Group Broad Agency Announcement DAAD05-02-T-0215*, March 5, 2002 (for submittals due no later than April 4, 2002), "R-904" at p. 21.

Note, there is considerable and growing dispute over best practices and other initiatives that national governments should adopt and implement to interdict funding and other support for international terrorists. While U.S. citizens may often assume that the United States is a leading advocate of the widespread enforcement of, for example, anti-money laundering rules, some European governments have a quite dif-

The USA Patriot Act of 2001[239] increased the authority of the federal police to conduct Internet surveillance by easing the standard of proof required for a court order and by providing the police with authority to conduct nationwide and roving electronic wiretaps (something the FBI had sought years ago in the Omnibus Counterterrorism Bill, introduced after the first World Trade Center bombing but never enacted).[240,241] In 2002, the Foreign Intelligence Surveillance Court granted a record number of searches and wiretap orders, a more than 30% increase over 2001.[242] In addition, the Federal Bureau of Investigation has made widely reported use of its "Carnivore" software to monitor e-mail and web-surfing sessions.[243]

---

ferent perception. Reportedly, senior German government officials criticize the governments of the United States and the United Kingdom for allegedly "hindering moves for tighter regulation of the activities of underground banking networks often used for channeling terrorist funds. . . ." See Williamson, Hugh, *US, UK "Hindering Moves" on Underground Banks*, FINANCIAL TIMES, June 18, 2003 at p. 3.

239. Uniting and Strengthening America by Providing Appropriate Tools Required to Intercept and Obstruct Terrorism (USA PATRIOT ACT) Act of 2001 (Pub. Law 107–56), October 26, 2001.

240. Schneier, Bruce, SECRETS & LIES: DIGITAL SECURITY IN A NETWORKED WORLD, John Wiley & Sons, Inc., 2000, p. 67.

241. However, note that reportedly "three states and 133 localities have adopted resolutions critical of the USA Patriot Act." Clymer, Adam, *In the Fight for Privacy, States Set off Sparks*, THE NEW YORK TIMES, July 6, 2003, p. 1 at p. 3.

242. The numbers granted were 1,228 in 2002, compared with 934 in 2001. Scheeres, Julia, *Feds Doing More Secret Searches*, Wired News, May 9, 2003, accessed at www.wired.com/news/politics/0,1283,58774,00.html, accessed on May 9, 2003. The article also reports that since its inception in 1978, the Foreign Intelligence Surveillance Court has "approved every FBI application it has received, despite disclosing last year in a report (PDF) that the agency had misled FISA [Foreign Intelligence Surveillance Act] judges in 75 cases" and notes that "Applications for FISA warrants receive less scrutiny than Title III wiretaps despite the fact that they are much more intrusive" in the extent of permitted physical searches of residences, automobiles, and belongings. The FISA court consists of seven District Court judges appointed by the Chief Justice of the U.S. Supreme Court. See, however, decision by the United States Foreign Intelligence Surveillance Court of Review in *In Re Sealed Case No. 02-001*, decided November 18, 2002, the first appeal ever from the FISA (and one brought by the United States Government), that resulted in a reversal of the FISA's imposition of restrictions on the government. See opinion accessed at www.cadc.uscourts.gov/common/newsroom/02-001.pdf.

243. Carnivore should not be confused with Echelon. Echelon is a global system for the interception of private and commercial communications, operating by means of cooperation proportionate to their capabilities among the U.S., the U.K., Canada,

In response to such developments, and to capitalize upon perceptions that such programs are unduly intrusive, several companies have developed and marketed "identity-shielding services" within the past year. Anonymizer Inc. (based in San Diego, with 90,000 subscribers at present) represents that its service provides complete protection from electronic snooping by the FBI; Steganos GmbH (based in Germany, with 500,000 users currently) provides an anonymous web-surfing product. Such products, however, have not been designed to address the FBI's "Magic Lantern" software (disclosed first in late 2001), which reportedly can circumvent "identity-shielding services" by tracking a user's actions through a recording of the user's keystrokes.[244]

1.14.7 Multi-Lateral Initiatives Increase Scope and Depth of Due Diligence Obligations.

Multi-lateral initiatives, such as the Financial Action Task Force ("**FATF**"), appear to be moving toward a significant change in policy. They are departing from the historical registration of underground banking organizations, and moving toward enhanced, active, regular supervision of such underground organizations. United States government officials are reportedly acknowledging that the "old view that freezing bank accounts was the main way to halt terrorist finances isn't enough . . . [because] freezing of funds has had only very limited impact."[245] FATF has published *40 Recommendations* on its website, including several that encourage increased access to online customer iden-

---

Australia, and New Zealand under the UK/USA Agreement, (see European Parliament Resolution on Echelon, November 7, 2002, and Report on the Existence of a Global System for the Interception of Private and Commercial Communications (ECHELON Interception System) (2001/2098(INI)). Carnivore is an FBI-operated mechanism, limited to use under a court order, for collecting electronic communications in the Internet about a specific user targeted in an investigation; the device is installed at the Internet Service Provider. The FBI reportedly claims that Carnivore "filters" data traffic and delivers to investigators only those "packets" that they are lawfully authorized to obtain (*i.e.* Carnivore eats all data, but only digests what it is lawfully permitted to retain). See *The Carnivore FOIA Litigation*, Electronic Privacy Information Center, accessed at www.epic.org/privacy/carnivore. Details about Echelon and Carnivore are classified.

244. Marciniak, Sean, *Web Privacy Services Complicate Feds' Job*, THE WALL STREET JOURNAL, July 3, 2003, p. B4.

245. Id.

tification information and thus to greater knowledge about cyberspace transactors and their activities. Although many of FATF's 40 recommendations (as drafted) apply expressly to "bank financial institutions," *Recommendation 8* urges broader application to non-bank financial institutions, particularly of FATF recommendations 10 through 29.[246] *Recommendations 10, 11* and *14* provide, respectively:

> "Financial institutions should not keep anonymous accounts or accounts in obviously fictitious names: they should be required . . . to identify, on the basis of an official or other reliable identifying document, and record the identity of their clients, either occasional or usual, when establishing business relations or conducting transactions (in particular opening of accounts or . . . performing large cash transactions)."

---

246. Financial Action Task Force, *40 Recommendations*, Recommendation 8, accessed at www1.oecd.org/fatf/40Recs_en.htm. Note that banks have been under increasing pressure since September 11, 2001, to apply "know your customer" policies, procedures, and controls. See, for example, *Customer Due Diligence for Banks*, Basel Committee Publication No. 85, October 2001, translations September 2002, posted by the Bank for International Settlements accessed at www.bis.org/publ/bcbs85.htm, which defers on money laundering recommendations to the FATF but offers guidance from a "wider prudential perspective." Such guidance includes that "Sound KYC [know your customer] policies and procedures are critical in protecting the safety and soundness of banks and the integrity of banking systems. . . . KYC safeguards go beyond simple account opening and record-keeping and require banks to formulate a customer acceptance policy and a tiered customer identification programme that involves more extensive due diligence for higher risk accounts, and includes proactive account monitoring for suspicious activities." Basel Committee Publication No. 85, Introduction, at paragraphs 3 and 4. The publication notes that the extent of robustness of KYC policies varies greatly among different countries. Publication No. 85, issued three months after the attacks of September 11, 2001, addressed the need for enhanced KYC policies to avert reputational, operational, and legal risks to banks from money laundering activities of their customers and those on whose behalf they act or with whom they transact. It urges banks to not only know the identity of their customers but also to monitor account activity to identify transactions that do not "conform with the normal or expected transactions for that customer or that type of account." Bulletin, Part III, paragraph 19, accessed at www.bis.org/publ/bcbs85.pdf. BIS emphasized the need for rigorous KYC procedures to mitigate risks posed by the increasing number of requests to open accounts by persons who do not present themselves for face-to-face interviews and who wish to use their accounts for electronic banking via the Internet or similar technology. Bulletin, Section 2.2.6, paragraphs 45–48, accessed at www.bis.org/publ/bcbs85.pdf.

"Financial institutions should take reasonable measures to obtain information about the true identity of the persons on whose behalf an account is opened or a transaction conducted if there are any doubts as to whether these clients or customers are acting on their own behalf . . ."

"Financial institutions should pay special attention to all complex, unusual large transactions, and all unusual patterns of transactions, which have no apparent economic or visible lawful purpose."[247]

On June 21, 2003, the FATF agreed on amendments to the *40 Recommendations*. These will cause many industrialized countries to tighten laws on money laundering. Among the amendments are certain changes that will cause anti-money laundering measures to be extended "from banks to lawyers, accountants, real estate agents, casinos and other sectors . . ."[248] For example, the agreed upon *40 Recommendations*, as amended, now provide that:

"The customer due diligence and record-keeping requirements set out in Recommendations 5, 6, and 8 to 11 apply to designated non-financial businesses and professions in the following situations:

Lawyers, notaries, other independent legal professionals and accountants when they prepare for or carry out transactions for their client concerning the following activities:

• buying and selling of real estate;

• managing of client money, securities or other assets;

---

247. Financial Action Task Force, *40 Recommendations*, Recommendations 10, 11, and 14, accessed at www1.oecd.org/fatf/40Recs_en.htm. In an Interpretative Note to Recommendations 11 and 15 through 18, FATF adds the following suggestion for the equivalent of an expanded due diligence investigation in cases of doubt:

"If, based on information supplied from the customer or from other sources, the financial institution has reason to believe that the customer's account is being utilized in money laundering transactions, the financial institution must comply with the relevant legislation, regulations, directives or agreements concerning reporting of suspicious transactions or termination of business with such customers." Accessed at www1.oecd.org/fatf/Interpnotes_en.htm#Recommendations%208%20and%209 %20(Bureaux%20de%20Change).

248. Williamson, Hugh, *Taskforce Sets Tough Money Laundering Rules*, FINANCIAL TIMES, June 22, 2003, p. 1.

- management of bank, savings or securities accounts;
- organisation of contributions for the creation, operation or management of companies;
- creation, operation or management of legal persons or arrangements, and buying and selling of business entities."[249]

The FATF amendments also address "anti-terrorism best practices to control underground banks, including the 'hawala' system often used by migrant workers to remit earnings to home countries."[250] Countries are obligated to begin to implement the changes immediately; external assessments of each country's progress is scheduled to begin late in 2004.

1.14.8 Increased Duty to Identify Financial Customers.

In response to the attacks of September 11, 2001, the United States enacted legislation, the USA Patriot Act, which added several sections to the Bank Secrecy Act ("BSA"). The new BSA sections require, among other things, that the Department of Treasury (in conjunction with certain federal agencies and commissions)[251] prescribe regulations setting minimum standards for customer identification by "financial institutions" at the time of account opening ("326 Regulations").[252] Sec-

---

249. Financial Action Task Force on Money Laundering, *The Forty Recommendations*, as amended June 21, 2003, accessed at www1.oecd.org/fatf/pdf/40Recs-2003_en.pdf.

250. Id.

251. The participating federal agencies are the Office of the Comptroller of the Currency (OCC), the Board of Governors of the Federal Reserve System (Board), the Federal Deposit Insurance Corporation (FDIC), the Office of Thrift Supervision (OTS), and the National Credit Union Administration (NCUA) (collectively, the "Agencies"). The participating federal commissions are the Securities and Exchange Commission and the Commodity Futures Trading Commission.

252. In particular, Section 326 of the USA Patriot Act required Treasury to promulgate, by no later than one year from the date of the Act's enactment, regulations that at a minimum "require financial institutions to implement, and customers (after being given adequate notice) to comply with, reasonable procedures for (A) verifying the identity of any person seeking to open an account to the extent reasonable and practicable; (B) maintaining records of the information used to verify a person's identity, including name, address, and other identifying information; and (C) consulting lists of known or suspected terrorists or terrorist organizations provided to the financial institution by any government agency to determine whether a person seeking to open an

tion 326 defines the term "financial institutions" expansively to include: "banks, savings associations, and credit unions; securities brokers and dealers; mutual funds; futures commission merchants and introducing brokers; and credit unions, private banks and trust companies that do not have a federal regulator." Subsequent guidance from Treasury (and other federal agencies and commissions) advises that the reach is, in fact, even broader.[253] The 326 Regulations require, at a minimum, that financial institutions implement "reasonable procedures for:

(i)   Verifying the identity of any person seeking to open an account, to the extent reasonable and practicable;

(ii) Maintaining records of the information used to verify the person's identity; and

(iii) Determining whether the person appears on any list of known or suspected terrorists or terrorist organizations."[254]

On July 17, 2002, Treasury issued its proposed 326 Regulations,[255] initially to take effect in November of 2002 (a deadline subsequently postponed).[256] In April of 2003, Treasury (jointly with the requisite

---

account appears on any such list." Uniting and Strengthening America by Providing Appropriate Tools Required to Intercept and Obstruct Terrorism *(USA PATRIOT ACT) Act of 2001*, Pub. L. No. 107-56, 115 Stat. 272 (2001), Section 326(a)(2). Note the Bank Secrecy Act is also known as the Currency and Foreign Transactions Reporting (31 U.S.C. Sections 5311-5330 and 12 U.S.C. Sections 1818(s), 1829(b), and 1951-1959). The implementing regulations are at 31 CFR 103.

253. The term "financial institutions" would also include, among others, investment companies, futures commission merchants, insurance companies, travel agents, pawnbrokers, dealers in precious metals, check-cashers, casinos, and telegraph companies. Agile, however, would not appear to come within Section 326. See *Customer Identification Programs for Banks, Savings Associations, Credit Unions and Certain Non-Federally Regulated Banks,* accessed at www.ustreas.gov/press/releases/reports/326final rulebanks.pdf, p. 4.

254. Pub. L. No. 91-508, 84 Stat. 1114 (1970) (codified as amended in various sections of 12 U.S.C., 15 U.S.C. and 31 U.S.C.), Section 326. See *Customer Identification Programs for Banks, Savings Associations, Credit Unions and Certain Non-Federally Regulated Banks,* accessed at www.ustreas.gov/press/releases/reports/326finalrulebanks. pdf.

255. See Department of Treasury, Office of Public Affairs, *Press Release: Treasury and Federal Financial Regulators Issue Patriot Act Regulations on Customer Identification,* July 17, 2002, accessed at www.ustreas.gov/press/releases/po3263.htm.

256. Treasury issued proposed rules in July 2002, but three months later Treasury advised "all financial institutions that they will not be required to comply with section 326 of the USA PATRIOT ACT or the proposed rules issued by Treasury and the federal

agencies and commissions) issued the final 326 Regulations.[257] As a result, financial institutions must verify the identity of a "customer" at the time such "customer" seeks to open an account. The 326 Regulations provide that "A bank must implement a written Customer Identification Program (CIP) appropriate for its size and type of business . . ."[258] The CIP is required to address situations "where, based on the bank's risk assessment of a new account opened by a customer that is not an individual, the bank will obtain information about individuals with authority or control over such account, including signatories, in order to verify the customer's identity."[259] The CIP must also include procedures for the bank to check each customer "on any list of known or suspected terrorists or terrorist organizations issued by any Federal government agency and designated as such by Treasury in consultation with the Federal functional regulators."[260] Clearly, that would include OFAC's SDN List. Banks covered by the 326 Regulations were required to comply by October 1, 2003.[261]

---

functional regulators on July 23 until final implementing regulations are issued and become effective." Treasury also advised that "The final rules will provide financial institutions with a reasonable amount of time in which to come into compliance. However, financial institutions are reminded that they must continue to comply with any existing obligation to guard against money laundering and the financing of terrorism through adequate customer identification procedures. *Financial institutions should already be taking basic steps to ensure appropriate customer identification.*" U.S. Department of Treasury, Office of Public Affairs, press release *"Treasury Department Provides Guidance on Compliance with Section 326 of USA PATRIOT ACT,"* October 11, 2002, accessed at www.ustreas.gov/press/releases/po3530.htm. [Emphasis added.]

257. See Treasury Press Release, April 30, 2003, accessed at www.ustreas.gov/press/releases/js335.htm.

258. *Customer Identification Programs for Banks, Savings Associations, Credit Unions and Certain Non-Federally Regulated Banks,* §103.121, p. 79, accessed at www.ustreas.gov/press/releases/reports/326finalrulebanks.pdf.

259. *Customer Identification Programs for Banks, Savings Associations, Credit Unions and Certain Non-Federally Regulated Banks,* Section 103.121(b)(2)(ii)(C), p. 44, accessed at www.ustreas.gov/press/releases/reports/326finalrulebanks.pdf.

260. Id, in re: "comparison with government lists."

261. Willemsen, James J., and Arquette, Lisa D., *Supervisory Insights: From the Examiner's Desk . . . ,* FDIC, accessed at www.fdic.gov/regulations/examinations/supervisory/insights/examiners_desk.html.

1.14.9 Increased Importance of Compliance Programs.

The quality of a company's compliance program both positions it for "mitigating factors" in the event of a violation and reduces its risk profile in some instances, leading to reduced review of its conduct by enforcement authorities. The Federal Deposit Insurance Corporation ("FDIC"), for example, modified its traditional approach to compliance examinations in 2003 (based "almost exclusively on reviewing actual banking transactions for adherence to regulatory and statutory requirements"), because its limited resources and the expansion of regulations had made it increasingly difficult for it to complete examination schedules and write meaningful reports.[262] It henceforth would conduct "risk-focused compliance examinations" combined with an "in-depth evaluation of a bank's compliance management system," described as "the confluence of directorate and management oversight, internal controls and compliance audits."[263] Instead of attempting to check actual transactions, the examination will assess certain qualities in the bank's compliance "system:" its identification of emerging risks, whether it remains current on changes in laws and regulations, how well its employees understand compliance responsibilities, the integration of compliance into its business operations, whether it reviews operations to ensure compliance, and whether it takes effective corrective action when violations of law occur or when it discovers weaknesses in its own compliance system.[264]

The emphasis of regulatory compliance examinations would now shift from seeking to identify actual violations to focusing on where their occurrence could be highly probable (in the event internal compliance reviews were insufficient). The FDIC has made clear that it considers one such risk area to be the issuance of new financial products and whether (in connection with such issuance) the bank's compliance

---

262. Jackwood, John M., *Compliance Examinations: A Change in Focus*, FDIC Supervisory Insights, accessed at www.fdic.gov/regulations/examinations/supervisory/insights/compliance.html.

263. Id.

264. Id.

officer has conducted a pre-issuance compliance review of such product.[265]

The FDIC's approach is revealing with regard to the rationale and implications of its revised strategy for examination. And we think it reflects an approach that other comparably understaffed agencies facing the expansion of regulations can be expected to implement in the near future:

> "Starting each compliance examination by looking for violations of federal consumer laws and regulations and then drawing conclusions about how a bank manages its compliance responsibilities did little to address operational weaknesses or prevent future violations. Under the new approach, examiners first establish a compliance risk profile that reflects the quality of the bank's compliance management system. . . . The revised examination report format places comments and conclusions about **board and management oversight, the compliance program, and the internal review program on the first page**, along with recommendations for corrective action. . . . Of critical importance, this approach will help **move compliance from the back room to the boardroom** by establishing a tone and climate that support the incorporation of compliance risk management into the way employees do business. . . . Effective compliance program management at a bank starts at the top—with the board of directors and senior management, who are responsible for the bank's management and control."[266]

1.14.10 Heightened Enforcement of the Access Control Laws.

Since the attacks of September 11, there is evidence that the U.S. Government has enforced the TSR, EAR and ITAR with increased rigor, and has shown increased willingness to impose heavy fines on companies that fail to cooperate with federal investigative authorities. One objective is clearly to interdict transactions that would support or otherwise benefit persons, entities or countries targeted by such regulations. Consistent with that objective, the OFAC has repeatedly added names

---

265. Id.
266. Id.

to the Specially Designated Nationals ("SDN") List over the course of the years 2001 through 2003. Additions, for example, between June 2003 and July 2004 included:

- Each of the persons on the Department of Defense's 55-person Watch List of former Iraqi government and military officials;[267]
- Numerous specially designated global terrorists;[268]
- Persons and entities targeted by the Zimbabwean Sanctions Regulations;[269]
- Persons targeted by Executive Order 13348 Blocking Property of Certain Persons and Prohibiting the Importation of Certain Goods from Liberia;[270]
- Persons and entities targeted by the Foreign Narcotics Kingpin Designation Act;[271] and
- Other parties (such as certain Balkan entities) for unspecified reasons.[272]

OFAC has continued to interpret its authority broadly and aggressively to block the property of persons named to the SDN List. On December 4, 2001, for example, OFAC listed as a "specially designated terrorist" (and thus added to the SDN List) the Holy Land Foundation for Relief and Development ("HLF"), the largest Muslim charitable foundation in the United States.[273] In consequence of such listing, OFAC

---

267. See *Recent OFAC Actions*, June 24, 2003, accessed at www.ustreas.gov/offices/eotffc/ofac/actions/20030624.html.

268. See *Recent OFAC Actions* June 10, 2004, accessed at www.ustreas.gov/offices/eotffc/ofac/actions/20040610.html. See also www.ustreas.gov/offices/eotffc/ofac/actions/20040112.html.

269. See *Recent OFAC Actions*, March, 2004, accessed at www.ustreas.gov/offices/eotffc/ofac/actions/20040302.html.

270. See *Recent OFAC Actions*, July, 2004, accessed at www.ustreas.gov/offices/eotffc/ofac/actions/20040723.html.

271. See *Recent OFAC Actions*, June 1, 2004, accessed at www.ustreas.gov/offices/eotffc/ofac/actions/20040601.html.

272. The HLF has also been on the Bank of England's "Sanctions List" since 2001.

273. See *Recent OFAC Actions*, June 30, 2004, accessed at www.ustreas.gov/offices/eotffc/ofac/actions/20040630.html. The granting of a General License permitting most previously prohibited transactions under the Libyan Sanction Regulations also led to the removal of many Libyan entities from the SDN List in April 2004. However, because Libya continues to be identified by the State Department as a country that has continuously supported international terrorism, there remains a broad range of U.S. origin

blocked all the assets of HLF, and further contended that such blocking order also barred the HLF from using its funds for any purpose, including the provision of humanitarian aid, unless expressly licensed by OFAC.[274] This is significant, because the authority granted to the President under the International Emergency Economic Powers Act ("IEEPA") contains a humanitarian exception for donation of articles such as food, clothing and medicine, if intended to be used to relieve human suffering.[275] HLF challenged OFAC's authority to issue such a blocking order. While the Court upheld OFAC's authority to issue the order, it concluded that OFAC had exceeded its statutory authority to the extent that it prohibited HLF from providing humanitarian donations of the aforementioned articles (food, medicine, etc.). Nonetheless, the Court agreed with OFAC that it had acted within its authority to prohibit HLF from making monetary contributions for humanitarian purposes. Although the Court did not explicitly say so, it appears that it agreed with OFAC's justifiable mistrust of the non-humanitarian use that such funds could be put to, particularly in light of the fact that its co-founder raises funds for Hamas, another organization designated by OFAC as a terrorist group.[276]

Similarly, on December 14, 2001, the Secretary of Treasury blocked all assets of Global Relief Foundation, Inc., an Illinois charitable corporation that conducts operations in approximately 25 countries, including Afghanistan, Iraq, Palestine (West Bank and Gaza) ("GRF"). OFAC subsequently named GRF to the SDN List, deeming it a terrorist organization, although GRF purports to be a humanitarian organization. GRF challenged the designation in a court suit, arguing that it was a U.S. corporation, and therefore its property could not be "property in which any foreign country or national thereof has any interest" for the purpose of Section 1702(a)(1)(B) of the IEEPA. While two of GRF's three directors were foreign nationals, that did not change the citizenship of the corporation. In December 2002, the Court of Appeals for the Seventh Circuit agreed with Treasury that IEEPA's reference to interests in property should be understood to denote beneficial rather

---

items for which exports and reexports to Libya that require a license from the BIS or the Directorate of Defense Trade Controls, some of which continue to have a presumption of denial.

274. See *Holy Land Foundation for Relief and Development v. John Ashcroft*, 219 F. Supp. 2d 57 (D.C., 2002) at p. 68.

275. See IEEPA, 50 U.S.C. § 1702(b)(2).

276. 219 F. Supp. 2d 57 at p. 64 and note 1 therein.

than legal interests, because the IEEPA was designed to give the President control over assets that might be used by enemy aliens. The Seventh Circuit's elaboration of its reasoning incorporates arguments made by Treasury, and suggests the substantial shift in judicial receptiveness to certain arguments since the attacks of September 11, 2001:

> "Consider for a moment what would happen if Osama bin Laden put all of his assets into a trust, under Illinois law, administered by a national bank. If the trust instrument directed the trustee to make the funds available for purchases of weapons to be used by al Qaeda, then foreign enemies of the United States would have an "interest" in these funds although legal ownership would be vested in the bank. The situation is the same if al Qaeda incorporated a subsidiary in Delaware and transferred all of its funds to that corporation—something it could do without any al Qaeda operative setting foot in the United States. What sense could it make to treat al Qaeda's funds as open to seizure if administered by a German bank but not if administered by a Delaware corporation under terrorist control. Nothing in the text of the IEEPA suggests that the United States' ability to respond to an external threat can be defeated so easily. Thus the focus must be on how assets could be controlled and used, not on bare legal ownership."[277]

U.S. persons engaged in cyberspace transactions or in cyber-driven transactions should not underestimate OFAC's interpretation of the broad reach of the TSR, in light of the positions it has recently taken, and in light of subsequent judicial action sustaining such positions.[278]

Moreover, the TSR's scope can be expanded extra-territorially by contract, as has been done between the Federal Reserve and certain overseas financial institutions. The Federal Reserve has entered into contracts with eight overseas banks in connection with special currency trading. Those contracts require that such facilities do not transact with any country targeted by any of the TSR's.[279] When one bank under Fed

---

277. *Global Relief Foundation, Inc. v. Paul H. O'Neill*, 315 F.3d 748 (7th Cir., 2002) at p. 752.

278. For example, in mid-2004, the U.S. fined several European companies (*e.g.*, the Italian airline, Alitalia, and the Spanish airline, Iberia) for violating the trade sanctions that target Cuba. See Moré, Inigo, and León, Antonio, *US Fines More European Companies over Cuba*, FINANCIAL TIMES, September 3, 2004, p. 4, and Moré, Inigo, *US Fines Spanish Airline Iberia for Breaking Embargo on Cuba*, September 2, 2004, p. 1.

279. See Kirchhoff, Sue, *Fed Imposes Fine of $100m on Swiss Bank UBS Accused of*

contract acted in violation of this promise, the Fed promptly abrogated its contract. The bank in question, UBS AG, publishes on its website its commitment to act against money laundering and funding of terrorist groups, a position consistent with the objectives of the TSR.[280] It further advertises its "top-tier advisory and executional capabilities . . . [in] foreign exchange."[281] However, UBS personnel circumvented the TSR over an extended period of time and sought to conceal their activities. Beginning in 1996, UBS operated an Extended Custodial Inventory facility in Zurich, Switzerland under its contract with the Fed. In the fall of 2003, however, the Fed discovered that UBS personnel had been providing U.S. dollars to four countries targeted by the TSR, "specifically, Cuba, Libya, Iran, and Yugoslavia,"[282] in violation of the terms of its Fed contract prohibiting transfers to countries targeted by the TSR.[283] The Fed further found that UBS' personnel intentionally concealed such illicit dealings by falsifying the monthly reports to the Fed. The Fed terminated its contract with UBS in October of 2003 and, although it did not charge UBS, it imposed a **$100 million** fine on it for transactions in U.S. dollar banknotes with those embargoed countries (in an aggregate U.S. dollar amount between $4 to $5 billion).[284] The extra-

---

Fund Transfers to Nations Under U.S. Sanction, USA Today, May 11, 2004, accessed at http://insurancenewsnet.com/article.asp?a = top_news&lnid = 207052185,   reporting "Under the terms of the Fed contracts, banks are not to deliver to or accept dollar bank notes from countries subject to U.S. economic sanctions."

280. See UBS AG website statement, *Fighting Money Laundering*:

"Fighting money laundering is one of the largest challenges currently faced by major international financial centers. Find a [sic] comprehensive information here on how UBS, official authorities and international organizations are actively preventing money laundering as well as the financing of criminal activity." Statement accessed at www.ubs.com/e/media_overview/media_switzerland/virtualpresskits/money_laundering.html.

281. UBS advertisement, *Is This the World's First Two-Person Financial Powerhouse? You and Us.* The New York Times Magazine, May 30, 2004, p. 9.

282. Board of Governors of the Federal Reserve System, *Order of Assessment of a Civil Money Penalty Issued upon Consent,* In the Matter of UBS, AG, May 10, 2004, accessed   at   www.federalreserve.gov/boarddocs/press/enforcement/2004/20040108/attachment.pdf.

283. O'Brien, Timothy L., *Lockboxes, Iraqi Loot and a Trail to the Fed,* The New York Times, June 6, 2004, p. 1 at p. 7.

284. Board of Governors of the Federal Reserve System, *Order of Assessment of a Civil Money Penalty Issued upon Consent,* In the Matter of UBS, AG, May 10, 2004, accessed   at   www.federalreserve.gov/boarddocs/press/enforcement/2004/20040108/attachment.pdf.

territorial reach (to activities in Zurich), the magnitude of the civil fine (exceeding any published for violations enforced by OFAC), the termination of the contract and the widespread adverse publicity (presumably for deterrent effect) make clear that the Fed did not accept the explanation by UBS that responsibility for the violations rested only with the employees (whom UBS fired). It also suggests a continuing intensification of enforcement policies for violations of the TSR and other export and reexport controls.[285]

Concern for enforcement of the TSR is certainly one reason why PayPal, the online payment service (and eBay affiliate), reportedly now requires each international customer to identify itself and to confirm its identity (and location in a country other than one targeted by the TSR) by providing PayPal with a copy of its driver's license, a utility bill from its home address and a document verifying its date and place of birth.[286]

Increasingly rigorous enforcement has also been undertaken by the BIS. As noted earlier, since the third quarter of 2002, the BIS has twice brought actions to impose successor liability. Its website's publication of recent actions reflects the following enforcement actions:

- Imposition of $200,000 fine on Flint Hill Resources L.P. to settle allegations of unauthorized exports of petroleum to Canada.[287]
- Entry of guilty plea by Bushnell Corporation for criminal violations of the EAR by unauthorized export of 500 night vision devices to Japan and 14 other countries. (Bushnell agreed to pay a $650,000 fine and to receive a five-year corporate probation.)[288]

---

285. Agile's General Counsel noted that a day after levying the fine on UBS, the U.S. Government imposed trade sanctions against Syria for its support of terrorism, and the same day the Treasury Department closed access to the American banking system for Syria's main state-owned bank, the Commercial Bank of Syria, for transactions used to finance terrorism and money laundering related to the Iraqi subversion of the United Nations' oil-for-food program. See O'Brien, Timothy L., *Lockboxes, Iraqi Loot and a Trail to the Fed*, THE NEW YORK TIMES, June 6, 2004, p. 1 at p. 7.

286. *Features Identifying PalPal's Customers to Enforce Trade Sanctions*, LawMeme, posting by Nimrod Koziovski on March 31, 2004, accessed at http://research.yale.edu/lawmeme/modules.php?name = News&file = categories&op = newindex&catid = 3.

287. Commerce Department, press release, *Commerce Department Fines Kansas Firm for Unlicensed Petroleum Exports*, June 3, 2003, accessible at www.bxa.doc.gov/news/2003/KansasFirmFined.htm.

288. Justice Department, press release, *Bushnell Corporation Pleads Guilty to Illegally Exporting Night Vision Equipment*, April 16, 2003, accessible at www.bxa.doc.gov/news/2003/Bushnell4_03.htm.

- Settlement with E.H. Wachs Company in response to a charging letter alleging 15 violations of the EAR, including unauthorized exports of pipe cutter machines and spare parts to Iran. (Wachs agreed to pay a $159,000 fine, and to accept a three-year ban on exporting any item from the United States that is subject to the EAR).[289]
- Guilty plea by Silicon Graphics, Inc. to two felony charges that the company violated the EAR by unauthorized exports of high performance computers to a Russian nuclear laboratory. Silicon Graphics agreed to pay a $1 million penalty.[290]

In the first seven months of 2004, the pace of BIS enforcement has continued to accelerate, as evidenced by reports of settlements posted on the BIS website. The table below summarizes the largest of those settlements (with an *asterisk* to indicate that the company "voluntarily self-disclosed" its violation, presumably resulting in a reduction of such penalty):

Figure 7. BIS Civil Penalties Settlement Reports[a]

Entity	Violation	Penalty
Emcore Corporation (New Jersey)	Charged with 71 violations of the EAR (between 1998 and 2003) related to export of Metal Organic Vapor Disposition tools to China and Taiwan, making of false statements to the U.S. government and violating conditions on export licenses.	$400,000*
Molecular Probes (Oregon)	Charged with having exported conotoxin and tetrodotoxin without export license in violation of the EAR on 97 occasions (between 1998 and 2002)	$266,750*
Morton International, Inc. (Illinois) and its	Charged with violations of the EAR concerning unlicensed exports and attempted exports of compounds	$647,500*

(continued)

---

289. Order, *In the Matter of E.H. Wachs Company, Inc.*, United States Department of Commerce, June 3, 2003, accessed at http://efoia.bis.doc.gov/ExportControl-Violations/E755.pdf.

290. BIS, press release, *Silicon Graphics Settles Criminal and Civil Charges That Computer Shipments Violated U.S. Export Controls,* January 7, 2003, accessible at www.bxa.doc.gov/news/2003/SiliconGraphics1_7.htm.

Figure 7. (Continued)

Entity	Violation	Penalty
affiliates Morton International S.A.S. (France) and Rohm andHaas (Japan)[b]	(controlled for chemical and biological reasons) to countries including Mexico, Singapore, Taiwan, India, Israel, Poland and Tunisia, with unlicensed exports of organo-inorganic compounds to Singapore and Taiwan, and 117 violations by reexporting such compounds to Taiwan and India.[c]	
New Focus, Inc. (California)	Charged with failing to obtain export licenses (between 1997 and 2001) for shipments of amplifiers to the Czech Republic, Singapore and Chile, and failing to obtain export licenses under the **"deemed export"** provisions of the EAR for two Iranian nationals and one Chinese national, who, in the course of employment in the U.S., were exposed to manufacturing technology controlled by the EAR.	$200,000*
Pratt & Whitney (Connecticut)	Charged with 42 violations of the EAR (between 1998 and 1999), including failing to obtain export licenses for controlled technical data, with violations of the **"deemed export"** provisions of the EAR for releasing controlled technology to foreign nations (of Germany, The Netherlands and Spain), and failing to obtain licenses for exports to China, Japan and Singapore.	$150,000*
Roper Scientific, Inc. (New Jersey)	Charged with exporting night vision cameras (in 2000) to numerous countries (including South Korea, Japan and Italy) in violation of the EAR.	$422,000*
Saint-Gobain Performance Plastics, Inc. (California)	Charged with exporting controlled valves and pumps to Israel and Taiwan without export licenses on 189 occasions (between 1998 and 2000), failing to file a shipper's export declaration and falsely indicating that shipments did not require an export license.	$697,5000

(continued)

Figure 7. BIS Civil Penalties Settlement Reports[a] (Continued)

Entity	Violation	Penalty
Suntek Microwave, Inc.[d]	Charged with failing to obtain a license for export of detector log video amplifiers (which have military applications) to the People's Republic of China.	$275,000 (and a 20-year denial of export privileges)

[a]BIS, press releases, 2004, accessed at www.bxa.doc.gov/news/index.htm.

[b]BIS, press release, *Illinois Company and Two Foreign Affiliates Settles [sic] Charges Relating to Illegal Exports*, February 24, 2004, accessed at www.bis.doc.gov/News/2004/MortonIntl2_24.htm.

[c]Id.

[d]BIS, press release, *Suntek Microwave, Inc. and Company President Settle Charges of Illegal Exports*, May 6, 2004, accessed at www.bxa.doc.gov/News/2004/SunTeckMay04.htm.

With respect to the Saint-Gobain settlement, the Assistant Secretary for Export Enforcement emphasized that "Cases such as this demonstrates [sic] the importance of voluntary self-disclosures. Consistent with BIS' recently issued civil penalty guidance, the penalty in this case could have been significantly less if the company had voluntarily self-disclosed the violations."[291] Moreover, in a case related to the enforcement action listed above, Suntek Microwave pled guilty to violating the EAR (for failure to obtain export licenses for Chinese nationals who worked at Suntek and were trained in the EAR-controlled manufacturing technology). This was the *first* criminal conviction in connection with a "deemed export" case under the EAR.[292]

From this evidence, it is clear that the OFAC and BIS are pursuing more aggressive enforcement of the TSR and EAR. Incurring liability under the EAR cannot, therefore, be "written off" as a cost of doing profitable business. It should be noted that the violations in several cases were not unwitting. The BIS notified Bushnell that its night scope equipment required a license for export. Violation in spite of such notification will ordinarily prompt criminal charges, as it did in that case.

The trend since 2000 shows a quantum increase in total civil penalties assessed by the BIS in 2002 and 2003 as compared with 2000 and 2001:

- Fiscal year 2000: total civil fines: $1,271,500
- Fiscal year 2001: total civil fines: $2,509,250

291. BIS, press release, *Saint-Gobain Settles Charges of Unlicensed Exports*, June 25, 2004, accessed at www.bxa.doc.gov/news/2004/StGobainPerf_June04.htm.

292. BIS, press release, *Suntek Microwave, Inc. and Company President Settle Charges of Illegal Exports*, May 6, 2004, accessed at www.bxa.doc.gov/news/index.htm.

- Fiscal year 2002: total civil fines: $5,266,500[293]
- Fiscal year 2003: total civil fines: $4,092,000[294]

An even sharper increase occurred in the imposition of criminal fines from 2002 to 2003:

- Fiscal year 2002: total criminal fines: $ 93,000
- Fiscal year 2003: total criminal fines: $3,410,322[295]

In the first six months of 2004, civil fines exceeded $3 million (75% of the total for fiscal year 2003).[296] These and other developments make it ever more likely that transactors will need to know whether their dealings in cyberspace (and those dealings facilitated or driven by communications and negotiations by electronic means) involve parties, entities, governments or government controlled entities potentially targeted by the TSR and EAR. If a party has reason to know a proposed transaction could bring it into dealings with a targeted party, government or other entity, it risks liability under the applicable TSR and EAR for failing to take active and immediate steps to avoid such dealings.[297]

The U.S. government's insistence that companies cooperate with federal investigations is well illustrated by actions taken by the SEC against Lucent Technologies (the nation's larger manufacturer of telecommunications equipment) ("Lucent"). The SEC accused Lucent and nine former and current employees of fraudulently reporting nearly $1.2 billion in revenue. Lucent and three of its employees agreed to settle with the government without admitting or denying wrongdoing. How-

---

293. *BIS Annual Report for Fiscal Year 2002*, at p. 12, accessible at www.bxa.doc.gov/ news/2003/AnnualReport/chapter3p.pdf. Note that since cases may take months or years to investigate and prosecute, the increases in these figures probably do not represent efforts made only in each of the reported years. Nonetheless, the trend in penalties these depict would seem likely to continue, or at least level off at a higher than previous plateau. We quote these figures to indicate chiefly that the risk is non-trivial and the penalties make it worth investing in enhanced due diligence to avoid incurring liability.

294. *BIS Annual Report for Fiscal Year 2003*, at p. 14, accessed at www.bxa.doc.gov/ news/2004/03annualrept.

295. Id.

296. The sum of the fines shown in Figure 7 herein.

297. The BIS has set as a goal for fiscal year 2004 to "refine its ability to target the most sensitive items and end users of the greatest concern" and to "enhance its ability to detect violations of the deemed export provisions of the EAR." *BIS Annual Report for Fiscal Year 2003*, at p. 14, accessed at www.bxa.doc.gov/news/2004/03annualrept.

ever, the SEC imposed a **$25 million** fine on Lucent for not cooperating with the investigation. The SEC explained that "Stiff sanctions and exposure of their conduct will serve as a reminder to companies that *only genuine cooperation* serves the best interest of investors."[298]

Companies seeking to avert risks should anticipate how and where failures could occur and use aggressive measures (more preemptive than the usual compliance policies) to ensure that they will qualify for mitigating factors and will distance themselves from aggravating factors.

---

298. SEC Associate Director of Enforcement, Paul Berger, quoted in Belson, Ken, *Lucent Fined $25 Million by S.E.C. in Fraud Case*, THE WALL STREET JOURNAL, May 18, 2004, p. C-1.

CHAPTER 2

Checkpoint: Trade Sanction Regulations

2.0 Agile's Transaction at Checkpoint TSR.

In pursuit of its national security and foreign policy objectives, the United States deploys and rigorously enforces economic sanctions in order to deny the targets of such sanctions the benefits of commerce and finance with U.S. persons. The TSR implement these sanctions with a depth of detail and breadth of coverage that U.S. firms often misunderstand and/or underestimate. The TSR are also often quite dissimilar, reflecting different policy objectives (such as containment, constraints on military capabilities or "regime change"), or alternately target a country's reliance on a certain trade or a certain export revenue stream (such as petroleum in the case of Iran), but consistently reflecting an analysis of the various ways and channels through which the target obtains a broad range of financial support. Thus, even sanctions that target a petroleum exporting country extend far beyond that trade sector in the scope of their prohibitions.

The TSR are often perceived as burdening U.S. businesses, imposing costs in compliance and in the form of lost economic opportunities which competitors in other countries can nonetheless pursue (if the sanctions are not multilateral and consistently enforced). Such costs, however, prove difficult to quantify and often have a disproportionate impact on different sectors of commerce because they are "often highly concentrated in one or two industries."[1] The impact can also be both

---

1. O'Sullivan, Meghan L., SHREWD SANCTIONS: STATECRAFT AND STATE SPONSORS OF TERRORISM, Brookings Institution Press, 2003, p. 21.

direct and indirect (adding to the cost of production) as is the case with embargoes of "cheap" oil. There continues to be considerable debate about whether sanctions "work," whether they achieve their stated objectives (and whether the collateral damage they cause to the target is justified in light of the real damage they cause to U.S. business interests). This debate is likely to continue, because the means for analyzing such issues remain inexact and are burdened by the difficulty of "separating correlation from causality."[2] In the case of Libya (which has renounced its pursuit of weapons of mass destruction), and of Iraq (whose military capabilities were found to have been severely eroded by sanctions),[3] each proved far more successful in retrospect than commonly believed during the period in which sanctions were enforced. Yet even these successes are easily dismissed or trivialized by critics, because the final results were not achieved solely as a result of the sanctions. Although export controls reflected in the EAR tend to enjoy multilateral support (particularly those that are anti-proliferation), the TSR are often controversial, because they are perceived as a uniquely U.S. device, deployed to serve objectives that many U.S. allies do not support. As a result, overseas firms often resist requests to identify where their conduct might, if performed by a U.S. person, contravene the TSR.

The TSR, of course, have the most dramatic impact on businesses and firms that have historically transacted with countries targeted by the country-specific TSR. Some, of course, are not country-specific but are aimed rather at terrorist entities or concentrate on a country's leaders (as in the case of Zimbabwe and Liberia). When the U.S. government imposed trade sanctions on Iraq, Iran and Libya, the firms with the largest in-country investments (or whose businesses were heavily dominated by transactions in or with one or more of those countries) suffered the greatest financial hardship when they were forced to cease such dealings immediately. Firms from other countries often seized the commercial opportunities that the U.S. firms were compelled to abandon. U.S. allies often do not join the United States in observing or enforcing such sanctions, or they do so much less aggressively. Firms in regions like the former Warsaw Pact countries were not burdened by such barriers to their transactions. Inevitably, when U.S. firms later sought to acquire companies in these regions, they found that one of

2. O'Sullivan, Meghan L., SHREWD SANCTIONS: STATECRAFT AND STATE SPONSORS OF TERRORISM, Brookings Institution Press, 2003, p. 31.

3. Lopez, George A., and Cortright, David, *Containing Iraq: Sanctions Worked*, FOREIGN AFFAIRS, July/August 2004, pp. 90–91.

the major risks was avoiding liability for contravening the TSR. By acquiring such companies, they put themselves and their senior management at risk of being involved in transactions prohibited to U.S. persons by the TSR. For this reason, Agile's Counsel treats the TSR diligence check with great care. Care is also required because penalties imposed under the TSR are severe and can apply to companies and/or senior management. The TSR require continuous monitoring because new TSR or amendments to existing TSR, or additions to the lists of sanctioned parties, often come into force virtually over night with no advance notice, yet require immediate compliance.

2.1 Definition of Targeted Country or Organization.

With a few notable exceptions, each TSR targets a country and its government. The most notable exceptions are the TSR that target stateless terrorist organizations, drug organizations and, in the case of Zimbabwe and Liberia, officials of such countries. Each TSR provides a definition of such country, government or organization. As we will see in the subsequent analysis of a hypothetical cyber-driven transaction, the definitions of "U.S. person" in these TSR tend to sweep far more broadly than transactors anticipate, commonly including overseas branches of U.S. companies, sometimes including their subsidiaries (in the case of TSR that target Cuba and North Korea), and often applying to such U.S. persons "**wherever located**" in the world. Since each set of TSR seeks to deny to its target the benefits of economic and financial transactions (particularly those related to exports from the United States and their reexport, and to services and technology provided by U.S. persons), transactors need to be aware *at the earliest possible time* of any dealings that might involve (even peripherally) a TSR-defined target.

One cannot assume that each TSR will define a country and its government in the same way, however. OFAC drafts the applicable TSR to reach whatever activities or interests of a particular target the U.S. government seeks to put pressure on, by interdicting specific benefits that might flow in specific circumstances to such targets from such activities or interests. For example, the Iranian Transactions Regulations ("ITR") contain a definition of "Government of Iran," notes that refer to persons determined by OFAC to fall within that definition, and definitions of other terms that expand the reach of the ITR. Certain terms with unusually broad or counter-intuitive reach include: "interest" (the

ITR target all property and "interest" in property of the Government of Iran), "entity owned or controlled by the Government of Iran," "goods or services owned or controlled by the Government of Iran," "Iranian-origin," "Iranian-origin services" and "services owned or controlled by the Government of Iran."[4]

As a result of such carefully "targeted" regulation, each TSR must be analyzed separately. Currently, the chief targets of the broadest TSR are:

(a) **Countries**—Burma (Myanmar), Cuba, Iran, Libya,[5] North Korea and Sudan;

---

4. 31 CFR §§ 560.304, 560.306, and 560.313.

5. The TSR that targeted Iraq and Libya have changed considerably during the writing of this book, and, with significant exceptions, have been substantially lifted or curtailed. With respect to Iraq, on May 7, 2003, the President of the United States issued Presidential Determination 2003-23, which, among other things, suspended the Iraq Sanctions Act of 1990, *except* Section 586E (concerning penalties). On July 30, 2004, the President issued Executive Order 13550, which, among other things, (1) terminated the national emergency pursuant to which the Iraq Sanctions Regulations had been promulgated by OFAC; (2) replaced the earlier national emergency with "the national emergency declared in Executive Order 13303 of March 20, 2003, and expanded in Executive Order 13315 of August 28, 2003;" (3) terminated OFAC's authority to accept applications for, and to issue licenses concerning, exports and reexports of U.S.-origin items to Iraq (and transferring authority for all such licensing to the BIS). See Executive Order 13550, July 30, 2004, accessed at www.ustreas.gov/offices/eotffc/ofac/actions/ 20040730.html. Note that such change in licensing jurisdiction does not diminish the continuing effect of prohibitions on dealing with Iraqi persons and entities named on OFAC's SDN List, as evidenced by OFAC's action on August 2, 2004, which added three holders of Iraqi passports and one commercial entity (in Thailand with apparent Iraqi connections) to the SDN List.

In conjunction with OFAC's July 30, 2004, action, the BIS published the same day in the *Federal Register*, the Interim Rule (for public comment) Export and Reexports for Iraq which, among other things, "significantly reduces the level of control over commercial exports to Iraq while retaining restrictions on the export of multilaterally controlled items and other sensitive items to Iraq in keeping with Iraq's new economic and security status. The licensing requirements and licensing policy reflected in this rule are consistent with UNSC Resolution 1483 (2003) and other relevant resolutions which lifted the comprehensive trade embargo imposed on Iraq *but retained certain restrictions including an embargo on arms and related materiel and their means of production.*" See 69 FEDERAL REGISTER 146, pp. 46070–46088, accessed at http:// a257.g.akamaitech.net/7/257/2422/06jun20041800/edocket.access.gpo.gov/2004/pdf/ 04-17532.pdf. [Emphasis added.] Therefore the Interim Rule retains substantial restrictions on exports and reexports to Iraq that are destined for inappropriate end

(b) Stateless organizations—those involved in narcotics trafficking and terrorism;

(c) Proliferation—of weapons of mass destruction and highly enriched uranium assets; and

(d) Senior officials of certain governments—Zimbabwe and Liberia.[6]

An early checkpoint in a cyberspace or cyber-driven transaction should therefore consist in assembling a complete list of all the countries in which any party to the transaction (directly or indirectly) has connections or dealings. Red flags—(or indications of risk points to a U.S. firm)—occur when the target of an acquisition sells, exports to, or has dealings with, companies in any TSR targeted country. In this instance, the checkpoint necessary to avert the risks of contravening prohibitions against dealing with such countries or firms of such countries requires considerable diligence.

For cyberspace transactors (websites that do business with visitors thereto), there will be an increased obligation to determine whether a prospective customer is located in a targeted country or is a member of a targeted organization. For cyber-driven transactions, the requisite due diligence should be directed at answering the basic question: What countries, governments, entities and/or organizations do the parties to the transaction have commercial (or other) dealings with, and who are they contemplating dealing with? As early as possible, a comprehensive list of all agents, vendors, customers and financial institutions with

---

uses or end users. As a result, parties exporting to Iraq (or to parties that will reexport to Iraq) should make a close review of the Interim Rule before negotiating the terms of such transactions.

Note that with respect to Libya, on September 20, 2004, President Bush issued an Executive Order that terminated the national emergency that had been declared against Libya. The President explained that he took this action because the situation that had given rise to that national emergency "has been significantly altered by Libya's commitments and actions to eliminate its weapons of mass destruction programs and its Missile Technology Control Regime (MTCR) class missiles, and by other developments." Executive Order, dated September 20, 2004, accessed at www.whitehouse.gov/news/releases/2004/09/20040920-5.html. That action also terminated the Libyan Sanction Regulations but did not modify the export controls that were imposed earlier in 2004 against Libya by the Department of Commerce. Moreover, the U.S. State Department continues to list the Libyan government as a supporter of international terrorism, and thus the TSR that target such countries still apply to Libya.

6. See on OFAC's website the hyperlink for "legal documents," accessed at www.ustreas.gov/offices/eotffc/ofac/legal.

whom the non-U.S. parties have any transactions or commercial dealings must be requested (together with addresses). Such requests will almost certainly have a significant chilling effect on the transaction and the business relationship. Although the non-U.S. party will probably want to scrutinize its own list internally, overseas parties are often reluctant to initiate a review of their customers and suppliers under U.S. law. However, they are more likely to consent if access is subject to a nondisclosure agreement. If the diligence discovers a transaction or agreement with a company in a targeted country or its government or with a targeted organization, the next inquiry should be how to proceed with the contemplated transaction without the U.S. person becoming involved in any dealing prohibited to U.S. persons. If the proscribed transaction involves the simple website purchase of a product or technology by a person from a targeted country, rejecting the transaction will often suffice. But a mechanism needs to be in place to identify such persons. If, however, the issue is how to proceed with a transaction, when one of the parties thereto has extensive financial dealings in a targeted country, negotiations may be required to ensure that the U.S. party is not dealing with, supporting, facilitating or providing assistance to, the targeted country, its government or an entity controlled by such government.

If the contemplated transaction is a joint venture or acquisition, the only reliable and effective solution will often be to require the overseas party to cease all current dealings and to disengage completely from any future dealings with the countries, governments and organizations targeted by the TSR. As might be expected, such remediation can present substantial challenges to those negotiating on behalf of a U.S. person, particularly since such disengagement must be completed prior to the signing of a definitive transactional agreement in order to avert the risk of contravening the TSR upon signing. The negotiations concerning the relevant representations and warranties will become one of the most important and controversial of the deal's checkpoints.

2.2 Identification of Persons Targeted by a TSR.

A second dimension of TSR scope concerns targeted "persons"—those whose property and interests in property are blocked under a particular TSR. OFAC maintains a list of persons it has so designated—

the Specially Designated Nationals ("SDN") List.[7] As OFAC's Director R. Richard Newcomb has observed:

> "In practice, an SDN of a target nation is typically a government body of that country, or a representative, agent, intermediary, or

---

7. Note that TSR implemented pursuant to the IEEPA do not contain the expression "specially designated national" or the acronym "SDN;" the expression occurs only in those authorized by the Trading with the Enemy Act. One finds the concept, nonetheless, in several of the TSR, including those targeting organizations (such as Specially Designated Terrorists) and those targeting certain countries (such as Burma, Iran, and Sudan). In the case of the Zimbabwe, the subject of the Presidential Executive Order of March 7, 2003, titled "Blocking Property of Persons Undermining Democratic Processes or Institutions in Zimbabwe," the Order was crafted to avoid targeting the country and instead targets the property and interests in property of 77 Zimbabwean government officials. See White House Web Site, Executive Order page accessed at www.whitehouse.gov/news/release/2003/03/20030307-11.html.

The March 7th Executive Order reflects an effort by the United States to apply sanctions already applied by several other governments. For several years the Government of Zimbabwe, headed by President Robert Mugabe had come under increasing criticism for human rights violations. As a result, on February 18, 2002, the Council of the European Union adopted Common Position 2002/145/CFSP, which introduced restrictive measures against the Government of Zimbabwe and "those who bear wide responsibility for serious violations of human rights and of the freedom of opinion, of association and of peaceful assembly." See Common Council Position, July 22, 2002, quoting and amending the earlier February 2002 Council Position, accessed at www.dnb.nl/sanctiewetgeving/pdf/zimbabwe/council_22_july.pdf. (The February 2002 Council Position targeted 72 Zimbabwean government officials.) On 25 July 2002, by Commission Regulation (EC) No 1345/2002, the Council of the European Union extended those sanctions: "to cover all remaining Cabinet Ministers, Politburo Secretaries, Deputy Ministers, Assistant Secretaries of the Politburo and Grace Mugabe, the spouse of Robert Mugabe." Bank of England Press Release, 25 July 2002, accessed at www.bankofengland.co.uk/pressreleases/2002/084.htm. On the same date, in conformance with that Commission Regulation, the Bank of England, on behalf of the UK's Treasury, froze the funds of those individuals. See Bank of England Press Release, 25 July 2002, accessed at www.bankofengland.co.uk/pressreleases/2002/084.htm. Similar action was taken by the Reserve Bank of Australia on 25 November 2002, and finally by the United States with the March 7th EO. Media Release, Reserve Bank of Australia, accessed at www.rba.gov.au/MediaReleases/2002/mr_02_20_annex.html. In addition, the Reserve Bank of Australia in the same order directed that: "All transactions involving the transfer of funds or payments to, by the order of, or on behalf of such persons are prohibited." As of this writing, we understand from a telephone conversation with an OFAC official that OFAC is preparing a set of Zimbabwe sanctions regulations that would implement President Bush's Executive Order of March 7, 2003. Such regulations probably require considerable research by OFAC into the ongoing commercial activities and relationships of the targeted individuals order to ensure that the scope of the reg-

front (whether overt or covert), often located outside the country which functions as an extension of that government. It may be a firm created by the government, or it may be a third-country company that otherwise becomes owned or controlled by the government, or that operates for or on behalf of the government.

Since governments of the target countries tend to operate their international fronts as interlocking networks of companies and key individuals, it is important to recognize that any identified SDN is treated for all sanctions purposes as an entity of that government. Moreover, another person owned or controlled by an SDN or which acts for or on the SDN's behalf is also, by definition, an SDN of that country, irrespective of location."[8]

The applicable TSR make clear that U.S. companies and persons are responsible for avoiding dealings with, and for blocking[9] any property of, such persons (including interests in property within, or that come into, their possession or control). In addition, they are also responsible for avoiding such dealings with any persons not on the SDN List who represent or work on behalf of, or for the benefit of, anyone so named. Here the analysis required for an effective checkpoint is simpler: counsel should obtain a list of all persons, entities and organizations with whom the parties to the contemplated transaction currently deal or plan to deal. If any are named on the SDN List, all commercial dealings with them by a U.S. person are prohibited.

In cyberspace transactions, it is imperative for the website operator to have a mechanism (often interdiction software) that blocks any proposed transaction with persons on the SDN List. Banks and other financial institutions that process millions of transactions per day use such software to avert transferring funds to any SDN List party. We

---

ulations will reach the desired objective. It should be noted that in this instance the U.S. followed the European lead in imposing sanctions. Note: OFAC published the Zimbabwe Sanctions Regulations on July 29, 2004. See 69 FEDERAL REGISTER 145, pp. 45246–42555, accessed at www.ustreas.gov/offices/eotffc/ofac/legal/regs/fr45246.pdf.

8. Newcomb, R. Richard; Berlack, Evan R.; Hunt, Cecil; and Wall, Christopher R., COPING WITH U.S. EXPORT CONTROLS 2002, Practicing Law Institute, 2002, p. 127.

9. The Iranian Assets Control Regulations (IACR) provide, for example, that "No property subject to the jurisdiction of the United States or which is in the possession of or control of persons subject to the jurisdiction of the United States in which on or after the effective date Iran has any interest of any nature whatsoever may be transferred, paid, exported, withdrawn or otherwise dealt in except as authorized." Such property is "blocked." 31 CFR §535.201.

think it inevitable that OFAC will require the use of comparable software or interdiction devices by all websites operated commercially by a U.S. person. Because the SDN List is updated continually, sometimes more than once a week, the checkpoint to address this risk must also be an ongoing one. In cyber-driven transactions (such as a merger or outsourcing), a U.S. party will need to employ at a minimum: a representation of non-dealing with SDN List parties, a warranty that all parties will use best efforts to avoid any such dealings in the future, and appropriate bring-down language to ensure that once the U.S. party signs a definitive transaction agreement it will not thereby be drawn inadvertently into dealing with an SDN Party or someone who represents it or works on its behalf.

2.3 Identification of Benefits OFAC Seeks to Interdict.

Each TSR specifies the kinds of benefits it seeks to interdict (before such benefits can reach the targeted country, government, organization or person). Such specification usually takes the form of a broad range of activities prohibited to U.S. persons (or to those acting on their behalf) and of specific obligations that U.S. persons are under to interdict or block any property or interests in property, of persons named on the SDN List (if such property or interests are within the U.S. person's control or possession, or come within its control or possession). Here too it is essential that counsel have a clear understanding of what kinds of actions and interactions its client's U.S. persons are likely to engage in during and after a transaction (if they anticipate serving as officers or directors of an overseas entity or any of its affiliates).

It is important that counsel understand the specifics of how the other parties to the transaction conduct their business as well. For example, if a party is selling goods to a country targeted by a TSR, and such activities must cease before the U.S. person acquires such company, the requisite cessation must include *all related activities* prohibited by the TSR. Thus, mere cessation of further (or future) sales or purchases will not suffice. The pre-transactional dealings (requests for bids, tender of bids, negotiations) must cease (as well as deliveries pursuant to previous sales, and follow-up (if any) related to previously delivered goods including, but not limited to, performance on service contracts or warranties).[10] In short, the entire logistics chain of such sales of product (and replacement parts) or purchases of supplies must be wrapped up. Otherwise, each subsequent shipment and payment of invoice would constitute a separate violation of the pertinent TSR. Unless counsel appreciates the "mechanics" of how goods, services, supplies and technical data are delivered in the ordinary course, it is likely to recommend insufficient remediation, leaving a U.S. person exposed to serious risks of contravening the TSR, EAR and/or ITAR. Partial compliance will, in all probability not be construed as "good faith" in the event of an enforcement action.

Counsel should anticipate that OFAC will interpret each TSR very broadly, pursuant to its mandate, and challenges to OFAC interpretations are usually (although not always) unsuccessful. The courts have given considerable deference to OFAC's interpretations (while noting that the courts retain the right at some point to interpret the limits of OFAC's lawful exercise of its powers). When counsel consider how to interpret the TSR and (when necessary) what remediation to recommend to avert violations or to halt belatedly discovered violations, it is important to remember the purpose of each TSR and its rationale. Each TSR is designed to promote the national security and foreign policy objectives of the United States in a unique geographic or geo-political context. The authority for many of the TSR, and for OFAC's implementation and enforcement, derives from a declaration of national emergency by the President of the United States under powers granted by the International Emergency Economic Powers Act ("IEEPA").[11] IEEPA gives the President broad powers to address any "unusual and extraordinary threat" to the national security, foreign policy or economy of the United States.[12]

In order to exercise this authority lawfully, the President is required to declare a national emergency to deal with the perceived threat. Such

---

10. Commonly overlooked follow-up include invoices, payments, requests for service, return of goods for warranty repairs, and spare parts procurements.

11. 50 U.S.C. 1701-1706. As noted earlier, other TSR are promulgated under the authority of the Trading with the Enemy Act, 50 U.S.C. App. 1-44. Note also that the Antiterrorism and Effective Death Penalty Act, Section 321 (18 U.S.C. 2332d) prohibit U.S. persons from engaging in financial transactions with any government whose country has been designated a supporter of international terrorism under Section 6(j) of the Export Administration Act (50 U.S.C. App. 2405). Violation of that prohibition is a criminal offense.

12. 50 U.S.C. §1701–1706.

a declaration of national emergency issues in the form of an Executive Order,[13] and freezes the property (and blocks any transfer of property or interests in property) of the targeted government or organization. IEEPA authorizes the President to control property within the dominion of the United States in which the relevant target has an interest.[14] Each TSR implements the related Executive Order(s), and customarily includes prohibitions on transfer, payment, export, withdrawal or other dealing in the target's property and interests in property.[15] The Congressional purpose in authorizing such blocking orders is frequently described by the courts as putting "control of foreign assets in the hands of the President, in part to allow him to use the assets as a bargaining chip in dealing with a hostile country."[16]

Companies have frequently underestimated the reach of such orders and of the related TSR, and have failed to appreciate the detailed analysis that OFAC undertakes of a broad range of the target's activities and interests in transactions (including payments owed and payments already made by the target) before it promulgates a particular set of complex and highly specialized TSR. These are not "boilerplate" prohibitions adapted on an *ad hoc* basis to each new target. For instance, when a U.S. manufacturer of furnaces destined for Iraq found that the Iraqi Sanction Regulations required it to freeze either the goods it manufactured for Iraq *or* any payments already received from Iraq for such goods, it filed suit, challenging OFAC's power to promulgate such a regulation, arguing that it was the only party with a continuing interest in payment (clearly, the original party retains a colorable interest in any moneys paid, if it does not receive the goods contracted for, or such goods are defective or do not conform to the terms or purpose for which purchased, or the full contract terms are not fulfilled).

---

13. For example, Iraq Executive Orders Nos. 12,722 and 12,724, published in 55 FEDERAL REGISTER 31803 and 55 FEDERAL REGISTER 33089, respectively.

14. IEEPA, for example, permits the executive branch to "investigate, regulate or prohibit . . . transfers of credit or payments . . . by . . . any banking institution, to the extent that such transfers . . . involve any interest of any foreign country . . . [and] transactions involving . . . any property in which any foreign country . . . has any interest." 50 U.S.C. §1702(a)(1).

15. For example, 31 C.F.R. 575.201(a).

16. *Itek Corporation v. The First National Bank of Boston*, 704 F.2d 1 (1st Cir., 1983) at p. 9, quoting *Dames & Moor v. Regan*, 453 U.S. 654 (1980) at 673, quoting *Propper v. Clark*, 337 U.S. 472 (1949) at 493.

Although the District Court agreed with the manufacturer, the Court of Appeals for the District of Columbia Circuit reversed, holding that, although Iraq might no longer have any interest in the down payment it had made to the U.S. manufacturer, it nonetheless still had "some interest in the goods for which the down payment was paid and some interest in the **transactions**." Thus the IEEPA did not forbid OFAC from enforcing its regulation against either the delivered down payment or the undelivered furnaces.[17] Although the U.S. manufacturer had already resold one of the furnaces to a third party, OFAC also instructed the manufacturer to "freeze the proceeds from that sale,"[18] on the rationale that the original recipient arguably retained a legal interest in goods for which a down payment had been made.

With such considerations in mind, we return to the second due diligence report that Agile's General Counsel received from U.S. counsel (hereafter referred to as "Counsel").

2.4 Mapping the TSR Risk Points of Agile's Transaction.

The second due diligence investigation of Troll, Brugge and Ijsselmeer turned up several potential areas of likely violations. In its report, Counsel categorized Agile's risk points geographically by region and country: Middle East (Iran, Sudan, Syria), Asia (Myanmar, North Korea), Africa (Zimbabwe and Liberia) and the Americas (Cuba). Counsel[19] reviewed each of these according to the type of prohibited activity (*e.g.*, agency agreement, commercial contract, financing arrangement, etc.). With particular attention to OFAC's recently published Enforcement Guidelines, Counsel then ranked the commercial activities according to the adverse impact (under the TSR) that completion or continuation of such activities would have, and assigned priorities according to how quickly Agile would need to take action to avert such risks. Counsel also prepared the foundation for a "non-contravention"

---

17. See *Consarc Corporation and Consarc Engineering, Ltd. v. United States Treasury Department, Office of Foreign Assets Control,* 71 F.3d 909 (D.C. Cir., 1995) at p. 914.

18. Id at p. 911.

19. Unless otherwise noted, references hereafter to "counsel" signify outside U.S. counsel to Agile, not Agile's general counsel nor its overseas counsel.

legal opinion. In the context of the latter, the diligence report also listed additional documents that Counsel would need to review, officials at Troll, Brugge and Ijsselmeer whom Counsel wanted to interview informally, and salient questions that should be pursued to ensure that the report followed up each of the "red flags" or risk points identified by the report.[20] Counsel also obtained what was represented to be a reasonably complete list of vendors, customers, banks, etc. with whom Troll, Brugge and Ijsselmeer regularly dealt.

Counsel then focused on three important circumstances:

(i)   After Closing, Agile partners would serve on the Board of Directors of Troll and Brugge;

(ii) Agile did not want such directors to recuse themselves from any Board deliberations involving business plans, long-term objectives and transactional agreements (because this would undermine Agile's business purpose in pursuing the acquisition); and

(iii) Agile wanted Troll to become an overseas branch of Agile, and Brugge, an overseas subsidiary of Agile.

Since the TSR predominantly (but not exclusively) prohibit activities by "U.S. persons," the key to this TSR checkpoint was to determine whether any activities by Troll, Brugge or Ijsselmeer would, at any time, be attributable to Agile, its branches or its partners and personnel (as "U.S. persons"). By examining the past, present and probable (or proposed) future activities of Agile in connection with Troll's, Brugge's and Ijsselmeer's business dealings, Counsel was able to determine where such dealings might draw Agile's "U.S. persons" into inadvertent contravention of the TSR.

Counsel's starting point for this inquiry was the definition of "U.S. person" provided in each TSR. In all but two TSR (those for Cuba and North Korea), the definition of "U.S. person" is roughly equivalent. Since Troll has extensive dealings in Iran, counsel considered the defi-

---

20. The TSR and EAR each contain provisions that make clear that a "U.S. person" is responsible for recognizing "red flags" of potential violations and for pursuing them. Ignoring "red flags" would, of course, be tantamount to having a *reason to know* and thus to be at risk of having a willful violation imputed if Agile disregards such "red flags."

nition of "U.S. person" under the Iranian Transactions Regulations ("ITR") to be illustrative (but not dispositive):

> "The term *United States person* means any United States citizen, permanent resident alien, entity organized under the laws of the United States (including foreign branches), or any person in the United States."[21]

Since Agile partners would serve on Troll's Board after Closing, any matter that came before that Board would thereafter involve Agile as a "U.S. person" pursuant to this definition. Since Troll would become a foreign branch of Agile at Closing, any dealings by Troll thereafter would be considered dealings by an extension of Agile as a "U.S. person." Cyber-transactors easily overlook the breadth of the TSR definition of "U.S. person." To a European, such breadth is often perceived (not unreasonably) as an extra-territorial reach (and over-reach) of U.S. law, an unjustifiable interference in the commerce and laws of another country, and an infringement of its sovereignty. European counsel often questions U.S. counsel's reasoning in response to this perception.

Agile's Counsel anticipates that his recommendation will provoke several typically raised counter-arguments. First, that the ITR do not apply to "subsidiaries" and therefore do not apply to Troll. The answer to this is straightforward: while it is accurate that the ITR (unlike those that target Cuba and North Korea) do not define "U.S. person" to include "subsidiaries," Troll will be a foreign branch of Agile, and will thereby become a "U.S. person" at Closing.

The second argument asserts that because Troll will remain a Norwegian company after Closing, its activities are beyond the reach of the ITR (given a reasonable reading). If this is not the case, Agile should reconsider making Troll an Agile branch, and make it instead an Agile subsidiary. Such a change would arguably remove Troll from the ITR definition of "U.S. person." But even if Agile were inclined to reconsider its corporate restructuring plans (which in most cases are driven by clear and well-thought out economic and tax benefits), that ultimately would not remove the crucial risk point for Agile: the involvement of its partners on the Troll Board of Directors, where they will constitute a majority of the Board. When Agile's partners enter a Troll board meeting, they do so as "U.S. persons." The Troll Board deliberations and decisions (including decisions to approve proposed transactions and to

---

21. 31 Code of Federal Regulations (CFR) § 560.314.

authorize Troll's entry into transactions) include the deliberation and decisions of such "U.S. persons." Those decisions are thus clearly attributable to Agile.

The third argument is attractive for its simplicity: Agile's Danish partners are Danes, not U.S. citizens. Counsel must be misrepresenting the breadth of the ITR definition of "U.S. person," and how can that possibly be in Agile's best interests? While this has some superficial appeal, such a literal construction of the ITR would make circumvention of its mandate child's play. It is clear from the ITR's express provisions, that, if Hamlet, Prince of Denmark had been elected as a partner at Agile, he would thereby become a "U.S. person" for the purposes of the ITR (and those purposes only), **because Agile is a US person.**

Fourth, surely even Danes purportedly qualified as "U.S. persons" pursuant to such definition cannot be violating the ITR, and even if they are, no court in Denmark will hold them liable for it. This argument assumes that such persons are beyond service of process of U.S. District Courts, and that what such "U.S. persons" do in their own country (and not in the United States) should not be of concern to OFAC. In any event, it should not cause Agile to incur liability. Unfortunately, this argument misses the underlying rationale of these regulations: as partners, with power to sign and bind on behalf of Agile, Agile's Danish partners must not commit acts that contravene the ITR. If they do, Agile has thereby contravened the ITR. Any doubt that geographic location is irrelevant to the ITR calculus is dispelled by repeated expressions in the ITR that specified actions by a "U.S. person" are prohibited *wherever located*. Examples in the ITR of such "U.S. person" ubiquity include:

- *Prohibited trade related transactions with Iran:* "no United States person, **wherever located**, may engage in any transaction or dealing in or related to . . . (2) Goods, technology, or services for exportation, reexportation, sale or supply, directly or indirectly, to Iran or the Government of Iran."[22]

- *Prohibited facilitation by United States persons:* " . . . no United States person, **wherever located**, may approve, finance, facilitate, or guarantee any transaction by a foreign person where the trans-

---

22. 31 CFR §560.206 (a). [Emphasis added.]

action by that foreign person would be prohibited by this part if performed by a United States person or within the United States."

As that second example demonstrates, approval of any transaction involving Troll by the Agile-controlled Board, if prohibited by the ITR will be prohibited to Agile's partners serving on the Troll Board.[23] These examples amply demonstrate that the scope of ITR prohibitions on dealings by U.S. persons is extremely broad.[24]

2.5 Problems Found at the Checkpoint for TSR that Target Iran.

The following activities by Troll, if performed by a "U.S. person," would clearly violate the ITR.

---

23. Counsel also is keenly aware that several factors will increase the likelihood of OFAC enforcing the ITR rigorously: (1) President Bush, in a State of the Union speech, named Iran's government as one of the "axis of evil" governments; (2) U.S. opposition to Iran's widely reported development of nuclear weapons; (3) increasing reports by the United Nation's International Atomic Energy Agency ("IAEA") of Iran's failure to comply with the Nuclear Non-Proliferation Treaty (of which Iran is a signatory); and (4) Iran's continuing support for terrorist groups such as Hezbollah. For a good discussion of Iran's "extensive program aimed at making and working with material that can be used in nuclear weapons" and its disagreements with the IAEA, see Sweet, William, *Iran's Nuclear Program Reaches Critical Juncture*, IEEE SPECTRUM, June 2004, accessed at www.spectrum.ieee.org/WEBONLY/resource/jun04/0604niran.html.

24. Since comprehensive treatment of the TSR (or even of the ITR) is precluded by constraints of space, we would emphasize that each TSR is tailored to its target, each expressly provides that it is separate from each of the others, and the provisions of each tend to be structured along the following lines: a first tier stating prohibitions, a second tier stating interpretations, a third tier (not always present) elaborating further prohibitions (often to highlight technologies of concern), a fourth tier promulgating general licenses and other exceptions, a fifth tier containing penalties for violations, and a sixth tier that refers the reader to specially targeted persons and entities (which for all TSR are collected in what is known as the Specially Designated Nationals and Blocked Persons (or SDN) List, continuously available on OFAC's website and updated frequently (sometimes several times a month). See current SDN List accessed at www.ustreas.gov/offices/eotffc/ofac/sdn/t11sdn.pdf.

Cautionary note: when using the Acrobat search function for the SDN List one should *not* set any search term within quotation marks (double inverted commas) as one commonly does with Lexis or Google and similar databases: doing so will result in no matching terms. Searching without such punctuation will result in matching terms.

2.5.1 Activity: Sale of Troll Products to Third Parties for Reexport to Iran.

Troll sells software, often from its website, to parties in other Middle East countries whom it knows from correspondence will be re-selling such products to customers in Iran and to Iranian government controlled entities in their own countries.

➤ *Prohibited Conduct:* At Closing, or after signing the definitive purchase agreement ("DPA"), if Agile's partners are involved in approving, deliberating or facilitating such activity, each such sale would bring Agile into violation of ITR Section 560.204, which prohibits:

> "Sale, or supply of any goods, technology, or services to person in a third country undertaken with knowledge or reason to know that:
>   Such goods, technology, or services are intended specifically for supply . . . reexportation, directly or indirectly, to Iran or the Government of Iran; . . ."[25]

2.5.2 Activity: Sale of Troll Products to Third Countries for Incorporation into Other Products for Delivery to Iran.

Troll sells software modules for inclusion in systems made in Eastern Europe for customers in Iran. Such customers are known by Troll not to be the exclusive customers for such systems, but from year to year 65–80% of the sales of such systems are to Iranian corporate customers and the Iranian government.

➤ *Prohibited Conduct:* Such percentages suggest a predominance of such sales to Iranian customers. At Closing, or after signing of the definitive purchase agreement ("DPA"), if Agile's partners are involved in approving, deliberating or facilitating such activity (whether in online sales or otherwise), each such sale would bring Agile into violation of

---

25. 31 CFR §560.204 (a).

ITR Section 204, which *prohibits* "sale, or supply of any goods, technology, or services to person in a third country undertaken with knowledge or reason to know that:

> (b) Such goods, technology, or services are intended specifically for use in production of, for commingling with, or for **incorporation into goods**, technology, or services to be directly or indirectly supplied . . . exclusively or **predominantly** to Iran or the Government of Iran."[26]

2.5.3 Activity: Reexportation of Troll Products by Persons Other than United States Persons.

Since the fall of the Berlin Wall, Troll has had extensive dealings with high tech companies in countries that were formerly part of the Warsaw Pact, particularly those in countries known for weapons production (*e.g.*, Poland and Rumania). Two Troll software products that are sold to a Polish corporate customer incorporate technologies licensed from vendors in the United States. Counsel was provided with copies of contracts and related correspondence that might shed light on the dealings linked to those contracts. E-mails between Troll and the Polish customer indicate that one of Troll's software products will be incorporated by the Polish customer into a turnkey system and then sold to a branch of Bank Meli located in Dusseldorf, Germany. The U.S. technology incorporated into the final product will not be transformed, but will remain a separate encryption module.

The second Troll product has been packaged with software designed by the Polish customer and sold to several parties. Purchase orders include: (i) Foundation Secours Mondial in Brussels, Belgium; (ii) Holborn European Marketing Company Limited in Larnica, Cyprus; (iii) Stichting Wereldhulp—Belgie, V.Z.W. in Brussels, Belgium; and (iv) Mitsukura Trading Company Limited in Chuo-Ku Kobe, Japan.

For those customers, the encryption module containing US technology was similarly unmodified. For Stichting and Mitsukura, the

---

26. 31 CFR §560.204 (b). [Emphasis added.]

value of such technology constituted less than 10% of the final sale price, while for the others (including additional customers in Iran), the value constituted more than 20% of the final sale price. Delivery is pending to each of these customers. Some of the merchandise will be shipped by truck, some by sea, and some will have final software updates transmitted by e-mail.

➤ *Prohibited Conduct:* At Closing, and probably at signing of the DPA as well, Agile will come into violation of several TSR. The release of Troll software (online or otherwise), containing technology exported from the United States, constitutes a reexport under ITR Section 560.418, which prohibits such reexport if "made with knowledge or *reason to know*" that the technology is intended for Iran or the Government of Iran.[27] A bank in Dusseldorf may seem far removed from Iran, with no apparent connection to the Government of Iran. However, the ITR defines "*Government of Iran*" to include "Any entity owned or controlled directly or indirectly" by that government, and any entity designated by the Secretary of Treasury to be such an entity.[28] Such designations can be found on the SDN List, toward the end of which is a special section entitled "Iran." A prefatory notice states: "The following banks are owned or controlled by the Government of Iran. Transactions with them are severely restricted."[29] "Bank Meli" is named on the SDN List (together with its Dusseldorf Branch), thereby equating it with the Government of Iran, and making any participation by Agile partners in support of it a reexport in violation of the ITR.[30]

---

27. 31 CFR §560.418. [Emphasis added.]

28. 31 CFR §560.304. The breadth of the definition is particularly appropriate for the Government of Iran in view of the fact that most of the 340 companies listed on the Tehran stock exchange are "affiliated to the government and most buyers [of their shares] are institutions that are also tied to the government." Bozorgmehr, Najmeh, and Khalaf, Roula, *Iran's Stocks Shrug off Worries with 47% Increase,* FINANCIAL TIMES, July 3, 2003, p. 5.

29. SDN List, p. 104, accessed at www.ustreas.gov/offices/eotffc/ofac/sdn/t11sdn.pdf, accessed on June 26, 2003.

30. Section 560.418 contains an exemption for technology or software that meets the definition of "information and informational materials" in Section 560.315, but Troll's software would not come within such definition.

➤ *Prohibited Conduct:* Continuation and completion of each of the sales to the other customers would also cause Agile to violate the ITR. If, as of the Closing, Troll has not yet become a branch of Agile, sales to the Iranian customers would nonetheless violate ITR Section 560.205, as a reexportation from a third country "by a person *other than* a United States person," undertaken with knowledge or reason to know such reexportation is intended specifically for Iran.[31] While there is a *de minimis* exception for sales with insignificant dollar values, it contains several restrictions, including:

- The U.S.-origin goods, technology, or services must be *substantially transformed* into a foreign-made product outside the United States (which did not occur for Troll's encryption module).[32]

If such U.S.-origin items do not meet that first condition, then they must meet *all* of the following conditions:

- U.S.-origin goods, technology, or services must constitute less than 10% of the total value of the foreign-made product to be exported from a third country;[33]
- U.S.-origin goods (excluding software) must comprise less than 10% of the foreign-made good (excluding software);[34]
- U.S.-origin software must comprise less than 10% of the foreign-made software;[35]
- U.S.-origin technology must comprise less than 10% of the foreign-made technology; and,
- If the end-product is complex, made of a combination of goods (including software) and technology, the aggregate value of all U.S.-origin goods (including software) and technology in the foreign-made end product **must be less than 10%** of the **total value** of the foreign made product;[36]

---

31. 31 CFR §560.205(a).

32. 31 CFR §560.205(b)(1).

33. 31 CFR §560.205(b)(2). Care must be taken to review, however, the other restrictions that apply. This exception is not what it appears if one reads only §560.205, because it is further limited by §560.420, as we explain in the main text.

34. 31 CFR §560.420(a).

35. 31 CFR §560.420(b).

36. 31 CFR §560.420(d).

Only the reexports to two of the specifically identified customers, Stichting and Mitsukura, would appear to come within that narrow exemption, and further investigation would be required to confirm that such exports met all the restrictions for that exemption to apply.[37] Even for these two, however, there are other remaining impediments:

- Even if the U.S.-origin item meets all the above-conditions, a re-exportation of it to Iran or the Government of Iran is **prohibited** if the foreign-made end product is destined to end uses or end users prohibited under regulations administered by other U.S. government agencies (*e.g.,* the EAR and ITAR).[38]

- In addition, if such reexport is not prohibited under the ITR, such reexport may nevertheless require authorization by the Departments of State, Commerce, or other agencies of the U.S. government.[39]

Although Stichting and Mitsukura are located in countries that have been United States allies for decades, each such customer is named on the currently effective SDN List.

If Troll is not certain that it will complete performance of the respective contracts before the Closing of its acquisition by Agile, then such performance thereafter will be a clear violation of ITR Section 560.418. OFAC strongly opposes completion of transactions by U.S. persons with any party named on the SDN List, and the ITR expressly prohibits U.S. persons from dealing with such persons.

The ITR create an additional risk for Agile's partners. If under the Agile/Troll agreement, Troll *becomes a branch* of Agile at Closing, or if Agile partners become members of Troll's Board of Directors soon after the Closing, Agile must ensure that Troll or the U.S. persons on its Board do not contravene the ITR limits on *export or supply* of goods or technology to Iran or the Government of Iran "**by a *United States person* wherever located**." Here again there is a *de minimis* exemption, but it is even narrower than the one for reexports to Iran or the Government

---

37. There is also an exemption for release of technology or software by a U.S. person to Iranian customers if such technology or software meets the definition of information and informational materials in Section 560.315. For guidance, see first, 31 CFR §560.418, and Note thereto.

38. 31 CFR §560.420, Note 1.

39. 31 CFR §560.420, Note 2.

of Iran by third parties who are not U.S. persons. (Note that the prohibition is not just for such supply to Iran or the Government of Iran, but extends more broadly to encompass supply if "intended specifically or predominantly for Iran or the Government of Iran." In addition, the exemption does not apply to "services," but only to goods and technology.) For such export or supply to meet the *de minimis* exemption, the U.S. person who is exporting or supplying the U.S.-origin item(s) must have *ascertained that all of the following are the case*:[40]

- The U.S.-origin goods or technology must be for "substantial transformation or incorporation[41]" into a foreign-made end product in a country "other than the United States or Iran;"

- The U.S.-origin goods or technology must not have been subject to export license application requirements under *any* United States regulations in effect on May 6, 1995, or thereafter made subject to such regulations imposed independent of the ITR;

- U.S.-origin goods (excluding software) comprise less than 10% of the foreign-made goods;

- U.S.-origin software comprise less than 10% of the foreign-made technology;

- U.S.-origin technology comprise less than 10% of the foreign-made technology;

- The foreign-made end product is not destined to end uses or end users prohibited under regulations administered by other U.S.

---

40. Note that with such obligation to "ascertain" these facts, a U.S. person cannot seek to qualify his or her conduct within the *de minimis* exception by assuming such facts to be true. The TSR imposes an affirmative burden of enhanced due diligence to inquire and verify. Such burden is imposed, of course, because the U.S. person in these instances knows that the export or supply of U.S.-origin items is "intended specifically or predominantly for Iran or the Government of Iran."

41. Note that considerable care must be used in interpretation of the term "incorporation," and one cannot borrow the meaning from regulations issued by other U.S. agencies. As OFAC noted in a letter rejecting a party's claim to qualify for the *de minimis* exception for a U.S. export to a foreign country for reexport to Iran, "OFAC operates under different statutes from the Customs Service (and BIS), and the meaning of 'incorporation' for Customs' (and BIS') purposes may differ from that applied to export or reexport transactions subject to OFAC jurisdiction." *OFAC Letter*, 030331-FACRL-IA-02, March 31, 2003, p. 2, accessed at www.ustreas.gov/offices/eotffc/ofac/rulings/ia207007.pdf.

government agencies (*e.g.,* the EAR or ITAR), and is not intended for use in the Iranian petroleum or petrochemical industry (which the ITR define broadly to include "not only products uniquely suited for use in those industries" such as "oilfield services equipment," but also any for use in products such as "computers, office equipment, construction equipment, or building materials" that may have other uses but which are "intended specifically for use in the [Iranian] petroleum or petrochemical industries").

- In addition, if an item meets all of the above conditions, its export or supply by a U.S. person is **not** authorized if the foreign-made end product is of a type that other U.S. government agencies make ineligible for *de minimis* U.S.-origin content (*e.g.,* the EAR or ITAR).

- And lastly, if the item meets all the conditions for this exception, it may nevertheless require authorization by the U.S. Departments of State, Commerce or other agencies of the U.S. government.[42]

The ITR (like all other TSR) does not provide a great deal of guidance to parties involved in relational or other long-term (multi-month) contracts. The TSR were not drafted to contemplate the various stages of a commercial sale (including the negotiations preceding it and the logistical tail of shipment, transshipment, export and reexport that may be needed to perform it fully). Transactions that involve signings followed months later by closings are simply not addressed. There is, for example, no provision in any TSR that expressly prohibits a party from signing a contract to acquire a company then engaged in on-going business dealing with a party or parties on the SDN List, although one can find clear statements that would prohibit a U.S. person from owning or participating in the governance of such a company.

As a result, compelling arguments can be made that silence on such an important issue implies a policy that condones signing a definitive purchase agreement, provided that all dealings prohibited to U.S. persons cease before or at Closing. Such arguments, while superficially attractive, are not borne out by the enforcement history, however. OFAC takes the position that any economic support for parties named on the SDN List is prohibited by the ITR (and most of the other TSR). Similarly, support of any kind for the Government of Iran is explicitly pro-

---

42. 31 CFR §560.511(a), (b), and Note to §560.511. [Emphasis added.]

hibited by the ITR. When an acquirer signs a definitive purchase agreement, it thereby provides substantial support to the company it is acquiring. The prospect of the purchase may facilitate or otherwise enhance the target company's ability to perform its contracts, including those for or with parties targeted by the ITR.

While no single ITR prohibits Agile from signing the DPA, several provisions make clear that there is a substantial risk that Agile partners (especially those who will be involved in the interim in the governance of Troll, Brugge and Ijsselmeer) would necessarily be drawn into violations of the ITR. Since the ITR provide that "no United States person, wherever located, may approve, finance, **facilitate** . . . any transaction by a foreign person where the transaction by that foreign person would be prohibited" by the ITR "if performed by a United States person,"[43] any facilitation by Agile or its partners—such as advising Troll on any matter that arises in connection with contracts for customers named on the SDN List—would be a clear violation of the ITR.

Since the ITR prohibit any U.S. person, wherever located, from supplying goods, technology or services, if Agile's partners share their financial and commercial expertise with Troll in a way that directly or indirectly supports its performance of contracts for the customers named on the SDN List, such partners and Agile would thereby violate the ITR.[44] Such violations could foreseeably occur repeatedly between signing and Closing the DPA. Several other provisions in the ITR (and other TSR) reinforce this conclusion.[45]

---

43. 31 CFR §560.208.

44. 31 CFR §560.204.

45. Among the interpretative provisions in the ITR there appears the following example: "A United States person is engaged in a prohibited exportation of services to Iran when it extends credit to a third-country firm specifically to enable that firm to manufacture goods for sale to Iran or for an entity of the Government of Iran." 31 CFR §560.410. Arguments that suggest that signing a definitive purchase agreement does not provide substantial support for a company's performance of its outstanding contractual obligations simply overlook the transactional realities. Sellers want such agreements signed for reasons that always include the direct and indirect support that such signings provide immediately to the sellers. For example, the credit worthiness of a target company would be enhanced if it agrees to be purchased by a well-financed buyer, and the target company may not face pressure from certain creditors between the signing and the closing, thereby enabling it to devote increased resources to performance of its outstanding commercial contracts, including those for parties U.S. persons cannot deal with without violating the ITR and other TSR.

2.6 Risks Inherent in Letters of Credit ("L/C") and Stand-By Letters of Credit ("Stand-By L/C").

When reviewing Troll's relationships with financial institutions, counsel found two L/Cs and two Stand-By L/Cs in support of Troll software design and development contracts with two Sudanese customers, Blue Nile Packing Corporation ("Blue Nile"), a manufacturer of packaging paper goods, and Port Sudan Cotton and Trade Company ("Port Sudan Cotton"). These are not ordinary companies. Each appears on OFAC's SDN List and is a high profile party. While OFAC would not countenance violations of the Sudanese Sanctions Regulations,[46] it takes a particularly dim view of violations that occur in conjunction with SDN List parties. Bank of Khartoum Group, a Sudanese bank, issued the L/Cs for Troll's Sudanese customer in favor of Troll. Den Norsk Bank, a Norwegian Bank, confirmed the L/Cs. The L/Cs were in amounts equal to the aggregate amounts that the Sudanese customer would owe to Troll upon Troll's completion of milestones specified in the software development contracts. Den Norsk issued the Stand-By L/Cs for Troll for the benefit of its Sudanese customer. The Stand-By L/Cs were in amounts representing the down payments Troll had received at the start of each of the software development contracts, and could be drawn down in the event of a material breach by Troll in its performance of the software development contracts.

▶ *Prohibited Conduct.* Agile's acquisition of Troll will give it control and possession of what Troll controls and possesses. At the Closing of the acquisition, if Troll were still performing the software development contracts, Agile would be at risk of violating the Sudanese Sanctions Regulations ("SSR")[47] prohibiting, *inter alia,* exportation of services by an entity located in the United States ("including its overseas branches") to Sudan.[48] Such services are not only prohibited from being performed in Sudan, but also in Norway.

---

46. 31 C.F.R. Part 538, accessed at www.ustreas.gov/offices/eotffc/ofac/legal/regs/31cfr538.pdf.

47. 31 C.F.R. Part 538.

48. 31 C.F.R. §538.205 provides, in pertinent part: "exportation or reexportation, directly or indirectly, to Sudan of any goods, technology (including technical data, software, or other information) or services from the United States or by a United States person, wherever located . . . is prohibited."

Such prohibitions apply to services performed by U.S. persons "wherever located" (and Troll, as a future overseas branch of Agile, would be such a person), if such services are on behalf of a Sudanese entity with respect to its property interests or, in this case, relate to transportation of cargo to or from Sudan. The software at issue in this instance would facilitate export and cargo activities by Blue Nile and by Port Sudan Cotton.[49] Such services would also violate the SSR prohibition against performance by any United States person of any "contract . . . in support of an industrial, commercial . . . project in Sudan . . ."[50] by virtue of the fact that they support the commercial activities of Blue Nile and Port Sudan Cotton.

Disengagement from these contracts pose almost intractable problems, however. Troll could try to assign them, but software development contracts typically give the customers the right to withhold approval of such assignments. The customers, Blue Nile and Port Sudan Cotton, could be expected to bargain for substantial compensation and other remuneration in order to give their consent. In addition, Troll's unique skills may make it difficult to find a party ready, willing and able to take over its obligations. To the extent that Troll proprietary data are involved in the design and development project, and that Troll had intended to retain rights to such data, Troll itself will be highly reluctant to disengage. If the contracts are particularly profitable for Troll, that too will increase its reluctance to assign or disengage.

Assuming all such considerations can be resolved by the parties, issues relating to the payments Troll has already received and the outstanding L/Cs and Stand-By L/Cs still remain. If OFAC learns the details of Agile's acquisition of Troll and of Troll's commercial relationships with Blue Nile, Port Sudan Cotton and the Khartoum Bank Group (and

---

49. 31 C.F.R. §538.209, which prohibits "Any transaction by a U.S. person relating to transportation of cargo to or from Sudan." Note, for comparison, that OFAC has published on its website the redacted text of a reply by OFAC Director R. Richard Newcomb to a U.S. person's request for a license under which a U.S. subcontractor could conduct surveys and in-depth interviews with persons in Iran. OFAC's reply cited the Iranian Transactions Regulations, 31 C.F.R. § 560.204 prohibition, *inter alia*, of the direct or indirect exportation of U.S.-origin goods, services, or technology to Iran or its government. OFAC explained that the proposed conduct of surveys and interviews constitutes a prohibited export of services and that the license application, therefore, was denied. Ruling Number: 030424-FACRL-IA-03, April 25, 2003, accessed at www.ustreas.gov/offices/eotffc/ofac/rulings/ia042503.pdf.

50. 31 C.F.R. §538.207.

we assume that it will), it would not be unreasonable for it to take the position that Agile is obligated to block the payments Troll has received that will come within Agile's control upon Closing. Moreover, if at Closing Troll has any outstanding obligations to Blue Nile and Port Sudan Cotton under these contracts (such as warranty, maintenance and repair or replacement of goods lost in shipment), OFAC could contend that Blue Nile and Port Sudan Cotton continue to have an interest in their respective contracts and thereby in the payments received for performance of such contracts. If Blue Nile and Port Sudan Cotton are found to be front companies for the Government of Sudan, or are commercial entities of the Government of Sudan, then under SSR Section 550.201, no property (or interests in property) of the Government of Sudan that "hereafter . . . come within the possession or control of U.S. persons, including their overseas branches, may be transferred, paid, exported, withdrawn or otherwise dealt in."[51] Any transfer of such property by a U.S. person is "null and void."[52] The L/Cs and the Stand-By L/Cs would similarly represent property in which the Government of Sudan continues to have an interest (assuming that it controls Blue Nile and Port Sudan Cotton). If such financial instruments do not expire prior to Closing (and arguably prior to signing), they too must be assigned or terminated before any of Agile's U.S. persons are put at risk of dealing directly or indirectly with them in contravention of the SSR.[53]

2.7 Risks Inherent in Disengagement.

Troll's counsel invited Agile's Danish partners to assist in negotiating the recommended disengagements from activities identified as posing risks to Agile of violating the aforementioned TSR. Agile's counsel learned belatedly of the suggestion, when Agile's Danish partners returned from meetings in Trondheim, where they negotiated several such

---

51. 31 C.F.R. §538.201.

52. 31 C.F.R. §538.202.

53. Sometimes the courts have sustained OFAC's authority to freeze moneys drawn down under an L/C or Stand-By L/C (see *Itek Corporation v. The First National Bank of Boston* 704 F.2d 1 (1st Cir., 1983)), and sometimes they have held that OFAC's target no longer has an interest in the L/C and that independence principle of an L/C, therefore, must take precedence (see *Centrifugal Casting Machine Co., Inc. v. American Bank & Trust Co.*, 966 F. 2d 1348 (10th Cir., 1992)).

disengagement agreements with representatives of entities to whom the Iranian Transaction Regulations and Sudanese Transaction Regulations apply. Such negotiations began with e-mail correspondence, led to meetings in person, and continued thereafter by e-mail. Agile's Danish partners also reached tentative agreement with Troll's executives on the post-signing creation of three new subsidiaries to whom Troll proposed to assign the most valuable contracts that would otherwise pose problems under the ITR and SSR. The assignments would be executed three days after Closing of the DPA. Thereafter, any orders received from Iranian customers, or any transactional communications from the Sudanese customers, would simply be referred to one of these subsidiaries.

▶ *Prohibited Conduct.* Agile's participation in direct negotiations of an agreement for divestment has drawn it into violation of ITR Section 560.206 (which prohibits a U.S. person wherever located from engaging in any transaction or dealing in or related to goods, technology or services for . . . sale or supply to Iran), and of ITR Section 560.208 (which prohibits a U.S. person, wherever located, from approving or facilitating "any transaction by a foreign person" that a U.S. person would be prohibited from performing). This conduct also violates comparable provisions in the SSR.[54] If Agile's partners wished to participate in, or to oversee, such negotiations, they were required to obtain a license from OFAC prior to any such negotiations. Even negotiations for disengagement are arguably within ITR Sections 560.206 and 560.208.

The difficulties in discerning such risks argues for instituting checkpoints *before* negotiations reach such risk points, including checking the SDN List for the names of proposed transactional parties. However, since a violation has now occurred, the question becomes what should Agile do to remedy it? It should be remembered, in this context, that the number of violations will be computed by the number of such actions: since each e-mail transmitted and each individual meeting (including each transfer of interdicted information) constitutes an independent violation within a course of conduct that violates the ITR and the SSR, OFAC certainly will not view all such e-mails and meetings as one infraction, and has considerable charging discretion over the number of infractions it will claim to have occurred. (Each shipment of goods and each transmittal of valuable technical data will in all probability be treated by OFAC as separate infractions, because each provides

---

54. See 31 C.F.R. § 205 and §206, respectively.

benefits that the ITR are designed to interdict.) Agile and Troll must therefore be alerted to the risk of treating this as an "isolated oversight." In addition, and arguably more important, if the terms of the disengagements show an effort to preserve the benefits of the contracts for the parties targeted by the ITR and the SSR, OFAC could also conclude that Agile's partners have sought to evade the ITR and SSR. Each such act of evasion is a separate violation of the applicable regulations—the ITR or SSR.[55] The violations are therefore by no means trivial. A global solution to those and other violations (discussed below) will be required.

▶ *Prohibited Conduct.* The negotiation of a creative corporate solution (creating three Troll subsidiaries, assigning existing ITR and SSR prohibited contracts to them, and referring all future requests for contracts to them) would violate, for example, ITR Section 560.417, which expressly interprets the scope of violations under Section 560.208 (prohibited facilitation). Such prohibited facilitation occurs when a U.S. person (Agile) "Alters its operating policies or procedures, or those of a foreign affiliate, to permit a foreign affiliate to accept or perform a specific contract . . . or transaction involving Iran . . . without the approval of the United States person and such transaction by the foreign affiliate would be prohibited" by the ITR, if performed directly by a United States person.[56] Furthermore, the arrangement to refer future contracts to the subsidiaries would bring Agile into violation of a second provision of Section 560.208, which prohibits a U.S. person from referring to a foreign person "purchase orders, requests for bids, or similar business opportunities involving Iran or its government" and to which the U.S. person could not directly respond as a result of the ITR's prohibitions.[57] Numerous provisions in the SSR would also be violated.[58]

---

55. "Any transaction by any United States person . . . that evades or avoids, or has the purpose of evading or avoiding . . . any of the prohibitions contained" in the ITR is prohibited. 31 CFR §560.203.

56. 31 CFR §560.417(a).

57. 31 CFR §560.417(b).

58. See, for example, 31 CFR §538.407(c) (prohibiting the changing of policies or operating procedures of a foreign affiliate or subsidiary to enable it to enter into a transaction that could not be entered into directly by a U.S. person), 31 CFR §538.407(d) (prohibiting a U.S. person from referring to a "foreign person purchase orders . . . to which the U.S. person could not directly respond as a result of the

➤ *Ill-Advised, but Not Illegal Activity.* During the negotiations over remediation and disengagement, Agile's Danish partners, impatient with the resulting delays, consider a Troll proposal that Troll, on behalf of itself and its affiliates indemnify and hold harmless Agile and its partners for any violations. This would "solve" a multitude of risk management and timing issues, and seems to place the risk of noncompliance on the party best situated to supervise such compliance. In the context of corporate transactions, such risk shifting is not out of the ordinary and makes business sense. Risks are re-allocated all the time. Unfortunately, this solution (so often resorted to) is ill conceived in this specific context due to the regulations we are discussing. Indemnification will not protect Agile's partners, if the OFAC refers cases against them to the Justice Department, especially if Justice decides to seek prison terms for Agile's cognizant partners on any criminal charges. First (not to belabor the obvious), it is difficult to craft an indemnification against imprisonment. Second, indemnification, although not mentioned as an aggravating factor, could reasonably be viewed as "facilitating" behavior (and a violation in itself) as well as evidentiary behavior supporting a conclusion by OFAC that other independent violations were "willful," and OFAC could factor this into a determination of Agile's degree of "willfulness" or culpability. Indemnification of any violations of TSR caused by actions or inactions by Troll between the signing and the Closing could be interpreted by OFAC as evidence that Agile had reason to know (or knew) that TSR violations would occur, and sought indemnification as a remedy in the event of their discovery by OFAC. Agile should avoid this because it could severely discredit voluntary disclosure, if Agile decides such disclosure is necessary. In this manner, a quick fix is transformed into an incriminating circumstance as a result of the specific focus and mandate of these regulations. It should be remembered that the TSR are designed around, and engage in a tacit presumption of, circumvention.

By contrast, if the record shows that Troll proposed, and Agile rejected, such indemnification, then Agile is in a strong position to argue that it insisted that any risk of TSR violations be avoided as a condition for signing (which clearly would be deemed a mitigating factor, if Troll

---

prohibitions contained in this part"), and 31 CFR §538.407(a) (barring any unlicensed action by a U.S. person that assists or supports trading activity with Sudan by any person).

continued dealing with prohibited parties after such signing).[59] Similar considerations will arise when we consider indemnification for patent infringement.

2.8 Global Terrorists.

Mindful of Troll's extensive contacts in the Middle East, and Norway's greater tolerance for such transactions, Agile's counsel obtains from Troll a list of all persons and organizations with which Troll, Brugge and Ijsselmeer (and those acting as agents or otherwise on their behalf) have contracts and for which performance will not be complete prior to signing the DPA, or for which there exist executory contracts or contracts currently in negotiation or that are the subject of current or contemplated bids by Troll, Brugge or Ijsselmeer.

➤ *Prohibited Conduct.* Counsel compares the customer/transactor list to names on the SDN List. This confirms that Troll and Brugge have dealings with several individuals and organizations whose property and interests in property have been blocked, and who are identified on the SDN List by the acronym "SDGT." Such designation signifies that these persons or entities are specially designated global terrorists, such as: Hamas,[60] Hussein Mahamud Abdullkadir (Florence, Italy), Akida Investment Company Limited (Nassau, Bahamas),[61] Baraka Trading Company (Dubai, U.A.E.)[62] and Global Relief Foundation, Inc. (Bridgeview, Illinois).[63] Although other TSR apply, Agile's counsel notes that OFAC's June 6, 2003 promulgation of an interim final rule—the Global Terrorism Sanctions Regulations ("GTSR")—would also apply.

Under the GTSR, any property and/or interests in property of any person or organization identified by OFAC as an SDGT that are, or "hereafter come within the possession or control of U.S. persons including their overseas branches" are blocked.[64] (As OFAC explains,

---

59. Far better that Agile seek a representation from Troll that between signing and closing, if Troll happens to still be involved in dealing or to start dealings that might put Agile into violation of the TSR, cessation of such dealings is a condition for closing.

60. SDN List, p. 50, accessed at www.ustreas.gov/offices/eotffc/ofac/sdn/t11sdn.pdf, accessed on June 27, 2003.

61. Id, p. 5.

62. Id, p. 26.

63. Id, p. 47.

64. 68 FEDERAL REGISTER 109, p. 34198, to be a new section 31 CFR §594.201.

"Blocking" (also known as "freezing") is "simply a way of controlling targeted property. Title to the blocked property remains with the target, but the exercise of powers and privileges normally associated with ownership is prohibited without authorization from OFAC . . .")[65] Not only must Troll and its affiliates cease or disengage from all transactions and other dealings with such persons and organizations before Agile can sign the DPA, but, if any such person's property or interest in property comes into the possession or control of Troll, Brugge or Ijsselmeer after Closing, such property or interest in property must be blocked and reported to OFAC.

The GTSR contain no definition of "possession" or "control." Agile's counsel doubts that signing the DPA would evince possession or control over a SDGT's property merely because it was in Troll's, Brugge's or Ijsselmeer's control or possession. However, since the GTSR also prohibit any "U.S. person" from engaging in "any transaction or dealing in property or interests in property" of a person whose property is blocked under the GTSR (*i.e.,* property belonging to a SDGT),[66] were Agile to sign the DPA before Troll and its affiliates cease dealing in such property (or interests), Agile's partners and Agile would be at risk of contravening the GTSR. It would, therefore, be prudent for Agile to make such disengagements a pre-condition of signing *and to establish a mechanism for verifying such disengagement.*

2.9 Disengagements Required by Implementation of the Syrian Accountability and Lebanese Sovereignty Act of 2003.

Concurrently with the exploratory talks between Agile and Troll, the U.S. Congress enacted the Syrian Accountability and Lebanese Sovereignty Act of 2003 ("SALSA"). SALSA obligated the President of the United States to impose specified sanctions on Syria, if the President could not provide a certification that included, among other things, that the Government of Syria does not provide support for international terrorism.[67] Such certification was unlikely because the Department of

---

65. OFAC, *Frequently Asked Questions,* accessed at www.treas.gov/offices/eotffc/ofac/faq/index.html.

66. 68 FEDERAL REGISTER 109, p. 34200, to be a new section 31 CFR §594.204.

67. *Syria Accountability and Lebanese Sovereignty Restoration Act of 2003,* Pub. Law

State lists Syria as a supporter of international terrorism and criticizes its support, in particular, of the terrorist organization Hezbollah.[68] On May 11, 2004, acting on the authority conferred by the IEEPA and SALSA, President Bush issued an Executive Order to implement SALSA, imposing sanctions that included the following:

- The Secretary of State shall not permit the exportation or reexportation to Syria of any item on the U.S. Munitions List;

- The Secretary of Commerce shall not permit the exportation or reexportation to Syria of any item on the Commerce Control List, and with the exception of food and medicine, shall not permit exportation or reexportation of any product of the United States; and

- All property and interests in property of specified persons shall be blocked, including, for example, anyone significantly contributing (i) to the Government of Syria's provision of safe haven or other support for any person whose property or interests in property the United States has blocked for terrorism-related reasons (such as Hamas, Hezbollah, and Palestinian Islamic Jihad), (ii) the Government of Syria's military or security presence in Lebanon, or (iii) the Government of Syria's pursuit of the development and production of chemical, biological, nuclear weapons, or medium- and long-range surface-to-surface missiles.[69]

In 2003, when SALSA was signed into law, Agile had alerted Troll that if Troll, Brugge or Ijsselmeer were engaged in any transactions that might be targeted by SALSA, those would need to be examined closely by Agile before the signing of the DPA. Agile reminded Troll of the risks when, in early spring 2004, the newspapers began to report that it seemed probable that President Bush would implement SALSA in the near future.[70] The sanctions were much less comprehensive, however,

108-175, December 12, 2003, accessed at http://frwebgate.access.gpo.gov/cgi-bin/getdoc.cgi?dbname = 108_cong_public_laws&docid = f:publ175.108.pdf.

68. U.S. Department of State, *Sanctions on Syria: Implementing the Syria Accountability and Lebanese Sovereignty Act of 2003*, fact sheet, May 11, 2004, accessed at www.state.gov/p/nea/rls/32396.htm.

69. Executive Order 13338 of May 11, 2004, Sections 1(a) and (b), and 3(a)(i), (ii), and (iii).

70. See Marquis, Christopher, *U.S. Is Expected to Put Penalties on Syria*, THE NEW YORK TIMES, March 26, 2004, p. A-9, reporting that the U.S. Administration had hard-

than those imposed on Iran and Sudan. As implemented by Executive Order 13338 and a General Order of the BIS,[71] SALSA does not prohibit U.S. persons from investing in Syria, but U.S. firms that have operations in Syria cannot import goods from the U.S. to service their Syrian operations and will need to procure from suppliers outside of the United States. Troll had no contracts with Syrian entities, and as a precaution, made no new contracts with Syrian entities, but decided to continue to allow its affiliate Brugge to continue to perform existing pharmaceutical contracts there.

One of Brugge's contracts, arranged by one of its Middle East agents Iqbal Merchant (operating out of the United Arab Emirates), involved the provision of vaccination kits for animal disease control, specifically diseases contracted by animals such as dromedaries, goats, sheep and cattle. Brugge procured the vaccines from U.S. suppliers, added inoculation tools and instructions translated into Arabic, and sold them under contract to Syrian pharmaceutical firms in Damascus. In this manner, Brugge supplied vaccine kits for *sheep pox* and *goat pox virus* (diseases that are endemic in the Middle East).[72] Brugge also supplied vaccine kits for *bluetongue*, a virus most commonly found in fine-wool and mutton grades of sheep.[73]

> ➤ *Prohibited Conduct:* **Re-Export of Vaccines Prohibited by the EAR are Prohibited under the SALSA.** When the U.S. implemented the SALSA, Agile notified Troll, forwarded the State Department "Fact Sheet" on SASLA outlining the scope of the sanctions, and asked if Troll knew of any transactions that might contravene SALSA (on completion of Agile's acquisition of Troll, Brugge and Ijsselmeer). In response to

---

ened its position after concluding in February 2004 that Syria was "ferrying weapons from Iran to radical anti-Israel groups in Lebanon." The U.S. position may have also been in response to the fact that U.S. troops in Iraq were engaged in interdicting foreign fighters seeking to infiltrate across the Syrian-Iraq border in order to participate in uprisings in Iraq. See Marquis, Christopher, *Bush Imposes Sanctions on Syria, Citing Ties to Terrorism*, THE NEW YORK TIMES, May 12, 2004, p. A-10.

71. General Order Implementing Syria Accountability and Lebanese Sovereignty Act of 2003, 15 CFR Part 736, 69 FEDERAL REGISTER 94, pp. 26766–26768.

72. See The World Organization for Animal Health or OIE website, *Sheep Pox and Goat Pox*, updated April 22, 2002, accessed at www.oie.int/eng/maladies/fiches/A_A100.HTM.

73. See European Commission Health & Consumer Protection Directorate-General, Committee on Animal Health and Animal Welfare, *Possible Use of Vaccination against Bluetongue in Europe*, June 27, 2000, p. 8.

Troll's summary of Brugge's contracts, counsel requested copies of the contracts between Brugge and (i) its agent Iqbal Merchant, (ii) its U.S. suppliers of the vaccines and (iii) its Syrian customers. Troll objected to this request and, based on its reading of Executive Order 13338, asked why its pharmaceutical contracts did not fall within a clear exception for "medicines."

While such an exception is contained in Executive Order 13338, Counsel explained that the term "medicines" did not have a layman's meaning. When Agile ultimately reviewed the documents, it also noted that the U.S. suppliers had obtained licenses for export of the vaccines only to Norway. These licenses did not cover any reexport. This omission created additional compliance problems.

Agile explained its view as follows: the final rule published by the BIS includes two categories of "medicine" under the SALSA: (i) "medicines" that are classified as EAR99, which do not require a license for export or reexport to Syria; and (ii) all other "medicines" that are subject to EAR control. The rule further explains that "medicine is defined in part 772 of the EAR," the definitions section of the EAR.[74] Part 772 notes that "certain medicines, such as vaccines and immunotoxins, are on the Commerce Control List."[75] As such, those "vaccines and immunotoxins" required a license for export or reexport to Syria even before SALSA was implemented, and SALSA's subsequent implementation did not relax those controls. Under SALSA, one should anticipate closer scrutiny by the BIS of any request for a license to export or reexport such medicines to Syria.

On the Commerce Control List, ECCN IC991 covers vaccines against items controlled by ECCNs, including ECCN 352 for "animal pathogens." The Commerce Control List imposes controls on vaccines designed to treat the animal pathogens listed under ECCN 352, which include the animal diseases for which Brugge contracts to provide vaccines to its Syrian customers, namely "bluetongue" and "sheep pox virus." (While such a level of specificity may seem foolish, at first glance, it is important to remember the anti-proliferation (of weapons of mass destruction) and anti-terrorism rationales included in the EAR.)

---

74. General Order Implementing Syria Accountability and Lebanese Sovereignty Act of 2003, 69 Federal Register 94, p. 26767.

75. EAR, Part 772, definition of "Medicines," p. 17, accessed at www.access.gpo.gov/bis/ear/pdf/772.pdf.

Brugge's reexport of vaccines to immunize against those animal path-ogens thus does not come within the exception in SALSA, but remains controlled by the EAR. Both pathogens are controlled for reasons of chemical and biological weapons (CB) and anti-terrorism (AT). ECCN 352 notes that it controls those pathogens on the Country Chart for CB (column 1) and AT (column 1). In plain English, one looks at the Country Chart, finds the destination country, and sees if there is an "X" in the CB column 1 or AT column 1. For Norway, there is no "X" in AT column 1, but there is an "X" in CB column 1. To export this pathogen (or a vaccine to immunize against it) to Norway, one must first obtain a license from the BIS. (Vaccines for pathogens are con-trolled, because parties intent on the production, transfer or deploy-ment of biological weapons need the vaccine to protect themselves dur-ing such activities. Thus vaccine exports are as sensitive as exports of the pathogens themselves.) At the time that Brugge entered into its contracts with its U.S. suppliers of those vaccines, it had received some expressions of interest from several countries for its vaccine kits, but did not know which ones would actually sign contracts. Its suppliers apparently did obtain licenses for export of the bluetongue and sheep pox vaccines to Norway, but did not obtain licenses for reexport of those vaccines.

Agile's concludes that Brugge must notify its suppliers and, only if they can obtain licenses, would it be lawful under the EAR for Brugge (once acquired by Agile) to reexport the vaccines to Syria. However, the final rule cautions that, with very few exceptions not relevant here, "All license applications for exports or reexports to Syria are subject to a general policy of denial."[76] If the contracts will not be completed before the parties sign the DPA, Agile will not be comfortable signing, because it does not want its signature to be viewed as supporting or facilitating reexport in violation of the EAR. It is also concerned that products might be in the pipeline for shipment that would continue to flow after the scheduled Closing, and would compound the appearance of a vio-lation by Agile. Agile's concern is well-founded: newspaper articles have recently reported the arrival in Libya of a previously unreported ship-ment of sophisticated steel centrifuges for uranium enrichment, three months after Libya declared that it had abandoned its nuclear weapons

76. General Order Implementing Syria Accountability and Lebanese Sovereignty Act of 2003, 69 FEDERAL REGISTER 94, p. 26767.

programme.[77] Logistic tails tend to take much longer than anticipated to wind up completely, and Agile is unwilling to take such a chance.

Agile notifies Troll that it must cease doing business with its Middle East agent and must find a way to disengage from the contractual obligations. Pursuant to a periodic check of the names of Troll's transactional parties, Agile has discovered that OFAC has just added several names to the SDN List, including that of Troll's Middle East agent, Iqbal Merchant, identified by OFAC as a significant foreign narcotics trafficker or SDNTK. Troll dislikes being pressed into another disengagement, but it acknowledges the good fortune that it learned from Agile about Merchant's parallel activities, instead of from the Økokrim (Norwegian National Authority for Investigation and Prosecution of Economic and Environmental Crime).[78]

When Agile's Counsel asks whether Troll's counsel has spotted any "red flags" that should have alerted it to Merchant's narcotics dealings, counsel replies with the Norwegian adage: "all cats are grey in the dark."[79] However, Troll takes advantage of its *force majeure* clause with Merchant, terminating the contract on the ground that a government action (OFAC's placement of Merchant on the SDN List) constitutes an event of *force majeure*.

---

77. One example Agile sent included: Fidler, Stephen, *Centrifuges Shipped to Libya Could Reveal Clues about Khan Network*, FINANCIAL TIMES, May 29/May 30, 2004, p. 2.

78. The Økokrim, established in 1989, is a special unit for white-collar crime and is both a national police unit and a prosecution authority, as explained at its website, www.okokrim.no. The Økokrim investigates, among other violations, money laundering, stock market and securities violations, environmental, computer crimes (such as hacking), and information handling offenses. It was the Økokrim that investigated and prosecuted 19-year-old Jon Lech Johansen for copyright violation in reverse engineering a bypass of DVD DeCSS code protection. See *"DVD-Jon" Faces Retrial*, AFTENPOSTEN, January 20, 2003, accessed at www.aftenposten.no/english/local/article474756.ece.

As discussed in the introduction of this book, when Statoil ASA signed a consultancy agreement with a foreign consultant company, the Økokrim's Corruption Team initiated an investigation that led to Statoil being formally charged with violation of the Norwegian General Civil Penal Code provision concerning illegal influencing of foreign government officials. The Økokrim's scope includes cooperating with anti-terrorism efforts, as occurred when the U.S. government accused Mullah Krekar of planning terror actions (suicide missions) by signals distributed on the Internet—as a result of which the Økokrim confiscated large amounts of recordings of Mullah Krekar's activity on the Internet. See *CIA Misinformed about Ansar*, Nettavisen, January 8, 2004, accessed at http://pub.tv2.no/nettavisen/english/article170292.ece.

79. *I mørke er alle katter grå.*

> *Prohibited Conduct:* **Re-Export under a License Granted Prior to Implementation of SALSA.** Agile's General Counsel checks Agile's dealings for any that might no longer be lawful under SALSA's implementing order and regulations, and distributes a company-wide e-mail asking if any Agile aeronautical or other products are exported directly to Syria or are supplied to out-of-country recipients who might be reexporting to Syria. In connection with this, he drops in on the warranty repairs unit for aircraft parts and asks to see a list of parties that have returned parts for warranty repair. Seeing an acronym he does not recognize—*SAA*—he asks to review the transmittal documents. The warranty claim was filed by an aerospace firm in Toulon, France, on behalf of their customer, SAA—referred to variously in the documents as Syrian Arab Airline and SyrianAir. The submittals are dated March 22, 2004, and stamped "received" March 31, 2004. Agile has almost finished repairs, and is scheduled to ship them back to Toulon the next week. General Counsel is confident that the Toulon supplier will reexport the repaired parts to SAA, or will install them on SAA aircraft during a future overhaul or maintenance. The paperwork confirms as much, and Agile has previously obtained an export license from the BIS that covers reexport of the parts to Syria.

General Counsel confers by phone with outside counsel who asks the dollar value of the repairs (what Agile would have charged if the warranty period had expired) and whether the parts are safety-critical for the aircraft. The documents contain an aggregate repair cost of approximately $125,000 for two parts, and suggest that they are indeed safety-critical. Under these circumstances, the BIS's rule, or General Order on SALSA, "revokes" the authority to export or reexport to Syria under existing licenses. The General Order, however, permits the BIS to consider on a case-by-case basis, license applications for export or reexport of aircraft parts, because the President exercised a national security waiver under Section 5(b) of SALSA allowing BIS to make certain exceptions, including one for "parts and components intended to ensure the safety of civil aviation and the safe operation of commercial passenger aircraft." However, the total value of each approved license for aircraft parts essential to flight safety normally will be limited to no more than $2 million over the 24-month standard license term (except in the case of complete overhauls).[80]

Agile's General Counsel must decide whether to apply to BIS to grant a license for reexport under that exception. He would prefer not to

---

80. General Order Implementing Syria Accountability and Lebanese Sovereignty Act of 2003, 69 FEDERAL REGISTER 94, p. 26767. The U.S. Administration personnel

draw BIS' attention to Agile's indirect business with SyrianAir, nor to undertake the burden of the disclosures BIS might require before determining whether these circumstances justified a license exemption. The French customer in Toulon, however, has purchased a substantial quantity of Agile's products and has increased its orders despite the political differences between the two countries. The French aerospace firm was clearly within its contractual rights to request the warranty repair, rights that it paid additional compensation to receive, and will have good reason to react negatively to any suggestion of new conditions placed on repairs under warranty. For example, Agile could propose to condition its provision of repaired parts on receiving assurances that the Toulon company would not reexport the parts or install them on an SAA aircraft. Agile's General Counsel strongly doubts that the French firm would be willing to give such an assurance or to honor it if it did. Moreover, it will expect Agile first to try to obtain the requisite license for reexport by the French supplier to SAA. (Even if the French firm installs the parts on SAA aircraft during maintenance in Toulon, those aircraft are based at Damascus airport, and such installation would be viewed by the BIS as a reexport to Syria.)

In response to commercial practicalities, Agile files an application that makes clear that the parts will in all likelihood be reexported to the end-user, SAA, in Syria and that they are needed to ensure the safety of SAA's civilian aircraft. At the same time, General Counsel sends a memorandum to the warranty repair unit that they are to notify him on a going-forward basis each time they receive a warranty repair request for SAA. If the license is granted, he anticipates that it will contain the proviso that it cover no more than $2 million for the 24-month term of the license. He also anticipates that BIS will be slow to rule on the

---

who recommended and crafted this exception should be commended. Although there is irony in a post-9/11 anti-terrorist embargo that makes exceptions for the safe use of aircraft by a terrorist sponsoring government, little would be gained, and much would be lost, were an air tragedy to claim the lives of hundreds of Arab civilians because the U.S., in targeting Syria, cut off the supply of spares for U.S.-manufactured civilian aircraft. The Administration also added deft political nuance to SALSA by further broadening this "safety of civil aviation" exception to include "aircraft chartered by the Syrian Government for the transport of Syrian Government officials on official Syrian Government business." Here the concern seems to be to avert an accident that could destabilize or decapitate a government, and also to send a muted signal that the Administration has applied a measured response and has not sought by SALSA to implement any "regime change" policy. Whether such nuance will be appreciated in Damascus we cannot know, but the Administration deserves credit for sophisticated, sensitive refinements of SALSA that are not expressed or suggested in the text of the Act.

license, and that the French customer can be expected to question the delay. His recommendations, however, have steered Agile away from inadvertent violations of SALSA, and spared it the associated investigation time, fines, adverse publicity and related costs. He notes the ongoing need to audit Agile's compliance program to ensure that it will detect and avert such risks in the future.

2.10 Global Solution: Should Agile Voluntarily Disclose Violations Discovered by Enhanced Due Diligence?

Troll's counsel will no doubt oppose any action voluntarily to disclose violations discovered in the course of its diligence, fearing that the adverse publicity will cause problems with its best customer, the Norwegian MoD. In addition, Agile's own partners might initially resist a voluntary disclosure of the ITR violations to OFAC. Voluntary disclosure could prompt an investigation, and no Agile partner wants OFAC (and potentially the Justice Department) to have access to its documents, correspondence, files, internal communications, etc. There is arguably no specific requirement in the ITR to report such violations. (There are, however, other actions that require ancillary reporting under some TSR, such as the blocking of property. A client cannot avoid the reporting obligation by failing to block property deemed to be within its control, and OFAC would probably pursue more aggressive enforcement measures against failure to block substantial property, than against failure to report such blockage.) Agile's best interests may well rest in a prompt voluntary disclosure. Delay runs the risk that OFAC will learn of the violations "from another source." At that point, it will be too late to procure the substantial mitigating benefits of voluntary disclosure (including the 50% reduction in civil penalties). Failure to make a voluntary disclosure could also be viewed as violating the prohibition against evading the ITR, particularly if non-disclosure facilitates the completion of transactions that the ITR seek to interdict.

Agile may reasonably believe that by negotiating disengagement it effectively ensured that the disengagement would be thorough and would be completed before Agile signed the DPA. There are alternative, arguably more effective, methods that would not have drawn Agile into violations of the ITR. The question, from Counsel's and the Company's point of view, is of course how probable it is that OFAC will learn of the violations from "another source." Anyone who has trolled the World Wide Web for information knows that parties are often indiscriminate about disclosing transactions on their website. Troll's annual report could routinely be posted on Troll's website, together this time with references to Agile's arrangements for disengagement in full compliance with U.S. trade sanction regulations. The targeted SDN parties might also make use of the Web to post such disclosures for their own purposes (political as well as economic). When an official at OFAC reads the press releases of the signing of the DPA, its own web search could bring many facts to light that Agile believed would remain confidential. Other agencies of the U.S. government, by data mining and other global scans of the Internet, frequently intercept evidence of violations. The more serious the violations, the more compelling becomes the case in favor of voluntary disclosure. Moreover, inadvertent errors are often compounded (and appear willful) if followed by willful non-disclosure (particularly when OFAC has structured voluntary disclosure to provide substantial benefits).

Because willful violations will in all probability be referred by OFAC to the Justice Department for possible criminal prosecution, the situation presents one of the most difficult compliance issues for Agile—the choice between voluntary disclosure (which might precipitate an investigation) and remediation by Agile with no disclosure to OFAC. Agile's error was clearly not intended to circumvent the ITR and, although that would argue that disclosure poses a relatively low risk, there will always be institutional resistance to what is perceived as unnecessary or overzealous disclosure (with the concomitant risk of adverse publicity). We would note, however, that for companies who have a compliance policy in place prior to a violation of the TSR, any discrepancy between such policy and the company's subsequent conduct poses the risk of being deemed an "aggravating factor."

2.11 Risks from Laws Blocking Compliance with the TSR and Providing "Clawback" Remedies.

Agile's counsel has found no dealings between Troll, Brugge or Ijsselmeer and the targets of the Cuban Sanction Regulations ("CSR") or the U.S. Cuban Liberty and Democratic Solidarity Act of 1996 ("Helms-Burton").[81] Otherwise, Agile's Counsel would need to determine whether compliance with such laws would put Agile, Troll, Brugge and Ijsselmeer at risk of contravening laws passed in other countries that prohibit companies in their jurisdictions from complying with U.S. laws (specifically prohibiting dealing with the Government of Cuba). Unlike the TSR discussed above, the CSR extend their reach to subsidiaries of U.S. persons. The CSR prohibit dealings in property by "any person subject to the jurisdiction of the United States," if such dealings involve property in which Cuba or a Cuban national has "any interest of any nature whatsoever, direct or indirect."[82] Helms-Burton includes in its Title III, a provision strongly opposed by many U.S. allies: a right of action by U.S. citizens against foreign companies that traffic in U.S. assets expropriated by the Government of Cuba. Enactment of Helms-Burton caused a contretemps between the United States and many of its allies and trading partners, whose residual effects continue to the present. The European Union ("EU"), United Kingdom ("UK"), Canada and Mexico, among others, have legislation that prohibits cooperation or compliance with Helms-Burton.

European Council Regulation No. 2271/96 of November 22, 1996 (the "Blocking Statute") applies to all persons specified in its Article 11, including: (i) any natural person resident in the European Community and any national of a Member State, (ii) any legal person incorporated within the Community, and (iii) any natural person within the Community, including its territorial waters and air space, and in any aircraft or on any vessel under the jurisdiction or control of a Member State, **acting in a professional capacity.**"[83] (Despite its concerns with terri-

---

81. Helms-Burton, *inter alia,* gives U.S. citizens a right of action against foreign companies for damages caused by such companies' investment in U.S. property confiscated by Cuba.

Note that from January through November 2004, the Treasury Department has reportedly imposed penalties on 60 companies for violations of the Cuban Sanctions Regulations, including certain "high-profile fines" imposed on the Spanish airline Iberia (for transporting 480kg of Cuban cigars bound for Costa Rica via Florida) and on the German car manufacturer, DaimlerChrysler for exports by its Mexican subsidiary, DaimlerChrysler Vehículos Comerciales. See Moré, Iñigo, *DaimlerChrysler fine may damage US-EU relations,* FINANCIAL TIMES, November 16, 2004, p. 5.

82. 31 C.F.R. §515.201.

83. European Council Regulation No. 2271/96, Official Journal No. L309, 29/11/1996, Article 11 accessed at www.eurunion.org/legislat/extrel/cuba/cuba1.htm. [Emphasis added.]

torial waters and air space, the Blocking Statute does not specifically address a Member State's jurisdiction over its cyberspace.) The Blocking Statute provides, in relevant part:

> "No person referred to in Article 11 shall comply, whether directly or through a subsidiary or other intermediary person, actively or by deliberate omission, with any requirement or prohibition, including requests of foreign courts, based on or resulting, directly or indirectly, from the laws specified in the Annex [Helms-Burton and the Iran and Libya Sanctions Act of 1996 ("ILSA")[84]] or from actions based thereon or resulting therefrom."[85]

The Blocking Statute also provides for recovery of damages (including legal costs) caused by application of Helms-Burton and the ILSA (a remedy referred to as a "clawback").[86] Such clawback provides an opportunity for parties to recover in their own courts damages that might be caused, for example, by Helms-Burton's provision for suits against those who traffic in U.S. assets expropriated by Cuba. On April 11, 1997, the U.S. agreed with the EU upon a protocol for averting conflicts between the Blocking Statute and Helms-Burton (the "Understanding on Extraterritorial Legislation" or "Understanding"). The Understanding applies to both the Helms-Burton and the ILSA. Essentially, it states that the EU and US "agreed to disagree," while stepping up their efforts to develop agreed "Disciplines for Strengthening Investment Protection Against Expropriation." In the interim, a waiver of Title III of Helms Burton (the provision permitting suits against those who traffic in expropriated assets) has been granted to the EU.[87] A second Understanding, conditioned on Congressional approval, was reached in May 1998, but did not receive the requisite approval by Congress.[88] President Clin-

---

84. Pub. Law 104-172, August 5, 1996, accessed at http://frwebgate.access.gpo.gov/cgi-bin/getdoc.cgi?dbname=104_cong_public_laws&docid=f:publ172.104.pdf. Since the ILSA addresses only foreign support for Iran's petroleum industry, Agile's counsel was spared having to address conflicts between the ILSA and blocking laws prohibiting compliance with the ILSA.

85. European Council Regulation No. 2271/96, Official Journal No. L309, 29/11/1996 Article 5, accessed at www.eurunion.org/legislat/extrel/cuba/cuba1.htm.

86. Id, Article 6.

87. House of Commons, *Cuba and the Burton Act*, Research Paper 98/114, December 14, 1998, p. 37, accessed at www.parliament.uk/commons/lib/research/rp98/rp98-114.pdf.

88. Id. Note, however, that "Throughout the episode the EU was more concerned with the effects of the ILSA than Helms-Burton, not least because of the higher levels of trade and investment with Iran and Libya than with Cuba." House of Commons,

ton suspended Title III for successive six-month periods throughout his second term in office.[89] President Bush has repeatedly renewed the suspension.[90]

Canadian blocking legislation, the Foreign Extraterritorial Measures Act ("FEMA"), adopted by Parliament in 1984, took effect in 1985. Thus, except for amendments that came into force on January 1, 1997, FEMA (which predates Helms-Burton) covered several disputes between the U.S. and Canada such as the uranium cartel litigation, the Bank of Nova Scotia subpoenas case and the Siberian pipeline embargo.[91] The original FEMA authorized Canada's Attorney General (upon concurrence of the Minister of Foreign Affairs) to issue orders blocking compliance by "person[s] in Canada" with non-Canadian trade laws that "adversely affect" Canadian trade interests. When amended, it covered "all extraterritorial U.S. measures taken at all levels of government aimed at impeding trade between Canada and Cuba."[92] Such measures were defined to include the CSR and "any law, statute, regulation, by-law, ordinance, order, judgment, ruling, resolution, denial of authorization, directive, guideline or other enactment, instrument, decision or communication having a purpose similar to that of the Cuban Assets Control Regulations."[93] It contained the following broad prohibition:

"No Canadian corporation and no director, officer, manager or employee in a position of authority of a Canadian corporation shall,

Cuba and the Burton Act, Research Paper 98/114, December 14, 1998, p. 40, accessed at www.parliament.uk/commons/lib/research/rp98/rp98-114.pdf.

89. See U.S. Department of State, International Information Programs, *Text: Bush Informs Congress of Need to Renew Helms-Burton Title III Suspensions*, January 17, 2002, accessed at usinfo.state.gov/regional/ar/us-cuba/burton17.htm.

90. See, for example, U.S. Department of State, International Information Programs, *Text: Bush Informs Congress of Need to Renew Helms-Burton Title III Suspensions*, January 17, 2002, accessed at http://usinfo.state.gov/regional/ar/us-cuba/burton17.htm, and *Text: Bush Extends Suspension of Title III of Helms-Burton Act*, July 16, 2003, accessed at http://usinfo.state.gov/regional/ar/us-cuba/bush17.htm.

91. See Forsythe, Douglas H., *Canada: Foreign Extraterritorial Measures Act Incorporating the Amendments Countering the U.S. Helms-Burton Act*, 36 I.L.M. 111 (1997), accessed at www.asil.org/ilm/canada.htm.

92. Department of Foreign Affairs and International Trade, *Canada Amends Order Blocking U.S. Trade Restrictions*, January 18, 1996, accessed at www.canadiannetworkoncuba.ca/Documents/FEMA-96.shtml.

93. Foreign Extraterritorial Measures (United States) Order, 1992, accessed at www.canadiannetworkoncuba.ca/Documents/FEMA-96.shtml#Order.

in respect of any trade or commerce between Canada and Cuba, comply with an extraterritorial measure of the United States or with any directive, instruction, intimation of policy or other communication relating to such a measure that the Canadian corporation or director, officer, manager or employee has received from a person who is in a position to direct or influence the policies of the Canadian corporation in Canada."[94]

Though Agile's Counsel was spared the conflicting provisions of the CSR and Helms-Burton as well as the Canadian FEMA and other blocking laws, he nonetheless felt it necessary to maintain a checkpoint for such conflicting obligations in future transactions.[95] Norway has not enacted "blocking" legislation (otherwise substantial additional problems might have existed). There is considerable residual hostility towards Helms-Burton and, as a result, raising the issue of compliance with the TSR, EAR and ITAR often proves a flash-point in negotiations with overseas companies and their counsel.

2.12 Provision of Internet Connectivity Services to Iran.

Agile, like other providers of Internet connectivity services, was interested in providing such services to Iran. Pursuant to requests and inquires in this connection, OFAC published guidance on June 3, 2003,[96] noting that such services to Iran fall within the scope of the ITR (by virtue of providing services to persons in Iran, its government, or where the benefit is otherwise received in Iran). OFAC determined that such services to civilian customers in Iran could be authorized "on a case-

---

94. Id.

95. See also the United Kingdom's Protection of Trading Interests Act of 1980, 21 I.L.M. 834 (1982) and similar legislation enacted by Australia, Canada, France, and the Netherlands from the 1940's through 1980's. Muris, Timothy J., *The Interface of Competition and Consumer Protection* (prepared remarks of the Chairman of the Federal Trade Commission at the Fordham Corporate Law Institute's Twenty-Ninth Annual Conference on International Antitrust Law and Policy), October 31, 2002, footnote 28, accessed at www.ftc.gov/speeches/muris/021031fordham.pdf.

96. *Guidance on the Provision of Internet Connectivity Services*, 030606-FACRL-1A-07, June 3, 2003, accessed at www.treas.gov/offices/enforcement/ofac/rulings/ia060603.pdf.

by-case basis by specific license," but with certain limitations: the main purpose must be to benefit the people of Iran through increased access to information,[97] and the license applicant must state "or otherwise confirm" the following:

(i) That the specific Internet services such applicant would provide can be received in Iran using non-U.S. origin goods, technology and software that may be exported to Iran by non-U.S. persons without violating the ITR;[98]

(ii) That in connection with providing such services, no goods, technology or software will be exported directly or indirectly to Iran from the U.S., **or by U.S. persons, wherever located or by non-U.S. persons**, in violation of the ITR;[99]

(iii) That, in connection with providing such services, if the applicant wishes to do so through a third-country company, such company will not export or reexport, directly or indirectly, any goods, technology or software to Iran in violation of ITR §560.205.[100]

Any licenses OFAC might issue pursuant to this guidance would, in any event, not authorize a U.S. person to act as the "provider of end-user Internet or telecommunications services (including private network services offered via satellite) to Iran, the Government of Iran, or any person in Iran."[101] Thus OFAC takes the view that providers of such Internet services can interdict, and are responsible for preventing, the transmission or transfer of items (such as software) to parties in Iran. That the service provider must "otherwise confirm" the veracity of its compliance suggests that the service provider must be able to provide substantial documentation of its position in its license application. It is not possible to ascertain from the text of OFAC's guidance whether this reflects an increased awareness that such interdicting or blocking capabilities can be obtained and implemented by Internet service provid-

---

97. No doubt driven by U.S. foreign policy objectives, and the belief that such access to information from abroad in Iran may serve U.S. objectives.

98. In particular, ITR §§ 560.204 or 560.205.

99. In particular, ITR §§ 560.204 or 560.205. [Emphasis added.]

100. *Guidance on the Provision of Internet Connectivity Services*, 030606-FACRL-1A-07, June 3, 2003, accessed at www.treas.gov/offices/enforcement/ofac/rulings/ia060603.pdf.

101. Id.

ers, but it seems reasonable to infer that. Encryption services, in all probability, cannot be used to protect such provider from the need to comply with the ITR (as interpreted by OFAC's June 2003 guidance).[102]

Preliminary Action Items for Checkpoint TSR

- Map the risk points under the TSR by compiling a list of all countries whose entities are involved in the transaction or whose entities transact with the parties to the deal ("**Significant Countries List**")
- Compile a list of the target firm's affiliates, nationals (among its personnel), suppliers, customers, subcontractors, outsourcing parties, agents, freight forwards, financial institutions, carriers, visitors and other third parties with whom the target firm routinely transacts (including their chief officers) ("Significant Parties List")
- Note the countries of origin and in which they conduct business or operations.
- Check OFAC's website for a list of all countries currently targeted by the TSR and ascertain if any of those appear on the transaction's Significant Countries List.
- Treat each such country as a high risk point under the TSR.
- Check the names on the Significant Parties List against those that appear in each of the following relevant government lists:
  - ➤ OFAC's Specially Designated Nationals List
  - ➤ Embargoed Countries List (for TSR)
  - ➤ Terrorism List Countries (identified by State Department and thereby subject to the Terrorism Sanction Regulations)
- Compile a list of all end-user destinations for products, goods, technical data, and services sold, leased or licensed by the target firm and its affiliates.

---

102. Thus OFAC's position on this issue comes very close, although only implicitly, to the reasoning by the Seventh Circuit in its subsequent June 30, 2003, affirmance in *In Re: Aimster.*

CHAPTER 3

Checkpoint: Export Administration Regulations

3.0 Agile's Transaction at Checkpoint EAR.

The EAR implement U.S. export control policy on dual-use commodities, software and technology. "Dual-use" signifies items that have predominantly civilian use, but may also have military, proliferation or terrorism uses. The EAR also provide a "first line of defense" against the proliferation of weapons of mass destruction, and serve the ultimate goal of preventing U.S.-origin items from being diverted "into the hands of rogue nations, terrorists, and those who would use the goods and technologies" against the United States, its allies and countries with whom it has friendly relations.[1] Exports of items not otherwise controlled by other U.S. federal agencies are generally controlled by the Department of Commerce, primarily through the EAR (but note that many items are jointly controlled by the Departments of Commerce and State). The scope of such controls can be found primarily in the definition of what is "subject to the EAR" and in the EAR's enumerated "ten General Prohibitions." However, the EAR extends its controls in many unexpected (often inconsistent or unclear) ways that necessitate

---

1. Lichtenbaum, Peter, *International Smuggling Networks: Weapons of Mass Destruction Counterproliferation Initiatives*, testimony before the Senate Committee on Governmental Affairs Subcommittee on Financial Management, the Budget, and International Security, June 23, 2004, accessed at www.bxa.doc.gov/News/2004/PeterTmony6_23_04.htm.

a careful consideration of accepted assumptions about "export controls."[2] Examples of unexpected coverage by EAR include:

(i)   Export controls on domestic conduct—the EAR controls transfers or "releases" of technology, technical data and software *even if such items never leave United States territory*;

(ii) Export controls on overseas conduct involving U.S.-origin content: the EAR controls reexports of items manufactured overseas (if the products include more than a *de minimis* amount of U.S.-origin content and, in some instances, products if they have any amount of certain highly sensitive U.S.-origin content);

(iii) Export controls on overseas conduct involving a small number of products that contain no U.S.-origin content: the EAR controls exports by a "U.S. person" (such as an overseas branch of a U.S. firm) of certain items consisting wholly of non-U.S. origin materials when such items are intended for an end-user in Rwanda; and

(iv) Export controls that do not fit apparent definitions of the EAR's scope (so-called "catch all" controls): although the focus of EAR's controls is on the "dual use" items specified on the Commerce Control List ("CCL") in connection with the Enhanced Proliferation Control Initiative ("EPCI") (Part 744 of the EAR), these controls (which apply "[i]n addition to the license requirements for items specified on the CCL") require a license for export or reexport of *any item to any country* if the BIS has informed the U.S. person (or such person otherwise "*knows*" as defined in the EAR) that such item (product, service, technology, technical data or software) "will be used directly or indirectly" in specified conduct related to, among other things, **nuclear** activities, **maritime nuclear propulsion** end-uses, **missile** end-uses or **chemical** and **biological** weapons end-uses.[3]

---

2. Some lack of clarity is the unavoidable result of attempts to harmonize U.S. export controls with the multi-lateral control regimes in which the U.S. is a participant, such as the Nuclear Suppliers Group, the Missile Technology Control Regime, the Australia Group (chemical and biological nonproliferation), and the Wassenaar Arrangement (conventional arms and dual-use goods and technologies).

3. 15 C.F.R. §'s 744.2, 744.2, 744.4, 744.5 and 744.6.

The scope of EPCI controls is further expanded by the definition of "knows," which the EAR emphasizes includes "variants such as '*know*' and '*reason to know*' and *encompasses more than positive knowledge.*"[4] The various specified proliferation uses contain some exceptions (*e.g.,*

---

4. 15 C.F.R. §744.2(a), footnote 1. [Emphasis added.]

On October 13, 2004, the BIS published, for public comment in the Federal Register, a proposed rule to amend the EAR. See 69 Federal Register 60829, October 13, 2004. If adopted, the rule will make three substantial changes to the EAR:

- Redefine "knowledge" as applied to a person's responsibility to "know" of events or circumstances that suggest that a violation of the EAR is occurring or will occur;

- Enlarge the list of specified "red flags" (red flags are suspicious facts or circumstances that suggest a heightened risk of a violation of the EAR and trigger a party's affirmative duty to investigate to determine if action is needed to avert a violation); and,

- Offer a "safe harbor" from liability arising from knowledge-related provisions of the EAR.

The clarification of "knowledge" is the most important of these changes. Under the EAR, a party has an affirmative duty to "know" when its transactions or dealings would not comply with the EAR. The duty to "know" encompasses a party's actual knowledge that a circumstance exists or is substantially certain to occur, where a party has "reason to know" of such circumstance, and where a party is aware of a "*high probability*" of the existence of such circumstance or its future occurrence. Parties sometimes conclude that where there is less than a "high probability" or near certainty of a violation, they can proceed with the transaction. Such conclusion, however, will not comport with the BIS' interpretation of the EAR.

As explained in the proposed rule, the BIS sees *no difference* between circumstances that suggest a "*high probability*" that a violation will occur and circumstances that suggest "*more likely than not*" a violation will occur. To company executives and personnel, of course, there is a significant difference between a near-certitude (denoted by "high probability") and a barely overcome doubt (denoted by "more likely than not"). In an apparent effort to eliminate the discrepancy between the EAR's current definition of "knowledge" and the BIS' tightened interpretation of it, the BIS proposes to revise the definition: replacing the words "*high probability*" with the phrase "*more likely than not.*"

In the BIS' view, the revised definition makes no change in current policy; it is merely a "clarification of the current standard" and is consistent with existing BIS and industry practice. 69 Federal Register at 60831 As the BIS explains, "Fundamentally, BIS does not believe that moving to a 'more likely than not' formulation increases a company's responsibility with respect to knowledge." 69 Federal Register at 60831

The proposed redefinition, however, substantially lowers the "knowledge" threshold as understood and implemented in many companies' compliance programs and due

one may export or reexport items for nuclear activities to countries *specified on Supplement 3 to Part 744*).[5] Some of the provisions target certain end-use destination countries (*e.g.*, a license is required for export or reexport of an item "subject to the EAR," if the exporter "knows" such item "will be used in the design, development, production, stockpiling or use of chemical or biological weapons in or by a country listed in Country Group D:3," which as of April 2004 comprised 39 countries).[6] No license exceptions apply to the aforementioned EPCI controls.[7] Additional EPCI controls apply to items in order to preclude their diversion to terrorists and terrorist entities (as well as to certain encryption and microprocessor items). As noted in the discussion below, particular care is needed by pharmaceutical, medical, chemical and other firms to ensure compliance with the restrictions on the export and reexport of precursor items (those that can be used to make weapons of mass destruction) and most unexpectedly (but reasonably) a broad range of vaccines, antidotes and antitoxins that, if diverted, could be used to protect persons seeking to develop such weapons. It is an area that such firms need to revisit as the urgency for preventing such diversion continues to grow.

---

diligence standards. As a result, it expands the scope of a party's affirmative duty to "know" of facts and circumstances that suggest possible noncompliance with the EAR.

As if anticipating that companies will be surprised to learn that "high probability" and "more likely than not" are deemed to be equivalent, the BIS cautions that "companies with a strong compliance commitment are unlikely, even under the current definition, to proceed with transactions if they conclude that the circumstance of concern is 'more likely than not'." 69 Federal Register at 60829.

5. As of April 29, 2004, the countries to which such controls do not apply are chiefly certain NATO members and other close U.S. allies: Australia, Austria, Belgium, Canada, Denmark, Finland (not a NATO ally), France, Germany, Greece, Iceland, Italy (including San Marino and Holy See), Japan, Luxembourg, Netherlands, New Zealand, Norway, Portugal, Spain, Sweden, Turkey, and the United Kingdom. 15 C.F.R. §744.2, Supplement 3.

6. 15 C.F.R. §744.4(a). The Country Group D:3, found in Supplement No. 1 to Part 740 of the EAR contains 39 countries, including Afghanistan, Burma, Cuba, Egypt, India, Iran, Israel, Jordan, Libya, Oman, Pakistan, Qatar, Syria, Taiwan, Ukraine, Vietnam and Yemen.

7. Space constraints preclude a discussion of the many exceptions contained in the EAR, but there are four types that counsel should review: (1) items "not subject to the EAR;" (2) items not within the scope of the 10 General Prohibitions; (3) items that a Country Chart indicates are "NLR" (no license required); and (4) items that qualify for a License Exception (of which there are several).

3.1 Analytic Approach to EAR Compliance.[8]

Agile's second due diligence report approached the EAR checkpoint with four threshold questions:

(i) Prior to the signing of the proposed DPA, are any of Troll's, Brugge's or Ijsselmeer's products, services, technologies or activities "subject to" the EAR (including the EPCI);

(ii) Would any such items or activities become "subject to" the EAR from signing of the DPA through the Closing;

(iii) Would any such items or activities become "subject to" the EAR at Closing or thereafter?[9]

Parties often assume that the EAR apply only to tangible items, and then only to the subset of "dual use" items (those that have both a civilian and a military use). However, the EAR also apply to a broad range of activities by U.S. and non-U.S. persons, including to technologies and services, to commodities (because of their limited availability), to diversion of an export to an unauthorized ultimate destination and also, on occasion, to purely military items.[10]

---

8. The EAR were earlier authorized by the Export Administration Act of 1979 (EAA). From August 21, 1994 through November 12, 2000, the Act was in lapse. During that period, the President, through Executive Order 12924 and successive Presidential notices, continued the EAR in effect under the IEEPA (which results in different scales of penalties than the EAA. On November 13, 2000, the EAA was reauthorized, and it remained in effect through August 20, 2001. Subsequently, the EAA has been in lapse, and the President through Executive Order 13222 of August 17, 2001 (66 FEDERAL REGISTER 44025, August 17, 2001), as extended by the Notice of August 14, 2002 (67 FEDERAL REGISTER 53721, August 16, 2002), has continued the EAR in effect under IEEPA. See 68 FEDERAL REGISTER 35783, June 17, 2003.

9. "Subject to" the EAR is not an exclusive jurisdiction, and exports and reexports of such items and activities may be controlled also by other federal agencies. See 15 C.F.R. §734.2(a)(2).

10. See *United States v. Geissler*, 731 F. Supp. 93 (E.D.N.Y., 1990). Defendant U.S. person failed to obtain a required Commerce Department license while conspiring to cause the export to Iran of military aircraft tires for F-14 military aircraft. Usually such items would be controlled by being placed on the U.S. Munitions List, but in this instance the most relevant category on that list, Category VIII, "Aircraft, Spacecraft, and Associated Equipment" expressly excluded "aircraft tires," and thus excluded them

3.2 Checkpoint for Pre-Signing EAR Risks.

With respect to pre-signing risks of violating the EAR, Counsel reviewed both items and activities, since both come within the jurisdiction
of the EAR. Five categories of items are "subject to" the EAR:

(i) all items in the United States (whether or not they are made
here, once here, such items become subject to the EAR, even if
only transshipped through the United States);

(ii) all U.S.-origin items *wherever located*;

(iii) U.S.-origin parts, components, materials or other commodities
incorporated abroad into items made abroad, and U.S. origin
software or technology commingled with foreign software or
technology, *if* the U.S.-origin portion exceeds EAR specified *de
minimis* thresholds;[11]

---

from State Department jurisdiction. The court relied on an EAR provision that stated
that the EAR governed the licensing requirements for export of all commodities from
the Untied States unless controlled by another U.S. agency, found no other agency
retained control over F-14 aircraft tires, and deemed Commerce, therefore, to have
jurisdiction. The current EAR make clear that if aircraft, parts, accessories, and components do not appear on the Munitions List, all other such items "are under the export
licensing authority of the U.S. Department of Commerce." 15 C.F.R. §770.2(i).

The dividing lines between Commerce's and State's jurisdiction can become subtle,
if not obscure, because "dual use" is a policy that responds to continuously changing
national security and other priorities. One should not assume that Commerce is always
the "catch all" (i.e., that it controls only if others do not); it is sometimes the converse.
Thus, initial navigation systems for "civil aircraft" are controlled by Commerce, those
for any use other than "civil aircraft" are controlled by State (e.g., ship-borne use,
underwater use, ground vehicle use, space-borne use). See 15 C.F.R. 770.2(j). The EAR,
at times, make assumptions about "non-military" that few military officers would share.
For example, combat vehicles, whether or not armored, if designed for "specific fighting
function" are controlled by the State Department. Military vehicles not on the Munitions List are controlled by the Department of Commerce, although that category includes so-called "non-combat military purposes" such as troop transport (to the front,
from the front, during combat), equipment transport, and to bring "equipment over
land and road in close support of fighting vehicles and troops." 15 C.F.R.
§770.2(h)(1)(ii)(A) and (B).

11. The *de minimis* thresholds are set forth in 15 C.F.R. Section 734.4 and Supplement No. 2 of Part 734.

(iv) certain foreign made "direct products"[12] of U.S.-origin technology or software;[13] and

(v) certain items made by any plant or major component of a plant located outside of the U.S. that is a "direct product" of U.S.-origin technology or software.[14]

(There are additional EAR-related risk points that counsel should check. These are not covered by the "subject to" EAR categories, but nonetheless could entail liability for Agile. We mention a number of those briefly at the end of this chapter.)

Applying the above criteria, several Troll and Brugge products, services and technologies are potentially "subject to" the EAR **even prior to** the proposed signing of the DPA by virtue of their containing U.S.-origin software or technology commingled with foreign software or technology, or by virtue of being foreign made "direct products" of such software or technology. Such items do not fall outside the EAR for the following reasons:

(i) Some Troll or Brugge items (technology, software, services, and encryption products) intended for reexport contain U.S. origin technology and software that are not subject to the exclusive jurisdiction of another U.S. Government department or agency;[15]

(ii) Such items are not publicly available;[16]

(iii) Although none of the items are wholly of U.S.-origin (Troll does not buy and resell or distribute for any U.S. firm), nonetheless the items *might* incorporate more than the *de minimis* levels of U.S.-origin components, software or technology (discussed in detail below); and

(iv) For other Troll or Brugge produced items that might not exceed the *de minimis* levels of U.S.-origin components, software or

---

12. "Direct product" denotes the "immediate product (including processes and services) produced directly by the use of technology or software." 15 C.F.R. §734.3(4).

13. As described in 15 C.F.R. Section 736.2(b)(3).

14. As described in 15 C.F.R. §736.2(b)(3).

15. 15 C.F.R. §732.2(a).

16. 15 C.F.R. §732.2(b). See also 15 C.F.R. Part 732, Supplement No. 2, *Am I Subject to the EAR?*, January 2003.

technology, some are nonetheless captured by EAR General Prohibition Three (there are ten EAR General Prohibitions).[17]

With regard to Troll's or Brugge's activities, neither company currently employs any U.S. citizens. Prior to the proposed signing of the DPA, none of Agile's partners will have had any direct or indirect involvement in activities by Troll and Brugge, with one possible exception—the disengagement negotiations between Agile's Danish partners and representatives of the Iranian company customers of Troll. However, Agile's Danish partners did not release any technological data or information during such negotiations (in either conversation, documents or correspondence). In light of that fact, they did not "reexport" any items for the purposes of the EAR during such negotiations. Even if no items were exported, counsel must still be concerned that General Prohibitions of the EAR were not violated. Four of these apply to "U.S. persons" overseas (such as Agile's Danish partners).

One cannot assume that because Agile's Danish partners qualify as "U.S. persons" under the TSR, they will also be "U.S. persons" under the EAR. None of the definitions of "U.S. person" provided in any TSR applies directly in the EAR. The current EAR definition of "U.S. person" is comparable to those found in most of the TSR; however, the EAR applies one definition of "U.S. person" to three sections (Sections 744.6, 744.10, and 744.11), and a modified definition to portions of Section 740.9 (temporary imports and reexports, exports and reexports of items temporarily in the United States, and **exports and reexports of beta test software**), Section 740.14 (personal baggage of persons leaving the United States, etc.), Part 746 (embargoes and other special controls) and Part 760 (restrictive trade practices or boycotts).[18] For the purposes of Sections 744.6, 744.10, and 744.11 the term "U.S. person" is much the same as that found in the TSR (*e.g.,* the Iranian Transactions Regulations), and includes:

  (i) "Any individual who is a citizen of the United States, a permanent resident alien of the United States, or a protected individual as defined by 8 U.S.C. 1324b(a)(3);[19]

---

17. See 15 C.F.R. Part 736.2.

18. 15 C.F.R., Part 772, "U.S. person," May 2003, p. 3.

19. The reference to "a protected individual" does not appear in the TSR definitions of "U.S. person."

(ii) Any juridical person organized under the laws of the Untied States or any jurisdiction within the United States, **including foreign branches;**[20] and

(iii) Any person in the United States."[21]

Since Agile's office in Denmark is one of its "foreign branches," any actions on behalf of, or attributable to, that "foreign branch" by its Danish partners constitute actions by a "U.S. person"—Agile. What activities (other than export of items) are Agile's Danish partners barred from engaging in by the EAR's General Prohibitions? There are four such activities, and no exceptions to any of the four exist under the EAR:

(i) *Denial Orders*—they may not take any action prohibited by a "denial order," which denies export and other privileges to the persons to whom they are issued, and prohibits others from dealing in any respect with such persons with regard to exports or reexports, whether or not the items are subject to the EAR;[22]

(ii) *Proliferation Activities*—they may not, without a license from the BIS, engage in any of a broad range of activities (financing, contracting, service, support, etc.) that they "know" will assist in certain proliferation activities described in EAR Part 744 (relating, for example, to production of missiles or weapons of mass destruction);[23]

(iii) *Violate Orders*—they may not violate the terms of any license or any other order (including Denial Orders) issued under the EAR;[24] and,

(iv) *Knowingly Proceed to Violate the EAR* —they may not engage in any of a broad range of activities (sell, transfer, export, reexport, finance, order, or perform other service, etc.) with respect to any item subject to the EAR which is exported or to be

---

20. The TSR usually refer to "including overseas branches," but "overseas" and "foreign" are used without any suggestion of a difference in their meaning, although clearly "foreign" seems a more apt term for referring to Central and South American countries and Canada. [Emphasis added.]

21. Id.

22. General Prohibition Four (Denial Orders), 15 C.F.R. §736.2(b)(4).

23. General Prohibition Seven, 15 C.F.R. §736.2(b)(7).

24. General Prohibition Nine, 15 C.F.R. §736.2(b)(9).

exported (or reexported or to be reexported) "with knowledge" that a violation of the EAR, any order, license, license exception, etc. "has occurred, is about to occur, or is intended to occur in connection with the item . . . "[25]

Of those four, the activity that most concerns Counsel is the first—Denial Orders. No action by Agile's Danish partners may violate the terms of any "denial order." Since each such order is tailored to the targeted person (individual, company, organization), the best checkpoint is the published lists of recipients of denial orders: the **Denied Persons List.**[26] For example, if Agile's Danish partners had been negotiating with representatives of a party that has received such an order (*e.g.,* General Polyphase, Inc.) or anyone negotiating on its behalf, such negotiations would contravene the standard denial order[27] issued to General Polyphase that took effect October 30, 1997 and is not scheduled to expire until October 30, 2012. That order prohibits General Polyphase (of Tunis, Tunisia) and Adrian Attia (of Miami Beach, FL), together with "all successors, assignees, officers, representatives, agents, and employees," from participating in any way in any transaction involving the export or reexport of any item subject to the EAR or in "any other activity subject to" the EAR, including negotiating or otherwise being involved in any transaction involving export or benefits from exports from the United States. However, the portion applicable to all U.S. persons, is the following prohibition, which makes General Polyphase (and any other denied person) a "pariah" and imposes a broad obligation of due diligence on all U.S. persons:

"No person may, directly or indirectly, do any of the following:

A. Export or reexport to or on behalf of the denied person any item subject to the Regulations;

B. Take any action that facilitates the acquisition or attempted acquisition by the denied person of the ownership, possession, or control of any item subject to the Regulations **that has**

---

25. General Prohibition Ten, §736.2(b)(10).
26. The list can be viewed on the BIS website at www.bis.doc.gov/DPL/thedeniallist.asp. Changes are made on an ongoing basis. For example, 11 persons were added to the Denied Persons List on July 1, 2003. See "Recent Changes to the Denied Persons List," accessed at www.bis.doc.gov/DPL/recentchanges.asp.
27. Most denial orders tend to be of a standard form and scope.

been or will be exported from the United States, including financing or other support activities related to a transaction whereby the denied person acquires or attempts to acquire such ownership, possession or control;

C. Take any action to acquire from **or to facilitate the acquisition or attempted acquisition** from the denied person of any item subject to the Regulations that has been exported from the United States;

D. Obtain from the denied person in the United States any item subject to the Regulations with knowledge or reason to know that the item will be, or is intended to be, exported from the United States; or

E. **Engage in any transaction to service** any item subject to the Regulations that has been or will be exported from the United States and that is owned, possessed or controlled by the denied person, or service any item, of whatever origin, that is owned, possessed or controlled by the denied person if such service involves the use of any item subject to the Regulations that has been or will be exported from the United States. For purposes of this paragraph, servicing means installation, maintenance, repair, modification or testing."[28]

On comparing the names of the individuals and entities involved in the negotiations with the Iranian companies, Counsel ascertains that, although at least one Iranian company (CCC, Inc.) is named therein, none of the individuals or entities in the negotiations is named on the currently effective Denied Persons List. Further, none of those parties was negotiating on behalf of or for the benefit of any such party. Such diligence provides important background justification for decision-making should an inquiry be raised subsequently.

As an added precaution, Agile's Counsel can make a similar check of the entities on the Entity List. The Entity List contains the names of end users who "have been determined to present an unacceptable risk of diversion to [persons, entities or countries] developing weapons of mass destruction or the missiles used to deliver those weapons."[29] For

---

28. 62 FEDERAL REGISTER 59655, November 4, 1997. [Emphasis added.]

29. Accessed at the BIS website at www.bis.doc.gov/Entities/Default.htm, accessed July 5, 2003.

example, "For all items subject to the EAR" it is necessary to obtain a license to export or reexport such item to the "Moscow Aviation Institute."[30] The Entity List also provides citations to the published versions of the precise terms of each such restriction.[31] In each such instance, the notice advises that all license applications will be reviewed with a "presumption of denial."[32] Since Agile's Danish partners have been negotiating with representatives of Iranian companies, and no Iranian company appears on the currently effective Entity List (and since the negotiations did not involve the reexport of any item), the negotiations have not created a problem with respect to the Entity List. This conclusion does not, however, relieve Agile of the responsibility to watch for potential violations of the EAR.

3.3 Period From Signing Until Closing.

As with the TSR, Agile's decision to put its Danish partners on the Boards of Directors of Troll and Brugge, respectively, means that to the extent that any Agile partners become involved in either company's activities in the interim between signing and Closing, their actions on behalf of Agile could potentially contravene the EAR, if prohibited to U.S. persons. All such actions must therefore be undertaken only with a clear prior understanding of any applicable limitations or restrictions. Counsel might consider preparing bullet point memoranda identifying risk points under the EAR during that interim period.

Risks

Encryption Re-Exports by Troll.

1. Activity.

The value of surveillance on encrypted communications is reduced substantially if the targets are alerted to such surveillance. A substantial

---

30. 15 C.F.R. Supplement 4 to Part 744, p. 12.

31. The license policy varies with the target: some are reviewed on a case-by-case basis, EAR99 items have a presumption of approval, and others have a presumption of denial.

32. 64 FEDERAL REGISTER March 26, 1999 14605.

commercial market exists therefore for products that facilitate the discovery of clandestine surveillance. One of Troll's newest products is designed to be incorporated in and to modify communications cable systems to detect such surreptitious surveillance. There is U.S.-origin technology in this Troll product. Such technology is "subject to" the EAR. The Commerce Control List includes it among "Information Security" items,[33] and categorizes it with an Export Control Classification Number ("ECCN") of "**5A002**."[34] An ECCN represents the following information:

First digit "0"–"9":   identifies the category in the CCL
The letter: Identifies which of five groups the item is listed under[35]
The other digits: Identify the reason for controlling the item.[36]

For the particular item(s) commingled in the Troll product, the ECCN represents the following: **5** (signifying Telecommunications and Information Security category); **A** (signifying equipment assemblies, or components) and **002** (signifying that it is controlled for national security. It is also controlled for Anti-Terrorism and Encryption Item purposes. An ECCN of "5A002" warrants close scrutiny of destination, end-user and end-use, as well as careful analysis of the applicable EAR. Since this item appears on the CCL with an ECCN, the item is not only "subject to" the EAR, but upon export will also be considered a "controlled U.S.-origin" item for the purpose of Counsel's analysis of its reexport by Troll (and after the Closing by Agile through its foreign branch).[37]

---

33. As such it is in CCL category 5. There are 10 categories on the CCL, numbered 0 through 9. The category number is the first digit in an item's ECCN. The categories are: 0—Nuclear Materials, Facilities, and Equipment; 1—Materials, Chemicals, Micro-organisms, and Toxins; 2—Materials Processing; 3—Electronics; 4—Computers; 5—(Part 1) Telecommunications, (Part 2) Information Security; 6—Sensors and Lasers; 7—Navigation and Avionics; 8—Marine; and 9—Propulsion Systems, Space Vehicles, and Related Equipment. See 15 C.F.R. Part 774.

34. 15 C.F.R. Supplement No. 1 to Part 774, p. 3.

35. The five categories are: A—Equipment, Assemblies and Components; B—Test, Inspection and Production Equipment; C—Materials; D—Software; and E—Technology. 15 C.F.R. §738.2(b).

36. 15 C.F.R. §738.2(d)(1). Reasons for control include AT—Anti-Terrorism; CB—Chemical & Biological Weapons; CW—Chemical Weapons Convention; EI—Encryption Items, NS—National Security, etc. See 15 C.F.R. §738.2(d)(2).

37. Note that for encryption software under other ECCN's the applicable rules differ substantially from those applied by ECCN 5A002. Software, for example, con-

➤ *Prohibited Conduct.* Counsel asked Troll to provide a description of the U.S.-origin technology, the likely ultimate destinations, end-users and end-uses, and a computation of the percent of U.S.-origin technology in this product (based on the value of such technology compared with the projected sale price). On computation, the controlled U.S.-origin content is determined to constitute 24%. For most destinations, most products, most end-users and most end-uses, the EAR contains an exception for goods that are 25% or less commingled, controlled U.S.-origin technology (the *de minimis* threshold). For all the ultimate destinations identified by Troll's counsel, the EAR would not apply to reexport.[38] However, for certain countries there is a much lower *de minimis* threshold of 10%, and there are also several instances where there is no *de minimis* exception (such as "Aircraft of the type described in ECCN 9A991 [*e.g.,* military and de-militarized aircraft such as Cargo aircraft (C-45 through C-118 inclusive, and C-121 or Trainers bearing a "T" designation and using piston engines, when such aircraft incorporate a CSIS [commercial standby instrument system] integrating a QRS11-00100-100/101 sensor").[39]

The operative concern in the context of Agile's contemplated acquisition is whether any of the ultimate destination countries for the Troll product could potentially include Iran, or whether any ultimate end-user could include an Iranian entity (as defined). In this instance, there is in fact a confidential proposed sale to two Iranian customers: an Iranian bank in Germany (the bank was apparently concerned about the possibility that German authorities might be monitoring its communications), and a closely held Iranian company's office in Hamburg. On review, the actual percentage of controlled U.S.-origin content in the product was restated as 2.4%, due to an earlier clerical error. However, even this seemingly insignificant percentage did not obviate the

---

trolled for EI reasons under ECCN 5D002 and eligible for export under what is known as the "retail" or "source code" provisions of license exception ENC, can be made eligible for *de minimis* treatment upon request to the BIS as part of an encryption review request. See 68 FEDERAL REGISTER 35784, June 17, 2003. This and other variations make it necessary for exporters of encryption products to carefully review on a case-by-case basis each such product under the applicable EAR (whether the encryption product or software is embedded in other items or in the form of text depicting the source code).

38. 15 C.F.R. §734.4(d)(3), January 2003.
39. 15. C.F.R. §734.4(a)(3)(ii).

problem. According to the final rule promulgated by the BIS on June 17, 2003: **"There is no *de minimis* level for foreign-made items that incorporate U.S.-origin items controlled for 'EI' [Encryption Item] reasons under ECCN 5A002 . . . ."**[40] Since the Troll product would commingle a U.S.-origin item controlled for EI under that ECCN, any reexport of such item in the Troll product (regardless of destination) would require a license (from the Department of Commerce), if such reexport was scheduled to occur after the Closing of Agile's acquisition of Troll. Furthermore, the proposed reexport to an Iranian company would constitute a "deemed release" of the technology to the bank's Iranian national employees, and thereby to Iran itself.[41] If such sale occurred after the Closing, it would require a license (for which there would be a presumption of denial). With respect to the proposed sale (and reexport) to the Iranian bank, this not only poses a risk under the EAR, but is also clearly prohibited by the Iranian Transactions Regulations.[42]

---

40. See 15 C.F.R. §734.4(b), January 2003, and 68 Federal Register 35784, June 17, 2003. [Emphasis added.]

41. See 15 C.F.R. §734.2(b)(2) that provides that "export" of any technology or software (other than encryption source code and object code software, addressed under 15 C.F.R. §734.2(b)(9)) includes any "release of technology or software subject to the EAR in a foreign country" and "any release of technology or source code subject to the EAR to a foreign national. Such release is deemed to be an export to the home country or countries of the foreign national." 15 C.F.R. §734.2(b)(2).

42. This transaction had not been disclosed in discussions concerning the ITR and exemplifies the way a fact thought to have been checked thoroughly at the TSR checkpoint may escape discovery but be found at the EAR checkpoint (and *vice versa*, since these checkpoints are not sequential, but recurrent).

Note that the source of this controlled U.S.-origin encryption technology—a company in the United States—would be at risk of violating the EAR if Troll proceeds with the proposed reexport in the absence of a Commerce Department license: that, of course, is not the responsibility of Agile or its Counsel, not directly. However, recall under General Prohibition 10 that a U.S. person may not do a broad range of activities with respect to an item subject to the EAR with knowledge that in connection with such transaction a violation of the EAR has or is about to occur. If Agile's Danish partners direct or advise Troll to complete the proposed reexport prior to the Closing, and if Agile is aware or has reason to know that no license for reexport of that technology has been issued, then the BIS could argue that by giving such direction as a condition for signing the DPA, Agile thereby violated General Prohibition 10. We think that the scope of General Prohibition 10 probably does not reach as far as certain prohibitions in the TSR against any facilitation of targeted transactions, but the tendency of business executives to try to solve problems can lead to too risky an involvement by a U.S. person in solutions that involve activities that would contravene the EAR (or the TSR). BIS's

The DPA would have to include a representation and/or warranty to the effect that, as of the signing date and going forward (presumably with a "bring-down" at Closing), Troll, Brugge and Ijsselmeer will not engage in any transaction that could result in a post-Closing reexport of any products containing controlled U.S.-origin items constituting more than the applicable *de minimis* amount(s). Serious consideration should also be given to precluding such activity as of the signing date, in order to avert the risk that a deal made by Troll with one of its out-of-country customers prior to Closing might result in a reexport after Closing. Presumably, the economic costs to Troll in lost business opportunities must also be weighed in determining which course of action to pursue, but counsel's role is to provide a "risk analysis" on which company officers can base their business decisions, so that such risks can be balanced against unnecessary interference with the ongoing economic enterprise. Faced with such risks, and an evaluation of the probability of their occurrence, the acquirer may determine that disengagement is the most practical and effective solution. In many instances, simply winding up certain dealings prior to Closing will be the better course, because the risk of a violation is acceptably low and is necessary to avoid disrupting ongoing commercial activities or relations (that do not pose a risk).

The warranty would further preclude Troll and its affiliates from engaging in any transaction that could result in a reexport after Closing of any item that contained controlled U.S.-origin technology or software controlled for "EI" purposes under ECCN "5A002,"[43] unless a license had first been obtained. Note that overseas counsel are not likely to agree to a broad agreement concerning non-contravention of any applicable EAR. In view of the EAR's complexity and the nuances of its application to specific commercial activities, it is reasonable for them

---

interpretation would probably be shaped by the seriousness of the violation (the sensitivity of the U.S.-origin item, and whether the ultimate delivery would be to a pariah country, pariah end-user, or for a pariah end use of the applicable EAR). BIS's actual position would be uncertain. Our purpose in mentioning it is not to advocate an unduly aggressive interpretation but to draw attention to the kind of activity in which negotiations can bring U.S. persons unwittingly close to a violation by engaging too extensively in the remediation efforts that should be confined to the party on the other side of the table.

43. Such representation and warranty would also have to cover items controlled for EI purposes for ECCN's 5D002 or 5E002 on the Commerce Control List, if applicable to Troll's or Brugge's reexports.

to refuse to do so or to ask for the most limited and fact specific language. Moreover, boilerplate language on such issues is inherently unreliable and ill-advised. For a sensitive item like the one under discussion, (controlled for "national security" reasons), the EAR Country Chart makes clear that a license for reexport would be required for many destinations, ranging from the targeted countries under the EAR (*e.g.*, Cuba, Iran, and Sudan) to countries not targeted by any comprehensive embargo (*e.g.* Costa Rica and Zambia). Early review will aid in identifying a potential risk (and evaluating its probability of delaying the transaction).

2. Activity.

As a result of budget re-allocations in the Royal Norwegian MoD, Troll has begun to explore the commercial opportunities for marketing and selling online some of its encryption products that incorporate controlled U.S.-origin encryption software. It has been developing broadcast encryption that would efficiently permit information to be broadcast "to a dynamically changing group of users allowed to receive the data,"[44] while excluding those not entitled to receive such data. Troll's potential customers include many in EU countries where privacy rules are much more restrictive than in the United States. For that reason, Troll has sought to develop a "tracing algorithm" that would trace and find persons who may have contributed their decryption keys to an illicit decryption box (permitting nonpaying customers to receive decrypted broadcasts intended only for paid subscribers). Troll's product would avoid the need to identify such persons (thereby complying with stringent privacy rules), but would seek to disable the illicit decryption box (a technology called "trace-and-revoke software").[45] For use in such product, Troll has purchased a "symmetric algorithm" that employs a key length of 128 bits from a U.S. company in New York City, and proposes to make the commingled end-product available on its website. Ads for the product have been uploaded to the website, but the start date for sales is still to be scheduled. Such sales could begin either before or after the Closing (of Agile's acquisition of Troll), but

---

44. Naor, Dalit, and Naor, Moni, *Protecting Cryptographic Keys: The Trace-and-Revoke Approach*, COMPUTER, July 2003, p. 48. Our conception of this Troll product is derived from the Naors' very interesting article.

45. The term is borrowed from Naor, Dalit, and Naor, Moni, *Protecting Cryptographic Keys: The Trace-and-Revoke Approach*, COMPUTER, July 2003, p. 48.

will certainly begin after the anticipated signing of the DPA. The symmetric algorithm will constitute approximately 20% of the final value of the end product.

For a more select group of customers, Agile will bundle that software with a program incorporating encryption software which (at Troll's request) was specially designed by a U.S. firm to reduce compromising emanations of information-bearing signals. This bundled product will not be available from Troll's website, but rather will be customized on-site by Agile and Troll technicians for certain customers who will in turn produce second generation encryption software products. The custom designed software from the United States company, combined with the symmetric algorithm, constitutes 40% of the value of the end product.

➤ *Prohibited Conduct.* The symmetric algorithm that Troll is proposing to sell out of country (and thereby reexport) from its website is "subject to" the EAR with an ECCN of **5D002** (information security software) as software having the characteristics or performing the functions of equipment controlled by "5A002."[46] Moreover, it is not controlled like other software, but is treated under the EAR in the same manner as an ECCN 5A002 item.[47] What this means is that it is controlled for reasons of national security and anti-terrorism and as an encryption item.[48] As such, the percentage of controlled U.S.-origin content is irrelevant: **there is no *de minimis* threshold for encryption software categorized as 5D002**.

Despite the liberalization of U.S. export controls on encryption software in recent years, certain encryption software—that controlled for EI purposes—constitute items transferred from the U.S. Munitions List to the CCL in 1996,[49] and remain a subject of concern at the State Department's Directorate of Defense Trade Controls. Of particular concern are Troll's plans to sell (and thereby reexport) the controlled U.S.-origin asymmetric algorithm from its website.

---

46. See 15 C.F.R. Supplement No. 1 to Part 774, Category 5D(a), May 2003, p. 5.
47. See 15 C.F.R. Supplement No. 1 to Part 774, Category 5D, Note, May 2003, p. 4.
48. Id.
49. See 15 C.F.R. Supplement No. 1 to Part 774, Category 5D, License Requirements, May 2003, p. 4.

Unfortunately, the EAR guidelines are not clear in this area. The EAR provide that making such encryption software accessible to persons outside the United States "including transfers from . . . Internet file transfer protocol and World Wide Websites" constitutes an export "**unless the person making the software available takes precautions adequate to prevent unauthorized transfer of such code.**"[50] The EAR specifies what would constitute "precautions *adequate* to prevent" unauthorized transfers: "such precautions for Internet transfers" of products such as encryption software, certain encryption source code and general purpose encryption toolkits "shall include such measures as" the following:

(i) The website's access control system must check the address of every system outside of the U.S. or Canada "requesting or receiving a transfer" and must verify that such system "do[es] not have a domain name or Internet address of a foreign government end-user (e.g. ".gov," ".gouv," "mil" or similar addresses);"[51]

(ii) The website's access control system must provide "every requesting or receiving party with notice that the transfer includes or would include cryptographic software subject to export controls under the Export Administration Regulations, and anyone receiving such a transfer cannot export the software without a license or other authorization;"[52] and

(iii) Every party that requests or receives a transfer of the encryption software "must acknowledge affirmatively that the software is not intended for use by a government end-user" (as defined in EAR Part 772),[53] and that such party "understands the cryp-

---

50. 15 C.F.R. §734.2(b)(9)(ii). [Emphasis added.] Note that software controlled for EI reasons under ECCN 5D002 on the CCL does not qualify for exemptions from the EAR, as may publicly available technology and software if they meet certain requirements. See 15 C.F.R. §734.3(b)(3).

51. 15 C.F.R. §734.2(b)(9)(iii)(A). The precaution is suggestive, but counsel should note that many overseas government e-mail addresses do not have such conspicuous markers. For example, certain Norwegian government e-mail addresses are simply of the form ____@c2i.net. Hence prudent companies will not limit such precautions to the EAR's current suggestions, which are not intended as an exhaustive list.

52. 15 C.F.R. §734.2(b)(9)(iii)(B).

53. The EAR defines "government end-user" as applied to encryption items to include, *inter alia*, "any foreign central, regional or local government department, agency or other entity performing governmental functions." It includes government

tographic software is subject to export controls" under the EAR and "anyone receiving the transfer cannot export the software without a license or other authorization."[54]

No one can seriously believe, however, that implementation of such mandated precautions will prevent unauthorized transfer to a variety of persons that the U.S. Government does not want to acquire such software. For example, assuming that the visitor to Troll's website did not log on from a proscribed address (such as ".gov"), any person currently subject to an EAR "denial order" or otherwise named on OFAC's SDN List could give the requested affirmative acknowledgement simply by clicking appropriately, and could proceed to purchase and download encryption software controlled under 5D002. Clearly this is one of the serious omissions in the transfer of control of encryption software from the State Department to the Commerce Department. While the former is primarily concerned with national security, the latter is more concerned with promoting economic growth. (As commentators have noted, "the State Department is generally considered much less sensitive to commercial considerations than the Commerce Department.")[55] The result is a regulation that imposes formal compliance exercises and costs, but does little to prevent the unauthorized transfer of sensitive technologies. The EAR states that the "BIS will *consider* acknowledgments in electronic form, provided they are adequate to assure legal undertakings similar to written acknowledgements."[56] Even if the import of the phrase "assure legal undertakings" were clear, its enforcement is wholly impracticable. In addition, "adequate precaution" provisions invite the website operator to shift the legal obligation from itself (where the burden reasonably belongs) to the user who is much less likely to understand the applicable law, and has no incentive to comply (as enforcement action will seldom, if ever, be brought against him).

---

research and other similar institutions involved in Munitions List production or distribution. It expressly excludes, however, a variety of other institutions such as "banks and financial institutions." Note, however, that transfer of such encryption software to an Iranian bank would be prohibited, not by the EAR (although such banks are government controlled) but by the applicable Iranian Transactions Regulations, since such banks appear on OFAC's SDN List.

54. 15 C.F.R. §734.2(b)(9)(iii)(C).

55. *Nunn-Wolfowitz Task Force Report: Industry "Best Practices" Regarding Export Compliance Programs,* July 25, 2000, p. 3.

56. 15 C.F.R. §734.2(b)(9)(iii)(C). [Emphasis added.]

Website compliance purportedly driven by such provisions is highly porous and virtually ineffective. One current website attempts to conform to the EAR's requirements with the following inquiry:

> "Are you or the computer(s) you are operating in Iraq, Iran, Libya, North Korea, Sudan, Syria, or Cuba right now? o Yes o No
>
> Do you acknowledge affirmatively that you understand that the requested software is subject to export controls under the Export Administration Act and that you may only export or reexport the software under the laws, restrictions and regulations of the U.S. Bureau of Industry and Security or foreign agencies or authorities. o Yes o No"[57]

Few U.S. citizens could in good faith answer "yes" to the second question, because it requires the purchaser to have knowledge of the applicable regulations and substance of the EAR.[58] We are forced back on the first lesson of law school: a right is illusory without an effective remedy. In this context, a representation is illusory without an effective enforcement scheme. The purchaser has no incentive to familiarize himself with applicable law. This is the seller's task. We believe the BIS will reconsider the efficacy of such provisions as the technologies to block transfers to countries and end-users targeted by the EAR, TSR and ITAR become more widely known, and as such technologies prove economic and effective against counter-measures (particularly if the federal government translates homeland security into rigorous enforcement of restrictions, including those against unauthorized transfers of sensitive technologies).

---

57. A university research department's website, accessed on July 6, 2003. Out of respect for the institution we do not provide the URL.

58. To the university website operator's credit, if one happens to click "no" in answer to one of the questions and then click the button signifying that the answers above are correct, a web page appears under the title "Cryptographic Software Access Denied." Rather uselessly, however, the visitor is then coached to correct the problem by being told further down on the page that while his or her answers indicate that under the EAR they are not permitted to download the software, they should "Please check to make sure that you answered all the questions accurately," thereby coaxing if not inviting the unsuccessful truth teller to become a successful liar in order to receive permission to download the encryption software. At that point, a different web page appears, describing the export license exception granted by the BIS to the product, reminding the visitor that the software can be exported without a license to all countries except "Iran, Iraq, North Korea, Libya, Sudan, Syria, and Cuba" and providing below the FTP (file transfer protocol) hyperlinks to commence the download.

In any review of the adequacy of compliance precautions in connection with website sales of encryption software, an important focus for counsel must be the EAR country restrictions for encryption software. Agile's counsel should focus specifically on the provisions that state:

> "You may not knowingly export or reexport source code, corresponding object code or products developed with this source code to a country in Country Group E:1 [which currently lists Cuba, Iran, Libya, North Korea, Sudan and Syria]."[59]

Those restrictions apply to encryption software controlled for ECCN 5D002, *even if* it would otherwise qualify under the EAR as "publicly available" under ECCN 5D002, and if it would be considered publicly available under EAR §734.3(b)(3) (as well as the corresponding object code resulting from the compiling of items that would otherwise be covered by such source code).[60] For such software, EAR Section 734.13(e) expressly authorizes exports and reexports without review of encryption source code. Recall, however, that the software purchased by Troll from a U.S. company would not qualify as "publicly available" under the applicable EAR. A later subparagraph in the same section further modifies the restrictions for online releases of publicly available encryption software, even when controlled under ECCN 5D002:

> "Posting of source code or corresponding object code on the Internet (e.g., . . . World Wide Web) where it may be downloaded by anyone would not establish "knowledge" of a prohibited export or reexport . . . In addition, such posting would not trigger "red flags" necessitating the affirmative duty to inquire under the 'Know Your Customer' guidance provided in Supplement No. 3 to part 732 of the EAR."[61]

---

59. 15 C.F.R. §740.13(e)(4). Note the inclusion of Syria in this prohibition, which is not the target of a comprehensive TSR but is subject to restrictions under the TSR that target countries that support international terrorism. Note also that although the President by Executive Order has lifted all but the penalties provision of the Iraqi Sanctions Regulations, and the BIS has issued an Interim Rule modifying the EAR with respect to exports and reexports to Iraq, there continue to be restrictions on certain transfers of encryption items to Iraq. As always, a party should review both the EAR and TSR before agreeing to export any item potentially controlled by such regulations. The party should also give careful consideration to the fact that in any transaction the facts learned from due diligence at one checkpoint often providing illuminating clues and "red flags" at the other checkpoint.

60. 15 C.F.R. §740.13(e)(1).

61. 15 C.F.R. §740.13(e)(6).

This provision makes no mention of taking precautions adequate to prevent unauthorized transfer of such code (which the EAR expressly apply to exports of encryption software categorized under ECCN 5D002, that do not qualify for the "publicly available" exception). It is easy to overlook the earlier restriction, or to conclude that the two provisions conflict and, therefore, that the least restrictive controls (ordinarily a good rule of thumb for reading any regulation drafted in the course of extended negotiation by committee). In this instance, however, *they do not conflict.* This is merely a clarification. If encryption software, controlled under ECCN 5D002 (and thus controlled for reasons including national security and anti-terrorism) qualifies as "publicly available," it can be released without the precautions required for software that does not qualify for that exception. Moreover, the EAR will not impute "knowledge" of a prohibited transfer from the posting of such source code on a website.[62]

Because Troll's trace and revoke software do not qualify as "publicly available" (under ECCN 5D002), if Troll intends to proceed with sales of this software, it must implement precautions "adequate" to prevent reexports prohibited by the EAR prior to Closing. Moreover, since even publicly available encryption software controlled under ECCN 5D002 cannot knowingly be transferred to Cuba, Iran, Libya, North Korea, Sudan or Syria,[63] suitable representations and warranties should be included in the DPA to avert the risk that Troll or Brugge will engage in releases—from their websites, by e-mail or through other digital media—to anyone in those countries, or to their nationals (remembering that a "deemed release" to a national will constitute an export or reexport to that person's home country).

With respect to the custom designed encryption software, the contemplated arrangement—that Agile experts will modify such product

---

62. If the website operators are U.S. persons and the website employs geo-locating technology, the operator may thereby be at heightened risk of having imputed to them that they "knew or should have known" of a prohibited export or reexport. Such knowledge may come to be regarded as a red flag. If so, the operator would then have an affirmative duty to make further inquiries about the ultimate destination, end-user, and end use of its product.

63. Note that Iraq, until July 30, 2004, was among the list of prohibited destinations, but it has been removed as a result of the BIS's publication of an Interim Rule on Exports and Reexports to Iraq. See 60 FEDERAL REGISTER 146, July 30, 2004, p. 46070 at p. 46075.

at the customer facilities—arguably runs afoul of the EAR prohibition that U.S. persons may not (without BIS authorization) provide:

> "Technical assistance (including training) to foreign persons with the intent to aid a foreign person in the development or manufacture outside the United States of encryption commodities and software that, if of United States origin, would be controlled for EI reasons under ECCN 5A002 or 5D002."[64]

Unless appropriately licensed, the proposed use of Agile experts to provide such services will have to be cancelled. In addition, Agile must reconsider its plans to provide technical services to Troll for the development of Troll's encryption products for the Royal Norwegian MoD, and will have to obtain licenses for all such activity in advance. The prohibition does not exempt such assistance, **even when it is provided to nationals of a NATO ally.**

3. Activity—Reexport of Software for Explosive and Detonator Detection.

With the assistance of Brugge, Troll has developed specially designed software to be used in equipment deployed by Norwegian police and peacekeepers for the detection of explosives and detonators and the presence of explosive residues. Some of this software commingles software purchased from a company in Utah. Troll has developed two grades of the device, one for Norwegian personnel, and a less sensitive version for incorporation in equipment to be offered for sale to airports throughout the Middle East. Troll has signed one contract with the agency responsible for security at Damascus International Airport in Syria and completed negotiation of a second, for sales of the software to be incorporated (loaded) in on-site equipment by the ultimate end-user. Troll anticipates signing a similar contract with Dey and Melli Sakhteman, the main Iranian contractors for the construction of Imam Khomeini International Airport in Iran.[65]

▶ *Prohibited Conduct.* The BIS issued an interim rule amending the EAR (effective on April 3, 2003) to expand the scope of explosives detection equipment to include the kind that Troll's software would help to operate.[66] In the same interim rule, the BIS amended the EAR to

---

64. 15 C.F.R. §744.9(a).

65. See the website for the Airport Industry, accessed at www.airport-technology.com/projects/tehran.

66. 68 FEDERAL REGISTER 16208, April 3, 2003.

expand controls on the export and reexport of such equipment, imposing regional stability ("RS") controls, and further clarifying the already applicable anti-terrorism ("AT") controls, on this equipment.[67] Such equipment is controlled under ECCN 2A983.[68] Software that is specifically developed for use in equipment controlled under ECCN 2A983 is, in turn, controlled under ECCN 2D983.[69] Both the software and the equipment are controlled for reasons of regional stability and anti-terrorism.

Under section 6(j) of the Export Administration Act of 1979, the U.S. Secretary of State has designated Cuba, Iran, Libya, North Korea, Sudan, and Syria as countries whose governments are supporters of international terrorism.[70] The EAR's anti-terrorism control provisions require prior license for any exports or reexports of software controlled under ECCN **2D983** to any such designated country. As a result of the operation of these provisions, Troll's contract for sale of the trace and revoke software to Syria cannot be performed after the Closing of Agile's acquisition of Troll without the appropriate license. Applications for a license to export or reexport such software for all end-users in Syria "will generally be denied."[71] In addition, the application will have to be submitted (and an answer received) prior to the Closing of the Agile/Troll transaction, and preferably before the signing of the DPA, since it will impact certain representations and warranties by Troll in the DPA. In spite of the fact that the "contract sanctity date" for sales of software controlled under ECCN 2D983 to Syrian customers was "March 21, 2003"[72] (one month after Troll and the Syrian

---

67. Id.

68. 15 C.F.R. Part 774, Supplement No. 1, May 2003, p. 5.

69. 15 C.F.R. Part 774, Supplement No. 1, May 2003, p. 41.

70. 15 C.F.R. Part 742, Supplement No. 2, Section (a), May 2003, p. 1, as amended, however, by the BIS's proposed Interim Rule published in 69 FEDERAL REGISTER 146, July 30, 2004, p. 46070. Exports without a license are prohibited to any group identified by the Secretary of State as a foreign terrorist organization. For example, on July 12, 1999, the Commerce Department imposed a 20-year denial of all U.S. export privileges on a Lebanese, naturalized U.S. citizen for attempted export to Lebanon of a thermal imaging camera whose ultimate end-user would be Hezbollah, an organization that the State Department has designated as a foreign terrorist organization. A criminal indictment has been issued against the individual who is currently a fugitive. See BIS Selected Case Summaries *Thermal Imaging Camera Intercepted on Its Way to Hizballah*, accessed at www.bxa.doc.gov/Enforcement/CaseSummaries/Camera2Hizballah.html.

71. 15 C.F.R. Part 742, Supplement No. 2, Section (c)(40), May 2003, p. 19.

72. 15 C.F.R. Part 742, Supplement No. 2, Section (c)(40)(ii), May 2003, p. 19.

entity signed their contract), the future sale is **not** exempted from the
license requirement. BIS determines the applicable contract sanctity
date at the time the party submits its application together with the
relevant supporting data (in this instance, the contract and evidence
of the date of its signing).

Since no deliveries have occurred as yet, it is extremely unlikely that
the BIS would grant the license. Two other factors make denial a virtual
certainty: (i) since the contract is with an entity of the Syrian government, the Terrorism List Governments Sanctions Regulations would
prohibit such transaction;[73] and (ii) the Secretary of Commerce is required to bar the exportation or reexportation to Syria of any item on
the Commerce Control List (with the exception of food, medicine, and
commercial air safety equipment) under the Syrian Accountability and
Lebanese Sovereignty Act of 2003.[74] (See discussion of the Act above in
Section 2.9.)

A comparable license requirement applies for exports and reexports
of such software to Iran. Again, the express policy is that application
for a license "will generally be denied."[75] The contract sanctity date for
reexports by non-U.S. persons to Iran was also March 21, 2003. Since
the software contract has not yet been signed, Troll should disengage
from further negotiations before Agile signs the DPA, and Agile should
obtain appropriate representations and warranties from Troll that it has
completed such disengagement and will not resume such negotiations.
(**Note:** provisions of the Iranian Transactions Regulations would also
prohibit the performance of such contract.)[76]

4. Activity—Reexport of Controlled Toxin in Form Not Specified on Commerce Control List—Successor Liability.

Brugge became a Troll subsidiary as a result of an acquisition by
Troll of certain partnership interests in Brugge in February 2003. In
2002, Brugge assisted in setting up a pharmaceutical production plant

---

73. See Executive Order 13224, September 23, 2001, accessed at www.ustreas.gov/
offices/eotffc/ofac/sanctions/t11ter.pdf, and 31 C.F.R. §596.201, accessed at
www.ustreas.gov/offices/eotffc/ofac/legal/regs/31cfr596.pdf.
74. Executive Order 13338 of May 11, 2004, Sections 1(a) and (b), and 3(a)(i), (ii),
and (iii). Although there are other exceptions implemented in Executive Order 13338,
such as for commercial airline safety, it is doubtful that they would be interpreted to
include explosives detection equipment for use by the Syrian government.
75. 15 C.F.R. Part 742, Supplement No. 2, Section (c)(40)(i), May 2003, p. 19.
76. 31 C.F.R. §§ 560.204 and 560.205.

for development of immunotoxins and related diagnostic kits. The products were supplied by a company in Warsaw, Poland to Polish troops deployed in NATO operations, and were used to protect against weapons-grade biotoxins. Products sold in this connection included a deadly nerve poison, tetrodotoxin ($C_{11}H_{17}N_3O_3$), found in Japanese puffer fish. Brugge had purchased it in the form of tetrodotoxin citrate from a U.S. company. No export license was obtained. The U.S. company explained that, although numerous human pathogens and toxins are controlled by the EAR, there was no listing on the Commerce Control List for "tetrodotoxin citrate." Because the U.S. company concluded that the EAR was not applicable (and no license was required), it did not notify Brugge of any limitation on reexports. Brugge interpreted this absence as an implied permission to reexport without further licensing. Similar reexports are planned pursuant to the project development contract that Brugge currently has with the Polish firm.

➤ *Prohibited Conduct.* Given U.S. concern over proliferation of precursor chemicals (and similar substances that could potentially be used by terrorist organizations), Counsel reviewed the reexport of this toxin and found that "tetrodotoxin" is controlled on the Commerce Control List under ECCN **1C351**,[77] which controls toxins. Moreover, **immunotoxins** are controlled under ECCN **1C991**. A check of the Country Chart confirmed that export of "tetrodotoxin" to Norway would require a license, in spite of the fact that there was no listing for "tetrodotoxin citrate." The issue then was whether the BIS would take the view that an unlisted citrate containing a controlled toxin was nonetheless subject to the EAR and similarly controlled under the same ECCN as the unamalgamated toxin. If this were the case, Agile could be liable for subsequent reexports by Brugge of "tetrodotoxin citrate," and could incur successor liability for previous reexports of that product by Brugge upon Closing.

Because it was reasonable, and indeed highly probable, that BIS would take the position that the citrate form was also controlled, there was a substantial open-ended risk of liability. In an analogous fact pattern, BIS issued charging letters to Sigma-Aldrich Business Holdings ("SABH") and two subsidiaries, Sigma-Aldrich Corporation ("SAC") and Sigma-Aldrich Research Biochemicals ("SARB"), alleging exports of "tetrodotoxin citrate" without the required license, making false or

---

77. 15 C.F.R. Part 774, Supplement No. 1, "1C351."

misleading statements, and failure to maintain records. The BIS action argued that SABH and SAC should be held liable as successor entities for violations committed by SARB prior to SARB's sale of its partnership interests to SABH and SAC as well as for violations that occurred thereafter. The partnership interests in question had been transferred four years earlier. BIS was not only willing to pierce the corporate veil, but was willing to construe "successor liability" extremely broadly. A subsequent decision by an administrative law judge held that successor liability can be applied under the EAR on the rationale that the terms "company" or "association" include successors and assigns. The EAR evince a clear intent to provide remedies beyond the "persons" who violate the EAR, and thus sweep broadly enough to include their successors as "related persons." Moreover, the judge compared the export of tetrodotoxin in a citrate buffer to export of the toxin in "packaging material." The citrate merely facilitated export, and therefore did not change the essential nature of the product being exported. Pursuant to this reasoning, the judge found that the "packaged" citrate also required a Commerce Department license if export entailed any destinations listed in the Charging Letters (countries in Asia and Europe).

On the issue of whether SABH and SAC assumed such liability by purchasing the partnership interests, the judge acknowledged that, under traditional rules, asset purchasers were not liable unless one of four exceptions applied: (i) express assumption of liability; (ii) a transaction that amounts to a *de facto* consolidation or merger (on a "successor in interest" theory); (iii) the purchaser is a "continuation" of the seller; or (iv) the parties entered into the transaction fraudulently to escape liability. However, because such exceptions were designed to prevent a corporation from "escaping its liabilities merely by changing hats," and not to address the security concerns of the EAR, the judge added a broadened "substantial continuity" exception to the traditional rules. Under this exception, the judge noted several relevant factors in making a determination of on-going liability: whether the successor (i) retains the predecessor's employees, supervisory personnel and production facilities, (ii) continues to produce its products, (iii) keeps its business name, (iv) keeps its assets and general business operations, and (v) holds itself out to the public as the predecessor corporation. If several of these occur, a finding of successor liability would not be unreasonable. Without such a rule, it would be too easy to evade liability by a purely formalistic change of name. While "substantial continuity" of a commercial enterprise has historically required knowledge of the potential liability, the judge further noted that at least one court had held that such knowledge could be inferred from the facts and totality of circumstances. Such inference could be drawn if each of the five factors were found in the transaction.[78] The judge found all five factors in the Sigma-Aldrich case.

On the question of successor liability in the acquisition of partnership interests, the judge found that the Purchase Agreement mentioned the transfer of partnership units only, not of assets, obligations or liabilities. Ordinarily, parties would not be considered successors in interest if that were the full statement of the facts: "An entity that holds partnership units in another company is not liable for that company's wrongdoing, unless it can be shown that the partners were controlling the operations of that company."[79] However, the judge relied on testimony that the predecessor had also sold all its assets and businesses to the successor company, although there was no evidence of consideration. He concluded that an issue remained as to whether the predecessor "gratuitously transferred its assets," or such assets had been acquired by the successors before being transferred. Before a hearing could be held on this issue, Sigma Aldrich agreed to settle the charges by paying a fine of $1.76 million.[80]

That decision suggests that: (i) exports of "tetrodotoxin citrate" to Brugge in Norway had required a license, (ii) reexports of the substance by Brugge to Poland required a license (since the Country Chart shows that exports and reexports of "tetrodotoxin" are controlled to Poland), and (iii) since Agile's acquisition possesses the same factors cited by the administrative law judge for application of the successor liability doctrine (including the fact that Agile would acquire all assets of Troll and Brugge), there is a strong likelihood that the BIS would hold Agile liable for such violations as a successor in interest, if such reexports continue beyond the Closing. Agile should therefore persuade Troll to cause Brugge to disengage from the relevant contract prior to signing the DPA.

---

78. The judge also reasoned that the doctrine of successor liability could apply even if the BIS did not issue charges against the predecessor corporation.

79. *In the Matter of: Sigma-Aldrich Business Holdings, Sigma-Aldrich Corporation; and Sigma-Aldrich Research Biochemicals, Inc.*, August 29, 2002, accessed at www.bis.doc.gov/Enforcement/CaseSummaries/Sigma_Aldrich_ALJ_Decision_02.pdf, at p. 13.

80. BIS, *Sigma Aldrich Pays $1.76 Million Penalty to Settle Charges of Illegal Exports of Biological Toxins*, press release, November 4, 2002, accessed at www.bis.doc.gov/News/2002/SigmaAldrichPays4Acquisition.htm.

The purpose of pursuing a *pre-signing* disengagement is not to avert successor liability, but rather to (i) reduce the number of potential violations (each shipment would be a prohibited reexport), (ii) reduce the probability that product ordered pre-Closing would slip through to post-Closing shipments, (iii) provide a demonstrable record that Agile had done its utmost to minimize the potential harm contemplated by the EAR control of such reexports, and (iv) in the event of charges, position Agile to discuss the issues with the BIS in the most beneficial posture. As with other transactions found in the earlier due diligence review, it is important that Agile not violate EAR General Prohibition 10 by knowingly financing a violation of the EAR, since Agile would know that violations had occurred, could occur post-Closing and would be occurring after signing, unless pre-signing disengagement was timely put in place. Care must be taken to ensure that the logistical tail of the Brugge/Polish company project has been completely wound up. (The BIS appears to have implemented successor liability more recently in its January 2003 charging letters against Boeing.)[81]

These EAR examples illustrate how risk points can escape counsel in the United States, if due diligence reports merely summarize a company's commercial dealings.[82] A statement such as "Troll produces encryption products and anti-terrorist technologies" does not provide sufficient intelligence for counsel to interpret the activities on the ground that determine the location and magnitude of the risk points for potential violations of the TSR, EAR and ITAR. Under pressure to meet customer demands, companies may solve problems in a commercially efficient manner while unwittingly violating the EAR, TSR or other Access Control Laws.

Consider the following "common business practice" scenario: Iran Air places an order with the German-based company, Fluke Germany,

81. U.S. Department of State, *Press Release*, January 02, 2003, accessed at www.state.gov/r/pa/prs/dpb/2003/16309.htm.

82. It is important to monitor revisions of the EAR as they appear in the FEDERAL REGISTER in order to ensure that new risk points are identified. For example, the Revision of Export Controls for General Purpose Microprocessors, 68 FEDERAL REGISTER 1796, January 14, 2003 (codified at 15 C.F.R. Parts 744 and 774), created a new license requirement applicable to the export and reexport of general purpose microprocessors in instances where the exporter or reexporter knows (*or has reason to know*, or is informed by the BIS) that such microprocessor is intended or will be used by a "military end-user" or otherwise for a "military end-use" in a country of concern for national security reasons. There is a presumption of denial for any such license applications.

for three advanced signal generators. The purchase order clearly states: "Please ship to Iran Air Frankfurt Airport for reforwarding to Tehran, Iran." Fluke Germany cannot fill the order from inventory and requests its affiliate, Fluke Holland, to obtain the product. However, it too is out of stock, and in turn requests the product from the manufacturer in the United States, Fluke USA, which forwards the signal generators as requested. All invoices among the suppliers bear a destination control statement: "These commodities were licensed for ultimate destination Fed. Rep. Germany. Diversion contrary to United States law is prohibited."[83] Fluke Germany, pursuant to the original purchase order, delivers the products to Iran Air in Frankfurt, but the accompanying invoice no longer contains the destination control statement, and bears no indication of a license authorization, license limitation or caution against "diversion." After a few days, Iran Air ships the product to Iran. At the time in question, the EAR clearly required that no person in a foreign country (or in the United States) reexport certain products from an authorized country of ultimate destination, or export the product from

---

83. As with the EAR requirements for "adequate protections" against unauthorized transfer, such statements tend to be more formalistic than informative: it is very unlikely that a company not involved in military sales (and thus not as accustomed to "end user certificate" requirements) would understand anything by the statement "Diversion contrary to United States law is prohibited"—just as a U.S. citizen would be unlikely to understand a sign on the German Autobahn that proclaimed: "Disregard of flashing high beams is prohibited." Destination control statements often go unnoticed, and even when noticed they are seldom understood by the personnel in another country. However, in "due diligence" investigations, seeing such statements in some documents and not in others should be early alerts to easily overlooked risk points under the EAR, TSR, and ITAR. In cyber-driven transactions, if due diligence does not drill down to such mundane documents as purchase orders, it is virtually impossible to verify compliance with, or risk points under, the EAR, TSR and ITAR. Requesting access to, and time for review of, such documents can drive up transactional costs and bring clients to the not uncommon impasse with counsel: requests to do it "quick and dirty" accompanied by the unexpressed insistence that it be "quick, thorough and squeaky clean."

Checkpoints will not be funded if they prove to be transactional chokepoints whose justification is lost on clients trying to complete a deal. As enforcement tightens, and as agencies such as OFAC make increasing use of websites to disclose the names of violators and the penalties assessed against them, client concerns that EAR, TSR, ITAR and patent checkpoints are unnecessary or not justified by the cost may diminish. But whether or not such threats seem to subside, clients will inevitably challenge the necessity of deep U.S. compliance checks when the deal is governed by a foreign jurisdiction's domestic law and subject chiefly to the regulatory agencies of that jurisdiction or others linked to it such as EU regulatory jurisdiction.

the United States with the knowledge that it would be reexported from the authorized country of ultimate destination, unless a license had been obtained.[84] None of the Fluke companies complied with this requirement, nor did Iran Air. Five years passed without the parties questioning the legitimacy of the transaction. The Commerce Department then instituted administrative proceedings against Iran Air, but not against any of the Fluke company violators. On review, the Circuit Court upheld Commerce's authority to impose strict liability for civil violations, noting that one court had upheld the imposition of criminal sanctions on a "near strict liability basis."[85]

3.4 Additional EAR-Related Risk Points.

As noted at the start of this chapter, there are additional EAR-related risk points that Agile's Counsel also checked independently, because they would not be discovered in a routine review of simply the five mentioned categories of items "subject to" the EAR, but they could entail liability for Agile. We mention a number of them briefly here.

➤ *Prohibited Conduct*—**Participation in, or Failure to Report a Request to Participate in, an EAR-Prohibited Boycott.** The EAR contain a set of provisions that bar "U.S. persons" from engaging in conduct that cooperates with an EAR-prohibited boycott or discrimination ("Anti-boycott Regulations" or "ABR"). The ABR definition of "U.S. person" refers to the following:

> "Any person who is a United States resident or national, including individuals, domestic concerns [partnership, corporation, association, etc.], and 'controlled in fact' foreign subsidiaries, affiliates, or other permanent foreign establishments of domestic concerns."[86]

---

84. See *Iran Air v. Kugelman*, 302 U.S. App. D.C. 174 (D.C. Cir., 1993).

85. Id, at note 7, referring to *United States v. Shetterly*, 971 F.2d 67, 73 (7th Cir. 1992), holding that 50 U.S.C. App. § 2410(a) "requires only that the criminal defendant 'knowingly exported . . . a controlled commodity, without obtaining the appropriate export license' and does not require that 'the exporter know [] that a license is required.'"

86. 15 C.F.R. §760.1(b).

The ABR reaches activities of a "U.S. person" only if they occur within interstate or foreign commerce of the United States, a difficult determination when reviewing the activities of a "controlled-in-fact" foreign affiliate of a U.S. firm. Recitation of general rules are often unreliable for such determinations; the rules for making such determinations on a case-by-case basis are quite detailed. The potential scope of the ABR's extra-territorial reach is clearly illustrated by the explanatory ABR provision, which states in relevant part:

> "The action of a domestic concern in **specifically directing** the activities of its controlled in fact foreign subsidiary, affiliate, or other permanent foreign establishment **is an activity in United States commerce.**"[87]

In addition, a transaction, for example, between a "controlled-in-fact" foreign affiliate and a foreign person involving goods or services (including information) acquired from a person in the United States "is in United States commerce," if any of several conditions is met, including if the goods or services were acquired to fill an order for a person outside of the United States or to meet "anticipated needs of specified foreign customers." Thus, if the "controlled-in-fact" foreign affiliate places such orders for items from the U.S. to fulfill present or anticipated obligations as a supplier, the activity is within U.S. commerce and within the reach of the ABR.

Unlike conduct prohibited by other previous sections of the EAR (or the TSR), which are not violated unless the U.S. person engages in the proscribed activity, the ABR impose a reporting requirement that is triggered if the U.S. person (or an entity it controls-in-fact) receives a request to comply with, further or support such activity. (Such reports must be filed quarterly.) Thus the U.S. person is obligated both to refuse to participate in *and* to report to the Department of Commerce the request to participate. (Note: the Ribicoff Amendment to the 1976 Tax Reform Act also requires U.S. taxpayers to report "operations" in, with, or related to, a boycotting country or its nationals, and any requests received to participate in or cooperate with an international boycott.)[88]

There are six categories of ABR-prohibited conduct that apply when such conduct by a U.S. person occurs in interstate commerce or U.S. foreign commerce:

---

87. 15 C.F.R. §760.1(d). [Emphasis added.]
88. See Internal Revenue Code, Section 999.

- **Refusing to do business** in or with a boycotted country or a "blacklisted" company (e.g., a company of the boycotted country);[89]
- **Refusing to employ or otherwise discriminating** against U.S. persons (individuals, entities, or personnel of such entities) on the basis of race, religion, sex, national origin or nationality;[90]
- **Furnishing information or knowingly agreeing to furnish information:**
  - ➤ about the race, religion, sex, national origin or nationality of U.S. persons (individuals, entities, or personnel of such entities);[91]
  - ➤ about the U.S. person itself or any other person regarding their "past, present, or proposed business relationships" with or in "a boycotted country," a business, national or resident of such country, or "[w]ith any other person who is known or believed to be restricted from having any business relationship with or in a boycotting country;"[92] or
  - ➤ about "whether any person is a member of, has made contributions to, or is otherwise associated with or involved in the activities of any charitable or fraternal organization which supports a boycotted country."[93]
- **Paying, honoring, confirming, or otherwise implementing a Letter of Credit** that contains a condition or requirement that a U.S. person is prohibited from complying with by the ABR.[94]

Note: The ABR expands the reach of the Letter of Credit provision by several additional provisions, three of which deserve particularly close attention:

First, no U.S. person shall, as a result of application of this provision, "be obligated to pay, honor, or implement" a Letter of Credit;[95]

---

89. 15 C.F.R. §760.2(a).
90. 15 C.F.R. §760.2(b).
91. 15 C.F.R. §760.2(c).
92. 15 C.F.R. §760.2(d).
93. 15 C.F.R. §760.2(e).
94. 15 C.F.R. §760.2(f)(1).
95. 15 C.F.R. §760.2(f)(1).

Second, compliance with this provision "shall provide an absolute defense in any action brought to compel payment of, honoring of, or other implementation of a letter of credit, or for damages resulting from failure to pay or otherwise honor or implement the letter of credit;"[96] and

Third, a Letter of Credit implemented outside the United States by a U.S. person located outside the United States "will be presumed to apply to a transaction in U.S. commerce."[97]

If Troll or any of its affiliates has been asked by any third party (supplier, customer, shipping entity, etc.), in connection with a sale, purchase or transfer of goods or services (including information), to enter into an agreement that would involve Troll or its affiliates in any of those actions, Agile needs to consider whether, upon the Closing, Troll or its affiliates would be viewed as *intentionally (not inadvertently)* performing agreements that involved the ABR-prohibited conduct. It should also consider whether any such requests to further or support such conduct are likely to occur (since receipt of such requests must be recorded, expressly rejected, and reported quarterly to BIS).

Thus, if Troll is receiving *draft versions* of purchase orders, shipping documents, Letters of Credit, correspondence concerning issuance or confirmation of such Letters of Credit, supply agreements, sale agreements, agent agreements, etc. that contain terms that contravene the ABR, Agile must anticipate the post-Closing risks such documents entail: Agile or its "controlled-in-fact" foreign affiliates (Troll, Brugge, or Ijsselmeer) would be viewed as performing such agreements, or as receiving post-Closing requests to engage in or support the ABR-prohibited conduct (and thus would have the burden of reporting such requests and responding to investigative follow-up inquiries by the BIS).

Although the primary target of the ABR-prohibited conduct is usually Israel (including its citizens, companies and all vessels flying its flag), the ABR also prohibits such conduct when the target is Taiwan (and the request to engage in or support the boycott originates with the People's Republic of China), or when the target is India or Pakistan, or any other country with which the U.S. has good relations. The Depart-

---

96. 15 C.F.R. §760.2(f)(5).
97. 15 C.F.R. §760.2(f)(9).

ment of Commerce, Office of Anti-boycott's website offers the following illustrations:

- A **purchase order** states: "Goods of Israeli origin not acceptable."
- **Letters of Credit** include the conditions that: "A signed statement from the shipping company, or its agent, stating the name, flag and nationality of the carrying vessel and confirming . . . that it is permitted to enter Arab ports;" or "Importation of goods from Israel is strictly prohibited by Kuwait import regulations; therefore, certificate of origin covering goods originating in Israel is not acceptable."
- A **contract** includes a warranty that: "The seller warrants that no supplier or manufacturer or any part of the product is precluded from doing business with Saudi Arabia under the terms of the Arab boycott regulations."
- A **repair order** includes a provision that: "Invoices must be endorsed with a certificate of origin that goods are not of Israeli origin and do not contain any Israeli material and are not shipped from any Israeli port."[98]

In Agile's enforcement of this checkpoint, it would be well advised to require Troll and its affiliates to start a routine practice to record all such requests, to take formal action in response to each such request, to document (in correspondence, meeting minutes, etc.) each such action, to ensure that these practices are instituted on or prior to the signing of the DPA, and to preserve such records in a manner that will keep them accessible for the statutory period of five years subsequent to receipt of the request.[99] The ABR checkpoint is one more instance in which overseas companies can be expected to have no prior experience in rejecting or monitoring requests, instructions, or contractual correspondence that, if accepted by a U.S. person, would entail liability for such person. Agile's review for ABR risks is again best done early—on the first diligence review of the documents at Troll and its affiliates (including relevant e-mail). In our experience, the most problematic documents, however, will be those related to issuance, confirmation and

---

98. BIS, Office of Antiboycott Compliance, *Examples of Boycott Requests,* accessed at www.bxa.doc.gov/antiboycottcompliance/oacantiboycottrequestexamples.html.
99. 15 C.F.R. §762.2(b)(32) and §762.6(a).

extension of Letters of Credit. Given the provisions noted, remediation of these may necessitate pre-signing amendment or other action to ensure that completion of such action does not expose a U.S. person to liability, or cause a delay in the contemplated cross-border transaction (merger, acquisition or outsourcing).

3.4.1 Activity: Export, Reexport or Transfer of Items Controlled by Two or More U.S. Government Agencies or Agencies Other than BIS.

Jurisdictional overlaps, particularly between items controlled by the Departments of Commerce and State, continue to be unresolved. For example, some items on the Commerce Control List also appear on the U.S. Munitions List (which usually means that State has jurisdiction). Formal transfers of items from the jurisdiction of one agency to that of another frequently take place (as occurred in 2002, with regard to "space qualified" items such as components for satellites and space stations). Other departmental jurisdictions that should be reviewed (depending on the transaction) include: the Departments of State, Treasury and Energy, the Environmental Protection Agency, the Nuclear Regulatory Commission and the U.S. Patent and Trademark Office ("PTO"). If a U.S. person intends to file a patent application, or amendment, modification or supplement thereto in a foreign country or with a foreign governing body (such as the EU), and such filing would entail the export or reexport technology "subject to" the EAR, permission must be obtained not from the BIS but from the PTO.[100]

➤ *The Prohibited Conduct:* **Export, Reexport or Transfer of Items Subject to Implicit or Non-Obvious Control by the EAR.** The structure of the EAR can lead the reader to think that the text of one provision provides a comprehensive rule for export, reexport or transfer of an item (including technology, software or information), and will not alert the reader (with a caution or cross-reference) to other prohibitions that nonetheless apply to such conduct regarding such item. Examples include the following:

---

100. See 15 C.F.R. §734.3(b)(1)(v) and 37 C.F.R. Part 5.

- The Ten General Prohibitions do not exhaust the EAR's description of prohibitions.

- The exception to General Prohibition Two—that a U.S. person may not export, reexport or export from abroad any foreign-made item (including software or technology) that incorporates more than a *de minimis* amount of controlled U.S.-origin items—can lead the reader to infer reasonably that if its item qualifies for that exception no license is required. However, Part 734's description of the five categories of items "subject to" the EAR, refers to both foreign incorporation of controlled U.S.-origin items that exceed the *de minimis* amount *and* to some items that do not exceed the *de minimis* amount—items that are "subject to" the EAR when exported or reexported in any quantity as described in 734.4(a).[101] (See our discussion above, of Troll's encryption item.)

- The calculation of *de minimis* amounts (detailed in Supplement No. 2 to EAR Part 734) fails to mention an exclusion set forth earlier in that Part, specifically that "Commodities subject only to short supply controls are not included in calculating U.S. content."[102]

- There are inconsistent provisions describing the coverage of the EAR, leaving one to conclude that the most prudent course is to ensure compliance with the most rigorous provision (rather than risk having to argue to the BIS that a failure to comply resulted from an inconsistency—an argument that perforce must acknowledge knowledge of the more rigorous provision). In addition, although we reviewed five categories "subject to" the EAR, based on a review of Part 734, that Part is not comprehensive. Moreover, the EAR's suggested guidance, that a party check the transaction by asking a series of questions,[103] will not necessarily lead one to all the exceptions and inconsistencies.

Just as efforts to complete commercial transactions (and not forfeit immediate economic opportunities) can result in unwitting violations that entail strict liability, so pressure to complete cyber-driven transactions (such as mergers, acquisitions, outsourcings and joint ventures)

---

101. 15 C.F.R. §734.3(a)(3)(i).

102. 15 C.F.R. §734.4(e).

103. The questions are "What is [the item]? Where is it going? Who will receive it? What will they do with it? and What else do they do?" They are found at 15 C.F.R. §732.1(a)(1).

can result in unwitting failure to understand the full scope of the commercial activities that generate the greatest risk points under the Access Control Laws.[104] For Agile, as a defense contractor, several such risk points result from the ITAR, which we will now review.

---

104. There are important exceptions to the Iranian Transactions Regulations that have either been affirmed by the courts in recent decisions or clarified by OFAC in 2004. For example, the Institute of Electrical and Electronic Engineers (IEEE) applied to OFAC in 2003 to clarify that IEEE's peer review and publication of scholarly works from its members in Cuba, Iran, Libya, and Sudan would not be violating the applicable TSR programs that target those countries. The effort required several written submissions by IEEE to OFAC, a "summit conference" in Washington, D.C., in February 2004 attended by OFAC officials and representatives of many of the academic and scholarly publishing entities, and further meetings at OFAC's offices. The result was a favorable determination issued by OFAC in a letter to IEEE's counsel on April 2, 2004.

The difficulty in obtaining the decision turned on OFAC's initial view that the exception for import of informational materials did not permit peer review and editing of manuscripts because that resulted in prohibited substantive alternations or enhancements of informational material by U.S. persons prior to its final importation for publication. However, as IEEE made clear, and eventually persuaded OFAC, IEEE's peer reviewers may spot problems in a submitted paper and may advise the paper's author of the nature and extent of those problems, but they do not substantially rewrite or revise the manuscript to remedy those problems. To make that distinction clear to OFAC required considerable deliberation and discussion. It also demonstrated how careful parties must be when seeking to act within the terms of an express exception to the TSR. And it demonstrated the value of conferring with good counsel and approaching OFAC in advance, rather than inferring that OFAC will necessarily adopt a view of activities that seem obvious to a party but only because that party is deeply involved in its own activities which OFAC may have little opportunity to understand unless properly approached. See OFAC Interpretative Ruling Number 040405-FARCL-1A-15, accessed at www.ustreas.gov/offices/eotffc/ofac/actions/20040405.html.

We would add that the investment in a proactive approach to OFAC is almost certainly far less costly and burdensome to litigating the issues as occurred in *Masood Kalantari v. NITV, Inc.*, 352 1202 (9th Cir, 2003). That copyright infringement case required the court to decide whether the Iranian Transactions Regulations prohibited the commercial importation of movies from Iran, the copyright of such movies, or the assignment to a U.S. person of the exclusive rights to copyright, distribute and exhibit the movies in North America. The court held each of those activities came within express exceptions to those regulations for importation of information and informational materials "whether commercial or otherwise," the filing and prosecution of copyrights, and incidental transactions related thereto. On those grounds, the Ninth Circuit reversed the District Court, which had held that plaintiff lacked a valid assignment or authority to obtain a valid copyright of the Iranian films it had procured. The fact that such argument persuaded the trial court but resulted in a reversal by the Ninth Circuit suggests that the plaintiff TV producer and promoter of Iranian cultural events in the U.S. would have been spared such costs and risks if it had applied in advance to OFAC for a clarification.

CHAPTER 4

Checkpoint: International Traffic in Arms Regulations

4.0 Agile's Transaction at Checkpoint ITAR.

Defense acquisitions present particularly severe regulatory challenges. Cross-border defense acquisitions create additional layers of compliance not customarily found in non-defense acquisitions. The most important derive from compliance with national security protections, as set forth in defense trade controls (which for the United States is the ITAR).

The ITAR comprises a hierarchy of controls, including several levels of defense items, categorized by their military significance and their potential to protect or undermine national security (if diverted or released to unauthorized persons, entities or nations). All such items are deemed "defense articles."[1] The controls contained in the ITAR with respect to items on the U.S. Munitions List are far more stringently enforced than the EAR (with respect to items on the Commerce Control List). This is because the consequences of unauthorized transfer or release of such defense articles and technical data is potentially catastrophic from a national security perspective.

The ITAR's control of the release or transfer of "technical data" (which covers oral, written and electronic transfers) is designed to create sanctions against careless electronic transmission of such data (*e.g.,* e-mail, instant messaging, posting of data on websites or storing files

---

1. 22 CFR §120.6.

on portable, high density media, such as keychain drives, iPods, CD-ROMs, DVDs, etc.).[2] It should be remembered that technologies that enhance communication[3] also facilitate unauthorized electronic disclosure. The exigencies of the electronic age place enormous pressure on compliance procedures, especially if electronic technologies have not been recalibrated to prevent inadvertent release of ITAR-controlled technical data. The ITAR does not expressly require such recalibration, but it encourages it through the incentives created by the legal presumptions and potential defenses arising from its presence (or absence). Since ITAR prohibits unauthorized exports, each firm that handles ITAR-controlled technical data has a continuous obligation to anticipate such risks and to avert them by auditing and improving its ITAR compliance procedures. In short, as the means of communication improve, firms must enhance their means of interdicting unauthorized communication (and transfer) of technical data. Otherwise, such firms will inevitably contravene the ITAR. While that principle also applies to the EAR and TSR, it applies with particular precision, heightened diligence and enhanced scrutiny to the ITAR and its efforts to maintain the most rigorous U.S. export controls on "defense"-sensitive data.[4]

The following table highlights those controls applied by the ITAR that are considerably more strict than those applied by the EAR. A number of these will be explained in detail later in this section:

---

2. For example, in the opinion of an astrophysicist and retired weapons scientist, the breakdown in information security and the problem of missing data at Los Alamos National Laboratory, "Most likely . . . lies in the proliferation of ever-smaller and easy-to-lose computer storage devices that hold ever more information." See Blumenthal, Ralph, *Idle at Los Alamos: A Weapon Lab as Its Own Worst Enemy*, THE NEW YORK TIMES, July 22, 2004, p. A-12, reporting views of Charles Keller. As of this writing, the reported proposed solution to the problem is to bar the use of portable disks and other storage devices from the laboratory. CNN, *Next on CNN*, broadcast on CNN on July 24, 2004 at 3:10 PM.

3. For example, mobile phones that have integrated still or video cameras. As of August 2004, 20% of all mobile phones sold have integrated cameras. See Flynn, Laurie J., *The Cellphone's Next Makeover: Affordable Jukebox on the Move*, THE NEW YORK TIMES, August 2, 2004, p. C-4.

4. We would expect that such controls will increasingly apply to homeland security sensitive data.

Figure 1. Comparison of EAR and ITAR

EAR	ITAR
Provides a *de minimis* exception for items that consist of less than 10%, in value, of U.S.-originated content (although exception does not apply to certain items under certain controls such as encryption items controlled by ECCN 5A002)	No *de minimis* exception
Licenses exports and reexports	Licenses exports only.
Do not require end-user certificates	Requires end-user certificates (that items will not be reexported without US permission)
Does not require U.S. citizens to report when they have reason to believe that someone is violating the EAR	Requires reporting of all known violations and attempts to violate ITAR
Does not require producers or exporters of "dual use" items to register	Requires all producers and exporters of "defense articles" to register with U.S. Government – also requires anyone who modifies an item for military application to register
Does not require formal agreements between exporter and end-user of "dual use" technical data	Requires formal Technical Assistance Agreements between exporter and recipient of defense related technical data, and that they not come into force before the Directorate of Defense Controls approves the agreement
Controls exports to many countries for a variety of reasons (antiterrorism, anti-proliferation of WMDs, etc.), but applies no complete embargoes	Controls exports of defense articles all countries, and applies complete arms embargoes to many countries.
Places few limits on who may export "dual use" items (and only bars exporting by persons who the BIS has deprived of their exporting privileges)	Places several limits on who may export "defense articles" and "defense services"
Issues general licenses for exports of certain items	No general licenses
Does not regulate political campaign contributions or commissions pay in relation to any contract for "dual use" items	Requires reporting of political campaign contributions or commissions, above a threshold amount, paid in relation to any contract for defense articles or services

Certain defense articles require even more rigorous controls by virtue of "their capacity for substantial military utility or capability."[5] The ITAR expressly acknowledges this risk and labels such defense articles "significant military equipment" or "SME."[6] An asterisk precedes each such item on the USML.

In turn, certain SME require a heightened level of scrutiny as a result of the magnitude of the investment in their research and development ("nonrecurring costs") or their production. These are labeled "major defense equipment," and are defined by the ITAR as "any item of significant military equipment . . . on the U.S. Munitions List having a nonrecurring research and development cost of more than $50,000,000 or a total production cost of more than $200,000,000."[7]

The EAR is permitted to list all known "dual use" items without the risk of compromising U.S. national security, because the existence of such items is well known from their civilian use. Listing them as dual use (having military potential) does not disclose to potential adversaries any useful information about how to modify or use them to harm U.S. interests. By contrast, if the USML listed all known defense articles in the U.S. arsenal (including those not yet deployed, but under development or on the drawing boards), the USML would certainly compromise U.S. national security. For this reason, the ITAR has a bifurcated policy of controls: it controls items whose existence it discloses by placing them on the USML; and it controls items whose existence it does not disclose or acknowledge, but whose potential or future developments it anticipates. The latter expresses its policy of applying controls to items that may be designated in the future as defense articles or defense services. Hence, the ITAR's policy for designating what it controls includes the following:

"An article or service may be designated or determined in the future to be a defense article (see §120.6) or defense service (see §120.9) if it:

(i) Is specifically *designed, developed, configured, adapted, or modified* for a military application, and

   (a) Does not have predominant civil applications, and

   (b) Does not have performance equivalent (defined by form, fit and function) to those of an article or service used for civil application; or

---

5. 22 CFR §120.7.
6. 22 CFR §120.7.
7. 22 CFR §120.8.

(ii) Is specifically *designed, developed, configured, adapted, or modified* for a military application, and has significant military or intelligence applicability such that control under this subchapter is necessary."[8]

If an item has been developed, adapted or modified for a military application, and as such does not have predominant civilian applications (and is not equivalent in performance to articles or services that have civilian applications), the Directorate of Defense Trade Controls (the "Directorate")[9] may designate it as a "defense article" or "defense service," and subject it to ITAR controls. Such controls apply even if the item has yet to appear on the USML (or may in fact never appear). This policy reflects the assumption that national security should trump civilian applications. To this end, subparagraph (b) overrides the rule enunciated in subparagraph (a). If an item has been developed, adapted or modified for a military application and, as such, its purpose or use, whether military or *"intelligence"* (a term not defined in the ITAR), is sufficiently significant that control by the ITAR is necessary, the Directorate may disregard its civil applications and subject it to control by the ITAR (again, even if the item has yet to appear on the USML or may never appear). The list of defense articles and services on the USML is much shorter than the list of dual-use items on the CCL, but the terms of the USML sweep far more broadly, in order to extend its reach to the widest possible variety of items without risking inappropriate specificity. The USML has 22 categories, the last of which is titled "Miscellaneous Article." This last category extends the reach of the USML (and thus the scope of the ITAR) by purporting to cover: "Any article not specifically enumerated in the other categories of the U.S. Munitions List which has substantial military applicability and which has been specifically designed or modified for military purpose."[10]

The reach of the USML is further extended by appending to each of its categories a statement that "technical data" and "defense services"[11]

---

8. 22 CFR §120.3. [Emphasis added.] To remove any doubt that any other considerations might outweigh national security, the ITAR adds that the "intended use of the article or service after its export (i.e., for a military or civilian purpose) is not relevant" to a decision on whether the ITAR controls that item.

9. In this Chapter, in order to reduce the number of acronyms we are substituting the term "Directorate" for "DDTC" (the term used in the previous chapters).

10. 22 CFR §121.1, Category XXI, "Miscellaneous Articles." [Emphasis added.]

11. "Defense services" includes such activities as design, development, testing,

directly related to the items in that category are also included in such category (without enumeration). Transactions that are cyber-driven are most likely to require close monitoring to prevent the unauthorized export of such "technical data" and "defense services."

It is important to recognize that the defense trade controls employed by U.S. allies differ in many important ways from the ITAR, because such differences can create misconceptions about the scope of compliance during cross-border negotiations. To begin with, in comparison to U.S. controls, other nations' controls are less comprehensive in their application or scope and less rigorous in their enforcement. Although nations tend to resemble one another in their concerns regarding national security, they often deviate from one another in important ways in what they regard as a threat to such security. This is reflected in the precautions embodied in their defense trade controls. (We need only reflect on the fact that two World Wars have been fought on European soil to understand that their perception of the vulnerability of their borders differs from that of the United States.) Agile needs to be alert to such differences, since its pursuit of Troll will require compliance with a variety of dissimilar defense control regimes (those of Norway, Canada, The Netherlands and, because of Agile's marketing plans for its anti-terrorist technologies, the United Kingdom (the "U.K.")). These differences are particularly pronounced with regard to control of disclosure or electronic transfer of technical data from nationals of one country to those of another (inside and outside the originating country).

As a result, nationals from Norway or the U.K. can make disclosures to U.S. persons, consistent with their defense export controls, but reciprocal disclosures by U.S. persons under similar circumstances (or in the same meeting) may be prohibited by the ITAR. Since technical personnel engaged in problem solving meetings, or exploring potential cooperation may exchange information or expertise, may provide technical advisory services, or may make proposals that are not primarily focused on observing the strict limits of the ITAR, it is extremely important for U.S. defense firms to ensure that personnel are trained in and reminded of the boundaries that must be observed in such meetings (whether conducted face-to-face or electronically by video conference, e-mail or other means of transmission).

---

maintenance, repair, operation, and destruction of defense articles. See 22 CFR §120.9(a)(1).

To illustrate the risks, we will consider two technology transfer scenarios. In the first, Agile, Troll and a U.K. firm each have received subcontracts related to the JSF (Joint Strike Fighter) on which they are to collaborate. Each has among their engineering staff nationals of The Netherlands. The project manager at each company asks his respective general counsel whether a license will be needed to talk about (or show diagrams of) the JFS technical data to the Dutch national engineers. The second scenario involves the same facts, but the U.K. firm proposes that representatives from each company arrange a meeting to exchange technical data, either in the United States, the U.K. or Norway. Again the project managers at each company ask their counsel about the constraints on transfers of information or any controlled technology to foreign nationals of the other two companies, depending upon where the meeting takes place.

To both inquiries, Agile's U.S. counsel must answer that there are serious constraints on such transfers or "releases" under the ITAR. A license would be required before any exchange can lawfully take place. When a U.S. person "releases" ITAR controlled technical data to a foreign national, either within the United States or abroad, the U.S. person thereby "exports" that data. The ITAR defines "export" to be any of five activities, including among others: "Disclosing (including oral or visual disclosure) or transferring technical data to a foreign person, whether in the United States or abroad."[12] (Note that, unlike the EAR which defines a transfer of controlled data to a foreign national within the United States as a "deemed export," the ITAR makes no reference to "deemed export," and simply defines such releases as an "export" that requires a license. While the EAR provides for licensing of exports and reexports, the ITAR applies a stricter regime: it provides licenses solely for "export;" any reexport or retransfer is strictly prohibited. Thus the ITAR defines "*reexport*" and "*retransfer*" as proscribed activities. Such retransfer would constitute "the transfer of defense articles or defense services to an end use, end user or destination not previously authorized.")[13]

By contrast, counsel to the U.K. firm would probably not see significant constraints on such transfers, although he might add a precautionary caveat for "other" circumstances. Unless the technical data relates to a weapon of mass destruction (which it does not), a U.K. firm

---

12. 22 CFR §120.17.
13. 22 CFR §120.19. [Emphasis added.]

does not need a license to transfer controlled technical data to Dutch or other foreign nationals residing in the United Kingdom. Under Parliamentary Order 2003 ("Order 2003"), the contemplated "transfer" would fit one of the definitions, namely a "transfer by non-electronic means . . . from a person or place within the United Kingdom."[14] There is no prohibition in Order 2003 on the transfer by non-electronic means of technical data to a foreign national residing in the United Kingdom.[15] The U.K. Department of Trade & Industry issued a Supplementary Guidance Note that clarified the rationale behind this: "The approach in the controls is based on the concept of exports or transfers from the United Kingdom to overseas, not on nationality."[16] Even more remarkably, Order 2003 places the obligation of obtaining a license on whomever exports or transfers from the United Kingdom, even if that person is a foreign national and received such technical data from someone else in the United Kingdom. As the Supplementary Guidance Note points out: "if you transfer the technology or software to anyone, whether a foreign or U.K. national, within the United Kingdom, and that person subsequently exports the technology or software out of the United Kingdom, they must obtain an appropriate license." But there is an important caveat. Order 2003 provides that:

> "No person shall transfer by any non-electronic means any software or technology to a person or place within the United Kingdom where . . . he is aware that such software or technology is or may

---

14. *Export of Goods, Transfers of Technology and Provision of Technical Assistance (Control) Order 2003*, Statutory Instrument 2003 No. 2764, Section 2, "transfer," accessed at http://216.239.39.104/search?q = cache:NeMFOuWi5UIJ:www.legislation. hmso.gov.uk/si/si2003/20032764.htm + %22statutory + instrument + 2003 + No. + 2764%22&hl = en. Order 2003 came into force on May 1, 2004.

15. Order 2003 actually uses the term "technology," not technical data, but defines technology similarly to mean "information (including but not limited to information comprised in software and documents such as blueprints, manuals, diagrams and designs) that is capable of use in connection with the development, production or use of any goods." *Export of Goods, Transfers of Technology and Provision of Technical Assistance (Control) Order 2003*, Statutory Instrument 2003 No. 2764, Section 2, "technology," accessed at http://216.239.39.104/search?q = cache:NeMFOuWi5UIJ:www.legislation. hmso.gov.uk/si/si2003/20032764.htm + %22statutory + instrument + 2003 + No. + 2764%22&hl = en.

16. See UK Department of Trade & Industry, Export Control Organisation, *Supplemental Guidance Note on the Transfer Abroad of Controlled Military Technology and Software by Electronic Means*, November 10, 2003, last updated June 4, 2004, accessed at www.dti.gov.uk/export.control/publications/sgnintangible.htm.

be intended, in its entirety or in part, for any relevant use, if he has reason to believe that such software or technology may be used outside the European Community."[17]

The phrase "any relevant use" contains a potentially broad reference to weapons of mass destruction ("WMDs") and missile delivery systems for WMDs, because it is defined to mean:

"Use in connection with the development, production, handling, operation, maintenance, storage, detection, identification or dissemination of chemical, biological or nuclear weapons or other nuclear explosive devices, or the development, production, maintenance or storage of missiles capable of delivering such weapon;"[18]

Thus, if the non-electronic transfer of technology relates to WMDs, then each of the participants at the meeting (or those who will be speaking or showing hard copy of technical data) must ascertain whether any of the other persons in the meeting (whether U.K. or foreign nations) intends or may be intending to use such technical data "outside the European Community." Unlike the ITAR (which makes a firm responsible for those it entrusts with technical data), Order 2003 remains dangerously ambiguous about who would be responsible, if two attendees at the meeting, one a U.K. national the other a Dutch national, both resident in the United Kingdom, decided to transfer the technology to parties outside the European Community. If the technology did not relate to WMDs or a missile delivery system for WMDs, there would be no obligation by the U.K. firm to obtain a license for the non-electronic transfer of technology at this meeting. If the technology did relate to WMDs but the U.K. firm was unaware of any intention by a participant in the meeting to make subsequent use of the technology for such purpose, there would be little the U.K. firm could do to ensure that no transfer of data would occur either by an attendee or someone to whom it might subsequently transfer the data for a prohibited use—to produce, operate, maintain, etc. WMDs. Order 2003 apparently does not prohibit such transfers when the transferor is unaware of any intention

---

17. *Export of Goods, Transfers of Technology and Provision of Technical Assistance (Control) Order 2003*, Statutory Instrument 2003 No. 2764, Section 9(3), accessed at http://216.239.39.104/search?q=cache:NeMFOuWi5UIJ:www.legislation.hmso.gov.uk/si/si2003/20032764.htm+%22statutory+instrument+2003+No.+2764%22&hl=en.

18. Id, Section 2, "any relevant use."

to use the data for "any relevant use" (WMDs or missile delivery systems).

As for the meeting in the United Kingdom, although all presenters will know that representatives attending on behalf of Agile and Troll will eventually leave the European Community, since the meeting will not touch on WMDs or their missile delivery, the U.K. firm does not need to obtain a license for the non-electronic transfer of technical data about the JSF. But what of the "export" of the data by the Agile and Troll representatives? *They*, in fact, need to obtain a license from the U.K. Department of Trade and Industry.

When reviewing the original concerns in the context of applicable Norwegian defense trade controls (assuming the meeting were to occur in Norway), counsel to Troll would identify certain constraints on the transfer of such data under a cautious interpretation of the applicable laws and regulations. Such caution derives from the lack of guidance in the Norwegian export laws and regulations, whose texts are quite general, and do not provide illustrative examples. The implementing regulations for the Norwegian export controls clearly require permission of the Foreign Ministry for exports of technology and all forms of technical information regarding products on Norway's two strategic items lists (one for "dual-use," and one for weapons, ammunition and other military material). These expressly require such permission for "intangible transfers."[19] In light of these provisions, Troll would be required to obtain a license from the Royal Norwegian Ministry of Foreign Affairs to share technical information at such meeting.[20]

As has become clear from this example, if the parties convene their meeting in the United States or Norway, the host company is responsible for obtaining licenses for any controlled technical data that might be released to the foreign national visitors by someone within the host country (*e.g.,* by a U.S. person in the United States). If the meeting occurs in the United Kingdom, the attendees from Agile will need to obtain at least two kinds of licenses: one from the Directorate of Defense

19. *Ministry of Foreign Affairs Ordinance of 10 January 1989 to Implement Export Regulations for Strategic Goods, Services and Technology*, Para. 1(c) and (d), accessed at www.nisat.org/export_laws-regs%20linked/Norway/regulations_of_10_january_1989.htm.

20. See also *Report by the Royal Norwegian Ministry of Foreign Affairs, Submitted to the Storting (Parliament)*, June 18, 1999, accessed at www.nisat.org/export_laws-regs%20linked/Norway/export_report_for_1998.htm.

Trade Controls to authorize releases of ITAR controlled technical data by Agile's representatives to Troll's representatives and to the British firm's representatives; and one from the U.K. Department of Trade & Industry to authorize the Agile attendees to export, from the United Kingdom to the United States, the ECA 2002 controlled technical data that they receive from the British firm during the meeting.

What if, instead of meeting, the project managers propose to transfer the technical data electronically through the Internet? Will a license be required under those circumstances? An electronic transfer will not obviate the need for a license if such electronic transfer originates in the United States; consent to transfer by the appropriate authorities would still be required. The ITAR treats as an "export" any electronic transfer (through telephone, cellphone, fax, e-mail, video conference, VoIP,[21] etc.) to a party outside the United States, or to a foreign national within the United States.

By contrast, the European Union Code of Conduct on Arms Exports, adopted on June 11, 1998, does not prohibit or otherwise control electronic transfers of military technical data. Recent efforts to include such controls in that Code of Conduct have thus far been unsuccessful.[22] Prior to the ECA 2002, the UK government controlled only the tangible transfer of military technology (*e.g.,* an export of military hardware), and the electronic transfer of dual use technologies. Remarkably it did *not* control (and thus did not prohibit) the electronic transfer of military technology. One could not carry it, but one could lawfully e-mail it.[23]

---

21. Voice over Internet Protocol.

22. The EU's latest effort, in 2003, simply "endorsed the importance of considering effective legal controls on electronic transfers of the software and technology associated with items on the common list, which is already done in certain Member States," and "agreed to pursue its deliberations on this issue, taking into consideration the work done in the dual-use area." *Compendium of Member States Agreed Practices within the Framework of the Code of Conduct,* OFFICIAL JOURNAL OF THE EUROPEAN UNION, December 31, 2003, Section II(3), p. 2, accessed at http://europa.eu.int/eur- lex/pri/en/oj/dat/2003/c_320/c_32020031231en00010042.pdf.

23. U.K. Department of Trade and Industry, *Supplementary Guidance Note on the Transfer Abroad of Controlled Military Technology and Software by Electronic Means,* November 10, 2003, last updated June 4, 2004, accessed at www.dti.gov.uk/export.control/publications/sgnintangible.htm. See also U.K. Department of Trade and Industry, *United Kingdom Strategic Export Controls: Annual Report 2003,* p. 1, accessed at www.fco.gov.uk/Files/kfile/Full_Report_03.pdf. **Note:** That has now been rectified by the secondary legislation under the ECA 2002, so that the transfer or export from the U.K. of all controlled military and dual-use technology and software, by any means whatsoever, is now prohibited unless authorized by an appropriate license.

Even with enactment of ECA 2002, the United Kingdom has left significant loopholes in its defense trade controls that the ITAR has been careful to close. If a U.S. person conveys any defense technology to a foreign national (outside or inside the United States) by telephone, the ITAR treats such transfer as an export which requires a license. If someone in the United Kingdom conveys military technical data by telephone (or other electronic means such as fax, e-mail, video conferencing, etc.) to a foreign national in the UK, that method of transfer is not deemed an export under ECA 2002. ECA 2002 prohibits electronic transfers only if they are "to a person or place outside the United Kingdom."[24] (Canada similarly controls electronic transfers only geographically, that is, only if the data will leave Canada, and does not have a "deemed export" rule. By contrast, Australia has no controls for electronic transfers of technical data, except those related to WMDs, and does not have a "deemed export" rule.)

Moreover, if someone in the United Kingdom conveys military technical data by telephone to someone outside the United Kingdom, such transfer constitutes an export only if "the transfer involves reading out the contents (whether in part or whole) of a document containing controlled technology or describing its contents in such a way as to achieve substantially the same result."[25] Thus if the disclosing person obtains the information not from a document, but from highly sensitive discussions among researchers or military personnel, the electronic transfer of such information to someone outside the United Kingdom is not treated as an export, and is not controlled by, ECA 2002.[26]

For U.S. companies that are responsible for the use and subsequent reexport of defense articles and technology by recipients overseas, it is important to be aware of such foreign loopholes, because they can ex-

---

24. *Export of Goods, Transfers of Technology and Provision of Technical Assistance (Control) Order 2003*, Statutory Instrument 2003 No. 2764, Section 6(1), accessed at http://216.239.39.104/search?q = cache:NeMFOuWi5UIJ:www.legislation.hmso.gov.uk/si/si2003/20032764.htm + %22statutory + instrument + 2003 + No. + 2764%22&hl = en.

25. U.K. Department of Trade and Industry, *Supplementary Guidance Note on the Transfer Abroad of Controlled Military Technology and Software by Electronic Means*, November 10, 2003, last updated June 4, 2004, accessed at www.dti.gov.uk/export.control/publications/sgnintangible.htm.

26. Prior to 1998, Norway did not control electronic transfers of intangible technology. See *Report by the Royal Norwegian Ministry of Foreign Affairs, submitted to the Storting (Parliament)*, June 18, 1999, accessed at www.nisat.org/export_laws-regs%20linked/Norway/export_report_for_1998.htm.

ercise the requisite level of caution while the data is under their control, but cannot guarantee that its subsequent handling by foreign entities (while fully compliant with their own laws) will comply with U.S. laws. Such loopholes and other differences (including enforcement policies) between defense export controls in the United States and in the United Kingdom have hindered efforts by the governments of the two countries to negotiate and gain approval of a waiver to the ITAR for sale of some unclassified defense equipment from the United States to the United Kingdom (particularly in the context of the JSF program).[27] Congressional opposition to the ITAR waiver is expressed in a House of Representatives Committee on International Relations Report, dated May 1, 2004, that includes a detailed comparison of the military export controls in key areas for the United States and United Kingdom and notes critically, for example, that for "intangible transfers" while the U.S. controls such transfers *"by any means"* (under the ITAR), the U.K. "Controls *oral and visual transfers only for WMD;* Controls for all items when by electronic means and telephone [only] to extent a controlled document is read out."[28]

Several of the major U.S. and U.K. contractors have dedicated considerable efforts to determining the best ways to engage in transatlantic collaborative work on projects, without contravening the applicable laws and regulations and while maintaining the requisite level of security, particularly where nationals from different countries may have access to project computers, and where (as on the JSF) the majority of the work is done across borders, electronically, through a virtual private network. The corporate sponsors of those efforts, known as the Transatlantic Secure Collaboration Program ("TSCP"), are trying to solve several challenges simultaneously: how to deal with transfers of sensitive

---

27. See Chutner, Andrew, *U.K. Tries to Rein In Technology Transfers,* DEFENSENEWS, December 1, 2003, p. 4. Other hindrances included the announcement on July 10, 2003, that U.S. federal agents were investigating 18 U.S. firms for alleged illegal exports of ITAR-controlled items to a U.K. company (Multicore), which itself had been under investigation by U.S. officials since December 1999 for allegedly conspiring to illegally purchase (and reexport to Iran) Hawk missile components and fighter jet parts. See Svitak, Amy, *U.S. Leaders Wince at Iran-U.K. Charges,* DEFENSENEWS, July 14, 2003, p. 4.

28. *U.S. Weapons Technology at Risk: The State Department's Proposal to Relax Arms Export Controls to Other Countries,* report of the Committee on International Relations of the United States House of Representatives, May 1, 2004, 92-549PDF, Appendix 11, p. 121.

data electronically; how to segregate and secure data; how to encrypt data and carefully transfer it back and forth across the Atlantic; how to protect intellectual property rights (particularly patent and proprietary data rights) among the team partners; how to control access to portions of the data; and how to label or tag the data such that senders and recipients will know its security classification, what intellectual property claims must be respected, and whether the data is licensed for transfer or a license condition restricts or bars its transfer.[29]

Agile must therefore take precautions to ensure that its personnel do not assume that, because Norway, The Netherlands and the United Kingdom are NATO allies, they therefore have comparable controls on defense articles and technical data.[30]

Another important difference between the ITAR and defense controls applied by NATO allies (with the exception of the United King-

---

29. See *A Framework for Secure Collaboration across US/UK Defense,* Version 1, March 5, 2003, accessed at www.afei.org/pdf/5mar2003_Final_Design.pdf, and *Translantic Secure Collaboration Program (TSCP) Final Design Document (Phase 2),* Version 1.0, April 21, 2004, accessed at www.afei.org/pdf/040421_Final_TSCP_Phase_2_Design.pdf. The corporate sponsors of the first document were Rolls-Royce, BAE Systems, General Dynamics, Lockheed Martin Corporation, and Raytheon Company. They were joined in sponsoring the second document by Airbus/EADS, Boeing Company, CAE, Northrop Grumman, Smiths Aerospace, and Westland Helicopters (the "Sponsoring Companies").

30. U.S. and U.K. officials have been negotiating a waiver of the ITAR that would permit transfers between the two countries of unclassified defense equipment, but as of this writing it has not been approved by the two governments. See Chutner, Andrew, *U.K., U.S. to Ease Rules on Mutual Defense Sales,* DEFENSENEWS, May 26, 2003, p. 1. Moreover, the prospects for such waiver appear to be diminishing. There is strong opposition to it by the House Armed Services Committee. In addition, the EU is considering lifting its arms embargo on China, and in response, the U.S. House of Representatives has threatened to restrict the sale of U.S. military equipment and technologies to European allies. See Alden, Edward, *US Threat to Restrict Arms Sales to Europe,* FINANCIAL TIMES, May 14, 2004, p. 4.

As of this writing, officials of the Bush administration have reportedly "agreed to back away from National Security Presidential Directive 19 . . .," the order President Bush had issued to relax export control for close allies in the war against terrorism. See Matthews, William, *Waffling on Trade Waivers for U.K.,* DEFENSENEWS, August 2, 2004, p. 1. The efforts to grant such waivers have been further complicated by legislation proposed by Chairman of the House Armed Services Committee, Representative Duncan Hunter, that would severely restrict the DoD's ability to purchase defense materiel from foreign suppliers. See Spiegel, Peter, *Weapon Hawk's Push against Foreign Suppliers Makes American Defence Contractors Nervous,* FINANCIAL TIMES, July 31–August 1, 2004, p. 4.

dom) is that the ITAR has a much longer list of countries to whom export and reexport of ITAR controlled items is prohibited.[31] It is U.S. policy to deny export licenses to certain countries, including: Belarus, Cuba, Iran, North Korea, Syria, and Vietnam.[32] There are also countries against which the United States maintains an arms embargo, including: Burma, China, Haiti, Liberia, Rwanda, Somalia, Sudan and the Democratic Republic of the Congo.[33] Finally, any country identified by the State Department as having repeatedly provided support for acts of international terrorism is also subject to denial of an export license for defense articles, specifically Cuba, Iran, North Korea, Sudan and Syria.[34] Unlike the EAR and the TSR, the ITAR impose both a duty to avoid engaging in transactions to export controlled items to such countries as well as a duty to report: "Any person who knows or has reason to know" of a proposed or actual sale, or transfer, of defense articles, services or data to any of the aforementioned countries "must immediately inform the Office of Defense Trade Controls."[35]

In our discussion of the ITAR, we have focused on risk points that traditional contractors may inadvertently contravene, or that new entrants to the defense and homeland security community may fail to recognize or appreciate, because such risk points do not commonly occur in consumer transactions. Such risk points also occur when a party overlooks recent changes in the applicable rules, or encounters a new regulatory regime in a cross-border transaction with a country with which it has not previously transacted business.[36] Ideally, a firm's Gen-

---

31. The U.K.'s Order 2003 includes Schedule 3, which lists 18 countries to which, under Section 11, an aircraft or vessel cannot be exported. Section 11 adds three additional countries. But unlike the ITAR, this does not constitute a complete ban on exports of all defense articles to such countries.

32. 22 CFR §126.1(a).

33. Id.

34. 22 CFR §126.1(d). As of this writing, the sanctions and bans that target Iraq and Libya are undergoing revision. Note that the ITAR automatically bans transactions in defense items whenever the United Nations Security Council mandates an arms embargo, and U.S. persons anywhere must avoid entering into transactions that would contravene such ban.

35. 22 CFR §126.1(e).

36. To keep the discussion manageable, we omit for now the host of issues unique to classified projects, sales of classified defense articles and transfers of classified military information. Such information is restricted to military use. National security requires its protection, and access to it is restricted by its designation as confidential, secret, or top secret set forth in Executive Order 12356, and it is subject to the rules of the National Disclosure Policy. There are eight categories of such information: (1) Organization,

eral Counsel and outside counsel should reinforce each other's efforts to anticipate and pre-emptively address such risk points.[37]

4.1 Agile's Interest in Leveraging Troll's Skills in Defense and Homeland Security Technologies.

Agile's interest in acquiring Troll derives in part from its desire to obtain some of the overseas unclassified subcontract work for the Joint Strike Fighter ("JSF") program, and in part from a conviction that Troll has technological capabilities that would enable Agile to compete successfully for future homeland security contracts. Agile has been encouraged by the U.S. military to acquire Troll, because there is some discomfort with the multiple locations at which work is proceeding on the JSF. They also believe that Agile's expertise will improve Troll's quality of performance and make it a better candidate for subcontract work (although Agile believes that significant benefits will also flow from Troll to Agile as is usually the case in a strategic merger or acquisition). Agile is attempting to position itself based on its projections of how the industry will develop.

Agile would like to arrange conferences (face-to-face meetings in Norway, or video conferences) between technical personnel from Agile

---

Training, and Employment of Military Forces; (2) Military Material and Munitions; (3) Applied Research and Development Information; (4) Production Information, including (a) Manufacturing Information (more sensitive than Build-to-Print or Assembly Information), (b) Build-to-Print Information (more sensitive than Assembly Information), and (c) Assembly Information; (5) Combined Military Operations, Planning, and Readiness; (6) U.S. Order of Battle; (7) North American Defense; and (8) Military Intelligence. INTERNATIONAL PROGRAMS SECURITY HANDBOOK, Chapter 3, accessed at www.fas.org/sgp/library/ipshbook. The three categories of production information reoccur in unclassified projects but not involving such sensitive information.

37. Agile and Troll are both working on classified projects, such as the Joint Strike Fighter, but we think the issues of the unclassified portions of such projects are sufficient for our objectives of exploring the challenges that cyber-driven transactions encounter. Contact with classified projects or information will seldom, if ever, occur in the ordinary course of commercial transactions. The controls on access to classified projects and information will require a company to qualify itself accordingly, and as a result of such qualifying it is very unlikely that a company will venture inadvertently into violations applicable to classified projects and classified information. We therefore limit discussion to compliance requirements for non-classified defense articles and technical data and to compliance with ITAR controls on such items and information.

and Troll to explore collaborative cooperative pursuit of DHS contracts for antiterrorist technologies as well as work on the JSF. In the course of such collaborative efforts, Agile and Troll will need to exchange manufacturing technology. A due diligence check of ITAR issues that might arise in the conduct of such communications, technical exchanges and proposed export of defense articles and information would be a prudent precaution in this context. Because of the time pressure created by the highly competitive nature of defense contract bidding, such meetings will need to proceed on an expedited schedule. It is therefore essential to put the checkpoints in place and to bring personnel up the diligence learning curve prior to any such meetings. Several risk points deserve close attention, and Agile's personnel must be alerted to these in advance, including the following:

➤ *Prohibited Conduct:* **Export of Technical Data Without a License.** The projected discussions will cover the JSF and certain components that the two companies may collaborate in producing, a number of which are stealth-related. The JSF, a developmental multi-role jet aircraft, is designed solely for military application. It does not appear by name on the USML, but clearly falls within Category VIII (a) "Aircraft . . . specially designed, modified, or equipped for military purposes." In addition, although the term "stealth" does not appear anywhere on the USML, it does appear in an annex thereto, in the Missile Technology Control Regime at §121.16, where it is described as follows:

> "Materials, devices, and specially designed software for reduced observables such as radar reflectivity, ultraviolet/infrared signatures on acoustic signatures (i.e. stealth technology), for applications usable for the systems in Item 1 or Item 2 (see §121.1, Category XIII (e) and (k)), for example:
>
> (a) Structural material and coatings specifically designed for reduced radar reflectivity;
>
> (b) Coatings, including paints, specially designed for reduced or tailored reflectivity or emissivity in the microwave, infrared or ultraviolet spectra . . ."[38]

While neither of the categories referenced in that listing (Category XIII (e) or (k)) are aircraft, those are provided merely as examples and

---

38. 22 CFR §121.16, Item 17, Category II.

are not intended to be exhaustive. Clearly "stealth" technology, as applied to a military aircraft, is within the contemplation of (and subject to control) by the ITAR.

Agile's engineers will not bring any hardware to the meetings with Troll, and will limit their presentation to documents, drawings, illustrations, software, etc. Counsel's first concern is for the potential export of "technical data" in connection therewith, which the ITAR defines, in relevant part, as:

> "Information other than software . . . required for the design, development, production, manufacture, assembly, operation, repair, testing, maintenance or modification of defense articles. This includes information in the form of blueprints, drawings, photographs, plans, instructions and documents."[39]

In any meeting Agile has with foreign nationals (*e.g.*, with Troll's Norwegian engineers) whether such meeting occurs abroad or in the United States, and in the course of any communications between Agile's and Troll's engineers (by phone, video conference, fax or e-mail), there is the substantial risk that Agile will thereby "export" JSF "technical data." Such communications fall within one of the ITAR definitions of "export:" "Disclosing (including oral or visual disclosure) or transferring technical data to a foreign person, whether in the United States or abroad." The ITAR makes it unlawful to "export or attempt to export from the United States any . . . technical data . . . for which a license or written approval is required by this subchapter without first obtaining" such license or approval from the Directorate.[40] Willful violations are punishable by imprisonment for not more than 10 years (for each count), or a fine not to exceed $1 million (for each count), or both.[41]

The ITAR requires a license for the "oral, visual or documentary disclosure of technical data by U.S. persons to foreign persons."[42] This requirement applies regardless of the manner of transmittal of the technical data.[43] Such license would not be required, if the technical data to

---

39. 22 CFR §120.10(a)(1). "Technical data" also include classified information relating to defense articles and defense services, information covered by an invention secrecy order, and software as defined in §121.8(f).
40. 22 CFR §127.1(a)(1).
41. 22 CFR §127.3.
42. 22 CFR §125.2(c).
43. Id.

be transferred was "sold, leased or loaned by the Department of Defense to a foreign country" under the Foreign Military Sales ("FMS") program pursuant to a Letter of Offer and Acceptance authorizing such transfer and meeting certain criteria.[44] At this stage in the JSF program, there is no Letter of Offer and Acceptance in place, because no sale of the aircraft have yet occurred. Thus, Agile's activities (the contemplated transfers to Troll) cannot qualify for this exception. Alternatively, a party can apply for approval of a Technical Assistance Agreement (discussed below), which involves more labor by counsel, but has a greater likelihood of being approved, since the ITAR suggests a preference for such agreements over licenses for the transfer of technical data.

Agile's engineers cannot be expected to recognize the distinction between non-export and export, because they will effectively engage in an "export" each time they disclose technical data. This is likely to occur during telephone discussions and email exchanges even at a very preliminary stage in setting the agenda for face-to-face meetings and video conferences. The cautious course is thus to obtain a license to cover export of such technical data, and to review carefully the full scope of what could potentially be "exported." Over-inclusion in this context is far preferable to omission. **The license application should be reviewed carefully to ensure that it does not inadvertently make any untrue statement of a material fact or omit a material fact that thereby makes the license misleading.** Such acts are also violations of the ITAR.[45]

If the Directorate issues the license, its conditions and qualifications (if any) must be reviewed carefully, because Agile's personnel must adhere strictly to each such condition. For example, if the license authorizes the showing of blueprints developed by Agile related to the JSF, it could foreseeably add the condition that "no U.S. Air Force drawings may be exported."[46] The ITAR makes it unlawful "[t]o violate any of

---

44. 22 CFR §126.6(c). The criteria include: that the transfers occur only during the effective period of the Letter of Offer and Acceptance ("LOA") and the implementing FMS contract; the LOA must specifically identify such technical data; the transfer cannot be to any country to which the ITAR bans such transfers (unlikely, given that no LOA would be issued for such a country); and that the U.S. person responsible for the transfer "maintains records of all transfers in accordance with Part 122 of the ITAR. 22 CFR §126.6(c) 1 through 6." In addition, the transfer must be made by the relevant foreign diplomatic mission or its freight forwarder, which would again, not cover Agile's contemplated transfer to Troll.

45. 22 CFR §127.3(b).

46. Defense contractors not infrequently lose sight of the "provisos" or "limita-

the terms or conditions of licenses or approvals."[47] General Counsel should consider issuing an explanatory memo, prior to any substantive communications between Agile's and Troll's engineers, detailing the rules and restrictions that must be followed. And counsel should follow up with a briefing employing hypotheticals to demonstrate the scope

---

tions," such as "all releases of software must be reviewed and approved by the Department of Navy." For example, in February 2003, Condor Systems—a California-based defense contractor that specializes in the design and manufacture of signal intelligence and electronic warfare systems and products (some installed on U.S. and allied navy submarines)—demonstrated a prototype of one of its signal processor systems to Forsvarets Materielverk, the military procurement agency for the government of Sweden and principal contractor for the manufacture of the A-17 submarine for the Swedish Navy. The kind of signal processor Condor makes appears on the U.S. Munitions List, which sets forth 21 categories of defense articles and services that are subject to export licensing controls under the ITAR. Unless an exemption applies, the ITAR require an export license for any such item *to all destinations.*

In April 1996, Condor applied for a "demonstration license" to show the prototype in a trade show in Stockholm, Sweden. The former Office of Defense Trade Controls (ODTC) granted a license but included twelve "limitations and provisos," each a limitation on the scope of the license. The limitations included that "Rubidium timing standard" must not be "offered/discussed" by Condor. Condor violated the prohibition. It compounded the problem later by representing in an export license application for the system that the model for the Swedish Navy would contain only "commercial off-the-shelf" software, which was untrue. The software had been developed in conjunction with the U.S. Navy exclusively for use in United States Navy programs, and it had not been approved by the U.S. Navy as an "off-the-shelf" product.

Condor pled guilty to two counts of making false statements to United States Government officials. The company was placed on a three-year probation (probably reflecting the fact that the U.S. Navy needed to receive product support from Condor) and was ordered to pay a fine of $1 million. See press release by the United States Attorney's Office, Northern District of California, February 10, 2003, accessed at www.usdoj.gov/usao/can/press/html/2003_02_10_condor.html.

Note that the ITAR do not apply only to licensing of exports of defense articles, but also to brokering of transactions for such articles or services and to registration of persons engaged in the manufacture or export of defense articles. The sensitivity to the meaning of "export" that one must have when interpreting the EAR is required to an even greater extent when interpreting the ITAR: show or tell a foreign national in the United States anything controlled by the ITAR, and one has thereby exported it to their country and done so in violation of the ITAR if done without a valid license. Even the performance of defense services for foreign nationals constitutes an "export" under the ITAR. While the Defense Department has been making vigorous attempts to encourage new U.S. entrants to the defense contract community, including a relaxing of its interpretations of applicable intellectual property rules, each such company that performs work for the DoD must take great care to comply with the ITAR.

47. 22 CFR §127.1(a)(4).

and limitations of the license. The ITAR makes clear that the party to whom the license is granted "is responsible for the acts of employees, agents, and all authorized persons to whom possession of the licensed defense article or technical data has been entrusted regarding the operation, use, possession, transportation and handling of such defense articles or technical data abroad."[48] Although that provision does not explicitly say so, it also covers the use and handling of technical data within the United States.

Although not required by the ITAR, it would be highly advisable for Agile to keep records of each transfer of the technical data in tabular form, listing, for example, the transfer dates, who made the transfers, the kind of technical data transferred, the recipients and the mode of transmittal.[49] Counsel could might consider reviewing the minutes of important meetings and e-mail logs. The Directorate has the right to inspect the records that are required to be maintained by all registrants with its office, and such records must be maintained for five years. In the event that a question arises concerning a transfer of technical data, or an investigation is commenced, a carefully maintained record of all technical data transfers will facilitate a defense against allegations of

---

48. 22 CFR §127.1(b).

49. 22 CFR §122.5(a) and (b). The records that ITAR does require a registrant to maintain are records concerning the "manufacture, acquisition and disposition of defense articles; the provision of defense services; and information on political contributions, fees, or commissions furnished or obtained . . ."

Note that the *omission of a requirement to keep records of transfers of technical data* is a rare instance in which the ITAR seems out of step with the risks posed by electronic transfers facilitated by the Internet. It is also a rare instance in which the ITAR is less restrictive than the export controls imposed by the U.K., which require that certain records be maintained "in respect of transfers of all controlled technology by electronic means." The guidance provided adds that "we are not requiring records to be kept of every e-mail to a particular end-user if a transfer takes place over a prolonged period. It is sufficient to identify the technology transferred, the dates between which it was transferred, and the identity of the end-user." However, when intangible transfers are made under an Open General License, the U.K. requires the following records be kept: a description of the technology sent (type and what it is to be used for), details of the recipient, date of the transfer or period of time of the transaction, and any other records which the license itself may require be kept. Such records must be kept for three years. See U.K. Department of Trade & Industry, Export Control Organisation, *Supplementary Guidance Note on the Transfer Abroad of Controlled Military Technology and Software by Electronic Means,* November 10, 2003, last updated June 4, 2004, accessed at www.dti.gov.uk/export.control/publications/sgnintangible.htm.

wrongdoing, and arguably demonstrates the seriousness, good faith and integrity of the compliance program in place.

It is useful in this context for counsel to standardize and simplify record keeping to encourage contemporaneous recording. E-mails that transfer technical data can either be copied or saved to a folder reserved to store such records.[50] This will automate the recording of sender, recipient, date and possibly subject line. Some companies store e-mails from counsel in a "privileged" folder. The same could be done for technical transfers. Such storage would also facilitate counsel's conduct of ITAR compliance audits, which will need to be done on a regular basis. An investigation by State or DoD agencies will inevitably request such emails. The more orderly their retention, the more likely that personnel will be found to have complied with the ITAR's restrictions on transfers of technical data. Contemporaneous record keeping also serves as a continuous reminder of the ITAR's restrictions and may also act as a check on "loose" drafting.

➤ *Prohibited Conduct:* **Export of Technical Data Without a Technical Assistance Agreement.** The ITAR treats a U.S. person's transfer of ITAR-controlled technical data to a foreign national both as an "export" and a provision of a "defense service." In such instance, the Directorate will sometimes consider granting a license for the transfer of technical data.[51] It is more probable, however, that a firm like Agile will find it must apply for (and obtain) Directorate approval for provision of a "defense service." The ITAR defines "defense service," in relevant part, as:

"(i) The furnishing of assistance (including training) to foreign persons, whether in the United States or abroad in the design, development, engineering, manufacture, production, assembly, testing, repair, maintenance, modification, operation, demilitarization, destruction, processing or use of defense articles;

(ii) The furnishing to foreign persons of any technical data controlled under this subchapter . . . whether in the United States or abroad. . . ."[52]

---

50. A company should consider tight restrictions on, or prohibition of, instant messaging, since instant messaging poses substantial security risks. See discussion of such problems in Chapter 6 on information security.

51. 22 CFR 124.1(a).

52. 22 CFR §120.9(1) and (2).

Unlike the process to obtain a license, the process to obtain approval to furnish a "defense service" requires the drafting of a formal agreement between Agile and Troll (what the ITAR terms a "Technical Assistance Agreement" ("TAA")), which must be submitted to the Directorate, and which cannot come into force without the Directorate's prior written approval.[53] In addition, certain technical data cannot be transferred under a TAA. For example, while assembly of defense articles can be included, transfer of production rights or manufacturing knowhow cannot. Such technical data can only be conveyed under a Manufacturing License Agreement.[54]

The ITAR requires that a TAA contain six statements the texts of which are set forth in ITAR §124.8 and must be replicated verbatim (not paraphrased) in the TAA. Counsel summarizes the six statements to familiarize Agile with the agreements and understandings it will need to negotiate with Troll. (During the negotiation of these, the parties representing Agile must be careful to avoid transferring any technical data covered by the TAA). The six statements include:

- The Directorate's approval of the TAA must be received before the TAA can come into force;
- The TAA is subject to all U.S. export control laws and regulations (which would include the EAR, TSR, and ITAR);
- The parties' obligations under the TAA shall not modify the performance of any obligations any parties thereto have to the U.S. government under prior contracts;
- The U.S. Government, by approving the TAA, incurs no liability for patent infringement;
- All provisions in the TAA that refer to the U.S. Government and the Department of State remain binding on the parties after termination of the TAA;,
- And (most important for Agile and Troll) any technical data or defense service exported under the TAA from the United States,

---

53. 22 CFR §124.1(a). Note that such approval must be obtained even if the provision of "defense service" will not include a transfer of "technical data," as may occur when providing a defense service to repair or destroy a defense article abroad. Note also that if Agile obtains approval of a TAA, Agile is thereby exempt from the requirement to obtain a license for the export of the technical data covered by the TAA.

54. 22 CFR §120.21.

and any defense article produced or manufactured with such data or service, "may not be transferred to a person in a third country or to a national of a third country except as specifically authorized" in the TAA, unless the parties have obtained the Directorate's prior written approval. (What is known as an "end-use assurance.")[55]

Since the Directorate can require changes to the TAA, parties should submit only a final, unsigned version.[56] The ITAR specifies substantial disclosures that must be provided to the Directorate in the text of the formal transmittal letter.[57] If the Directorate approves the TAA, the U.S. applicant must either furnish the Directorate with a signed copy of the TAA within 30 days of its execution or, if the parties elect not to sign the TAA, notify the Directorate of that fact within 60 days of such decision.[58] The applicant must also notify the Directorate not less than 30 days prior to the TAA's expiration, and inform the Directorate of the continuation of any "foreign rights" or of the "flow of any technical data to the foreign party."[59]

The ITAR thus requires parties to monitor their efforts to conclude or to terminate a TAA, and to provide the Directorate with the information it needs to maintain supervision of the "flow of technical data" under that TAA. The term "flow," although not defined, unmistakably

---

55. 22 CFR §124.8 (1) through (6).

56. Note that approval often requires interagency coordination. It may also require notification to Congress. For example, any TAA that involves the manufacture abroad of "significant military equipment" must be notified to Congress (by the Department of State), regardless of the value of the data to be transferred. 22 CFR §124.11 See also Arms Export Control Act, §36(d). Other notifications are triggered when the transfer exceeds certain value thresholds.

57. 22 CFR §124.12 (a). Such additional disclosure includes: (1) identification of the U.S. Government contract under which the technical data was "generated, improved, or developed and supplied to the U.S. Government;" (2) whether the technical data derives from any bid or other proposal to the U.S. Government; (3) the military classification of the technical data; and (4) any patent application that discloses any of the subject matter of the technical data covered by an "invention secrecy order" issued by the U.S. Patent and Trademark Office.

58. Thus, the ITAR does not permit parties to negotiate a TAA, obtain Directorate approval of it, and then abandon the TAA without notice to the Directorate: in short, they must make a decision, one way or the other, to sign or not to sign and then provide the Directorate the appropriate information.

59. 22 CFR §124.12(b)(3).

includes electronic transfers of technical data, and those too must be reported to the Directorate as the termination date of the TAA approaches. This is one of many record keeping requirements imposed by the ITAR that does not appear under the other U.S. export controls (nor under those of Norway, the European Union or the United Kingdom).

Once the need for a TAA has been established, its negotiation and drafting will become a pacing task of the acquisition, and should be recognized as being part of the structuring process of the transaction, although other issues can be addressed separately and will not be influenced by the terms of the TAA. TAA's tend to be unusually time-consuming. A recent RAND study disclosed that two major contractors for the JSF—Lockheed Martin and BAE Systems—had been working closely to develop TAA's to enable BAE to have access to some proprietary technologies related to the production of its portion of the work. Such TAA's have occasionally taken "in excess of nine months" to complete.[60]

A TAA can require such extended time because the more the product is evolving, with developing technology or developing applications, and the more sensitive the data (in terms of security classification and proprietary rights), the more the TAA tends to be a "moving target," one whose contours will inevitably keep changing. The negotiations, therefore, tend to be unpredictable, with provisional agreement on certain terms becoming irrelevant, or of diminishing importance, for the following reasons:

- The end-users see a change in the nature of the threats that the weapon system was initially conceived to address, and request that the design changes accordingly;

- Such design changes can require further stretching of the technological envelope, and thus the technical content of the TAA must be revised to match it;

- The U.S. and U.K. technology control and disclosure policies and procedures continue to evolve;[61]

---

60. Cook, Arena, Graser, Pung, Sollinger, and Younossi, *Assembling and Supporting the Joint Strike Fighter in the UK: Issues and Costs*, RAND Europe (prepared for the United Kingdom's Ministry of Defence), 2003, pp. 115–116. accessed at www.rand.org/publications/MR/MR1771.

61. For example, the U.K.'s enactment of ECA 2003 and issuance of the implementing Order 2003.

- Technology that might not have been releasable at the start of the negotiations, can abruptly become releasable, and jurisdiction for its control can shift (in the United States) from the State Department to the Commerce Department (or vice versa);
- In the case of the United States and United Kingdom, the current efforts to obtain Congressional approval of an ITAR-waiver for transfers of unclassified technical data could change the terrain of TAA's for the JSF considerably.

In Troll's case, there will be the added problem of foreign nationals and dual nationals employed by Troll (each foreign national is required to sign a nondisclosure agreement that must be provided to the Directorate).[62] If the U.S. Government believes that the technical data is "currently sensitive" (another moving target), it may require a background check of each foreign national. Moreover, dual nationals from any country proscribed or targeted by ITAR Section 126.1 "will not be authorized."[63] At present, that includes 12 countries. As a result, Troll cannot employ on work covered by the TAA any dual nationals from China, Iran or Belarus, for example.[64]

BAE and Lockheed Martin reportedly have sought to reduce the TAA preparation time by negotiating overarching TAA's (*i.e.,* covering the transfer of technologies required to produce the JSF's rear fuselage and empennage), and then implementing a disclosure process called the "TAA Staircase," whereby transfer of those technologies is agreed upon through successive amendments to the overarching TAA. As the RAND study describes it:

"Each amendment is envisioned to remove some restrictive provisos and to allow progress towards a level of disclosure to enable a successful development and operational testing programme."[65]

62. See Department of State, *Guidelines for Preparing Agreements,* October 2003, Section 10, p. 37, accessed at http://pmdtc.org/docs/agbook.pdf. The key sentence affirms: "I hereby certify that such data will not be further disclosed, exported or transferred in any manner, to any other foreign national or any foreign country without the prior written approval of the Office of Trade Controls Licensing, U.S. Department of State."

63. Id, p. 39.

64. 22 CFR §126.1(a).

65. Cook, Arena, Graser, Pung, Sollinger, and Younossi, *Assembling and Supporting the Joint Strike Fighter in the UK: Issues and Costs,* RAND Europe (prepared for the

Nonetheless, the RAND study foresees serious delays to the project if the technology transfer issues are not resolved expeditiously, and recommends that the U.K. government give the issue "immediate attention and commence advance planning."[66] Although Agile and Troll have a simpler task (they do not intend to transfer classified technical data), other issues complicating and prolonging the process will be similar, but will have to be resolved under much greater time pressure. While a U.S. prime contractor can make up lost time by putting pressure on its subcontractors, Agile and Troll cannot report to the prime contractor that their "problems negotiating the TAA's have caused the project schedule to slip" in order to gain similar leverage.

➤ *Imprudent Activity:* **Export of Technical Data Under a TAA Without Verifying the Recipient's Capability to Abide by Restrictions of the TAA and ITAR.** By requiring non-transfer to third parties as a condition of the TAA signed by both the U.S. and foreign national parties, the ITAR extends its jurisdiction extra-territorially over the conduct abroad of Agile and of Troll (and their respective personnel, representatives, and agents). By further requiring that the verbatim text in the ITAR be included in the TAA, the ITAR leaves no room for parties to negotiate language that could dilute its controls. Agile should make clear to Troll the responsibilities it undertakes by signing the TAA so that its representatives do not mistake such provisions for boilerplate. Agile should also verify that Troll has the internal policies and procedures in place to ensure that it will fulfill its obligation to prevent any transfer to a person in a third country (or to a national of a third country who may be visiting Norway or be a resident of Norway).

Verification is a relatively painless and cost-effective step, and it encourages personnel responsible for monitoring compliance with the ITAR to discover potential violations before damage is irrevocable. A good starting point for determining the seriousness of Troll's existing compliance regime is those provisions in the ITAR that Troll is not likely to be unaware of, including the text that the ITAR requires to be included in the TAA. A simple checklist approach to this is to ask the series of questions set forth below. Each question, takes as its premise, that Troll's signing of the TAA obligates it to comply with the ITAR,

---

United Kingdom's Ministry of Defence), 2003, pp. 117. accessed at www.rand.org/publications/MR/MR1771.

66. Id.

and that it will need to modify its export control policies and procedures in accordance with such obligation:

(i) What procedures does Troll intend to implement to discover if any Troll personnel, who will have received or had access to ITAR-controlled technical data, have violated the ITAR by mishandling such data?

(ii) What procedures does Troll intend to implement to discover if ITAR-controlled data is being handled in ways that increase the probability of ITAR violations?

(iii) What mechanisms does Troll intend to implement to ensure that its senior officers receive prompt report of any violation of the ITAR by personnel of Troll or its affiliates?

(iv) What mechanisms does Troll intend to implement to ensure that Agile's senior officers receive prompt report of any violation of the ITAR by personnel of Troll or its affiliates?

Agreement on the TAA should be conditioned on Troll's implementation of such procedures.

In the absence of such analysis and procedures, a subsequent violation by Troll that comes to the attention of the Directorate will find Agile hard pressed to persuade federal authorities that it took seriously its obligations under the ITAR. While the ITAR does not explicitly require Agile to undertake such diligence, it does set forth a set of expectations that must be met by firms found to be in violation of the ITAR who seek to persuade the Directorate to consider "mitigating factors." It is also in Agile's economic interest to increase the probability that the proposed transaction will be completed timely (that is, without the regulatory delays, concomitant costs and uncertainty of an investigation and/or enforcement action). Just as there have been significant recent changes in OFAC's and BIS' mitigating and aggravating factors (and a similar tightening of the U.S. Sentencing Guidelines), there is a comparable emphasis in the ITAR on the consideration the Directorate will give to such factors. Such diligence is relatively simple and cost effective, can be structured into any pre-transaction checklist, facilitates the timely consummation of the transaction and, in the event of enforcement, demonstrates good faith, allowing a company like Agile to position itself in the event of a violation. It will also help Agile to persuade Troll to take precautions that will reduce the likelihood of a violation.

The ITAR's guidance appears in Section 127.2 which many companies would arguably prefer to disregard, because it invites action (voluntary self-reporting) that many officers understandably find unpalatable. In that section, the ITAR expresses a general policy of actively encouraging voluntary disclosure to the Directorate when firms "believe they may have violated the Arms Export Control Act, the ITAR or any license or approval issued thereunder."[67] In exchange, the ITAR promises that self-disclosure "may be considered a mitigating factor," when the Directorate considers what administrative penalties (if any) to impose.[68] If the self-reported violation merits a referral to the Department of Justice ("DoJ") for consideration of criminal prosecution, there is no assurance that voluntary self-reporting will have any mitigating effect on the DoJ. The ITAR obligates the Directorate to notify DoJ of the voluntary self-disclosure, but the DoJ "is not required to give that fact any weight."[69] The Directorate will only consider voluntary self-reporting as a mitigating factor if: it receives such report *prior* to the time any U.S. Government agency "obtains knowledge of either the same or substantially similar information from another source and commence[s] an investigation or inquiry that involves that information," and that is intended to determine if there has been a violation of the Arms Export Control Act, the ITAR or any license or approval granted thereunder.[70] Unlike similar provisions in the EAR and TSR, the ITAR presses for a report even if the firm is not certain that it has committed a violation. The ITAR threshold for a report is the firm's belief that it "may" have violated an applicable law or rule and is often perceived by firms as premature or anticipatory. The rationale in such seemingly "over-zealous" enforcement is of course the concern for national security, and

---

67. 22 CFR §127.12(a).

68. Id.

69. 22 CFR §127.12(b)(3). In light of the 2004 amendments to the U.S. Sentencing Guidelines and the Thompson Memo that preceded them, voluntary self-reporting would only have a chance of being weighed as a mitigating factor if the firm also gave sufficient "cooperation" to DoJ; *i.e.,* helped identify all culprits in the firm and, if pressed to do so, waived attorney-client privilege and attorney work product protections. The ITAR, at least, is candid in its holding out no assurance that self-reporting will mitigate penalties if criminal violations have indeed occurred, although there is probably a sharp distinction to be drawn between self-reporting of an *attempt* to violate and of the *commission* of a violation: both contravene the ITAR, but the report of the former, if it thereby prevents an unauthorized release or export, would seem to have the best chance of being weighed a mitigating factor.

70. 22 CFR §127.12(b).

this explains why such reporting can only be effective if made prior to a substantial violation or pattern of violations. The ITAR notes: "Failure to report such violation(s) may result in circumstances detrimental to U.S. national security and foreign policy interests."[71] The pressure by other countries to gain unauthorized access to U.S.-controlled defense technology was amply evidenced in a 2004 DoD Inspector General Audit ("IG Audit") that disclosed the findings of the DoD's Defense Security Service annual study, *Technology Collection Trends in the U.S. Defense Industry 2003* (presenting a summary of reports of suspicious foreign activity). As the IG Audit explained, in the calendar year 2002, "818 incidents of suspicious activity were reported from 84 countries;"[72] moreover, such incidents:

"Continue to increase from year to year with information systems, sensors and lasers, and electronics among the most targeted technologies. The extent of foreign interest in and methods of collection for those technologies have [sic] changed over the years, from passive attempts to more sophisticated activities. Some of the top methods used for gaining access to targeted technology are as subtle as requests for scientific and technical data, attempts to acquire technology, and inappropriate conduct by foreign nationals during visits to U.S. facilities."[73]

The IG Audit noted the consequences when such efforts to acquire U.S.-controlled *unclassified* technical data succeed:

"Unauthorized access to unclassified export-controlled technology could allow foreign nations to counter or reproduce the technology and thus reduce the effectiveness of the program technology, significantly alter program direction, or degrade combat effectiveness."[74]

Such risks warrant a policy of stringent controls. Unfortunately, the IG Audit found that deficiencies in DoD contract policies and moni-

71. Id.
72. Department of Defense, Office of Inspector General, *Export Control: Export-Controlled Technology at Contractor, University, and Federally Funded Research and Development Center Facilities,* Audit Report (D-2004-061), March 25, 2004, p. 3, accessed at www.dodig.osd.mil/audit/reports/fy04/04-061.pdf.
73. Id.
74. Id, p. 13.

toring of DoD-funded contracts failed to prevent unauthorized access to such technology by foreign nationals.[75] It concluded that:

"DoD does not have adequate processes to identify unclassified export-controlled technology and to prevent unauthorized disclosure . . . Until DoD program managers are held accountable for identifying export-controlled technology and are assured that facilities obtain authorized approval or have controls in place to protect the export-controlled technology, DoD will be at increased risk of other nations countering or reproducing the technology, thus reducing its effectiveness."[76]

Unfortunately, even classified export-controlled technology needs substantially improved protections as evidenced by the three instances of such data "going missing" from the nuclear weapons laboratory at Los Alamos, New Mexico ("Los Alamos Laboratory"), including a data loss involving the laboratory's "weapons physics division"[77] (later reported to be the discovery, on July 7, 2004, of the loss of at least two computer disks containing sensitive weapons information)[78] and the concurrent discovery that secret information at the Los Alamos Laboratory "was repeatedly transmitted over an unclassified e-mail system."[79]

Consistent with its policy of more stringent controls, the ITAR also establishes more demanding criteria and requirements for self-reporting. While the EAR leaves the form of such report in the discretion of the reporting party, any self-report under the ITAR must follow a precise, two-step procedure. *First*, the person or firm should notify the Directorate "as soon as possible after the violation(s) are discovered;"[80] and *second*, it must "conduct a thorough review of all export-related transactions where violation(s) are suspected."[81] Such reporting (prior to conducting a "thorough review") may seem counter-intuitive and premature. However, a well-designed compliance program should ideally be structured to respond early, because the ITAR requires early

75. Id, pp. 5, 13–17.
76. Id, p. 17.
77. Chang, Kenneth, *Los Alamos Missing Secret Data*, THE NEW YORK TIMES, July 10, 2004, p. A-13.
78. Vartabedian, Ralph, *Classified E-Mail Left Nuclear Lab*, LOS ANGELES TIMES, July 16, 2004, p. A-1.
79. Id.
80. 22 CFR §127.12(c).
81. Id.

reporting to limit the potential harm that can be done by the suspected violation(s). To achieve that objective, the ITAR requires that a party's report (which must be in writing) provide extensive information, including:

- "A precise description of the nature and extent of the violation (e.g., an unauthorized shipment, doing business with a party denied U.S. export privileges, etc.);"
- "[A] thorough explanation of why, when, where, and how the violation(s) occurred;"
- Complete identities and addresses of all persons involved;
- Export license numbers, if applicable;
- USML descriptions, quantities, and characteristics of the commodities or technical data involved; and
- Corrective actions, if any, already undertaken.[82]

The report must also provide copies of documents that substantiate it.[83] The ITAR allows (but does not require) the Directorate to consider other information to determine how much mitigating credit a firm should receive. The implication however is that, unless voluntary self-reporting occurs, a firm will be given little (if any) mitigating credit. If it does occur, any enhancement of mitigating credit will depend on the answer to specifically enumerated questions:

- Whether the transaction would have been authorized had proper application been made;
- Why the violation(s) occurred;
- The degree of cooperation with the ensuing investigation;
- Whether the firm has instituted or improved an internal compliance program to reduce the likelihood of future violations; (Note: this is another instance in which the ITAR requires such immediate and far-reaching reaction to discerned violations that an adequate response is only probable if it has been designed into the firm's compliance program.)

---

82. 22 CFR §127.12(c)(2).
83. 22 CFR §127.12(d).

• Whether the person making the disclosure did so with the full knowledge and authorization of the firm's senior management. (If not, then the ITAR emphasizes that a firm will not be deemed to have made a voluntary self-report.)[84]

Because the ITAR puts great emphasis on voluntary self-reporting, and conditions any such report on the "full knowledge and authorization of the firm's senior management," the most reliable (and arguably the only reliable) course of action that Agile (or any similarly placed firm) can take to position itself to qualify for mitigating credit, in the event of a violation of the ITAR by a foreign entity with which it has a TAA in force, is to conduct its own diligence. This will ensure that the foreign entity (Troll) has implemented procedures to: (i) detect violations and attempted violations; (ii) report them immediately to the senior management of the foreign entity; and (iii) report them immediately to the senior management of Agile. Agile's counsel recommends that the four verification questions previously listed be addressed to Troll. In that way, Agile can assess Troll's readiness to fulfill its obligations under the TAA, and can provide specific guidance to Troll to bring its compliance procedures within the ITAR requirements. While Troll may object to the extra-territorial reach of U.S. law over its export controls, Agile must be prepared to answer such concerns in the interests of completing the transaction (and to demonstrate how early compliance can be effected with minimal disruption to business practices in place and minimal cost relative to a later enforcement action). It can also argue credibly that such defense controls protect Agile's home country and Troll's.[85] Because most parties in the "defense technology"

---

84. 22 CFR §127.12(b)(3)(i)–(v). Thus if a whistle-blower within a company notifies the Directorate of a violation, such company would not be deemed to have made a voluntary self-report.

85. To argue against such controls by equating them with the U.S. use of military force is sophistry. The ITAR serves to prevent advanced military technology from reaching parties who would use it not only against U.S. persons and interests but also Europeans and any others they might select as a susceptibly soft target. The attacks on the trains in Madrid on March 11, 2004, vividly demonstrate that any country is a potential target of terrorism and that for terrorists, any justification, however flimsy, will suffice. For example, one of the "justifications" broadcast for the Madrid train bombings was the Spanish expulsion of the Moors in 1498. By that measure, the history of any country contains enough transgressions to satisfy any terrorist in need of a justification for a "retaliatory" attack.

However, the task of U.S. counsel seeking to persuade an overseas counsel of the

field are "repeat" players, these issues are going to come up inevitably, if not in this transaction, then in another because the concerns exist throughout the law and regulatory schema applicable to this field.

▸ *Prohibited Conduct:* **Non-compliance with End-User Assurance or Certificate.** Agile has a second important reason for reviewing Troll's activities. If there is a potential problem, it will usually relate to a violation of the end-use assurance that the technical data covered by the TAA "may not be transferred to a person in a third country or to a national of a third country except as specifically authorized" in the TAA without the Directorate's prior written approval. If Troll's internal procedures are not adequate, its personnel run the risk of contravening this end-use assurance.

Two risks predominate in Troll's handling of the technical data it receives from Agile, and Agile needs to address each in close consultation with Troll.

Insecure Storage of Data. First, Troll may assume that its procedures for securing its trade secrets and complying with Norwegian export controls will suffice to comply with the ITAR. In all probability, they will not. Many companies still use traditional protections that have not been updated to address the increasing risks posed by digital media and

need to comply with the ITAR is hampered by reports that enable critics of the U.S. government to claim it applies a double-standard: one for conduct expected of nations friendly to it (comply with the ITAR) and one for conduct that it insists it is free to pursue to detect and interdict terrorists. An example of the latter is the substance of a recently leaked government lawyers' report that espoused the position that: "In order to respect the president's inherent constitutional authority to manage a military campaign . . . (the prohibition against torture) must be construed as inapplicable to interrogations undertaken pursuant to his commander-in-chief authority." (The parenthetical text appears in the original document.) See Bravin, Jess, *Pentagon Report Set Framework for Use of Torture,* THE WALL STREET JOURNAL, June 7, 2004, p. A-1 at p. A-17.

Note, too, that the Directorate understands that its controls are imperfect, but that perfect control—non-export—is not feasible nor beneficial. As Robert Maggi, the Directorate's Director, recently observed in testimony before a Congressional committee: "The only sure way to eliminate the proliferation risk of U.S. defense exports is to never allow U.S. defense articles and services to leave our shores. This is an untenable policy and it would not make us more safe and secure." *Testimony of Robert W. Maggi before the Subcommittee on National Security, Emerging Threats, and International Relations of the House of Representatives Committee on Government Reform,* March 9, 2004, p. 7, accessed at http://reform.house.gov/UploadedFiles/maggi%20testimony.pdf.

cyberspace. If Troll receives all technical data from Agile on CD-ROMs or DVDs, and secures such data appropriately, then the existing safeguards are probably sufficient (pending Troll's use of the data). However, it is clear that Troll cannot use such data without loading it onto a computer. At that point, personnel will ordinarily load it onto a hard drive. If Troll has only password protection limiting access to that drive, the data is not secured against unauthorized access and transfer. If the computer in question is connected to the Internet, the data is exposed to unauthorized access by cyber-intruders. Few firms have reliable means (such as intrusion detection mechanisms) to determine if hackers have penetrated their Internet-linked computers.[86] Such data should therefore be kept off all computers linked to the Internet (including those linked indirectly through a firm's intranet), and a more secure means than password security should be employed to limit internal access, which is the source of the most serious risks to the data assets.[87]

Procedures Derived from Norway's End-User Declarations. Second, like many defense firms, Troll can be expected to have implemented security procedures derived from its experience with its home nation's export controls. These are the controls that "bite" the most frequently, and therefore get the most attention. Agile is willing to contemplate an on-going business alliance with Troll in part because Troll is an experienced contractor for the Royal Norwegian Ministry of Defence. Troll is already substantially "up the learning curve" in terms of doing this kind of business and there will be fewer front-end costs of bringing it "up to speed." However, Troll has not been a subcontractor for any DoD project so its compliance sensitivities must be recalibrated. Agile must ascertain how familiar Troll is with DoD and ITAR terminology. To the extent that Agile can use existing compliance with some "re-tooling" this will substantially limit time, cost and resistance of re-tooling for U.S. compliance. Troll has probably never signed a TAA with a U.S. firm, and is thus unfamiliar with an "end-user assurance" that complies with the ITAR standard. However, the latter is similar to a Norwegian "end-user declaration," with a number of important differences that must be highlighted.

---

86. See discussion of "intrusion detection" mechanisms in Chapter 6 on the checkpoint for information security.

87. In addition, security measures for access and authentication should be regularly reviewed and enhanced in order to ensure they remain sufficient safeguards against the improved capabilities of potential external and internal risks.

As a negotiating strategy, start with familiar concepts and introduce
bullet-point differences in order to foster agreement expeditiously. The
important differences for our transaction are as follows: the ITAR "end
user assurance" applies more stringent controls than the Norwegian
"end-user declaration." For example, the Norwegian end-user declaration is provided by the intended recipient of defense materiel, confirms that such person is indeed the recipient, and describes where the
materiel is to be installed and used. It also affirms that the materiel will
not be resold without the prior consent of Norwegian authorities.[88]

Under the ITAR by contrast," *the recipient must affirm that it will
not "transfer" (rather than "not sell") the ITAR-controlled technical data.*
The difference in scope of these two terms cannot be overstated. It is
also not intuitive. A Norwegian company would not ordinarily provide
another party with technical data, unless it was selling it to that party.
But the ITAR sweeps more broadly than the transactional terminology
implies. A "transfer" within the contemplation of ITAR is not transactional and not necessarily between "arm's length" parties. The real
concern of this terminology is who inside Troll will have access to, or
be entrusted with, the data. The Norwegian end-user declaration pays
no attention to the internal risk.

This last point becomes important when we consider the make-up
of Norway's (non-national) immigrant population. During the Iranian
Revolution, Norway accepted a significant number of Iranian refugees.
As of January 1, 2002, about 88,000 Iranian refugees were living in
Norway, 28% of the total immigrant population in Norway. Any such
person who is not a Norwegian citizen becomes a "prohibited recipient"
of the technical data under the ITAR.

The Norwegian end-user declaration treats foreign nationals in other
countries with far greater trust than does the ITAR's end-user assurance.
Many immigrants and foreign nationals work at defense contractors
and companies that produce homeland security technologies. Agile itself
has many on its staff. But Agile is careful to limit access to its ITAR-
controlled technical data. Its foreign nationals cannot access such data
without a license or other approval from the Directorate, because such
unauthorized access would be an "export" in violation of the ITAR.

---

88. See, for example, "Documentation Requirements," *Report by the Royal Norwegian Ministry of Foreign Affairs, Submitted to the Storting (Parliament)*, 18 June 1999,
accessed at www.nisat.org/export_laws-regs%20linked/Norway/export_report_for_
1998.htm.

This distinction is analogous to traditional security clearances. Employees in "sensitive" industries routinely have different levels of access to sensitive data. Troll presumably limits access to its Norwegian military technical data solely to its Norwegian personnel (and to those with appropriate security clearances) when the information is deemed sensitive. There is a high probability that the ITAR would require Troll to recalibrate its policies and procedures for internal handling of technical data received from Agile to conform to the ITAR standard as well. Troll would also have to recalibrate those policies and procedures to ensure that it did not transfer the technical data to any foreign nationals at other Norwegian firms (as could easily occur during meetings or visits to Troll's facilities).

Moreover, the U.S. Government can also be expected to do a background check of Troll as part of what is known as the "Blue Lantern" program. Under this program, the Directorate makes inquiries to verify that the intended end-user of technical data can be entrusted with such data. Blue Lantern refers to pre-licensing and post-shipment checks to ensure that technologies with military application are not diverted into the hands of end-users inimical to the national security of the United States. Blue Lantern is a risk management tool and in Troll's case, it could be expected to be deployed as a "front-loaded" check preceded by the following verifications:

- Troll and its subsidiary Brugge (together with their listed officers and directors) would be checked against a comprehensive watchlist maintained by the State Department (a list that includes over 50,000 names provided by law enforcement, intelligence, the DHS and other sources);[89] and
- The Directorate's licensing officers would check the proposed TAA for any indicia of suspicious transactions.

The Blue Lantern checks would follow. Because Troll would be an unfamiliar end-user to the Directorate, it would ask (the Embassy in Oslo) for a full explanation of the history of the company, its role in the particular project for which the TAA was proposed and its relation-

---

89. *Testimony of Robert W. Maggi before the Subcommittee on National Security, Emerging Threats, and International Relations of the House of Representatives Committee on Government Reform,* March 9, 2004, p. 10, accessed at http://reform.house.gov/UploadedFiles/maggi%20testimony.pdf.

ship with (and performance for) the Royal Norwegian Ministry of Defence.[90] If the check returned negative or questionable information about Troll, the Directorate would determine whether it should resolve the case as unfavorable (prompting a denial of the TAA) or as favorable. Blue Lantern runs checks on roughly 400 cases per year.[91] In the fiscal year 2003, the Directorate initiated 413 checks that resulted in 76 unfavorable cases—18.4% or almost one in five. However, since the technical data to be covered by the TAA relates primarily to aircraft structures, the more relevant figure is the percentage of unfavorable checks involving aircraft spare parts at risk of diversion to prohibited countries. Twenty-four percent of those checks resulted in unfavorable cases.[92]

The rationale for this increased vigilance is that embargoed countries may seek spare parts to increase the operational readiness of their military aircraft inventories. While Troll is not seeking to import aircraft spare parts, the latter figure suggests that the Directorate will make a more thorough check in circumstances where there is a greater motivation for diversion. In fiscal year 2001, a Blue Lantern pre-license check prevented potential misuse of warfare training technical data, when it found that the purported end-user in Asia could not be confirmed.[93] In Troll's case, the risk of an unfavorable determination is low, due to its lack of inclusion of commodities like spares, and because it already enjoys a "favored" relationship with the Royal Norwegian MoD. However, the Blue Lantern check of Troll is likely to be extremely thorough, because Troll is seeking to be a subcontractor on a highly sensitive project (the JSF or F-35). Countries that are not close U.S. allies will be looking for ways to learn the performance characteristics and composition of the stealth aircraft parts.[94] For that reason, implementing the additional precautions to improve Troll's compliance policies and procedures will improve Troll's chances of receiving a favorable Blue Lantern pre-license check. By contrast, if Troll employs foreign nationals

90. Id, p. 16

91. End-Use Monitoring of Defense Articles and Defense Services—Commercial Exports, 2001, accessed at www.pmdtc.org/docs/End_Use_FY2001.pdf.

92. Id, p. 17.

93. End-Use Monitoring of Defense Articles and Defense Services—Commercial Exports, 2001, accessed at www.pmdtc.org/docs/End_Use_FY2001.pdf

94. Preventing the diversion of such information improves the survivability and mission success for the aircrews of such aircraft. For similar reasons, when the Israeli Defense Forces developed "reactive armor" for their tanks and other vehicles, they kept it a secret for years, and only the capture of one of their vehicles caused its disclosure.

from ITAR-embargoed countries and does not appropriately restrict access to technical data, Troll would almost certainly will be rejected by the Blue Lantern check. It is highly preferable, from a purely business perspective, to invest in compliance rather than lose a valuable JSF sub-contract and the technology transfers that would accompany it.

It would also be advantageous for Troll to compile a list of all its suppliers and customers, the names of their officers and directors, and of their agents and representatives (particularly if any are located in, or reportedly transact in, ITAR-embargoed countries). These should be checked against the U.S. State Department's list of statutorily "debarred parties." If Troll suspects a match, it should investigate carefully and thoroughly. The ITAR prohibits transacting with such parties, and although Troll would not be violating the ITAR at this time by such transaction, it could not continue such a relationship after signing the TAA. (Troll should also check the prohibited parties lists, such as OFAC's SDN List and BIS' Denied Persons List, Entity List and Unverified List.) Agile's acquisition of Troll could not proceed without Troll's disengaging from such relationships and dealings.

➤ *Prohibited Conduct:* **Making Proposals to Foreign Nationals With Respect To Significant Military Equipment Without Prior Approval or Notification.** There is one final caution on the checklist for commencement of detailed discussions between Agile's and Troll's technical personnel. If Agile is considering the possibility that Troll will manufacture any Agile products (as might occur, if Agile receives a JSF sub-contract for work that could be improved or expedited by Troll's designing of the hardware or performing in-country assembly for aircraft destined for the Royal Norwegian Air Force), and this possibility will be discussed at the up-coming meetings, then General Counsel should consider applying to the Directorate for approval. This approval is separate from the TAA for transfer of technical data (which was not tied to the JSF). While the JSF does not appear on the USML, aircraft appear on it in Category VIII (a), a listing preceded by an asterisk.[95] Such an annotation designates it as Significant Military Equipment or SME. Technical data directly related to the manufacture or production of aircraft are also deemed SME.[96] Directorate approval is needed before Agile (a U.S. person) may make a "proposal" or "presentation designed to

---

95. 22 CFR §121.1, Category VIII(a).
96. 22 CFR §121.1, Category VIII(i).

constitute a basis for a decision on the part of" Troll (a foreign person) to enter into a manufacturing license agreement or technical assistance agreement for production or assembly of SME, regardless of the dollar value or the foreign country (there is no exception for Norway as a NATO country).[97]

The ITAR defines the terms "proposal" or "presentation" broadly to mean, with respect to ITAR-controlled technical data:

> "the communication of information in sufficient detail that the person communicating that information **knows or should know** that it would permit an intended purchaser to decide . . . to enter into the . . . technical assistance agreement."[98]

If, for example, an Agile engineer were to describe key parameters of the technical data, the capabilities that Troll would gain by obtaining it and how soon it could be available for delivery, that description would constitute a Section 126.8 "proposal" or "presentation." To make such a proposal or presentation "willfully" without Directorate approval constitutes a criminal violation of the ITAR. To attempt to make one "willfully," or to conspire to make one, without Directorate approval, also constitutes a criminal violation of the ITAR. The ITAR does, however, permit Agile to advertise its possession of the technical data, and to hold preliminary discussions to ascertain the market potential. To lawyers, there may be a bright line between talks to ascertain the market potential of selling data to Troll and talks that permit Troll to decide if it should enter into the TAA, but to technical personnel (such as engineers) the distinction is anything but bright. The forthcoming Agile/Troll talks could easily move between expressions to sound out the scope of Troll's interest (market potential) and expressions to inform it enough to whet its appetite for Agile data. It asks too much of technical personnel to insist that they discern the ITAR distinction between market "scoping" and market making. Agile should seek the Directorate's approval, even if the predominate purpose of the talks is expected to be testing the market. An excess of care before the fact is far preferable to the subsequent need for a voluntary self-disclosure in response to an inadvertent "transfer" violation. Failure to apply for such approval

---

97. 22 CFR §126.8(a)(3).
98. 22 CFR §126.8(b).

could also lead to Directorate disapproval of a license, agreement or sale under the FMS program. There is no need to risk such disapprovals.

Agile should plan well in advance to apply for such approval, because the Directorate must receive the seven requisite copies of the letter application at least 30 days before Agile makes the proposal or presentation to Troll.[99] In view of Troll's need to improve its compliance policies and procedures, however, the 30 day notice period will not delay the transaction, but will in fact buy Troll time to put its house in order, and can be presented in this light.

➤ *Prohibited Conduct:* **Circumventing the ITAR by Changing Policies or Operating Procedures of an Overseas Affiliates in Order to Perform Transactions Prohibited to U.S. Persons.** The publication of an OECD[100] report in April of 2004 prompted Troll's officers to raise an additional concern with the officers of its subsidiary Brugge. The report found a perception among the senior officers of Norwegian companies doing extensive business abroad that solicitation of bribes by foreign nationals in the country where business was transacted was a major issue. An earlier report had found that 10% of the top leaders of Norway's 95 largest companies had been "exposed to solicitations for bribery/grease payments," and 60% believed that "corruption was necessary to get into markets or to win contracts in developing countries."[101] While major companies were aware that Norwegian law imposed criminal penalties for payment of bribes, medium to small company officers were largely unaware of such laws, and knew only that such payments were not tax deductible.[102]

Troll has increased its compliance attention to such laws in response to two recent developments: (i) amendments to Norway's Penal Code that tightened the anti-corruption laws (effective from July 4, 2003), and (ii) highly publicized violations of the new law committed by Statoil ASA ("Statoil"), when it elected not to terminate by the effective date of the new anti-corruption law an agreement that was made illegal by

---

99. 22 CFR §126.8(c)(2).
100. Organisation for Economic Co-Operation and Development.
101. OECD Directorate for Financial and Enterprise Affairs, *Report on the Application of the Convention on Combating Bribery of Foreign Public Officials in International Business Transactions*, Working Group on Bribery in International Transactions: Norway Phase 2, April 12, 2004, p. 6, accessed at www.oecd.org/dataoecd/3/28/31568595.pdf.
102. Id, p. 10.

such law. The latter violations resulted ultimately in substantial adverse publicity for Statoil, the resignation of its CEO and chairman, and a $2.9 million fine imposed by the Økokrim.[103]

Troll's officers therefore have sought an assurance from Brugge that, in its pursuit of contracts in the Middle East and East Africa, its personnel have not made any payments in violation of Norway's anti-bribery laws. They raised the subject in a meeting concerning Agile's inquiries regarding the participation of foreign nationals from countries proscribed by the ITAR.

At that meeting, Troll discovered that such payments were routinely made by Brugge in Sudan (a country torn by civil war) as a cost of positioning itself to do future business. Brugge had on-going contracts in Sudan, one of which was viewed as an opportunity to position Brugge to expand its business there. In conjunction with that contract, Brugge had hired two Sudanese nationals to work at its offices in Norway.

Troll's officers cautioned that the two Sudanese nationals would have to be excluded from any collaborative projects with Agile, and that Brugge should take steps to deny them access to any ITAR-controlled technical data that Agile might transfer to Troll and that Troll might share with Brugge.[104]

There was an additional issue, however. Troll's counsel had recently told Agile's counsel that Brugge had no dealings with Sudan, because his preliminary inquiries revealed no such dealings. When Agile's Counsel was subsequently informed of the Sudanese contracts, he advised that such contracts would have to be added to those Troll would be required to disengage from or, in this instance, cause its subsidiary to wind up. Troll's counsel proposed an alternative that would enable Brugge to retain the benefits of its hard earned position in the Sudanese market. After Closing, Brugge would create an offshore subsidiary to which would be transferred the contracts in question, and which would be solely responsible for performing those contracts. Because Agile intended to put U.S. persons on the Board of Directors of Troll, none would sit on the Board of Brugge. Creation of a Brugge subsidiary,

---

103. The Norwegian National Authority for Investigation and Prosecution of Economic and Environmental Crime, accessed at www.okokrim.no. See the introduction to this book for a fuller discussion of the Statoil case.

104. It is important to ensure that the precautions apply to computers and networks that could be used by such persons to access such data.

counsel reasoned, should insulate the U.S. persons from any involve-ment in the Sudanese dealings.

Unfortunately, while such reasoning is valid under many regulatory regimes, it is not effective under the laws at issue here. Adding another corporate layer or remove would not limit the reach of the Sudanese Sanctions Regulations (or SSR). Moreover, the SSR (like the Iranian Transactions Regulations) contain an unusual prohibition, as follows:

> "No U.S. person may change its policies or operating procedures, or those of a foreign affiliate or subsidiary, in order to enable a foreign entity owned or controlled by U.S. persons to enter into a transaction that could not be entered into directly by a U.S. person . . ."[105]

Brugge's actions could foreseeably be imputed to Agile's objection to the transactions. Moreover, if ITAR auditing personnel asked why Brugge had created the new subsidiary at precisely the time that Agile was completing its acquisition, Brugge would be required to disclose that Troll's ownership prompted the creation of the new subsidiary. Even if Agile did not actually direct the change in corporate structure, its presence would be perceived as the precipitating cause for the change. While this is arguably a conservative reading of the SSR prohibition, it is the better position to avoid all reasonably foreseeable risks of violating the trade sanction regulations, because such violation can severely bur-den a transaction, or prevent its consummation due to impractical delay or too onerous costs, and can put the U.S. party's officers at a high risk of personal liability.

Sometimes a due diligence inquiry at one checkpoint unearths the suggestion of a problem that should have been found at another check-point. In this instance, a problem that should have been detected at checkpoint TSR, was instead found at checkpoint ITAR. One risk of due diligence checks, when performed by the large staffs customarily assigned to transactions, is that tasks are allocated to different personnel no one of whom is aware of (or reviews) the prohibitions and require-ments of all the applicable rules. Assigning smaller specialized teams minimizes the need for repetitive competence and reduces the risk of such problems and facilitates better coordination. Moreover, in the course of such diligence reviews, important inquiries should be made in person, not in question-and-answer e-mails that encourage imme-

---

105. 31 CFR §538.407(c).

diate response without further inquiry. Such electronic communications prevent the sender from checking the recipient's understanding and increase the probability of misunderstood instructions going undiscovered. Over-reliance on such e-mail exchanges also reduces the probability that lawyers will probe officers or press complex inquiries, and encourages a kind of "asked and answered" mentality. The benefits of face-to-face meetings during due diligence were reinforced when Agile's counsel approached the issue of whether Troll and its affiliates were in compliance with applicable laws for the protection of privacy and of personal data. This is our next checkpoint.[106]

---

106. Although not a cross-border issue, we note that Agile's General Counsel will comply with the ITAR requirement that within five days of "the establishment, acquisition, or divestment of a subsidiary or foreign affiliate" it will notify the Directorate by registered mail. 22 CFR §122.4(a).

CHAPTER 5

Checkpoint: Personal Data Protection

5.0 Agile's Transaction In Light of the Personal Data Protection Laws of Multiple Jurisdictions.

The EAR, TSR and ITAR have one unifying principle: if the item is U.S.-controlled, then access to it by non-U.S. persons ultimately requires U.S.-government consent (in the form of a license or an exception from the license requirement). The "gold standard" for such laws tends to be the U.S. laws and regulations (as we noticed in our review of the ITAR). Personal data protection laws have a quite different unifying principle: if such information is controlled by an applicable law, then access to it ultimately requires consent of the data subject (the person to whom such data relates and who can be identified directly or indirectly by use of such data). The "gold standard" for such laws tends to be EU Directives (such as those on Personal Data and on Electronic Transmissions), but other countries (such as Canada) have comparable personal data protection schema (and in the Canadian case, some of its provinces have personal data protection laws whose relationship with Canada's national laws remains unclear and uncertain). U.S. firms that operate globally probably devote more attention and resources to compliance with personal data protection laws than any other of the Access Control Laws. U.S. firms that are less accustomed to engaging in cross-border transactions are often surprised at the rigidity of the personal protection laws: if a transaction or contemplated introduction of a company practice would contravene such laws, there are seldom any suitable exceptions, loopholes or interpretations that can diminish the burden of compliance. Compliance on an *ad hoc* basis is unnecessarily time-consuming and costly, and yet, since there is no one standard that will meet all such regulations, a certain extent of *ad hoc* compliance is unavoidable.

Many firms prefer to adopt personal data protection policies and practices that will substantially reduce the amount of compliance needed to meet the requirements of any given state's personal data protection laws. Firms that transact globally typically encounter personal data protection problems when they seek to centralize in their U.S. offices information about their personnel overseas (or across the United States/Canadian border).[1] However, since the United States does not have a national and comprehensive personal data protection law, the laws of EU Member States (implementing the EU Directives) prohibit the transfer of such information to the United States, because such transfers of personal data can occur only to non-EU countries that provide an "adequate" level of privacy protection (a standard the United States currently does not meet). For such transfers from an EU Member State to the United States (even if only an internally among branches of the same firm), certain conditions must be met such as the requirements set forth in the U.S.-EU "Safe Harbor Framework" ("Safe Harbor") (a mechanism which enables the EU to certify that participating U.S. companies meet the EU requirement for adequate privacy protection). That Framework, for example, requires adherence to certain principles related to:

Notice (to the data subjects concerning the collection, purpose and use of their personal data; where they should address inquiries concerning such data, etc.);

Choice (giving the data subjects an opportunity choose whether their personal information will be used for a purpose beyond or contrary to the purposes for which it was initially collected and whether it will be disclosed to third parties; **Note:** for "sensitive" information an "opt-out" is inadequate, the choice must be an "opt-in" if such information will be used for a purpose other than that for which it was collected or will be disclosed to third parties);

---

1. See Scheer, David, *Europe's New High-Tech Role: Playing Privacy Cop to World*, The Wall Street Journal Online, October 10, 2003, accessed at http://online.wsj.com/ PA2VJBNA4R/article/0,,SB106574949477122300-search,00.html.

Onward Transfer (that such data will not be transferred to third parties unless such parties have subscribed to the Framework or enter into a written agreement with the disclosing organization to provide the same level of privacy protection for such data);

Security (that organizations creating, maintaining, using or disseminating such data will implement "reasonable precautions" to protect it from loss, misuse and unauthorized access, disclosure, alternation and destruction);

Data Integrity (that organizations will ensure that for its intended use the data is complete, accurate, and current);

Access (that data subjects will have "reasonable access" to the data about them and if they find it contains inaccuracies, they can correct, amend or delete it, except where providing such access would impose a burden disproportionate to the risks to the data subjects' privacy); and

Enforcement (that there are a "readily available and affordable independent recourse mechanisms" to ensure that a data subject's complaints will be investigated and resolved, that procedures have been implemented to verify an organization's compliance with the Framework, and that sanctions for violations are sufficient to ensure compliance).[2]

For large firms to come into compliance with the Safe Harbor can be a prodigious task, and even for smaller firms the task will require substantial effort. General Motors, for example, to update its internal electronic company phone book had to devote months to "mapping where the phone book might be used and by whom," and then had to notify its European employees that their office numbers would be sent to headquarters in the United States and that they could opt for a third-party mediator if they objected (none did), and then had to have each of its approximately 200 affiliates execute data sharing agreements that included provisions prohibiting the misuse such phone numbers.[3] Such

2. U.S. Department of Commerce, *Welcome to Safe Harbor*, accessed at www.export.gov/safeharbor/index.html.

3. See Scheer, David, *Europe's New High-Tech Role: Playing Privacy Cop to World*, The Wall Street Journal Online, October 10, 2003, accessed at http://online.wsj.com/PA2VJBNA4R/article/0,,SB106574949477122300-search,00.html.

companies usually find it necessary to appoint a Chief Privacy Officer to oversee such efforts on an on-going basis.

Agile's acquisition of Troll will include Troll's majority interest in the joint venture Ijsselmeer, which has the significant potential to market a growing portfolio of anti-terrorist technologies (biometric and thermal imaging detection, identification, and cryptographic authentication, thick-polymer sensors, M2M and RFID tracking devices, personal gateways and Japanese patented robotic devices) to government security agencies and commercial entities. During the months of exploratory talks, Troll disclosed only cursory information concerning Ijsselmeer, because Ijsselmeer had objected to any such disclosures until the prospects of the acquisition improved substantially. To reduce its start-up costs, Ijsselmeer had historically not filed for patents to protect many of its proprietary technological inventions. Instead, it had relied on trade secret protections (at the risk that in the interim other companies would file for and obtain patent protection for the same inventions). In its view, the less it disclosed about its inventions, the better it would be able protect them. As a result of this business decision, Ijsselmeer was reluctant to entrust any proprietary information to a U.S. company that had the resources to exploit rapidly Ijsselmeer's technological insights and innovations, and that would almost certainly do so in the event that the acquisition talks broke down. Ijsselmeer's thrift, mistrust and circumspection (the strategies of a start-up protecting its turf) would eventually cost Agile dearly, because these kept Agile from discerning a host of privacy and personal data protection compliance risks. Finding such violations at a later stage in the acquisition made correction difficult to plan and execute as well as unnecessarily costly.

5.1 Ijsselmeer's Collection and Processing of Personal Data.

Ijsselmeer's technologies are in various stages of development towards commercialization. The company's research and development strategy had been to push its technologies into prototypes and then test those prototypes in varying environments. Ijsselmeer tested its biometric detection prototypes in two environments: in a controlled laboratory setting (where human subjects volunteered for brief sessions, in connection with which they signed written consents to have their personal data gathered by the prototype devices); and in an uncontrolled setting at transportation hubs (railway stations, ferry ports, bus and tram stops, subways) where none of the human subjects gave prior consent, or even knew that potentially sensitive personal data was being gathered. The biometric detection tests were conducted in cities in The Netherlands, Canada and Japan. The tracking devices, M2M (machine-to-machine) and RFID (radio frequency identification), were tested on bicycles in Oslo, on buses in Tromsø, Norway,[4] and in "smart license plates" on vehicles on Highway 401 between Toronto and Guelph, Canada.

Ijsselmeer unobtrusively videotaped the use of its prototypes in both the laboratory and the transportation hub settings. In both settings, the subjects were unaware that they were being taped.

Members of Ijsselmeer's teams (and Troll) received reports of the prototype tests, which included raw and processed biometric data linked to the identity of the subject from whom it was obtained. (This linkage turned such data into "personally identifiable information.") Ijsselmeer circulated these test reports (and the sensitive personal data packages) into and out of The Netherlands, Norway, Canada and Japan.

As part of its due diligence, Agile asked to review all test and other reports that might provide assessments of the effectiveness and limitations of Ijsselmeer's technologies. It asked that these be transmitted by e-mail or otherwise express mailed to its offices in the United States (noting that all such transmittals would be kept confidential under the terms of the nondisclosure agreement between Agile and Troll and their respective affiliates and agents).

However, Agile's European counsel cautioned that the request for such reports should be reviewed under applicable privacy and personal data protection laws and regulations before being complied with.[5]

---

4. Ijsselmeer is not the first company to deploy smart tracking devices on bicycles and buses. Rusken, a bicycle rental company, uses M2M technology to keep track of its bicycles in Oslo and ensure their return to their racks (see Budden, Robert, *The Rise of the Talking Machines*, FINANCIAL TIMES, May 26, 2004, p. 11). Similarly, Volvo Mobility Systems has deployed Linux-powered tracking technology on the buses in the northern city of Tromsø, transmitting every 30 seconds the details of each bus's progress via the GPRS cellular link—information relayed to electronic displays at every bus stop so passengers can determine how long they must wait before the next bus arrives at their stop (non-trivial information in a city where the sun does not rise in the depth of winter and prevailing temperatures are frigid). See Handford, Richard, *Cold, Dark Days at the Bus Stop*, FINANCIAL TIMES, February 18, 2004, p. 11.

5. The creation of biometric databases, when linked to personal identifiable information, raises privacy concerns. Such concerns over biometric databases are likely to emerge in countries that test biometric technologies and implement such technologies

Agile's U.S. counsel was aware of the European Parliament Directive on the protection of individuals' privacy with regard to the processing of personal data and the free movement of such data ("Directive on Personal Data")[6], and of the European Parliament Directive on the processing of personal data and the protection of privacy in the electronic communications sector ("Directive on Electronic Transmission")[7]. However, his understanding of the Directive on Personal Data was limited to news discussions of efforts by the United States and the European Union to reach accords on pre-flight disclosure of personal data ("Airline Passenger Data Agreement")[8], and of the burdens that large U.S. corporations encountered in transferring personal data from their European to their U.S. entities or in connection with transfers between European companies. He understood that the Directive on Electronic Transmission replaced and amplified an earlier directive (that barred the transmission of personal data outside the European Union unless the recipient country's protections for personal data met the standards set by the EU Directives) extending such limitation to electronic transmissions of such data.[9] This directive also requires protection of the confidentiality of the content of communications and, upon completion of such communication, deletion of the traffic data (such as dialing, routing and addressing, except for limited purposes such as billing). Because the Directive on Personal Data mandates that Member States

---

to secure borders and to create unique means of identifying individuals for commercial transactions.

6. EU Directive 95/46/EC of the European Parliament and of the Council of 24 October 1995.

7. EU Directive 97/66/EC of the European Parliament and of the Council of 15 December 1997.

8. See Mitchener, Brandon, *EU Governments Are Set to Approve Airline-Data Deal*, THE WALL STREET JOURNAL, May 5, 2004, p. A-12. The EU and U.S. finally signed the accord on May 29, 2004, allowing the U.S. to continue to receive information in advance on airline passengers, which started on an interim basis in March 2003. The accord permits U.S. Customs and Border Protection to collect 34 items of personal information (e.g., name, address, and credit card information). The accord has an initial period of three and a half years. *US and EU Sign Air Passenger Data Deal*, FINANCIAL TIMES, May 29/May 30, 2004, p. 2.

9. *EU Directive 2002/58/EC of the European Parliament and of the Council of 12 July 2002 Concerning the Processing of Personal Data and the Protection of Privacy in the Electronic Communications Sector*, OFFICIAL JOURNAL L. 201, July 31, 2002, at 37–47 (replacing EU Directive 97/66/EC).

enact legislation to implement its provisions,[10] Danish counsel provided a summary, but also recommended that Agile's General Counsel engage Dutch counsel for guidance on the applicable Dutch law implementing the Directive on Personal Data.

Agile's Danish counsel also highlighted the following key points concerning the Directive in relation to Ijsselmeer's handling of personal data in its summary:

- The Directive defines personal data to mean "any information relating to an identified or identifiable natural person" (referred to as the "data subject").[11]

  ➤ Agile should focus, in Ijsselmeer's case, on its technology's capacity to create information about an "identifiable" natural person, *i.e.,* "one who can be identified, directly or indirectly, in particular by reference to . . . one or more factors specific to his physical, physiological, mental, economic, cultural or social identity."[12]

- The Directive applies to both the automatic and non-automatic processing of personal data.

  ➤ Agile should focus, in Ijsselmeer's case, on its technology's capacity to perform automatic processing of personal data, especially since the Directive defines "processing of personal data" very broadly, and encompasses features of processing easily overlooked; the Directive defines such processing, in pertinent part, as "any set of operations . . . performed on personal data . . . such as collection, recording, organization, storage, adaptation or alternation, retrieval, consultation, use, disclosure by transmission, dissemination or otherwise making available, alignment or combination, blocking, erasure or destruction."[13]

- It should be noted that while Ijsselmeer is the obvious "controller" of the processing of personal data, Troll is also a "controller." To the extent that Agile's agreement with Troll gives Agile any pre-

---

10. The implementing legislation is required to harmonize the rules applicable in each Member State with the standards set in the Directives.

11. Directive on Personal Data, Article 2(a).

12. Id.

13. Id., Article 2(b).

Closing rights to participate in decisions concerning the "purposes and means of" Ijsselmeer's processing of such data, Agile too becomes a "controller" under the Directive.

- Certain categories of personal data cannot be processed unless the controller clearly qualifies for an exception. Such categories include: "personal data revealing racial or ethnic origin, political opinions, religious or philosophical beliefs, trade-union membership, and the processing of data concerning health or sex life."[14]

  ➤ Agile should focus, in Ijsselmeer's case, on its technology's capacity to process data revealing "racial or ethnic origin . . . [and] data concerning health. . . ."

- Counsel should give particular attention to the Directive's conditions for transfer of personal data to third countries, which may only occur if: (i) "the third country in question ensures an adequate level of protection,"[15] or (ii) such transfer qualifies for one of the exceptions. Only one of those exceptions would appear to be available to Ijsselmeer, namely "the data subject has given his consent unambiguously to the proposed transfer."[16]

  ➤ Agile should focus on finding out whether Ijsselmeer has met the applicable Dutch legal requirements for "consent" of the "data subjects." It should not accept any suggestions of "*implied*" consent (which would ordinarily not meet those requirements and would, in any event, be difficult to document and prove if Dutch authorities were to investigate Ijsselmeer).

It is important for Agile to learn in greater detail how Ijsselmeer has handled personal data, and what, if anything, it may not have done to comply with Dutch data protection laws and regulations. Clearly Agile needs to verify the substance of Ijsselmeer's technologies in the context of the proposed acquisition in order to make a commercial assessment of: how close they are to being commercialized; whether they can help position Agile to compete for DoD and DHS contracts for anti-terrorism technologies and subcontracts for the DHS "virtual borders" program; and whether those technologies offer any marketable advantages

---

14. Id., Article 8(1).
15. Directive on Data Protection, Article 25(1).
16. Id., Article 26(1)(a)

in "data mining." Such assessments are routine, in the context of a strategic acquisition, and regulatory diligence can often "piggy back" on the business diligence.

General Counsel must map risk points and checkpoints to ensure that the transaction can proceed without challenge by the Dutch authorities and without Agile incurring liability. Like other companies encountering foreign data protection laws for the first time, Agile has assumed that the United States has privacy protections comparable to other modern democracies, and that it will need to make few adjustments to accommodate whatever privacy (and personal data protection) regulations may exist in The Netherlands, Norway, Canada and Japan. Such views are not accurate either with respect to U.S. privacy laws or with respect to the privacy protections required by the laws of those countries.

When Agile's Danish counsel flagged privacy and personal data protection as the areas in which she anticipated compliance problems that might delay the transaction, she underscored the radically different agendas underlying United States and European privacy and data protection laws. Agile's officers and directors (like their counterparts at other U.S. firms) perceive privacy and related data protection laws as involving: (i) security of their firm's proprietary information, (ii) protection of their firm's computers from unauthorized access by hackers in cyberspace, and (iii) a patchwork of isolated, specialized activities governed by technical laws that do not extend to Agile's current operations (*e.g.*, protections of: patient's personal information, individually identifiable information of customers of financial institutions, and data stored by California companies and firms doing business in California that would be subject to the California Database Protection Act of 2001, to cite just a few). European privacy and data protection laws are at once more comprehensive in their scope and more detailed in the protections they afford. This perhaps reflects the "sunshine" bias in favor of the fewest limitations on access to information that inheres in the uniquely American concept of popular democracy. It no doubt reflects (on the European side) the experience with the pernicious use of government collected personal data for the Holocaust in countries such as The Netherlands.

But it also expresses the significant current debate over the extent to which security laws and regulations, seeking to prevent acts of terrorism and to ensure public safety, may encroach privacy rights, and the underlying tension evidenced in those debates concerning the relationship between security and privacy. The question is most often posed as whether increased security and tougher security laws (and their implementation by law enforcement officials) will result in decreased respect for privacy and privacy rights, or in better protection of those rights? Recent commentators have taken the view that "in times of war and other crises, the need for security inevitably threatens our commitment to liberty" and privacy.[17] But this is hardly a new debate. Alexander Hamilton warned against such risk:

> "Safety from external danger is the most powerful director of national conduct. Even the ardent love of liberty will, after a time, give way to its dictates. The violent destruction of life and property incident to war, the continual effort and alarm attendant on a state of continual danger, will compel nations the most attached to liberty, to resort for repose and security to institutions which have a tendency to destroy their civil and political rights. To be more safe, they, at length, become willing to run the risk of being less free."[18]

James Madison (when arguing in favor of adoption of the Constitution) saw the vanity of imposing "constitutional barriers to the impulse of self-preservation," but argued that the nation should avoid when possible the "necessity and the danger" of such impulse. He reasoned:

> "The means of security can only be regulated by the means and the danger of attack. They will, in fact, be ever determined by these rules and by no others. It is in vain to oppose constitutional barriers to the impulse of self-preservation. . . . [a wise nation] does not rashly preclude itself from any resource which may become essential to its safety, [and] will exert all its prudence in diminishing both the necessity and the danger of resorting to one which may be inauspicious to its liberties."[19]

---

17. *Safeguarding Privacy in the Fight Against Terrorism,* Report of the Technology and Privacy Advisory Committee, March 2004, p. 7, accessed at www.mipt.org/pdf/Safeguarding-Privacy-Fight-Against-Terrorism.pdf.

18. Hamilton, Alexander, THE FEDERALIST PAPERS, No. 8, accessed at www.yale.edu/lawweb/avalon/federal/fed08.htm.

19. Madison, James, THE FEDERALIST PAPERS, No. 41, accessed at www.yale.edu/lawweb/avalon/federal/fed41.htm.

However, he opposed those measures aimed at silencing dissent during war that would not protect the nation from the dangers of war. In a letter to Jefferson on the Alien and Sedition Acts, he observed:

"The management of foreign relations appears to be the most susceptible of abuse, of all the trusts committed to a Government, because they can be concealed or disclosed, or disclosed in such parts & at such times as will best suit particular views; and because the body of the people are less capable of judging & are more under the influence of prejudices, on that branch of their affairs, than of any other. *Perhaps it is a universal truth that the loss of liberty at home is to be charged to provisions agst. danger real or pretended from abroad.*"[20]

Still other commentators have considered the tension between security and liberty to be an illusory conflict, arguing that "Without security, you can't have privacy."[21]

In the United States, such debates have focused more recently on "data mining" and the questionable use of mined personal data use by the DHS and DoD in connection with programs like the unfortunately named "Total Information Awareness" project funded by DARPA (a project retitled in May of 2003 as "Terrorism Information Awareness"). Data mining (or techniques that make similar use of personal information concerning U.S. persons to detect and deter terrorism) occurs in several U.S. Government programs including the Financial Crimes Enforcement Network (a Treasury project), the "Know Your Customer" rules (a BIS policy), the MATRIX (Multistate Anti-Terrorism Information Exchange system linking the DHS with the law enforcement

---

20. Madison, James, *Letter to Thomas Jefferson,* May 13, 1798, accessed at www.constitution.org/jm/17980513_tj.htm. [Emphasis added.] Unfortunately, as seen in McCarthyism, appeals to the need to defend the nation against external threats can lose sight of Madison's caution of the "danger of resorting" to means that are "inauspicious" to liberty, and prove Madison's observation that "A bad cause seldom fails to betray itself." Madison, James, THE FEDERALIST PAPERS, No. 41, accessed at www.yale.edu/lawweb/avalon/federal/fed41.htm.

21. Remarks of Richard Clarke in Goth, Greg, *Richard Clarke Talks Cybersecurity and JELL-O,* IEEE SECURITY & PRIVACY, May/June 2004, p. 14. Other commentators concur: "Privacy considerations are necessarily interwoven in security because the privacy of data is directly dependent upon security—without security there is no privacy." Westby, Jody R., Editor, INTERNATIONAL GUIDE TO CYBER SECURITY, American Bar Association, Privacy & Computer Crime Committee, Section of Science and Technology Law, 2004, p. 19.

data bases in several states), and the Computer-Assisted Passenger Pre-screening System (a DHS project reportedly terminated in July 2004).[22,23] A DoD sponsored Report, *Safeguarding Privacy in the Fight Against Terrorism* (the "Safeguarding Privacy Report"), concludes that, while data mining is a vital tool for fighting terrorism, it can present "significant privacy issues."[24] However, a Separate Statement to that Report, is careful to draw a distinction between the privacy issues raised by data mining and other pre-eminent "constitutional rights such as freedom of speech, freedom from racial discrimination, freedom from religious discrimination, and freedom to participate in the political process," because

> "If privacy is a subject of the magnitude of liberty, free speech, freedom from racial or religious discrimination, etc., then particular governmental action with respect to such actions' constitutionality is measured by 'strict scrutiny' [under footnote four in the 1938 case of *United States v. Carolene Products Co.*], but if privacy is not within the Constitution, or even if it is, but is not in the category of 'liberty,' 'racial discrimination,' etc., then particular governmental action with respect thereto requires a mere rational basis for such actions not to violate the Constitution. Valid constitutional concepts and distinctions, like appropriate words in intellectual discourse, are wise persons' counters especially when called upon to advise Cabinet Secretaries."[25]

---

22. Note that while the DHS reportedly announced that CAPPS 2 was "dead," a DHS spokesman also observed that "the administration continues to move forward on an automated aviation passenger prescreening system to replace the existing antiquated airline system, to better manage risk and be more efficient." Dow Jones Newswire, *US Govt "Reshaping" Air Passenger Screening System-NY*, Wall Street Journal Online, July 16, 2004, accessed at http://online.wsj.com/article/0,,BT_CO_20040716_001579-search,00.html?collection = autowire%2F30day&vql_string = %27Prescreening + System%27%3Cin%3E%28article%2Dbody%29.

23. *Safeguarding Privacy in the Fight Against Terrorism*, Report of the Technology and Privacy Advisory Committee, March 2004, p. viii, accessed at www.mipt.org/pdf/Safeguarding-Privacy-Fight-Against-Terrorism.pdf. There are those who view the post-9/11 pursuit of security as creating a "surveillance-industrial complex." See *The Surveillance Industrial Complex Report*, ACLU, www.aclu.org/surveillance/, p. 6.

24. Id.

25. *Separate Statement of William T. Coleman, Jr.*, at pp. 68–69, in *Safeguarding Privacy in the Fight Against Terrorism*, Report of the Technology and Privacy Advisory Committee, March 2004, accessed at www.mipt.org/pdf/Safeguarding-Privacy-Fight-Against-Terrorism.pdf. That privacy is not accorded the same rank as the other constitutionally protected rights mentioned by Coleman can be perceived if one considers

We would object to the presumption that, simply because the right to privacy is a "penumbral" right, rather than an "enumerated" right, means that it does not enjoy the same validity and protection afforded other "fundamental" rights.

Even acknowledging that such a debate exists in the U.S., it is not mirrored in the views of the European Community toward privacy and personal data protection. In the United States, the lack of a comprehensive law for the protection of privacy (or of personally identifiable data) and the arguments over the constitutional status of a right to privacy, contrast sharply with the legislated protections of right to privacy under Dutch law, for example. Privacy is not only an explicit right under the Dutch Constitution but, in implementing the Directive on Personal Data, Dutch law creates a two-tiered system of protections, one for sensitive personal data, and one for all other personal data, a distinction quite alien to U.S. business executives and their counsel, who are often surprised to find U.S. allies in Europe and Canada insisting on much greater protection for personal privacy than is commonly afforded in the United States.

5.2 Compliance with the Dutch Personal Data Protection Act.

To understand the scope of the Dutch privacy protection laws, Agile engages Dutch counsel in Eindhoven (where Ijsselmeer has its Netherlands offices) and learns the following. Unlike the U.S. Constitution, which makes no mention of a "right to privacy," the Constitution of the Kingdom of the Netherlands (Nederlandse Grondwet) grants its citizens an explicit right to privacy. Article 10 states, in pertinent part:

> "(1) Everyone shall have the right to respect for his privacy . . .
> (2) Rules to protect privacy shall be laid down by Act of Parliament in connection the recording and dissemination of personal data.
> (3) Rules concerning the rights of persons to be informed of data recorded concerning them, of the use that is made thereof, and to have such data corrected shall be laid down by Act of Parliament."[26]

---

how many might in certain circumstances agree with Patrick Henry's view "Give me liberty or give me death" and then imagine how few, if any, would agree if he had said instead "Give me privacy or give me death."

26. Constitution of the Kingdom of the Netherlands, Article 10, accessed at

Efforts to protect The Netherlands from terrorism since September 11, 2001 have provoked some of the same debates voiced in the United States concerning the proper balance of security and privacy. The Dutch data protection authority (*College Bescherming Persoonsgegevens* or CBP), in its Annual Report in 2002, expressed worries that security interests were subverting privacy interests in debates among Dutch administrators and politicians:

> "Security was the primary focus of political and public debate in 2002. Amid the general calls for greater decisiveness, supervision and control, various prominent administrators and politicians made a caricature of privacy. Privacy protection was portrayed as an impediment to public safety; privacy legislation therefore required reform. In November, the administration proposed that everyone over the age of twelve should have a legal obligation to identify themselves. It was also suggested that, with a view to aiding the fight against crime and terrorism, all telecommunication traffic data should be retained for an extended period. The Dutch Data Protection Authority (DPA) is very concerned that a simplistic introduction of greater police powers could seriously undermine the rights and interests of ordinary citizens. Furthermore, the Dutch DPA strongly refutes the notion that privacy protection acts as a barrier to the resolution of social problems by hindering cooperation between various authorities. It is the Dutch DPA's conviction, borne out by experience, that privacy protection is one of the success factors for effective government."[27]

The applicable Dutch law (*Wet bescherming persoonsgegevens* or the Personal Data Protection Act) contains provisions that Ijsselmeer was either unaware of or inattentive to, and a number of its practices clearly contravene the Act. As a result, Ijsselmeer cannot transfer its test reports

---

www.oefre.unibe.ch/law/icl/nl00000_.html. Article 13 of the Dutch Constitution also prohibits violation of the privacy of "correspondence" and of "telephone and telegraph," subject to exceptions provided by the Dutch Parliament.

27. CBP Annual Report 2002, accessed at www.cbpweb.nl/en/documenten/en_jv_2002sum.htm.

Note: the security vs. privacy debate in The Netherlands has been transformed by the reaction of the Dutch government and public to the assasinations of Pim Fortuyu (on May 5, 2002) and Theo Van Gogh (on November 2, 2004). See Kuper, Simon, *Trouble in Paradise*, FINANCIAL TIMES, December 4, 2004, accessed at http://news.ft.com/cms/s/c21efce6-459-11d9-8fef-00000e2511c8.html.

to a U.S. location pursuant to Agile's commercial diligence request until Ijsselmeer corrects those noncompliant practices and takes certain actions to qualify itself, under the Personal Data Protection Act, for lawful transfers of personal data to the United States. The following risk points emerge from discussions with counsel.

5.2.1 Activity.

Ijsselmeer does not have in-house legal counsel. In its "cost-saving" start-up mode, it has paid little attention to whether its research and development of biometric products, prototypes and testing has brought it within the scope of the Dutch Personal Data Protection Act ("PDPA"). However, because it links the biometric information it derives to information that clearly identifies the data subject, Ijsselmeer's biometric devices undeniably make use of "personal data," defined under the PDPA as "any information relating to an identified or identifiable person."[28] In fact, its biometric devices engage in almost every kind of "processing of personal data" described or contemplated by the PDPA, which defines such processing as "any operation or set of operations concerning personal data, including in any case the collection, recording, organization, storage, updating or modification, retrieval, consultation, use dissemination by means of transmission, distribution or making available in any other form, merging, linking, as well as blocking, erasure or destruction of data."[29] The PDPA uses the term "responsible party" instead of "controller" to identify the persons who "alone or in conjunction with others, determines the purpose of and means for processing personal data."[30] Ijsselmeer and its majority investor Troll are for now the sole responsible parties, but only as long as Agile does not participate in any determination of the purpose and/or means for Ijsselmeer's processing of personal data—something that Agile's Counsel needs to be particularly vigilant about.

Moreover, the PDPA applies not only to Ijsselmeer's processing of personal data in The Netherlands,[31] but also to any processing "by or

---

28. PDPA, Article 1(a), accessed at www.cbpweb.nl/en/structuur/en_pag_cbp.htm.
29. PDPA, Article 1(b).
30. PDPA, Article 1(d).
31. PDPA, Article 4(1).

for" a responsible party who is not established in the European Union but who makes use of automated means situated in The Netherlands.[32] In the past, Ijsselmeer's divisions in Canada and Japan have remotely processed personal data from Dutch data subjects through linkages to Ijsselmeer's computers in Eindhoven. Troll, on the other hand, has not. With that in mind, Agile's Counsel and Dutch counsel go through a checklist of risk points under the PDPA, initially focusing exclusively on Ijsselmeer's processing of personal data.

➤ *The Prohibited Conduct*—**No One Appointed to Act for Ijsselmeer under the PDPA.** Dutch counsel asks Ijsselmeer's chief information officer ("CIO") to identify who at Ijsselmeer is designated to act on its behalf in accordance with the PDPA. Ijsselmeer has made no such appointment or designation, in spite of the fact that the PDPA requires that such a person be designated and prohibits the processing of personal data until that condition is met.[33]

Ijsselmeer should immediately designate an officer to serve in that capacity and thereby be the "responsible party" for purposes of the PDPA. Although Ijsselmeer does not have to report this noncompliance to the Dutch Data Protection Authority, it should prepare for possible future disclosure by internally recording when the appointment takes effect and which processing of personal data preceded or followed that date. The Dutch Data Protection Authority may consider relevant that Ijsselmeer pursued more than cosmetic compliance once it recognized the oversight.

➤ *The Prohibited Conduct*—**Processing Proceeded Without Notice to the Dutch Data Protection Authority and Without Adequate Measures to Protect Personal Data.** Counsel asks if anyone at Ijsselmeer notified the Dutch Data Protection Authority that Ijsselmeer intended to process personal data with its biometric devices (because no processing of personal data is permitted under the PDPA prior to submittal of such notification).[34] Again, no one at Ijsselmeer was aware of this requirement. Ijsselmeer will need to compile a list of the kinds of processing of personal data that are undertaken by all personnel in the organization (not simply during testing of the biometric devices), and determine if any are exempt from notification under the Dutch Check-

---

32. PDPA, Article 4(2).
33. PDPA, Article 4(3).
34. PDPA, Article 27(1).

list Exemption Decree (which specifies 40 categories that are exempt from the notification requirements of the PDPA). Category 28 for "Scientific research and statistics"[35] might arguably be available for the research portion of Ijsselmeer's processing.[36] However, the tests of its prototypes would probably not qualify as "scientific research," because the goal of such testing is to determine commercial viability.

The appropriate notice must be drafted and forwarded promptly to the Dutch Data Protection Authority. Such submittal must be on a specified Notification Form, filled out in Dutch and signed by the "responsible party."[37] In addition, each individual method and act of processing of personal data will require a separate Notification Form, which will probably mean that several such forms will be required to be submitted by Ijsselmeer.

In addition, the form requires the following information:

• Name and address of the responsible party;

• The purpose(s) of the processing;

• A description of the categories of data subjects and data categories relating thereto;

---

35. Dutch Data Protection Authority, *Categories Exempt from Processing*, accessed at www.cbpweb.nl/en/structuur/en_pag_melden.htm.

36. Note that the Working Party (the independent European Union Advisory Body on Data Protection and Privacy) has expressed strong reservations about the use of biometric data in visas and residence permits. Thus it seems probable in the near future that some other exemptions may be added to the Dutch Checklist Exemptions for biometric data used in visas and residence permits. As the Working Party noted in its report in August 2004, "the growing interest in the application of biometric identification techniques calls for an extremely careful analysis of the legality of processing such data for identification purposes, since biometric data intrinsically involve genuine risks for the persons concerned if they are lost or used for purposes other than those for which they were intended. In particular, there is a not inconsiderable risk that an individual whose digital fingerprints have been collected does not otherwise communicate his or her real identity, particularly if the circumstances under which the fingerprints were collected do not guarantee perfect reliability; the hijacked identity would then be permanently associated with the digital fingerprints in question." *Opinion of the Article 29 Data Protection Working Party on the Inclusion of Biometric Elements in Residence Permits and Visas*, adopted on August 11, 2004, p. 4, accessed at http://europa.eu.int/comm/internal_market/privacy/docs/wpdocs/2004/wp96_en.pdf.

37. Dutch Data Protection Authority, *Correct Notification*, accessed at www.cbpweb.nl/en/structuur/en_pag_melden.htm.

- The recipients or categories of recipients to whom the data may be supplied;
- The planned transfers of data to countries outside the European Union; and
- A general description allowing a preliminary assessment of the suitability of the planned measures to guarantee the security of such processing.[38]

While Ijsselmeer's CIO is reluctant to disclose the purpose of the processing, this need not involve the disclosure of any proprietary information. Ijsselmeer will need to identify as possible recipients of data outside the European Union, parties (who need not be named) in Norway, Canada, Japan and the United States, and will have to provide a general description of the measures it proposes to take to guarantee the security of the processing. While Ijsselmeer has a policy of strict confidentiality (including nondisclosure agreements required of all personnel, the securing of all test results in locked file cabinets, etc), it does in fact routinely download and store sensitive personal data on its computers. As noted earlier, when computers are linked to the Internet, security precautions must be taken (including the deployment of software or hardware that can detect unauthorized access, either externally from the Internet or internally by persons not cleared to access such data) to ensure the "sanctity" of stored data (including its accuracy, which can be compromised by hackers or other cyber-intruders).

Ijsselmeer's computers are linked to the Internet on a broadband DSL line, but its system has never been infected with a virus. It restricts access by requiring use of a password entry system. Because Ijsselmeer uses only one password for its entire system—"IJSSEL77"—hacking software readily available on the Web (such as Lophtcrack) could easily enable a hacker to penetrate Ijsselmeer's security. With no procedures in place for checking unauthorized access, Ijsselmeer could very well have had its computers penetrated without its knowledge. In short, Ijsselmeer's cybersecurity for sensitive personal data is superficial at best.

The PDPA requires that:

"The responsible party shall implement *appropriate technical and organizational measures* to secure personal data against loss or against any form of unlawful processing. These measures shall *guar-*

---

38. PDPA, Article 28.

antee an appropriate level of security, taking into account the state of the art and the costs of implementation, and having regard to the *risks associated with the processing and the nature of the data to be protected.* These measures shall also aim at preventing unnecessary collection and further processing of personal data."[39]

Since Ijsselmeer collects, processes and stores copious quantities of sensitive personal data on its computers (and since the biometric data includes genetic information), the appropriate security measures should provide the highest level of security[40] protection against unauthorized access. It would be advisable to have a cybersecurity specialist scan its Internet-linked computers for embedded malwares that compromise computer security features in four ways:

Confidentiality (allowing unauthorized access to data),

Integrity (allowing unauthorized changes to the system state or data residing or passing through such system),

Availability (allowing unauthorized access to a system resource), and

Control (granting privileges to unauthorized users, enabling a subsequent confidentiality, integrity or availability violation).[41]

Counsel recommends that Ijsselmeer move its biometric personal data to computers not linked to the Internet, and that it implement an identity management authentication system to guard against unauthorized access, following the accepted wisdom:

"So the rule for cybersecurity is not to count on opponents not coming, but to rely on having ways of dealing with them; not to count on opponents not attacking, but to rely on having what cannot be attacked."[42]

---

39. PDPA, Article 13. [Emphases added.]

40. The Dutch Data Protection Authority recognizes four categories of risk to personal data. The highest is for large quantities of sensitive data that undergo complex processing—which well describes Ijsselmeer's processing of personal data. See Dutch Data Protection Authority, *Protection Levels for Personal Data,* accessed at www.cbpweb.nl/en/structuur/en_pag_publ.htm.

41. Bace, Rebecca, and Mell, Peter, *Intrusion Detection Systems,* SP 800-31, National Institute of Standards and Technology, November 2001, p. 40, accessed at http://csrc.nist.gov/publications/nistpubs/800-31/sp800-31.pdf.

42. The original quotation, using "military operations," is from Tzu, Sun, THE ART OF WAR, translated by Thomas Cleary, Shambhala, 1991, pp. 64–65.

The original issue remains, however, of Ijsselmeer's having processed personal data without having first given notice to the Dutch Data Protection Authority. Prompt notice avoids a recurrence of the problem, but does not cure the violations that have already occurred. The Authority can impose a penalty for each violation, including a fine of up to EUR 4,500.[43] Such fine is required to reflect the gravity and duration of the violation.[44] In extreme cases, criminal proceedings may be initiated (by criminal enforcement authorities, not by the Dutch Data Protection Authority).[45]

The PDPA is silent on whether a company is required to report its own violations, as well as on whether the Authority will consider lenient treatment for companies that do voluntarily report their violations. However, the Dutch Data Protection Authority emphasizes on its web site that:

> "A fine can also be imposed if you have incorrectly or incompletely reported your data processing and/or if you fail to report changes (in time). Periodically, the Dutch DPA will subject notifications from specific sectors or of specific processing to a further investigation."[46]

Thus, once Ijsselmeer files the requisite notifications for each form of processing of personal data, it should anticipate that at some point the Dutch Data Protection Authority will investigate the accuracy of its notifications. Such investigation will almost certainly uncover the fact that Ijsselmeer submitted such notifications without disclosing that it had processed personal data before making such filings. Agile's counsel concurs and concludes that Ijsselmeer will need to make a full disclosure to the Dutch Data Protection Authority. However, Ijsselmeer can be expected to be understandably resistant to such course of action because it does not want to invite fines, adverse publicity or the possibility of criminal proceedings.

In reality, there is almost no possibility of criminal proceedings, because no one at Ijsselmeer was aware of the PDPA's requirements. They therefore could not have deliberately violated such provisions and,

---

43. Dutch Data Protection Authority, *Fines,* accessed at www.cbpweb.nl/en/structuur/en_pag_melden.htm.

44. PDPA, Article 66 (1) and (3).

45. PDPA, Article 66 (5).

46. Dutch Data Protection Authority, *Fines,* accessed at www.cbpweb.nl/en/structuur/en_pag_melden.htm.

under the PDPA, only "Responsible parties who deliberately commit an offence . . . shall be punished with a prison sentence for a maximum of six months. . . ."[47] The Authority is not permitted to impose a fine "where responsible parties give a reasonable explanation as to why they cannot be regarded as responsible" for the violation.[48]

Dutch counsel would like to explore any mitigating circumstances that may exist for Ijsselmeer as well, but Ijsselmeer's CIO sees no benefit to this course of action. In the process of advising any client in this field the burden will be on counsel to make the case for early and full disclosure. The rationale is simple. Disclosure allows the company to go forward with a clean slate and to limit or mitigate its liability and the disruption of any on-going inquiry as to past violations. It also provides a credible posture from which to make the argument of inadvertence and lack of "intent" or "willful violation." Once a violation has been discovered, if disclosure is not timely made, there is arguably a prima facie case for intent to violate.

Agile's Counsel confers with Agile's partners, then sets up a conference call linking Troll's counsel, Agile's Dutch counsel and Ijsselmeer's Chief Executive Officer ("CEO") and CIO. Agile's Counsel explains that Agile will not sign a definitive acquisition agreement until Ijsselmeer has come into full compliance with the PDPA, including a disclosure to the Authority of all violations. Ijsselmeer's officers predictably refuse to put themselves in peril in order to reduce Agile's risks. Troll attempts to persuade Agile that these issues can be sorted out between signing and Closing. However, Agile does not want the Dutch authorities to take the view that, by signing and then influencing the development of Ijsselmeer's technologies, Agile's partners might thereby become "responsible parties" under the PDPA for the purposes of Ijsselmeer's processing of personal data. Agile suggests that Troll consider divesting itself of its interests in Ijsselmeer. Troll might be willing to do that, but only *after* Agile signs the acquisition agreement. This is understandable, because Troll is being asked to forfeit a valuable asset with no certainty that the transaction requiring such forfeiture will in fact be consummated. This is the crux of all such pre-signing negotiations. In all such situations where divestiture (or compliance) precedes signing, counsel will face an uphill burden of persuasion and must therefore be able to argue forcefully the cost of non-compliance or late compliance. Deals

47. PDPA, Article 75(2).
48. PDPA, Article 66(2).

fail at the eleventh hour with some regularity, and it is counsel's role not simply to advise on the law, but to provide useful guidance on how to balance or evaluate the cost versus the benefit in foregoing lucrative business opportunities in reliance on a deal that may never occur. Agile's Counsel suggests the compromise that Agile and Troll revisit the issue once Agile determines whether Ijsselmeer's operations (and Agile's need to receive test reports containing personal data) pose any other serious personal data compliance issues.

➤ *The Prohibited Conduct*—**Prohibited Processing of Sensitive Data.** Some of the biometric data indicia that Ijsselmeer collects include race (skin color), health (scars from disease or injuries, problems like cataracts detected in iris scans), genetic information and whether the person has an elevated temperature (a thermal scan that Ijsselmeer developed for public health authorities in Asia to check in-bound passengers for early symptoms of SARS, etc.). The PDPA generally prohibits processing such sensitive data, unless Ijsselmeer's processing qualifies for one of four exceptions.[49]

One of the exceptions for processing racial data is controversial and might not suffice, because such processing is permitted where it is carried out "with a view to identifying data subjects and only where this is essential for that purpose."[50] However, this exception should be Ijsselmeer's last recourse.

---

49. PDPA, Article 16. Note as a general rule that the PDPA prohibits processing of personal data without the unambiguous consent of the subject, unless such processing comes within one of four exceptions:

"b. the processing is necessary for the performance of a contract to which the data subject is party, or for actions to be carried out at the request of the data subject and which are necessary for the conclusion of a contract; the processing is necessary in order to comply with a legal obligation to which the responsible party is subject;

c. the processing is necessary in order to protect a vital interest of the data subject;

. . .

e. the processing is necessary for the proper performance of a public law duty by the administrative body concerned or by the administrative body to which the data are provided, or

f. the processing is necessary for upholding the legitimate interests of the responsible party or of a third party to whom the data are supplied, except where the interests or fundamental rights and freedoms of the data subject, in particular the right to protection of individual privacy, prevail." *Personal Data Protection Act*, Article 8, accessed at http://home.planet.nl/~privacy1/wbp_en_rev.htm.

50. PDPA, Article 18(1)(a).

A more reliable and more easily proved exception allows such processing in circumstances where it is carried out with the "express consent of the data subject."[51] Ijsselmeer obtained signed consents from every data subject who participated in the tests of its biometric devices conducted in its Eindhoven laboratories. However, the consent form itself is deficient in at least two respects. First, while it details the kinds of personal data that will be collected by Ijsselmeer's biometric devices, it says little about how they will be linked to information that identifies the subject from whom they were collected, or how they will be processed and subsequently handled. Second, the consent form inaccurately describes (and misrepresents) the purpose of the processing as "scientific research to improve the sensitivity and accuracy of measuring devices."[52]

The CIO explains that Ijsselmeer's concern for secrecy and its desire to protect its trade secrets requires that the purpose be both vague and misleading in order to prevent any of the data subjects from publicly disclosing Ijsselmeer's efforts to enter the security market. Unfortunately, the statute requires that the form must accurately and reasonably inform the data subject of the purpose(s) for which the personal data is being collected and processed. Anything less would fall short of the PDPA requirement that consent be "unambiguously" given. Consent becomes ambiguous if the data subject does not accurately understand the purpose.

To the extent that the consent form gives a misleading explanation of its purpose, it risks contravening the PDPA requirement that "Personal data shall not be further processed in a way incompatible with the purposes for which they have been obtained."[53] In addition, it risks

---

51. PDPA, Article 23(1)(a).

52. Ijsselmeer must also ensure that its collection and processing of personal data meet other standards under the PDPA, including (1) that "personal data shall not be kept in a form which allows the data subject to be identified for any longer than is necessary for achieving the purposes for which they were collected or subsequently processed;" (2) that "personal data may be kept for longer than provided under (1), where this is for historical, statistical or scientific purposes, and where the responsible party has made the necessary arrangements to ensure that the data concerned are used solely for these specific purposes;" (3) that "personal data shall only be processed where, given the purposes for which they are collected or subsequently processed, they are adequate, relevant and not excessive;" and (4) that "[t]he responsible party shall take the necessary steps to ensure that personal data, given the purposes for which they are collected or subsequently processed, are correct and accurate." *Personal Data Protection Act*, Articles 10 and 11, accessed at http://home.planet.nl/~privacy1/wbp_en_rev.htm.

53. PDPA, Article 9(1).

violating the PDPA's prohibition on excessive collection of data for the purpose, since the PDPA states: "Personal data shall only be processed where, given the purposes for which they are collected or subsequently processed, they are adequate, relevant and **not excessive**."[54] Ideally, new consents should be drafted, and the data subjects asked to re-execute them.

When the CIO implements privacy procedures, she will also need to develop a formal agreement between herself and whoever has responsibility for processing Ijsselmeer's trove of personal information. Such agreement should set limits on the processing of such personal information and establish standards for security to protect the information from unauthorized access, removal or tampering.

Because videotaping of the performance of the biometric devices in public places created a permanent tape (not merely a transient record) to allow researchers to compare the results over several periods of time during the development of the devices, Ijsselmeer must notify the Authority of such videotaping. The use of such devices in public (without the express permission of the Authority and consent of the data subjects) also violates the PDPA, and the videotaping arguably constitutes video surveillance in a public place, requiring notice to the Authority under the Hidden Camera Surveillance Act, 2003.[55]

▶ *The Prohibited Conduct*—**Transfers of Personal Data to the United States.** Assuming that Ijsselmeer can bring its activities into compliance with the PDPA (a considerable assumption at this stage of the negotiations), the proposed transfer of the test reports (pursuant to Agile's routine pre-acquisition due diligence request) would require careful planning, in order to overcome the obstacles to such transfer imposed by the PDPA on transfers of personal data.[56] The PDPA provides that:

---

54. PDPA, Article 11(1). [Emphasis added.]

55. In addition, the EU's Data Protection Working Party published in 2004 its *Opinion 4/2004 on the Processing of Personal Data by Means of Video Surveillance,* which emphasizes that under the Directive the processing of personal data by video surveillance requires "unambiguous consent." See the *Opinion* at p. 6, accessed at http://europa.eu.int/comm/internal_market/privacy/docs/wpdocs/2004/wp89_en.pdf.

56. The notice required of Ijsselmeer before it started to process personal data includes, among the required particulars, "the planned transfers of data to countries outside of the European Union." *Personal Data Protection Act*, Article 28(1)(e), accessed at http://home.planet.nl/~privacy1/wbp_en_rev.htm.

"Personal data which are subject to processing or intended for processing after they have been transferred, shall only be transferred to a country outside the European Union in the case that, without prejudice to compliance with the provisions of this Act, *that country guarantees an adequate level of protection.*"[57]

Although the PDPA provides criteria for making such an assessment,[58] a decision by the Dutch Data Protection Authority in April of 2004 makes clear that the United States does not guarantee an adequate level of protection for the data subjects' personal data. In that decision, the Authority investigated BREIN, the Dutch entertainment industry's anti-piracy association. BREIN was sharing personal data with its counterparts in the United States. The Authority determined that such sharing violated the PDPA. A spokesperson for the Authority observed:

"The US does not maintain a suitable level of [privacy] protection. The passing on of information is in principle forbidden, unless the recipient organization meets a high protection level (the 'safe harbour' principles), or has received appropriate permission from the [Dutch] minister of justice."[59]

---

57. PDPA, Article 76(1). [Emphasis added.]

58. See PDPA, Article 76(2).

59. Figueiredo, Joe, *Authority Declares Sharing of Piracy Data with US Partners Illegal*, DMEurope.com [Digital Media News for Europe], April 29, 2004, accessed at www.dmeurope.com/default.asp?ArticleID = 1650. The data that BRIEN had transferred included name, address, bank account number, and IP address. Consistent with that finding by the Authority is the opinion by the EU's Data Protection Working Group's finding issued in its *Opinion 2/2004 on the Adequate Protection of Personal Data Contained in the PNR of Air Passengers to Be Transferred to the United States' Bureau of Customs and Border Protection (US CBP)* that concluded that it could not make a "favorable adequacy finding" concerning the transfer of air passenger data from the EU to the United States Bureau of Customs and Border Protection. See *Opinion*, January 29, 2004, accessed at http://europa.eu.int/comm/internal_market/privacy/docs/wpdocs/2004/wp87_en.pdf.

Note, however, that as of this writing, the European Parliament has voted to refer to the European Court of Justice a draft agreement between the European Commission and the United States on air passenger data. Under the draft agreement, 34 different items of air passenger information could be collected by U.S. Customs and Border Protection officials prior to take-off of such passengers' aircraft for the United States. See *NewsBriefs*, IEEE SECURITY & PRIVACY, May/June 2004, p. 16.

The PDPA would not bar Ijsselmeer from transferring personal data to Agile in the United States, if Ijsselmeer qualified the transfer for one of the six exemptions to the PDPA. However, only one such exemption seems relevant to our fact situation: if the data subjects give their prior unambiguous consent to such transfers. Ijsselmeer would need to obtain an executed consent from each data subject whose personal data appears in the test reports that Agile has requested. Moreover, it is crucial that the consent be drafted to comply with the potential uses that Agile intends to make of such data. If Agile intends to use such data for a purpose other than one specified in the consent, Ijsselmeer would have to obtain a fresh consent from each data subject or risk contravening the PDPA requirement that: "Personal data shall not be further processed in a way incompatible with the purposes for which they have been obtained."[60]

Thus far, Agile's examination of the risk points at Checkpoint Privacy suggest that negotiations will be needed to accommodate three conflicting positions: (i) Agile's unwillingness to take on the risk of becoming a "responsible party" for personal data previously processed by Ijsselmeer; (ii) Ijsselmeer's unwillingness to disclose its previous violations (in the hope that no subsequent investigation by the Authority will discover its contraventions); and (iii) Troll's unwillingness to choose (prior to Agile signing a definitive acquisition agreement) between divesting itself of its interests in Ijsselmeer and exercising the authority it has (as the majority interest in Ijsselmeer) to direct compliance by personnel who may quit rather than comply. Agile's Counsel remains convinced, however, that Troll's owners will eventually intervene and order Ijsselmeer to make a full disclosure to the Authority, since anything less will provide no cover, if the Authority finds the violations during a later investigation. Troll's interests are aligned with Agile's in this regard, and it is important that counsel focus on this in its analysis. Troll too will want to avoid having liability under the PDPA damage its reputation. The question remains, of course, whether Ijsselmeer could continue to be successful if certain of its key officers resign rather than let Ijsselmeer disclose its noncompliance to the Dutch Data Protection Authority.

Having assessed the scope and magnitude of privacy compliance

---

60. PDPA, Article 9(1).

issues under Dutch law, Agile's Counsel now turns to similar assessments under Canadian, Norwegian and Japanese law.

5.3 Compliance with Canada's Personal Information Protection and Electronic Documents Act ("PIPEDA").

Having closed his discussion with Ijsselmeer's CIO on impediments to transfers of data from The Netherlands to the United States, Agile's Counsel considers whether Ijsselmeer's possible transfers of personal data to Canada (as well as to Norway and Japan) comply with the Dutch Data Protection Law and with the applicable laws of the transferee jurisdictions. He must also consider whether there are further impediments to transfers of the same data from those jurisdictions to the United States, and whether the laws of those jurisdictions or of The Netherlands remain impediments. Agile's Counsel engages a Canadian solicitor ("Solicitor") from a firm in Ottawa as privacy counsel, and emphasizes the need to alert Agile's partners to important differences in the broad reach of different jurisdictions' privacy laws.

The Solicitor provides Agile's Counsel with a report of a study (commissioned by the Ontario Information and Privacy Commissioner) comparing Canadian and U.S. corporate attitudes and motivations on the protection of their customers' privacy. It confirms the gap between U.S. views that such laws can be ignored and Canadian insistence on conscientious enforcement. Canadian businesses reportedly view their privacy practices as "an opportunity to improve relations with customers." By contrast, U.S. businesses view their privacy practices as a legalistic burden, and compliance as an onerous but necessary requirement for avoiding civil lawsuits.[61] Other findings of the study are reflected in Figure 1 below:[62]

---

61. Hamilton, Tyler, *U.S., Canadian Firms Worlds Apart on Privacy*, TORONTO STAR, May 24, 2004, accessed at www.thestar.com/NASApp/cs/ContentServer?pagename = thestar/Layout/Article_Type1&c = Article&cid = 1085351408746&call_pageid = 968350072197&col = 969048863851.

62. Id.

Figure 1. Comparison of Attitudes on Protection of Customers' Privacy

Privacy Practice	Canadian Firms	U.S. Firms
Assign a senior executive as firm's privacy officer	75%	50%
Believe "good privacy practices" are linked to customer trust and brand loyalty	61%	17%
Conduct: (i) privacy training programs (ii) privacy awareness activities for new employees	82% 71%	50% 43%
Focus of concern when seeking to protect customer data	Concerned with: (i) insider misuse of data; (ii) ensuring third-party partners and suppliers respect privacy policies.	Concerned with: protecting data from outsiders.

In short, U.S. firms seem to view privacy protections as something to be accomplished by investments in other, more commercially justified objectives: protection of the firm's assets from external threats (which might include malicious hackers, competitors engaged in industrial espionage or this month's malware-of-the-moment). Canadian firms, by contrast, seemed more concerned with abuses by their own personnel, who might misuse their legitimate access.

The differences between Canadian and U.S. approaches to privacy and security are likely to be one focus of a review ordered by the British Columbia ("BC") Privacy Commissioner on the impact of the U.S.A. Patriot Act on British Columbia's plans to contract out its government Medical Services Plan to an American company. The BC Privacy Commissioner wants the review to ascertain if the Patriot Act affects "the privacy of ordinary British Columbians by allowing their personal information to be seized by the FBI in B.C." in connection with "the outsourcing of public services to U.S.-linked services."[63] Specifically, the BC Privacy Commissioner intends to examine the following questions:

> "(i) Does the USA Patriot Act permit USA authorities to access personal information of British Columbians that is, through the outsourcing of public services, in the custody or under the control of USA-linked private sector service providers? If it does, under what conditions can this occur?

> (ii) If it does, what are the implications for public body compliance with the personal privacy protections in the FOIPP Act [British Columbia's *Freedom of Information and Protection of Privacy Act*]? What measures can be suggested to eliminate or appropriately mitigate privacy risks affecting compliance with the FOIPP Act?"[64]

The BC Privacy Commissioner's goal is to release an advisory before August 13, 2004.

---

63. *Patriot Act Probe Begins*, CBC News British Columbia, May 28, 2004, accessed at http://vancouver.cbc.ca/regional/servlet/View?filename=bc_privacy20040528.

64. Office of the Information & Privacy Commissioner for British Columbia, *Request for Submissions: Assessing* USA Patriot Act *Implications for Privacy Compliance under British Columbia's* Freedom of Information and Protection of Privacy Act, May 28, 2004, accessed at www.oipcbc.org/news/21120publicinvite.pdf.

Note: the report, *Privacy and the USA Patriot Act: Implications for British Columbia Public Sector Outsourcing*, accessible at www.oipcbc.org/news/21120publicinvite.pdf, was finally released in October 2004 after submission of this book for publication. A description of the report will be provided in a future supplement to this book. A key finding presented by the report was "[t]here was general consensus that US authorities could, at least under some circumstances, use powers enacted by the USA Patriot Act to make orders for access to personal information located in Canada that is involved in outsourcing of public body functions to a US linked contractor." *Privacy and the USA Patriot Act*, at p. 12. Similarly, the report noted, "if personal information is located outside British Columbia, it is subject to the law that applies where it is found, regardless of the terms of the outsourcing contract. . . . There is general consensus in the submissions that the FIS Court could, under FISA, order a U.S. corporation to produce records held in Canada by its Canadian subsidiary. There is no general consensus, however, about whether the FIS Court would make such an order in the face of a Canadian law prohibiting disclosure." *Privacy and the USA Patriot Act*, at pp. 117–118.

However, before *Privacy and the USA Patriot Act* was released, the British Columbia government, in October 2004, amended the British Columbia Freedom and Information Privacy Act ("FOIPP Act") to protect files and increase privacy protections. The amendments, as explained by a Canadian commentator, included:

Differences between Canadian and U.S. views of privacy can also be observed in the Canadian restrictions on access to, and use of, social security numbers ("SSNs") as compared with the lack of such restrictions in the United States. A U.S. General Accounting Office report on the routine collection and use of SSNs by the U.S. private sector concludes that the SSN is the "key piece of information" enabling many private sector entities (consumer reporting agencies, information brokers or resellers and health care organizations) to conduct their businesses and deliver services to their customers.[65] Such entities rely on the SSN as the key identifier and verifier of a person (making it extraordinarily sensitive data, although it is not a concept mentioned by the GAO report), and use it as a link to information they accumulate about that individual. They also frequently resell such information (together with the SSN) to other entities. The GAO has found that it can obtain such information (including the SSN) from the websites of Internet-based information resellers merely for payment of a fee, with no restrictions on its collection, use or disclosure. Such activity, if conducted in Canada, would contravene PIPEDA. In the United States, by contrast, the patchwork of laws that impose privacy restrictions creates only limited safeguards in certain industries and states.[66]

- "Placing restrictions on public bodies and service providers storing, accessing or disclosing personal information outside Canada;
- Extending the restrictions that already apply to public bodies to public employees, service providers and employees and associates of service providers;
- Requiring public bodies and service providers to report any foreign demand for disclosure of personal information not covered by the *FOIPP Act* . . .
- Protecting 'whistle-blowers' who report a foreign demand for information;
- Creating offences for violation of the new privacy protection provisions, including fines of up to $500,000 for a corporation, up to $25,000 for a partnership or individual service provider and up to $2,000 for an employee."

Riley, Thomas B., *Security vs. Privacy: A Comparative Analysis of Canada, The United Kingdom, and The United States – An Update of Issues: October 2004*, November 1, 2004, www.electronicgov.net/pubs/research_papers/slp/Sec&PrivUpdateOct04.pdf and Gowlings: *Privacy Briefing Newsletter*, October 15, 2004, vol. 3, no. 21, www.ppt.gc.ca/publications/pdfs/ar_o2_e.pdf

65. GAO, *Social Security Numbers*, GAO-04-11, January 22, 2004, p. 1.

66. Examples include (1) the Gramm-Leach-Bliley Financial Services Modernization Act of 1999, 15 U.S.C. §§ 6801-6810, 6821-6827, which creates a new definition of personal information that includes SSNs and imposes limits on when financial institutions (*e.g.*, banks, credit unions, insurance companies, and securities and com-

It is unclear to Agile whether Canadian law will be viewed by the European Union as providing sufficient privacy protections to meet the standards required to permit transfers from a Member State of the European Union to Canada. (Recall the Dutch determination that such protections in the United States are not sufficient; recall also that Agile's Board had declined recommendations to invest in the measures needed to qualify for the "Safe Harbour" exception by virtue of which qualified companies can be recipients of personal data transferred from a firm in an EU Member State to a firm in the United States).

A European Commission Decision, rendered three years before the Canadian federal privacy law ("PIPEDA")[67] came into full effect,[68] made the following observations of PIPEDA in the context of EU privacy requirements:

- "[T]he Canadian Act will extend to every organization that *collects, uses or discloses* personal information in the course of a *commercial activity. . . .*[69]

---

modities brokers firms) may disclose such non-public information to non-affiliated third parties (it also creates criminal penalties for anyone who fraudulently seeks access to such information); (2) the Health Insurance Portability and Accountability Act, Pub. L. No. 104-191 (1996) (codified in 42 U.S.C.), which protects the privacy of what it defines as protected health information that includes SSNs and which similarly limits when health care organizations and health care providers can disclose such information to others without the patient's consent; and (3) the Drivers Privacy Protection Act that prohibits any person from knowingly obtaining or disclosing personal information contained in a state motor vehicle record (including the SSN) for any use not expressly permitted by that law. Interestingly, the GAO found that as result of the Drivers Privacy Protection Act, the online resellers of personal information have ceased to glean SSNs from drivers licenses, but there remains a multitude of other ways to obtain SSNs without contravening a federal law. See GAO, *Social Security Numbers*, GAO-04-11, January 22, 2004, pp. 14–17. California enacted in 2001 a law that restricts private sector use of SSNs, prohibiting companies and persons from, for example, posting or publicly displaying SSNs or requiring "an individual to transmit his or her social security number over the Internet unless the connection is secure or the social security number is encrypted" " Cal. Civ. Code §1798.85. A somewhat similar law comes into effect in Missouri on July 1, 2006 (2003 Mo. SB 61).

67. Personal Information Protection and Electronic Documents Act.

68. January 1, 2004.

69. Commission Decision of 20 December 2001, *Pursuant to Directive 95/46/EC of the European Parliament and of the Council on the Adequate Protection of Personal Data Provided by the Canadian Personal Information Protection and Electronic Documents Act*, 2002/2/EC, p. 2, accessed at http://europa.eu.int/eur-lex/pri/en/oj/dat/2002/l_002/ l_00220020104en00130016.pdf. [Emphasis added.] The opinion also notes a number of entities to which PIPEDA does not apply, including those "to which the Federal Privacy

- "The Canadian Act covers all the basic principles necessary for an adequate level of protection for natural persons. . . ."
- "The applications of these standards is guaranteed by judicial remedy and by independent supervision carried out by the authorities, such as the Federal Privacy Commissioner invested with powers of investigation and intervention."
- "[T]he provisions of Canadian law regarding civil liability apply in the event of unlawful processing which is prejudicial to the persons concerned."[70]

The Commission Decision concluded that, for the purposes of the Directive on Personal Data, "Canada is considered as providing an adequate level of protection for personal data **transferred** from the Community to recipients subject to" PIPEDA.[71] However, the Solicitor cautioned against relying on that Decision, because it is subject to reconsideration by its own terms: the European Commission "shall evaluate the functioning of this Decision on the basis of available information, three years after its notification to the Member States and report any pertinent findings to the Commission . . . including any evidence that could affecting the finding in Article I of this Decision that protection in Canada is adequate. . . ." The Decision is, therefore, scheduled for review in 2004, and Agile will need to position its transaction to avoid being impeded, if such review concludes that Canadian protections are not adequate in light of subsequent judicial decisions and Privacy Commissioner rulings.

If Agile continues to insist on reviewing the test reports containing the sensitive personal data, it needs to consider whether to obtain the added insurance of written consents from the data subjects for such transfers, since new consents will in any event be required under Dutch law to authorize the new use of the personal data. To solicit and obtain such consents would involve a disproportionate effort with highly uncertain results.

There is another alternative: Ijsselmeer could determine whether there is a cost-effective way to anonymize the personal data, or to delete

---

Act applies, or that are regulated by the public sector at a provincial level" as well as "non-profit organizations and charitable activities unless they are of a commercial nature."

70. Id.
71. Id.

or encode the link between the biometric data and personally identifiable information. Its data would then arguably fall outside the scope of the Dutch Personal Data Protection Law. (Several EU members take the position that "anonymized data are not personal data and that their data protection laws do not restrict the processing of such data,"[72] and that such data can be freely transferred. The Dutch Personal Data Protection Law does not mention "anonymization," but does mention "blocking" and "deletion." Ijsselmeer should take steps to ensure that if it transfers the anonymized data, it does not release the original data set to Agile or any of its affiliates through any other route, since such release would enable Agile to de-anonymize the data and would create the impression of a willful effort to circumvent the Dutch Personal Data Protection Law.)

The Canadian Solicitor also directs Agile's attention to the fact that even where an adequate level of protection exists for a data transfer, there is a second condition that must be met (as noted in the Community's Decision on PIPEDA), namely that "the Member States' laws implementing other provisions of the Directive *are complied with prior to the transfer.*"[73] This is a double-edge sword: in light of Ijsselmeer's contraventions of the Dutch Data Protection Law, its transfer of personal data to its co-venturers in Ontario, Canada may well have failed to comport with the Dutch Data Protection Law's provisions for such transfer. In addition, for all future transfers, Ijsselmeer cannot rely on a blanket permission to transfer to Canada, but must come into compliance with the Dutch Data Protection Law. Numerous notices will be required to the Dutch Data Protection Authority, and these may well attract the attention of the Authority. It would be imprudent to think the Authority would not want an accurate history of Ijsselmeer's processing of personal data.

At this juncture, given the rapidly magnifying compliance burden, the obvious question is: does Agile really need to obtain the test reports (with their contents of sensitive personal data) directly from Ijsselmeer, or can it more safely, swiftly and with fewer compliance problems, obtain the same information from copies already in Ijsselmeer's Ontario, Canada offices? There is the possibility that PIPEDA will not apply, since

---

72. Such EU members include Spain, France, the U.K., and Germany. See Baker, Stewart; Kuilwijk, Kees; Chang, Winnie; and Mah, Daniel, *Anonymization, Data-Matching and Privacy: A Case Study*, December 2003, p. 8.

73. Id., p. 1.

none of the data subjects of the biometric device tests appear to live in Canada. The Solicitor suggests that they put on hold the question of disclosure of Dutch personal data across the Canadian border, and simply map out the risk points for Ijsselmeer's personal data already in Canada (including that collected and processed) that Agile might want disclosed to it (he notes that PIPEDA sometimes speaks in the European terms of "transfer" of data, when transfer is to a third party for processing,[74] but often speaks more broadly in terms of "disclosure" of data).[75]

▶ *Prohibited Conduct:* **Failure to Appoint an Individual to Ensure Ijsselmeer's Compliance with PIPEDA.** Like their colleagues in Eindhoven (at Ijsselmeer's home offices), the Ijsselmeer (Ontario) officers appointed no one to be Ijsselmeer-Ontario's privacy officer or otherwise to be "accountable for the organization's compliance" with PIPEDA. Ijsselmeer's Canadian operations include among its officers several senior research fellows from the Canadian College of Medical Geneticists in Ottawa, Ontario. Initially no research fellow was willing to be designated as the firm's privacy officer.

The Solicitor explains that PIPEDA applies to "organizations" (including an association, person, partnership or trade union),[76] and that, by virtue of their relationship to Ijsselmeer, all of Ijsselmeer's personnel potentially come within PIPEDA. Whether Ijsselmeer (including its participating researchers or administrators) is subject to PIPEDA will turn on whether it is involved in a "commercial activity," which PIPEDA defines broadly as:

---

74. PIPEDA, Clause 4.1.3.

75. In situating Ijsselmeer's offices in Toronto, Ontario, we have simplified the issue, but hasten to point out that several Canadian provinces have enacted privacy statutes that to various extents displace PIPEDA. The actual relationship between each of those relatively new statutes and PIPEDA, which only came into full force on January 1, 2004, is unclear and uncertain. We caution that if a party comes within the jurisdiction of a province that has enacted a privacy law, such as Alberta, or a health care data law, that great care be taken to consider its relationship to PIPEDA and to the other provinces' privacy laws, particularly if there are transfers to third parties in those other provinces. Since the purpose of our discussion is to illustrate the need for a privacy checkpoint in cross-border transactions, we think it reasonable for this discussion to review only PIPEDA and to alert the reader to the need to be cognizant of the other applicable privacy laws enacted by certain Canadian provinces.

76. See PIPEDA, § 2(1), definition of "organization."

"any particular transaction, act or conduct or any regular course of conduct that is of a commercial character. . . ."[77]

Ijsselmeer's efforts to develop, prototype and commercialize anti-terrorism technologies clearly bring it (and its personnel) within the definition of commercial efforts designed towards business transactions. Such activities are undeniably within the scope of PIPEDA. The immediate issue is whether they wish to delegate to someone other than a non-research fellow the responsibility for being the firm's privacy officer.

When a research fellow does agree to assume responsibility, his duties are described as follows: unlike his counterpart at Ijsselmeer (Eindhoven), he would be expected to implement policies and practices to give effect to PIPEDA's principles, including procedures to:

(i)   protect personal information;

(ii) receive and respond to complaints and inquiries;

(iii) train staff and communicate information to employees about Ijsselmeer's privacy policies and practices; and

(iv) develop information that explained these policies and practices.[78]

Ijsselmeer (Ontario), however, does not have the notification burden that Ijsselmeer (Eindhoven) failed to fulfill. There is no provision in PIPEDA that personal information cannot be processed without prior notification of the Privacy Commissioner. The Dutch appear to insist on a more centralized approach, but do not set as high a standard for consent.

➤ *Prohibited Conduct:* **Failure to Obtain Individuals' Consent for Collection, Use and Disclosure of their Personal Information.** The Solicitor suggests that they first consider the collection of personal data by Ijsselmeer (Ontario) directly from subjects located in Canada, and begin the legal review by focusing solely on the terms of PIPEDA.[79] Ijsselmeer's biometric devices have been developed to increase the ability to identify a specific person based on progressively smaller indicia.

77. PIPEDA, § 2(1), definition of "commercial activity."

78. PIPEDA, Clause 4.1.4.

79. The province of Ontario has not enacted its own general privacy legislation, but has enacted the Health Information Protection Act, effective November 1, 2004.

This has the effect of broadening the data that are covered by PIPEDA, which applies to any data that identifies a person or by which a person's identity can be inferred (but does not include the name, title or business address or telephone number of an employee of an organization).[80]

Ijsselmeer (Ontario) has collected what PIPEDA refers to as "personal health information,"[81] which PIPEDA defines as applicable to several kinds of such information, the most relevant to Ijsselmeer's activities is:

"Information concerning the physical or mental health of the individual; . . ."[82]

From the description of the biometric devices (and the linkage of the biometric information collected by such devices to data that identifies the data subject), however, it becomes clear that Ijsselmeer (Ontario) has been collecting both "personal information" and an important subset of such information, "personal health information." Under PIPEDA, this information is considered sensitive.[83]

Ijsselmeer (Ontario) has obtained "consents" from the subjects from whom it obtained such "information" as part of the tests of the biometric devices, and has employed a standard consent form. This form is based on one that they received from Ijsselmeer (Eindhoven) and is the same one that Agile's Counsel reviewed. The purpose statement is therefore misleading without further inquiry. The Solicitor thinks that the consent is defective under PIPEDA as well, for several reasons:

- Unlike the Dutch Data Protection Law which merely requires that consent be "unambiguously" given, PIPEDA emphasizes that the

---

80. PIPEDA, § 2(1).
81. Id.
82. Id., definition of "personal health information." One might ask if biometric data includes information about the "health of the individual." In Ijsselmeer's research, it does. Ijsselmeer seeks to determine physical traits from genetic sequences identified in nuclear and variable mitochondrial DNA. Such information would include hair, eye color, body weight, shape, and height, as well as health indicators such as genetic disease (*e.g.,* diabetes) and other medical identifiers. Eventually, Ijsselmeer intends that with such identifiers it can distinguish sequences to determine the number of contributors to a DNA sample obtained from typical surfaces such as a handrail or doorknob.
83. PIPEDA, Clause 4.3.4, which provides, in pertinent part, that "some information (for example, medical records . . .) is almost always considered to be sensitive, any information can be sensitive, depending on the context."

"knowledge and consent" of the individual are required for "collection, use, or disclosure of personal information."[84] The requisite knowledge cannot be demonstrated, if the consent is characterized by ambiguous or misleading information concerning its purpose or the use to which such personal information will be put. PIPEDA requires that the consent be "meaningful," *i.e.*, the purposes must be stated "in such a manner that the individual can reasonably understand how the information will subsequently be **used or disclosed**."[85] Thus, by not accurately stating how the information would be used, Ijsselmeer failed to comply with PIPEDA. Moreover, unlike the Dutch Data Protection Law, PIPEDA explicitly prohibits any misleading of the individual from whom an organization seeks consent, and the prohibition leaves no room for ambiguity: "Consent shall not be obtained through deception."[86]

• Moreover, Ijsselmeer's units circulated the test results among their respective offices by e-mail. Thus information collected from the test subjects in Ontario has already been transferred to Ijsselmeer (Eindhoven) and Ijsselmeer (Tokyo) where the test results were compared and correlated with those obtained at those other facilities. The initial consent form used by Ijsselmeer (Ontario) made no mention of intended transfers of the individual's personal information across Canadian borders to other units of Ijsselmeer, and a later version of the consent form simply contained an "opt-out" box that individuals could check if they opposed having their personal information transferred to third parties. Where consents were not obtained prior to the transfers out of Canada, the transfers contravened PIPEDA. In light of decisions by Canada's Privacy Commissioner concerning the inappropriateness of "opt-out" consents where sensitive data is involved,[87] even

---

84. PIPEDA, Clause 4.3.

85. PIPEDA, Clause 4.3.2.

86. PIPEDA, Clause 4.3.5. That same clause, in fact, gives as its example a health-care illustration: "an individual would not reasonably expect that personal information given to a health-care professional would be given to a company selling health-care products, unless consent were obtained." In addition, Clause 4.4.2 provides that "personal information be collected by fair and lawful means is intended to prevent organizations from collecting information by misleading or deceiving individuals about the purpose for which the information is being collected. This requirement implies that consent with respect to collection must not be obtained through deception."

87. See PIPED Act Case Summary #42, *Air Canada Allows 1% of Aeroplan Mem-*

the later versions of the consents would probably be found defective.

One might argue that there was no transfer, because the personal information remained internal to Ijsselmeer. It merely circulated and, while it left Canada, it never left the company. This argument will probably not carry the day, however, because PIPEDA controls the transfer of information from Canada to other countries, regardless of whether such transfer is among a company's divisions or affiliates or to recipients outside of the company.

PIPEDA does allow for implied consent, in limited circumstances, but for data that is sensitive, implied consent would not be prudent, and would probably not comply with PIPEDA.[88] In the event of a complaint, it is more likely than not that Canada's Privacy Commissioner or a court will find that such implied consent fails to comply with PIPEDA. Further, implied consent will not support an argument that the consenting individuals gave their implied consent for any division or unit of Ijsselmeer to review such results. And "implied consent" should be avoided, where the information at issue includes sensitive data. Ijsselmeer (Ontario) is fortunate that its practices did not provoke a complaint. Once the news of the acquisition breaks, the officers should anticipate that one of the individuals who signed the consent form will

---

bership to "Opt out" of Information Sharing Practices, March 11, 2002, accessed at the Privacy Commissioner of Canada website at www.privcom.gc.ca/cf-dc/cf-dc_020320_e.asp, where the Commissioner determined that information about individuals' purchasing habits and preferences was "sufficiently sensitive to warrant obtaining positive or 'opt-in' consent, as opposed to negative or 'opt-out' consent, from the individuals concerned." The Commissioner also noted that PIPEDA does not allow for "token compliance" in obtaining consent, and that in some instances the descriptions provided to individuals were "so vague and open-ended as to render any consent invalid"—and thus found the complaint was "well-founded." Note that this determination was foreshadowed almost a year earlier when the federal Privacy Commissioner stated, in a press release, that "opt-out" may not be appropriate where sensitive personal information is concerned. See Privacy Commissioner of Canada, preliminary finding, news release, July 18, 2001, The Privacy Commissioner of Canada, George Radwanski, Today Sent the Following Letter to Air Canada with Regard to Complaints Received by This Office," accessed at www.privcom.gc.ca.

88. See PIPEDA, Clause 4.3.4, which states, in pertinent part, "In determining the form of consent to use, organizations shall take into account the sensitivity of information."

contact Ijsselmeer (Ontario) to inquire what is being done with his or her personal information.

Because PIPEDA does not allow organizations engaged in commercial activity (who use personal information for that activity) to build a wall of silence between an individual and the information he or she has consented to let the organization collect and use, Ijsselmeer's personnel will have to answer any such inquiry, and cannot stand on their non-disclosure agreements. To be sure, Ijsselmeer has substantial duties to keep such information confidential from third parties (particularly since it is sensitive information),[89] but part of the privacy officer's duties include making Ijsselmeer's privacy policies and practices accountable, open and accessible to individuals who provide it with personal information. Ijsselmeer must create a formal procedure to ensure that when an individual requests it, Ijsselmeer provides the following within a reasonable time and at minimal cost to the individual:[90]

- The existence, use and disclosure of his or her personal information, as well as access to it (provided that in doing so, the personal information of others is not thereby disclosed, which in Ijsselmeer's case might pose difficulties);[91]
- An opportunity to challenge the accuracy and completeness of such information and, if erroneous or incomplete, to have it appropriately amended;[92]
- If the individual remains unsatisfied with the organization's resolution of such challenge, the organization must record the substance of the individual's challenge and dissatisfaction;[93]
- Whether the organization has any personal information about the individual and, if so, the source of it;[94] and
- A procedure for withdrawal of any consent given by the individual for the collection, use or disclosure of his or her personal information.[95]

It should be noted that much of the information that Ijsselmeer

---

89. See PIPEDA, Clause 4.7: "Personal information shall be protected by security safeguards appropriate to the sensitivity of the information."
90. PIPEDA, Clause 4.9.4.
91. PIPEDA, Clause 4.9.
92. Id.
93. PIPEDA, Clause 4.9.6.
94. PIPEDA, Clause 4.9.1.
95. See PIPEDA, Clause 4.3.8.

gathers is stored in coded form. PIPEDA nonetheless requires that requested information be provided or made available "in a form that is generally understandable," and specifically provides, as an example, that "if the organization uses abbreviations or codes to record information, an explanation shall be provided."[96] If technical jargon makes the explanation impenetrable to anyone outside the biomentric research field, Ijsselmeer must include an explanation of such information to make it understandable to lay persons.

To ensure that data subjects understand clearly the purpose for which their data is collected, and to minimize the likelihood that data subjects will find it necessary to make inquiries about the use of their data, the Solicitor recommends that Ijsselmeer (Ontario) develop an improved consent form and use it for all future collections, uses and disclosures of personal information. With regard to the personal information already transferred without consent to Ijsselmeer's offices in Eindhoven and Tokyo, he recommends that Ijsselmeer's privacy officer develop guidelines and implement procedures to govern the retention of personal information[97] and its destruction.[98] Under those guidelines, Ijsselmeer should destroy, erase or make anonymous (strip of personal identification data) all personal information contained in the test reports or in any other records that Ijsselmeer circulated among the three offices. (He points out, however, that PIPEDA's policies do not apply to the data outside of Canada, unless there is an agreement between the transferor and transferee, and that his recommendation is narrowly designed solely to reduce Ijsselmeer's risks of violating PIPEDA by inadvertent disclosure or retention of data longer than necessary.) He also recommends that Ijsselmeer review any forms that it requests from data subjects to make certain that such forms avoid collecting any personal information (unless necessary to the research).

Counsel's recommendation to destroy or anonymize the data in the test reports, however, substantially reduces the value and efficacy of the testing and research results, because such personal information is necessary to measure (and validate) improvements in the ability of the biometric devices to detect and authenticate identities. The Solicitor's recommendation would compel the creation of new data bases and new baselines for measurements, and would substantially delay developments that would advantage Ijsselmeer in the race to market with these

---

96. PIPEDA, Clause 4.9.4 and Clause 4.10.2.
97. PIPEDA, Clause 4.5.2.
98. PIPDEA, Clause 4.5.3.

new technologies. This is a textbook example of the need to develop realistic compliance strategies that do not over-burden the economic rationale of the activities to which they are attached, but that make a good faith effort to understand and observe the laws and regulations applicable to that activity. Otherwise, the regulatory tail can end up wagging the business dog. It may be that future business endeavors will have to be structured from inception with an eye toward compliance, but this will necessarily have a chilling effect on research and development and on individual economic enterprise at a micro-level and on the efficient allocation of capital on a macro level. From the point of view of national policy, we may be forced to choose between enhanced security and bottom-line competitiveness in a global economy. The tension is of course between closing porous borders for security reasons and opening them for economic ones.

Agile's Counsel is also worried about the timely and responsible destruction of information. American corporate record retention rules require that destruction occur only at scheduled times, and not in response to a discovery of wrong doing (thereby appearing to be a destruction of evidence that could form the basis an enforcement agency claim of obstruction of justice).[99] Obstructing an investigation or destroying personal information subject to an access request is an indict-

---

99. One of the challenges to Agile's General Counsel are these cultural and legal differences in response to error, oversight, blunders, and violations: cures that are not permitted in The Netherlands, and that might be provocative in the U.S., might in some instances be quite appropriate in other legal systems such as Canada, depending on the circumstances. The PIPEDA requirement that "Personal information that is no longer required to fulfill the identified purposed should be destroyed, erased, or made anonymous" may be one such circumstance—not for the purpose of covering up violations but for mitigating the wrong that might continue to be compounded if such data continued to be stored, processed, used for new purposes, or transferred without obtaining the requisite consent in advance.

We point out these differences advisedly and caution against inferring license from them, but we think that another of the blind spots that cyber-driven transactions tend to create is an awareness of such differences that tends to come out more clearly and completely in face-to-face meetings, for which there is no adequate substitute however much we pretend that such substitutes are provided in correspondence by e-mail or communication by telephone. Face-to-face meetings also tend to find more nuanced solutions to such problems far more rapidly than telephone or e-mail exchanges, which in our experience tend to encourage entrenchment, especially by counsel with limited imagination or who are accustomed to bullying their path through transactional negotiations.

able offense. However, destroying personal information before any request for it arises, and in the course of fulfilling an organization's policies on limiting the duration of storing personal information, is **not** a violation but a requirement of PIPEDA.

Our inquiry began by asking whether Agile can obtain these reports and, if not, whether it can get the information it needs in an alternative manner that is not "compliance intensive." Once again, economic and business exigencies must be weighed. Until Agile has scrutinized the test reports, it will not have an adequate basis for evaluating the purchase price allocable to Troll's investment in Ijsselmeer or, more importantly, for evaluating whether it should even be willing to purchase Ijsselmeer. Technical personnel at Agile are satisfied that, if the personal information could be redacted (or anonymized), the test reports would provide sufficient information to permit evaluation of: the capabilities of the various devices, their potential commercialization, and any potential infringement of patents in the European Union, Canada, Japan and the United States.[100] If appropriate consents are obtained on tests conducted between signing and Closing, Agile could review such reports with the personal data included.

Ijsselmeer (Ontario)'s research fellows remain concerned about whether such redacting or anonymizing can be done on an expedited and cost effective basis without compromising the data base (recall that a substantial part of the real economic value of the research and development is currently dependent on the integrity of the test results; damage to the latter will impact marketability dramatically and cause a substantial loss in bottom line "good will"). Counsel revisits the question of whether the personal data transferred from The Netherlands to Canada can be transferred directly to Agile (sparing Agile the need to get the reports from Ijsselmeer (Eindhoven)). The impediment to this strategy is that PIPEDA does not state that "personal information" is limited to information collected from persons within the territories of Canada. Counsel reads PIPEDA as applicable to any "personal information" from outside Canada that comes into the possession of an organization doing business in Canada. Two conclusion follow from this interpretation.

First, Ijsselmeer (Ontario) has contravened PIPEDA to the extent that it has used any personal information received from Ijsselmeer (Eindhoven) for which, under Dutch law, the data subject did not con-

---

100. See discussion in Chapter 7 of these Checkpoint Patent issues.

sent to such transfer or such use. Even if Ijsselmeer (Eindhoven) now obtained after-the-fact consent from each such data subject for those transfers and uses, retroactive consent is not expressly permitted by (and arguably not acceptable under) the Dutch Data Protection Law. PIPEDA might permit retroactive consent by a Canadian organization to *transfer* personal information, but Ijsselmeer (Ontario) cannot get retroactive permission to *use* personal information. In short, even if curing the problem of nonconsensual collection of the personal data were possible in The Netherlands, that would still fail to cure the problem of non-consensual transfer to Canada. Ijsselmeer (Ontario) is not entitled to have used the personal information transferred from Ijsselmeer (Eindhoven). Since the transfer was not consented to by the data subjects, PIPEDA would not allow such use. Any other interpretation would encourage circumvention of the EU Member States' implementation of the EU Personal Data Directive. PIPEDA leaves little doubt on this point:

> "When personal information that has been collected is to be used for a purpose not previously identified [and the defective Dutch consents fall into such a description], **the new purpose shall be identified prior to use.** Unless the new purpose is required by law, the consent of the individual is required before information can be used for that purpose."[101]

Second, since the personal information received from Ijsselmeer (Eindhoven) cannot be used by Ijsselmeer (Ontario) without contravening PIPEDA, the same reasoning precludes Ijsselmeer (Ontario) from transferring it to any third party, but particularly to Agile in the United States (where the adequacy of protection of personal data has already been deemed by Dutch legal authorities to be insufficient for the purposes of the Dutch Data Protection Law). Although PIPEDA does not speak in these terms, Ijsselmeer (Ontario) should think of the personal information received from Ijsselmeer (Eindhoven) as received *in trust*—Ijsselmeer (Ontario), therefore, has a duty, under PIPEDA, to accord it the same protection as it would have if collected in Canada.

---

101. PIPEDA, Clause 4.2.4. [Emphasis added.] See also PIPEDA, Clause 4.5, which provides, in pertinent part: "Personal information shall not be used or disclosed for purposes other than those for which it was collected, except with the consent of the individual or as required by law."

Two questions remain: (i) whether Ijsselmeer (Ontario)'s new consents should reference the possibility of transfer to, and use of the information by, a United States firm; and (ii) whether, during the interim between such transfer and the announced signing of the definitive acquisition agreement, PIPEDA would require disclosure of the identity of the recipient company (in response to an individual inquiry about the end-use of personal data) or whether the requirements of PIPEDA would be trumped by the non-disclosure agreements prohibiting any mention of the transaction until issuance of a joint press release. In the Solicitor's view, PIPEDA requires that consents be broad enough to cover transfer "out of Canada" to a potential recipient in another country (provided that such transfer would only be done subject to a comprehensive personal information transfer agreement including, among other things, a requirement that the recipient abide by PIPEDA in the manner described in such agreement). Agile will need to come into similar compliance before Closing, if it intends to request and receive any of the personal information collected by Ijsselmeer before Closing.

This leaves Agile with the choice of foregoing such information or qualifying itself to receive and use it. The choice will probably depend largely on economic and business considerations. However, Agile might also solve the problem by having the research results tabulated and interpreted by a competent research entity in Canada who would then forward the statistical correlations to Agile. Alternatively, Agile could have Ijsselmeer (Ontario) provide a statistical digest and a representation as to its accuracy with a warranty by Troll to re-evaluate the price if the representation is breached.

More problematic is the issue of what (if anything) can be disclosed, if an individual asks for the identity of the recipient company before that has become public information. PIPEDA states that: "In providing an account of third parties to which it has disclosed personal information about an individual, an organization should attempt to be as specific as possible."[102] The statutory exceptions to such specificity do not afford a shelter where the organization providing such account could identify the recipients who have received such information.[103] PIPEDA obligates an organization to identify the recipient if it knows

---

102. PIPEDA, Clause 4.9.3.

103. On this issue, see discussion in Platt, Priscilla; Hendlisz, Lise; and Intrator, Daphne, PRIVACY LAW IN THE PRIVATE SECTOR: AN ANNOTATION OF THE LEGISLATION IN CANADA, Canada Law Book Inc., 2003 at p. PIP-203.

it. Ijsselmeer (Ontario) clearly knows the recipient to be Agile. PIPEDA is silent about the effect that a non-disclosure agreement could have on whether an organization may refuse to disclose such information (or delay for a reasonable period) the disclosure of the recipient's identity. Agile can avoid the problem by expressly requiring that no personal information in Ijsselmeer (Ontario)'s possession be transferred to it until after the contemplated acquisition of Troll has been publicly announced.

It is important at this juncture to understand the cost of non-compliance and to review the potential sanctions for violations as these will certainly be factored into any business analysis (if only tacitly). If an individual files a complaint concerning misuse of personal data, the matter would first be investigated by Canada's Privacy Commissioner (who functions as an ombudsman), who is required to file a report within a year. If the complainant (or party complained about) is not satisfied with the Commissioner's report, the party may apply to the Federal Court, which, in addition to other remedies, may order an organization to correct its practices to comply with certain sections of PIPEDA (not all sections are mandatory), order an organization to publish notice of any action taken or proposed to be taken to comply with PIPEDA and award damages to a complainant, "including damages for any humiliation . . . suffered."[104] Ijsselmeer (Ontario) could be ordered to comply, to make disclosures that could prove quite embarrassing and adverse to its reputation (and to that of Troll and Agile), and to pay damages. Similar concerns could also emerge concerning Ijsselmeer's testing of tracking devices and its use of hidden cameras to record the test results in public places. (However, there is no requirement under PIPEDA for a company to disclose contraventions in the absence of any complaint.)

➤ *Prohibited Conduct* (**In Some Circumstances**): **Video Recording Without the Individuals' Prior Consent.** Ijsselmeer has made video recordings of individuals (during tests of the biometric devices) and of the tracking devices attached to vehicles. The former clearly involve personal information captured in a video recording. Although PIPEDA is silent on whether license plate numbers constitute personal information, the video recordings of the tests superimpose the names of the test subjects on the bottom of the screen. This has resulted in a video

---

104. PIPEDA, § 16.

record that links their name and their vehicle license plate numbers, thereby coming within PIPEDA's definition of personal information. In addition, because the video recordings captured images of individuals who were not part of the research, such recordings intruded on their privacy within the scope of PIPEDA's protections. PIPEDA's definition of a "record" includes "pictorial or graphic work, photograph, film, microform, sound recording, [and] videotape."[105] Consent should have been obtained for the videotaping, in light of the reasoning in recent decisions by the Privacy Commissioner of Canada.

In one such case, a company had tried for two years to accommodate an employee's unique workplace requirements to overcome his complaints of limitations resulting from a medical condition. When an independent assessment supported a finding that the employee was not accurately representing the state of his health, the employer hired a private investigation firm to conduct video surveillance of the employee (away from work), which found him engaged in activities he claimed to be incapable of. The company fired him, and (in what can only be described as "chutzpah") he brought a complaint alleging that the company had collected his personal information by way of video surveillance in violation of PIPEDA. The Assistant (Privacy) Commissioner noted that the company relied on an exception to the requirement for consent, Paragraph 7(1)(b) which (in her description) states that "an organization may **collect** personal information without the knowledge or consent of the individual *only* if it is reasonable to expect that the collection with the knowledge or consent of such individual would compromise the availability or the accuracy of the information and the collection is reasonable for **purposes related to investigating a breach of an agreement or a contravention of the laws of Canada or a province.**"[106] The Assistant Commissioner noted at the outset that the Office of the Privacy Commissioner considers video surveillance:

---

105. PIPEDA, §2(1), definition of "record."

106. Office of the Privacy Commissioner of Canada, *PIPED Act Case Summary #269*, April 23, 2004, accessed at www.privcom.gc.ca/cf-dc/2004/cf-dc_040423_e.asp. [Emphases added.] The Commissioner also noted that an exception to the requirement for consent to use such information "is provided in paragraph 7(2)(d), which allows an organization to use personal information without the individual's knowledge or consent only if it was collected under paragraph 7(1)(b)." Thus the threshold and key question was whether the company's collection of such information came within the 7(1)(b) exception.

"To be an extremely privacy-invasive form of technology. The very nature of the medium entails the collection of a great deal of personal information—information that may concern innocent third parties, that may be extraneous, or may lead to judgements about the subject that have nothing to do with the purpose for collecting the information in the first place. [And that] . . . resorting to video surveillance, especially on employees away from the worksite, must be considered only in the most limited cases."[107]

The Assistant Commissioner noted, however, that in this instance the company had substantial evidence to support its suspicion that the employee had broken the "relationship of trust;" that it had exhausted all other means of obtaining the information it required in "less privacy-invasive ways;" and that there was substantial evidence to support the company's position that it resorted to video surveillance to determine if the employee was violating his employment contract by misrepresenting the state of his health. The Assistant Commissioner therefore accepted the company's reliance on the exception to consent in paragraph 7(1)(b), and accordingly concluded that the complaints were "not well founded."

The Assistant Commissioner, however, added "further considerations" that provide guidance of value to Agile and Ijsselmeer (Ontario). She recommended that the company formalize the steps it took by developing policies and practices that are "privacy conscious." These should take into account the following:

- Video surveillance is a last resort and should only be contemplated if all other avenues of collecting personal information have been exhausted;
- The decision to undertake video surveillance should be made at a very senior level of the organization; and
- The private investigator [or anyone conducting such surveillance] should be instructed to collect personal information in accordance with the *Act* [PIPEDA], and should be especially mindful of Principle 4.4 [which stipulates that collection of personal information shall be limited to that which is necessary for the purposes identified by the organization].[108]

With these in mind, Ijsselmeer (Ontario)'s video recording would

107. Id.
108. Id.

not come within the exceptions to PIPEDA's requirement for prior consent. Since such recordings also collected personal information of individuals beyond those involved in the study, they did not comply with PIPEDA Principle 4.4, limiting collection of personal information to that necessary for the purposes identified by the organization.

It should be remembered that PIPEDA was enacted, in part, to enable Canada to qualify as a country that EU Member States would regard as providing adequate protection of personal data in order to allow it to receive such information from persons in Member States. The EU's emerging views of the application of the EU Directive on Personal Data are therefore relevant to any discussion of its scope, because they might influence how the Privacy Commissioner interprets PIPEDA in similar circumstances (despite differences between PIPEDA and each of the EU Member States' laws implementing the Directive on Personal Data).

In February of 2004, in connection with debate (at the European Community level and in individual EU Member States) concerning increased recourse to "image acquisition systems in Europe for the past few years" and in order to "identify prerequisites and limitations applying to the installation of equipment giving rise to video surveillance as well as the necessary safeguards for data subjects," the EU's Data Protection Working Party issued an opinion that "concerns surveillance aimed at the distance [sic] monitoring of events, situations and occurrences. . . ."[109] The EU Working Party took a view of videotape surveillance of persons in public or publicly accessible places that is consistent with that expressed by Canada's Assistant Privacy Commissioner. The Working Party observed that an individual in transit through such places "may well expect a lesser degree of privacy, but not expect to be deprived in full of his rights and freedoms as also related to his own private sphere and image."[110] The Working Party emphasized the risk that video surveillance could interfere with the individual's right to free movement:

> "Data subjects have the right to exercise their freedom of movement without undergoing excessive psychological conditioning as regards their movement and conduct as well as without being the subject of detailed monitoring such as to allow tracking their movement

---

109. Article 29 Data Protection Working Party, *Opinion 4/2004 on the Processing of Personal Data by Means of Video Surveillance*, February 11, 2004, 11759/02/EN WP 89, accessed at http://europa.eu.int/comm/internal_market/privacy/docs/wpdocs/2004/wp89_en.pdf.

110. Id., p. 6.

and/or triggering 'alarms' based on software that automatically 'interprets' an individual's supposedly suspicious conduct without any human intervention—on account of the disproportionate application of video surveillance by several entities in a number of public and/or publicly accessible premises."[111]

The opinion concludes that the Directive on Personal Data applies to such surveillance videotaping, with the result that the video images "must be processed fairly and lawfully," "must be used in accordance with the principle that data must be adequate, relevant and not excessive" and "must be kept for a limited period." Processing of personal data by means of video surveillance must also meet one of the enabling conditions such as "unambiguous consent [of the data subject], necessity [sic] for contractual obligations, for compliance with a legal obligation, for protection of the data subject's vital interests . . ."etc.[112] By the same reasoning, video surveillance must meet the other requirements of the EU Directive on Personal Data, including:

- Providing the appropriate safeguards for processing of sensitive data;
- Security of processing operations;
- Notification of processing operations; and
- Transfer of data to third countries.[113]

In short, collection of personal information by video surveillance, without the prior consent of the individuals involved, if done in the course of a commercial activity, would provide strong grounds for an investigation by the Privacy Commissioner. It is highly probable that the Commissioner would find Ijsselmeer's video surveillance in violation of PIPEDA, and would find support for that view in decisions rendered by the Assistant Privacy Commissioner (and in the EU Working Party opinion). The safest course for Ijsselmeer is the destruction

---

111. Id.

112. Id.

113. Id., pp. 6–7. The opinion notes, on p.11, in a country-by-country review, that in The Netherlands, a change in the Penal Code, recently approved by the Lower House of the Dutch Parliament and effective from January 1, 2004, "extends the scope of the criminal offense of making pictures of places accessible for the public without informing them . . .".

of the records. But, as noted earlier, this should be done pursuant to formally implemented procedures to avoid any appearance of wrong-doing.[114] Ijsselmeer (Ontario) should avoid any further non-consensual video recording of its tests, in light of the fact that the Assistant Privacy Commissioner considers video surveillance to be an "extremely privacy-invasive form of technology." The same policy should be adopted by Ijsselmeer (Eindhoven), in light of the Data Protection Working Party opinion and Ijsselmeer's compliance problems under the Dutch Data Protection Law. It should, in short, conduct its biometric research less intrusively and in keeping with the Dutch proverb *De kat uit de boom kijken* ("The cat looks on from the safety of the tree").

The importance of the video surveillance issue will probably increase in the near future, as a result of the trend towards the substantial pro-liferation of powerful, inexpensive sensors, including radio-frequency identification (RFID) tags embedded in consumer products that can then track the purchaser, biometric sensors for identification and au-thentication, Global Positioning System devices that can track individ-uals, and most invasive of all, minute surveillance devices that rely on image acquisition systems. As one commentator recently explained:

> "[I]n step with Moore's Law . . . Cameras will become hugely more [sic] effective and ubiquitous when they get to be so small that they are hard to see with the unaided eye. Absolutely nothing in the physics of this technology precludes that kind of miniaturization. At the University of California, Berkeley, researchers such as Kris-tofer Pister and David Culler, as well as companies like Crossbow Technology Inc., in San Jose, Calif., and Dust Networks, Berkeley, Calif., are already developing technology they call **smart dust— cubes of silicon the size of ants' heads that each host a sensor, a processor, and wireless-communications hardware**. A decade or so from now, these kinds of devices could well spread vision into every nook and cranny of our world."[115]

---

114. Whether video could be anonymized is an open question, and hence destruc-tion is preferable. Obscuring the faces may leave other personally identifiable features visible and thus might not achieve anonymization. For example, if a military uniform shows the name of the soldier above a pocket, obscuring the soldier's face would not anonymize the video of that soldier in uniform.

115. Goldstein, Harry, *We Like to Watch*, IEEE SPECTRUM, July 2004, p. 34. [Em-phasis added.]

If systems such as "smart dust" are marketed and become popular in countries that apply personal data protection laws comparable to those in the EU and Canada, then the Working Group's caution concerning the over-proliferation of such devices will need to be heeded by counsel advising the developers and users of such technologies:

"The over-proliferation of image acquisition systems in public and private areas should not result in placing unjustified restrictions on citizens' rights and fundamental freedoms: otherwise citizens might be actually compelled to undergo disproportionate data collection procedures which would make them massively identifiable in a number of public and private places."[116]

➤ *Prohibited Conduct:* **Inadequate Protection for Sensitive Data.** A serious issue arises in connection with the destruction of the records: Ijsselmeer (Ontario) has taken few measures to secure the records (with the exception of the test reports of the biometric devices and tracking devices). Such precautions should be added to the list of policies and procedures to be instituted for Ijsselmeer (Ontario), because PIPEDA explicitly requires security safeguards (proportional to the sensitivity of the information) to protect personal information against "loss or theft, as well as unauthorized access, disclosure, copying, use, or modification. Organizations shall protect personal information regardless of the format in which it is held."[117]

Destruction of personal information raises more subtle security issues. Ijsselmeer needs to identify and trace all records of each individual's personal information—whether in photocopies (such as the test reports circulated to Eindhoven and Tokyo), video tapes or digital storage media. Ijsselmeer (Ontario) should not simply discard any of the records in the ordinary course, but instead should first comply with PIPEDA's requirements for care "in the disposal or destruction of personal information, to prevent unauthorized parties from gaining access to the information."[118]

---

116. Article 29 Data Protection Working Party, *Opinion 4/2004 on the Processing of Personal Data by Means of Video Surveillance*, February 11, 2004, 11759/02/EN WP 89, p. 4, accessed at http://europa.eu.int/comm/internal_market/privacy/docs/wpdocs/2004/wp89_en.pdf.

117. PIPEDA, Clause 4.7, 4.7.1, and 4.7.2.

118. PIPEDA, Clause 4.7.5.

There is a rich lexicon of English words that denote destruction of digital data. However, digital data destruction is seldom so thorough as to leave no trace. Much of it remains in a form that can be recovered with advanced data recovery technologies.[119]

In light of the sensitivity of the information, Ijsselmeer (Ontario) should consider replacing the hard drives that contain such data, and engaging a security firm to render such drives reasonably unreadable. Ijsselmeer (Ontario) should carry out these activities in an organized way such that it can evaluate at any given time (with a high degree of certainty) whether it still retains control over records of a particular individual's personal information.

5.4 Checking Compliance with Privacy Laws in Japan.

Agile's Counsel completes his survey of privacy checkpoints by consulting next with counsel in Tokyo and then again with Agile's Danish counsel who is familiar with Norway's privacy regulations. Ijsselmeer (Tokyo) anticipates that by late spring of 2005 it will meet the qualifying conditions requiring it to implement policies and procedures to come into compliance with the Japanese Law for the Protection of Personal Information[120] (whose provisions apply to private businesses starting on May 30, 2005) ("PPIL"). The PPIL is not a privacy law, but applies to any entity that has gathered a certain volume of personal information collected in a "personal data base or the like." The PPIL focuses on personal databases, rather than items of personal information, and defines "personal data base or the like" to mean:

> "A collection of information containing personal information that falls into either of two categories:
>
> (i) A collection of information systematically arranged in such a way that specific personal information can be retrieved by a computer; or,

---

119. For an excellent discussion of the limits to security technologies, see Schneier, Bruce, SECRETS & LIES: DIGITAL SECURITY IN A NETWORKED WORLD, John Wiley & Sons, Inc., 2000, pp. 240–254.

120. Law No. 57 of 2003.

(ii) Any other collection of information designated by a Cabinet order as being systematically arranged in such a way that specific personal information can easily retrieved otherwise."[121]

The PPIL defines an "entity handling personal information" to mean an entity using a personal database or the like for its business,[122] and defines "personal data held" to mean personal data that an entity handles and has the authority to disclose, correct, add, delete, suspend use of or erase.[123]

This Law limits the use that a company may make of such personal data, by requiring the "entity handling personal information" to specify the purpose of its use ("Purpose of Use") as "strictly [clearly] as possible," and further requires that such entity not use such information for any purpose beyond that stated in the Purpose of Use.[124] Strict adherence to the Purpose of Use is thus a crucial requirement that Ijsselmeer (Tokyo) must observe (if it becomes an entity handling such data), and regular audits would be advisable to ensure that company practices or the practices of certain personnel do not depart from the specified Purpose of Use. It would probably also be advisable for Ijsselmeer (Tokyo) to draft such Purpose of Use as broadly as possible (while respecting the requirement for clarity), so that it has room to adjust practices without having to modify the Purpose of Use on each occasion.

An entity handling personal information must also comply with certain fair information principles, including:

- Not acquiring information by unfair means;
- Promptly notifying the data subject of the Purpose of Use, or otherwise announcing such Purpose;
- Keeping the personal data up to date and accurate, and securing it against damages, loss or unauthorized disclosure ("leakage");[125]
- Not supplying personal data to third parties without the prior consent of the data subject except in narrowly defined circum-

121. Law No. 57 of 2003, Article 2.
122. Id.
123. Id.
124. Law No. 57 of 2003, Article 15.
125. Id., Article 25 and 27.

stances (*e.g.,* where consent would be difficult to obtain and the information is needed to protect "life, body or property of an individual"); and

• Ceasing to use the data's subject's personal data upon request.[126]

The PPIL requires Ijsselmeer to give prior disclosure of the purpose for which it collects such information, to obtain consent before disclosing it to third parties, and (apparently) to give notice to the subject individual of any change in the purpose for which the information will be used as well as *any change in the personnel who manage such information.*[127] It is not surprising that, in a culture that places great emphasis on long-term relationships, a change in managers of personal information is regarded as a critical change warranting notice to the subject individuals. The goal is for Ijsselmeer (Tokyo) to implement a privacy compliance program that will conform to the Japanese privacy law when it comes into effect. Counsel would also like it to avoid the public embarrassment suffered by other Japanese companies that have allowed substantial personal information to be disclosed publicly.[128]

Of particular importance to Agile, the PPIL provides that *in the event of a merger or acquisition, the acquirer may only use personal information it obtains from the target company for the Purpose of Use that the target company collected such information.* Otherwise the acquirer must obtain a new consent from each of the data subjects.[129] Agile should therefore coordinate with Ijsselmeer (Tokyo) in drafting the Purpose of Use to

---

126. *Violations of Consumer Privacy: A Steady Stream in the Media 1998–2003,* PRIVACY & AMERICAN BUSINESS, November 2003, pp. 17–18, accessed at www.ey.com/global/download.nsf/US/Japanese_Consumer_Privacy_Law/$file/P&ABJapanSpecialIssue.pdf.

127. Woriton, Amy E., *Asia Opts for EU-Style Privacy,* PRIVACY IN FOCUS, June 2003, accessed at www.wrf.com/publications/publication.asp?id = 143056272003, and *Japan Passes Privacy Protection Law,* USA TODAY, May 23, 2003, accessed at www.usatoday.com/tech/news/2003-05-23-privacy-japan_x.htm.

128. In 1999, Japanese media reported that an NTT employee sold personal information of about 1,000 NTT customers to a private investigation agency. In 2003, the son of a former employee of Mainichi Shimbun attempted to auction customer data removed by the employee from that newspaper company. *Violations of Consumer Privacy: A Steady Stream in the Media 1998–2003,* PRIVACY & AMERICAN BUSINESS, November 2003, p. 8, accessed at www.ey.com/global/download.nsf/US/Japanese_Consumer_Privacy_Law/$file/P&ABJapanSpecialIssue.pdf.

129. Id., p. 18.

ensure that it is broad enough to cover Agile's intended use of such data without having to obtain additional consents.

More problematic for Agile is the PPIL Law requirement for the entity using a personal data base to obtain the consent of each data subject prior to any transfer to a third party. The PPIL Law does not make clear whether a company's affiliates are a third party (requiring consent prior to transfer). The Japanese government may clarify that issue before the PPIL comes into force. The issue is particularly important for Agile, because the PPIL (unlike PIPEDA and the Dutch Personal Data Protection Act) does not distinguish between transfers inside Japan and those across its borders to other countries. Thus for Ijsselmeer (Tokyo) to continue to transfer personal information will require either an interpretation of the PPIL that internal cross-border transfers are not considered to be to third parties, or it must obtain consent prior to making such transfers. The issue will not turn, however, on whether such information is or is not "sensitive." The PPIL does not distinguish between sensitive and non-sensitive data[130] (as do PIPEDA and the Dutch Personal Data Protection Act), and thus the transfer of sensitive personal data will not impose an additional compliance burden for Ijsselmeer (Tokyo).

While Ijsselmeer (Tokyo) pursues robotics research, its location in Japan positions Ijsselmeer to market its vehicle tracking devices in the Japanese market (a market that has historically been difficult for non-Japanese companies to enter). An excellent opportunity for its products is presented by the Ministry of Transportation's plan to issue "smart" license plates, beginning in 2004.[131] Agile would prefer to pursue such opportunities without compliance problems arising from the PPIL, particularly its provision that upon request from a data subject an entity must cease using that subject's personal information.

5.5 Checking Compliance with Privacy Laws in Norway.

Agile's counsel has three fundamental privacy law issues to take up with Troll's counsel: (i) whether Troll will rectify Ijsselmeer's noncom-

---

130. Id., p. 23.

131. *Privacy and Human Rights 2003: Country Reports, Japan,* accessed at www.privacyinternational.org/survey/phr2003/countries/japan.htm.

pliance with Dutch and Canadian privacy laws; (ii) whether Troll has complied with Norwegian privacy law with respect to personal data transferred to it from Ijsselmeer; and (iii) whether Troll will provide Agile with personal information about certain of its officers and key employees, such that Agile can assess them and the chances that they will be able to obtain security clearances to work on Agile's classified projects. On the first issue, Troll is reluctant to force compliance on the Dutch personnel of Ijsselmeer (a result of both cultural aversion and a recognition that the Dutch personnel are likely to respond poorly to pressure). This is a business decision, not a legal one, and its resolution will turn on the "corporate culture" more than on any other single factor.

On the second issue, Agile's Danish counsel has informed Agile that Norway's privacy law, the Personal Data Act[132] (and its implementing Personal Data Regulations)[133] is remarkably comprehensive, in fact, much more so than the Dutch or Canadian privacy laws. The penalties for violation of Norway's Personal Data Act, if committed willfully or through gross negligence are severe: fines or imprisonment for a term not exceeding one year or both, but in "particularly aggravating circumstances," a sentence of imprisonment not exceeding three years may be imposed.[134] Unlike Ijsselmeer, Troll is an experienced company that has probably been careful to comply with the Personal Data Law to ensure that it does not jeopardize its contractual relations with the Royal Norwegian Ministry of Defence.

➤ *Prohibited Conduct:* **Storage and Use of Personal Data Received from Outside Norway from Data Subjects Without Properly Obtaining Their Consent.** Troll was not aware of Ijsselmeer's inattention to privacy laws. Troll was therefore unaware that when it received Ijsselmeer's test reports containing sensitive biometric data it took control of such information without the data subjects' consent. Such sensitive personal information qualifies as "personal data" under Norway's Personal Data Law, which defines it broadly as "any information and assessments that may be linked to a natural person," and as "sensitive personal data" under that Law, because it contained information of "racial or ethnic origin" and "health."[135] Norway's Personal Data Law

---

132. Act of 14 April 2000 No. 31 relating to the processing of personal data, accessed at www.datatilsynet.no/lov/loven/poleng.html
133. Regulations on the processing of personal data (Personal Data Regulations).
134. Act of 14 April 2000 No. 31, § 48.
135. Act of 14 April 2000 No. 31, §2(1) and §2(8).

("PDL") is similar to PIPEDA in this regard: it does not address the issue of obligations for personal information received from outside of Norway.[136] The PDL applies to "controllers" (persons who determine the purpose of processing personal data and which means are to be used), but only to those who are "established in Norway" or, if "outside the territory of the EEA,"[137] those who make use of equipment in Norway (in which case the controller must have a representative in Norway).[138] Troll's Chief Information Officer ("CIO") fulfilled the duties of its appointed "controller." Troll's CIO was not aware that the reports contained personal, let alone, sensitive personal data.

Troll's engineers uploaded the CD-ROM containing the test data and personal data onto Troll computers. Such uploading constituted "storage" under the PDL, one form of "processing." Troll's engineers then compared the test results with other reports in their system, a second form of "processing," since "processing of personal data" is defined as "any use of personal data, such as collection, recording, alignment, storage and disclosure or a combination of such uses."[139] The PDL does not address the question of whether Dutch law or Norwegian law should be applied to determine whether consent for such processing was properly obtained from data subjects not located in Norway. The PDL, however, has more rigorous requirements for consent than the Dutch Personal Data Protection Act, which requires only an explanation of the purpose for the collection of the information and "unambiguous" consent.

The Norwegian PDL dictates what the controller must (on his own initiative) inform the data subject of before seeking consent: the name and address of the controller and of his representative (if any); the purpose of the processing; whether the data will be disclosed and if so, the identity of the recipient; the fact that the provision of data is voluntary; and any other circumstances that will enable the data subject to exercise his rights under the PDL "in the best possible way" (*e.g.*, in-

---

136. Instead, the Personal Data Law considers the issue of transfers only "to other countries." See Act of 14 April 2000 No. 31, §§ 29 and 30.

137. The EEA, or European Economic Area, was created by agreement in 1992 between the European Union and several other countries, only three of which eventually participated in the Single Market without undertaking the full responsibilities of membership in the EU. The three countries are: Norway, Iceland, and Liechtenstein.

138. Id., §4.

139. Id., §2(2).

forming him or her of the right to demand that inaccurate data be rectified, etc.).[140] In that context, the PDL defines "consent" as "any freely given, **specific and informed declaration** by the data subject to the effect that he or she agrees to the processing of personal data relating to him or her."[141] Since Ijsselmeer (Eindhoven) deliberately misled the data subjects about the purposes for its collection and use of their information, and did not disclose that the information would be transferred to Troll, the consent they gave (if evaluated by the Norwegian PDL) would fall far short of the requisite "specific and informed declaration" of agreement. Clearly Troll has violated the PDL by storing the personal information without proper consent.

▶ *Prohibited Conduct:* **Processing Sensitive Data Without a License from the Data Inspectorate.** Troll's use of the information has constituted further violations, because it occurred without consent, and because it constituted processing that exceeded the limits of what Troll had set forth in the statutorily required notification to the Norwegian Data Inspectorate. Such notice must be given not later than 30 days prior to commencement of processing, and new notification must be given prior to processing that exceeds the limits set forth in the initial notice.[142] In addition, since the biometric information from Ijsselmeer processed by Troll was sensitive data, the Norwegian PDL required Troll to have first obtained a *license* from the Norwegian Data Inspectorate (not a requirement for personal data "which have been volunteered by the data subject," but in light of the deceptive means by Ijsselmeer to procure consents, the Data Inspectorate could reasonably view such data as not truly "volunteered" by the data subjects).[143]

---

140. Act of 14 April 2000 No. 31, §19. Such notification by the controller is not required only if there is no doubt that the data subject already has the required information.

141. Id., §2(7). [Emphasis added.]

142. Id., §31. The PDL requires that the notice provide a substantial disclosure by the controller to the Data Inspectorate, including: when the processing will begin; identity of the person with day-to-day responsibility for fulfilling the obligation of the controller; the purpose of the processing; an overview of the categories of personal data that are to be processed; the sources of the personal data; the legal basis for collecting the data; the persons to whom the personal data will be disclosed, including recipients in other countries, if any; and the security measures relating to the processing. The task virtually compels an organization to implement procedures otherwise required by the PDL. See Act of 14 April 2000 No. 31, §32 (Content of the notification).

143. Id., §33. The required license is not a paper formality. The PDL requires that an assessment be made as to whether the disadvantages of such processing outweigh

Fortunately, no complaints had been received, nor have any requests for information been made by any of the Dutch data subjects. And there is no requirement that compels voluntary self-reporting of a violation of the PDL. There is also no requirement concerning how a controller should proceed to destroy such information. Most importantly, there is no requirement for testing whether such destruction permitted recovery of the data.

Troll should therefore destroy (or anonymize) the personal data, and most importantly, do so before Ijsselmeer takes any action, so that if a Dutch data subject learns of the transfer and contacts Troll, Troll can truthfully respond that it no longer possesses the data and has not transferred it to any third party. This means, of course, that Agile's request for the test reports should be denied, as such transfer would preclude Troll from asserting that it had destroyed and not transferred such data. Transfer to the United States would clearly require consent of the data subjects, because Norway's Data Inspectorate could be expected to conclude that the United States was not a country that ensured the required "adequate level of protection of the data."[144] Troll's counsel is confident that the information has not been transferred to any third party nor accessed without authorization. Troll carefully observes Norway's Personal Data Regulations, which are unusual in the depth of detail they provide with respect to the security measures that controllers must implement to protect personal data.[145]

On the question of Agile's request for personal information regarding Troll's personnel (including performance evaluations), the parties have agreed to negotiate a data transfer agreement that would specify the purposes for the transfer, limit the uses Agile could make of the information, and set conditions for protection of the information. The agreement would have to be disclosed to each of the personnel whose personal information Agile sought and, unless such persons agreed to such transfer and subsequent use, Troll would not be able to provide

---

considerations that favor the processing. See Act of 14 April 2000 No. 31, §34 (Decision as to whether to grant a license). Moreover, if granted, the license may lay down conditions for processing to limit the disadvantages the processing would otherwise impose on the data subject. Act of 14 April 2000 No. 31, §35 (Conditions laid down in the license).

144. Act of 14 April 2000 No. 31, §29. See also Personal Data Regulations, §6.2 (Data Inspectorate's assessment of the level of protection in third countries), which only came into force from January 1, 2004.

145. We review some of those provisions in Chapter 6 on information security.

Agile with their personal information. That too would need to be clearly expressed in the data transfer agreement.

Agile had anticipated that the most difficult provisions for it to agree to (because they would require a change in its own internal policies) would concern the **security measures to protect the confidentiality of the personal information**. Agile has comparable measures in place to secure the classified data it receives or generates in relation to its U.S. government contracts, but it could not readily adapt those to the protection of personal information. Agile will need to establish new policies quickly, because the more clearly the agreement specifies such protections, the more likely it is that Troll's personnel will give their consent to the requested transfers. Such problems could entail extensive changes in policies and procedures. It is important that the lead-time for this not be underestimated or the timetable for the acquisition will slip. Because acquisition timetables are usually calibrated to key regulatory dates, any slippage can have severe economic consequences. One such timetable these parties must address is approval of the acquisition by Norway's Competition Authority.

5.6 Norwegian Regulatory Review of Agile's Acquisition vs. U.S. Review of Norwegian Acquisition of High Tech Firm—Checkpoint CFIUS.

Agile and Troll have kept their acquisition talks confidential, but have determined that under the Regulation on the Notification of Concentrations that came into force on May 1, 2004 ("Concentrations Regulation"), they must give notice of the contemplated acquisition to the Norway's Konkurransetilsynet or Competition Authority. Such notice gives the Konkurransetilsynet the opportunity to review the acquisition, under Norway's Competition Act, to determine if the acquisition will create or increase a significant restriction on competition. If the Konkurransetilsynet makes that determination, it will intervene, and either prohibit the transaction or issue a conditional approval (*e.g.*, requiring divestiture of certain assets or activities in order to remove the negative effects on competition).[146]

---

146. Konkurransetilsynet, *The Rules on Control of Concentration*, p. 3, accessed at

Until the Konkurransetilsynet makes its determination, the parties will not be permitted to implement the acquisition.[147] If, however, the "undertakings" (the parties to the acquisition) have a combined annual "turnover" (revenue) of less than 20 million Norwegian Kroner ("NOK"), or if only one of the parties (Agile or Troll) has annual "turnover" in excess of NOK 5 million, then their transaction would be exempt from such notification requirement.[148] The audited financials for the last fiscal year for Agile and for Troll show that each has an annual "turnover" of over NOK 500 million, and that the two companies combined have a "turnover" well in excess of NOK 1 billion. Notification is therefore mandatory. They have a choice as to the form of notice: a short form standardized notification or a longer "complete" notification. Troll's counsel recommends the latter. Although complete notification requires disclosure of more information, it offers the substantial advantage that certain deadlines for the Konkurransetilsynet to complete its review start to run earlier.[149]

---

www.konkurransetilsynet.no/archive/Internett/vedlegg/english/control_concentrations.pdf.

147. Id.

148. *Regulation on Concentrations*, Section 2, accessed at www.konkurran setilsynet.no/internett/index.asp?strUrl = 1005157i.

149. Konkurransetilsynet, *The Rules on Control of Concentration*, p. 3, accessed at www.konkurransetilsynet.no/archive/Internett/vedlegg/english/control_concentrations.pdf. Complete notification requires disclosure to the Konkurransetilsynet of the following:

"a. Contact information for the parties to the merger or the undertaking(s) acquiring control.

b. Description of the concentration.

c. Description of the undertakings concerned and undertakings in the same corporate group.

d. Description of the markets affected by the concentration.

e. Description of the market structure of the affected markets.

f. Information on the most important competitors, customers, and suppliers of the undertakings concerned in the affected markets.

g. Account of any barriers to entry in the affected markets.

h. Account of any efficiency gains.

i. Information on whether the concentration is subject to the control of other competition authorities.

j. The most recent version of the agreement establishing the concentration, including enclosures.

k. The most recent annual reports and annual accounts of the undertakings concerned." *Regulation on Concentrations*, Section 2, accessed at www.konkurrans etilsynet.no/internett/index.asp?strUrl = 1005157i.

338   Checkpoints in Cyberspace

Troll's counsel has another reason for recommending complete notification. He expects that the Konkurransetilsynet would have eventually required the companies to file a complete notification. A recently completed acquisition of a U.S. high tech firm, Isosceles Fabrikant, Inc. ("Isosceles"), by a Norwegian defense and maritime corporation Birke Gruppen ASA ("Birke"[150]), has encountered an unexpected post-Closing U.S. government review, referred to in the Norwegian press as an "Exon-Florio" review. He anticipates that the Konkurransetilsynet will subject Agile's proposed acquisition to close scrutiny, if the U.S. government orders the unwinding of Birke's acquisition of Isosceles.

Troll's counsel asks how the U.S. government can wait until after completion of an acquisition to challenge it, and on what grounds it could legally order the unwinding of the Isosceles/Birke deal. Agile's Counsel explains that a post-Closing review rarely occurs. He does not know why it occurred on this occasion, but speculates that the cause may be Isosceles' unique position in the U.S. defense community. Isosceles manufactures nanoclay composites by a process that is new and difficult to control. Isosceles' products are used in fabricating wing and fuselage components to reduce their sharp angles, friction with the ambient air and susceptibility to increases in surface temperature, all features that are crucial to reduce, if not eliminate, the radar signature attributable to the shape, structure and composition of the F-22 and the F-35 (Joint Strike Fighter). Isosceles' components help to make these new fighter aircraft "stealthy" and help to diminish their prodigious weight (a chronic problem during development of new fighter aircraft). Most important, Isosceles is the sole source supplier of those crucial components. It (like Agile) has a Facility Security Clearance under the Department of Defense Industrial Security Program, and significant portions of its technologies and their application to the F-22 and F-35 are "black-box:" they require a security classification of "Secret" in order for personnel to have access to the work and its technical data.

Agile's Counsel infers that neither Birke nor Isosceles filed for an Exon-Florio review, as they could have done prior to the Closing of their transaction, which would have obviated the possibility (and surprise) of a post-Closing review. The authority for exercise of such extraordinary power over transactions rests in Section 5021 of the Omnibus Trade and Competitiveness Act of 1988 (the "Exon-Florio" provision), which amended Section 721 of the Defense Production Act

---

150. *Birke* means *birch* in Norsk. **Note:** *The Birke/Isosceles acquisition is inverted for our hypothetical.*

of 1950, and provided authority to the President to *suspend or prohibit* any foreign acquisition, merger or takeover of a U.S. corporation. To exercise that authority, the President must determine that:

(a) There is credible evidence that the foreign person acquirer that would exercise control after the transaction *might take* action that threatens U.S. national security (a term that remains undefined in the statute and that leaves the Executive Branch considerable discretion to interpret and enforce);[151]

(b) That existing provisions of law, not including the International Emergency Economic Powers Act [under which the President declares emergencies that lead to the TSR], do not provide adequate and appropriate authority to protect U.S. national security from the threat posed by the transaction.

As explained by the implementing regulations ("Section 721 Regs"), the principal purpose of Section 721 is to authorize the President to suspend or prohibit any merger, acquisition or takeover by a foreign person of a U.S. person (engaged in interstate commerce), when in the President's view "the foreign interest exercising control over that [U.S.] person might take action that threatens to impair the national security."[152] Foreign companies, seeking to acquire U.S. defense contractors or high tech companies that have DoD contracts, therefore, often consider filing a voluntary notice with the Committee on Foreign Investment in the United States ("CFIUS") to obtain clearance, or to have advance notice of what conditions the CFIUS might impose for clearance, thereby averting the risk of disrupting the transaction or causing post-Closing divestments.[153] (The CFIUS is an inter-agency committee,

---

151. We know of no case in which Section 721 authority has been used to challenge an acquisition on only indirect threats to U.S. national security. Moreover, the implementing regulations and the illustrative examples they contain do provide some limits to the credible interpretation of "national security." In practice, however, the President would not find his authority seriously questioned if he determines that U.S. national security is at risk, particularly in the post-9/11 era.

152. 31 CFR 800.101.

153. The GAO, however, in a 1995 study concluded that Exon-Florio was not a sufficient protection of U.S. technology, because too many parties did not file voluntary notices and CFIUS, on its own initiative, was not adequately closing the gap: "We [the GAO] found that many foreign investments occur in high-technology or defense-related industries that were not reported to CFIUS. While the significance of the gap is unclear, it does suggest that the CFIUS process alone cannot be relied on to surface transactions posing potential national security concerns." In a footnote, the GAO added that the

chaired by the Secretary of Treasury, and includes among its members the Departments of State, Commerce and Defense.)

From the next calendar day after a voluntary notice has been "accepted" (not merely received),[154] the CFIUS has a 30-day period to review the acquisition to determine if it involves foreign control and whether there are national security concerns that warrant further investigation.[155] If the CFIUS makes an affirmative finding on both issues (foreign control and national security risk), the Committee initiates a 45-day investigation. At its conclusion, the Committee submits a report and recommendation to the President of the United Sates. The President has 15 days to decide whether or not to take action.

The timing for filing a voluntary notice, however, requires more nuanced considerations, not the least of which is the need to defer such filing to the point at which the parties are reasonably certain that there will be no material changes in the transaction from their description of it in the voluntary notice. The CFIUS has authority, in the event of a "material change in the transaction as to which notification has been made" to reject the voluntary notice.[156] If the parties want to pursue a CFIUS review, they must re-start the entire process and face more rigorous scrutiny.

In addition, the parties to the transaction need to coordinate the filing of a voluntary notice carefully. Such notice can be filed by just one party to the transaction, by both parties separately at different times, or by both parties jointly. A failure to coordinate such filings (if the parties file separately, or only one of them files) can result in discrepancies prompting the Staff Chair to delay acceptance of the notice in order to obtain clarifications or information not submitted as required.[157]

U.S. government has "other mechanisms to safeguard national security, such as export control laws and industrial security regulations that protect classified facilities." GAO report, *Foreign Investments*, GAO/NSIAD-96-12, December 21, 1995, p. 7.

154. Receipt should not be mistaken for "acceptance" of a voluntary notice. Such notices do not compel a CFIUS review. Instead, the Committee, acting through the Staff Chair, may (1) reject voluntary notices not complying with 31 CFR §800.402; (2) delay the start of the review period until a compliant notice is received; or (3) decline to analyze the national security considerations because the Committee finds that the transaction is not actually subject to section 721. 31 CFR § 800.403.

155. 31 CFR §800.404. If the 30th day of that period is not a business day, then the review period closes on the next business day thereafter.

156. 31 CFR §800.404.

157. See 31 CFR 800.402(b)(2). That regulation further provides that "[w]here necessary to obtain such information, the Staff Chairman may inform the non-notifying

The voluntary filing requires the provision of extensive information concerning the parties, the proposed transaction and the acquirer's post-acquisition plans, and often exceeds what the parties (especially the acquirer) are willing to disclose. A filing of voluntary notice requires disclosure to the CFIUS of, among other information:

(i) With respect to the company to be acquired, and any entity of which it is a parent that is also being acquired, each contract (identified by agency and number) currently in effect (or that was in effect within the past five years) with an agency of the Government of the United States involving any classified information, technology or data, and the name, office and telephone number of the contracting officer[158] (an example of precisely the kind of information Birke, the Norwegian company, would not be able to provide if it made a filing independently of Isoceles, the company it seeks to acquire);

(ii) Whether the U.S. person being acquired produces products or technical data subject to the EAR and, if applicable, the relevant Commerce Control List number and a description of the technical data[159] (another example of information Birke would be unlikely to be able to provide, and which CFIUS would therefore request of Isoceles);

(iii) The plans of the foreign person acquirer for the U.S. person target company, with respect to (a) reducing, eliminating or selling research and development facilities, (b) changing product quality, (c) shutting down or moving offshore facilities which are within the United States or (d) consolidating or selling product lines or technology[160] (many foreign acquirers would be reluctant to disclose such information accurately to their target company, let alone to CFIUS).

Furthermore, as the Committee has noted in comments to the Section 721 Regs, when a party files a voluntary notice by itself, and has

---

party or parties that notice has been initiated with respect to a proposed transaction involving the party, and request that certain information set forth in this section, as specified by the Staff Chairman, be forwarded to the Committee within seven days after such request by the Staff Chairman."

158. 31 CFR 800.402(b)(3)(iv).
159. 31 CFR 800.402(b)(4)(i).
160. 31 CFR 800.402(b)(5)(ii).

the burden of answering questions about the other party "to the extent known or reasonably available to it," that does not limit its obligations. Thus a filing by one party often commits the other to making disclosures:

> "When a party giving notice is unable to answer fully a question pertaining to the other party, *it is not excused by the words 'to the extent known or reasonably available to it, from submitting a complete and accurate filing,* as has evidently been assumed by some parties. The [CFIUS] committee expects that in such a case either the party giving notice will obtain the assistance of the other party or parties, or that the latter independently will make a filing to the Committee, supplying the relevant information. In any case, the Committee will delay beginning the initial thirty-day review period until the filing is complete with respect to both parties . . . the Staff Chairman . . . when necessary, will contact directly the party or parties that did not file the notice and request that information responsive to Sec. 800.402 be filed within seven days of the receipt of the request."[161]

Certain features of Birke's acquisition of Isosceles increased the chances that if the CFIUS had received and accepted a voluntary notice it would have determined that the transaction necessitated Section 721 action. The threshold for a finding of national security threat is high, and the CFIUS tends to rely primarily on an assessment by the Department of Defense ("DoD"). Although guided in part by criteria in the Section 721 Regs, the DoD will consider whether the company being acquired is a sole-source supplier to the DoD, whether it has classified contracts and whether the diversion of critical technologies is a risk.[162]

Isosceles fits the three criteria that the DoD tends to focus on in determining whether there is a potential threat to national security. Isosceles is the sole source supplier of a patented composite airframe component, its subcontracts for the F-22 and F-35 are classified, and diversion of its technologies would create a substantial risk. The fact that Troll is located in a NATO country does not remove that risk, nor

---

161. 31 CFR Part 800, Appendix A, Preamble to Regulations on Mergers, Acquisitions, and Takeovers by Foreign Persons, as amended, comment on §800.402. [Emphasis added.]

162. The GAO reports those to be among DoD's salient criteria. See GAO report, *Foreign Investments*, GAO/NSIAD-96-12, December 21, 1995, p. 6.

does the fact that Norway is a partner and contributor to the F-35 (Joint Strike Fighter) program.

As Birke discovered, review of the acquisition of a U.S. firm by a foreign person can be initiated by the CFIUS after the Closing of such transaction and, if warranted, the CFIUS will make recommendations that, if accepted by the President of the United States, will result in an order that the acquisition or merger be blocked, allowed to continue only on the meeting of certain conditions, or if already concluded, to nonetheless be undone.[163]

Press reports suggest that the CFIUS members have viewed Birke's acquisition unfavorably as a result of transactions Birke has done with Iranian and other parties targeted by the TSR (which Treasury has detected on its own initiative). Birke's position is that it has merely followed the example set by French companies that are eagerly pursuing business opportunities in Iran (e.g., Renault, Alcatel, PSA Peugeot Citroën, Air France and Société Générale).[164] There is growing concern too regarding whether Isosceles' technologies should be entrusted to the control of foreign person involved in such dealings, particularly since that, in turn, would raise the risk of diversion of classified U.S. technologies to countries identified as supporting international terrorism.[165]

---

163. See 31 CFR 800.401(c), which states: "No agency notice, or review or investigation by the Committee [CFIUS] shall be made with respect to a transaction *more than three years after the date of conclusion of the transaction, unless the Chairman of the Committee,* in consultation with other members of the Committee, *requests an investigation.*" [Emphasis added.] Thus to protect national security, the CFIUS have the legal authority in the regulations to initiate an investigation even more than three years after "conclusion of the transaction." And since the term "conclusion of the transaction" is not defined in the regulations, the CFIUS could also interpret that to not occur until all post-closing actions contemplated in the acquisition or merger agreement had been completed (e.g., post-closing audits of performance and adjustments of purchase price accordingly are often provided for and could be interpreted reasonably as the actual "conclusion of the transaction").

164. Daragahi, Borzou, *France Steps up Its Investments in Iran,* THE NEW YORK TIMES, June 23, 2004, p. W1 and W7. For example, as reported in that article, Air France has resumed flights to Tehran (after seven years), Renault is to make a large-scale, long-term investment (its first in Iran since 1979), and Alcatel has signed multi-million dollar contracts to provide high-speed Internet service in Iran and communications for offshore oil and gas platforms.

165. As the GAO succinctly noted: "Because U.S. defense strategy relies on the deterrent effects of technological rather than numerical superiority, concern about foreign investment focuses on the U.S. government's ability to identify technologies crucial to defense systems and to act to preserve and promote U.S. leadership in them." GAO report, *Foreign Investments,* GAO/NSIAD-96-12, December 21, 1995, p. 2.

In Birke's case, the CFIUS determined that a Section 721 investigation was required by the end of the initial 30-day review period, because the CFIUS had serious misgivings about Birke's acquisition of Isosceles. The CFIUS therefore initiated a Section 721 review on its own motion. It requested information from Isosceles and from Birke. As the CFIUS proceeded through the 45-day investigation period, it attempted to ascertain whether Birke's acquisition of Isosceles posed an unacceptable threat to U.S. national security. (If the CFIUS so concludes, it would report that determination to the President, who would then have 15 days in which to make a final decision.) More recent reports suggest that the CFIUS, upon completing its review, appeared ready to recommend a decision to the President of the United States to block the transaction or set conditions that Birke would probably find unacceptable.

In discussions among Isosceles, Birke and the CFIUS Chair, it became clear that Birke did not want the adverse publicity of appearing to be willing to pose a security risk, but remained convinced that it could provide the assurances (and implement the security measures) needed for an agreement with CFIUS on an arrangement that would address all of the CFIUS' concerns.

(The issues raised in this scenario are reminiscent of the CFIUS' rejection of the proposed acquisition of Global Crossing by Singapore Technologies Telemedia and Hutchison Whampoa (controlled by Li Ka-shing, a Hong Kong billionaire), causing a 20-month delay and forcing Whampoa out of the deal.[166] The CFIUS investigation was prompted by

---

166. In early 2002, Global Crossing, a fiber-optic carrier, filed for Chapter 11 bankruptcy-court protection. Singapore Technologies Telemedia (SST) and Hutchison Whampoa (Whampoa) planned to acquire Global Crossing for $250 million. SST and Whampoa filed a voluntary notice with the CFIUS, which did not result in approval but in expressions of concern by the CFIUS that effectively blocked the deal. The concerns centered on the risk that Global Crossing's 100,000 miles of fiber optic networks—which carry voice and data and were relied upon by the U.S. government for some of its communications—could be compromised by reported links between Whampoa and the Chinese government. More precisely, there were concerns that China would be able to tap U.S. government or corporate traffic to carry out surveillance or to pilfer trade secrets. There were also concerns that foreign ownership of the fiber-optic network would limit the U.S. government's ability to conduct wiretaps and other electronic surveillance. "[P]reventing other countries from tapping such lines—while ensuring that U.S. intelligence services can still do" so is reportedly a high priority for the U.S., and motivated CFIUS' action in this case. See Dreazen, Yochi J., *Who Can Tap Undersea Wires Is Key to Merger*, THE WALL STREET JOURNAL, July 17, 2003, p. B1.

Proposals put forward by Whampoa to insulate Global Crossing, leaving Whampoa

DoD opposition to the proposed $1.6 billion acquisition of Silicon Valley Group Inc. by Dutch firm ASM Lithography Holding NV.)[167]

Eventually, Birke, Isosceles and CFIUS reached an accord, the terms of which were not publicly disclosed, but the result of which was that the transaction was not unwound. The CFIUS terminated its investigation and took no further action on the matter. In light of this, Troll and Agile proceed with their plan to file a complete notification with the Konkurransetylsynet, which, before the expiration of the review period, determines that no intervention is required.

Two other areas receive attention from Agile's counsel, and supplement the list of corrective measures: information security and patents, which we review in that order.

---

as only a passive investor, were not acceptable to the CFIUS, which issued a letter announcing it would start a 45-day period investigation. (Whampoa had even gone as far as hiring senior Pentagon adviser Richard Perle to assist in persuading the DoD to withdraw its opposition, but without success.) At that point, Whampoa withdrew its bid, and yielded its share to SST. DoD opposition to the acquisition continued, and it took SST several months before it could obtain CFIUS approval. To obtain it, SST had to make several concessions, including requiring as many as 10 network engineers to obtain U.S. security clearances, agreeing that all customer and network data would be stored in the United States, a "network security agreement," and engaging a third party to audit the compliance with such agreements. See Berman, Dennis K., and Dreazen, Yochi J., *Global Crossing Deal May Hit Snag*, The Wall Street Journal Online, July 9, 2003, accessed at http://online.wsj.com/PA2VJBNA4R/article/0,,SB1057715422714 42300-search,00.html?collection = autowire%2Farchive&vql_string = cfius%3Cin%3E%28 article%2Dbody%29, and Berman, Dennis K., *Bush Is Expected to Approve Deal to Buy Global Crossing*, The Wall Street Journal Online, September 9, 2003, accessed at http://online.wsj.com/PA2VJBNA4R/article/0,,SB106307111960491000-search,00.html? collection = autowire%2Farchive&vql_string = cfius%3Cin%3E%28article%2Dbody%29.

167. The DoD opposition was unusual in that it objected not to an existing critical supplier, but to a company that was merely a potential supplier to the DoD in the area of precision optics and semiconductor technologies. The U.S. company made photolithography machinery for projecting integrated-circuit patterns onto silicon wafers, thermal systems that deposit chemicals to provide insulation to silicon wafers, and precision optical parts such as mirrors and lenses used in satellite and aerial reconnaissance by the U.S. government. Such activities helped prompt strong Congressional opposition that influenced the CFIUS review. See Simpson, Glenn R., The Wall Street Journal Online, *Pentagon Moves to Postpone Deal for Silicon Valley Group*, March 8, 2001, accessed at http://online.wsj.com/PA2VJBNA4R/article/0,,SB98398244122006884 7-search,00.html?collection = autowire%2Farchive&vql_string = cfius%3Cin%3E%28 article%2Dbody%29.

CHAPTER 6

Checkpoint: Information Security

6.0 Agile's Transaction at Checkpoint Information Security.

When Marco Polo made his perilous journeys across largely uncharted regions of Persia, he credited the Tartar lordship with enforcing sufficient security to make merchants willing to risk the journey along the empire's trade routes:

> "Were it not for fear of the government, that is the Tartar lordship . . . they [the people of these kingdoms] would do great mischief to traveling merchants. The government imposes severe penalties upon them and has ordered that along all dangerous routes the inhabitants at the request of the merchants shall supply good and efficient escorts from district to district for their safe conduct on payment of two or three groats for each loaded beast according to the length of the journey. Yet for all that the government can do, these brigands are not to be deterred from frequent depredations. Unless the merchants are well armed and equipped with bows, they slay and harry them unsparingly."[1]

Trade route security is notoriously difficult to predict, and tends to involve taking unquantifiable risks. Plying a trade route requires a busi-

---

1. Polo, Marco, THE TRAVELS, Penguin Books, translated by Ronald Latham, 1958, p. 61.

ness assessment: weighing one's tolerance for risk against the contingent "promise" of profits.

The trade route of cyberspace has enabled users, such as Agile and Troll, to accumulate valuable information stored in digital files, but has also exposed them to external security risks (intrusions that may corrupt data, embed malwares or steal intelligence and other data). In addition, it has created new forms of internal security risks (as personnel circumvent security measures to gain unauthorized access to information assets or create vulnerabilities that outsiders can exploit to release sensitive data whose value critically depends on its being kept secret). In cyberspace, as in other trade routes, security is notoriously illusory, and shortlived at best.[2]

Information security—the effort to protect a firm's information assets and resources—bedevils officers and directors. It has often come up in recent meetings of Agile's partners and of Troll's directors with inconclusive results. Rapid cycles of technological advance in the design and development of cyber communication (and of malwares to exploit

---

2. A related trend that is beyond the scope of this book is the use of state-sponsored cyberforce. As one commentator keenly observes, "Those who rely upon the benefits of the Internet and the World Wide Web create vulnerabilities for themselves. . . . [S]tates and businesses must also be concerned about those who unlawfully penetrate, or hack into, intranets and computer systems closed to the public. With their open architecture, the Internet and the World Wide Web are ideally suited for *asymmetrical warfare* and corporate espionage. They can be used by states and nonstate actors to *anonymously* pry into a state's public, sensitive, and classified computers; to collect a wide range of government and business information; to manipulate data; to deceive decision makers; to influence public opinion; and to even cause physical destruction from remote locations abroad. . . . [A] dedicated and persistent hostile threat can gain access to almost any Internet-linked information infrastructure of any state in the world. The technology of CyberSpace adds new meaning to over-the-horizon warfare. Execution of an organized, large-scale attack can begin anonymously with the stroke of a single key on a computer keyboard, with commands being delivered around the world at the speed of light." Sharp, Sr., Walter Gary, CYBERSPACE AND THE USE OF FORCE, Aegis Research Corporation, 1999, pp. 17 and 19. Sharp also notes the discrepancies between domestic law and the laws applicable to state use of cyberforce: "When one state hacks into another state's computer systems it is very likely engaging in acts that are unlawful under the law of the territorial state, but under international law, the hacking state may be engaging in a lawful act of espionage that may not be considered a use of force. . . . The right to respond in anticipatory self-defense does not apply to the penetration of *all* government computer systems during peacetime, but it should apply presumptively to those sensitive systems that are critical to a state's vital national interests." Sharp, CYBERSPACE AND THE USE OF FORCE, pp. 127–129 (bold text in original).

it) often persuade senior management that they cannot understand information security and cannot apply their judgment and common sense to control it. Such factors also tempt them to seek a way to purchase (with one investment) one "global" impregnable solution.[3] The tendency is to put "front-end" loaded resources into constructing fortress-like defenses, then to become complacent with regard to the persistent and annoying upgrade notices (and the recommendations by a CIO to invest in improvements to address recent disclosures of vulnerabilities and of concomitant threats designed to exploit them).[4] As the GAO observed in a report in May of 2004, even in critical infrastructure industries (such as banking and finance, chemical, health care, and petroleum) it is difficult to address cybersecurity consistently and thoroughly

> "Unless it makes business sense to do so—that is, the investment is cost-beneficial. Typically this means that investments must generate revenue, save or avoid costs, or increase productivity. In some cases, IT [information technology] investments are undertaken for non-quantitative reasons, such as strategic impact or because such investments are necessary to protect critical infrastructure important to protect national security. While most companies realize that information security breaches are bad for business, in some cases, information security managers find it difficult to justify investments in security based only on the fear of attacks. . . . Organizations have limited resources—people and money—and consequently, they typically focus on improving cybersecurity only to the extent that those security needs are necessary to continue their business operations or are demanded by their customers . . . [A]n entity is best served by taking a risk-based view that considers all the risks that the entity faces . . . According to its own prioritization of these risks, the entity may determine the threat of cyber attacks to be a significant risk

---

3. Discussion often invokes terms such as "silver bullet" and "holy grail."

4. Part of the problem (that usual goes unnoticed by boards of directors) is that as Cynthia Irvine observes, "for poorly-built systems, an attacker always has the advantage," that it is futile to attempt to "address the asymmetric threat that the attacker poses through vigilance and repairs to inherently flawed systems," and that so long as such systems continue to be produced, repairing them will only address their "superficial weaknesses" and doom the systems' owners to the "Sisyphean purgatory of penetrate and patch." Irvine, Cynthia, *Teaching Constructive Security*, IEEE SECURITY & PRIVACY, November/December 2003, p. 59.

that it must mitigate. At this point, the entity can proceed to implement countermeasures to mitigate the risk of cyber attacks, based on its analysis of the cost-effectiveness of the countermeasures."[5]

Regardless of the priority an entity assigns to the risks of internal breaches of security and of cyber attacks and to mitigating such risks, information security is like dental work: *it requires continuous monitoring and improvement to keep pace with the evolving risks and the recurrent decline of internally enforced precautions.* The U.S. Defense Information Systems Agency cautions federal agencies to remember that "securing any network is a continual process that requires staying abreast of the latest vulnerabilities that may exist in network infrastructure components, server operating systems, and applications deployed throughout the enterprise."[6]

Certain developments since the early 1990's make continuous improvements in security an imperative for companies involved in defense contracting and homeland security, or any other industry in which a corruption of data could have catastrophic consequences (*e.g.*, telecommunications, air and rail transportation, petroleum producers, chemical and pharmaceutical makers, financial institutions, food suppliers, etc.). Prior to the widespread storage of sensitive data on company computers, corruption of one document would ordinarily not impact other documents or other storage locations. However, with the use of the computer (and the backup media of tapes, diskettes, CD-ROMs, etc.) as a storage medium, and the advent of networking, the risk of damage to the storage device or the storage media threatens to deny the user access to all data in the storehouse, or to infect interconnected storage devices, causing an ever-widening loss of or damage to data.

As storage media have increased in capacity, companies have commensurably increased the amount of data they store in one location.[7] A person seeking unauthorized access no longer needs to go from one

---

5. GAO, *Technology Assessment: Cybersecurity for Critical Infrastructure Protection,* GAO-04-321, May 2004, pp. 68–70.

6. Defense Information Systems Agency—Field Security Operations, *Voice Over Internet Protocol (VOIP) Security Technical Implementation Guide* (Unclassified), Version 1, Release 1, January 13, 2004, p. 19, accessed at http://csrc.nist.gov/pcig/STIGs/VoIP-STIG-V1R1R-4PDF.pdf.

7. Such data storehouses are, moreover, potentially accessible from any of several locations around the world.

file or warehouse to another. The intruder merely needs to click open a directory to gain access to the entire system of sensitive data. And such information is extremely portable. It can be cyber-transmitted or downloaded onto disks, making theft increasingly difficult to discern, because no visible evidence of "breaking and entering" is left behind. Indeed, the thing stolen is left behind. (In addition, the stored data is often well indexed and cross-referenced and capable in some instances of being rapidly searched for all occurrences of a word or integer, making it relatively easy for an intruder to locate crucial information.) One thin platter will hold literally volumes of sensitive data. Similar improvements make even this description obsolete as a status report (but not as trend report). For example, if Sony and TOPPAN Printing succeed in commercializing what they refer to as the "Blu-Ray" disc, the storage capacity will take another quantum leap, as such discs reportedly have a 25 gigabyte capacity.[8] Thus the traditional cycle of advances in the protective shield being closely followed by improvements in the sword take on greater significance in information security, because the failure of the shield leads to ever-increasing potential losses, damage or corruption of data and of the systems that depend on such data.

Information security has risen in importance for the federal government, because terrorist threats to homeland security include the threat of cyber-attack. Defense contactors, such as Lockheed Martin and Titan, expanded in the 1990's into information technology ("IT"), especially classified IT, and after 9/11, enhanced their offerings to the federal government in information security.

Other major changes affecting information security have come through increased "networking" of company computers on the Internet. Linking computers to the Internet has opened virtual backdoors in every company, allowing its data storehouse computers to be linked to the Internet. Intruders no longer needed physical access to the company's premises or to its data storehouse: Internet access abroad opened the possibility of access to any such company's sensitive data storehouse. The greater the bandwidth, the faster any intruder can remove large quantities of sensitive data. Concentration of data has inevitably brought concentration of bandwidth. Intruders enter unobserved, examine a computer without being noticed and remove copies of data

---

8. See Sony, *TOPPAN and Sony Successfully Develop 25GB Paper Disc,* press release, April 15, 2004, accessed at www.sony.net/SonyInfo/News/Press/200404/04-0415E.

files without having to change, delete or remove those files. In the hard-copy era, the advent of photocopying (and improvements in small cameras) facilitated the pilfering of documents without notice. The Achilles heel of information security systems in most companies now is their virtual ignorance of the undetected comings and goings of unauthorized personnel and intruders. Many do not have intrusion detection systems (*i.e.*, "software or hardware systems that automate the process of monitoring the events occurring in a computer system or network, analyzing them for signs of security problems . . . [which are] attempts to compromise the confidentiality, integrity, availability, or to bypass the security mechanisms of a computer or network").[9] Such organizations often also do not have intrusion prevention systems. An NIST study notes that intrusion detection systems are particularly helpful in discerning and reporting three kinds of computer attacks:

(i) *Scanning attacks*—in which "an attacker probes a target network or system by sending different kinds of packets" in order to learn many of the target system's characteristics and vulnerabilities, including sometimes an output of a list of hosts or IP addresses that probably will be vulnerable to attack;[10]

(ii) *Denial of service attacks*—usually involving one of two types, "flaw exploitation" that "exploit a flaw in the target system's software in order to cause a processing failure or to cause it to exhaust system resources . . . ." or "flooding" that dispatch to a "system or system component more information than it can handle" and thereby overwhelm it or monopolize its network connections;[11] and

9. Bace, Rebecca, and Mell, Peter, *Intrusion Detection Systems*, NIST Special Publication, p. 5. Intrusion detection systems can target a host but usually target network traffic (by reading network packets, comparing their content against pre-specified signatures or unique characteristics of known attacks and known anomalous network traffic, and, upon finding a match, generating an alert). Targeting such traffic, however, is ineffective if the organization does not continually update its signatures to "reflect lessons learned from attacks on itself and others, as well as developments in attack tool technologies" and properly "tune" its system (create signatures that can successfully distinguish between normal network traffic and potentially malicious traffic). See FFIEC, INFORMATION SECURITY (IT EXAMINATION HANDBOOK), December 2002, p. 69, accessed at www.ffiec.gov/ffiecinfobase/booklets/information_security/information_security.pdf.

10. Bace, Rebecca, and Mell, Peter, *Intrusion Detection Systems*, NIST Special Publication, p. 41.

11. Id., p. 42.

(iii) *Penetration attacks*—in which the attacker seeks to gain control of a system through "unauthorized acquisition and/or alteration of system privileges, resources or data."[12]

Some organizations who do have intrusion detection defenses fail to keep them up to date, while others ignore the seemingly endless parade of alarms they generate thinking they are "false alarms."[13] Fewer still have any reconnaissance detection systems. Yet since most intrusions from the Internet start with reconnaissance and reconnoitering of the targeted computer system, a company's defense systems either need to be extended to detecting such early warning signs, or the company should cease leaving its data warehouse linked to the unguarded portals of cyberspace.

Boards of Directors increasingly recognize the importance of information security. As European commentators have observed:

"For corporate boards, the existence of a crisis management plan and a data back-up system is no longer sufficient. Recent years have seen a dramatic increase in board-level recognition of the importance of corporate security policies in securing both physical and intellectual assets—and ultimately safeguarding shareholder value. According to the Institute of Chartered Accountants in England & Wales and The Risk Advisory Group, more than half of all com-

---

12. Id., p. 43. Other types of attacks, noted by the GAO, include: *distributed denial of service* (characterized by its use of a coordinated attack from a distributed system of computers rather than a single source and its use of worm to disperse the attack), *exploit tools* (used to determine vulnerabilities and gain unauthorized entry into systems), *logic bombs* (in which a programmer sabotages a system by inserting code to cause a program to perform a destructive action upon occurrence of a triggering event), *sniffer* (a program that intercepts packets of data en route and examines them for sensitive information they transmit, such as passwords), *Trojan horse* (a computer program that conceals embedded harmful code), and, of course, *worms* (programs that reproduce by copying themselves from one system to another across a network and, unlike a computer virus, do not require human intervention to promote or continue their propagation). GAO, *Technology Assessment: Cybersecurity for Critical Infrastructure Protection*, GAO-04-321, May 2004, p. 29.

13. The GAO in May of 2004 noted that an intrusion detection system has limitations that include being "prone to false positives and false negatives." GAO, *Technology Assessment: Cybersecurity for Critical Infrastructure Protection*, GAO-04-321, May 2004, p. 46.

panies now report that they review [information security] risks every board meeting or once a quarter."[14]

Given such developments, the paradox of information security is that the compelling desire to achieve it co-exists with an equally compelling desire to enjoy its achievement without further investment of funds or vigilance.

It's well known that orderly systems tend towards disorder and chaos.[15] Security and security systems abide by a similar law. Stated simply: *Security lapses.*[16] If this premise is used as a starting and end point, one cannot view information security as a one-time investment, nor as a structure that needs no improvement as the operative risks and parameters change. Having become sensitive to the potential for such lapses, Agile must now try to determine where they are most likely to occur in its operations, and must institute procedures to remediate the problem (if not to prevent it) and to increase the chances of early detection. Such detection increases the chances of containing it before significant damage is done to valuable information assets.

If an information security system overlooks the simple ways that security lapses, it is designed from its inception with critical vulnerabilities that can ultimately be exploited, particularly when the information has utility and value (as can be assumed, if a company has taken the time to collect, assemble and enhance it). Moreover, such vulnerabilities propagate rapidly. Security lapses tend to exist at all levels of an organization. Senior officers often have sensitive data on a PDA (personal digital assistant) in their pocket, on the hard drive of a laptop, and on a keychain drive in a brief case, each a much less secure form of storage. On repeated occasions, the head of the Central Intelligence Agency took home on a laptop copious quantities of data classified as "top secret," in violation of the agency's security protocols, demonstrating the very real risk that even the most security conscious personnel can have an artificial and unrealistic sense of the security of portable data.

---

14. Murray, Sarah, *Facing a New World of Risk,* FINANCIAL TIMES, special supplement titled "Understanding Corporate Security," July 14, 2004, p. 3.

15. Second law of thermodynamics.

16. As commentators have observed: "Any organization's security level is not static; it slowly degrades over time as hardware, software, people, and threats change." White, Greg, and Conklin, Art, *The Appropriate Use of Force-on-Force Cyberexercises,* IEEE SECURITY & PRIVACY, vol. 2, no. 4, July/August 2004, p. 33 at p. 37.

Security lapses tend to occur for reasons we are often reluctant to acknowledge, and that provide cover for such lapses. For example, it is insuperably hard for personnel to remain attentive to security for prolonged periods (or even for more than short intermittent intervals). Personnel often mistake an uneventful period for impregnability bestowed by the existing security system. They compound that mistake by assuming that security must be effective because no one is aware of any failure or breakdown. If an information security system is only as good as its most easily exploited vulnerability, the most ubiquitous weak point is the failure to discern when security lapses have occurred, when external threats appear in reconnaissance sweeps of a computer system linked to cyberspace, or when intrusions or leaks have taken place. Audits (that include testing) would reduce that risk, but good audits are not inexpensive. Moreover, companies generally dislike investments in audits, underfund them and do so, in part, because a "good audit" is viewed as one that finds no problem, that reports good news. After a few "good news" reports, the need for further investment in audits is questioned, and the audits become less frequent or less rigorous and eventually cease. A comparable tendency occurs in testing, even in what is referred to as "red teaming" (the engagement of a team to conduct attack exercises against a company to assess the quality of its security and make appropriate improvements):

> "All too often, red teaming devolves into a feel-good exercise in which simple security problems are discovered (the so-called low-hanging fruit) and fixed; improved security is then declared even though only the most rudimentary testing has taken place. This kind of red teaming (almost undeserving of the name) is not helpful."[17]

The problem stems not only from inadequate deployment of intrusion detection systems, but the all-too-human tendency to think that if one knows of no problem, then none must exist. As a Canadian security specialist noted, if users have not been adequately trained to recognize security risks "they will still leave sticky notes under the mouse [containing passwords and IDs] . . ."[18] or, as other commentators observed,

---

17. Arce, Iván, and McGraw, Gary, *Why Attacking Systems Is a Good Idea*, IEEE Security & Privacy, vol. 2, no. 4, July/August 2004, p. 17 at p. 18.

18. Wheelwright, Geof, *Sharing the Load across the Network*, Financial Times, special supplement titled "Understanding Corporate Security," July 14, 2004, p. 12, quoting Canadian Imperial Bank of Commerce security specialist Debbie Gerace.

employees will fail to "question a phone call from someone claiming to work in the IT [information technology] support department asking for user names and passwords," and thereby disclose information that compromises system security.[19] Audits of information security should be designed to find security vulnerabilities and lapses in established policies and procedures before such vulnerabilities are exploited. The more impregnable the security system appears, the more critical it is to probe it for hidden vulnerabilities in its structure and in the ways personnel use (and misuse) it.[20] Moreover, learning the profile of new types of attacks should be a high priority, because "the only way to properly defend a system against attack is to understand what attacks look like as deeply and realistically as possible."[21]

Often the most overlooked weak points in a security system (and therefore some of its most exploitable vulnerabilities) exist where the elaborate precautions are presumed to be self-enforcing mechanisms. Information security procedures are tedious and repetitive, and more often "honored in the breach." Human inattentiveness undermines the electronic precautions that, if rigorously observed, would catch many potential lapses. What remains are security precautions whose effectiveness tends to be exaggerated or rendered ineffective by human oversight or error. For example, a company invests in encryption to secure files it stores on its computers' hard drives and disks. Personnel reason that encrypted information is indecipherable to intruders and unauthorized users, so there is less need to follow more burdensome precautions, like locking doors or not leaving computers on and linked to the Internet overnight or limiting access to truly authorized personnel (which fails the moment one employee or officer asks someone else to do a task for him on a computer and "lends" his password or security

19. Murray, Sarah, *Facing a New World of Risk*, FINANCIAL TIMES, special supplement titled "Understanding Corporate Security," July 14, 2004, p. 3.

20. Our observations apply even to seemingly "watertight" security systems such as those adopted by global companies that confidently rely on public key encryption and issuance to each user of a unique digital certificate to provide "strong authentication for network access, and when needed, application access" and the ability to protect (through encryption) sensitive business information, especially when doing business via the Internet." Guida, Richard; Stahl, Robert; Bunt, Thomas; Secrest, Gary; and Moorcones, Joseph; *Deploying and Using Public Key Technology: Lessons Learned in Real Life*, IEEE SECURITY & PRIVACY, vol. 2, no. 4, July/August 2004, p. 67.

21. Arce, Iván, and McGraw, Gary, *Why Attacking Systems Is a Good Idea*, IEEE SECURITY & PRIVACY, vol. 2, no. 4, July/August 2004, p. 17.

number to permit the necessary access). Unfortunately, adoption of a safeguard tends to obscure the hazards unique to it, because the people who have promoted its adoption often do not want to reveal its hazards or may not be aware of or fully understand them.

Remarkably, amidst the post-9/11 concerns for security against terrorist risks, internal information security at the Los Alamos National Laboratory (a nuclear weapons facility operated by the University of California) appears to have become lax or to have broken down completely. In July 2004, Department of Energy ("DoE") officials are investigating the following lapses, each symptomatic of a serious discrepancy between security imperatives and conduct by the Laboratory personnel:

- Two computer disks containing sensitive weapons information were missing;
- 19 electronic storage devices with classified data were missing;
- Secret information was repeatedly transmitted over an unclassified e-mail system; and,
- Lab employees engaged in "widespread disregard of security procedures."[22]

As a consequence, the DoE halted all work at the Laboratory (except work critical to national security), and such problems contributed to DoE's decision to "put up for bid all lab management contracts that have been held uncontested for more than 50 years" by the University of California (including Los Alamos, Lawrence Livermore and Berkeley National Labs).[23]

There are hidden risks in the most sophisticated information security systems. For example, if the company stores its valuable data on unencrypted disks, and an intruder or electronic malfunction corrupts the data, there are often means of recovering the data. However, if the company stores its data on encrypted disks, subsequent corruption makes the encrypted data utterly useless; it cannot be recovered. "Thus, while data stored on an encrypted disk is more secure, it is also at greater

---

22. Vartabedian, Ralph, *Classified E-Mail Left Nuclear Lab*, LOS ANGELES TIMES, July 19, 2004, p. A-1.

23. Proctor, Charles, and Su, Nancy, *Los Alamos Lab Work Halted*, DAILY BRUIN, July 19, 2004, pp. 1 and 4.

risk of loss."[24] Moreover, since encryption tends to make the daily use of data much more cumbersome, security lapses may occur merely in personnel failing to open and close a file properly.

Similarly, a Chief Information Officer might assume, without checking, that a proposal to store data in higher capacity media (if cost effective) would warrant approval. The choice between preserving data on CD-ROMs and DVDs would thus seem to come down to a preference for higher capacity, provided the company has devices that can read the storage media. But as museum conservators know, long term storage assumes that years later the object will not have deteriorated due to a failure to consider the stresses imposed by the environment and the storage container. Few companies consider whether their storage media will be "unreadable" by electronic means after several years. Information security requires close attention to such issues. The choice of a storage medium is not merely between media that differ in capacity; it is also a choice between media that differ in fragility (or preservability). The higher capacity DVD (despite error checking and correcting mechanisms in the recording devices) contain smaller bits of data than are stored on CD-ROMs. Smaller bits of data are more vulnerable: tiny scratches, dirt and debris more easily obscure or ruin the disc's surface, making it impossible for them to be read. Books and documents do not suddenly change from text rich to empty blank surfaces. They can take a remarkable amount of abuse from those who use them, and from poor storage techniques. DVD tolerate little abuse. Personnel used to grabbing disks and thoughtlessly entering them into a device-tray will find later that data they thought they could access is suddenly unreadable. Other factors that can make information stored on DVD's inaccessible—and that deserve to be part of the information security calculus—include:

- Gravity can deform DVDs stored in jewel cases that only support the disc at the hub (the edges tend to sag), and once deformed they unbalance a high-speed DVD drive;
- Unduly stiff supports for DVDs in cases can require so much force to release the DVD that again, the requisite force to free them also deforms the disc;

---

24. Mosuch, Frank, and Hillson, Susan B., *Technical Security Measures*, in DATA SECURITY AND PRIVACY LAW, edited by Kevin P. Cronin and Ronald N. Weikers, 2003, at p. 3–22.

- Extreme temperatures, and rapid cycling of temperatures (which may be useful when performing burn-ins of hardware to identify infant mortality in such units) substantially shorten the readable-life of a DVD disc;
- Excessive humidity also shortens the life of the disc;
- Storing discs in paper sleeves tends to mar the disc surface with tiny scratches that can render data unreadable;
- Unlike a CD-ROM which is one unit of plastic, a DVD is made by bonding two polycarbonate discs together which can delaminate and are more easily damaged by bending and flexing;[25]
- Whereas prerecorded CDs and DVDs (of music or video) "have physical indentations—little pits—that represent digital bits of information," many writeable CDs and DVDs are instead "coated with a layer of dye, and a laser burns the requisite pattern of bits into it."[26] That dye, however, can fade with time, and some makers' disks fade faster than others, with no indication on the packaging or labels;
- Moreover, the faster the recording speed of the burner, the sooner the recorded data will be affected by decay of the storage media surface (a problem that can be mitigated by recording only on CDs coated with a virtuous metal such as gold that does not react with air, water, or light).[27]

Storage stresses must be part of any security analysis.[28] Prudent investment in information security should be proportional to the value

25. See Labriola, Don, *DVD Rot, or Not?* PC MAGAZINE, June 22, 2004, pp. 76–77.

26. Gomes, Lee, *Beware the Fading Dye: Writeable CDs, DVDs Vary a Lot in Quality,* THE WALL STREET JOURNAL, June 21, 2004, p. B-1.

27. Id. Reportedly some of the problem can be diminished by slower recording speeds and using media that are coated with a thin layer of a metal that does not react with air or water, such as gold (but not silver). For comprehensive discussion of storage issues related to CDs and DVDs, see Byers, Fred R., *Care and Handling of CDs* and *DVDs—A Guide for Librarians and Archivists,* NIST Special Publication 500-252, October 2003, accessed at www.iti.nist.gov/div895/carefordisc/CDandDVDCareandHandling Guide.pdf

28. The point to be emphasized is that each media has its storage issues, and those need to be evaluated before committing a firm's trove of sensitive data to long-term storage that may prove, years later, to have been a compromise of the information's security by exposing it to storage and environmental stresses. Such evaluation should also consider adoption of preservation systems that can absorb or "scavenge" oxygen, reduce humidity, and diminish the effects of acids and other corrosive substances. Such systems (such as Mitsubishi Gas Chemical Company's "RP System") are increasingly used to protect foods, certain sensitive military components, artifacts in museums, and may well be adaptable for protecting digital media and the data recorded on their

of the asset that needs protection. The more sensitive and valuable the data (and the more the company's reputation depends on its protection), the higher should be the level of security precautions adopted to protect it (including the auditing and routine improvements to those precautions). In short, **protect most what matters most**. Agile's partners support investments in information security, in part, because anything less trifles with national security, and in part, because they do not want to open the newspaper one morning and learn that due to a security lapse, Agile's information assets have been plundered or corrupted.

Unfortunately, few technologies guard against risks from insiders, the source of the highest risks. As reported in the 2002 CSI/FBI survey, 70 percent of successful attacks originate from inside the fortified network boundary.[29] As the GAO explains, "Insiders may not need a great deal of knowledge about computer intrusions because their knowledge of a victim system often allows them to gain unrestricted access to cause damage to the system or to steal system data. The insider threat also includes outsourcing vendors."[30] Such attacks succeed by exploiting the inherent weakness of computer security systems: their reliance on safeguards that work by allowing or denying extensions of trust. As explained by security commentators:

> "The issue is trust. Insiders must be trusted to do their jobs; applications must be trusted to perform their tasks. The problem occurs when insiders—be they users or applications—intentionally or unintentionally extend trust inappropriately. There is often a large gap between the rights we believe we are extending to another person, application, or component and the rights that are actually granted.
>
> A large part of the challenge of digital security is that there is little correspondence between typical real-world trust relationships and cyber-trust relationships. While the real world has numerous examples of partial trust, many [network] architectures rely on complete trust to function."[31]

---

metallic layers, particularly if such data has been recorded not for daily or monthly retrieval but instead for long-term storage for disaster recovery purposes or software escrows.

29. Thompson, Herbert H., and Ford, Richard, *The Insider, Naivety, and Hostility: Security Perfect Storm?*, ACM QUEUE, vol. 2, no. 4, June 2004, p. 59.

30. GAO, *Technology Assessment: Cybersecurity for Critical Infrastructure Protection*, GAO-04-321, May 2004, p. 24.

31. Id., pp. 60 and 62.

For example, when company personnel receive a draft agreement attached to an e-mail they can only read it by extending trust to that attached file, a trust that opening it will not infect or otherwise damage their computer system and its stored data. They cannot exercise mitigated or partial trust to reduce that risk. Scanning files with anti-virus software, for example, does not apply mitigated trust, because such scans will only detect known viruses and offer no protection against unfamiliar new viruses. Thus such software too works by an all-or-nothing trust: if an unfamiliar virus is not detected, the user proceeds to extend total trust, opens the file, and unleashes the virus in the system. Such software does not permit the user to extend partial trust to the file (to open it partially or have a glimpse at its contents). As a result, "User and administrator naivety contribute significantly to the insider threat. The all-or-nothing trust models that pervade both software and network architectures make it likely that a user will inadvertently extend privilege to a malicious user or application."[32]

Of the ten most common viruses reported in 2003, four (including the most common one) did not exploit vulnerabilities in system software but took advantage instead of a user whose actions extended misplaced absolute trust (*e.g.,* opening a file attached to an e-mail).[33] Training and reminders can reduce such errors, but they will inevitably recur due to security lapses. And the consequences for information security on a digital system tend to have extended ramifications, because the trust extended by one user often allows a malware access to an entire network whose architecture has no means of rescinding such trust before the damage is triggered. If the malware is a "sleeper" whose damage becomes apparent only at a later time when it is subsequently activated, the damage will only be discovered when programs start to operate aberrationally, and even then considerable time may pass before personnel realize that these are symptoms of a serious problem spreading through the network.

The Sponsoring Companies of information security architecture in connection with collaborative work on the JSF (an architecture dubbed the "DMZ design") discussed their security priorities in 2003 in *A Framework for Secure Collaboration Across US/UK Defense* ("Framework for Secure Collaboration").[34] These companies focused on indicia like

---

32. Id., p. 64.
33. Id.
34. The "Framework" is described as "a business-driven initiative to provide guide-

a company's track record (*e.g.,* lack of export violations) as the key indicator of what precautions should be in place.[35] They acknowledged that "within the universe of 'Sensitive' [classified] data . . . some data will require more protection than others"[36] and that, in a collaborative environment (in which several companies are working on the same defense project), the security policy structure is secure only to "the level of the weakest participant's policy."[37] For this reason, they sought to establish guidance on the minimum set of security mechanisms that a JSF contractor would need in order to have confidence that it would not violate export controls. They proposed three successively higher levels of assurance earned by security policies and mechanisms (dubbed "Bronze," "Silver" and "Gold"). But they also advocated that a contractor's track record (not national security concerns arising from the nature of the information handled) should determine the level of investment in security. They explained their reasoning:

> "The DMZ design does not associate levels of data sensitivity with the Bronze, Silver, and Gold assurance levels. Rather, it associates those assurance levels with the tolerance for risk that an organization is willing to accept (i.e. risk management). That tolerance may be a function of several variables: past performance, a growth strategy for new business offerings, or simply an assessment of good business practices. For instance, a company with a near perfect export control record that currently has set many of the enabling policies at the Bronze level of assurance may remain at that level without a need to make investments to reach the Silver assurance level."[38]

---

lines regarding policies, procedures, and mechanisms for the secure sharing of electronic information among international defense companies and their governments. Such guidelines will help facilitate the requirements for increasing collaboration and through life contractor logistic support in an increasingly regulated environment." *Background Information on the Program for Secure Collaboration across the Transatlantic Defense Community,* 2003, accessed at www.afei.org/news/Background_Info_SCE_Program.pdf. The Sponsoring Companies initially were Rolls-Royce, BAE Systems, General Dynamics, Lockheed Martin Corporation, and Raytheon Company. They were joined in phase 2 of the project by Airbus/EADS, The Boeing Company, CAE, Smiths Aerospace, and Westland Helicopters.

35. Sponsoring Companies, *A Framework for Secure Collaboration across US/UK Defense,* version 1.0, March 5, 2003, p. 37, accessed at www.afei.org/pdf/5mar2003_Final_Design.pdf.

36. Id.

37. Id., p. 36.

38. Id., p. 37.

Agile's counsel are skeptical of this approach, because it reflects business advantages possessed only by the largest defense contractors, treats quite imperfect records of compliance by such companies as if they were flawless, and encourages companies to defer investing in improved information security until a failure (and potential compromise of national security) makes such investment compelling.

It is remarkable that the Sponsoring Companies of the Framework for Secure Collaboration received the tacit blessing of the U.S. DoD for that approach, because it is inconsistent **on its face** with the recent enforcement guidelines issued by Treasury for the TSR, by the BIS for the EAR, and by the Sentencing Commission for the U.S. Sentencing Guidelines. Allowing information security to be dictated by a firm's "tolerance of risk" assumes that the only party at risk for a failure in information security is the company that possesses the sensitive information. That approach might have appeal in the U.S. commercial realm where companies' self-interest can be presumed to motivate adequate compliance. But it is highly flawed when the true "beneficiary" of the protections is a third party (or third parties) who has little or no ability to control the day-to-day handling of its data (and interests). The third-party beneficiary model is evident in the EU and Canada protocols for handling personal data. Those personal data protection laws and regulations would not condone the "risk tolerance" approach of the Framework for Secure Collaboration, because such laws are designed to protect the privacy of the individual identifiable by such information.

It would be too easy to conceal otherwise actionable negligence or misconduct under the rubric of a high tolerance for risk, in the absence of laws designed to discipline (with the threat of debarment from lucrative business) those firms whose rhetoric of risk tolerance amounts to little more than a pretext for the injudicious, careless or even reckless mishandling of private information. Moreover, the approach is antithetical to the purposes of the ITAR and the EAR, which is to avert the risk of diversion of sensitive technologies into the hands of persons and countries that seek to harm U.S. persons, interests and national security. Here the "third party" is national security. In this context, the "tolerance for risk" to those interests would argue compellingly for a "zero tolerance" policy when determining the level of information security (particularly in light of the unique vulnerability of digital information). We should not wait until highly sensitive data has been released illegally or corrupted before management is expected to invest in a high level of information security.

Although protection of national security should motivate the investment in information security, the Sponsoring Companies argue for a modified self-interest test—what drives each company's security policy should be its aversion to penalties:

> "If a company has had a series of violations or incidents in recent history, then there may be a business imperative for further investment to avoid fines, imprisonment, the revocation of export licenses, a denial of export privileges, and exclusion from practice in the defense industry (i.e. debarment) . . . The DMZ design is built around the fundamental assumption that business imperatives determine the exposure to risk a company will tolerate."[39]

The difficulty with this reasoning is that most economic enterprises see their "benefit" in temporal terms: a long-term, ill-defined and not easily quantified goal, like the protection of national interest is weighed against the short-term, highly-visible "hit" to the bottom line of upgrading information security. In these economic analyses, the longer-term, less quantifiable goals always lose to the dollars and cents on paper. The "risk-tolerance" position is akin to saying "**if we can tolerate the risk, the nation can too**." Because a number of the Sponsoring Companies are among the few remaining large prime defense contractors to survive the consolidations in the 1990's, the U.S. Government may fine them, but it cannot afford to deny itself their services. It is only the second and third tier defense contractors who face the risks of a denial of export privileges or debarment, not the giants like Boeing, Lockheed-Martin or Raytheon. Such one-sided "inelasticity" makes any risk analysis highly suspect and hardly impartial. A more likely motivation for the largest, publicly owned defense contractors would be to the threat of damage to reputation and the accompanying drop in stock price. Privately owned Agile, however, cannot afford to be viewed as a security risk when pursuing JSF contracts. Moreover, the longer an organization postpones implementing appropriate security measures, the more costly it will be finally to deploy them, because so many features of the company's security will need to be reviewed and revised accordingly.

We should note in passing that enactment of certain U.S. laws imposes information security duties on certain companies in particular sectors (none of which happen to be Agile's). Each contributes to the evolving maze of information security regulation. Within that maze,

---

39. Id.

companies increasingly find themselves at risk of being potentially held liability for failures of their security precautions to meet one or more disparate legislated standards (or for failure to meet a standard that may subsequently be "implied" by a court of law from the language or context of a private contract that includes significant commitments for information security).[40] For example:

- Agile is not a "financial institution" (a category which includes a broadly defined group of non-bank entities), and it does not come within the scope of the *Gramm-Leach-Bliley Financial Services Modernization Act of 1999*,[41] and thus is not subject to the Federal Trade Commission promulgated Safeguards Rule,[42] effective May

---

40. Thomas Smedinghoff keenly observes: "Three legal trends are rapidly shaping the information security landscape for most companies. They are:

- "an increasing recognition that providing information security is a corporate legal obligation;
- "the emergence of a legal standard against which compliance with that obligation will be measured; and
- "a new emphasis on a duty to disclose breaches of information security.

While the law is still developing, and is often applied only in selective areas, these three trends are posing significant new challenges for most businesses." Smedinghoff, Thomas J., *Security & Surveillance: Trends in the Law of Information Security*, BNA INTERNATIONAL WORLD DATA REPORT, vol. 4, no. 8, August 2004, p. 1.

As commentators have noted, to the extent that statutory information security obligations, such as contained in the Health Insurance Portability and Accountability Act or Gramm-Leach-Bliely Act, are "clearly applicable to the activities covered by a contract, a court could imply a private contractual requirement to comply with these obligations. Such implied contractual obligations could substantially lessen the comfort that companies might otherwise draw from the fact that these statutes do not provide a private right of action." Baker, Stewart, and Shenk, Maury, *A Patch in Time Saves Nine: Liability Risks for Unpatched Software*, October 2003, accessed at www.steptoe.com/publications/274a.pdf.

41. 15 U.S.C. §§ 6801-6810, 6821-6827. Not being a "financial institution" also spares Agile the burden of complying with numerous other information security regulations in that industry: "In fact, in the financial industry alone there are over 200 laws, regulations, and government bulletins, alerts, and other guidance documents addressing the information security obligations of financial institutions." Smedinghoff, Thomas J., *Security & Surveillance: Trends in the Law of Information Security*, BNA INTERNATIONAL WORLD DATA REPORT, vol. 4, no. 8, August 2004, p. 2. A list of those laws, regulations and other documents is accessible at www.ffiec.gov/ffiecinfobase/resources/re_01.html.

42. 67 FEDERAL REGISTER 36493, May 23, 2002, codified at 16 CFR Part 314, ac-

23, 2003, with its requirement that each covered institution establish a comprehensive security program to ensure that customer
information receives sufficient security and confidentiality.

---

cessed at www.ftc.gov/os/2002/05/67fr36585.pdf. Although the FTC designed the Security Rule to be a flexible standard, the Rule requires that the information security
plan ("ISP") for each "financial institution" include among its safeguards certain elements, which in all probability will come to be viewed as a minimum best practice
standard for ISPs, not only of "financial institutions" but for other companies that
gather, process, store, or transmit sensitive information or data over which they must
maintain tight control. Those minimum safeguards include:

- designate one or more employees to coordinate the ISP;
- identify reasonably foreseeable internal and external risks to the security, confidentiality, and integrity of customer information that could result in the unauthorized disclosure, misuse, alternation, destruction, or other compromise of such
  information, and assess the sufficiency of any safeguards in place to control these
  risks;
- ensure that such risk assessment includes consideration of risks in each relevant
  area of operations, including—(1) employee training and management; (2) information systems (including network and software design, information processing, storage, transmission, and disposal); and (3) detecting, preventing, and
  responding to attacks, intrusions, or other systems failures;
- design and implement information safeguards to control the identified risks and
  regularly test or otherwise monitor the effectiveness of the safeguards' key controls, systems, and procedures; and
- evaluate and adjust the ISP in light of the results of such testing and monitoring,
  any material changes to operations or business arrangements, or any other circumstances that the institution knows or has reason to know may have a material
  impact on its ISP.

See 16 CFR §314.4.

Agile will also not be subject to (but should find instructive for its information
security planning) the proposed *Interagency Guidance on Response Programs for Unauthorized Access to Customer Information and Customer Notice* issued by the Office of the
Comptroller of the Currency, Office of Thrift Supervision, Board of Governors of the
Federal Reserve System and the Federal Deposit Insurance Corporation. See 69 *Federal
Register* No. 155 at p. 47954, August 12, 2003, accessed at www.mortgagebankers.org/
industry/docs/03/68fr47954.pdf. The proposed Guidance provides the interpretation by
those agencies of Section 501(b) of the Gramm-Leach-Bliley Act, and describes their
expectations that each financial institution "develop a response program to protect
against and address reasonably foreseeable risks associated with internal and external
threats to the security of customer information maintained by the financial institution
or its service provider." 68 *Federal Register* at p. 47955. The Guidance notes that "A
response program should be a key part of an institution's information security program.
Having such a program in place will allow the institution to quickly respond to incidents

- Agile is not a health care provider or other covered entity, and does not come within the scope of the *Health Insurance Portability and Accountability Act* ("HIPAA").[43] It is, therefore, is not subject to HIPAA's detailed Security Rule.[44] That rule requires the covered entities to protect the confidentiality and integrity of certain kinds of health information by limiting access to computers containing sensitive information, and by deploying encryption technology and audit trail procedures. The HIPAA Security Rule is useful, however, because it provides a concise checklist of issues that can be adapted to other systems containing sensitive information. To the extent that Agile can demonstrate that its security compares favorably with the requirements of the HIPAA Security Rule, it will have at least one formal benchmark to present to its partners, when they review Agile's budget for information security improvements in connection with its acquisition of Troll.

- Agile is not a public company; it does not come within the scope of the *Sarbanes-Oxley Act of 2002* ("SARBOX"), and thus its partners do not face the risk of shareholder suits under SARBOX. Some commentators suggest that shareholders "could arguably complain [under SARBOX] of a breach of fiduciary duty in circumstances in which company officials knew (or perhaps should have known) of a security vulnerability but failed to address it adequately with the result that confidential data were lost."[45] Other commentators have noted that when the Securities and Exchange Commission

---

involving the unauthorized access to or use of customer information in its own customer information systems that could result in substantial harm or inconvenience to a customer." 68 *Federal Register* at p. 47959. Agile will need to anticipate the emerging trend this foreshadows, namely of a duty to warn third parties when a breach of security may cause damage to their confidential data or other information—a duty that may also extend to Agile's service providers (and thus should be addressed in its contracts with such providers).

43. Pub. L. No. 104-191 (1996), codified in sections of 42 U.S.C.

44. See 45 CFR Parts 160, 162, and 164, 68 FEDERAL REGISTER 34 at pp. 8334–8381, February 20, 2003. Effective date, April 21, 2003. Covered entities, with the exception of small health plans, must comply with the Security Rule by April 21, 2005; small health plans must comply with the Security Rule by April 21, 2006.

45. Raul, Alan Charles; McNicholas, Edward R., and Dwyer, Julie, *Information Security: An Overview of Legal Considerations on Securing Data in Cyberspace*, CIPERATI (a cyberspace and IP law newsletter), vol. 1, issue 1, April 2004,

("SEC") issued rules to implement Section 404 of SARBOX, those rules defined "internal control over financial reporting" to include:

"Those policies and procedures that . . . (3) Provide reasonable assurance regarding prevention or timely detection of unauthorized acquisition, use or disposition of the registrant's assets that could have a material effect on the financial statements."[46]

They suggest that the SEC could interpret the "reasonable assurance" obligation to extend to controls on information security, at least with respect to companies that suffer a material adverse effect on their business as the result of an information security breach.[47]

- Agile is not a California company, and to date, has not done any business in California. It therefore does not come within the scope of the California Security Breach Information Act, which went into effect on July 1, 2003.[48] That Act imposes a duty on California companies and companies doing business in California (and that own or use computer data that includes personal information of their customers) to report to such customers any security breach that compromises certain of their personal information (*e.g.*, social security number, license plate number, etc.).[49]

---

46. *Management's Report on Internal Control over Financial Reporting and Certification of Disclosure in Exchange Act Periodic Reports*, 68 FEDERAL REGISTER 36,636, 36,640 (June 18, 2003). As other commentators observe, "Sarbanes-Oxley Act requires senior management of public companies to attest to the internal controls and integrity of their financial information. Its provisions regarding data retention and document alteration and destruction also impact security programs. Beyond specific legal requirements, a corporation's officers and directors have a fiduciary duty to the corporation and shareholders to use reasonable care to protect the corporate digital assets and to manage risks and potential liabilities that can flow from security breaches. This includes compliance with contracts, non-disclosure agreements, collaborative arrangements, and shared network usage agreements (such as between manufacturer and distributor). Where corporate officers and directors are sufficiently negligent, they may be subject to derivative shareholder suits." Westby, Jody R., INTERNATIONAL GUIDE TO CYBER SECURITY, American Bar Association, Privacy & Computer Crime Committee, Section of Science & Technology Law, 2004, pp. 24–25.

47. See Baker, Stewart, and Shenk, Maury, *A Patch In Time Saves Nine: Liability Risks for Unpatched Software*, October 2003, accessed at www.steptoe.com/publications/274a.pdf.

48. Cal. Civ. Code § 1798.82, accessed at www.leginfo.ca.gov/calaw.html.

49. Agile also would not come within the scope of an act passed by California's legislature (and currently awaiting signature by the state's governor), A.B. 1950, which requires a business that owns or licenses personal information about a California resi-

- Agile uses its website (at www.agilewing.com) for procurement of supplies, advertising its product lines and making information available to investors, but does not use the site to buy or sell to consumers, does not collect personally identifiable information from consumers and thus does not collect any such information from California residents.

   As a result, it does not come within the broad scope of the California Online Privacy Protection Act of 2003, effective from July 1, 2004 ("OPPA"). OPPA applies to operators of a website or online service, who use such site or service for "commercial pur-

---

dent "to implement and maintain reasonable security procedures and practices appropriate to the nature of the information, to protect the personal information from unauthorized access, destruction, use, modification, or disclosure," and, if such business discloses personal information about a California resident to a "nonaffiliated third party" to require by contract that such entity "maintain reasonable security procedures and practices appropriate to the nature of the information, to protect the personal information from unauthorized access, destruction, use, modification, or disclosure." California Assembly Bill, No. 1950 (to be added to Section 1798.81.5 of the California Civil Code) accessed at www.steptoe.com/publications/316f.pdf. The legislation defines "personal information" to mean (when not encrypted or redacted) an individual's "first name or first initial and his or her last name" in combination with social security number or driver's license number or California identification card number or credit card information (such as the account number, card number in combination with any required security code, etc.).

The legislation would not apply to "covered entities" subject to HIPAA, or to any business "that is regulated by state or federal law providing greater protection to personal information than that provided" by this legislation, provided such business is in compliance with such laws (*i.e.,* if in compliance with such other laws, the business is deemed to be in compliance with this California legislation). The difficulty facing companies seeking to ensure their compliance with A.B. 1950 is that the legislation provides no definition or metric to guide companies seeking to determine what level of security protections are "appropriate to the nature of the information." Such a provision would appear to require increasingly stringent safeguards for increasingly sensitive information, but if a breach occurred, such a determination might be closely scrutinized by California enforcement officials.

Agile would also not come within the scope of the recently enacted S.B. 1506 (which has been signed by the state's governor), which makes it a criminal violation for anyone who: "knowingly electronically disseminates all or substantially all of that commercial recording or audiovisual work to more than 10 other people without disclosing his or her e-mail address, and the title of the recording or audiovisual work is punishable by a fine not exceeding two thousand five hundred dollars ($2,500), imprisonment in a county jail for a period not exceeding one year, or by both that fine and imprisonment." California S.B. 1506, accessed at http://info.sen.ca.gov/pub/bill/sen/sb_1501-1550/ sb_1506_bill_20040921_chaptered.html.

poses," and who collect personally identifiable information "through the Internet from individual consumers residing in California who use or visit the commercial website or online service."[50] Since the Act defines such information to include information typically required to conclude an online transaction (name, address, e-mail address, phone number, social security number),[51] website operators who transact with consumers residing in California (regardless of where the website is hosted or where the operator is headquartered) must comply with the Act's requirements, including: "conspicuously" posting a privacy policy on its website;[52] explaining the categories of personally identifiable information that the site collects from consumers; identifying the third parties with whom such information may be disclosed to or shared; and describing the process by which consumers can review and request changes to the information collected about them, the effective date of the policy, and the process by which the operator will notify consumers of material changes to that policy.[53]

It is this last requirement that will probably require the closest attention to avert violations of the Act. Inherent in it is a requirement that the website operator ensure that its privacy policy and its actual practices (in the collection and use of personally identifiable information) remain congruent. This will require at a minimum that staff members do not adopt practices that deviate from the posted privacy policy, that counsel be alerted when practices need to be changed so that the privacy policy can be amended, *and* that timely notification of such amendments be issued or

---

50. California Business & Professions Code, §22575(a). However, Agile will need to consider whether its risk management needs to address the information security required to make electronic signatures enforceable: "[U]nder some laws, electronic signatures are enforceable in certain cases only if appropriate security is used. . . . [L]aws in the United States, such as the Uniform Electronic Transactions Act (enacted in 46 states), and Uniform Commercial Code Article 4A (enacted in all states), recognize the role of information security as a basis for allocating risk of loss and liability." Smedinghoff, Thomas J., *Security & Surveillance: Trends in the Law of Information Security*, BNA INTERNATIONAL WORLD DATA REPORT, vol. 4, no. 8, August 2004, p. 2.

51. California Business & Professions Code, §22577(a). Note that the Act defines "personally identifiable information" to mean such information collected online by the operator "from that individual and maintained by the operator in an accessible form . . . ."

52. California Business & Professions Code § 22575(a).

53. California Business & Professions Code § 22575(b).

distributed *before* implementing the new practices. Maintaining privacy practices in congruence with posted privacy policies is remarkably difficult in companies that need (for sound business reasons) to adjust their business practices rapidly, and on an on-going basis, in order to capitalize on emerging opportunities. For example, in the *Tower* case (discussed in Section 1.9 above and in more detail later in this chapter), the errant revision of software caused the violative discrepancy between policy and practice.

Hence it is imperative that the personnel responsible for changing practices confer promptly with counsel to review the potential for such discrepancies and to avert the costs, disruptions and distractions that result from violations. The Act provides no explicit remedies (but can be used as the basis for a civil suit), and (fortunately for firms) it provides violators with a 30-day window in which to come into compliance after being notified of non-compliance.[54] The latter safeguard is only helpful, however, if a firm is careful to apprise its personnel of the significance of such notices, and quickly routes all such notices to an officer with the authority to cure the non-compliance. Moreover, personnel should be aware that the Act is quite precise and specific concerning the standards for a "conspicuously" posted privacy policy (*e.g.,* the policy must appear on the site's home page or "first significant page after entering the website" or be accessible from such location by an icon hyperlink provided the icon contains the word "privacy" and the icon uses "a color that contrasts with the background color of the web page . . .").[55]

Agile's General Counsel has learned from his enhanced diligence that the acquisition of Troll imposes the obligation to ensure that Agile's information security measures up to certain other statutory standards.[56]

---

54. California Business & Professions Code § 22575(a). Note that to violate the Act, an operator must be in non-compliance with its requirements "knowingly and willfully" or "negligently and materially." See § 22576.

55. California Business & Professions Code § 22577(b).

56. However, to the extent that Agile's interest in Troll includes acquiring ownership of trade secrets that Troll might posses, Agile might find it prudent to extend its diligence into a check of Troll's measures to protect its trade secrets, since if those have not been sufficient the information may not qualify as a trade secret under U.S. law.

Moreover, as one commentator recently observed, "[R]ather than telling companies what specific security measures they must implement, developing law requires companies to engage in an ongoing and repetitive process that is designed to assess risks,

Agile conducts a risk assessment of its information security annually, performs audit tests of its information security (probing for vulnerabilities, lapses, etc.) and updates its information security plan based on the findings of such risk assessments and audits.[57]

---

identify and implement appropriate security measures responsive to those risks, verify that they are effectively implemented, and ensure that they are continually updated in response to new developments. . . . Key to the new legal standard is a requirement that security be responsive to a company's fact-specific risk assessment. . . . They must be responsive to the particular threats a business faces, and must address its vulnerabilities. . . . [F]irewalls and intrusion detection software are often effective ways to stop hackers, but if a company's major vulnerability is careless (or malicious) employees who inadvertently (or intentionally) disclose passwords, then even those sophisticated security measures, while important, will not adequately address the problem." Smedinghoff, Thomas J., *Security & Surveillance: Trends in the Law of Information Security*, BNA INTERNATIONAL WORLD DATA REPORT, vol. 4, no. 8, August 2004, p. 3.

57. Note that testing that should be a routine part of such audits is not a "one-size-fits-all" activity and must be calibrated to reflect the skill, expertise, and experience of a company's personnel. Otherwise, inexperienced or inexpert personnel will fail and learn little, and highly skilled personnel will not have their mettle (in a potential crisis) tested and their hidden vulnerabilities discovered. As commentators have observed: "If the organization under test has not sufficiently grown in its security development, a technical penetration test—especially a red teaming event—always results in the red team successfully penetrating the site and won't lead to any significant improvements. An organization must crawl before it can run. . . . [L]ook at the annual computer defense exercise event conducted between the [U.S. military's] service academies and selected invitees. This training event has evolved over the years, increasing in difficulty as students have increased their ability to defend the network. This matching of exercise level to defender capability is a key factor in successfully deploying this type of event." White, Greg, and Conklin, Art, *The Appropriate Use of Force-on-Force Cyberexercises*, IEEE SECURITY & PRIVACY, vol. 2, no. 4, July/August 2004, p. 33 at p. 35.

For additional guidance on audits of information security, the Corporate Governance Task Force Report includes among its recommendations that, where practical, "each independent organizational unit [of a company] should perform a regular evaluation to validate the effectiveness of its information security program." Corporate Governance Task Force Report, *Information Security Governance: A Call To Action*, April 2004, p. 16, accessed at www.google.com/search?q = %22corporate + governance + task + force + report%22&ie = UTF-8&oe = UTF-8. The report further recommends that the evaluation "be performed by an internal auditor or independent external auditor, and it should include:

- "Testing the effectiveness of information security policies, procedures, and practices of a representative subset of the organizational unit's information systems
- An assessment of compliance with the requirements of [the report] . . . and related information security policies, procedures, standards, and guidelines."

It has also identified risk points generated by the proposed trans-action in the course of its enhanced diligence. These offer a good start-ing point for evaluating the strength of the existing system and potential compliance issues. In addition, a spot audit might focus on the following:

- Is there a readily accessible record of known or suspected breaches of Agile's information security?

- Based on that record, or on procedures that address incident re-ports and responses to security breaches, what is the average time elapsed between vulnerability or weakness discovery and imple-mentation of corrective action?[58]

- Is there a readily accessible record of Agile's improvements in sys-tem security for the past two years that links the improvement

---

It also recommends that a senior executive summarize the results of such evalua-tions in a report to the board of directors or similar governance entity, and similarly, chief executive officers of companies should have an annual information security eval-uation conducted, review the evaluation results with appropriate staff, and submit a report of the evaluation to the board of directors. Corporate Governance Task Force Report, *Information Security Governance: A Call To Action*, April 2004, pp. 9 and 16–17, accessed at www.google.com/search?q = %22corporate + governance + task + force + report%22&ie = UTF-8&oe = UTF-8. This would also appear to be required by the reporting and certification provisions of SARBOX.

58. Agile's counsel derives these questions from NIST SP 800-55 *Security Metrics Guide for Information Technology System*, 2003, p. 45, accessed at http://csrc.nist.gov/publications/nistpubs/800-55/sp800-55.pdf. Note that any such list presumes that the company or organization has first conducted a comprehensive inventory of its digital systems and performed a risk management assessment of those systems. The difficulty, however, of laying that proper foundation has proved a significant challenge to com-panies and government agencies. For example, the DHS Inspector General concluded in September 2004 that DHS's own information security remained seriously deficient because, in part, it lacked "an accurate and complete system inventory" and those responsible for identifying required program and system information continue to lack a sufficient understanding of fundamental definitions of programs and systems. As a result, the DHS Inspector General noted that DHS needs to strengthen its agencywide information security procedures with respect to: "(1) wireless technologies according to NIST SP 800-48; (2) protecting critical infrastructures from cyber vulnerabilities and threats; (3) remote access to DHS' systems; (4) vulnerability scanning; (5) penetration testing; (6) incident detection, analysis, and reporting; (7) security configuration poli-cies and procedures; (8) specialized security training; and (9) IT security training costs." DHS Office of Inspector General, *Evaluation of DHS' Information Security Program for Fiscal Year 2004*, OIG-04-41, September 2004, p. 7, accessed at

with the reason for its implementation and identifies its cost? If so, what improvements did Agile find it necessary to implement—ranked in order of their cost?[59]

- Has an Agile audit tested the system security (a) to determine if the security improvement has introduced subsequent processing problems, and (b) to determine if the improvement rectified the problem that prompted it?[60]

- If Agile tests its system, what precautions does it take to control and limit the risks from such tests to data integrity, confidentiality and system availability (as well as to the sensitive information of the tests and test results)? As the Federal Financial Institutions Examination Council ("FFIEC") has cautioned:

"Because testing may uncover nonpublic customer information, appropriate safeguards to protect the information must be in place. Contracts with third parties to provide testing services should require that the third parties implement appropriate [security] measures . . . . Management is also responsible for ensuring that employee and contract personnel who perform the tests or have access to the test results have passed appropriate background checks, and that contract personnel are appropriately bonded. . . . **Since knowledge of test planning and results may**

---

59. Counsel does not assume that the more costly the improvement the more important it was to implement, but rather, the greater an improvement's cost the more justified it had to be in order to be included in the information security budget. Counsel wants to see what issues have drawn Agile's attention since such issues may need to be checked in the enhanced due diligence review. Counsel also recognizes that each cross-border acquisition does not trigger a need to do an information security review, but since this is Agile's first foray into a cross-border acquisition the need to do an initial review in this context is justified, and the added costs can be viewed as an investment in security provided for subsequent, similar transactions.

60. See NIST SP 800-55 *Security Metrics Guide for Information Technology System,* 2003, p. 49, accessed at http://csrc.nist.gov/publications/nistpubs/800-55/sp800-55.pdf. Note also that counsel may find it prudent to adopt safeguards set forth in the British standard BS7799, which provides guidelines for safeguarding an organization's information assets. BS7799 has two parts: a standard code of practice, providing default guidelines on types of security controls to safeguard an entity's assets, and a management standard specification for what is termed Information Security Management Systems. Information concerning BS7799 can be accessed at www.gammassl.co.uk/bs7799/works.html, www.thewindow.to/bs7799 and at www.ukas.com/information_centre/technical/technical_bs7799.asp.

facilitate a security breach, institutions should carefully limit the distribution of their testing information. . . . Management should also consider requiring contractors to sign nondisclosure agreements and to return to the institution information they obtained in their testing."[61]

- If Agile relies heavily on password protection has it recently checked such protection for three of the most common deficiencies in the use of passwords? (*i.e.,* (i) failure to disable or change default vendor accounts and passwords (thereby denying a malicious use access to administrative privileges), (ii) easily guessed passwords (such as names of relatives and integers that match birthdates), and (iii) "storage or transmission of user accounts and passwords with weak or no encryption."[62] Note that, as the GAO has reported, there is often a persuasive reason for the reluctance to use complex passwords or to adopt strong password practices, namely "their use could hinder a rapid response to safety procedures during an emergency. As a result, . . . weak passwords that are easy to guess, shared, or infrequently changed are reportedly common in control systems [of critical infrastructures]. Sometimes a default password or even no password at all is used.")[63]

- Has Agile checked each of its personnel, as well as each of its partners, to determine if they routinely (or occasionally) leave the premises with any portable devices and storage media—laptops, PDAs, flash memory units, etc.—and, if so, has Agile checked whether its information security procedures are consistently followed in taking such units off-premises? (*i.e.,* does sensitive data leave the premises on insecure devices despite policies that might prohibit or limit such conduct?)

- What percentage of persons who use such portable devices have access to Agile's sensitive information?[64]

---

61. FFIEC, Information Security (IT Examination Handbook), December 2002, p. 79, accessed at www.ffiec.gov/ffiecinfobase/booklets/information_secruity/information_security.pdf.

62. GAO, *Technology Assessment: Cybersecurity for Critical Infrastructure Protection,* GAO-04-321, May 2004, pp. 79–80.

63. Id., p. 78.

64. This question begs a more sensitive question that counsel can only hint at,

- What percentage of data transmission facilities in the organization have restricted access to authorized users?[65]
- What percentage of laptops and other portable devices have encryption capability for sensitive files?[66]
- What percentage of used media are reliably sanitized before reuse or disposal?[67]
- In view of record retention rules (required for example by the EAR, as noted below), what percentage of critical data files and operations have an established backup frequency?[68]
- For the same reason, what percentage of systems have a contingency (disaster/recovery) plan?[69]
- Are restrictions in place on who is permitted to perform maintenance and repair activities?[70]
- What percentage of systems generate audit trails that provide a trace of user actions?[71]
- If Agile is considering creating an interconnection between its computers and those overseas of Troll (and perhaps of Brugge and Ijsselmeer), has Agile prepared an interconnection security agreement between itself and an overseas entity? (Such agreement specifies the technical and security requirements for establishing, operating and maintaining the interconnection.)[72] For example, (a)

---

namely does Agile have any mechanism it uses, however informally, to monitor and detect when any such person may show signs of being under great strain or stress, may be unusually moody for a prolonged period, or may have been observed to have been seemingly "living beyond their means"? Since many information security risks originate internally, often with disgruntled personnel or persons unable to cope with some emotional or financial crisis, the more sensitive the information an organization possesses (especially for national security or company proprietary rights), the more there is a need for some system to alert staff to such problems. Agile's counsel knows of no formal security system guidance on this subject—and senses that such guidance tends to wish away such problems—but that is precisely why they cannot be ignored. There are, of course, serious privacy issues implicated by any effort to monitor morale among personnel. The issue is beyond the scope of this book but warrants attention.

65. See NIST SP 800-55 *Security Metrics Guide for Information Technology System*, 2003, p. 59, accessed at http://csrc.nist.gov/publications/nistpubs/800-55/sp800-55.pdf.

66. Id., p. 61.

67. Id., p. 64.

68. Id., p. 65.

69. Id., p. 67.

70. Id., p. 70.

71. Id., p. 96.

72. NIST SP 800-47 *Security Guide for Interconnecting Information Technology Sys-*

will firewalls be installed between the two company's intranets? and (b) how will the security incident response teams of the two companies be coordinated?[73]

- Does Agile have a person responsible for ensuring the prompt downloading of security patches, and if so, what is the average (and the longest) time Agile has taken during the past two years to download, check and install such patches on its computer systems (including those that are linked to its portable computers, such as laptops and PDAs)?[74]

- Does Agile have a regular plan for auditing the security stance of all its systems, to verify such things as current versions of software, current patch levels and system security settings set as defined by corporate security standards? (These are tasks that information technology staff routinely undertake.)

- Does Agile audit for mundane problems or routine systems mismanagement that can fail to contain a seemingly insignificant or non-major local problem (and that can propagate through an organization's network because personnel have not been trained to respond to prevent such events from triggering a virtual chain reaction)?

The GAO in May of 2004 emphasized that "it is important to recognize that up to the present, many of the most costly and disruptive cyber events have not been caused by malicious cyber attacks, but instead originated with mundane problems or routine systems mismanagement."[75] GAO cited, as evidence, the findings of the joint U.S.-Can-

---

tems, August 2002, pp. 3-5 through 3-6, accessed at http://csrc.nist.gov/publications/nistpubs/800-47/sp800-47.pdf.

73. The Federal Financial Institutions Examination Council (FFIEC) cautions that "[e]xcessive reliance on a single control could create a false sense of confidence. . . . Financial institutions should design multiple layers of security controls and testing to establish several lines of defense between the attacker and the asset being attacked. To successfully attack the data, each layer must be penetrated. With each penetration, the probability of detecting the attacker increases." FFIEC, INFORMATION SECURITY (IT EXAMINATION HANDBOOK), December 2002, p. 14, accessed at www.ffiec.gov/ffiecinfobase/booklets/information_security/information_security.pdf.

74. Agile's counsel adds a footnote to General Counsel to alert him to the increasing likelihood that companies might incur liability for failing to download and install security patches within a short period of time after the vendor makes them available on its website.

75. GAO, *Technology Assessment: Cybersecurity for Critical Infrastructure Protection*,

ada Power System Outage Task Force which investigated the causes of the August 14, 2003 blackout the damage from which was estimated at between $7 billion and $10 billion. The Task Force concluded that the outage resulted from a chain of mishaps, "starting with a malfunctioning monitoring and control system" deployed by power grid operators in Ohio and that could not cope with higher than normal demand for power which triggered not only a local blackout but, due to the interconnectedness of the power grid it spread to Canada, New York and elsewhere on the U.S. East Coast where remedial actions could not be taken because personnel could not understand what was happening. GAO summarized such evidence as pointing to what it called the "mundane cybersecurity threat" whose chief features it described as including:

- "Inadequate system monitoring and control tools;
- Unplanned growth of a large, complex, system with external interdependencies;
- A combination of seemingly unlikely external factors;
- Lack of a well-defined stakeholder responsible for overall robustness; and
- Operator confusion and mistakes."[76]

The GAO expressed concern that these "mundane cybersecurity threats" receive little attention yet are "emerging as a serious risk," because they place computer-operated systems into an entity's critical roles (as well as such roles for the nation's economy and military), that such systems "are growing through an unplanned, organic process of accretion, without any sort of global plan, and without a well-defined entity

---

GAO-04-321, May 2004, p. 34. In addition, the threats posed by disgruntled employees (especially during mergers and acquisitions) remains among the most severe threats to a company's information security. As recently reported, "The greatest security risk facing large companies and individual Internet users over the next 10 years will be the increasingly sophisticated use of social engineering to bypass IT security defenses, according to Gartner. In an announcement Sunday, the research company defined social engineering as 'the manipulation of people, rather than machines, to successfully breach the security systems of an enterprise or a consumer.' This involves criminals persuading a user to click on a link or open an attachment that they probably know they shouldn't." Kotadia, Munir, *Old Scams Pose the 'Greatest Security Risk,'* CNET News.com, November 1, 2004, accessed at http://news.com.com/2100-7349_3-5435199.html.

76. Id., p. 35.

with clear responsibility for security and reliability" and that such critically positioned systems are "intrinsically hard to analyze or monitor, so that even if the nation were to mandate that they be controlled, the science for doing so would often be lacking" and makes such systems "tomorrow's terrorist target."[77]

6.1 Risk of Liability for Breach of, or Deficiencies In, Information Security.

Counsel acknowledges that no firm can simply implement corrections to its system (patches) without first ensuring that they will not introduce new problems or create system conflicts that can bring down the firm's networked computers.[78] However, there is an increasing likelihood of liability, if a firm does not implement a patch before its system is hacked and confidential information assets are compromised, corrupted, lost or stolen. As a result, software customers (including banks and other financial institutions, hospitals, "first responders," telecommunications providers, aerospace firms and manufacturers of products such as chemicals, plastics and pharmaceuticals) increasingly face an

---

77. Id., p. 35. Teaching students of software design to identify and eliminate vulnerabilities so that they to learn to assess systems for potential misuse is also necessary because, as commentators have observed, the evolution of misuse is occurring more rapidly than the development of countermeasures. At some institutions, where the instructors can accept and fulfill a duty to monitor a student's trustworthiness, it makes good sense to teach students to understand the attacker's strategies, tactics, and philosophy. As Colonel Don Welch and Major Ron Dodge observe, "Because the attack-understanding philosophy provides so many advantages, it has become the prevailing philosophy at the US Military Academy. All our graduates will one day be in positions of responsibility for information systems security. By knowing the ways in which systems could be attacked, they will have much greater success protecting and defending them." Welch, Don, and Dodge, Ron, *Information Assurance the West Point Way*, IEEE SECURITY & PRIVACY, September/October 2003, p. 65.

78. As GAO's director of information security issues recently observed, "Patch management is a critical process used to help alleviate many of the challenges involved with securing computing systems from attack. A component of configuration management, it includes acquiring, testing, applying, and monitoring patches to a computer system." GAO Testimony, *Information Security: Agencies Face Challenges in Implementing Effective Software Patch Management Processes*, statement of Robert F. Dacey before the Subcommittee on Technology, Information Policy, Intergovernmental Relations and the Census, House Committee on Government Reform, June 2, 2004, p. 3.

unenviable Hobson's choice: install a recommended security patch immediately (at the risk of creating a severe incompatibility with one's existing software), or postpone installing the patch (at the risk of being sued for negligently failing to take the precautions necessary to protect confidential information or to avert damage to third parties' systems).

The risk of such liability is no longer hypothetical or speculative. And it increases rapidly with increases in the sensitivity and quantum of confidential information gathered, stored and used by a commercial firm. A brief review of recent cases illustrates the emerging trend of increased liability for failures to provide either required or promised (expressly or implicitly) information security.

The cases also reveal six additional trends that substantially expand the scope of information security risks:

(i)   Advances in payload capability;

(ii) Enhanced stealthiness;

(iii) Launching of pre-emptive exploits (striking previously undisclosed vulnerabilities);

(iv) Posting of stolen source code on the World Wide Web (facilitating non-commercial discovery of vulnerabilities in such code);

(v)   Wireless expansion of targets (linking devices to the Internet exposes such devices to intrusions from the Internet); and

(vi) Imputing of liability for insufficient security (in the absence of a breach of security).

A brief explanation of each trend will improve our understanding of some of the ramifications of decisions by courts and federal enforcement agencies.

First, the payloads carried by malwares (that can be imbedded in a system by a hacker or an "intrusive code" from the Internet) are increasingly capable of causing severe and widely dispersed damage to computers, networked systems and the valuable data stored on them, communicated through them and processed by them. For example, the Witty Worm,[79] which began to spread on March 19, 2004, was the first

---

79. The name "Witty" derives from the code of its payload, which contains the phrase "(.) insert witty message here (,)." Levy, Alias, and Arce, Iván, *The Spread of the Witty Worm,* IEEE SECURITY & PRIVACY, vol. 2, no. 4, July/August 2004, p. 46.

"widely propagated Internet worm to carry a destructive payload,"[80] and to infect "a host population that was proactive about security—they were running firewall software"[81] (in particular, Internet Security System's products—BlackICE and RealSecure).[82] The victims' systems firewall software contained a vulnerability that the Witty Worm exploited, thereby infecting hosts on internal networks. The Witty Worm's payload was unusually destructive: it eventually crashed the infected machines "(and often permanently) deactivate[d] each infected host."[83] Although the vulnerable population was "only" approximately 12,000 computers, it did so at a relatively rapid rate: infecting 110 hosts in the first 10 seconds, 160 in the first 30 seconds, and infected a majority of its victims worldwide within 45 minutes (about 30 minutes longer than the SQL Slammer worm took to infect its victims).[84] It accomplished this feat approximately 36 hours after the firewall software maker disclosed the vulnerability.[85]

Witty reflects substantial skill, malice, and "knowledge of the practical and theoretical state-of-the-art in worm construction and computer security:"[86] (i) it sent itself to random IP addresses with random destination ports, enabling it to penetrate firewalls;[87] (ii) it contained no significant bugs, implying pre-release testing;[88] and (iii) the author

---

80. Id.

81. Id., p. 48.

82. Schneier, Bruce, *The Witty Worm: A New Chapter in Malware*, COMPUTERWORLD, June 2, 2004, accessed at www.COMPUTERWORLD.com/securitytopics/security/virus/story/0,10801,93584,00.html.

83. Levy, Alias, and Arce, Iván, *The Spread of the Witty Worm*, IEEE SECURITY & PRIVACY, vol. 2, no. 4, July/August 2004, pp. 48–49.

84. Id., p. 47.

85. As explained by Bruce Schneier, "Security company eEye Digital Security discovered the vulnerability in ISS's BlackICE/RealSecure products on March 8 [2004], and ISS released a patched version on March 9. Eeye published a high-level description of the vulnerability on March 18. On the evening of March 19, about 36 hours after eEye's public disclosure, the Witty worm was released into the wild." Schneier, Bruce, *The Witty Worm: A New Chapter in Malware*, COMPUTERWORLD, June 2, 2004, accessed at www.COMPUTERWORLD.com/securitytopics/security/virus/story/0,10801,93584,00.html.

86. Weaver, Nicholas, and Ellis, Dan, *Reflections on Witty: Analyzing the Attacker*, 2004, accessed at www.icsi.berkeley.edu/~nweaver/login_witty.txt.

87. Schneier, Bruce, *The Witty Worm: A New Chapter in Malware*, COMPUTERWORLD, June 2, 2004, accessed at www.COMPUTERWORLD.com/securitytopics/security/virus/story/0,10801,93584,00.html.

88. Weaver, Nicholas, and Ellis, Dan, *Reflections on Witty: Analyzing the Attacker*, 2004, accessed at www.icsi.berkeley.edu/~nweaver/login_witty.txt.

has a mastery of "worm-lore" evidenced by the fact that the malicious payload severely damaged each infected host without slowing the worm's propagation and dispersal.[89] As commentators observed:

> "Witty demonstrated that any minimally deployed piece of software with a remotely exploitable bug can be a vector for wide-scale compromise of host machines without any action on the victim's part. The practical implications of this are staggering: with minimal skill, a malevolent individual could break into thousands of machines and use them for almost any purpose with little evidence of the perpetrator left on most of the compromised hosts."[90]

In addition, as noted by the GAO's Director of Information Security Issues,

> "The sophistication and effectiveness of cyber attacks have steadily advanced. . . . The director of the CERT Centers has estimated that as much as 80 percent of actual security incidents go unreported, in most cases because

> • There were no indications of penetration or attack,
> • The organization was unable to recognize that its systems had been penetrated, or
> • The organization was reluctant to report the attack."[91]

Ironically, the U.S. government's increasing reliance on computer systems to protect homeland security makes the reliability of such security dependent on keeping it impermeable to intrusive malwares. Regrettably, that condition has not been met, as evidenced by the fact that on September 22, 2003 the State Department's electronic system for "checking every visa applicant for terrorist or criminal history failed

89. Id.

90. Shannon, Colleen and Moore, David. *The Spread of the Witty Worm*, 2004, accessed at www.caida.org/analysis/security/witty/. No humans had to open attached files to cause Witty to spread.

91. GAO Testimony, *Information Security: Agencies Face Challenges in Implementing Effective Software Patch Management Processes*, statement of Robert F. Dacey before the Subcommittee on Technology, Information Policy, Intergovernmental Relations and the Census, House Committee on Government Reform, June 2, 2004, p. 5.

worldwide for several hours . . . . Because of a computer virus . . . . "[92] The virus rendered the Consular Lookout and Support System of 12.8 million records (from the FBI, State Department, U.S. immigration, drug-enforcement and intelligence agencies) inaccessible, with no backup system immediately available. Access was restored within a few hours, but in the interim the U.S. was forced to cease issuing visas.[93] Moreover, the GAO's survey in 2004 of patch management by 24 federal agencies found inconsistent patch management policies that leave such agencies at increased risk of attacks that exploit software vulnerabilities in their systems for the following reasons:

- Eight agencies had no patch management policy;
- Ten agencies did not have patch procedures in place;
- Fifteen agencies do not have any patch testing policies in place; and,
- Only four agencies monitor all of their systems on a regular basis.[94]

As payloads improve, so do their delivery systems (each taking advantage of improvements in the trade route's bandwidth—its speed and capacity). Improved payload and delivery requires that information security be addressed as an ever-vigilant and on-going *process*. Unfortunately, the inventors of malwares probably achieve far greater economies of scale from their investments in research and development than do the owners of the systems their inventions are designed to attack. Certain payloads and delivery systems originate in what can be called the "creative hacker community:" their inventor creates them as "trial balloons" to see what he can accomplish. Ultimately, the greatest risk comes from state support of such efforts. Effective defenses and responses to such risks, and developing the justifications to obtain budgets to improve such defenses and responses, are not keeping pace with improvements in payload and delivery systems. One reason is that firms

92. Bridis, Ted, *State Dept. Says Computers Hit by Virus*, State Department, September 23, 2003, accessed at www.newsday.com/news/politics/wire/sns-ap-state-computer-virus,0,3362483,print.story?coll = sns-ap-politics-headlines.

93. Id.

94. GAO Testimony, *Information Security: Agencies Face Challenges in Implementing Effective Software Patch Management Processes*, statement of Robert F. Dacey before the Subcommittee on Technology, Information Policy, Intergovernmental Relations and the Census, House Committee on Government Reform, June 2, 2004, pp. 11–12.

(as well as the military) respond best to tangible threats: a new product enters the market and competitors quickly respond; militarize a border (mobilize radar and photo detectable assets) and the neighboring countries quickly take notice. However, intangible risks—an improved payload and delivery system of malicious code—gives no advance notice of its presence, except perhaps if the developers start to brag or "chatter" over the Internet about the capabilities they have developed.

While some communication technologies attract what Timothy Wu refers to as a "high chatter to deployment ratio" (where "the volume of talk about the technology exceeds, by an absurd ratio, the actual number of deployments"),[95] such ratio is not replicated in pre-deployment developments of malwares. Firms therefore must attempt to reinforce their information security without having the tangible evidence to justify such investments (and at the risk that a mere investment in anti-virus software will only protect them against the "known and already deployed" threat, not against those under development that have not been released "in the wild"). In the meantime, the financial incentives to develop malicious code continue to grow "as financially motivated individuals look to break into computer systems and take advantage of other's computer resources to spam, install adware, create bot networks to threaten and blackmail websites, or steal sensitive financial information. The lure of money is changing the computer security playing field."[96]

Second, a further improvement in malwares is in their enhanced stealthiness. A remarkably large number of firms do not know that their systems have been penetrated, because the intruder or intrusive malware has not changed anything on the system. Data may have been reviewed without leaving a trace. Data may have been copied without triggering an alarm. Defenses may have been reconnoitered in the absence of scan detectors, leaving the firm none the wiser and not alerted to the need to shore up its information security safeguards. As security researchers have observed:

95. Wu, Timothy, *Broadband Policy: A Broadband Policy User's Guide*, OPEN ARCHITECTURE AS COMMUNICATIONS POLICY, Center for Internet and Society, Stanford Law School, 2004, p. 233 at p. 235, accessed at http://cyberlaw.stanford.edu/blogs/cooper/archives/002272.shtml.

96. Levy, Alias, and Arce, Iván, *Approaching Zero*, IEEE SECURITY & PRIVACY, vol. 2, no. 4, July/August 2004, p. 66.

"After breaking into a system, attackers usually install *rootkits* to create secret backdoors and cover their tracks. Unlike the name implies, rootkits don't provide root access. Instead, they arm attackers with stealth on already compromised systems. Stealthy operations hide processes, files, and connections that let an attacker sustain long-term access without alerting system administrators."[97]

Enhanced stealthiness is not solely an Internet-related issue: it reoccurs in software development that has been subcontracted (domestically) or outsourced (overseas), and results in modules that may contain surreptitiously embedded code that may covertly compromise a capability or be triggered by a processing event or by an instructive signal. The more mission critical the software, the greater the potential harm (*e.g.,* software in air traffic control systems, in military command and control systems, or in civilian and military airborne systems).

Third, historically there has been a complacency enhancing cycle between the discovery of vulnerabilities and the launching of malware to exploit them. A software maker would discover a vulnerability in code it had already sold; it would work for months to develop a security patch to correct the vulnerability (although sometimes it might not rate the vulnerability a priority and that would extend the time before a patch would be developed). It would then release the corrective patch, thereby disclosing publicly the existence and nature of the vulnerability, and a clock would start to run: customers would have a limited but unspecified amount of time to download the patch, test their systems for its use, install it, test their systems for problems resulting from such integration, and then ensure that all the firm's systems (desktop, laptop, and other portable devices) had received the requisite corrective security patch. Eventually, time would run out: malware exploiting the vulnerability would be deployed and start to circulate or propagate through the Internet (and through firms' intranets). This "window of vulnerability" initially lasted for several months, but recently it has been reduced to several weeks, and then days (and finally with the Witty Worm—36 hours). This trend presages discovery of a vulnerability by the maker of malware *before* discovery by the maker of the software, and deployment of the malware *before* the maker of the software can take pre-emptive or preventative action. Such an occurrence is referred to as a *zero day vulnerability*.[98]

---

97. Ring, Sandra, and Cole, Eric, *Taking a Lesson from Stealthy Rootkits*, IEEE Security & Privacy, vol. 2, no. 4, July/August 2004, p. 38.

98. Levy, Alias, and Arce, Iván, *Approaching Zero*, IEEE Security & Privacy, vol.

Worms that can exploit a web browser that is integrated with an operating system, enabling the attacker to take control of the penetrated systems, should be anticipated, since the capabilities to create them already exist. Such browsers ordinarily include considerable amounts of "re-used" code, originally written before security had become a priority and thus not "baked in" to such code.[99] The economy of "reusing" code, from a time when security was not given sufficient attention, creates substantial opportunities for the creators of malwares. Moreover, the time required for any deployed malware to spread world-wide has been reduced to a few minutes. In the case of the "SQL Slammer" worm in January 2003, ten minutes was required for it to circumnavigate the trade route of cyberspace.[100] Unfortunately, software makers are reluctant to discuss or to disclose what they know (and what they reasonably fear they do not know) about such developments, which leaves commercial firms relatively unaware of such risks, their magnitude and their potential cost.

Fourth, there appears to be a rising incidence in the theft and posting of software maker's proprietary source code. In February of 2004, hackers posted code from Microsoft's Windows operating system. In May of 2004, a portion of the Cisco Systems Inc. software, part of its Internet

---

2, no. 4, July/August 2004, p. 65. Note: Although the Witty Worm may have originated in a *zero-day vulnerability,* analysts of the worm and evidence of its authorship think that the timing of its release, coming so closely after the release of the security patch, argues against the probability that its author independently discovered the firewall software vulnerability. See Weaver, Nicholas, and Ellis, Dan, *Reflections on Witty: Analyzing the Attacker,* 2004, accessed at www.icsi.berkeley.edu/~nweaver/login_witty.txt.

99. We note in passing that the practice of reusing code is legally perilous, because it risks infringing on the original code author's copyright in such code.

100. Metz, Cade, *Is Microsoft to Blame?,* PC MAGAZINE, August 3, 2004, p. 73 at p. 74, quoting Cooperative Association for Internet Data Analysis. See also GAO, *Technology Assessment: Cybersecurity for Critical Infrastructure Protection,* GAO-04-321, May 2004, pp. 30 and 32 (noting that in the same time 10-minute period the Slammer worm infected more than 90 percent of vulnerable systems by doubling in size every 8.5 seconds).

The speed with which hackers take advantage of reported flaws is increasing, reducing the time that software makers have to develop and deploy a corrective patch. For example, on October 19, 2004, a tool was posted online to test Web browsers; on October 26, 2004 the tool identified a bug in Microsoft's Internet Explorer; on November 2, 2004 sample code that exploits that vulnerability was posted by a programmer; and on November 9, 2004 that code was used to spread the Mydoom worm throughout the world. Bank, David, *Mydoom Worm Renews Debate On Cyber-Ethics,* THE WALL STREET JOURNAL, November 11, 2004, p. B-1.

Operating System installed on every unit of Cisco equipment, was stolen and published on the Web.[101] Such publications provide unauthorized parties an opportunity to scrutinize code for potential vulnerabilities and, if they find any, to develop malwares that exploit such vulnerabilities. Since Cisco-manufactured routers are a highly reputable and important device for improving information security at companies that possess valuable data, a breach in the security of such devices would pose considerable risk to its customers. Moreover, if such thefts and publications continue to occur, there is an increasing probability that makers of malwares will exploit vulnerabilities early, magnifying the resultant damage.

Fifth, the advent of new technologies and their deployment tends to occur both with little appreciation of their risks to privacy and to information security. The long ramp up to the deployment of "3G" (or broadband capabilities in mobile phones) combined with the wireless linking of earlier generation mobile phones and of PDA's and other portable devices to the Internet and, most recently, the addition of Voice Over Internet Protocol ("VoIP")[102] has considerably expanded the number of devices that malware can target. What makes that numerical increase significant is that such devices contain increasingly large data bases of highly sensitive or confidential information (the memory capacity of such devices has also expanded as has the speed with which data (including pilfered data) can be downloaded onto them). However, users of such devices tend to carry their pre-Internet habits into their use of devices linked to the Internet and, as a result, do not adequately consider the information security risks to which they expose such data when they download or copy it from an older model to a new one with Internet capabilities. In late July 2004, for example, a Gartner report cautioned that "disk-based MP3 players, such as Apple's iPod, and digital cameras with smart media cards, memory sticks, compact flash and other memory media" pose significant security risks to companies, because these small portable storage devices can be walked into a company (thereby bypassing its firewalls). They can thus introduce malwares

---

101. Thurm, Scott, *Cisco Software Apparently Stolen, Giving Hackers Glimpse into Code,* THE WALL STREET JOURNAL, May 18, 2004, p. B-9.

102. VoIP is a process that enables the transfer of voice data over a "packet switched network" and thereby allows a personal computer user to place long-distance telephone calls through the Internet rather than through a "circuit switched network" used by traditional landline telephones.

and, because they typically use high speed connections such as USB and firewire, they can be used to steal data at much greater speeds than achievable with downloads to CDs.[103] As such developments demonstrate, when new technologies (like the iPod) achieve dramatic commercial success, it is easy to overlook the security risks that they pose. Companies will be understandably reluctant to "ban" such devices (Gartner's recommendation), since that would interfere with the efficiencies provided by portable devices. Moreover, the diminutive size of such devices makes any such policy difficult to enforce.

Sixth, as detailed below, there is an increasing willingness of enforcement agencies and courts to impute liability for deficient information security, sometimes on the grounds of alleged "deceptive practices" (without an intention to deceive, which historically had to be proved if deceit was alleged), sometimes on the grounds that a breach of security is no longer a necessary predicate of (and need not be proved to establish) liability for insufficient safeguards of information security. To business executives (and their legal counsel), such arguments are counterintuitive and may appear "far fetched." However, such reasoning is increasingly relied on by reputable institutions—including the Federal Trade Commission. This is a rare instance in which developments in the law seem to anticipate an innovative technology that "leap frogs" previous capabilities. Imputing liability in the absence of a breach (but on evidence of deficient information security safeguards) can arguably be justified as a response to the anticipated deployment of malwares that will exploit such deficiencies, if given the opportunity. This potential liability is one of the most difficult for Agile to address, but a review of recent cases suggests that it should be addressed without delay.

One case involved liability imposed for failure to implement a corrective patch in a timely manner. Early in the morning of January 25, 2003, the telecommunications provider, Verizon-Maine ("Verizon"), detected an abrupt increase in Internet traffic and diagnosed the cause: a "worm" was propagating itself with accelerating rapidity. Later dubbed the "Slammer Worm," it scanned servers that it attacked for other vulnerable devices, then sent itself to the new device—a process that was rapidly repeated. The increased traffic imperiled Verizon's Operational Support System ("OSS"), and Verizon decided that an external quar-

---

103. Donoghue, Andrew, *Analyst: iPods a Network Security Risk*, CNET News.com, July 6, 2004, accessed at http://news.com.com/Analyst+iPods+a+network+security+risk/2100-7355_3-5258588.html.

antine process was needed to ensure the safety of its networks and systems. It therefore brought down all the OSS interfaces for the purpose of accelerating isolation and recovery from the worm attack. It promptly notified the Competitive Local Exchange Carriers ("CLECs") by e-mail of the event (and one by phone). Verizon kept its OSS interfaces offline for the remainder of Saturday and Sunday until 6 PM in order to inspect, identify and remove infected devices from service and, where needed, to patch, test and reconnect devices. Two days off-line, however, reduced Verizon's measurable performance or metrics for that month, and obligated it to provide the CLECs a rebate it computed to be $62,000. Verizon computed that, if it could obtain a waiver of the monthly performance metric from the Maine Public Utilities Commission ("Maine Commission"), the rebate would be reduced to $18,000. Verizon filed for such waiver. Responsive comments (in opposition) were filed by AT&T Communications of New England and WorldCom ("Respondents").[104]

Verizon maintained that it had reacted swiftly to the worm attack, that such attack was beyond its control, that the attack negatively affected its ability to meet the performance metrics and that it should, therefore, be granted a waiver from these metrics. Respondents did not challenge Verizon for its conduct during the worm attack, but assailed it for having been caught "unprepared" by the attack. From October 16, 2002 through the date of the attack (January 25, 2003), Verizon failed to take measures that would have prevented the attack from succeeding. In early October 2002, Microsoft had publicly disclosed the vulnerability in Security Bulletins, labeled it "critical" (the highest warning level), released corrective security patches by October 16, 2002, and urged customers to apply the patch in an "especially timely manner." From that date, until three months later when the attack occurred, Verizon had 15 occasions on which it could have tested and deployed this security patch, and thus, even granting Verizon's contention (that installing patches requires considerable amount of testing and evaluation to ensure that unforeseen interoperability problems do not occur), Verizon had ample opportunity to protect its OSS and maintain its performance standards.[105]

104. *Inquiry Regarding the Entry of Verizon-Maine into the InterLATA Telephone Market*, Docket No. 2000-849, 2003 Me. PUC LEXIS 181, April 30, 2003, pp. 1–2.
105. Id., pp. 2–3.

The Maine Commission concluded that Verizon "did not take all reasonable and prudent steps available to it," because although "Microsoft initially notified network administrators of a potential problem with the Slammer Worm at least six months before the attack actually occurred," and had issued security patches three months prior to the attack, Verizon chose not to install the appropriate patch.[106] The Respondents also demonstrated that their systems were largely unaffected by the worm attack, because they had installed the Microsoft patch. Therefore, the Maine Commission determined that Verizon should be held accountable for its failure.[107]

The *Verizon-Maine* decision will probably be repeated in other industries by other adjudicators, but with the added context of the six above-mentioned trends. Advances in payload capacity will result in damage far more widespread and costly than that experienced by Verizon-Maine. Enhanced stealthiness may prevent the victimized firm from detecting the attack as early as Verizon-Maine did. If the deployer of the malware has found an undisclosed vulnerability, it may succeed in launching an attack at a time when there is no security patch available and none that could be developed quickly enough to contain or limit the ever-widening propagation and dispersal of damage. Verizon-Maine could quarantine its OSS by bringing it down for two days (on a weekend), time it used to install and test the patch. In the absence of a patch, an attack during the business week would do far greater harm, and would compel firms to decide between quarantining their systems (disconnecting them from the Internet) or leaving such systems vulnerable to re-occurrences of the attack or to hybrid forms that might be part of the malware's payload. Such attacks, in the absence of a security patch, could quickly spread to the wireless devices now linked to the Internet. Finally, the adjudicator of any resulting controversy would have to adjust sharply downward any time deemed to be reasonable for installation of patches. The *Verizon-Maine* case did not pose a risk to the OSS developer (Microsoft), but rather to its customer (who no

---

106. Id., p. 3.
107. Id., p. 4. Recently decided cases concerning the U.S. Department of Interior's breach of fiduciary duties as evidenced by *deficiencies in digital security* of its computers suggest that company directors could similarly be held liable for breach of their fiduciary duty of care for serious deficiencies in their company's digital security. For discussion of those federal court decisions, see Trope, Roland L., *Directors' Digital Fiduciary Duties*, IEEE Security & Privacy, JANUARY/FEBRUARY 2005. p. 000.

doubt did not anticipate that it could be held accountable for failing to patch its leased software in a timely manner).

Software makers should anticipate that they too will eventually be at risk in similar circumstances for failing to discover a vulnerability in their wares, or for failing to develop a patch in a timely manner (in light of the trend of sharply reduced time between the discovery of a vulnerability and the launching of an attack to exploit it). Software makers, however, have a potential defense that could immunize them against liability for terrorists' cyber-attacks that penetrate or exploit a vulnerability in their wares. But they must apply *long in advance* to qualify their products for such immunity. The protection is provided by the so-called SAFETY Act (the Support Anti-Terrorism by Fostering Effective Technologies Act of 2002), which entitles products, upon review and approval by the Department of Homeland Security ("DHS"), to be designated a "Qualified Anti-Terrorist Technology" ("QATT"), and upon further review and approval by DHS (to confirm that the product meets specifications), to be "certified" and thereby entitled to the "government contractor defense" (whether sold to a government or non-government customer). If a software maker's wares (or any other firm's products or services) earn the DHS designation as a QATT and receive "certification," the seller is *immune from tort liability arising out of any failure of the product or service in connection with a terrorist attack or an effort to recover from such attack.*[108]

The purpose for offering such immunity was to encourage firms to invest in developing anti-terrorist technologies without exposure to massive tort recoveries if the technology failed to perform as expected during a terrorist attack. Surprisingly, few companies have taken advantage of the SAFETY Act's offer. 500 applications were expected during the first year of the Act, but eight months after the Act went into effect, DHS had received only 19 applications. *The Act also applies to non-U.S. firms,* but very few overseas firms are aware of the Act, although most are keenly aware of the risks of tort liability for firms that sell products into the United States. DHS, at present, takes several months to determine whether to grant designation and certification of technologies, products and services submitted to it for review. In June

---

108. For more detailed discussion, see Trope, Roland, *Guarding Against Terrorism— and Liability*, IEEE Spectrum, January 2004, accessed at www.spectrum.ieee.org/careers/careerstemplate.jsp?ArticleId = i010604.

of 2004, it granted the first such designations and certifications as follows:

Figure 1. Initial Designations and Certifications Under the SAFETY Act[a]

Vendor	Product/Service Technology	Use
Michael Stapleton Associates	SmartTech	PC-based system that can be linked to any X-ray machine to screen packages for explosive devices.
Michael Stapleton Associates	Bomb-detection canine teams	Detect explosive devices.
Teledyne	Mobile Fluid Jet System or "Water Sabre"	Reduced in size, mobile device to cut metal—to be used remotely from up to 1,000 feet away to cut into suspect containers.
Northrop Grumman	Mail "sniffer"	To sniff envelopes as they pass through high-speed sorting machines at post offices to detect trace amounts of biological toxins such as anthrax.
Lockheed Martin	Computer based data mining	Computer system that analyzes informaion from multipe sources and processes it for "near real-time" threat analysis.

[a]See Block, Robert and Lunsford, J. Lynn, *U.S. Gives Liability Protection To Antiterror Firms*, THE WALL STREET JOURNAL, June 18, 2004, p. B-2.

Note: Agile has included in its enhanced diligence a review of each technology produced by the target companies (Troll and its affiliates) to ascertain if any might qualify for SAFETY Act protection, in which case it will expedite submission of application for each to DHS for SAFETY Act designation as a QATT and for certification as an "Approved Product for Homeland Security." Such products will thus have immunity from tort liability in connection with terrorist (including cyber-attacks), and can be marketed with an "Approved Product" label.

The three additional cases on information security concerned charges by the Federal Trade Commission ("FTC") and settlements entered into by it. The FTC enforces an omnibus consumer protection statute (Section 5 of the FTC Act), which provides that "unfair or deceptive acts or practices in or affecting commerce are declared unlawful."[109] To date, the FTC has taken enforcement action in the field of information security against companies that it alleged made explicit or implicit promises to take appropriate steps to protect sensitive information provided by consumers. The FTC further alleged that the defendant companies' security measures were inadequate, and their promises were, therefore, "deceptive acts or practices" in violation of Section 5. In 2003 and 2004, the FTC, in its third, fourth and fifth cases targeting companies that "misrepresent the security of consumers' personal information" reached settlements, respectively, with designer clothing and accessory marketer, Guess, Incorporated ("Guess"), with Tower Records, Inc. ("Tower"), and with educational product seller Gateway Learning Corp. ("Gateway").[110]

In the *Guess* case, the FTC charged that the company exposed consumers' personal information (including credit card numbers) to "commonly known attacks by hackers," and that it "didn't use reasonable or appropriate measures to prevent consumer information from being accessed at its website, Guess.com."[111] Guess had represented to visitors to its website that "This site has security measures in place to protect the loss, misuse, and alteration of information under our control," and that "All of your personal information, including your credit card information and sign-in password, are stored in an unreadable, encrypted format at all times."[112]

The FTC noted that Guess did not, in fact, store personal information in an unreadable, encrypted format at all times, and that those limited security measures Guess did in fact implement failed to protect

---

109. 15 U.S.C. § 45 (a)(1).

110. The two earlier enforcement actions were against Eli Lilly (see Final Decision and Order at www.ftc.gov/os/2002/05/elilillydo.htm) and Microsoft (see Final Decision and Order at www.ftc.gov/os/2002/12/microsoftdecision.pdf).

111. Federal Trade Commission, *Guess Settles FTC Security Charges; Third FTC Case Targets False Claims about Information Security,* June 18, 2003, accessed at www.ftc.gov/opa/2003/06/guess.htm, accessed on February 12, 2004.

112. Id.

against Structured Query Language injection attacks enabling a visitor to Guess' website in February of 2002 to "read in clear text credit card numbers stored in Guess' databases . . ."[113] The settlement with the FTC required Guess to implement a comprehensive information security program for Guess.com and its other website, and to have that program certified as meeting or exceeding the standards in the Consent Order by an independent professional within a year, and biannually thereafter. The certification must specifically attest that Guess' security program is effective and provides reasonable assurances that the security, confidentiality and integrity of personal information is protected.[114] Also, for a period of five years, Guess must maintain, and upon request make available to the FTC for inspection and copying, a print or electronic copy of each document relating to compliance. Such records expressly include "a sample copy of each different print, broadcast, cable, or Internet advertisement, promotion, information collection form, web Page, screen, e-mail message, or other document containing any representation regarding"[115] Guess' online collection, use and security of personal information from or about consumers. Those and other tasks ordered by the FTC will impose a burdensome transactional diligence and open-ended costs on Guess well into the foreseeable future.

In the *Tower* case, the FTC alleged that the company's commercial website (where it markets and sells music and video recordings and other entertainment products) collected personal information (name, billing address, shipping address, e-mail address and phone numbers) from buyers of its products, subject to the following representations of privacy and confidentiality:

> "Tower Records.com is committed to safeguarding your privacy online. We will never share your personal information with anyone for any reason without your explicit permission.

*   *   *

---

113. Id.

114. Federal Trade Commission, *In the Matter of Guess, Inc. and Guess.com Inc.,* Agreement Containing Consent Order, File No. 022-3260, accessed on February 12, 2004 at www.ftc.gov/os/2003/06/guessagree.htm.

115. Id.

We use state-of-the-art technology to safeguard your personal information. . . .

* * *

Your TowerRecords.com Account information is password-protected. You and only you have access to this information. . . . While we strive to protect your personal information, TowerRecords.com cannot ensure or warrant the security or services, and you do so at your own risk. . . ."[116]

In November and December of 2002, Tower redesigned the "check out" feature of its website, and rewrote the software code for the "Order Status" application, but failed (inadvertently) to include any "authentication code" to limit access and ensure that only the authorized customer could view a customer's "Order Status" information. As the FTC described the security consequences:

"The omission of authentication code. . . . created a commonly known and reasonably foreseeable vulnerability in the Order Status application often referred to as 'broken account and session management.' *Any visitor to the Tower website who entered a valid order number in the Order Status URL could view certain personal information* relating to other Tower consumers. . . . The vulnerability lasted for eight days and was exploited by a number of visitors. . . . *[P]ersonal information relating to approximately 5,225 consumers was accessed by unauthorized users. . . .*"[117]

Under the terms of the Settlement, Tower agreed that: it would "not misrepresent" the extent to which it maintained and protected the privacy, confidentiality or security of its customers' personal information; that it would establish, implement and maintain a "comprehensive information security program that is reasonably designed" to protect such information; that it would document such program, designate employees to coordinate and be accountable for its information security program; that it would identify the material risks to the security, confidentiality and integrity of its customers' personal information; and that it

---

116. Federal Trade Commission, Complaint, *In the Matter of MTS, INC., d/b/a Tower Records/Books/Video*, Order, File No. 032-3209, accessed at www.ftc.gov/os/ca-selist/0323209/040602comp0323209.pdf.
117. Id. [Emphasis added.]

would regularly test and monitor these safeguards. In addition, biannually for ten years, Tower has agreed to obtain an assessment and report from a qualified independent third-party professional, reviewing its safeguards, their appropriateness, and whether they surpass the FTC's standards (as set forth in the Settlement), and certifying that Tower's security program is operating with sufficient effectiveness to provide reasonable assurance that the security, confidentiality and integrity of its customers' personal information will be protected.[118]

In the *Gateway* case, the FTC alleged that Gateway, a marketer and seller of the "Hooked on Phonics" brand products for learning math and reading had made the following privacy representations on its website:

> "We at Gateway Learning Corporation are committed to protecting the privacy of our visitors, and we treat any information you share with discretion, care and respect. . . .
>
> We do not sell, rent or loan any personally identifiable information regarding our consumers with any third party unless we receive a customer's explicit consent. . . .
>
> We do not provide any personally identifiable information about children under 13 years of age to any third party for any purpose whatsoever. . . .
>
> If at some future time there is a material change to our information usage practices that affect your personally identifiable information, we will notify you of the relevant changes on this Site or by e-mail. You will then be able to opt-out of this information usage . . . ."[119]

Gateway made those representations continuously from the year 2000 through June of 2003, but deviated from those representations in April of 2003 by starting to rent personal information provided by consumers at its site (without seeking or receiving any form of consent from such consumers) and included in the information it rented the age range (0–5 years old, 2–5 years old, and 6–10 years old) and gender of its consumers' children for use by marketers in targeting parents.[120]

---

118. Federal Trade Commission, Final Decision and Order, *In the Matter of MTS, INC., d/b/a Tower Records/Books/Video,* Docket No. C-4110, May 28, 2004, accessed at www.ftc.gov/os/caselist/0323209/040602do0323209.pdf.

119. Federal Trade Commission, Complaint, *In the Matter of Gateway Learning Corp.,* 043047, p. 2, accessed at www.ftc.gov/os/caselist/0423047/040707cmp0423047.pdf.

120. Id., pp. 2–3.

Two months later, while continuing to make the earlier privacy representations, Gateway disclosed (only on its site and not by e-mail) that "we may provide your name, address and phone number . . . to reputable companies whose products or services you may find of interest. If you do not want us to share this information with these companies, please write to us . . . or e-mail us. . . . "[121] Gateway did not disclose that it had already shared such information, nor did it acknowledge that it also shared the personally identifiable information about its customers' children. Subsequent changes to its posted privacy representations continued to fail to disclose those relevant facts that would have revealed it to be acting in breach of such representations. The FTC therefore deemed Gateway's representations to be false or misleading. The FTC also noted that Gateway's retroactive application of its revised privacy policy "caused or is likely to cause substantial injury to consumers that is not outweighed by countervailing benefits to consumers . . . and *is not reasonably avoidable by consumers.* The practice was, and is, an unfair act or practice."[122]

In the Consent Agreement, the FTC required Gateway to avoid such misrepresentations, to refrain from applying changes to its privacy policy concerning collection of personally identifiable information from consumers "before the date of the posting" of a notice of such changes unless it has received an express affirmative "opt-in" consent from such consumers, to pay a fine, and further remedies including (i) for a period of five years to maintain and provide upon request to the FTC a copy of each different privacy statement posted on its site, a sample of each different consent form it uses, and all invoices, communications and records relating to the disclosure of personally identifiable information to third parties (a burdensome record keeping obligation) and (ii) to give the FTC 30-days notice of any change in the corporation to which the Agreement would apply (thereby making clear that a successor entity would continue to be under the obligations of the Consent Agreement).[123]

The *Guess, Tower* and *Gateway* cases illustrate that governmental regulatory agencies are prepared to hold commercial firms liable for failing to provide adequate protection for the confidential information

---

121. Id., p. 4.
122. Id., p. 5. [Emphasis added.]
123. Federal Trade Commission, Agreement Containing Consent Order, *In the Matter of Gateway Learning Corp.*, 043047, pp. 4–5, accessed at www.ftc.gov/os/caselist/0423047/040707cmp0423047.pdf

entrusted to them by their customers that they invited by promises of
security. Such agencies may thereby create, by analogy, a variant of the
traditional business invitee rule (Tort Law), which holds commercial
entities to the highest duty of care to individuals whom they have invited
to do business with them. With respect to customer invitees and the
confidential information that businesses solicit and obtain from them
as a pre-condition of doing business, such businesses will be treated as
owing the highest duty of care, and will be held strictly liable for security
failures that cause loss, theft, damage, alteration of, or unauthorized
access to, such information. If that is an accurate description of the
emerging trend, companies will have a low "risk tolerance" for information security failures. Recent pronouncements by the FTC will add
impetus to this trend, by emphasizing *three key principles* that guide its
enforcement policies with respect to a vendor who breaches its own
online representations to safeguard the privacy of its customers' personal information:

- First, "a company's security procedures should be appropriate for
  the kind of information it collects and maintains. . . . It is highly
  problematic when a company inadvertently releases sensitive personal information due to inadequate security procedures."[124]
- Second, "not all breaches of information security are violations of
  FTC law—the Commission is not simply saying 'gotcha' for security breaches. . . . Instead, the Commission . . . [seeks] to determine whether the breach resulted from the failure to have procedures in place that are reasonable in light of the sensitivity of
  the information."[125]
- And, third, "There can be law violations without a known breach
  of security,"[126] a position the FTC adopts in the belief that com-

---

124. *Cybersecurity and Consumer Data: What's At Risk for the Consumer,* prepared
statement of Hon. Orson Swindel, Commissioner, Federal Trade Commission, hearing
before the Subcommittee on Commerce, Trade, and Consumer Protection of the Committee on Energy and Commerce, House of Representatives, First Session, November
19, 2003, pp. 12, accessed at www.access.gpo.gov/congress/house.

125. Id.

126. Beales, Howard, Director of the FTC Bureau of Consumer Protection, *Information Security—Challenges for Consumers and Businesses,* prepared statement of the
Federal Trade Commission before the Subcommittee on Technology, Information Policy, Intergovernmental Relations, and the Census, Committee on Government Reform,
U.S. House of Representatives, June 16, 2004, at p. 11, accessed at www.ftc.gov/os/2004/
06/040616cybersecuritytestimony.pdf.

panies cannot wait for a breach before implementing appropriate safeguards for information security. As the FTC explains: "Particularly when explicit promises are made, companies have a legal obligation to take reasonable steps to guard against threats before a compromise occurs."[127]

Companies engaged in cross-border transactions will face additional risks, if their software security is riddled with vulnerabilities.[128] The

---

127. Id., p. 12. In testimony before a House subcommittee, FTC Commissioner Orson Swindle added to those principles, noting: "[T]he Commission has come to recognize several principles that should govern any information security program. First, information security is an ongoing process of assessing risks and vulnerabilities: no one static standard can assure appropriate security, as security threats and technology constantly evolve. Second, a company's security procedures must be reasonable and appropriate in light of the circumstances. Such circumstances include the company's size and complexity, the nature and scope of its activities, and the sensitivity of the consumer information it handles. . . . Implementation of these principles requires a business to develop a security plan and make security monitoring and oversight part of their regular operations . . . Information security planning should include: identifying internal and external risks to the security, confidentiality, and integrity of consumers' personal information; designing and implementing safeguards to control these risks; periodically monitoring and testing the safeguards to be sure they are working effectively; adjusting security plans according to the results of testing or changes in circumstance; and overseeing the information handling practices of service providers who have access to the personal information." Swindle, Orson, *Prepared Statement of the Federal Trade Commission before the Subcommittee on Technology, Information Policy, Intergovernmental Relations, and the Census, Committee on Government Reform, U.S. House of Representatives on Protecting Information Security and Preventing Identity Theft,* September 22, 2004, pp. 3–4, accessed at www.ftc.gov/os/2004/09/040922infosecidthefttest.pdf.

128. Note that the enforcement risks arise not only from federal agency review but, in the U.S. and Canada (among others), from state and provincial agency review. For example, in October 2003, the retailer Victoria's Secret entered into a settlement agreement with the New York State Attorney-General's Office to pay a penalty of $50,000 in order to resolve charges that Victoria's Secret violated New York state laws concerning deceptive business practices, false advertising, and fraudulent business activities. The charges arose from the fact that although Victoria's Secret website represented that it maintained customer data in "private files on our secure Web server" and that "we provide stringent and effective security measures on our website," a security flaw existed in the site from August through November 2002 that permitted the names, addresses, and orders of more than 560 customers to be made available to anyone who manipulated customer identification numbers and order numbers to access customer records. See Schwartz, John, *Victoria's Secret Reaches a Data Privacy Settlement,* The New York Times Online, October 21, 2003, accessed at http://query.nytimes.com/gst/abstract. html?res = F3091FFD355A0C728EDDA90994DB404482&incamp = archive:search.

information that may be leaked, accessed or pilfered without authorization, may bring them into contravention of much more stringent laws in the U.S. (the EAR and ITAR) and abroad (the privacy and personal information protection laws and regulations of countries such as The Netherlands, Norway, and Canada).[129]

Some commentators, however, have argued that the damage inflicted by the Witty Worm, and the fact that it exploited a vulnerability in an intrusion detection product (a firewall's software) within a day of publication of that vulnerability, should cause a re-evaluation of the assumption that security can be achieved, by practices such as good patch management by end users. They contend that:

> "The patch model for Internet security has failed spectacularly. . . . When end users participating in the best security practice that can be reasonably expected get infected with a virulent and damaging worm, we must reconsider the notion that end-user behavior can solve or even effectively mitigate the malicious software problem and turn our attention toward both preventing software vulnerabilities in the first place and developing large-scale, robust, and reliable infrastructure that can mitigate current security problems without relying on end-user intervention."[130]

---

129. Some vendors play down the risks while at the same time offering subdued cautions that enable them to say they urged speed and caution simultaneously. As one website notes: "Typically, a patch can be installed over the top of an existing program, but again this will depend on the supplier and the nature of the patch." The Software Patch, accessed at www.softwarepatch.com. Some commentators overlook the potential liability and encourage an analysis merely of the costs in labor hours to implement patches before installing them. (See Lindstrom, Pete, *A Patch in Time*, INFORMATION SECURITY, February 2004, accessed at http://infosecuritymag.techtarget.com/ss/0, 295796,sid6_iss326_art580,00.html.) But they also overlook the transactional costs of losing system operations during a critical point in a transaction or during a period when a developer needs to reduce schedule delays not extend them with downtime of the system.

130. Levy, Alias, and Arce, Iván, *The Spread of the Witty Worm*, IEEE SECURITY & PRIVACY, vol. 2, no. 4, July/August 2004, p. 49–50.

Transactional counsel must also increase their awareness of the intersection of information security and a potential litigant's duties to preserve all accessible electronic information that may be relevant to such litigation, duties that are increasingly viewed as attaching prior to the filing of a lawsuit. Such duties therefore may attach at a time when transactional or corporate counsel is advising a client without the assistance of litigation counsel to alert them to such duties. Failure to fulfill such duties can prompt opposing counsel to allege spoliation of evidence and seek sanctions, including an instruction of an adverse inference to a jury (see *Zubulake V* 2004 U.S. Dist. LEXIS 13574,

Such arguments attempt to generalize from an exceptional occurrence. The enforcement cases brought by the FTC, for example, illustrate clearly that commercial entities that promise to provide security

---

S.D.N.Y., 2004) or preclusion of witnesses who failed to comply with record preservation obligations or a fine (see *United States of America v. Philip Morris USA Inc.*, Civil Action No. 99-2496, D.D.C, 2004, accessed at www.dcd.uscourts.gov/99-2496ai.pdf, where the District Court imposed a monetary sanction in the amount of $2,750,000).

If a company suffers a breakdown in its information security during a period when it is under an obligation to have implemented a "litigation hold" (suspending the operation of its document retention/destruction procedures), it may find that information and records it was obligated to preserve have thereby been damaged, destroyed, or rendered all but irretrievable except at exorbitant expense to recover the damaged digital files. A company that maintains weak information security procedures will probably also find it difficult to prove that an information security breach caused such damage or loss, and even if it can carry that burden of proof, it may then find itself confronted with allegations that its information security reflected an indifference to its duties to preserve relevant information and records. The scope of these duties may surprise many transactional counsel who tend not to become involved in such issues. In the *Zubulake* discovery decisions, District Court Judge Scheindlin has given careful thought and analysis to the issue and set forth what may well become an emerging standard for such duties in a decision on two main issues—counsel's obligation to ensure that relevant electronically stored information is preserved by giving the client clear instructions to preserve such information and a client's obligations to heed such instructions. As Judge Scheindlin explained:

> " 'Once a party reasonably anticipates litigation, it must suspend its routine document retention/destruction policy and put in place a 'litigation hold' to ensure the preservation of relevant documents. As a general rule, that litigation hold does not apply to inaccessible backup tapes (e.g., those typically maintained solely for the purpose of disaster recovery), which may continue to be recycled on the schedule set forth in the company's policy. On the other hand, if backup tapes are accessible (i.e., actively used for information retrieval), then such tapes *would* likely be subject to the litigation hold. [citation to *Zubulake IV.*]
>
> "A party's discovery obligations do not end with the implementation of a 'litigation hold'—to the contrary, that's only the beginning. Counsel must oversee compliance with the litigation hold, monitoring the party's efforts to retain and produce the relevant documents. Proper communication between a party and her lawyer will ensure (1) that all relevant information (or at least all sources of relevant information) is discovered, (2) that relevant information is retained on a continuing basis; and (3) that relevant non-privileged material is produced to the opposing party.... To do this, counsel must become fully familiar with her client's documents retention policies, as well as the client's data retention architecture. This will invariably involve speaking with information technology personnel, who can explain system-wide backup procedures and the actual (as opposed to theoretical) implementation of the firm's recycling policy. It will also involve communicating with the 'key players' in the litigation, in order to understand how they stored information. . . .

will be held liable, if those promises prove misleading or deceptive, regardless of the cause of the security breach. While software makers have recently promised to dedicate more resources to reduce such vulnerabilities in their products, the fact remains that, as software contin-

---

A lawyer cannot be obliged to monitor her client. . . . At the same time, . . . a party cannot reasonably be trusted to receive the 'litigation hold' instruction once and to fully comply with it without the active supervision of counsel." *Zubulake V*, 2004 U.S. Dist. LEXIS 13574 (S.D.N.Y., 2004) at pp. 31–32 and 38.

These and other issues relating to the "discovery of electronically stored information" are the subject of proposed amendments to the Federal Rules of Practice and Procedure recommended by the Advisory Committee on Federal Rules of Civil Procedure, released for public comment in August 2004, and accessed at www.uscourts.gov/rules/comment2005/CVAug04.pdf. The report of the Advisory Committee highlights technical aspects of electronically stored information that can be easily overlooked by counsel accustomed to thinking of documents solely in hard copy or who underestimates the dynamic nature of digital records:

"Electronically stored information may exist in dynamic databases that do not correspond to hard-copy materials. Electronic information unlike words on paper, is dynamic. The ordinary operation of computers—including the simple act of turning a computer on or off or accessing a particular file—can alter or destroy electronically stored information, and computer systems automatically discard or overwrite data as a part of their routine operation. Computers often automatically create information without the operator's direction or awareness, a feature with no direct counterpart in hard-copy materials. Electronically stored information may be 'deleted' yet continue to exist, but in forms difficult to locate, retrieve, or search. Electronic data, unlike paper, may be incomprehensible when separated from the system that created it. *Report of the Civil Rules Advisory Committee*, August 3, 2004, p. 3.

The Advisory Committee recognized that as the technology has changed, the language traditionally used to refer to the objectives of discovery has been rendered obsolete: the traditional concept of a "document" cannot be stretched to accommodate all forms of "electronically stored information." Those forms include not only the surface text, but also such information as may include "embedded data (earlier edits that may be hidden from a 'paper' view of the material or image displayed on a computer monitor) and metadata (automatically created identifying information about the history or management of an electronic file.)" *Report of the Civil Rules Advisory Committee*, p. 8. If the proposed amendments are adopted, transactional counsel will need to become familiar with them in order to ensure that appropriate actions and precautions are taken if a transaction moving towards closure also starts unmistakably moving towards a reasonable anticipation of litigation.

In addition, counsel will need to anticipate the emergence of new technologies that the proposed rules might not accommodate. For example, an underlying assumption of the *Zubulake* decisions and the proposed rules is that electronically stored information is both durable (difficult to delete) yet dynamic (easily modified or damaged by automatic overwrite operations of a computer system). Neither those

ues to become exorbitantly large and complex, it will inevitably contain hidden vulnerabilities including the risk of a *zero-day vulnerability*. In the meantime, companies should not assume that liability can be avoided by pointing to a vulnerability in a security precaution. Heightened diligence is a more appropriate response.

Agile's counsel must determine what information security obligations Agile incurs (directly for information stored in its computers from any source, and indirectly for information transferred to and stored in the computers at Troll, Brugge and Ijsselmeer) in the course of entering into an agreement to acquire Troll and its affiliates. To facilitate this analysis, he makes a list of the kinds of valuable, sensitive information that Agile has stored in its computers and for which certain laws, regulations and/or agreements impose obligations on Agile to avert breaches in its information security. There are, of course, other kinds of information, but the electronically transferred, processed and stored information concerns him most. His concern is to identify the standards that the applicable laws and regulations expressly dictate, or that are implied by the need to meet collateral obligations. As a check on his analysis, he compares his conclusions to the security standards for trans-Atlantic collaborative work on the JSF developed by the Sponsoring Companies,[131] to the requirements of HIPAA's Security Rule, and to the

---

court decisions nor the proposed rules contemplate emails that would not be initially preserved by the transmitter's system or would be accessible to the recipient unless overwritten or degraded by the system. However, recent reports point to new technologies that will either create no record of the transmittal or will make the email inaccessible due to a post-receipt withdrawal of permission to decrypt an encrypted e-mail. For example, users of the RIM Blackberry (or "Crackberry"), if not supported by enterprise server software (back in the office), will reportedly not have a record saved of what they sent: such persons "will have to settle for a system in which your e-mail (including AOL or Hotmail) is wirelessly auto-forwarded every 15 minutes, to your phone (and to a special website, for your traveling convenience). When you return to your Mac or PC, *you'll have no indication that you replied, composed, filed or deleted messages on your BlackBerry.*" Pogue, David, *For BlackBerry Users, a New Way to Write*, THE NEW YORK TIMES, p. G-1 at G-7 [Emphasis added.] The post-receipt encryption technology has reportedly been developed by Microsoft and IBM, enabling the sender to send encrypted e-mail and to embed in it a date and time limit to the decryption authorization, "which includes the right to print and copy." The report notes that "there may be little practical difference between a document that has been deleted and one that is out of reach because it is encrypted." Sinrod, Eric J., *The Legal Implications of Self-destructing E-mail*, USA TODAY, September 22, 2004, accessed at www.usatoday.com/tech/columnist/ericjsinrod/2004-09-22-sinrod_x.htm.

131. See, for example, Sponsoring Companies, *A Framework for Secure Collabora-*

guidance provided by the Commerce Department's National Institute of Standards and Technology Publications ("NIST") on information security.[132] These provide extremely thorough checklists for improving information security.

6.2 Information Security Obligations Imposed by the EAR—Issues Raised by Outsourcing.

The EAR contain no formal requirement for ensuring "information security." However, any information or other item controlled by the EAR that can be stored in digital form on a computer or other digital media imposes on the U.S. person that possesses such data the obligation to ensure that its information security precludes the unauthorized export and "deemed export" of such information. The EAR does not provide guidance on the level of precautions that a U.S. person must implement to fulfill such obligation. Instead, it mandates the occurrence that must be avoided: unauthorized transfer or export in violation of the EAR.[133] Agile should therefore ensure that no digitally stored items

---

tion across US/UK Defense, Version 1.0, March 5, 2003, accessed at www.afei.org/pdf/5mar2003_Final_Design.pdf.

132. NIST, through its Information Technology Laboratory (ITL), develops tests, test methods, reference data, and technical analyses to advance the development productive use of information technology. ITL has issued a series of publications on information security, including: NIST SP 800-16, *Guide for Developing Security Plans for Information Technology Systems;* NIST SP 800-27, *Engineering Principles for Information Technology Security (A Baseline for Achieving Security)*; NIST SP 800-47, *Security Guide for Interconnecting Information Technology Systems;* NIST SP 800-55, *Security Metrics Guide for Information Technology Systems;* and NIST SP 800-61, *Computer Security Incident Handling Guide.* NIST publications can be accessed at www.nist.gov.

133. Although one Commerce Control List Category—Category V—applies to "Telecommunications and 'Information Security,'" it does not provide Agile's counsel with any insight into the levels and precautions needed by Agile nor impose any additional information security obligations. It just establishes controls over items in that category, such as certain kinds of encryption.

Note also the information security obligations that must be addressed by the outsource vendor. As Smedinghoff points out: "As companies move to outsource an ever-increasing array of business processes, government regulators are focusing their efforts on requirements that ensure the security of the corporate information that will be under the control of the outsource provider. In many cases laws and regulations imposing information security obligations expressly cover the use of third party outsource providers. This is particularly true in the financial sector, and under the various E.U. data

controlled by the EAR can be accessed from cyberspace. The rationale for such an extreme blanket exclusion is that the current evaluations of existing vulnerabilities reported by software and firmware vendors, and of actual intrusions experienced by companies, make clear that such linkage poses an unnecessary risk. Agile should also ensure that no such items are downloaded onto portable devices that personnel can remove from its premises.

For certain "sensitive" exports, the EAR does impose precise security requirements. One such export that Agile contemplates making to Troll is high performance computers and related software.[134] As an inducement to Troll, Agile has proposed that the parties collaborate on designing a replacement for fly-by-wire software. Such software would need to be tested on high performance computers. The Joint Strike Fighter ("JSF" or "F-35"), like many U.S. developmental aircraft, has exceeded its weight budget (similar problems afflicted the ill-fated A-12 and the F-22).[135] As a result, project management has probably been compelled to issue directives for weight reduction solutions. The end-user will not want to reduce armament or weapon load capacity. One solution is to replace heavy and hard-to-maintain hydraulic actuation of flight controlled surfaces with actuation by a new electro-hydrostatic

protection laws. Thus, laws are recognizing that it is absolutely essential that any out-sourcing agreement impose information security obligations on the outsource provider in a manner designed to ensure that the data will be protected in a manner that satisfies the legal obligations." Smedinghoff, Thomas J., *Security & Surveillance: Trends in the Law of Information Security*, 4 BNA INTERNATIONAL WORLD DATA REPORT 8 (August 2004), p. 2.

134. High performance computers, or HPCs, can process prodigious quantities of complex calculations at substantially higher speeds than the common desktop computer. They do so by tightly integrating multiple processors with application and system software over a high-speed network. More specifically, they use multiple processors to perform parallel processing. Agile's programmers segment the computational aspects of the problem, and distribute the segments to different processors for concurrent processing. Completing several tasks concurrently, instead of sequentially, enables fly-by-wire (and the new power-by-wire) operations that require real-time computational resources provided by HPCs. Fly-by-wire was first introduced on the F-16. Power-by-wire may be introduced on the JSF.

135. Early in 2004, the manufacturer's design projections "determined that the jump-jet version of the aircraft was between 2,500lb and 2,800 lb (1,136kg-1,272kg) too heavy." Odell, Mark, *Lockheed Insists New Jet Will Fly*, FINANCIAL TIMES, July 20, 2004, p. 21. The same article notes that the weight problem has delayed a decision by the U.K.'s Royal Navy on ordering two new aircraft carriers that are to be designed launching and landing of the JSF.

flight control and power system that will substantially improve flight-by-wire. The prime contractor terms this new system "power-by-wire," and estimates that it will reduce gross takeoff weight by 6%.[136]

Since Agile manufactures hydraulic systems that "power-by-wire" would render obsolete and could displace from the JSF design, Agile hopes to position itself to be a subcontractor for the new systems and the software required to operate them. Troll recommends outsourcing some of software effort to a firm that it has worked with since 1997 in the island city of Bombay, renamed Mumbai,[137] the commercial capital of India ("MumbaiSoft"). Such outsourcing raises important questions under the EAR and its information security requirements, specifically: (i) what license (if any) will be needed, if Agile exports high performance computers ("HPCs") and related software to Troll in Norway; (ii) what license (if any) will be needed for their reexport to India; and (iii) what information security conditions will such license(s) impose on Agile, Troll and MumbaiSoft.

Before Agile can export HPCs (including the related software and technology) for a power-by-wire system to certain countries, it will have to obtain a license from the BIS, as a result of the strategic and proliferation significance of such items. Unlike many licenses, one for HPCs will almost certainly contain a long list of conditions imposed on the U.S. exporter (Agile) and the ultimate consignee and end-user. The EAR license requirements for HPCs are not reflected in the Country Chart. Instead, EAR Section 742.12 divides destination countries into three categories: Tiers 1, 3, and 4 (Tier 2 has ceased to exist and its countries have been moved to Tier 1).[138] The EAR contains a blanket prohibition on export of HPCs to Tier 4 countries (*i.e.,* Cuba, Iran, Libya, North Korea, Sudan and Syria).[139] Exports of HPCs to Tier 1 countries qualify for an exemption from the license requirement.[140] Norway is a Tier 1 country.[141] Agile will, therefore, require no license to export HPCs and related software to Troll. By contrast, exports of HPCs that have a CTP[142]

---

136. *Power by Wire*, AVIATION TODAY, June 12, 2004, accessed at www.aviation-today.com/cgi/av/show_mag.cgi?pub = av&mon = 0501&file = 0501flybywire.htm.

137. By Act of Parliament in 1997 the city of Bombay was renamed Mumbai. The city continues to be referred to by most people as Bombay.

138. 15 CFR §742.12(a)(2).

139. Id. As amended by the BIS's issuance of the proposed Interim Rule on Exports and Reexports to Iraq, which removed Iraq from the list of Tier 4 countries. See 69 FEDERAL REGISTER 149, July 30, 2004, p. 46070 at p. 46076.

140. 15 CFR §742(b)(1).

141. 15 CFR 740.7(c).

142. The acronym CTP is defined in the EAR to mean "composite theoretical

of greater than 190,000 MTOPS to Tier 3 countries require a license.[143] Since India is a Tier 3 country,[144] Agile will need to obtain a license for reexports of HPCs and related software to MumbaiSoft.

Although relations between the United States and India have improved markedly in the aftermath of 9/11, India and Pakistan occupy a unique position among the Tier 3 countries. There is a *presumption of denial* for all exports of HPCs to any Indian and Pakistani entities determined to be involved in nuclear, missile or military activities included in Supplement No. 4 to part 744 (referred to as the "Entity List").[145] Agile will need to scrutinize MumbaiSoft's relationships with the military-industrial entities of India in order to determine the applicability of this section. Any such relationship would be viewed by the BIS as posing a risk of diversion and could trigger a denial of the license.

Agile's counsel cautions that even if MumbaiSoft does not have any such high-risk relationships, a license application to reexport HPCs to it will still not result in an unqualified license. Instead, any such license will almost certainly contain "safeguard conditions," many of which require that enhanced information security measures be implemented by Agile (as U.S. exporter) and by MumbaiSoft (as ultimate end-user in India).

In the event Agile decides to apply for a license to reexport HPCs and related software to MumbaiSoft, Agile must submit a "security plan" to the BIS, signed by MumbaiSoft and by the export authorities in India. The "security plan" must contain specific elements that the BIS will impose as conditions to the license issued for that export. The EAR provides a list of 36 safeguard conditions (many with multiple subparts) that the BIS can add to the license, and that would apply information security precautions to the computer, its software and the related technical data. Such safeguard conditions could, for example, require the following of MumbaiSoft and Agile:

- Agile will assume responsibility for providing adequate security against physical diversion of the computer during shipment to MumbaiSoft (*e.g.*, using the most secure route possible—this pre-

---

performance," which is a measure of a computer's processing performance in units of MTOPS, or "millions of theoretical operations per second." See 15 CFR §772 definition of "composite theoretical performance."

   143. 15 CFR §740.7(d).
   144. 15 CFR §740.7(d).
   145. 15 CFR §742.12(b)(3)(iii).

cludes using the services or facilities of any country in Tier 4 (*i.e.*, Cuba, Iran, Libya, North Korea, Sudan, and Syria)).

- Upon delivery to MumbaiSoft, there will be **no reexport or intracountry transfer** of the computer without the prior written authorization of the BIS.

- The computer [*i.e.*, the HPC] will be used only for those activities approved on this license and reexport authorization.

- Agile shall only export software with the computer that supports the approved end-uses specified in this license.

- Agile will station security personnel[146] at MumbaiSoft's computer facility to ensure that the appropriate security measures are implemented.

- Agile's representatives shall be present when certain key computer functions are being carried out (*e.g.*, the establishment of new accounts, the assignment of passwords, the random sampling of data, the generating of daily logs, the setting of limits to computer resources available to users in the development mode).

- Agile's representatives shall perform all maintenance of the HPC system.

- Spare parts kept on site will be limited to the minimum amount. Spares will be kept in an area accessible only to Agile's representatives. Agile's representatives will maintain a strict audit system to account for all spare parts.

- The computer will be equipped with the necessary software to: permit access to authorized persons only, detect attempts to gain unauthorized access, set and maintain limits on usage, establish accountability for usage, and generate logs and other records of usage. This software will also maintain the integrity of data and program files, the accounting and audit system, the password or computational access control system, and the operating system itself.

- No computer will be networked to other computers outside MumbaiSoft's computer center without prior authorization from BIS.

---

146. The EAR does not specify whether such personnel must be U.S. citizens, but it would seem highly irregular and risky for a U.S. exporter of an HPC to a Tier 3 Country to delegate such responsibilities completely to nationals of a Tier 3 Country.

- There will be no direct input to the computer from remote terminals.
- The source code of the operating system will be accessible only to Agile's representatives. Only those individuals will make changes in this source code.
- MumbaiSoft will also cooperate with the U.S. Government or Agile's officials concerning the physical inspection of the computer using facility, on short notice, at least once a year and will provide access to all data relevant to computer usage.
- Agile will station representatives at MumbaiSoft's computer facility, or make such individuals readily available, to guide MumbaiSoft's security personnel in the implementation and operation of the security measures.
- Under guidance by the Agile personnel that Agile must station at MumbaiSoft's facilities, MumbaiSoft's security personnel must undertake certain measures (applicable to the computer, the software, and related technology and thus any technical data), which measures include:

  > Housing the computer system in one secure building and protecting it against theft and unauthorized entry at all times;

  > The establishment of a system to ensure the **round-the-clock supervision** of computer security;

  > The inspection, if necessary, of any program or software to be run on the computer system in order to ensure that **all usage conforms to the conditions of the license**;

  > The inspection of any output generated by the computer to determine whether the program runs or output conform with the conditions of the license;

  > The inspection of usage logs daily to ensure conformity with the conditions of the license and the **retention of records of these logs for at least a year**;

  > Nationals from any Computer 4 country (*e.g.*, Cuba, Iran, Libya, North Korea, Sudan, and Syria)[147] shall not be permitted, among other things, to:

---

147. See 15 CFR §742.12(a)(2). The Computer 4 rules prohibit nationals from those countries accessing any high performance computer "physically or computationally." See 15 CFR §740.7(b)(2).

❖ Access the computers;

❖ Have passwords or ID's used to access the restricted computers;

❖ Have any work done on their behalf on the restricted computers.[148]

Thus Agile's General Counsel should review in detail what reexports Agile intends to make to MumbaiSoft, and should ensure that Agile understands the potential range of security requirements that may be imposed. As illustrated by the high performance computer security provisions, the list can be exhaustive and burdensome. That Agile could be required to station highly trained personnel to enforce the security provisions of the license will increase the costs considerably, and demonstrates once again the unusually broad extraterritorial reach of U.S. export control. Counsel notes that Agile should anticipate that MumbaiSoft's officers and directors will not welcome such safeguards. They may well view the conditions as offensive and obtrusive, especially the stationing of Agile's personnel in MumbaiSoft's facilities and the intrusive monitoring to ensure information security.

The EAR also imposes record keeping obligations, which, in turn, imply obligations to maintain information security that will ensure the preservation of those records, the integrity of the information they contain, and the ready access to such records in the event of an audit or investigation. At least 43 sections of the EAR contain record keeping provisions.[149] For all exports, EAR Section 762.2 imposes the requirement that several records be kept, including:

• Export control documents
• Memoranda;
• Notes;
• Correspondence;
• Contracts;
• Invitations to bid;
• Books of account;

---

148. 15 CFR §742, Supplement No. 3.
149. A handy list appears at 15 CFR §762.2(b).

- Financial records; and,
- Restrictive trade practice or boycott documents[150] and reports.[151]

The EAR requires that the U.S. person must retain the "original records" in the form in which that person received or prepared them. The EAR relieves the U.S. person of the duty to retain the "original record" if they meet certain conditions ensuring that the BIS has access to an exact image of the original. Some of the permitted methods involve storing the records in digital media:

> "The regulated person may use any photographic, photostatic, miniature photographic, micrographic, automated archival storage, or other process that completely, accurately, legibly and durably reproduces the original records (whether on paper, microfilm, or through electronic digital storage techniques)."[152]

To create and retain any record other than the "original record," however, the regulated person must ensure that its computer and information security systems meet nine conditions. Those conditions include:

- When displayed on a viewer, monitor, or reproduced on paper, the records must exhibit a high degree of legibility and readability.
- The system must preserve the initial image (including both obverse and reverse sides of paper documents) and record all changes, who made them and when they were made. This information must be stored in such a manner that none of it may be altered once it is initially recorded.
- The regulated person must establish written procedures to identify the individuals who are responsible for the operation, use and maintenance of the system.
- The regulated person must keep a record of where, when, by whom, and on what equipment the records and other information were entered into the system.[153]

These records must be retained for a period of five years from the latest of certain events, including the date of export, any known reexport

---

150. Example: a proposed purchase order in which the overseas entity requests a representation that the U.S. person will not ship its goods on a vessel flying the Israeli flag or registered in Israel. To comply with such request would contravene the EAR. Moreover, the EAR imposes a duty to report each instance to the BIS.

151. 15 CFR §762.2.

152. 15 CFR §762.5(b).

153. 15 CFR §762.5(b).

or any termination of the transaction.[154] Losing track of records contravenes the requirement. Failing to keep the records free from corruption or damage contravenes the requirement. That records could be
tampered with, severely damaged or destroyed by hackers or malware
entering from the Internet, underscores the importance of counsel's
recommendation to keep such records on a computer or storage device
that is not linked to cyberspace.

6.3 Information Security Requirements Imposed by the TSR and ITAR.

Parties who engage in any transaction subject to any of the TSR
must keep a full and accurate record of each such transaction (whether
effected under a license or otherwise), and must retain such records for
reexamination for at least five years after the transaction.[155] If requested
by the Director of OFAC, the party must furnish under oath complete
information related to such transactions. Agile's information security
needs to cover all documents that OFAC could request on such occasions: books of account, contracts, letters or other papers connected
with any such transaction.[156]

Similarly, all U.S. persons that are required by the ITAR to register
with the Directorate of Defense Trade Controls must maintain records
concerning the "manufacture, acquisition, and disposition of defense
articles" for a period of five years from the expiration of the license or
other approval.[157] Agile has complied with such requirements since its
registration with the Directorate.

---

154. 15 CFR 762.6(a).

155. 31 CFR §501.601.

156. 31 CFR §501.602. To avert the burdens of such record keeping is another
reason to require Troll to complete disengagements, as requested, before Agile signs the
DPA.

157. 22 CFR §122.5(a). If a registrant triggers any of the reporting requirements
for political contributions or commissions, records of such payments must also be
retained. The Directorate can require that the records be kept longer than 5 years.

It is important to note that any U.S. company that modifies a product—hardware
or software—for a military use incurs the obligation to register with the Directorate
and thereby also incurs the record keeping obligations. It remains to be seen whether
companies that modify products for homeland security will be deemed thereby to have
come within the parameters of the ITAR if such items appear to thereby have a quasi-
military purpose. The line between BIS and Directorate licensing jurisdiction over such
items requires careful review by U.S. manufacturers and exporters. For example, the

6.4 Information Security Requirements Imposed by Personal Data Protection Laws.

From the diligence review of Troll, Brugge and Ijsselmeer, counsel notes that Troll should pose no additional information security problems, because it appears already to be compliant with the detailed requirements of Norway's Personal Data Act. (The information security requirements for compliance with personal data rules in Norway are more detailed and comprehensive than any required by Norway's export controls.) Norway's Personal Data Regulations require measures to "prevent the danger of loss of life and health, financial loss or loss of esteem and personal integrity, and to protect the confidentiality, availability and integrity of the data."[158] Moreover, those Regulations require

---

Directorate has licensing jurisdiction for chemical and biological protective and detection equipment specifically designed, developed, modified, configured, or adapted for military applications (see 22 CFR part 121, category XIV(f)), as is commercial equipment that incorporates components or parts controlled under that category unless those components or parts are: (1) integral to the device; (2) inseparable from the device; and (3) incapable of replacement without compromising the effectiveness of the device, in which case the equipment is subject to BIS's licensing jurisdiction under ECCN 1A004.

Note, however, that on May 6, 2004, the BIS issued a final rule revising the Commerce Control List, including a revision that imposed national security (NS2) and antiterrorism (AT1) license requirements on items under ECCN 1A004, such as (1) gas masks, filter canisters, and decontamination equipment therefore designed or modified for defense against biological agents or radioactive materials adapted for use in war or chemical warfare agents; and (2) protective suits, gloves, and shoes (similarly designed or modified for such uses). The new rule explains that in this entry the phrase "adapted for use in war" means "Any modification or selection (such as altering purity, shelf life, virulence, dissemination characteristics, or resistance to UV radiation) designed to increase the effectiveness in producing casualties in humans or animals, degrading equipment, or damaging crops or the environment." The new rule also notes that "Protective equipment and components are classified as 1A004 if they have been tested and proven effective against penetration of BW/CW [biological warfare/chemical warfare] agents or their simulants . . . for use by emergency responders or evacuees in chemical, biological, radiological or nuclear environments . . . even if such equipment or components are used in civil industries as mining, quarrying, agriculture, pharmaceuticals, medical . . . ." See 69 FEDERAL REGISTER 88, p. 25312 at p. 25313, May 6, 2004. That such distinctions require so much detail to explain suggests the inherent difficulty of separating the DDTC's and BIS's licensing jurisdiction over such items and the need to be wary of assuming BIS control when DDTC's more rigorous control may apply.

158. Personal Data Regulations, Section 2-1.

that, where any such dangers exist, the firm must address them with
plans and "systematic measures" that are "proportional to the probability and consequence of breaches of security."[159] The Personal Data
Regulations require Norwegian companies to do each of the following
to ensure information security:

- Prepare a formal information security strategy;[160]
- Conduct risk assessments to determine the probability and consequences of security breaches;[161]
- Adopt measures to prevent unauthorized access to equipment
  used to process personal data and to prevent unauthorized access
  to any equipment of significance for data security;[162]
- To **encrypt** any personal data that must be transferred electronically through a transfer medium that is beyond the physical control of the firm's data controller (or protected in other ways when
  confidentiality is necessary);[163]
- Adopt security measures that prevent unauthorized use of the information system and make it possible to **detect** attempts to make
  such use (each of which must be recorded);[164]
- Conduct security audits regularly that document any unforeseen
  use of the information system (referred to as a "discrepancy");[165]
  and,
- To eliminate the cause, and prevent the recurrence, of any such
  discrepancy, and, if the discrepancy resulted in an unauthorized
  disclosure of personal data where confidentiality was necessary, to
  notify Norway's Data Inspectorate.[166]

Norway's information security requirements clearly contemplate
electronic and Internet risks, and obligate a firm to take such measures
as are necessary to protect against them.

159. Id.
160. Id., § 2-2.
161. Id., § 2-4.
162. Id., § 2-9.
163. Id., § 2-11.
164. Id., § 2-14.
165. Id., § 2-5.
166. Id., § 2-6.

By comparison, the Netherlands' Personal Data Protection Act provides remarkably little specific guidance on information security, noting only in general term:

> "The responsible party shall implement appropriate technical and organizational measures to secure personal data against loss or against any form of unlawful processing. These measures shall guarantee an appropriate level of security, taking into account the state of the art and the costs of implementation, and having regard to the risks associated with the processing and the nature of the data to be protected. These measures shall also aim at preventing unnecessary collection and further processing of personal data."[167]

Canada's PIPEDA is slightly more specific than the Netherlands' law, but provides far less guidance than Norway's. PIPEDA requires that "security safeguards" protect personal information against "loss or theft . . . unauthorized access, disclosure, copying, use, or modification" regardless of the format in which a company stores or holds the information."[168] PIPEDA (unlike Norway's laws) provides no guidance on the handling of occurrences of unauthorized uses or attempted uses. Instead, PIPEDA merely recommends that more sensitive information be safeguarded by a higher level of protection (but even that is not mandatory).[169] On specific information security measures, PIPEDA merely recommends the use of technological measures such as "passwords" (an obsolete and inadequate protection) and "encryption" (which may provide little protection if the encryption level is low).[170]

The penchant for over-reliance on "passwords" as a safeguard, when combined with inadequate controls to govern their issuance and use, turns "passwords" into a hidden vulnerability. A recent security breach illustrates the problem. In late June of 2004, the Chief Executive of Marks and Spencer (the UK retailer that was the target of a takeover attempt) sought to retrieve his phone records from his mobile phone service provider, MMO_2. MMO_2 asked him to provide his "password." He had never received a "password," and apparently told that to MMO_2, but was told that "someone using his name had established one a week

---

167. Personal Data Protection Act, Section 13, accessed at http://home.planet.nl/~privacy1/wbp_en_rev.htm.
168. PIPEDA, Clause 4.7.1.
169. PIPEDA, Clause 4.7.2.
170. PIPEDA, Clause 4.7.3.

earlier."[171] This suggests that the Chief Executive's confidential phone records were disclosed without authorization, because the issuance of "passwords" by the service provider was not sufficiently secure. An MMO_2 spokesman explained the slip: "in order to gain access to the records, a determined imposter would have to be armed with sufficient information about the person they were impersonating."[172] Such explanation makes clear on its face that the service provider's security was not designed to resist efforts by a "determined imposter." Such a party, armed only with "information" about a company's chief executive, succeeded in causing the service to issue a "password" (that entitled its user to privileged access to confidential records). That the service provider claimed that the imposter "would only have access to standard billing information" fails to make clear the scope and substance of such information and whether it, in turn, could draw significant inferences about other undisclosed acquirers or bidders that, in a disputed takeover, could compromise confidentiality at several levels of the transaction. More importantly, from such information one can ascertain if there is a "white knight," which is valuable insider information. As the Financial Times report points out: the Chief Executive's "phone records are significant because [of] the, [UK] Financial Services Authority,[173] which is looking into insider dealing in M&S [Marks & Spencer] shares."[174]

6.5 Recommendations from the DMZ Design.

To the extent that Agile deems it necessary to improve its information security, the guidance in the EAR (noted above) and in the DMZ

---

171. Petzlik, Charles; Saigol, Lina; and Hargreaves, Deborah, *Takeover Battles: M&S Chief Hit by Breach of Security*, FINANCIAL TIMES, June 30, 2004, p. 19.

172. Id.

173. The Financial Service Authority is an independent non-governmental body given statutory powers by the Financial Services and Markets Act 2000. The Crown's Treasury appoints its Board. The statute defines its objectives as: "maintaining confidence in the financial system; . . . promoting public understanding of the financial system; . . . securing the appropriate degree of protection for consumers; . . . and reducing the extent to which it is possible for a business carried on by a regulated person to be used for a purpose connected with financial crime." Financial Services Authority, accessed at www.fsa.gov.uk/objectives.

174. Petzlik, Charles; Saigol, Lina; and Hargreaves, Deborah, *Takeover Battles: M&S Chief Hit by Breach of Security*, FINANCIAL TIMES, June 30, 2004, p. 19.

Design will provide good checks on what it has in place and on its proposed improvements. Agile's General Counsel suggests that Agile consider the following suggestions from the DMZ Design (the "Gold" level):

- Regularly scan the system for vulnerabilities at all levels, and ensure that as new ones are identified they are posted in real time throughout the system;
- Ensure that anti-virus updates and security patches are received immediately, and promptly checked and implemented;
- To the extent that Agile engages in collaborative work with Troll, ensure that the notification of any incidents of unauthorized access or use (and any attempts, including reconnaissance scans) are shared across the collaborative system;
- Ensure that Agile's and Troll's intrusion detection systems monitor critical internal networks and hosts as well as perimeter networks and hosts;
- To restrict execution privileges of mobile code, automate configuration management of the system's code;
- Note that, to the extent that Agile may monitor personnel in its affiliates outside of the U.S., it needs to check with legal counsel in advance to ensure that it is not violating privacy or personal data protection laws by such activity;
- Consider establishing a computer forensics team to gather information on incidents so that appropriate disciplinary or legal action can be taken against violators (but again, such team should only be established after conferring with counsel on procedures, particularly for the proper gathering and retention of evidence);[175]
- Recognize that, in a multi-national collaborative network, Agile will need to address problems of identifying, authenticating, and authorizing users by a delegated administrative solution (with Agile handling its own and Troll handling its own); the problem becomes acute, of course, if there is reexporting of HPCs to MumbaiSoft in India;[176]

---

175. Sponsoring Companies, *A Framework for Secure Collaboration across US/UK Defense*, Version 1.0, March 5, 2003, pp. 50–51.

176. Id., p. 64.

- Consider end-to-end encryption of defense related work by encrypting data during storage on servers, databases, storage area networks (although no one product currently can handle all of those), and (as of this date) require 156-bit or better encryption unless prohibited by local law;[177]
- Ensure that Agile's and Troll's intrusion detection alarms (at network and operating system level) notify security personnel and system administrators in real time at both companies; note that this problem becomes acute if MumbaiSoft is in the picture;
- Note that, as the Framework shrewdly points out, "In many cases, organizations have implemented" intrusion detection systems ("IDS"), "but do not respond to security events when" such systems alert administrators and analysts; the resulting "breakdown in the human chain and in the policies and procedures regarding escalation of security events can render an IDS useless."[178]

6.6 Adjust Precautions to Minimize Risks from the Expanded Use of Highly Vulnerable Telecommunications Technologies—Instant Messaging and VoIP.

New telecommunications technologies often enter the market without built-in security (partly because vendors may have deferred investments in security until the technology proves profitable, and partly because the security risks often are not well recognized until the technology is widely used). As usage of such unprotected technologies expands, these technologies add substantial vulnerabilities to an organization's computer systems. For that reason, Agile's Counsel is concerned with the lack of security inherent specifically in two of these technologies: instant messaging ("IM") which tends to be introduced unofficially by an organization's personnel, because they find it easy to use, effective in real-time and convenient, and Internet telephony or VoIP, which tends to be introduced officially by an organization's management, because VoIP offers potentially large cost savings and provides

---

177. Id., p. 69.
178. Id., pp. 73–74.

efficiencies not available from traditional telephone communications as part of a single package. (We will provide brief explanations of each with two caveats: first, VoIP which started out as a relatively simple technology has rapidly become quite complex, as successive generations of development offer enhanced features and equipment to handle all the calls of a global organization; and second, advising clients on security issues related to such new and complex technologies requires counsel to familiarize itself with the technology. At the same time, counsel must find ways to minimize the technical learning curve for clients who will have little patience for technical details but will require a foundation in it to appreciate the nature of the new security risks.)

Instant Messenging. IM originated in 1996 as a software that users could download for free from the Internet and has subsequently become a popular way for members of communities and social groups to communicate with one another. IM is best understood in comparison to its closest alternative, e-mail. To communicate by e-mail, a user types a message in an e-mail window and clicks the SEND button to dispatch it. Unless one employs intrusive software (discussed earlier), one does not know if the recipient is "in," or "online," or whether they received it or read it (until one receives a reply).[179] E-mails are stored on the sender's and receiver's computer systems (as well as on intermediary computers). E-mails tend to be written without revision, editing, and often in haste, thereby creating a document that, if reviewed in a subsequent investigation or litigation, will have the appearance of a formal writing but in fact evidence an almost non-reflective discourse (which in many cases has proved problematic for the sender, and sometimes for the recipient if they did not reply and dispute or disagree with the sender's message).

By contrast, to communicate by IM, a user opens a "session," sees who else on their "buddy list" is online, types a message (that is usually much shorter, uses more undefined acronyms, is less grammatical, and shows even less reflection than an e-mail message), and hits ENTER thereby transmitting the message to the selected online recipient who quickly receives a signal indicating that an IM transmittal has arrived at their computer. Although e-mails can be sent simultaneously to many recipients, the user can only attend to one e-mail message at a time. With IM, however, a user can simultaneously have open multiple sessions and be exchanging messages with several online interlocutors (reading the message from one, while typing a message to another).

179. Even the device of confirming receipt can be blocked by the recipient.

(Note, however, that unlike a chat room where several online users can type messages that will appear in the same window, IM sessions remain bilateral.) IM has several advantages over e-mail: once the parties open an IM session, the sender knows the recipient is online (and is not in doubt as to whether the message is being received and likely to be read); the communication is faster and more like a dialogue than is possible with e-mail; most IM software is free and easily downloaded from the Internet; it enables persons to communicate over long distances in dialogue that far more closely approximates a long-distance telephone conversation (without the charges); and IM facilitates the creation of communities of users (whether of co-workers, colleagues, friends, etc). It also offers a subtler benefit: a distance and detachment that enables persons to converse by IM who otherwise do not converse (*e.g.,* two co-workers who might not talk in the workplace or two students who do not talk at school often do so easily when communicating by IM).

IM usage (and non-usage) reflects a generation gap: many high school and college students and a company's younger employees use IM, whereas until recently most business executives did not use it, many were unfamiliar with its features, and few were aware of the broad extent of its use in the workplace. As a result, its use tended to enter an organization through the youngest personnel and could be widespread in an organization without senior management being aware that personnel were using it frequently for a large variety of official and unofficial purposes. By mid-2004, however, 92% of North American companies were reportedly using IM (although such report fails to make clear whether such usage is official, unofficial or a blend of both).[180] Most of those companies use a consumer version of IM (such as MSN Messenger, Yahoo Messenger or AOL Instant Messenger). As corporate usage has increased it has created a market for makers of software to enable organizations to "secure, archive and manage their employees' instant message traffic."[181]

IM, however, also has several disadvantages, most of which pose serious, often overlooked or underestimated risks to an organization's information security and thus increase its exposure to liability. Since records of IM are retained at the source, destination, and intermediary

---

180. Nasaw, Daniel, *AOL Withdraws from Part of Instant-Messaging Market*, The Wall Street Journal Online, June 21, 2004, accessed at http://online.wsj.com/PA2VJBNA4R/article/0,,SB108768030939842015-search,00.html.

181. Id.

computers, such records at a company can be the target of investigatory or litigation discovery requests. A company may, therefore, be taking an official position in an investigation or in litigation papers or trial testimony only to be impeached with the text of IM records that contradict such position. Senior management can, in good faith, express a belief that e-mail or IM records refutes. This has happened frequently in recent litigation when one party introduces emails of the other party into evidence. We think the risks posed by such records will probably be greater with IM records, because while e-mails are often carelessly written (or written without sufficient awareness and care for how they might be interpreted by a judge, jury, or arbitrator in a future litigation), IM communications are usually even worse in that respect. The speed with which they are written and exchanged leaves little or no time for reflection (to delete an excessive or exaggerated position or remove an incautious opinion). Their ungrammatical utterance, use of incomplete sentences, and heavy reliance on undefined acronyms makes them rife with ambiguities that can be distorted or misinterpreted subsequently by federal enforcement officials and triers of fact.

The fact that certain communities of IM users may adopt and standardize (in their communications) a set of acronyms does reduce such risks. For example, one IM provider, AOL, posts an *Acronym Dictionary* at its website[182] but that does not "fix" or "freeze" the meaning of the listed acronyms nor prevent the customary inventing of new acronyms "on the fly" by IM users. Since contracts can now be formed online (and are enforceable under the federal E-Sign Act), and since negotiations often occur by e-mail and by IM (both of which can be used to transmit attached files containing draft contracts), the use of IM acronyms in such communications can expose a company to unexpected commitments, agreements, and liability.

If a vendor's representative uses IM to offer a discount for a follow-on sale of spares and receives the following IM response from the customer, "WFM CID TIA," it might not be immediately obvious to the customer's legal counsel that the customer just expressed in shorthand the potentially enforceable contractual message "Works For Me. Consider It Done. Thanks In Advance." Of course, if the seller's IM communication opened with "DQMOT" (Don't Quote Me On This) and closed with "BICBW" (But I Could Be Wrong), the risk of enforceability

---

182. AOL Instant Messenger, *Acronym Dictionary*, accessed at www.aim.com/acronyms.adp?aolp = .

might be substantially reduced or at least more controversial. If such utterances occur in the context of potential violations of the Access Control Laws, the risks created by such ambiguities far outweigh the benefits of using acronyms and IM, notwithstanding assurances by the vendors (such as AOL's cheery encouragement in the use of its Dictionary and the listed acronyms, "Get your message across quickly and save yourself some keystrokes, too. Refer to this handy chart for the most commonly used acronyms among AIM users and before long, you'll be communicating faster than ever with friends, family and colleagues.")[183] When one considers the care that counsel take to define terms in definitive acquisition agreements, it is at a minimum perilous to have company personnel and officers negotiating the text of such agreements by use of IM and its unique diction and acronymic lexicon (where we doubt that anyone ever cites any dictionary, offline or online, to ensure a clear understanding of such acronyms, and the pace of communication would not permit discussion of such terms but instead encourages users to press on and hope that previous misunderstandings, if immediately important, will get clarified by further exchanges).

We would also emphasize that acronyms, unless formally defined in a discourse or document, can become contentious and controversial in subsequent litigation. In the defense industry, the acronym "N/A" often appears in hastily drafted contracts, progress and status reports and other significant correspondence, often without the recipient being aware (particularly if they are overseas) of the range of possible meanings that the sender may later elect to claim he "intended," since N/A can arguably mean "Not Applicable," "Not Avoidable," "Not Available," or "Not Agreed."[184]

Organizations, moreover, are often unaware of the extent to which their personnel use IM for official and unofficial communications at work. Even if an organization locks out or otherwise precludes the

---

183. Id.

184. Thus with the adoption of IM, one can foresee acronyms invented that mean one thing the day they are sent but are claimed to mean something quite different during an investigation. For example, in the context of IM communications during recurrent failures of flight critical USAF software in acceptance tests, the acronym TTITTF might have been intended and understood in the original message to mean "Terminate Tests Its Too Tough To Fix" (i.e., cease testing this module but don't report the problem to the government customer) and later be claimed by the sender or recipient to have actually meant "Time to Tell It To The Feds" to purportedly encourage disclosure of the problem to the customer.

downloading of IM software into its computers, its personnel can usually access IM by sending messages directly from a Web browser and thereby introduce unanticipated vulnerabilities into an organization's computer system that tend to remain unnoticed by management until an IM vulnerability results in a recognized security breach. Unfortunately, many security breaches that result from the use of IM remain undetected. Users are often not aware when others access their messages. Moreover, users seldom attempt to authenticate the identities of others in an IM session, and there is, in fact, no consistent and reliable way to verify the identify of IM senders, exposing users (and their organizations) to hijackings of their IM sessions or to participating in sessions that can result in the unauthorized release of sensitive information inadvertently to strangers.

One potential of harm from IM was illustrated in May of 2002 when the CERT Coordination Center issued a warning that intruders were tricking unsuspecting users into "downloading and executing malicious software, which allows the intruders to use the systems as attack platforms for launching distributed denial-of-service (DDoS) attacks," and reported that tens of thousands of systems had been compromised by such attacks.[185] Other sources of potential harm from IM are inadvertently introduced when the prospective user downloads the requisite IM software or when an experienced user downloads an upgrade of such software, because increasingly such software comes "bundled" inextricably with so-called "adware" that often functions as "spyware." For example, AOL offers a security caution to its IM users that, if they receive an IM communication that asks them to "check out" certain links (such as www.buddylinks.net) they should disregard it because,

> "This link takes users to a website that asks them to download a game. If the user agrees to download the game, the website also installs a secret "adware" program on the user's machine that can deliver unwanted advertisements and promotions. The adware program will also send the same link out to every person on the user's Buddy List—spamming their friends and associates with a link to the same adware."[186]

---

185. Cert Coordination Center, *Social Engineering Attacks via IRC and Instant Messaging,* Cert Summary CS-2002-02, May 28, 2002, accessed at www.cert.org/summaries/CS-2002-02.html.

186. AOL Instant Messenger, *Online Security/Safety FAQ,* accessed at www.aim.com/help_faq/security/faq.adp?aolp = .

However, in April of 2004, AOL entered into an agreement to offer WeatherBug software in two forms in upgrades of its IM software: in one version, users receive WeatherBug at no cost (but also apparently with no option to decline it) and will receive ads as a result of adware embedded in WeatherBug; in an optional version, users *pay* to receive WeatherBug *without* adware.[187] AOL and WeatherBug, however, offer divergent interpretations concerning the advertisements: AOL sells an ad-free version of WeatherBug, but otherwise provides a version that will direct ads to the user; WeatherBug, on its website, insists that it is not adware:

> "Nor is WeatherBug adware—we are scrupulously careful about the inalienable rights of our consumer and business users, and adhere to the strictest standards that currently exist relating to meaningful notice, informed consent and user control. Read our Bill of Rights."[188]

We think such inconsistencies will prove problematic for organizations whose employees may be using such products. Moreover, unless an organization's employees all purchased the ad-free version, the organization's computers will inevitably receive substantially increased traffic from such advertisements, thus slowing down system performance and increasing the risks from malwares. AOL acknowledges there are risks from malware due to vulnerabilities in related software, as it explains in a posted response to a Frequently Asked Question "Are there any known security issues that might affect AIM [AOL's IM software]?:"

> "A security hole in the Windows version of Internet Explorer allows a malicious website to run dangerous code on your computer if you visit that website. The attacker can then control your computer, and sign on with your AIM Screen Name if your password is stored (although your password would not actually be revealed). If you think your computer has been compromised, you should immediately change all of your AIM passwords here. All users should

---

187. Naraine, Ryan, *AIM 5.5 Adds WeatherBug*, Earthweb, April 19, 2004, accessed at www.instantmessagingplanet.com/public/article.php/3342301.

188. WeatherBug, *Not Spyware, Not Adware*, accessed at http://ww3.weatherbug.com/aws/notspyware.html.

immediately install the security patch, available from Microsoft at http://www.microsoft.com/technet/security."[189]

In July of 2004, however, the Federal Deposit Insurance Corporation ("FDIC") expressed much greater concerns with respect to IM security risks when it circulated a Financial Institution Letter cautioning that since IM was not originally developed for commercial use "it lacks standard security features, "[190] and explained:

"The lack of built-in security, the ability to download files and the built-in "buddy list" of recipients create an environment in which viruses and worms can spread quickly. . . . This threat has additional risks to the workplace network because public IM does not travel through a central server where traditional corporate anti-virus protection software is located. . . . [Moreover] IM transmits unencrypted information . . . on the Internet and may be accessed by anyone. . . . The risks associated with the use of IM include revealing confidential information over an unsecured delivery channel, spreading viruses and worms, and exposing the network to backdoor Trojans which are hidden programs on a system that perform a specific function once users are tricked into running it. IM is vulnerable to denial-of-service attacks, hijacking sessions and legal liability resulting from downloading copyrighted files"[191]

Even if an organization attempts to configure its network "firewalls" to block all IM that stratagem will probably not block IM completely, because IM has what is known as a "port crawling" or "port agile" feature that enables IM transmitted messages to locate and travel

189. AOL Instant Messenger, *Online Security/Safety FAQ*, accessed at www.aim.com/help_faq/security/faq.adp?aolp = #issues.

190. Dow Jones Newswires, *FDIC: Banks Should Restrict Use of Instant Messages*, July 21, 2004, The Wall Street Journal Online, accessed at http://online.wsj.com/article/0,,BT_CO_20040721_008815-search,00.html?collection = autowire%2F30day&vql_string = instant + messaging%3Cin%3E%28article%2Dbody%29.

191. FDIC, *Guidance on Instant Messaging*, July 21, 2004, p. 1, accessed at www.fdic.gov/news/news/financial/2004/fil8404a.html. The FFIEC cautions that IM can cause the introduction of malicious code into an organization: "Typically malicious code is mobile, using e-mail, Instant Messenger, and other peer-to-peer (P2P) applications, or active content attached to Web pages as transmission mechanisms." FFIEC, INFORMATION SECURITY (IT EXAMINATION HANDBOOK), December 2002, p. 53.

through any port that has not been blocked.[192] To mitigate the risks introduced by IM, the FDIC offered the following recommendations:

- "Establish a policy to restrict public IM usage and require employees to sign an acknowledgement of receipt of the policy.
- Consider implementing an intrusion detection system to identify IM traffic. . . .
- Create rules to block IM delivery and file-sharing.
- Consider blocking specific IM vendors.
- Ensure a strong virus protection program [and] . . . a strong patch (software update) management program.
- Include the vulnerabilities of public IM in information security awareness training."[193]

Surprisingly, the FDIC Letter does not mention the risks of adware and spyware from IM, although such risks appear to be increasing as IM providers seek to generate revenues from the otherwise "free" IM software. Note that while sometimes the distinction between "adware"

---

192. FDIC, *Guidance on Instant Messaging*, July 21, 2004, p. 4, footnote 2, accessed at www.fdic.gov/news/news/financial/2004/fil8404a.html.

193. Id., p. 2. Other IM security risks include: (1) IM messages tend to be sent in clear text, and are thereby susceptible to interception by hackers; (2) they often use TCP/IP port 80 for communications that tend to be left open by firewalls to facilitate Web browsing; and (3) antivirus software is often not configured to check and interpret IM-transmission protocols, only Web traffic. Lawton, George, *Instant Messaging Puts on a Business Suit*, IEEE COMPUTER, March 2003, p. 15. Symantec officials have expressed concerns that IM systems are vulnerable to attack by a worm and that such an attack could "spread to half a million machines in 30 or 35 seconds." Metz, Cade, *The IM Security Threat?*, PC MAGAZINE, August 17, 2004, p. 20.

In addition, IM's casual nature encourages users to be less than professional in their communications. Their messages, on one hand, often "go uncaptured by any corporate database, making them unauditable;" on the other hand, however, users overlook the fact that even when their transmitting system does not retain a copy, any of the participants in their IM conversation can "copy and paste the entire chat onto a notepad or Word document, and some IM services allow you to archive entire messages." *Our Hottest Security Tips: Sage Advice for Protecting Corporate Assets in a Dangerous World*, COMPUTERWORLD Executive Bulletin, November 2004, pp. 13–14. The unintended consequences of such actions can include that other parties to a litigation would have copy of communications from a company's staff but the company itself would not have copy, which could provide opposing counsel with records it could use to surprise and undermine a witness' position in depositions and cross-examinations.

and "spyware" expresses little more than a difference between a critic's perspective (calling it spyware) and a vendor's perspective (calling it adware), there is more often the understanding that spyware can be used by third parties to conduct surveillance on a user's sessions on the Internet and on their computer, *e.g.*, recording "confidential passwords used for online banking or pilfer sensitive information leading to identity theft."[194] Commercial firms should also be considering those risks when reviewing policies on the use, restriction or prohibition of IM. We would also emphasize that since corporate officers would never agree (in our experience) to have their negotiations of a transaction tape recorded or videotaped, they should bear that reservation in mind when reviewing policies for IM, because IM records may create a similar record of online negotiations.[195]

VoIP. Voice over Internet Protocol (or VoIP) refers to a combination of hardware and software that enables users to conduct telephone conversations over the Internet (a digital data medium) instead of over traditional telephone lines (an analog voice transmission medium). The technology first appeared in 1995 (when Vocaltec, Inc. marketed Internet Phone Software), which made possible telephony from one desktop or laptop computer to another, with the signal sent and received by modems at the source and destination.[196] VoIP is a technology whose basic technical aspects need to be understood in order to appreciate the security risks it poses. Since VoIP is a significant change in telephony communications, it is best understood by comparing it to the traditional telephone system. In its simplest form, traditional telephony involved a

---

194. Bobelian, Michael, *The Spyware War*, THE NEW YORK LAW JOURNAL, May 6, 2004, p. 5. Note that in March of 2004, Utah enacted broad anti-spyware legislation. See Schwartz, John, and Hansell, Saul, *The Latest High-Tech Legal Issue: Rooting out the Spy in Your Computer*, THE NEW YORK TIMES, April 26, 2004, p. C-3. See also Clyman, John, *Antispyware*, PC MAGAZINE, August 3, 2004, p. 89, which makes the sensible recommendation (that users often ignore): "When you install a new application, read the end user license agreement (EULA) carefully. . . . But shareware and freeware often pack a spyware payload, which should appear in the EULA." P2P software often contains embedded adwares and spywares.

195. With respect to such negotiations, if the officers of the company later know or should know that a litigation or investigation is reasonably likely to occur, they would have a duty to preserve all relevant evidence, including the IM records of such negotiations. Such records may prove as valuable to prosecutors and opposing counsel as email records have been in recent litigations.

196. Dvorak, John C.; Pirillo, Chris; and Taylor, Wendy, ONLINE! THE BOOK, Prentice Hall, 2004, p. 679.

one-to-one link from a source phone to a destination phone. However, that description omits an important feature: the nature of the link. If we are not careful, we may think of traditional telephony as merely an electrical form of two tin cans connected by a wire.

When a user lifts the receiver to initiate a call, he hears a dial tone that signifies that a *circuit* has been opened from his phone to the telephone carrier's local office. When the user dials the number of the destination phone (local or long distance), the telephone carrier's local office routes the circuit through a switch to the destination phone. When the recipient of the call lifts the receiver, the circuit is complete and open between the source and destination phones. This voice transmission mode uses an analogue signal, and is referred to by the method used by the carrier to complete the circuit, *i.e.,* "circuit switching." The traditional telephony system is referred to as a "plain old telephone system" ("POTS"). POTS is valued by users for its clarity and seeming lack of interruptions—it replicates the voice without introducing time lags that would create ambiguity and confusion. Note, however, that it is also an inefficient system, in that the signal tends to be in one direction at a time, which is not a problem for users since they tend to adhere to a convention in which not more than one user speaks at a time (even in a conference call). While the circuit is open throughout the duration of the call, there is relatively a small amount of signal transmitted.

To use traditional telephony for long-distance calls, a telephone call uses what is known as the "Public Switched Telephone Network" ("PSTN") whereby a call initiated by a source phone, routed to the local carrier's office, is then linked to a long-distance carrier (who charges a fee for each such connection), and then to the destination's carrier and onto the destination phone. The addition of the long-distance carrier does not, however, change the form of the signal—it remains a purely analog voice signal.

By contrast, when a user places a call through the use of VoIP, the analog voice signal must be converted into a digital signal and divided into data packets,[197] so that it can be transmitted in the same manner

---

197. A packet is a block of data that includes in its package the addressing and other information necessary for its delivery. Devices such as routers and switches move packets inside a network and between networks. In a network (that uses the Transmission Control Protocol/Internet Protocol or TCP/IP) each server or computer is assigned an IP or numeric address, which is its unique address. See GAO, *Technology Assessment: Cybersecurity for Critical Infrastructure Protection*, GAO-04-321, May 2004, p. 38.

as other data (e-mails and any attached files) from a source computer to a destination computer via the Internet. VoIP thus does not involve the local carrier's "circuit switching." Instead, it uses what is referred to as "packet switching."

When a caller uses VoIP, he may initiate the call with a variety of instruments (a POTS, a mobile phone, an Internet Protocol phone ("IP Phone"), a wireless LAN phone, or a software-based phone in a computer ("Soft Phone") running client software). If he is using a calling card, he may first dial a special code, to route the call to a VoIP service, and then add the long distance number of the destination phone. If he is using an IP Phone or Soft Phone, the special code is usually unnecessary, because the call will be routed automatically to the VoIP service. When he speaks, the voice analog signal is sent to a source IP voice gateway (often provided by the VoIP service company, and located either within the caller's company, at the local phone company's offices or at another location). This first stage of the signal's journey can use either the traditional PSTN or a private IP telephony network. The source gateway converts the analog voice signal into a digital signal, removes or cancels the echo (inherent in traditional voice telephony), compresses the signal (so that it can be sent quickly enough to keep latency to a minimum), translates it into IP packets, and routes it for transmission over a telecommunications network (which most commonly will be the Internet) to an IP voice gateway nearest to the destination phone. This destination gateway reverses the process, reassembling the voice packets, uncompressing them and converting them from digital back to an analog voice signal. It then routes the signal through the destination's local PSTN to the destination phone. The user at the destination phone hears the sender's analog voice signal. (Note that the entire process can be internal to a global company, with the transmissions occurring over the company's intranet, or it can be over a service provider's broadband network.)[198]

However, depending on the quality of the service, there may be pauses or brief interruptions which can be distracting and, if accompanied by omissions of part of the voice signal, can cause confusion or misunderstandings. The delays and losses occur for several reasons: (i) data transmissions over the Internet do not occur continuously, but in bursts at indeterminate intervals (unlike voice, which tends to be a

---

198. See Belson, Ken, *Web Phone Service May Have It All, Except Many Users*, THE NEW YORK TIMES, July 25, 2004, Section 3 (Sunday Business), p. 7.

relatively continuous flow), causing "jitter" or variations in the arrival time of the voice packets; (ii) efforts to reduce "jitter" (often by holding the fastest transmissions, thus allowing the packets to be delivered in their original sequence) can cause longer delays between deliveries of packets and unintended pauses in the voice; (iii) transmissions of data over the Internet (during peak load periods or periods of congestion) often result in loss or partial loss of data packets (to rectify such problems systems may send redundant information). Moreover, if a system of limited bandwidth is occupied by transmission of a large data file, this can also cause voice packets to drop out or be delayed.[199]

The potential cost savings in the use of VoIP result from: (i) the bypassing of traditional circuit-switched networks (particularly if the VoIP service does not use PSTN); (ii) the consolidation of equipment (if IP phones replace traditional phones and enable users to employ one network for transmission of both voice and data); and (iii) utilization of excess bandwidth. It also creates the possibility for adding features unavailable through traditional telephony (such as advanced multimedia transmissions).[200]

---

199. Dvorak, John C.; Pirillo, Chris; and Taylor, Wendy, ONLINE! THE BOOK, Prentice Hall, 2004, p. 678–681, 684, 690, and 692; and Gralla, Preston, HOW THE INTERNET WORKS, 7th edition, QUE, 2004, pp. 120–121. Note that VoIP bypasses the long distance carrier (and its associated charges). If the call begins with the dialing of a special number (before the long distance number) the routing of the call will also bypass the PSTN. This account still oversimplifies the process. For additional explanation of how VoIP works, see sources quoted above in this footnote.

Note that VoIP can reduce a call's confidentiality and its integrity. As explained by KPMG's Zarrella and McNally, "Traditional telephony operating over a dedicated PSTN network does not require encryption. A confidentiality breach in the traditional network generally requires physical connection to the network to eavesdrop on conversations from selected lines. . . . With VoIP, the nature of the underlying protocol makes it relatively easy to identify calls from a particular location from anywhere in the direct network. Tools to enable eavesdropping are widely available and encryption of voice traffic is the essential means to combat this. . . . An example of the potential implication of not encrypting is having a user's phone banking details (account number or pin tones) intercepted across the network. . . . A dedicated VoIP VPN can be used to encrypt data over disparate locations; however, if encryption is not performed between the appropriate endpoints (for example, between gateways instead of between handsets), the encryption might not be effective." Zarrella, Egidio, and McNally, Peter, VOICE OVER IP: DECIPHER AND DECIDE: UNDERSTANDING AND MANAGING THE TECHNOLOGY RISKS OF ADOPTION, KMPG International, 2004, p. 14.

200. Dvorak, John C.; Pirillo, Chris; and Taylor, Wendy, ONLINE! THE BOOK, Prentice Hall, 2004, p. 678.

The widely reported advent of VoIP (the launch of broadband Voice over Internet Protocol) for transmission of consumer voice communications services in North America, Europe and Asia has been matched by the much less reported investment in what is termed "enterprise VoIP" or "LAN (local area network) telephony" supported by the leading networking equipment manufacturers (Cisco Systems, Avaya, Nortel Networks and Mitel Networks). The magnitude of corporate investment in "enterprise VoIP" is projected by Cisco Systems to exceed $30 billion in the period from 2004 to 2008.[201] Organizations (ranging from health care service providers to aerospace companies such as Boeing) have elected to replace their land line traditional telephones with company-wide "enterprise VoIP" to achieve cost savings, to shift all voice traffic to an internal corporate data network, and to take advantage of advanced features available with VoIP such as " 'follow-me' telephone services and extensive call logging and management," as well as the possibility of integrating video and other multimedia group applications.[202]

As of this writing, new second-generation "enterprise VoIP" equipment is entering the market, accompanied by what is referred to as "Second-generation VoIP based on Internet standards–SIP, Soap and Simple."[203] Regardless of whether an organization adopts a first or second generation VoIP, there is the high probability that it will fail to recognize the need for a concomitant analysis of the increased vulnerability it thereby incurs in its information security. However, the implementation of an enterprise VoIP will inevitably be far more complex, involving additional equipment such as routers, Ethernet switches, telephone gateways and servers linked together to create VoIP network boundaries and to provide interfaces to other networks. (Since these boundaries and interfaces will probably be among the major sources of VoIP vulnerabilities, counsel will eventually need to develop a method of explaining them.)

Agile is considering replacing its traditional telephone systems with second-generation enterprise VoIP (partly to follow Boeing's lead in the aerospace industry and partly because it has learned that Troll already makes extensive, although not company-wide, usage of enterprise VoIP). It is therefore necessary for counsel to develop a checklist of

---

201. Taylor, Paul, and Budden, Rob, *Save a Packet on Phone Calls*, FINANCIAL TIMES IT Review, July 21, 2004, p. 6.
202. Id.
203. Id.

VoIP risks, by reviewing trouble-shooting recommendations posted on the websites of VoIP vendors (such as Cisco), and by reviewing the valuable resources provided by the National Institute of Standards and Technology's Computer Security Division's publications, particularly the 2004 U.S. Defense Information Systems Agency ("DISA") publication designed to assist in the improvement of security for DoD information systems—the *Voice Over Internet Protocol (VoIP) Security Technical Implementation Guide*—which the DoD refers to as the "STIG."[204] Many of the security concerns arise from the design of the network supporting the VoIP environment. Explaining the risks that arise from VoIP requires a basic understanding of the change that VoIP makes in such networks.

Cisco's website acknowledges risks in using its VoIP service and the need to prepare for what it refers to as the "emergencies" that can result:

"Router crashes, buffer leaks, router hangs, and high CPU utilization can cause major delays. Get prepared for such potential emergencies and more with a troubleshooting guide."[205]

Unfortunately, the site merely provides a sequence of hyperlinks that cause the visitor to anticipate that it will find (with a mouse-click) a web page providing a "troubleshooting guide" or resources from which to construct such a guide. Perhaps these hyperlinks are a "work in progress," but the site does not acknowledge that, and thus the visitor finds only, with each click, the following (the hyperlinks are the underlined text):

"Recommended Readings
Instructive books and articles categorized by specific technologies"[206]
"Recommended Readings
Find articles, books, and other technical resources about networking technologies.

---

204. DISA Field Security Operations, *Voice Over Internet Protocol (VoIP) Security Technical Implementation Guide*, Version 1, Release 1, January 13, 2004, accessed at http://csrc.nist.gov/pcig/STIGs/VoIP-STIG-V1R1R-4PDF.pdf.

205. Cisco, *IP Telephony/VOIP Troubleshooting*, accessed at www.cisco.com/en/US/tech/tk652/tk701/tech_troubleshooting.html.

206. Id.

Command Reference"[207]
"Command Reference
Downloads
Command Reference
Table of Contents
Cisco IOS Command Reference
allow-connections

. . .

debug voip ipipgw

. . .

media (dial peer)
zone cluster remote . . ."[208]

Thus, the hyperlinks' promise of a troubleshooting guide points, in fact, to a cyber-mirage that leads the visitor to merely a page of technical commands, and fails to provide guidance on measures to avoid the "emergencies" that Cisco warns will result from "major delays" caused by "router crashes, buffer leaks, router hangs, and high CPU utilization." (Cisco deserves credit for acknowledging those problems, but companies need better metrics in order to decide on the impacts such "major delays" might have on their communications and operations.) One can find elsewhere on Cisco's website further acknowledgement of VoIP performance risks which, depending on their manifestation in a user's system, might also pose information security risks. For example, on a page offering guidance to overcome quality of service ("QoS") problems, Cisco emphasizes that different calls may utilize substantially different quantities of bandwidth, that such differences need to be analyzed and minimized, and then explains that ultimately:

> "With VoIP, the main things to look for when troubleshooting QoS issues are dropped packets and network bottlenecks that can cause delay and jitter.

---

207. Id.
208. Cisco, *IP Telephony/VOIP—Troubleshooting—Commands*, accessed at www.cisco.com/en/US/tech/tk652/tk701/tech_recommended_readings09186a00801d0822.html#1033249.

Look for:

- Interface drops
- Buffer drops
- Interface congestion
- Link congestion"[209]

Agile's counsel notes those risks (including the resources that may be required to continuously tweak a VoIP system to provide the desired and promised performance), but finds a more informative and easier to understand resource in the DISA's STIG.

The STIG emphasizes that VoIP has certain performance weaknesses that can be overcome, but only by taking additional precautions. For example, VoIP has often appeared to provide a degraded quality of voice transmission due to time-lags (pauses) that can confuse callers (*e.g.*, by making them think the other party has stopped speaking, or by altering the intended intonation). This problem, known as "latency in voice transmission" is much more noticeable in voice communications than the similar problem of "latency in data transmissions" (when one computer sends data packets to another). As a result, if an organization's network is to provide a smooth transmission of voice and data, it must treat voice and data traffic differently, be able to prioritize these two different types of traffic, provide a guaranteed throughput level (for voice), and ensure that voice packets receive priority over data packets in order to achieve the required quality of service.

The DISA's STIG identifies vulnerabilities in systems that rely on VoIP or enterprise VoIP and offers recommendations to mitigate an organization's exposure to such risks, including the following:

- *Vulnerability:* Since voice is being transmitted in packets over the Internet and is not protected the way traditional telephony or POTS communications are from eavesdropping and wire tapping, *it is vulnerable like e-mails to interception at many points prior to delivery to its destination.*

---

209. Cisco, *Troubleshooting and Debugging VoIP Call Basics*, accessed at www. cisco.com/warp/public/788/voip/voip_debugcalls.html.

➤ *Recommendation:* Deploy VoIP systems and components on their own logically different, dedicated networks that are *not* shared with the local data network.[210]

- *Vulnerability:* Since VoIP often involves the replacement of traditional phone hardware by so-called "soft phones" hosted by a desktop computer and that must reside on the data segment, these "soft phone" hosts are susceptible to any external or internal attack on the organization's computer system. They are more vulnerable to attacks due to the increased number of possible entries into the system (such as the Operating System, resident applications, and enabled services, each of which can be vulnerable to viruses and worms). Thus "soft phones," if used, *create a conduit for malicious attack against the voice transmissions pose a serious risk to the VoIP* environment, and *they pose the risk that if a virus or worm "crashes" an organization's computer network it will no longer have the alternative of communicating by POTS* (which usually continue to operate during such attacks and crashes).

  ➤ *Recommendation:* Ensure that "soft phones" are permitted only where their intended use has been identified and the inherent risks have been reviewed and precautions taken to minimize such risks. (Counsel adds his own suggestion that Agile retain traditional telephony as a critical backup system.)

- *Vulnerability:* To overcome "latency in voice transmissions," a VoIP system needs to "open" four ports[211] in a network's firewalls *for each call initiated or received.* "Opening a range of ports this large would surely compromise any network."[212]

  ➤ *Recommendation:* Compartmentalize the VoIP servers to isolate and protect them from unauthorized access. There are two methods to accomplish this. One solution involves limiting the range of ports that may be used for VoIP traffic; but this method has the drawback that it does not avoid the need to

---

210. DISA Field Security Operations, *Voice Over Internet Protocol (VoIP) Security Technical Implementation Guide*, Version 1, Release 1, January 13, 2004, p. 21, accessed at http://csrc.nist.gov/pcig/STIGs/VoIP-STIG-V1R1R-4PDF.pdf.

211. Two ports for signaling and two ports for transmitting and receiving user information.

212. DISA Field Security Operations, *Voice Over Internet Protocol (VoIP) Security Technical Implementation Guide*, Version 1, Release 1, January 13, 2004, p. 24, accessed at http://csrc.nist.gov/pcig/STIGs/VoIP-STIG-V1R1R-4PDF.pdf.

open four ports for each call, and as call traffic rises in an organization during the work day, the number of ports opened (and vulnerabilities created in the firewalls) rises rapidly to an unacceptable level. The other solution involves having the firewall "broker" all VoIP calls, and has the drawback that it takes considerable time to configure and must be altered each time a VoIP user is added or removed from the system. The STIG recommends that firewall controls be placed "in front of all networks and components supporting VoIP servers," and thus inevitably requires additional equipment and time to configure and check it.

- *Vulnerability:* Since the network servers that support VoIP (and thus the organization's telephone system) are mission critical for the organization's operations, and since such servers contain sensitive information (such as the logging of all calls), these servers need to be viewed as being vulnerable to any malware that could affect the system's computers.

  - ➤ *Recommendation:* Place such servers and components on a separate network protected by a "VoIP aware firewall" and dedicate them solely to VoIP operations.[213]

A review of white papers published by some VoIP vendors reveals other critical information security risks to companies that converge their telephony and data communications into a VoIP system, because "Deploying voice applications on the converged infrastructure exposes the applications to new threats of disclosure, integrity, and denial of service. Each threat and threat category highlight the potential for the loss of significant tangible and intangible business value."[214] Avaya's white paper on security identifies the following risks:

- Threat of disclosure of private, confidential conversations through "eavesdropping:"

  "In the data world eavesdropping involves sniffing network packets for data that can be interpreted in real-time or saved for later

---

213. Id. Also, see Kuhn, Richard D., Walsh, Thomas J., and Fries, Steffen, *Security Considerations for Voice Over IP Systems*, NIST Special Publication 800-58, January 2005, accessed at http://csrc.nist.gov/publications/nistpubs/800-58/SP800-58-final.pdf, published as this book was going to press.

214. Avaya, *Security in Converged Networks*, white paper, February 2003, p. 5, accessed at www1.avaya.com/enterprise/whitepapers/msn1841.pdf.

analysis or playback. In the converged space, the new eavesdropping threat involves sniffing voice conversations. The probability of being vulnerable to eavesdropping increases as voice applications move to converged networks because shared IPnetworks are directly accessible with wider user access and thus are easier to sniff for traffic than are traditional voice networks."[215]

• Threats to integrity of stored data:

"Integrity threats are threats based on the insertion of bogus content into files or communication streams. Attackers may insert malicious or misleading data into unprotected files. When read or executed with the assumption that the files have integrity, the corrupt files may disrupt system operation. Attackers may also change the contents of data as they are transferred resulting in the improper interpretation of the data. Another integrity threat involves an attacker spoofing the identity of a valid user. When successful, the imposter may gain access to proprietary information or systems and operate with the full privileges of the impersonated user."[216]

• Use of modems for remote access (thereby creating security hole in defense perimeter):

"A particularly challenging situation exists when an unauthorized modem is attached to an employee workstation enabling a bridge between the public phone network and the enterprise data network. An attacker can gain access to the enterprise data network by finding the modem, perhaps by war dialing, and taking control of the victim's computer. The unauthorized bridge represents a vulnerability to the enterprise network."[217]

Recent reports suggest that authors of malwares have started to target VoIP systems:

215. Id.
216. Id., p. 6.
217. Id., p. 9. Note that Avaya's warranty for its VoIP products specifies, among its exclusions, "failure to implement all new releases to Software provided under the Agreement"; *i.e.,* its warranty is conditioned on the user implementing all patches Avaya releases (although the warranty is remarkably vague about how quickly a user must implement such "new releases" in order to retain coverage of the warranty). *Avaya US Warranty Policy,* 01/16/03, p. 2, accessed at http://support.avaya.com/elmodocs2/prodtran/Warranty_Policy_011603.pdf.

"[A] branch of a major insurer in the Northeast with about 1,000 Internet [VoIP] phone lines lost voice service for eight business hours because a worm jammed its servers, costing the company hundreds of thousands of dollars. In another case, a worm infected the voice and data systems at a bank branch also in the Northeast that had 500 Internet phone lines, disabling the company's trading floor, leaving it with about a million dollars in losses, according to the company's security provider."[218]

In both instances, the firms subsequently installed software to block intruders (by tracking their behavior and rejecting malicious packets).[219] It is unclear, however, whether there is a currently available solution to protect VoIP systems from hackers seeking to tap them and eavesdrop on the conversations. Reportedly, it is easier to tap into VoIP systems than to wiretap traditional phones. Although commercial VoIP services provide some security measures, if a hacker succeeds in penetrating a user's computer and placing a malicious program in it, he could thereby read e-mail messages and listen to VoIP calls, a risk that grows substantially if the penetrated computer is operated by a company that manages its VoIP system internally.[220]

Since VoIP is an emerging technology, whose protocols are still being developed and have not been fully standardized, and since the equipment is also undergoing rapid development and enhancement, there will be many additional security issues that will be discovered as VoIP usage expands. One of the most important security issues will probably arise from the new capabilities that VoIP can provide such as logging of all calls. In any government investigation of a firm, or in civil litigation with other parties, such records could be the subject of discovery requests. Counsel at companies that adopt VoIP with such capabilities should carefully review the record retention policies, and alert management to the fact that retention of such records pose certain risks, but that any deletion of such records must be part of a routine disposal of records and must be capable of being halted not merely at the first notice of a pending investigation or litigation (*e.g.,* receipt of a subpoena), but much earlier when it becomes "foreseeable" that such records may be

---

218. Belson, Ken, *Hackers Are Discovering a New Frontier: Internet Telephone Service,* The New York Times, August 2, 2004, p. C-4.

219. Id.

220. Id.

needed or requested for "official proceedings" by courts or agencies (such as OFAC, the BIS or the Directorate).[221]

6.7 Adjust Precautions to Avert Worst-Case Risks from Cyber-Attacks.

Increasingly, threats to information security are posed by terrorist groups and intelligence agencies of nation-state adversaries of the United States and its allies. There is, for example, the risk that such groups could launch a multi-platform, polymorphic worm that could propagate itself first through the Internet, then through a defense firm's gateways, and finally throughout its corporate intranet.[222] In August of 2003, the Welchia worm infested the Navy Marine Corps Intranet (that links approximately 100,000 users), depriving it of 75% of its capacity.[223]

A potential state-adversary already enjoys five advantages that it could leverage to cause widespread damage:

(i) Cyber-security continues to be underfunded and mismanaged at many companies;

(ii) Until recently, few if any software vendors put a high priority on designing and testing their wares to remove vulnerabilities from the Internet (here again the effort is underfunded and mismanaged);

(iii) The recent announcements of critical vulnerabilities by many software vendors evidences the likelihood that much of the software code installed on company computers has many critical vulnerabilities that the vendors have yet to discover, creating opportunities for a state-adversary to discover vulnerabilities not yet known or not yet patched by the vendors;

(iv) Even the announcement by vendors of a vulnerability does not

---

221. For further explanation of the statutory source of this obligation in the obstruction of justice laws, see discussion in the Conclusion.

222. For excellent discussion of this risk, see Weaver, Nicholas, and Paxson, Vern, *A Worst-Case Worm*, May 5, 2004, accessed at www.dtc.umn.edu/weis2004/weaver.pdf.

223. Messmer, Ellen, *Navy Marine Corps Intranet Hit by Welchia Worm*, NetworkWorldFusion, August 19, 2003, accessed at www.nwfusion.com/news/2003/0819navy.html.

result in widespread, rapid patching by firms; for example, although the vulnerability exploited by the Blaster worm was announced a month before the worm struck, it nonetheless infected at least 8 million systems (for which patches had not been timely installed); and,

(v) There currently exists no mechanism that can alert users as rapidly as a well-designed worm could propagate.

In short, a state-adversary seeking to target the U.S. with a worm would have the advantage of being inside our "decision loop," and thus able to cause continuing cycles of damage faster than we could orient our systems to address the problem, decide on the best course of action, and take the required action. Whoever has the tightest "decision loop" tends to enjoy the advantage in such confrontations, and here the advantages continue to accrue to the state-adversary.

Building on such advantages, if a state-adversary could support the development and testing of such a worm, the risks would be much greater than anticipated (or contingently prepared for) by most companies. As recently explained by commentators,[224] a state-adversary could fund the research and testing needed to enhance the worm's effect in the following ways:

(i) Discover unreported (zero-day) vulnerabilities in widely used operating system software code (which might require theft of the code, something a state-adversary could support through its intelligence entities);

(ii) Design a never-before-encountered exploit of those vulnerabilities;

(iii) Package the exploit on a self-propagating worm;

(iv) Design the worm's payload to attack a variety of platforms; and

(v) Design the payload to initially avoid detection (by installing itself in an operating system's boot block for later activation by a programmed date).

Current estimates are that a well-designed, rigorously tested worm could affect a large population of Internet servers in a few minutes,

---

224. Weaver, Nicholas, and Paxson, Vern, *A Worst-Case Worm*, May 5, 2004, accessed at www.dtc.umn.edu/weis2004/weaver.pdf.

spread through gateways into company intranets in a few hours, and in near-real time completely infect each such intranet.[225] Once dispersed through a company's intranet, the worm could, when activated, initially overwrite random sectors on computer hard drives, thereby corrupting data, and could then direct the computer to erase the disk.

Agile's current defenses against such a worm are no better than any other company's. Agile cannot prevent the worm from afflicting computers nationwide, but it can take precautions to be among the few more likely to remain unaffected, or if affected, not seriously damaged. Since the worm could be dispersed by e-mail, Agile needs to ensure that it does not place undue reliance on an intrusion detection system that uses signature-based methods (ones that need to recognize the worm in order to block it). In a worst-case scenario, there would not be time to deploy the requisite block.

A worm's payload could also include the means to infect the BIOS— the Basic Input and Output System that allows a computer to turn on and check itself. Most computers now have the capacity to have their BIOS updated by a flash program—one loaded into the computer that quickly updates the BIOS. If done incorrectly, the upgrade can disable the computer. If done by a worm designed to install an incorrect BIOS, the result will similarly disable the computer. Most computers now allow such flash upgrades of the BIOS with programs sent by the vendor through the Internet, *i.e.,* the computer's BIOS includes a jumper or switch that, on leaving the factory, is by default set to allow such flash upgrades and, unfortunately, to allow a worm to do a flash corruption of the BIOS.[226] Agile could consider opening each of its computers and setting those switches to the "off" position, requiring manual clearance of future upgrades.[227]

225. Id., p. 5.
226. Id., pp. 7 and 10.
227. Agile should also give serious consideration to requiring that its personnel avoid using Microsoft's Internet Explorer as their Web browser. There are increasing reports of vulnerabilities or security holes in Internet Explorer that make it easier for viruses, spyware, and other malwares to penetrate a computer (and thereby compromise a company's networks). Although Microsoft has recently issued its Service Pack 2 to reduce those vulnerabilities, it has not eliminated them, and some firms have found that Service Pack 2 is so incompatible with their existing systems that they cannot implement it. Moreover, Internet Explorer reportedly contains more vulnerabilities than other browsers, in part because of its design. In addition, a Symantec study of viruses and hacking activity reports "a fourfold rise in the number of new viruses attacking Windows computers, to 4,496 during the first half of 2004, the largest increase the company has ever documented." The study further reports that the favorite target of

Agile should also ensure that its information security policies are upgraded in response to these risks (and that it regularly conducts unannounced or unscheduled audits to verify their successful implementation). For example, at many companies the written policy requires nightly backups of all significant data; however, the actual practice may be much less frequent. The real need for backups should reflect how

---

these malwares were e-commerce companies and small businesses, because of the "attractiveness of their vast stores of credit-card numbers and other information," and that "[a]ttackers also became much more aggressive in their efforts to exploit vulnerabilities in Web-application software." Richmond, Riva, *Money Increasingly Is Motive for Computer-Virus Attacks*, THE WALL STREET JOURNAL, September 20, 2004, p. B-5.

Commentators increasingly urge that Web users switch from Internet Explorer to other, more secure browsers such as Firefox, Mozilla, Netscape, or the Norwegian-designed Opera. See Mossberg, Walter S., *Mossberg's Mailbox*, THE WALL STREET JOURNAL, September 9, 2004, and Leavitt, Neal, *Scob Attack: A Sign of Bad Things to Come?*, IEEE COMPUTER, September 2004, p. 18. Illustrative of the vulnerabilities of Internet Explorer was the June 2004 attack, launched by a Trojan horse (a non-replicating program that hides malware inside data or Web pages) and dubbed "J.S.Scob.Trojan" ("Scob"), which compromised over 630 different Web servers that hosted millions of infected Web pages during the attack. Scob targeted all Windows versions and all Internet Explorer versions. Scob presented a new threat: users did not need to open an attachment in order for their systems to be infected—they merely had to visit a contaminated website and their system would thereby become infected. Five days after its launch, Scob's dispersal was finally diminished when officials shut down the Russian website from which it was launched.

The unique vulnerabilities of Internet Explorer ("IE") that Scob exploited (and that other malwares can be expected to exploit) include the following: "IE has certain technologies and design features not found in other browsers, like ActiveX, security zones, [and] proprietary DHTML . . . Vulnerabilities related to these technologies and design decisions typically don't affect other browsers since they don't implement these technologies or use the same design choices." Leavitt, Neal, *Scob Attack: A Sign of Bad Things to Come?*, IEEE COMPUTER, September 2004, p. 18, quoting Art Manion (Internet security analyst with the US Computer Emergency Readiness Team, US-CERT). To avoid viruses and spyware, as one commentator recently observed, there are basically two choices: (1) "The single most effective way to avoid viruses and spyware is simply to chuck Windows altogether" in favor of Apple's operating system (Mac OS X) and Apple's Safari browser, because "[t]here has never been a successful virus written for Mac OS X . . . there is almost no spyware written for Mac OS X, . . . there is no spyware that targets the Mac . . . [and] the Mac is invulnerable to viruses and spyware written for Windows . . . ;" and (2) retain Windows, attempt to diminish the risks through firewalls, antivirus programs, etc., but nonetheless discontinue use of Internet Explorer in favor of other browsers (noted above). Mossberg, Walter, S., *How to Protect Yourself from Vandals, Viruses If You Use Windows*, THE WALL STREET JOURNAL, September 16, 2004, p. B-1.

much data the firm can afford to lose. A financial institution should be backing up data far more frequently than just nightly. Counsel recommends that any critical work be backed up on portable flash memory or similar devices as the work progresses throughout the day. Counsel also recommends adapting a suggestion offered by the Nunn-Wolfowitz Task Force by ensuring that company personnel understand senior management's commitment to information security. That Task Force reasoned that the degree of senior management commitment is "potentially correlated with the degree of involvement by the Board of Directors."[228] We recognize that few companies think that compliance (in export controls or information security) warrants regularly scheduled Board of Director time and attention. However, negative audit findings or reports of contravention of the Access Control Laws or a breach in information security will almost certainly demand such time and attention, but will in all probability receive it too late to avert the damage to the company and its reputation. Moreover, Directors and senior officers who do not routinely involve themselves in such issues are at heightened risk of mismanaging a crisis intertwined with such issues (as occurred in senior management's dubious responses to the anti-corruption crisis at Statoil). We therefore concur with the Task Force's suggestion that "one way for a company to sustain a strong and very visible management commitment is to give a Board committee process-level oversight of export compliance functions [and, we would add, information security functions], similar to the Audit Committee's oversight of financial matters," a role that could be performed by any of several Board Committees (Executive, Operations, Compliance or Audit).[229]

Agile should continue to adhere to its basic precepts for shoring up information security: treat security as an ongoing process, not only to detect intrusions and attempts, or to identify vulnerabilities, but to determine where Agile's personnel may be acting in ways that cause security lapses. By doing so, Agile may hope to minimize, but not completely avoid, the dual problems of "right-hand-to-sinister hand" (diversion) and "sinister-hand-to-right-hand" (embedded malicious code).

---

228. *Nunn-Wolfowitz Task Force Report: Industry "Best Practices" Regarding Export Compliance Programs*, July 25, 2000, p. 9.
229. Id.

CHAPTER 7

Checkpoint: Patent

7.0 Agile's Transaction at Checkpoint Patent.

Agile advertises many of its products on its website, and has software products available for download from that website. The Agile servers are located in New Jersey. As part of the merger, Agile contemplates consolidating the Troll, Brugge and Ijsselmeer information systems operations with its own. In particular, for cost saving and control purposes, all web-based transactions will be routed through the Agile servers in New Jersey. Agile's Counsel is aware that various computer-implemented inventions and business methods are patentable in the United States,[1] but believes that no patent infringement issue is raised by routing the transactions through New Jersey for two reasons:

(i) U.S. patent law is territorial—it does not cover activities occurring outside the boundaries of the United States and its possessions; and

(ii) European patent law expressly prohibits patent protection for both methods of doing business and "programs for computers."

Since the web-based transactions resulting from the merger with Troll and Brugge will for the most part originate in Europe and be

---

1. See *e.g., State Street Bank & Trust Co. v. Signature Financial Group, Inc,* 149 F.3d 1368 (Fed. Cir. 1998).

completed it Europe, patent infringement issues would not appear to be a problem.

Like all simple answers, this conclusion is probably wrong. U.S. patent law is territorial, but that does not mean that any activities that take place at least in part outside the U.S. are free from infringement claims. Direct patent infringement is defined in 35 USC § 271(a) as territorial:

> "Except as otherwise provided in this title, whoever without authority makes, uses, offers to sell, or sells any patented invention, *within the United States* or imports into the United States any patented invention during the term of the patent therefore, infringes the patent."

To illustrate how this would apply to a computer implemented, business method patent, consider one claim of Amazon.com's "one-click" patent:

A method of placing an order for an item comprising:

  (i) Under control of a client system,

  (ii) Displaying information identifying the item; and

  (iii) In response to only a single action being performed, sending a request to order the item along with an identifier of a purchaser of the item to a server system;

  (iv) Under control of a single-action ordering component of the server system,

  (v) Receiving the request;

  (vi) Retrieving additional information previously stored for the purchaser identified by the identifier in the received request; and

  (vii) Generating an order to purchase the requested item for the purchaser identified by the identifier in the received request using the retrieved additional information; and

  (viii) Fulfilling the generated order to complete purchase of the item

  (ix) Whereby the item is ordered without using a shopping cart ordering model.

In the case of a Troll customer in Austria placing an order through the Troll website, elements "a"–"c" and "h" are performed in Europe, while all or portions of the remaining elements could be performed in Agile's servers in New Jersey. At a minimum, given Agile's desire to route all transactions through the New Jersey servers for control purposes, at least some of the steps must be performed, at least in part, in New Jersey.

Does partial performance of some of the elements of this claim in the United States constitute using the invention within the United States, for purposes of 35 USC § 271? The statute literally requires using the "patented invention" within the United States. Using only parts of the invention in the United States would not seem to fall within the scope of § 271(a). Case law can be read to support such a construction. In *Rotec Industries v. Mitsubishi Corp.*,[2] the U.S. Court of Appeals for the Federal Circuit[3] (hereinafter "Federal Circuit") was faced with a situation where certain activities occurred in the United States, but the bulk of the infringement (if any) occurred overseas. The court held that an offer to sell less than a complete invention did not violate § 271(a), relying on *Deepsouth Packing Co. v. Laitram Corp.*[4]

In *Deepsouth* the U.S. Supreme Court had held that export of the components of a patented invention for assembly abroad did not constitute infringement of a U.S. patent on the assembled combination. In response, Congress enacted 35 USC § 271(f), which made it a violation of U.S. patent law to supply such components for assembly abroad. The Federal Circuit in *Rotec* concluded that *Deepsouth* was still good law with respect to claims arising out of § 271(a), stating:

> "One may not be held liable under § 271(a) for 'making' or 'selling' less than a complete invention."[5]

One would think the same rule would apply to "using" the invention, so *Deepsouth* and *Rotec* would seem to protect Agile from liability where, for control purposes, only a part of the invention is performed in the United States. One would probably be wrong.

---

2. 215 F.3d 1246 (Fed. Cir. 2000).

3. The U.S. Court of Appeals for the Federal Circuit has jurisdiction over all appeals where jurisdiction below arose out of the patent laws, as determined by the well-pleaded complaint rule. See 28 USC § 1295. The Federal Circuit does not necessarily have jurisdiction over all patent appeals, however, since the patent issue may arise as the result of a counterclaim. In the latter situation, the appeal goes to the regional circuit court of appeals. *Holmes Group, Inc. v. Vornado Air,* 535 U.S. 826, 122 S.Ct. 1889 (2002).

4. 406 U.S. 518 (1972).

5. 215 F.3d at 1252, n.2.

Several U.S. cases stand for the proposition that a transnational system can infringe a United States patent where the "control point" of the system is physically within the United States. (Recall that Agile wants to route all Troll and Brugge transactions through its New Jersey servers for control purposes.) In *Decca Ltd v. United States*,[6] the accused system was a navigational system for ships and aircraft that required the use of three radio broadcast stations. Two of the stations were in the United States, but one was in Norway. Without the Norwegian broadcast station, there could be no infringement, because the patent claims required at least three stations. The U.S. Court of Claims concluded, however, that the accused system, as a whole, was present in the United States because the master station that coordinated and monitored the entire system was located within the United States. That is, because the system's "control point" was in the United States, the entire system was present in the U.S. for patent infringement purposes.

The reasoning in *Decca* was based upon the earlier U.S. Patent Office Board of Interference decision in *Rosen v. NASA*.[7] In *Rosen* an accused system included multiple satellites, in space, monitored from a control point in the United States. The Board of Interferences held that the accused system should be viewed as a single integrated system and its location, for purposes of patent law, should be based on the location of the system's control point.[8]

---

6. 544 F.2d 1070 (Ct. Cl. 1976).

7. 152 USPQ 757 (1966).

8. Note that intellectual property protection during interplanetary exploration is the subject of the Intergovernmental Agreement (IGA), negotiated among the five Space Station Partners (Partners) and the bilateral Memorandum of Understanding that NASA negotiated with each of its Partners. Those agreements address treatment of intellectual property, including the exchange and protection of proprietary data. The IGA explains how the Partners will use and protect their respective intellectual properties, a delicate and difficult task in light of the substantial differences in each Partner's domestic intellectual property laws. Relevant U.S. statutes include the Space Act of 1958, as amended, which addresses patentable inventions. Perhaps most interesting for participants in cyberspace and cyber-driven transactions are the two documents that set forth how crew members from the Partners will handle proprietary data during interplanetary travel: (1) the Space Station Procedures for the Protection of User Intellectual Property; and (2) the International Space Station Crew Code of Conduct. For example:

"For purposes of determining the country of inventorship, a territorial approach based on the ownership/registry of elements was established. Therefore, an activity occurring on an element is deemed to have occurred in the territory of the Partner

Decca and *Rosen* could be dismissed as old cases from admittedly lower tribunals, but their analysis has been followed more recently (although with opposite results). For example, in *Hughes Aircraft Co. v. United States,*[9] the United States Court of Federal Claims applied the "control point" analysis to the question of whether a spacecraft, the Ariel 5, infringed a U.S. patent. The Ariel 5 was built in England and launched from Kenya by a team of Italians. One of the experiments aboard the Ariel 5 involved transmitting data to a NASA station in the United States for analysis. The court found that, although the NASA station provided the central communications link for tracking and data acquisition services, the NASA station did not direct, control, or monitor the spacecraft. Lacking a domestic control point, the court held that the Ariel 5 was not "used" within the United States, and hence did not infringe.

More recently, the U.S. District Court for the District of Massachusetts applied the "control point" analysis. In *Freedom Wireless, Inc. v. Boston Communications Group, Inc.,*[10] the accused system was a Canadian wireless telephone system that relied upon a prepayment/billing system in the United States for completion of "prepaid" wireless calls. Specifically, prepaid wireless telephone calls were received by a wireless tower located in Canada, transmitted to a switching office located in Canada, identified there as being a "prepaid" call and then rerouted to a prepaid billing/verification system in the United States. If the call was verified, it was then connected to a Canadian local carrier. The signal processing done in the United States by the billing/verification system was admittedly an "essential component" of the accused Canadian system. The District Court concluded that although the U.S. component of the system was "essential," it was not the "control point" of the system. The U.S. component did not direct, control, or monitor the Canadian system in any way. It simply performed a verification task for the Canada system, and returned the (essential) verification information back to Canada. Since the U.S. component was not the "control point,"

---

who owns/registers that element." Office of the General Counsel of NASA, Intellectual Property and the International Space Station: Creation, Use, Transfer, Ownership, and Protection: Executive Summary, September 1999, accessible at www.hq.nasa.gov/ogc/iss/exec_summary.html.

9. 29 Fed.Cl. 197 (Ct. Fed. Cl. 1993).
10. 198 F.Supp.2d 11 (D. Mass. 2002).

there could be no infringement of the U.S. patent by the Canadian system. The District Court distinguished the *Decca* and *Rosen* cases by pointing out that the accused infringers in those cases were unquestionably present in the United States,[11] and a substantial portion of the systems involved were located within the United States. In *Freedom Wireless*, on the other hand, the court found:

> "This was a Canadian system that happened to extend into the United States, not a domestic system that happened to extend into Canada."[12]

Faced with the "control point" line of cases Agile's Counsel is forced to rethink the wisdom, and cost savings, of routing the Troll and Brugge transactions through Agile's New Jersey servers for control purposes.

Could the solution be to base the Agile servers in Europe, since both business methods and computer programs are expressly excluded from patent protection there?[13] That deserves a closer look. Article 52(2)(c) of the European Patent Convention (EPC) excludes from the scope of inventions:

> "Schemes, rules and *methods for* performing mental acts, playing games or doing business, and programs for computers."

But the law is not as clear as it appears. Article 52(3) provides:

> "The provisions of paragraph 2 shall exclude patentability of the subject matter or activities referred to in that provision only to the extent to which a European patent application or European patent relates to such subject matter or activities **as such**."

In construing these provisions, the European Patent Office Board of Appeals has generally required that the inventions have a "technical effect" for patentable subject matter to be present. But "technical effect" is not necessarily a precise term. For example, in *In re Sohei*,[14] the Technical Board of Appeal for the European Patent Office found patentable subject matter in a claim directed to a computer system for plural types of independent management including at least financial and inventory

---

11. In fact the defendant was the United States in both cases.
12. 198 F.Supp.2d at 18.
13. European Patent Convention, Article 52(2)(c).
14. Decision T 769/92, 1995 O.J.E.P.O. 525 (Tech. Bd. App. 1994), available at http://legal.european-patent-office.org/dg3/biblio/t920769ep1.htm.

management. The claims were generally directed to conventional computer elements, such as a display unit, an input unit, a memory unit, an output unit and a digital processing unit. The Board concluded that the invention, although it had software implemented and method of doing business features, was not excluded from patentability because technical considerations concerning solutions of the problem the invention solves were needed in order to carry out the invention.

In *Sohei*, the claims required, in addition to the conventional elements mentioned above, a "single transfer slip" having a unitary format, and a "file management" feature made possible by the unitary format. The Technical Board of Appeal found these to involve the requisite technical effect, stating:

> "There are two consequences of the unitary slip format: firstly, the operator input is facilitated in that always the same screen is displayed; secondly, when the transfer slips have been stored in the daybook file, the processor knows always where exactly to find data which are to be copied to other files. This latter feature makes it possible to update various files directly from the stored transfer slips without involving the operator; multiple inputs of redundant data are thus avoided."

The Board expressly disclaimed any reliance upon the "financial and inventory management" features, the meaning of the data, or the details of the transactions as providing the requisite "technical features."

Faced with the very real possibility of patent infringement claims in Europe on its software-implemented inventions, Agile must now reconsider. Troll has paid little attention to patents, because of the nature of its business, and Agile's Counsel has assumed that software-implemented inventions were not protectable in Europe. As a result, no due diligence has been performed to detect the existence of potential patent infringement problems. Is Agile acquiring a potential patent infringement liability? Counsel does not know, but should find out before Closing.

Another matter to reconsider is where the computer processing relating to the Troll and Brugge transactions acquired as a result of the merger should be done. Considerations of U.S. patent law clearly indicate that the control point of such processing should not be in the United States if the goal is to avoid U.S. patent problems. But could some non-control processing be done in the United States in order to avoid infringing European patents?

An intriguing answer can be found in the decision of the England and Wales Court of Appeal in *Menashe Business Mercantile Ltd. v. William Hill Organization Ltd.*[15] In *Menashe*, the patentee was enforcing a European patent in the United Kingdom. The claim in question was directed to, in relevant part,

> "A gaming system for playing an interactive casino game comprising a host computer, at least one terminal computer forming a player station, communication means for connecting the terminal computer to the host computer and the program means for operating the terminal computer, the host computer and the communication means . . . characterised in that the terminal computer is situated at a location remote from the host computer . . ."

The defense of William Hill Organization Ltd. was that the "host computer" required by the claims was not situated in the United Kingdom, but rather was located in Antigua or Curacao. The Court of Appeal was not persuaded. In a statement full of relevance to Agile's proposed merger, and any possible patent infringement that it is acquiring, the Court of Appeal stated:

> "The claimed invention requires there to be a host computer. In the age that we live in, *it does not matter where the host computer is situated.* It could be in the United Kingdom, on a satellite, or even on the border between two countries. *Its location is not important to the user of the invention nor to the claimed gaming system.*"

The Court's legal conclusion that the location of the host computer is legally irrelevant to the issue of patent infringement is of extreme importance to Agile. The acquisition of Troll may be exposing it to patent infringement liability in Europe no matter where Agile has its processing performed. Moreover, the reasoning supporting that conclusion, that the location of the host computer is not important to the user of the invention, or to the functioning of the invention, is probably true of most software-implemented inventions.

The Court of Appeal in *Menashe* recognized a fundamental difference between ordinary machines and computer-implemented inventions, stating:

---

15. 2002 EWCA Civ 1702 (2002), available at www.bailii.org/ew/cases/EWCA/Civ/2002/1702.html.

"In that respect, there is a real difference between the claimed gaming system and an ordinary machine. For my part I believe that *it would be wrong to apply the old ideas of location to inventions of the type under consideration in this case.*"

Where then is the proper venue for enforcing such a patent? The Court of Appeal held that the relevant location is that of the user, in this case the United Kingdom:

"If the host computer is situated in Antigua and the terminal computer is in the United Kingdom, it is pertinent to ask who uses the claimed gaming system. The answer must be the punter.[16] Where does he use it? There can be no doubt that he uses his terminal in the United Kingdom and it is not a misuse of language to say that **he uses the host computer in the United Kingdom. It is the input to and output of the host computer that is important to the punter and in a real sense the punter uses the host computer in the United Kingdom although it is situated in Antigua and operates in Antigua.** In those circumstances it is not straining the word "use" to conclude that the United Kingdom punter will use the claimed gaming system in the United Kingdom, even if the host computer is situated in, say, Antigua."

Agile's understanding of the risks of patent infringement have been fundamentally flawed. In order to determine the value of the merger, it is now imperative to estimate the potential liability for patent infringement, both in the United States and in Europe.

In investigating the patent issues more deeply, Agile's Counsel notices that 35 USC § 271(a) also prohibits *offering to sell* an invention in the United States. Would this apply to the advertising of Troll, Brugge and Ijsselmeer products on Agile's U.S. based website? It could. The Federal Circuit has held that traditional contractual analysis should be applied to determine whether an "offer to sell" for purposes of § 271(a) has occurred, stating:

"[A]n offer for sale, whether made before or after a patent is applied for, or after it is granted, requires no more than a commercial offer for sale. Both sections [35 USC §§ 102(b) and 271(a)] invoke the traditional contractual analysis. Therefore, we similarly define §

---

16. A "punter" in Britain is a person who gambles.

271(a)'s 'offer to sell' liability according to the norms of traditional contractual analysis."[17]

If Troll, Brugge and Ijsselmeer products are the subject of a commercial offer for sale on the Agile website in the United States, then the "offer to sell" prong of infringement of § 271(a) is implicated.

But surely, says Agile's Counsel, such an offer would not be an infringement unless the resulting sale also occurred within the United States.[18] Precedent, unfortunately, does not favor that position. In *Rotec Industries, supra,* the Federal Circuit analyzed whether the U.S. activities associated with a transaction constituted an offer to sell the invention. There was no question that the sale itself occurred outside the United States. The court eventually concluded that those U.S. activities did not constitute an offer to sell. Judge Newman, in a concurring opinion stated:

> "[T]he majority opinion necessarily accepts the critical premise that an 'offer to sell' made in the United States can constitute patent infringement even when the contemplated sale could not infringe the patent."[19]

The statute itself appears to support this position, stating that whoever "offers to sell, or sells any patented invention within the United States . . . infringes the patent."

The U.S. District Court for the District of Delaware has followed the apparent holding of the Federal Circuit in *Rotec.* In *Wesley Jessen Corp. v. Bausch & Lomb, Inc.,*[20] Bausch & Lomb had previously been enjoined

---

17. *Rotec Industries, Inc. v. Mitsubishi Corp.,* 215 F.3d 1246, 1254-55 (Fed. Cir. 2000).

18. Agile will also need to consider what currency will be used on Troll's and Brugge's websites. As noted by Rice and Gladstone, "when services are quoted in a currency other than that of the website's domicile, this would arguably be evidence of intent to reach that jurisdiction. Again, widely used currencies, such as the U.S. dollar, or generic currencies like the Euro, should not be considered evidence, taken alone, of targeting. As technology advances, the use of 'push' technology would likely be viewed as targeting activity that warrants specific jurisdiction in the location of the pushee." Rice, Dennis T., and Gladstone, Julia, An Assessment of the Effects Test in Determining Personal Jurisdiction in Cyberspace, 58 BUSINESS LAWYER 601, February 2003, at p. 653. Agile's General Counsel notes that Norway voted not to join the European Union and continues to use its national currency, the Kroner, not the Euro. Thus a choice of Kroner, to the exclusion of dollars or Euros, could have significant implications and would require deliberation by Agile's partners.

19. 215 F.3d at 1258.

20. 256 F.Supp.2d 228 (D.Del. 2003).

from infringing a U.S. patent. It exported the products (apparently after offering in the United States to sell them) and sold them overseas. The district court concluded that these activities could constitute an infringing "offer to sell" although no actual infringing sale took place in the United States, stating:

> "[T]he Court rejects Bausch & Lomb's argument that an 'offer to sell' can only take place if there is also an unlawful sale within the United States."[21]

There are district court cases to the contrary, but their validity is questionable in view of *Rotec.*[22]

Agile should rethink the value of making Troll, Brugge and Ijsselmeer products available for sale on its U.S. website. Part of its enhanced due diligence should include determining whether those products infringe any U.S. patents before they are offered for sale on the website.

Section 271(a) also prohibits the importation of any patented invention into the United States. Agile's Counsel by now is justifiably concerned that the various software products of Troll may, if downloaded into the United States, infringe one or more U.S. patents.

Counsel's concern with the various forms of infringement under § 271(a) arises in part because there is no intent requirement—patent infringement is actionable whether or not the infringer intended to infringe, or indeed whether or not the infringer knew about the patent. As the U.S. Supreme Court stated in *Florida Prepaid Postsecondary Education Expense Board v. College Savings Bank,*[23]

> "Actions predicated on direct patent infringement . . . do not require any showing of intent to infringe; instead, knowledge and intent are considered only with respect to damages."

Independent creation of an invention is no defense to a charge of patent infringement.[24] Agile's Counsel, therefore, cannot merely rely upon the assurances of Troll, Brugge and Ijsselmeer that they have not copied the inventions of others, or that they created their products

---

21. Id. at 234.
22. See *Cybiotronics, Ltd. v. Golden Source Electronics, Ltd.,* 130 F.Supp.2d 1152 (C.D.Cal. 2001); *Quality Tubing, Inc. v. Precision Tube Holdings Corp.,* 75 F.Supp.2d 613 (S.D.Tex. 1999).
23. 527 U.S. 627, 119 S.Ct. 2199 (1999).
24. *Kewanee Oil Co. v. Bicron Corp.,* 416 U.S. 470, 477 (1974).

without copying the inventions of others. Even if those assurances are true, they do not constitute a defense to patent infringement in the United States.

In Europe, the question of lack of infringing intent may constitute a defense in certain countries. For example, in Denmark, Ireland, Sweden and the United Kingdom, the defense of lack of intent is available, but is nullified if the patentee properly marked the patented goods with the patent number.[25] In France the defense is available even if the patented product was properly marked.[26] In Belgium and Germany no such defense is available.

Agile's Counsel also discovers that U.S. patent law contains another provision imposing liability with no requirement of intent. Section 271(g) of Title 35, United States Code, prohibits the importation, offer to sell, sale, or use of a product in the United States that is made overseas by a process patented in the United States. This section has two significant exceptions:

(i) Where the product is materially changed by subsequent processes; and

(ii) Where the product becomes a trivial and nonessential component of another product.

The direct application of § 271(g) is illustrated in *Bio-Technology General Corp. v. Genentech, Inc.*[27] In that case one of the claims at issue read as follows:

> "A method for producing human growth hormone which method comprises [1] culturing bacterial transformants containing recombinant plasmids which will, in a transformant bacterium, express a gene for human growth hormone unaccompanied by the leader sequence of human growth hormone or other extraneous protein bound thereto, and [2] isolating and purifying said expressed human growth hormone."[28]

The accused infringer performed its process in Israel and alleged that the product of its process was not "human growth hormone" as required by the patent claim, but instead was "insoluble met-hGH"[29]

---

25. See e.g. United Kingdom Patent Act 1977, § 62.
26. French Patent Law of 1968, Article 51.
27. 80 F.3d 1553 (Fed. Cir. 1996).
28. 80 F.3d 1553 at 1558.
29. hGH is a recognized abbreviation for "human growth hormone."

The Federal Circuit rejected that argument. The accused infringer further argued that the product of its process—met-hGH—was materially changed by a subsequent process into human growth hormone. The Federal Circuit again rejected the attempted distinction between met-hGH and human growth hormone, holding that there was no real difference between the two products, stating:

> "BTG therefore cannot maintain that the 'materially changed' exception to infringement applies, because the product made by the patented process is not changed at all, let alone 'materially changed.' The 'materially changed' exception of § 271(g) requires, at a minimum, that there be a real difference between the product imported, offered for sale, sold, or used in the United States and the products produced by the patented process."[30]

Counsel for Agile now realizes that the pharmaceutical products of Brugge (particularly the generic versions) need to be examined for patent infringement claims in the United States, although the products themselves will be made overseas.

But does § 271(g) also apply to the software products of Troll? Nothing in the statute precludes application to software process patents other than the requirement that a "product" exist that is made by the patented process. In the biotechnology context, at least one court has held that "information" cannot be the product made by a patented process for purposes of § 271(g). In *Synaptic Pharmaceutical Corp. v. MDS Panlabs, Inc.*,[31] the patent had obtained several process patents covering assays or tests for determining whether certain compounds will bind to certain living cells.

The processes were performed in Taiwan and the test results were sent to the United States. Although the test results were the intended output of the patented assays, the district court held that § 271(g) did not cover the results. The court was concerned that construing § 271(g) to cover results would lead to absurd resulting, stating:

> "A scientist who observes a patented test in a foreign jurisdiction and then returns home to the United States—with the memory of that test result in his mind—would, by his own journey, import a

30. 80 F.3d at 1560.
31. 2002 WL 32098065 (D.N.J. 2002).

'product which is made by a process' and would thus be liable under § 271(g)."[32]

Synaptic may be applicable to the Troll software products, allowing the results of Troll's programs to be freely imported even if the steps performed overseas by those products would infringe a U.S. patent if performed in the United States. But *Synaptic* does nothing to relieve Counsel's concern about the pharmaceutical products made by Brugge.

Agile's Counsel is now aware of the strict liability issues raised by U.S. patent law. There is some substantial, enhanced due diligence to perform.

---

32. Id. at *7. Thus, unlike the EAR with its recognition of "deemed exports," U.S. patent law does not, as yet, appear to recognize "deemed imports."

Conclusion

The value of Agile's enhanced diligence (as we have seen) depended in large part on the firm's willingness to undertake a comprehensive compliance review, and to use the "intelligence" produced by such review in a timely fashion to avoid potential obstacles to the successful completion of its acquisition. While such obstacles, and the risks that they can pose problems late in negotiations, may initially prompt counsel to wish it could "undiscover" them and avoid the obligations to probe and test the underlying facts, such a strategy (as we hope we have amply demonstrated) does not make economic sense. Had Agile pursued such a short-term course, it would have lost the crucial advantage of time, and the delay could have made it impossible for Agile to effect remediation measures rapidly enough to preserve the opportunity to acquire Troll. Having a comprehensive compliance program in place, and deploying the recommended checkpoints early gave Agile its best chance to keep those two timeframes (business acquisition or "transaction time" and regulatory compliance or "remediation time") from conflicting. Such a conflict will inevitably interfere with the long-term economic objectives of any company engaged in cross-border transactions (due to the accelerated pace of transactional business in an increasingly global economy).

It is therefore imperative to recognize the interdependence and interrelationship of these two time-frames, each creating a limited "window" of opportunity: transaction time (whose expiration prevents the deal from being done at all or, at a minimum, from being completed without exceeding its budget), and remediation time (whose expiration puts the acquirer and its officers at unacceptable risk of violations of the Access Control Laws). When counsel alerts its client to the need for remediation, it must make every effort to structure such remediation so that it does not undermine, or interfere with, the business initiatives of the ongoing enterprise. Because the cost of remediation is directly related to the delays in its pursuit or to oversights in a given compliance program, the better positioned a company is to react rapidly to a compliance issue, the better the chances will be that it can keep remediation time and costs to a minimum and manage it so that it does not destroy or over-burden economic opportunities. As the Nobel Laureate Nadine Gordimer once observed: "The first adjustment to any change must be to the time-frame imposed within it;"[1] Agile's counsel therefore needs to maintain a "forward-looking" compliance program, and (in the context of a transaction, but particularly a strategic acquisition like the one we have discussed) to persuade its acquisition partners to take the necessary corrective measures as early and as quickly as possible.

In our hypothetical, Agile was able to request and receive the necessary compliance measures. That, of course, does not always occur, and transactional exigencies can frequently push companies to ignore or postpone the inquiries that the Access Control Laws require when a party discerns potential compliance problems. Parties occasionally receive cautionary notices from the BIS alerting them of persons to avoid, but they cannot assume, in the absence of such notice, that they are justified in overlooking red flags (whether those that the BIS lists on its website or those that they receive internally from personnel expressing misgivings). Often it is not the subtlety of the issues that delays remediation, but the inconvenience that such remediation poses.

We recognize that some provisions of the Access Control Laws reflect an effort to anticipate the ingenuity and determination of targeted countries to circumvent embargoes and controls on the export of sensitive technologies. Evidence that emerged in 2004, of Iraq's circumvention of the oil-for-food rules and of Libya's circumvention of export controls to procure WMD[2] technologies, will undoubtedly prompt

---

1. Gordimer, Nadine, THE PICKUP, 1999, Penguin Books, p. 124.

2. The national security importance of respecting and enforcing the TSR were amply justified in March of 2004 when the Libyan government, in a declaration to the Organization for the Prohibition of Chemical Weapons (based in The Hague), acknowledged that in addition to pursuing the development of nuclear weapons it had made 23 tons of mustard gas "at Rabta, a production facility in the Libyan desert 75 miles southwest of Tripoli . . . [and] had kept the gas and a variety of chemical precursors intended for the production of sarin and other nerve agents at two storage facilities. . . . [and] had tested the gas as a weapon and made thousands of bombs to deliver the lethal agents as part of its chemical weapons program." Miller, Judith, *Libya Discloses Production of 23 Tons of Mustard Gas*, THE NEW YORK TIMES, March 6, 2004, p. A-5.

OFAC, BIS, and the DDTC to redouble their efforts to tighten regulations and enforcement policies accordingly.

However, there is an unrecognized yet compelling need for such regulations and policies to take into consideration the exigencies and business realities of the transactional markets. Cross-border deals need to proceed without undue impediments, if U.S. businesses are to function competitively in foreign, international and global markets. Otherwise, the legitimate desire to make our borders safe will gradually burden our participation in a global economy, move us toward "isolationism" in a world that is rapidly breaking down or reducing the significance of national borders.[3] Out of respect for the objectives pursued by OFAC, BIS and the DDTC, we have often argued in this book for conservative readings of the Access Control Laws, because we believe that proper management of remediation time will promote the successful completion of transactions without undue cost or unduly burdensome measures. However, we recognize that certain provisions in the Access Control Laws would benefit (and would be more likely to achieve their objective), if such laws also reflected an appreciation of the transactional burdens imposed by requirements that can be violated prior to Closing (and even prior to the signing of a definitive acquisition agreement).

We recognize that when laws over-burden the efforts of parties to pursue business opportunities the result is a steady erosion of compliance with such laws (through increasingly narrow interpretations by parties and their counsel). That is not to suggest that legitimate parties will attempt to find ways to transact with illicit or targeted parties. But the potential for inadvertent, unwitting or "expedient" violations in

---

3. As one commentator observed: "Just beyond the horizon of current events lie two possible political futures—both bleak, neither democratic. The first is a retribalization of large swaths of humankind by war and bloodshed: a threatened Lebanonization of national states in which culture is pitted against culture, people against people, tribe against tribe—a Jihad in the name of a hundred narrowly conceived faiths against every kind of interdependence, every kind of artificial social cooperation and civic mutuality. The second is being borne in on us by the onrush of economic and ecological forces that demand integration and uniformity and that mesmerize the world with fast music, fast computers, and fast food – with MTV, Macintosh, and McDonald's, pressing nations into one commercially homogenous global network: one McWorld tied together by technology, ecology, communications, and commerce. The planet is falling precipitantly apart *and* coming reluctantly together at the very same moment." Barber, Benjamin R., *Jihad v. McWorld*, The Atlantic Online, March 1992, accessed at www.theatlantic.com/politics/foreign/barberf.htm.

pursuit of important business opportunities is real. We cannot lose sight of the fact that significant wealth is generated by positioning business enterprises to pursue economic opportunities in emerging markets. But the creation of wealth must be balanced against the increasingly important need to safeguard national security. It has been estimated (in reports reviewed by the GAO) that $83 billion in wealth was lost when the Twin Towers fell.[4] The conclusion this compels is that until such laws are improved to address this tension, there will be a greater risk of noncompliance or partial, inefficient, after-the-fact "boot-strapped" compliance by companies and their officers. The real question that must be answered is: will noncompliance result from a legitimate party's failure to deploy and enforce transactional checkpoints because the ultimate cost of such compliance was economic non-viability? We believe that enhanced due diligence (through early deployment of transactional checkpoints) provides the best means for parties seeking to negotiate a practical, cost-effective solution that takes into account both the demands of the deal and the requirements of compliance.

Early deployment of transactional checkpoints is also warranted by the recent Justice Department trend to indict corporations and their officers, where personnel have been instructed to alter or destroy records, or were not properly instructed to preserve such records by timely interruption of document retention policies. Many lawyers mistakenly believe that "obstruction of justice" statutes obligate the preservation of records only upon receipt of a subpoena. Although some applicable provisions are triggered by receipt of a subpoena, a significant number come into effect much earlier when it becomes "foreseeable" that such records may be needed or requested for "official proceedings" by courts, Congress or agencies (such as OFAC, the BIS or the DDTC). The breadth of these obstruction of justice provisions should not be underestimated. For example, 18 U.S.C. §1512 (b) includes the following as predicate elements of an offense:

> "Whoever . . . corruptly persuades another person, or attempts to do so . . . with intent to . . . cause or induce any person to . . . alter, destroy, mutilate, or conceal an object [such as a document, an e-mail or other record] with intent to impair the object's integrity or availability for use in an official proceeding;"[5]

---

4. GAO, *Review of Studies of the Economic Impact of the September 11, 2001, Terrorist Attacks on the World Trade Center*, GAO-02-700R, May 29, 2002, p. 2, accessed at www.gao.gov/new.items/d02700r.pdf.

5. 18 U.S.C. §1512(b).

Section 1512 (f) broadens the reach of the statute, by extending it to an indefinite and indeterminate time prior to a pending action:

"(1) an official proceeding need not be pending or about to be instituted at the time of the offense;"[6]

Section 1512 (f) further broadens the reach of the statute, by expanding the universe of "objects" or records to include inadmissible or privileged materials:

"(2) the testimony, or the record, document, or other object need not be admissible in evidence or free of a claim of privilege . . ."[7]

The Sarbanes-Oxley Act of 2002 increases the risk of such violations, by adding the following provision to Section 1512:

"Whoever corruptly—

(i) Alters, destroys, mutilates, or conceals a record, document, or other object, or attempts to do so, with the intent to impair the object's integrity or availability for use in an official proceeding; or

(ii) Otherwise obstructs, influences, or impedes any official proceeding, or attempts to do so, shall be fined under this title or imprisoned not more than 20 years, or both."[8]

Thus, there is an unusually clear and compelling incentive for early detection and remediation of potential violations of the Access Control Laws (and particularly of the TSR, EAR and ITAR). Such early attention to compliance reduces the probability that company personnel will engage in conduct that might prompt an investigation (or other "official proceeding"), or otherwise take actions in the misguided belief that they are averting an investigation by deleting or altering records related to potential violations of the Control Access Laws. Clearly the most serious risk for Agile is not that its personnel will destroy documents (its compliance program trains personnel to be keenly aware of the impropriety of such action), but rather that its personnel may create records in the diligence phase that they believe can be subsequently altered or deleted.

---

6. 18 U.S.C. §1512(f)(1).
7. 18 U.S.C. §1512(f)(2).
8. Pub. L. No. 107-204, codified at 18 U.S.C. §1512(c).

An internal memo describing (albeit unwitting) conversations with a party named on OFAC's SDN List cannot simply be "redacted" or edited without potentially violating 18 U.S.C. §1512. A comparable e-mail by one of Arthur Andersen's in house counsel was introduced into evidence by federal prosecutors to support the charge of obstruction of justice under Section 1512. The e-mail stated in relevant part:

"Here are a few suggested comments for consideration.

- I recommend deleting reference to consultation with the legal group and deleting my name on the memo. Reference to the legal group consultation arguably is a waiver of attorney-client privileged advice and if my name is mentioned it increases the chances that I might be a witness, which I prefer to avoid.
- I suggested deleting some language that might suggest we have concluded the release is misleading."[9]

The more "forward-looking" a company's compliance is with the Access Control Laws, the lower the probability that its personnel will engage in conduct that while practical could later become grounds for a charge of obstruction of justice under Section 1512. The penalty for such conduct is breath-taking in its severity. Violations of the TSR can result in a fine and up to ten years imprisonment, but violations of Section 1512 can result in a fine and up to 20 years imprisonment. Agile's primary concern with potential violations of the Access Control Laws, as well as with the obstruction of justice statute, remains the risk of inadvertent violations. It has therefore adjusted its compliance program and its enhanced early diligence and remediation accordingly.

Our treatment of Access Control Laws has been selective, but we hope representative of the hidden risks that such laws create for cross-border transactions and such transactions in cyberspace. A notable omission from our discussion (and one that warrants inclusion in the recommended transactional checkpoints) is a review of the export control laws as they apply to or impact on enforcement of immigration control laws. Such issues arise when companies involved in producing or exporting EAR or ITAR controlled items employ foreign nationals,

---

9. E-mail from Nancy A. Temple, October 16, 2001, in Gillers, Stephen, ETHICAL CHALLENGES IN LEGAL PRACTICE, Association of the Bar of the City of New York, July 28, 2004, p. 18.

or seek to outsource production overseas or to other companies in the U.S. that employ foreign nationals, or enter into negotiations (as Agile has with Troll) with an overseas firm whose personnel include nationals from countries identified by the Department of State ("DoS") as providers of continuous support for international terrorism (*e.g.,* Iran or Sudan).

As part of its response to the attacks of September 11, the federal government increased its efforts to prevent diversion of sensitive technologies by reducing the risks that foreign nationals would gain access to such technologies by working at such companies. Therefore, in August of 2002, the DoS revised the Technology Alert List ("TAL"), which was originally designed to "help maintain technological superiority over the Warsaw Pact and was targeted at individuals from the Soviet Union and other Communist countries."[10] The same month, the DoS circulated a cable to U.S. Embassies and Consulates to provide additional guidance for the use of the TAL in cases that might fall under the purview of Immigration and Nationality Act ("INA") Section 212(a)(3)(a), which "renders inadmissible aliens who there is reason to believe are seeking to enter the United States to violate U.S. laws prohibiting the export of goods, technology or sensitive information from the United States."[11] The revised TAL consists of two parts: a Critical Fields List, identifying major fields of technology transfer concern,[12] and a DoS List of designated State Sponsors of Terrorism.[13] If a visa applicant's planned activities raise questions of possible ineligibility under INA Section 212(a)(3)(a), the consular post is instructed to submit a Security Advisory Opinion ("SAO") in the form of a Visas Mantis and "transmit the request by cable simultaneously to the Visa Office (VO)

---

10. Department of State, *Cable to U.S. Embassies and Consulates Abroad*, August 2002, para. 5, accessed at www.travel.state.gov/state147566.html.

11. Id., para. 1.

12. The main sections of the Critical Fields List are: A. Conventional Munitions; B. Nuclear Technology; C. Rocket Systems; D. Rocket System and Unmanned Air Vehicle Subsystems; E. Navigation, Avionics, and Flight Control Useable in Rocket Systems and Unmanned Air Vehicles; F. Chemical, Biotechnology, and Biomedical Engineering; G. Remote Sensing, Imaging, and Reconnaissance; H. Advanced Computer/Microelectronic Technology; I. Materials Technology; J. Information Security; K. Laser and Directed Energy Systems Technology; L. Sensors and Sensor Technology; M. Marine Technology; N. Robotics; and O. Urban Planning.

13. Department of State, *Cable to U.S. Embassies and Consulates Abroad*, August 2002, para. 7, accessed at www.travel.state.gov/state147566.html.

at the DOS, the FBI and interested agencies."[14] INA Section 212(a)(3)(a) renders ineligible for a visa any alien "who a consular officer knows or has reasonable ground to believe is seeking entry to the United States to engage solely, principally, or incidentally in any activity to violate or evade any law prohibiting the export from the United States of goods, technology, or sensitive information."[15] Such agencies conduct a review and submit responses to the DoS, which summarizes them and issues a response to the consular posts, with a determination of whether DoS objects to the issuance of the visa. Mantis checks take approximately 30 days, but can take longer if any interested agency "places a processing hold on the check."[16]

Several other changes to U.S. immigration laws and policies, scheduled to come into effect in 2004 and 2005, will severely affect foreign nationals seeking entry to the United States, even if only for business meetings, discussion of technical exchanges or collaborative work:

- By October 26, 2004, all U.S. consulates are required to have the capability to record fingerprints and photographs of most foreign nationals, to begin to issue visas containing biometric identifiers of the traveler and to enter such data in the US-VISIT data bases maintained by the DoS and the DHS;

- Effective October 26, 2004, foreign nationals seeking entry to the U.S. under the Visa Waiver Program (which permits citizens of specified countries to apply for admission to the U.S. "for ninety

---

14. Walsh, Tien-Li Loke, *The Technology Alert List, Visas Mantis, and Export Control: Frequently Asked Questions,* IMMIGRATION AND NATIONALITY LAW HANDBOOK 2004–2005, vol. 2, p. 418.

15. Department of State, *9 FAM 40.31 Exhibit I: Technology Alert List,* accessed at http://foia.state.gov/masterdocs/09fam/0940031X1.pdf.

16. Id., pp. 418–419. Moreover, the granting of a visa closes off one set of risks and opens another: those of a party overstaying the period granted by the visa. Under INS Section 212(a)(9)(B) a party who overstays and is unlawfully present for more than 180 days is confronted by severe penalties. If he leaves before overstaying a year and without undergoing a removal proceeding, he is denied entry to the United States for three years from the date on which he finally leaves. However, if his overstay extends to a year or longer, he is denied entry for 10 years. Agile will need to ensure that the foreign national personnel of Troll and its affiliates do not make such errors, if they are reassigned to work temporarily at Agile's U.S.-based entities. For discussion of the practical problems that such deadlines impose on applicants for change to another temporary status, see Mailman, Stanley, and Yale-Loehr, Stephen, *Managing Our Immigration Laws: We Have to Do Better,* NEW YORK LAW JOURNAL, June 28, 2004, p. 3 at p. 6.

days or less as nonimmigrant visitors for business or pleasure without first obtaining a . . . nonimmigrant visa . . . "[17]) will be required to possess and present machine-readable passports; and

• Effective October 26, 2005, such persons will also need to possess and present passports that contain biometric identifiers (unless their passports were issued prior to that date).

To comply, almost all foreign nationals who do not qualify for the Visa Waiver Program will find it necessary to undergo a visa interview and security check at a U.S. consulate, with the possibility of extended delays and denial.[18]

In the current enforcement environment, such proceedings and delays are increasingly probable. Here again the issue of transaction vs. compliance time arises. If Agile seeks to hold face-to-face meeting with representatives from Troll, Brugge and Ijsselmeer, it will likely find it far more convenient to conduct such meetings overseas in light of the potential difficulty of procuring visas for representatives from Troll and its affiliates (particularly if any are not Norwegian nationals).[19] Recall that, in Brugge's case, its personnel include foreign nationals from one of the designated State Sponsors of Terrorism (Sudan),[20] and with respect to such nationals, DoS applies "special scrutiny."[21] The potential problems do not cease upon issuance of a visa. A consular post (or at its request the Department of Commerce) may commence inquiries to determine if the U.S. employer of a foreign nation has measures in place to prevent such person from gaining unauthorized access to EAR and ITAR controlled items (including technical data and software) or allows such access without having obtained the requisite license.[22] As one commentator notes:

---

17. Patrick, Michael D., *Foreign Travelers Face Major Changes*, NEW YORK LAW JOURNAL, July 30, 2004, p. 3.

18. Id., pp. 3–4.

19. For brief discussion of such issue, see Dong, Nelson G., *Homeland Security and Technology Workers—The New Age of Export Controls*, TECHNOLOGY TRANSACTIONS, April 2004, pp. 1, 2, and 6.

20. Such states include Cuba, Iran, Libya, North Korea, Syria, and Sudan. Department of State, *Cable to U.S. Embassies and Consulates Abroad*, August 2002, Tab B, accessed at www.travel.state.gov/state147566.html.

21. Id., para. 7.

22. Walsh, Tien-Li Loke, *The Technology Alert List, Visas Mantis, and Export Control: Frequently Asked Questions*, IMMIGRATION AND NATIONALITY LAW HANDBOOK 2004–2005, vol. 2, p. 421.

"The issue is not whether an individual accessed the controlled technology, but whether the individual simply had access. Merely having access to the entire [computer/intranet] system [of a company] creates the possibility that the IT [information technology] support personnel could visually inspect the data and thus subject the company to a 'deemed export' violation. This issue is further complicated when companies outsource IT support, creating additional risks of export violations."[23]

The latter poses a striking risk, when one considers how much e-traffic is outsourced to Bangalore, India.

The problems inherent in Agile's traveling overseas have been discussed at length above. Similarly, if Agile outsources work to Troll that involves EAR or ITAR controlled technologies, and later resumes performance of such work in-house, it needs to ensure that in the interim it has not relaxed its information security in any way that would permit unauthorized foreign nationals access to such technologies. Note that the reach of the TAL extends beyond EAR and ITAR controlled technologies as a result of the addition of the following category (and the DoS guidance for its use):

"**Urban Planning**: Expertise in construction or design of systems or technologies necessary to sustain modern urban societies. (PLEASE NOTE: Urban Planning may not fall under the purview of INA Section 212 (a)(3)(a), U.S. technology transfer law, or any other U.S. law or regulation. However, Urban Planning is a special interest item and posts are requested to refer such visa application requests to CA/VO/L/C for further review.) Look for technologies/skills associated with:

- Architecture
- Civil engineering
- Community Development
- Geography
- Housing

---

23. Id., p. 424.

- Landscape architecture
- Land use and comprehensive planning
- Urban design"[24]

Foreign nationals at Troll would probably trigger Visas Mantis reviews as a result of their work respectively in stealth-related aircraft skin (TAL category "I. Materials Technology") and encryption (TAL category "J. Information Security"), while foreign nationals at Brugge and Ijsselmeer would probably trigger such reviews for their work in pharmaceuticals and biometrics (TAL category "F. Chemical, Biotechnology and Biomedical Engineering"). Fortunately for Agile, its checkpoints for the Access Control Laws (if properly implemented) should minimize the risks that its personnel will violate such laws. But its contemplated acquisition of Troll and its affiliates will pose serious risks and visas delays to the extent that Agile must have personnel of these companies enter the United States for meetings or work at its facilities.

We would also emphasize that, when dealing with companies whose countries have not participated in U.S. embargoes, and who have therefore had unrestricted access to business opportunities in countries targeted by such embargoes (a market imperfection whose upside economic benefits, by virtue of the artificially structured competition, are difficult to ignore), a U.S. firm should anticipate the high probability that activities prohibited to U.S. persons have had a long history, may be very important to the business portfolios of companies, and could easily draw U.S. persons into violations of the TSR, EAR and ITAR in the course of routine negotiations. As companies increasingly invest in ventures along the cyberspace trade route, they may appreciate Agile's experience and seek early deployment of appropriate checkpoints.

Cross-border cyberspace and cyber-driven transactions will bring U.S. companies into increasingly frequent dealings and transactions with companies and partnerships abroad that pose significant risks under the Access Control Laws. The risks derive, in part, from the combination of the broad reach of those laws and regulations and the high probability that the overseas persons are engaged in dealings and transactions that have not been filtered through compliance checkpoints to ensure observance of and attention to such laws and regulations. Agile's

---

24. Department of State, *Cable to U.S. Embassies and Consulates Abroad*, August 2002, para. 7, accessed at www.travel.state.gov/state147566.html.

investment in checkpoints will not be an attractive option to many participants in these transactions. The alternative, however, delaying meaningful investments in compliance until the risks of violations and of infringements matures into potential litigations—civil or criminal — argues strongly in favor of investments in early deployment and enforcement.

Remediation, once litigation has been commenced, will almost certainly be more burdensome and expensive. It will also put the company and its management and personnel on a virtual "war footing," often creating "siege mentality" and a misguided defensiveness that is deleterious to good judgment. We are not claiming this as a new insight, but it is remarkable how often management overlooks the fact that personnel can operate far below expectations during a pending investigation or litigation. Centuries ago, Xenophon (in his account of the Greek army's retreat from Persia) emphasized this loss of judgment in the heat of conflict, arguing that traversing a difficult terrain was far easier than traversing a level one when assailed or pursued by an enemy:

> "It is much easier to march uphill without fighting than to march on the level when one has enemies on all sides; and one can see what is in front of one's feet better by night, when one is not fighting, than by day, if one is; and rough ground is easier for the feet, if one is not fighting as one marches, than level ground is, when there are weapons flying round one's head."[25]

In short, the recommended checkpoints will seem most valuable when one understands clearly the real costs and far-reaching consequences of failing to deploy and enforce them. Risk management strategies like the one we are proposing will not necessarily have a direct impact on research, development, marketing or acquisitions, but the very real indirect impact can only be ignored at risk to a company's economic health. All such endeavors require a freedom to maneuver and think imaginatively that seldom can prevail (let alone thrive) in the hostile environment of litigation or investigations that contravention of the Access Control Laws can impose. Avoiding such distractions is a paramount objective for any company seeking to prosper in cyberspace. In Marco Polo's time there were decidedly different risks, and yet at that time as well the solution remained to set up a kind of checkpoint:

---

25. Xenophon, THE PERSIAN EXPEDITION, Book IV, Chapter 6 "*They Capture a Mountain*," Penguin Classics, translated by Rex Warner, 1949, pp. 203–204.

"[B]ands of travelers make a point of keeping very close together. Before they go to sleep they set up a sign pointing in the direction in which they have to travel, and round the necks of all their beasts they fasten little bells, so that by listening to the sound they may prevent them from straying off the path."[26]

Agile's experience in acquiring Troll, Brugge and Ijsselmeer will stand it in good stead for future transactions, provided it deploys the checkpoints early, enforces them stringently, and does not trivialize the risks that it discovers.

---

26. Polo, Marco, THE TRAVELS, Penguin Books, translated by Ronald Latham, 1958, p. 85.

Index

About the Authors

Roland L. Trope is a partner at Trope and Schramm LLP, resident in its New York City office, an Adjunct Professor in the Department of Law, United States Military Academy at West Point and in the U.S. Defense Institute for Security Assistance Management, Wright-Patterson Air Force Base, and co-editor of the Digital Protection Department in the journal *IEEE Security & Privacy*. In his practice he advises on cross-border transactions, export controls, trade sanctions, compliance with privacy regulations, defense procurements, intellectual property, and management of information security.

The views expressed in this book are solely those of the authors and do not reflect the official policy or position of the Department of the Army, Department of Defense, or the U.S. Government.

Greg E. Upchurch is a member at Husch & Eppenberger LLP, resident in its St. Louis, Missouri office. In his practice he advises on IP litigation, patents, trademarks, copyrights, and IP licensing. He is adjunct professor of law at Washington University in St. Louis. He is the author of the *Intellectual Property Litigation Guide* (West Group, 1995).